DEFENSE MECHANISMS

Theoretical, Research and Clinical Perspectives

ADVANCES IN PSYCHOLOGY

136

Editor:

G.E. STELMACH

ELSEVIER

Amsterdam – Boston – Heidelberg – London – New York – Oxford – Paris
San Diego – San Francisco – Singapore – Sydney – Tokyo

DEFENSE MECHANISMS

Theoretical, Research and Clinical Perspectives

Edited by

Uwe HENTSCHEL
Leiden University, The Netherlands

Gudmund SMITH
Lund University, Sweden

Juris G. DRAGUNS
The Pennsylvania State University, University Park, U.S.A.

Wolfram EHLERS
Private Practice, Stuttgart, Germany

2004

ELSEVIER

Amsterdam – Boston – Heidelberg – London – New York – Oxford – Paris
San Diego – San Francisco – Singapore – Sydney – Tokyo

ELSEVIER B.V.
Sara Burgerhartstraat 25
P.O. Box 211, 1000 AE
Amsterdam, The Netherlands

ELSEVIER Inc.
525 B Street
Suite 1900, San Diego
CA 92101-4495, USA

ELSEVIER Ltd
The Boulevard
Langford Lane, Kidlington,
Oxford OX5 1GB, UK

ELSEVIER Ltd
84 Theobalds Road
London WC1X 8RR
UK

First edition 2004

Library of Congress Cataloging in Publication Data
A catalog record is available from the Library of Congress.

British Library Cataloguing in Publication Data
A catalogue record is available from the British Library.

ISBN: 0-444-51263-2
ISSN: 0166-4115 (Series)

Transferred to digital printing 2007

PREFACE

Current attitudes toward psychoanalysis in its various guises range from credulous acceptance to blanket rejection. At this point, skepticism is more prevalent than enthusiasm. Critics often target the vague and speculative nature of psychoanalytic propositions. In particular, they allege that psychoanalytic constructs are couched in inherently nonfalsifiable terms, and as such fall outside of the range of science.

This is not the time or place to examine the merits of this critique. It must, however, be stated that defense mechanisms, which constitute the subject of this book, are generally considered to be among the most verifiable psychoanalytic concepts. The history of systematic research on defense mechanisms extends over at least seven decades. In the present volume, we have attempted to take stock of the current state of defense mechanisms, and examine the concept theoretically, empirically, and clinically. Its chapters bear witness to the variety and vitality of research approaches in this area. Defenses have been operationalized on the basis of responses gleaned during the perceptual process, projective scores and signs, clinical vignettes, observer ratings, self reports, and behavioral indices.

Research on defense mechanisms has addressed issues pertaining to personality functioning, social behavior, psychopathology, somatic disorders, child development, and the prediction of both maladjustment and of positive responses to a wide range of interventions. In fact, the concept of defense is germane to the entire gamut of complex human behavior, in its adaptive and maladaptive aspects.

The origins of this volume go back to 1993 when "The concept of defense mechanisms in contemporary psychology" was published. Ten years later, the authors have greatly updated and extended their coverage. Only the chapters by the two deceased authors, Paul Kline and Hans Sjöback, have been left unchanged. Many chapters have been thoroughly revised, some have been completely rewritten, and several new chapters have been added.

Defense mechanisms tend toward stability over time, even though there is some susceptibility to situational influence. Their temporal consistency highlights the potential of defense mechanisms for long term prediction of adaptive behavior. More generally, defense mechanisms are a part of the human information processing system, in its cognitive and psychophysiological aspects. In a comprehensive information processing system, which is only gradually being understood, defenses, with their cognitive, affective, and physiological aspects, are destined to play a pivotal role.

We have also attempted to encompass coping styles because of their close relationship to defensive operations. Yet coping has been a less controversial concept than defense, perhaps because its understanding is more compatible with common sense and is less beholden to contested psychoanalytic positions. In our judgment, the construct of defense does not rise or fall with the vicissitudes of psychoanalytic theory. We propose to examine it on its merits. Several chapters have provided underpinnings for new approaches for the validation of defense as a construct.

We are looking forward to defense mechanisms transcending the confines of its original theoretical framework. Thus, the phenomena of defense may be conceptualized from behavioral and other points of view. At the same time, we see no reason for rejecting the historically psychodynamic mainsprings of the concept. Optimally, both coping and defense may be conceptualized within the framework of an integrative theory of information processing.

This volume has been nurtured and sustained by the enthusiasm and persistence of its authors. It is gratifying that their commitment has been shared and supported by the publisher. We have enjoyed marvelous cooperation from the staff of Elsevier Science Publishers and we would like to extend our special thanks to Fiona Barron for her support and understanding throughout the publication process. We further would like to convey our appreciation to Mieke van der Voort who has very patiently prepared the layout.

We also gratefully acknowledge the financial support by GPS [Gesellschaft zur Förderung persönlichkeits- und sozialpsychologischer Forschung], Mainz, Germany.

As is often the case with multiauthored international volumes, as editors we were faced with the problem of balancing current standard English usage with the styles and practices rooted in a variety of traditions. We leave it to the readers to decide whether we have succeeded in this task.

The wealth of information in this volume and the complexity of its subject matter do not make for easy reading. Yet we hope that the volume will not be used only for reference. The thread that runs through it is the story of human adaptation in which defense and coping play a prominent part. It is our hope that readers will find ideas in it for reflection and discussion as well as for the extension of the continuing research effort.

Uwe Hentschel
Juris G. Draguns
Gudmund Smith
Wolfram Ehlers

Contents

Defense Mechanisms in Neuropsychological context

General Issues

Defense Mechanisms
U. Hentschel, G. Smith, J.G. Draguns & W. Ehlers (Editors)

Chapter 1

Defense Mechanisms: Current Approaches to Research and Measurement

Uwe Hentschel, Juris G. Draguns, Wolfram Ehlers and Gudmund Smith

Defense Mechanisms in a Casual Social Contact

Let us start out with the account of a recent chance encounter. One of this chapter's authors (U.H.) was seated next to an apparently homeless woman while riding on an underground train in Berlin. Unexpectedly, without any apparent pretext, she accosted him in a surly way by saying: "There are enough free seats around, so you don't have to sit here if the stench bothers you" (projection). There was indeed a strong smell of alcohol in the air, but the recipient of her remarks had not said a word about that or, for that matter, anything else. As the woman continued, she became friendlier and addressed her passive conversational partner more courteously and formally. In the process, she shared fragments of her life story, prompted only by a few brief interjected comments. Thus, she told that she had been married and had a grown-up daughter. Apparently, she also had a regular income. Why then did she rely upon the U-Bahn for warmth and shelter? Her subsequent comments provided no clues. Her speech and thought were intelligible and rational and her affect was appropriate, even though she did digress at times. There were clear signs of alexithymia as she experienced difficulties in expressing, labeling, and communicating her feelings. Moreover, some obtrusive negative features were noticeable, such as a brief but quite angry comment blaming her situation on what she saw as an excessive number of foreigners in Germany (projection). There was also self-pity, not about homelessness, but over her physical appearance and her unfulfilled wish for an operation of her jaw (turning against self, displacement). In a sudden outburst of anger she removed and threw away the bandage that was wrapped around her wrist (acting out).

What can be inferred from this random meeting? Let us venture three general, if tentative, conclusions. First, defense mechanisms, figuratively speaking, lie on the surface of human conduct, readily observable without the help of any explicit or standardized assessment procedures. Second, there may be a link between the nature and intensity of the defense mechanisms employed and the stresses currently or recently endured by a person. Third, defense mechanisms are likely to reflect, in Vaillant's (1977) phrase, a person's distinctive "adaptation to life" (p.6), or his or her formula of coming to grips with the challenges of living.

One of us was involved in a series of interviews with a small sample of urban German homeless men and women (Hentschel & Wigand, 1984). These procedures brought forth the ambivalence of the homeless toward the conventional middle-class lifestyle and the frequent intrusion of suicidal themes into their ideation. In retrospect, focusing our interviews upon the use of defense mechanisms may have shed more light on the processes underlying these persons' adaptive style.

In the rest of this chapter as well as in various chapters to follow, we shall attempt to delineate the construct of defense mechanism more precisely and to describe its impact upon various domains of behavior, ranging from deficits in attention deployment (Chapter 14) to psychopathology at different degrees of severity (Chapters 6, 9, 16, 17, 18, 19), somatic symptoms (Chapters 11, 20, 21, 22, 23, 24, 25, 26), and psychotherapeutic interventions (Chapters 9, 16, 17). The concept of defense mechanism has a history that extends over more than a century. In the ensuing sections, we shall trace its development from its origins to the present day. We shall also provide an introductory working definition that may help guide the reader throughout this volume.

From the Historical Roots of Defense Mechanisms to Contemporary Conceptualizations

In 1893 a new construct was introduced in psychology, that of repression (Freud, 1893/1964). At that time, the term "construct" still resided in psychology's preconscious, and. Freud did not call repression that. What he did was describe the manifestations of repression which he then proceeded to link to their antecedents and consequences. In Freud's (1893/1964) words, "the basis for repression itself can only be a feeling of unpleasure, the incompatibility between the single idea that is to be repressed and the dominant mass of ideas constituting the ego. The repressed idea takes its revenge however by becoming pathogenic" (Freud, 1893/1964, p.116). In his report on the case of Miss Lucie R., Freud asserted that it was primal repression that exerted an attraction on all other ideas or affects that were to be subsequently repressed: "When this process occurs for the first time there comes into being a nucleus and center of crystallization for the formation of a psychical group divorced from the ego - a group around which everything which would imply an acceptance of the incompatible idea subsequently collects" (Freud, 1893/1964, p. 123).

With this formulation, the concept of defenses was born. In his project for a neurologically based psychology, Freud (1954) also conceptualized a hypothetical neuronal network as a generalized model of defense. In the first phase of his construction of the ego apparatus, Freud (1894, 1896) described the role of repression and later that of defense in general in modifying traumatic ideas, with the potentially pathological mechanism of defense cutting off an unbearable idea from its affect. The same affect, however, which has not completely lost its strength, can become an unconscious source of energy for the formation of neurotic symptoms. A prominent example of an early unbearable idea is the incestuous impulse of the child directed at the parent of the opposite sex. In the ensuing steps of the sequence, the superego, evolving through identification with parental authority, was postulated to stimulate repression, with the possible result of infantile amnesia for these impulses. This process already constitutes a component of repression proper (or that of adult repression, starting after the formation of the superego), whereas primal repression was regarded by Freud as having a partially organic basis, as elaborated in his description of defense mechanisms by Paul Kline in Chapter 2.

In 1926, Freud (1926/1963) undertook to differentiate the concepts of repression and defense. Defense was to be the superordinate, inclusive concept; repression was destined to remain one of the mechanisms of defense, albeit the most important or even the prototypical one. Disagreement, however, continues as to whether repression is one defense mechanism among many or a pivotal component of the defensive structure (Fenichel, 1945; Madison, 1961; Matte Blanco, 1955; Sjöbäck, 1973). Of greater importance is the four-stage sequence proposed by Freud, consisting of the activation of an *impulse*, the experience of an intrapsychic *threat* over its expression, the mobilization of *anxiety*, and its eventual reduction upon the imposition of a *defense mechanism* (Freud, 1894/1964, 1926/1963, Sjöbäck, 1991). In the course of psychoanalysis, this sequence can be observed, albeit rarely in its entirety. What is obstructed from view is filled in on the basis of plausible first-order inference. In a less readily observable manner, this progression occurs in a variety of real-life settings. As such it constitutes an important manifestation of psychopathology of everyday life (Freud, 1901/1948; Jones, 1911), i.e., the intrusions of irrationality into the ideation and action of adequately functioning, rational human beings.

In the classical psychoanalytic view, defenses are directed against internal danger. Such a danger leads to the experience of intrapsychic conflict, usually between the superego and the id or between the ego and the id. The danger signal that activates the imposition of defenses is usually anxiety. However, the experiences of guilt or loss may also trigger defense mechanisms (Cramer, 1991; Fenichel, 1945; Sjöbäck, 1973). It is also recognized (Horowitz, 1986; Rycroft, 1968) that intense stress, such as danger to life and limb, can precede the imposition of a defense mechanism. There is ample clinical (e.g., Horowitz, 1986) and research (e.g., Vaernes, 1982) evidence in support of this position. Several chapters in this book attest to the complex interplay of physical illness and disability with the operation of defense mechanisms, in their discrete manifestations or in the form of more inclusive styles or patterns of defense. Moreover, shame has been identified as another important antecedent of defensive operations (Lewis, 1990; Westerludh, 1983). Outside of the psychoanalytic framework, it has been demonstrated that defense mechanisms are invoked in response to threats to self-esteem (Grzegolowska-Klarkowsla & Zolnierczyk, 1988), identity status (Cramer, 1995, 1997, 1998), objective self (Grzegolowska-Klarkowska & Zolnierczyk, 1990), and core personal beliefs (Paulhus, Fridlander, & Hayes, 1997). Thus, defense mechanisms are activated against a wide range of personally relevant threats. Freud's broadest formulation of defense encompassed "all forms of ego-protection against dangerous impulses" (Madison, 1961, p. 181). The emerging contemporary view, however, shifts the focus from the ego to the self and blends psychoanalytic insights with the findings of modern social psychology (Cramer, 2000). Thus, defenses do not have to provoked by an internal conflict; they may be aroused by whatever is perceived as dangerous to the person's survival, acceptance, and security in the social world.

Beside their often pathogenic consequences described in the classical psychoanalytic literature (e.g., Fenichel, 1945), defense mechanisms generate demonstrably positive effects. Thus, in a virtual monologue a girl (age 3.9) who had dreamed of a ghost ready to swallow her reassured herself by saying: "There are no ghosts, no, really not" (denial of a subjectively believed fact) and "when the ghost comes back my daddy will chase him away" (introjection). She added: "Ghosts really like people, don't they?" (reaction formation). These defenses clearly represent the child's *nonpathological* cognitive effort in seeking reassuring support against threatening dream images. This is an example of how the ego functions can counterbalance anxiety by means of defensive activity (Sandler, 1960) *without regressive tendencies*.

Defense Mechanisms as Part and Parcel of Everyday Life: Anna Freud's Contribution

Toward the end of Freud's career, a virtual catalogue of defense mechanisms had emerged. Their names were well known to practicing analysts, and their operations were routinely noted and often interpreted in the course of psychoanalysis. Yet, Freud never undertook the task of systematically sifting and integrating these accumulated observations on defense mechanisms into a comprehensive formulation. It remained for his daughter to do so. Her classical monograph (A. Freud, 1946) stands at the watershed between the formative period of psychoanalysis and the emergence of ego psychology.

Anna Freud (1946) described ten prominent defense mechanisms that had emerged from the psychoanalytic literature by that time: regression, repression, reaction formation, isolation, undoing, projection, introjection, turning against the self, reversal, and sublimation. Moreover, she specified the purposes of the defense mechanisms, their role in psychopathology and in healthy adaptation, and their maladaptive and adaptive consequences. A. Freud shifted the focus from psychopathology to adaptation. Defenses, she recognized, reduce or silence internal turbulence. However, they also help individuals cope with the demands and challenges of external reality. Even though the most spectacular instances of defense had come from the clinic, defenses are observed in psychologically unimpaired and nondistressed human beings. To be sure, a price is paid for reliance upon defense mechanisms. It is exacted in the form of reduced awareness of both self and environment. Spontaneity and flexibility in responding to challenges also suffer impairment.

Defense Mechanisms as Tools of Adaptation: George Vaillant's Contribution

Recent contributions recognize that defenses do more than reduce arousal. At their best, "defenses are creative, healthy, comforting, coping, and yet often strike observers as downright peculiar" (Vaillant, 1993, p.18). Quite often, they help bring about socially valued achievements. Vaillant (1977, p. 7) likened them to "an oyster [which], confronted with a grain of sand, creates a pearl." This recognition has stimulated the search for a chronological, developmental, or adaptive hierarchy of defenses. Vaillant (1977, 1992, 1993) proposed one such scheme by grouping defense mechanisms at four levels: I - psychotic mechanisms (delusional projection, denial, and distortion); II – immature mechanisms (projection, schizoid fantasy, hypochondriasis, passive aggressive behavior, acting out, and dissociation); III – neurotic defenses (isolation/intellectualization, repression, displacement, and reaction formation); and IV – mature mechanisms (altruism, suppression, anticipation, sublimation, and humor). At the lowest level, the mechanisms distort reality, at the highest, they bring about its integration with interpersonal relationships and feelings, At intermediate points, defenses alter distress and modify the experience of feelings, and they may appear odd, inappropriate, or socially undesirable from an outside point of view. It may be noticed that Vaillant placed most of the classical defense mechanisms as listed and described by A. Freud (1946) on Level III. Not coincidentally, these defenses were observed, named, and described in the course of psychoanalyzing neurotic patients. Vaillant's fourfold hierarchy has extended the concept of defense to both less and more mature levels of defense, thereby highlighting the pathological as well as the adaptive, and even creative, aspects of defense mechanisms. Its diagnostic relevance has been recognized by the inclusion of defense levels and individual defense mechanisms as a proposed axis in DSM-IV, the current version of the diagnostic manual of the American Psychiatric Association (1994).

Defenses: Theoretical, Observational, and Measurement Aspects

In contrast to a great many psychoanalytic constructs, defense mechanisms have always been clearly grounded in clinical observation. Proceeding from this empirical orientation, defense was conceptualized as a *behavioral observational construct.* Freud described what the psychoanalytic situation permitted him to observe and explained his observations as best he could, using his formidable literary and metaphorical gifts in the process. At no time, however, did he or other pioneering psychoanalysts attempt to quantify their observations, develop standardized measures, or use their emerging theoretical formulations in order to make predictions or advance and test hypotheses. Yet, Wundt's experimental laboratory was already in operation at the time, Sir Francis Galton was studying individual differences on a grand scale, and James McKeen Cattell had introduced the term "mental test." Nonetheless, the budding enterprise of experimental psychology, which was beginning to explore individual differences, failed to recognize the potential of systematic and controlled investigation of defense mechanisms. Thus, history of psychology took another course, and experimental study of defense mechanisms was not inaugurated until several decades later. In their quest for a new psychology, Freud and his adherents continued to amass experiences with neurotic patients in psychoanalysis, mostly in the form of case histories. Along with other psychoanalytic notions, defense was developing in this context, as it came to be embedded in the network of psychoanalytic concepts. This progression pulled defense mechanisms away from their empirical clinical origins as it favored speculation at the expense of cautious and plausible inference. An unfortunate byproduct of this trend has been a looseness of terminology in general and of definitions in particular.

The definition of defense mechanism in DSM-IV (American Psychiatric Association, 1994) reflects the current professional and scientific consensus on this topic:. "*Defense mechanisms* (or coping styles) are automatic psychological processes that protect the individual against anxiety and from the awareness of internal or external stressors. Individuals are often unaware of these processes as they operate. Defense mechanisms mediate the individual's reaction to emotional conflicts and internal and external stressors" (p. 751). Holmes (1984) posited three central features of defense mechanisms: avoidance or reduction of negative emotional states, distortion of reality to various degrees, from mild to blatant, and lack of conscious awareness in using defense mechanisms. From the aggregate of Freud's writings on the subject, Vaillant (1992) derived the following five principal characteristics of defense mechanisms:

1. Defense are a major means of managing instinct and affect.
2. They are unconscious
3. They are discrete (from one another).
4. Although often the hallmarks of major psychiatric syndromes, defenses are dynamic and reversible.
5. They can be adaptive as well as pathological (p. 4).

Specific defense mechanisms are described and introduced in Chapter 2. Anna Freud (1946) listed the ten major defense mechanisms that had been identified and described during the classical period of psychoanalysis, corresponding to Sigmund Freud's lifetime. And even in Anna Freud's monograph, on close scrutiny ten more mechanisms were found to be mentioned or described (Vaillant, 1993). In the intervening decades, numbers have burgeoned: to 22 major and 26 minor mental mechanisms proposed by Laughlin (1963), 39 by Bibring, Dwyer, Huntington, & Valenstein (1961), and 44 by Suppes and Warren (1975). Horowitz, Markman, Stinson, Fridhandler, and Ghannam (1990) described 28 distinct mechanisms, which they grouped on the basis of their outcomes, from successful adaptation to dysregulation and chaotic disruption. As yet, operational criteria have not been specified for this multitude of defensive operations, but the sheer numbers of these patterns of behavior testify to the variety of human self-protective devices.Defenses are the observable tip of the psychoanalytic iceberg. As such, they rest on a conceptual foundation which is hidden from view of both clinicians and experimenters. Conceptually pivotal, yet empirically demonstrable, defense mechanisms have been virtually destined to serve as the interface between psychological experimentation and psychoanalytic clinical observation. Still, a gulf remained to be bridged. Freud's theoretical formulations were based on extended observation of intensive and painful psychological experiences. Experimentation is of necessity limited in duration, and the ethical imperative of avoiding the infliction of harm severely restricts experimental manipulations. Moreover, defense mechanisms are often triggered by intense intrapersonal conflict. How can such experiences be reproduced under experimental conditions, except as "pallid facsimiles" (Kubie, 1952, p.708) of the clinical phenomena? Finally, psychoanalytic clinicians discovered the manifestations of defenses in the inextricable context of their antecedents and consequences. By contrast, the experimental reproductions of defense are limited to a small number of variables. The original objective of such experiments was simply to prove that repression – or another mechanism – existed. This objective was often pursued by normal volunteers performing tasks of limited duration and minimal personal relevance (cf, MacKinnon & Dukes, 1962). No wonder Freud remained skeptical! His response to one of the earliest proposed studies of repression is well known and often quoted: "I cannot put much value on these confirmations because the wealth of reliable observations on which these assertions rest make them independent of experimental verification. Still, it (experimental verification) can do no harm" MacKinnon & Dukes, 1962, p. 703). In retrospect, it is hard to say what these experiments collectively accomplished. Conclusions range from outspokenly negative (Holmes, 1978, 1985, 1990) to cautiously positive (Cooper, 1992; Erdelyi, 1990). Meanwhile, the focus of contemporary research effort has shifted to the investigation of how defense mechanisms can be measured and how they operate. The clash between psychodynamic concepts and traditional experimental methods may eventually be avoided with a more naturalistic approach, closer to real life circumstances, yet subject to the standardization of stimuli and quantification of observation. It is in this light that we shall later try to discuss the possibilities for the assessment of defense by means of self-report questionnaires.

In contemporary psychology, constructs are required to be operationalized, quantified, and measured. In recent decades, research on defense mechanisms has made progress toward meeting these standards. Advances have been achieved by means of experimental procedures, self-report scales, and projective techniques, as well as by research instruments specifically designed to tap defense mechanisms in the process of their emergence. The key criteria in measurement are reliability and validity, both of which are subject to quantitative determination. In this manner, quantitative information, independent of observers' judgment can be obtained about the stability, consistency, exactness, and similarity of test scores on relevant scales (construct validity), and of their usefulness in discriminating different groups (concurrent validity) and in predicting specific behaviors and performances (predictive validity). Within this framework, it is possible to calculate the standard error of measurement rather than be limited to subjective statements such as: "I think that this is true."

Psychometric principles are prominently exemplified by personality tests, especially of the true-false self-report variety. Cattell's (1945) personality tests are generally based on a representative list of descriptive terms which are used to define the underlying dimensions represented by these terms. In a similar manner, Guilford and Guilford (1934) established factor loadings for terms relevant to extraversion-introversion. The continued search by means of multivariate methods for an "adequate taxonomy" of personality descriptive terms has led to a robust solution by five basic factors (Digman, 1989; Goldberg, 1981) for which special tests have been developed (Costa & McCrae, 1989). They have been validated in several languages (Angleitner et al., 1990; De Raad, 1992). A degree of affinity has been established between the five-factor model and the circumplex models proposed by the adherents of interpersonal systems in personality diagnosis (Wiggins, 1982; cf. also Chapter 16). It is certainly true that the "big five" traits (openness, conscientiousness, extraversion, agreeableness and neuroticism [OCEAN]) cover a representative field of the culturally shared terms for personality description. Critics, however, have cast doubt on the validity of the lexical hypothesis for personality psychology (Block, 1995) and have objected to the use of laypersons' ratings of personality attributes (cf. Westen, 1996). In the present context the most important question, however, pertains to the hypothetical relationship of the "big five" to defense mechanisms. Later in this chapter we shall present some indirect, and for the most part negative findings relevant to this issue.

Wiggins (1973) made explicit several assumptions that underlie personality questionnaires:

1. Items are identical or similar in meaning for all respondents;
2. Persons can describe themselves accurately;
3. Honest answers are given by respondents to all test items.

However, personal freedom of expression is often considerably restricted by the use of standardized items which leave little room for spontaneity and invividuality. Situational (Magnusson & Endler, 1977) and process (Smith, 2001) aspects should also be taken into account. Even traditional trait theorists (Eysenck &

Eysenck, 1980; Herrmann, 1980} have never claimed that a given trait has the same impact under all conditions. Stagner (1977) has defined traits as generalized ways of perceiving a class of situations, which guide behavior in these situations. A dominant person can see, for example, a committee meeting as an opportunity to take charge whereas a submissive person would view it as a chance to let others make decisions, However, these behavior patterns would not necessarily generalize to other situations, such as family discussions. Epstein (1977) and Wittmann and Schmidt (1983) have suggested that prediction can be improved by using averages of repeated measures and by paying more attention to the reliability of criteria. A similar effect can be achieved by covering a broader spectrum of situations through the use of multiple behavioral criteria (Fishbein & Ajzen, 1974). However, the criteria employed should be relevant to the personality variables used as predictors (Monson, Hesley, & Chernick, 1982). These considerations can be applied in the same way to the use of defense mechanisms as predictors in empirical research, as Vaillant (1974) has already done in his study of consistency of adaptation across three decades.

How to integrate situational and process aspects with dispositions remains a challenge. In addition to the strategies already mentioned, Brunswik's (1955) functionalist approach has been favored, in particular, by percept-genetic researchers (cf. Chapter 7; Hentschel & Schneider, 1986; Hentschel & Smith, 1980). Its distinguishing characteristic is combining multiple predictors with several criteria not in a merely probabilistic but in a functional relationship. Beyond Brunswik's framework, it is generally recognized that both dispositions and situations must be conceptualized. Factor analysis is a prominent tool to that end, whereby a multitude of variables is reduced to a limited number of dimensions. Although prediction of specific acts has been attempted for a number of personality traits across a variety of situations, as discussed above, defense mechanisms, with rare exceptions (e.g. Henningsson, Sundbom, Armelius, & Erdberg, 2001; Sundbom & Kullgren, 1992), have not been included in such studies.

The Full Scope of the Defensive Process

Freud arrived at the core concept of the unconscious inductively, through conclusions from observations of his patients. He used this concept as a common denominator for very different phenomena like forgetting of familiar names, slips of tongue, dreams, and hysterical symptoms. The formation and use of the unconscious was a very important step in constructing Freud's complex model of the mind (Stagner, 1988). Its general aim was to describe behavior in terms of dispositions (e.g., fixation to a certain stage in the sexual development), situational aspects (e.g., fatigue), instigative causes (e.g., frustration), and fundamental, essential causes (e.g., unconscious conflicts). The model also allowed for the distinction between mental and material or reality-related causes in mental phenomena, e.g., the manifest content of a dream based on a recent perception as contrasted with its motivating source. Psychoanalysis thus clearly posits multiple causation of all observable behavior (Rapaport, 1960). With this perspective in mind, the criticism of an overly simple, rigorous, and straightforward operationalization of predictor and criterion variables is fully justified. To do justice to the complex psychoanalytic theoretical model, a complex research design combined with a complex model for the interpretation of empirical results is needed. The features that characterize most of the classical defense mechanisms are, of course, closely related to the psychoanalytic way of model building. In their original conceptualization, defense mechanisms were not evaluated against criteria based on test theory. When, however, defense mechanisms are incorporated into tests, the criteria by which psychometric measures are judged become fully applicable.

Defense mechanisms are embedded in a situational process that also has stable, structural and dispositional components. Seen purely within the framework of psychoanalytic theory, the following points seem to make an experimental or quasi-experimental approach preferable to the use of self-reports: the unconscious character of defense mechanisms; their causal relatedness to epigenetic stages and psychic complexes; their process character and their actual relatedness to other psychic processes; and, at least for the mechanisms at the lower end of a hierarchical conception (Vaillant, 1971), their observable deviation from normal behavior, with the potential implication of image distorting consequences and obstruction of adequate, reality oriented and adaptive, reactions.

At this point, we would like to emphasize the importance of the "internal milieu", as posited by Claude Bernard (cf. Robin, 1979), for the objective perception of the world. Potential distortions of veridical perception are often traceable to the organism's internal environment. The impact of internal organismic factors is clearly illustrated in the *act of touching*, which has been intensively studied within the *Gestaltkreis* (Gestalt region) framework by von Auersperg (1947, 1963a). Perception is linked to representational reality through what von Auersperg called "coincidental correspondence" In line with expectations based on hypothesis theory (Bruner, 1957), the respondent forms an idea of the whole object. Perceptual activity then proceeds through several phases of preconscious processing, akin to *microgenesis* as described in Chapter 7; the sequence culminates in labeling. This process, however, undergoes marked distortion when the temperature of the touching hand is lowered. Conductivity of the touched object facilitates he identification of the material of which it is made, such as wood, porcelain or metal. The first touching movement the actor usually gives an idea of the whole (hypothesis-theory). The perceptual action develops in different phases involving preconscious processes (*microgeneses;* cf. definitions in Chapters 5 and 7); the whole sequence receives confirmation through conscious labeling (retrograde determination). This process can be severely distorted when the temperature of the touching hand is lowered. Conscious representation is progressively restricted to the sensation of coldness, and neutral affect which typically accompanies tactile exploration gives way to negative sensations of coldness and even pain (von Auersperg, 1963b). Thus, subject and object come to be linked and almost fused. The dependence of perception of objects on the perceiver's internal organismic state holds true for all sensory modalities. According to percept-genetic theory (Smith, Kragh, & Hentschel, 1980), distortion of the visual image during the perceptual process frequently comes about as a result of defense mechanisms acting as filters, somewhat like the cold hand in the course of exploratory touching. Percept-genetic theory is focused upon process while clinical observation aims at grasping a phenomenon within its distinctive psychic complex at a point in time. This contrast applies to the two modes of studying defensive manifestations by percept-genetic and traditional clinical and psychometric means, respectively.

Vaillant (1971) presented the case of a hematologist as an example of displacement and intellectualization exerting a filter effect on behavior, as follows: "His professional responsibilities were exclusively clinical but recently he had made a hobby of studying cell-cultures. In a recent interview he described with special interest and animation an interesting lymphocyte culture that he was growing from a biopsy from his mother. Only very late in the interview did he suddenly reveal that his mother had died from a stroke only three weeks previously. His description of her death was bland and without noticeable concern." (p. 113). In this vignette the manifestations of defense are sharply delineated but the underlying process is not elucidated. How defenses unfold over time is discussed more extensively in Chapter 7.

It is worth emphasizing that defenses are not part of external reality. We reiterate Sjöbäck's fervent warning in Chapter 4 against reifying this concept. Instead, defense mechanisms are a construct that may be helpful in organizing and labeling a segment of the behavioral universe. None of the available methods for the detection of defense cover all of its manifold aspects. Moreover, each of them comes with its respective advantages and disadvantages.

Coping, Defending, and Cognitive Styles

Coping and Defending: Two Distinct and/or Overlapping Processes?

In several modern formulations, the concept of defense mechanisms has been extended over a wide spectrum of adaptiveness, maturity, and social value (Cramer, 1993; Vaillant, 1992, 1993). Still, one has to recognize that "we need defenses only when change in our lives happens faster than we can accommodate it" (Vaillant, 1993, p. 108). The alternative to defense is coping, understood as a process of adaptation that permits the person to work toward the attainment of his or her goals (Haan, 1977; Lazarus & Folkman, 1984; Vasiliuk, 1994) In the ideal case, coping involves the organization and integration of the person's accumulated experience and available resources; it is attuned to the characteristics and requirements of the outside world. A person's efforts at coping may or may not succeed in bringing about their desired outcomes; nonetheless they are often concerned with the means of attaining a realistic goal. Defenses, by contrast, abide by the imperative of reducing subjective distress. The contrast is prototypical between Anna Freud's ten mechanisms of defense – with the notable exception of sublimation (Fenichel, 1945; A. Freud, 1946) and the defenses placed by Vaillant (1992) at Levels II and III on the one hand and such modes of coping as logical analysis, empathy, and concentration on the other hand (Haan, 1977). The burden of the major typical defense mechanisms is shouldered in the form of self-deception, distortion of reality, and reduced social sensitivity. Notice, however, that there is considerable overlap between coping mechanisms and mature defenses which Vaillant (1992, 1993) assigned to Level IV. Even in this case, there is a subtle distinction. As described in biographical contexts, the mature defenses involve renunciation of goals rooted in fantasy and impulse, perhaps accompanied by resignation (Vaillant, 1993). Even so, in individual situations, coping and defending may be extremely difficult to extricate Thus, humor often combines the characteristics of both coping and defense. Chronologically, coping is the younger sibling of defense. The original observations of defensive manifestations go back to the early period of psychoanalysis; coping emerged as a theoretical construct more than half a century later (Haan, 1963; Kroeber, 1963).

Upon a thorough analysis of the two concepts, Cramer (1998, 2000) concluded that defense and coping can be differentiated on the basis of psychological processes, but not on the basis of outcome. To elaborate, she proposed that coping operations entail conscious processes whereas defenses operate outside of the person's awareness. The other difference pertains to intentionality. Coping revolves around the person's intentions, plans, means, and goals. Defenses, in keeping with their unconscious nature, are not directly related to the anticipated realization of a person's explicit objectives. Cramer also considered but rejected two other criteria. In her view, overlap prevails between coping and defending in their dispositional vs. situational sources nor can the two types of mechanisms be clearly distinguished on the basis of their positive vs. negative or adaptive vs. maladaptive character. At most, there is a difference in emphasis but not in kind. Others are more skeptical about the possibility of distinguishing the concepts of coping and defending (Erdelyi, 2001; Newman, 2001). Miceli and Castelfranchi (2001) have appended a subtler distinction in mental attitudes. Defense mechanisms involve manipulation of threatening representations, even to the point of making them disappear; revision, which is characteristic of coping, more consciously modifies the cognitive and emotional reaction to a painful situation without radically changing and thereby possibly distorting the perception of the stressful or painful situation. Over and above these proposed distinctions, coping and defending may also be differentiated on the basis of "how" versus "what" question. Coping may be seen as a strategy of how stressful events are managed whereas for defending the key question is what is repressed, isolated, projected, etc. To elaborate on the cardinal features of coping, Lazarus and Folkman (1984) have introduced the pivotal concept of appraisal as a crucial component of coming to grips with stress. Primary appraisal is initiated immediately upon the confrontation with a dangerous stimulus. Its goal is the recognition of danger and the assessment of its seriousness. In the course of secondary appraisal, the person takes stock of his or her resources in coping with the danger at hand. As proposed by Lazarus and Folkman stress management strategies encompass both problem solving and emotional coping devices which, however, are often difficult to separate from defense mechanisms (Cramer & Brillant, 2001). The gist of Lazarus's (1993) position can be summed up in the prayer of St. Francis of Assisi who asked for strength to change that which should be changed, acceptance of that which cannot be changed, and wisdom to know the difference.

Ursin, Baade, and Levine (1978) have specified that coping involves expectations of mastery of a challenging situation. "Coping is when the subject believes that he or she has the situation under control " (Ursin, Vaernes, Conway, Ryman, Vickers, Blanchard, & Blanchard, 1991, p.223). Proceeding from this tenet, the hypothesis is generated that positive outcome expectations would have the effect of lowering the arousal level.

Cognitive Styles and Defenses

An additional challenge pertains to the differentiation of defense mechanisms and cognitive styles. Both of these constructs constitute facets of individual adaptation that are embedded in the personality structure. Defenses are aroused by anxiety and other threats to the ego or the self. They aim at the reduction of personal distress and are germane to conflict resolution and restoration of psychic equilibrium. Cognitive styles are construed as generalized tendencies, habitually employed regardless of the emotional valence of stimuli or the person's affective state. Can an empirical relationship be established between defense mechanisms, for example, between the more primitive and global forms of defense and the cognitive style of field dependence (Witkin, Dyk, Faterson, Goodenough, & Karp, 1962)? The question about the existence and nature of the relationship between these two aspects of adaptation was first posed by Klein (1954) and was more recently investigated in a clinical sample by Hentschel (1980). He found seven distinct factors of cognitive control and four clusters of distinct defensive patterns, derived from the ratings of six defense mechanisms. In a complex set of relationships between these two types of variables, several of the seven cognitive patterns differentiated significantly among some of the patient clusters. In particular, links were established between the style of scanning and the defense of isolation, which provided cross-validation of earlier findings in a nonclinical sample by Gardner and Long (1962).

Defensive styles are influenced by the mode of attentional behavior (Messick, 2001). Cognitive styles thus can be regarded as basic predispositions for defensive reactions. As Holzman (1960) stated, there is "no repression without leveling" (p.339). Persons tending toward the assimilation of broad classes of stimuli rely upon a similar strategy in an emotional conflict by excluding painful impressions from consciousness. The hypothetical relationship between cognitive style and defense mechanisms has received partial validation

Empirical approaches to the measurement of defenses

General Considerations

What are the sources of information about defense mechanisms? How have they been obtained? Under five headings, we shall introduce the major methods of inquiry in current research on defense mechanisms. Investigation of defense mechanisms over the past century has resulted in the accumulation of a substantial amount of information. Still, a great many questions remain to be answered. In the ensuing sections, we shall attempt to move closer to these answers, on the basis of recent and current research approaches some of which are represented in the chapters of this volume

Clinical Observations

For Freud, psychoanalysis, based on free association, was a mode of therapeutic intervention and a method of data gathering. It is in and through psychoanalysis that he and his colleagues undertook to explore the impact of the unconscious upon behavior and experience. Clinical observations gathered in the analytic setting are of necessity private, confidential, qualitative, and complex. Accounts based on these data in the form of case histories, vignettes, and illustrations make up the foundation on which psychoanalytic formulations rest. This information is a rich source of leads and hypotheses. In the absence of quantitative and replicable data it lends itself poorly to conclusive confirmation or refutation of predictions. Psychoanalysts persist in their attempts to derive a maximal amount of information through clinical channels. For example, at the New York Psychoanalytic Institute a systematic effort was undertaken to pool clinical material on denial from case histories and to derive sound conclusions about it on the basis of group discussion and consensus (Moore & Rubenfine, 1969). Clinically derived qualitative information stands in a dialectical relationship to the newer, more objective and standardized, research methods. Clinical leads give rise to more formal data gathering by means of ratings, questionnaires or other systematic approaches, and findings so obtained are available for the application and modification of clinical practice as indicated. The dilemma with which investigators continue to be faced is, in Vaillant's (1993) words, "that what is measurable is often irrelevant and what is truly relevant often cannot be measured" (p. 118). The methods used by contemporary researchers, still to be described, represent their collective attempts at resolving this quandary.

Systematizing Clinical Data: Ratings

Clinical observations in their "raw" state have been systematized, objectified, and quantified by means of observers' ratings. These procedures have been principally applied to interview data (e.g., Jacobson, Beardslee, Gelfand, Hauser, Noam, & Powers, 1992). One of the earliest attempts to standardize the manifestation of defense was undertaken by Haan (1965) who developed Q-sort statements for ten coping and ten defense mechanisms. These ratings were based on transcripts of clinical interviews and observations. Vaillant (1992) extended Haan's Q-sort to the 18 mechanisms he investigated in his longitudinal projects. Earlier, Vaillant (1977) had constructed a rating system for 15 mechanisms of defense, to be scored as major, minor or absent. This system was found to have adequate interrater reliabilities; it demonstrated its criterion validity in a series of large-scale longitudinal studies (Vaillant, 1977, 1993). In the meantime, a number of other rating systems have been proposed and applied. The Defense Mechanism Rating Scale (DMRS) was introduced by Perry (1990). It features 30 ratings for discrete defense mechanisms and seven supraordinate scales. Its interrater reliabilities vary greatly across the scales for specific defense mechanisms and are quite low in several cases. DMRS is applicable for clinical interviews as well as for biographical vignettes. This system is described in Chapter 9, which also provides examples of its application. Ehlers' (1983) rating system encompassed 26 defense mechanisms, later reduced through factor analysis to five dimensions. These dimensions come close to corresponding to the classification system for defense mechanisms proposed by Anna Freud. Chapters 15 and 26 provide examples of the application of this instrument. One of the conclusions in Chapter 26 is that thorough training of the raters is indispensable for the application of this procedure.

Projective Techniques

A conceptual affinity links the rationale and the *modus operandi* of psychoanalysts and of the users of projective techniques. Projective test stimuli are ambiguous, responses to them are minimally constrained, and they provide the respondent with a lot of scope in imposing structure and meaning with less regard to social desirability than is true of self-report personality tests and greater opportunity for self-disclosure. In particular, projective tests lend themselves well to interpretation in terms of defense mechanisms, which in clinical settings, was widely practiced in the 1940's and 1950's. Some of the major test manuals (e.g., Rapaport, Gill, & Schafer, 1945) endeavored to provide guidance for this activity, which by and large tended to be pursued on the basis of testers' experience rather than research data. A major landmark in systematizing psychoanalytic interpretation of projective techniques was the appearance of Schafer's (1954) volume in which he spelled out a complex set of rules and principles, specifically for inferring the operation of various defensive operations from the Rorschach. Schafer's book, however, was mostly intended for the use of clinical practitioners rather than researchers. Its impact upon the utilization of the Rorschach test for research on defense mechanisms was limited, although Baxter, Becker, and Hooks (1963) converted Schafer's interpretive principles for projection, isolation, displacement, undoing, and denial into scorable research criteria. In recent research, three Rorschach indicators have assumed prominence: Rorschach Index of Repressive Style (RIRS) (Luborsky, Chris-Christoph, & Alexander, 1990), Lerner Defense Scales (LDS), and Rorschach Defense Scales (RDS) (Perry & Ianni, 1998). Each of these scales has been carefully validated and meaningfully applied to the identification of defenses in a variety of situations and with a variety of clinical and normal samples. Upon reviewing this research, Perry and

Ianni (1991) concluded that Rorschach responses may be less influenced by the examiner's technique than are interview data. The potential of these specialized defense measures remains to be realized, although the findings extant are promising in constructing defense indicators that are more sensitive than those that are based on interview data.

A major research effort has gone into developing, validating, and investigating indicators of projection, identification, and denial from TAT protocols (Cramer, 1991; Cramer & Blatt, 1993; Hibbard & Porecelli, 1998). Johnson and Gold (1995) constructed a new sentence completion test for the explicit of detecting defenses of different degrees of sophistication and maturity. In addition to preliminary norms, they have been able to discriminate between normal and psychiatrically hospitalized groups of respondents.

The projective approach, long derided for its alleged subjectivity and lack of sound validational data, appears to have obtained a new lease on life through the development of complex, theoretically derived indicators with a clear focus on specific defense-related criteria. Such "custom made" projective indicators provide an additional perspective for studying the manifold facets of a construct as complex as that of defense mechanisms. In this volume, Chapters 6 and 18 are largely based on projective techniques and deal with the Rorschach and TAT, respectively. Chapter 8 describes research with the Color Pyramid Test (CPT) (Schaie & Heiss, 1964), a projective test widely used in Germany, but as yet little known in North America.

Percept-Genetic Techniques

Projective techniques, personality scales, and observers' ratings share the feature of capturing the characteristics of a person at a moment in time. Defense mechanisms, however, unfold over a time span. Sandler and Joffe (1969) pointed to the parallels between perceptual microgenesis and the progressions of conflict, anxiety, and defense observed in psychoanalysis. This parallel is basic to the percept-genetic approach, developed to investigate "events over time" (Smith, 1957, p. 306). Its contribution to research on defense mechanisms is threefold. First, its originators (Kragh & Smith, 1970) have designed methods that permit the observation of defenses in their emergence. Second, they have developed operational definitions and scoring criteria for most of the prominent defense mechanisms. Third, they have accumulated massive amounts of data on these defense mechanisms and the conditions of their occurrence, Percept-genetic contributions are amply represented in this volume; Chapters 5, 7, 8, 13, 17, 19, 24, 25 deal with various aspects of the percept-genetic approach. Chapter 7 gives a methodological overview, that makes it unnecessary to go over the same ground at this point, especially since several additional recent surveys are available (e.g., Draguns, 1991; Olff, Godaert, & Ursin, 1991; Smith 2001). The prototypical percept-genetic instrument is the Defense Mechanism Test (DMT) (Kragh, 1985) which construes major Freudian defense mechanisms as distorted pre-recognition responses to threatening stimuli. Thus, the percept-genetic approach blends two traditions of investigation, the process oriented and the psychodynamic, in reproducing macrotemporal developments in micro-time.

Self-Report Scales

In the preceding sections, projective techniques, observers' ratings, and percept-genetic procedures were briefly introduced; in their several respective chapters, authors haveconsiderably amplified these introductory descriptions. The number and variety of self-report instruments necessitates a more extensive treatment. Indeed, their proliferation is paradoxical. Since defense mechanisms operate unconsciously, how can they be reported through an approach that is predicated upon direct and open self-disclosure? Instruments developed for this purpose represent their authors' attempts to resolve this dilemma.

Defense Mechanism Inventory: A Compromise Solution

Gleser and Ihilevich (1969) developed the Defense Mechanism Inventory (DMI) as a hybrid combining projective and psychometric features. Like projective tests, the DMI invites self-expression; leaning toward self-report personality scales, it structures response options. Gleser and Ihilevich proceeded from the assumption that a motivational conflict is necessary for a defense to be activated. In a procedure adapted from Rosenzweig's (1945) Picture Frustration Study, the DMI confronts the respondent generates brief stories in reaction to conflicts about authority, independence, sex, competition, and challenging reality situations. The DMI consists of ten stories featuring these five conflict areas. Responses are scored for five defense clusters: Turning Against Object, Projection, Principalization, Turning Against Self, and Reversal. Each of these scores is then assigned to one of the four following levels: action, feeling, thought, and impulsive fantasy. An impressive amount of research has been generated on the DMI in the United States (Cramer, 1988: Juni, 1982, 1994) Translations and adaptations have also been produced. In Germany, Hentschel and Hickel (1977) and Hoffmann and Martius (1987) worked on a direct translation of the DMI. More recently, Hentschel, Kiessling, and Wiemers (1998) kept DMI's format of conflict stories and multiple-choice answers, but modified story content and scoring.

The Inventory for Self-Evaluation of Defense Concepts (Ehlers & Peter, 1989) is also derived from DMI and is discussed below.

Two German Descendents of DMI

Hentschel, Kiessling, & Wiemers (1998) constructed the Questionnaire of Conflict Resolution Strategies (in German: Fragebogen zu Konfliktbewältigungsstrategien; FKBS) with the following changes by comparison to the DMI: Most of the stories were rewritten, with the explicit aim of keeping them close to daily experience; only two levels were scored, action and feelings and scored in a five-point scale Likert-type format for certainty of self-estimations. Unlike DMI, FKBS is scored for only five specific defense scales: Turning against Object, Turning against Self, Reversal, Intellectualization, and Projection. Internal consistencies range from. 78 to .90 and retest reliabilities over an eight-week period from .71 to .84. Further psychometric data as well as results from validation studies are reported in the test manual (Hentschel et. al., 1998) and in English by Hentschel, Ehlers, & Peter (1993). Empirical results with FKBS are reported in Chapters 14 and 23.

The Inventory for Self-Evaluation of Defense Concepts (in German: Selbstbewertung von Abwehrkonzepten, SBAK) was developed by Ehlers and Peter (1989). It is based on the psychoanalytic concept of reactivation of traumatic experiences, which can result in imposition of defenses. Conflict situations included in SBAK refer to helplessness, loss of love, castration anxiety, and disparity between pleasure and reality principles. SBAK comprises five scales: Rationalization, Denial, Turning Against Object, Regression, and Avoiding Social Contact. Its internal consistencies vary between .73 and .85. Further psychometric indices as well as the results of validation indices are reported in the test manual (Ehlers & Peter, 1989) and are summarized in English by Hentschel, Ehlers, & Peter (1993).

Attempts at Constructing Multidimensional Scales

Bond's Defense Style Questionnaire

Bond (1986a) embarked upon the construction of his Defense Style Questionnaire (DSQ) with the idea that self-report methods for registering principally unconscious processes could be useful. He argued (Bond, 1986b) that under certain circumstances, defenses can become conscious and, more important, that even if someone is not aware of his or her defense, the behavior connected with it may be obvious to the people in the surroundings and may eventually be reflected to the person. In this manner, such statements as, "People tell me that I often take my anger out on someone other than the one at whom I am really angry," describe displacement even if specific instances of displacement remain outside of the person´s awareness. Bond assumed that respondents can accurately comment on their characteristic style of dealing with conflicts: that is, they can provide self-appraisals of conscious derivatives of defenses (Bond, 1986a).

Bond's questionnaire of defense style comprises 88 items and is constructed with the aim of measuring 24 defenses. Factor analysis resulted in four factors which Bond (1986b) interpreted in relation to a maturity continuum, as follows: 1, maladaptive action pattern (e.g., regression, acting out); 2, image distorting (omnipotence, splitting, primitive idealization); 3, self-sacrificing (reaction formation, pseudo-altruism); and 4, adaptive (suppression, sublimation, humor). This maturational interpretation was supported by correlations between high-maturity indicators and ego strength and ego development scales. The unanswered question with this interpretation in relation to the construct validity of the scale is whether there is enough specific variance to interpret the four factors as qualitatively different phenomena and not just as four degrees of adaptation.

The Life Style Index

Plutchik, Kellerman, and Conte (1979) constructed the Life Style Index (LSI), on the basis of Plutchik's (1980) psychoevolutionary theory of emotions. According to that view, defenses are unconscious mechanisms for dealing with conflicting emotions, which may also be related to diagnostic categories. In the current version LSI has been limited to eight scales corresponding to the eight primary emotions in Plutchik's psychoevolutionary theory of emotions:

Trustful: Denial:	Distrustful: Projection
Timid: Repression:	Aggressive: Displacement
Discontrolled: Regression:	Controlled: Intellectualization
Depressed: Compensation:	Gregarious: Reaction Formation

In constructing these dimensions, ratings were obtained for defenses in various diagnostic categories, as well as for the appropriateness of the items. The maturity of the defenses and their direct and indirect similarity were also rated. Factor analysis was conducted to control the empirical overlap between the defenses. In Chapter 16 a more detailed report is presented on the development of the LSI, together with clinical studies on the prediction of readmission of schizophrenic patients, outcome of long-term psychotherapy, clinicians´ ratings of patients, prognosis in psychotherapy, and risk of suicide and violence.

Cognitive Orientation Self-report Inventory for Defense Mechanisms and Defense Mechanisms Questionnaire

Within their cognitive orientation (CO) framework, Kreitler and Kreitler (1976, 1982) conceptualized defense mechanisms as cognitive strategies for the resolution of internal conflicts. They differentiated defense mechanisms from strategies for the resolution of purely cognitive inconsistencies and from distress management (coping) strategies. Internal conflicts are mainly localized at the stage of planning one's action in response to a stimulus (What will I do?) and to the beliefs connected with such plans. A defensive program resolves the conflict by producing a new behavioral intent: through rationalization, denial, or projection. The questionnaire consists of four parts referring to norms (18 questions), general beliefs (11 questions), beliefs about self (12 questions), and goals (10 questions). It is a forced choice instrument with two or three response alternatives from which the respondent chooses one. A sample item is: "A person should try to guide his behavior according to logical rules which he can justify" (norms: rationalization). Kreitler and Kreitler also describe the role of cognitive programs, defined as defense mechanisms embedded in the complete input-output chain of human information processing. Thus, cognitive programs can be described as traces of defense within the meaning assignment process.

In two studies reported in Chapter 10, the Defense Mechanisms Questionnaire (DMQ) (Kreitler & Kreitler, 1972) was also used, in both cases as the dependent variable (i.e., as a criterion for the validation of the measure of defense within the CO questionnaire). The DMQ consists of seven prototypical situations in which common moral standards are violated, for example by not returning extra change given by mistake by a cashier at a grocery store. Each situation is followed by three options, expressive of. rationalization, denial, and projection, respectively. Each of these options is intended to represent possible explanations of the person's moral violation to self and to others. DMQ clearly has some projective features, but is embedded. in the context of the Kreitlers' distinctive cognitive approach to the assessment of defense mechanisms.

Other Approaches: Studying Defense Mechanisms Through Self-Expression

Under this heading, we have grouped several new and original approaches to the study of defense none of which have as yet been extensively investigated. The common denominator of these methods is that they are dependent on indirect or unobtrusive observation. Typically, information about the manifestations of defenses is obtained as a byproduct of another kind of activity while defenses are expressed without being elicited. Gottschalk and Gleser (1969) have developed a system of content analysis of verbal behavior for measuring respondents' psychological states. Respondents are asked to speak for five minutes about any interesting or dramatic life experience. Their accounts can be scored for defense mechanisms such as denial or displacement. The specific scales constructed for this purpose are presented in greater detail in Chapter 20. Moreover, the argument is advanced that several other scales not explicitly constructed for the purpose of assessing defenses may be relevant to defensive activity. The filter function of defense mechanisms once again comes into play in the relationship of hope scores of surgical patients to the maturity-immaturity dimension (Gottschalk & Hooigaard-Martin, 1986). Since content analysis of speech samples is a new and distinct approach, it is not surprising that correlations with defense scores on questionnaires are not very high (van der Zee, 1992). A new scale introduced by Bauer and Rockland (1995) utilizes segments of videotapes of psychotherapy sessions and is scored for twenty defense mechanisms. In this manner, raters' inference is minimized and their reliability is enhanced.

In Argentina, a computerized system of tremendous complexity for the content analysis of psychoanalytic transcripts and other texts has been developed by Liberman and Maldavsky (1975). Its core method, the so called David Liberman algorhythm (DLA), has been vigorously applied to the study of the vicissitudes of defenses in the psychoanalytic process, for the comparion of analysands with different diagnoses, of various phases of psychoanalysis, and of psychoanalytic vs. literary and rhetorical discourse (Maldavsky, 2003; Maldavsky, Cusien, Roitman, & Tate de Stanley, 2003). Information on the reliability and validity of the computer-based indicators obtained by means of the DLA has also been reported. In reference to specific defenses, Maldavsky et al. (2003) were able to demonstrate subtle differences between two varieties of denial, disavowal (Verleugnung) and repudiation (Verwerfung), on the basis of the comparison of several psychoanalytic transcripts and published literary texts by Jorge Luis Borges and Lewis Carroll. Maldavsky concluded, in line with psychoanalytic reasoning, that repudiation was more pathogenic than disavowal. Beyond this specific and subtle finding, the potential of ADL remains to be explored. Its attractive and unique feature is that it opens direct psychoanalytic data to objective and quantified scrutiny without intrusiveness or imposition of an extraneous procedure. In this respect, the procedures of the Argentine investigators show point of convergence with Ehlers' case-based psychoanalytic research in his chapter, which spans the range between factpr analytic data and qualitative psychoanalytic observations.

In a very different manner, Ozolins (1989) investigated non-communicative body movements in relation to defense mechanism scores on the DMT, and was able to demonstrate greater motoric expressiveness among repressors and increased motor rigidity among isolators. Somewhat similarly, repressors were rated to have more anxious facial expressions in response to affectively arousing stimuli than their low-anxiety counterparts (Asendorpf & Scherer, 1983). Milne and Greenway (2001) demonstrated a relationship between drawings and defense mechanisms, extending the leads that Erdelyi (1985) advanced on the basis of analysis of several works of art. Thus, a beginning has been made toward identifying defenses in speech samples, bodily activity, facial expressions and graphic productions; further work along these lines appears to be worth pursuing.

Theoretical and Empirical Implications of Regarding Defense as a Complex Construct

Correlation of personality factors as represented by the "Big Five" dimensions (McCrea & Costa, 1997) with defenses as assessed in self-report inventories has been found to be moderate, but only in one case; a product moment coefficient. of -.39 has been reported between agreeableness and turning against others (Hentschel, Ehlers & Peter, 1993). It is clear that defense mechanisms are independent constructs, well worth being investigated as such. However, the scrutiny of intercorrelations among the various defenses measures purporting to tap the same defense yields a somewhat disappointing, although not an entirely surprising, picture, As psychologists know only too well, two variables bearing the same or similar verbal label, are often correlated in a less than perfect manner. Such is the case with physiological, fantasy, projective, self-reported, and observer-rated indicators of anxiety. Closer to the topic of this chapter, there is no reason to expect a high correlation between repression scores on self-report scales and on the percept-genetic DMT (Kragh, 1985). Application of a complex model to the study of defenses would involve scrutinizing relationships between variables having a different label, relationships between variables with the same label at a higher level (second-order factors), and relationships among various sets of variables. The highest correlation coefficients would be expected between several self-report defense inventories. Unfortunately, there is no study to our knowledge of the relationships among all or at least most of the questionnaires purporting to investigate defenses.

Olff, Godaert, Brosschot, Weiss, and Ursin (1991) in The Netherlands studied the relationship between the translated versions of the five-story DMI and the LSI. In two samples, the overall score of defensiveness for the two inventories was used, and the respective coefficients were .52 and .55. It is debatable whether overall scores are the best descriptors of the relationship between the two inventories; in any case the resulting 30 percent of shared variance are not sufficient to permit us to speak of an identical construct. Vickers and Hervig (1981) found low convergent validity of the DMI with two other defense mechanism self-report inventories, and Cramer (1988) in her review of the DMI concluded that reversal is the only DMI scale that consistently produces expected relationships with the criterion variables, most of which pertain to scores on other questionnaires.

Another approach to the comparison of self-report defense scales and personality questionnaires, advocated by Heilbrun and Schwartz (1979), involves using defensive styles as moderator variables for the validity of personality scales. Heilbrun and Schwartz showed that, in some cases, the validity of personality scales is partially determined by defensive styles. There is little empirically based information available on the relationship between self-report defense scales and projective indicators of defense. A comparison of the DMI with the Blacky Defense Preference Inquiry produced significant results for two DMI scales (cf. Massong, Dickson, Ritzler, & Layne, 1982). Since correlations between scores on projective inkblot test scores and on self-report inventories generally tend to be low (e.g., Walsh & Betz, 1990), even in multivariate comparisons (Rimoldi, Insua, & Erdmann, 1978), there is no reason to expect more conclusive results for defense scales either. A more promising approach would involve studying the same target groups, possibly composed of uniform, carefully diagnosed neurotic patients, and comparing the contribution of the various measures to the differentiation of the groups, a technique which Hentschel and Balint (1974) introduced and applied under the namo of "structurogram."

In this volume, the two most frequently used types of measures are perceptgenetic techniques and self-report inventories. Therefore, the relationship between these two approaches assumes special relevance. In general, correlations are exceedingly low at the level of single variables. In a sample of 92 normal respondents, there were no significant correlations between the FKBS scales and the DMT variables. Canonical correlations between the DMT and the FKBS produced no significant results either. With an earlier version of the SBAK, four of the correlations with the DMT attained significance in a sample of 70 neurotic and psychosomatic patients (Gitzinger, 1988), a result that is hardly better than what would be expected by chance.

The Implications of the Complex Model Interpretation of Defense for Further Research

It is worth reiterating that the generally low correlations between single variables across different methods are an unsolved problem. A complex model interpretation offers a hypothetical conceptual solution. There is however no guarantee that it will meet with general acceptance. Verbal labels of variables sometimes seem to be "imprinted" in our minds, and systems that try to avoid these labels usually pay a price for it. One might speculate, for example, that Cattell´s (1965) system would have had greater impact if the author had not used his abstract index terms. Cattell's system with its oblique rotations, second-order factors, and complex equations for predicting actual behavior does show, however, that complex systems have a chance of acceptance if they are good. In reference to defense it seems nevertheless easier to "think" in terms of simple variables rather than consider beta weights of multiple regressions and coefficients of the structure matrices of canonical factors. Since factor analyses of various measures are likely to result primarily in method factors, factor analysis probably is not the optimal tool, even though it may be useful, especially in a confirmatory variant, for checking specific hypotheses, for example on the relationship of cognitive control principles to defense mechanisms (cf. Hentschel, 1980). There are now also a great many other multivariate methods that can be used for screening complex relationships (cf. SPSS, 1990).

Development of a fitting psychometric model of the relationship among the various methods for the identification of defenses is a highly desirable goal. Unfortunately, so far only little support has been obtained for a higher order statistical relation, for example, between self-reported and percept-genetic defenses. Eventually, collaboration between neuroscience and behavioral and computer disciplines can be envisaged as an ambitious but attainable goal. Neither behaviorism nor rule-based machine intelligence is able to explain brain function, but neuroscientists may benefit from using both the behavioral information in the actor's concrete situation and the command of computer technology in the analysis and reduction of immense quantities of data. By analogy, psychoanalysts could learn from differential psychology and statistics how to better organize their observational data on defense mechanisms in formulating prospective hypotheses instead of retrospective explanations. Harbingers of this trend include the development and application of the David Liberman Algorhythm by Maldavsky and his associates, which was briefly introduced earlier in this chapter, and the systematic use of primary psychoanalytic data in exploring the vicissitudes of defenses. At the same time, the operationalization of variables in experimental research, which is necessarily a formalized and reductionistic undertaking, should be informed by clinical observations. Experience in its context of occurrence and motivation, affected by potent unconscious influences, constitute the two foundations on which psychodynamic theorizing rests. Consequently, both contextual and unconscious factors should codetermine the empirical relevance of the concepts on which operational measures are based. The first step toward moving from speculation to objectivity should be the development of a sound and robust statistical model for the systematic mapping of similarities among the various ways of operationalizing a concept.. This mode of proceeding would enhance mutual learning and in the long run would help the concept of defense realize its promise and earn the place that it deserves in psychological theorizing, research, and practice.

We opened this chapter with the account of the defenses observed in a fleeting and random encounter, which is compatible with the clinical tradition. The concept of defense mechanisms has not only survived but prevailed, proceeding from subjective impressions through observational language to psychometric measurement. Both concurrent and predictive validity of various indicators of defense mechanisms upon systematic empirical study is quite impressive. However, there are unsolved problems pertaining to construct validity. We have already addressed this issue. If a grade were to be given for the conceptual adequacy of defense mechanisms as empirical constructs, the judgment would be that it has passed the test successfully.

References

American Psychiatric Association (1994). *Diagnostic and statistical manual of mental disorders. DSM-IV* (4th. ed.). Washington, DC: Author.

Anastasi, A. (1963). *Psychological testing* (2nd ed.). New York: Macmillan.

Angleitner, A., Ostendorf, F., & John, O.P. (1990). Towards a taxonomy of personality descriptors in German: A psycholexical study. *European Journal of Personality, 4,* 89-118

Asendorpf, .J. B & Scherer, K. R. (1983). The discrepant repressor: Differentiation between low anxiety, high anxiety, and repression of anxiety by autonomic facial-verbal patterns of behavior. *Journal of Personality and Social Psychology, 45,* 1334-1346.

Bauer, S.F. & Rockland, L. H. (1995). The inventory of defense-related behaviors – an approach to measuring defense mechanisms in psychotherapy: A preliminary report. In H.R. Conte & R. Plutchik (Eds.). *Ego defenses: Theory and measurement* (pp. 300-314). New York: Wiley.

Baxter, J., Becker, J., & Hooks, W. (1963). Defensive style in the families of schizophrenics and controls. *Journal of Clinical and Social Psychology, 5, 512-518.*

Bibring, G.L., Dwyer, T.F., Huntington, D.S., & Valenstein, A.F. (1961). A study of the psychological processes in pregnancy and of the earliest mother- child relationship. *Psychoanalytic Study of the Child, 16* , 62- 72.

Block, J. (1995). A contrarian view on the five-factor approach to personality description. *Psychological Bulletin* , *117,* 187-215.

Bond, M. (1986a). Bond's defense style questionnaire (1984 version) In G.E. Vaillant (Ed.), *Empirical studies of ego mechanisms of defense* (pp. 146-152). Washington, DC: American Psychiatric Press.

Bond, M. (1986b). An empirical study of defense styles. In G.E. Vaillant (Ed.), *Empirical studies of ego mechanisms of defense* (pp. 2-29). Washington, DC: American Psychiatric Press.

Bower, G.H. (1970). Analysis of a mnemonic device. *American Scientist, 58,* 496-510.

Bruner, J .S. & Postman, L. (1947). Emotional selectivity in perception and reaction *Journal of Personality, 16,* 69-77.

Brunswik, E. (1955). Representative design and probabilistic theory in a functional psychology. *Psychological Review, 62,* 193-217.

Bucci, W. (1985). Dual coding: A cognitive model for psychoanalytical research, *Journal of the American Psychoanalytic Association, 33,* 571-607.

Byrne, D. (1961). The repression-sensitization scale: Rationality, reliability, and validity. *Journal of Personality, 29* , 334-349.

Byrne, D. (1964). Repression-sensitization as a dimension of personality. In BA Maher (Ed) *Progress in experimental personality research. Volume 1*(pp. 169-220). New York: Academic Press.

Cattle, R.B. (1945). The principal trait clusters for describing personality, *Psychological Bulletin, 42* ,129-149.

Cattle, R.B. (1965). *The scientific analysis of personality..* Baltimore: Penguin.

Cooper, LA (1975). Mental rotation of random two-dimensional shapes., *Cognitive Psychology, 7,* 20-43.

Cooper, S.H. (1992). The empirical study of defensive processes : A review. In J.W. Barron, M.N. Eagle, & D.L. Wolitzky (Eds.) *Interface of psychoanalysis and psychology* (pp. 327-346). Washington, DC: Ameerican Psychological Association.

Costa, P.T., Jr. & McCrae, R.R. (1989). The NEO Personality Inventory (NEO-PI). In S.R. Briggs & J. Cheek (Eds.), *Personality measures.* Greenwich, CT: JAI Press.

Cramer, P. (1988). The Defense Mechanism Inventory: A review of research and discussion of the scales, *Journal of Personality Assessment, 52,* 152-164.

Cramer, P. (1991).,.*The development of defense mechanisms: Theory, research and assessment.* New York: Springer

Cramer, P. (1995). Identity, narcissism and defense mechanisms in late adolescence. *Journal of Research in Personality, 29,* 341-361..

Cramer, P. (1997). Identity, personality, and defense mechanisms: An observer-based study. *Journal of Research in Personality, 31,* 58-77..

Cramer, P. (1998). Coping and defense mechanisms: What's the difference? *Journal of Personality, 66,* 335-357..

Cramer, P. (2000). Defense mechanisms in psychology today. Further processes for adaptation. *American Psychologist, 55,* 637-646.

Cramer. P. & Blatt, S.J. (1993). Change in defense mechanisms following intensive treatment as related to personality organization and gender. In U. Hentschel, G.J.W. Smith, W. Ehlers, & J.G. Draguns (Eds.), *The concept of defense mechanisms in contemporary psychology* (pp. 310-320). New York: Springer Verlag.

Cramer, P. & Brilliant, M.A. (2001). Children's use and understanding of defenses. *Journal of Personality, 69,* 297-306.

Digman, J.M. {1989). Five robust trait dimensions: Development, stability, and utility, *Journal of Personality, 57,* 195- 214.

Draguns, J.G. (1984). Microgenesis by any other name. In W.D. Fröhlich, G. Smith, J.G. Draguns, & U. Hentschel (Eds.), *Psychological processes in cognition and personality* (pp. 3-13). Washington, DC: Hemisphere.

Draguns, J.G. (1991). Microgenetic techniques of personality assessment. In R.E. Hanlon (Ed.), *Cognitive microgenesis. A neuropsychological perspective* (pp.286-315). New York: Springer-Verlag.

Ehlers, W. (1993). The structure and process of defense in diagnosis of personality and in psychoanalytic treatment. In U. Hentschel, G. Smith, W. Ehlers, & J.G. Draguns (Eds.), *The concept of defense mechanisms in contemporary psychology* (pp. 253-274). New York: Springer-Verlag.

Ehlers, W., Gitzinger, I., & Peter, R. (1988). Experimental analysis of defense in a clinical setting. Paper presented at the XXIV International Congress of Psychology, Sydney, Australia.

Ehlers, W. & Peter, R. (1989). *SBAK Testhandbuch*[SBAK Manual]. Ulm: PSZ-Verlag.

Epstein, S. (1977). Traits are alive and well. In D. Magnusson & N.S. Endler (Eds.), *Personality at the crossroads: Current issues in interactional psychology.* Hillsdale, NJ: Erlbaum.

Erdelyi, M. H. (1985). *Psychoanalysis: Freud's cognitive psychology.* New York: Freeman.

Erdelyi, M. H. (1990). Repression, reconstruction, and defense: History and integration of the psychoanalytic and experimental framework. In J.L. Singer (Ed.), *Repression and dissociation* (pp. 1-31). Chicago: University of Chicago Press.

Erdelyi, M. H. (2001). Defense processes can be conscious or unconscious. *American Psychologist 56*, 761-762.

Eriksen, C. W. (1950). Perceptual defence as a function of unacceptable needs. Unpublished doctoral dissertation. Stanford University, Stanford, CA.

Eysenck, M. W., & Eysenck, H. J. (1980). Mischel and the concept of personality. *British Journal of Psychology* , *71,* 191- 204

Fenichel, O. (1945). *The psychoanalytic theory of neurosis.* New York: Norton.

Fishbein, M. & Ajzen, I. (1974). Attitude toward objects as predictors as single and multiple behavioral criteria., *Psychological Review, 81*, 59- 74.

Freud, A. (1937). *The ego and the mechanisms of defense..* London: Hogarth Press.

Freud, S., with Breuer, J. (1893). On the psychical mechanisms of hysterical phenomena: Preliminary communication. In *The standard edition of the complete psychological works of Sigmund Freud , Volume 3* (pp. 3-181). London: Hogarth Press.

Freud, S. (1894). The neuro-psychoses of defence. In: *The standard edition of the complete psychological works of Sigmund Freud, Volume 3* (pp. 45-61). London: Hogarth Press.

Freud, S. (1896). Further remarks on the neuro-psychoses of defence. In *The standard edition of the complete psychological works of Sigmund Freud, Volume 3*(pp. 162-185). London: Hogarth Press.

Freud, S. (1901/1948). *The psychopathology of everyday life.* New York: Macmillan.

Freud, S. (1911). Psychoanalytic notes on a autobiographical account of a case of paranoia (dementia paranoides). In. *The standard edition of the complete psychological works of Sigmund Freud, Volume 12*(pp. 9-79). London: Hogarth Press.

Freud, S. (1926). Inhibitions, symptoms and anxiety. In *The standard edition of the complete psychological works of Sigmund Freud, Volume 20* (pp. 87-172). London: Hogarth Press.

Freud, S. (1936). *The problem of anxiety.* New York: Norton.

Freud, S. (1954). The origins of psychoanalysis M. Bonaparte, A. Freud, & E. Kris (Eds.),:*Letters to Wilhelm Fliess, drafts and notes:1887-1902.* London: Imago.

Galton, F. (1883). *Inquiries into human faculty and its development.* London: Macmillan.

Gardner, R. W. & Long, R. I. (1962). Control, defence, and centration effect: a study of scanning behaviour. *British Journal of Psychology, 53,* 129-140.

Gitzinger, I. (1988). *Operationalisierung von Abwehrmechanismen: Wahrnehmungsabwehr und Einstellungsmessung psychoanalytischer Abwehrkonzepte* (Operationalization of defense mechanisms: Perceptual defense and attitude measurement of psychoanalytical defense concepts) Unpublished diploma thesis. University of Freiburg, Germany.

Gitzinger, I. (1990). Perceptual and linguistic coding of defense mechanisms in a clinical setting. PPmP Diskjournal, 1. no.1, 197 (*Psychotherapie, Psychosomatik, Medizinische Psychologie, 40*)].

Gleser, G.C. & Ihilevich, D. (1969). An objective instrument for measuring defense mechanisms., *Journal of Consulting and Clinical Psychology, 33,* 51-60.

Goldberg, L.R. (1981). Language and individual differences: The search for universals in personality lexicons. In L. Wheeler (Ed.), *Review of Personality and Social Psychology, Volume 2* (pp. 141-165). Beverly Hills, CA: Sage.

Gottschalk, L.A. & Gleser, G.C. (1969). *The measurement of psychological states through the content anlysis of verbal behavior.* Berkeley, CA:: University of California Press.

Gottschalk, L.A. & Hoigaard-Martin, J. (1986). The emotional impact of mastectomy. *Psychiatric Research, 17,* 153-167

Grzegolowska-Klarkowska, H. & Zolnierczyk, D. (1988). Defense of self-esteem, defense of self-consistency: A new voice in an old controversy. *Journal of Social and Clinical Psychology, 6,* 171-179.

Grzegolowska-Klarkowska, H. & Zolnierczyk, D. (1990). Predictors of defense mechanisms under conditions of threat to the objective self: Empirical testing of a theoretical model. *Polish Psychological Bulletin, 21,* 129-155.

Guilford, J.P. & Guilford, R.B. (1934). An analysis of the factors in a typical test of introversion-extraversion, *Journal of Abnormal and Social Psychology, 28,* 377-399

Haan, N. (1963). Proposed model of ego functioning. Coping and defense mechanisms in relation to IQ change. *Psychological Monographs, 77,* 1-23.

Haan, N. (1965). Coping and defense mechanisms related to personality inventories *Journal of Consulting Psychology, 29,* 373-378.

Haan, N. (1977). *Coping and defending.* New York: Academic Press.

Heilbrun, A.B. & Schwartz, H.L. (1979). Defensive style and performance on objective personality measures. *Journal of Personality Assessment,43,* 517-525.

Hentschel, U. (1980). Kognitive Kontrolprinzipien und Neurosenformen (Cognitive control principles and forms of neurosis). In U. Hentschel &

G. Smith (Eds.), *Experimentelle Perssoenlichkeitspsychologie. Die Wahrnehnung als Zugang zu diagnostischen Problemen.* (pp. 227-321). Wiesbaden: Akademische Verlagsgesellschaft.

Hentschel, U. (1984). Microgenesis and process description. In W.D. Fröhlich, G. Smith, J.G. Draguns, & U. Hentschel (Eds.), *Psychological processes in cognition and personality* (pp. 59- 70). Washington, DC: Hemisphere.

Hentschel, U. & Balint, A. (1974). Plausible diagnostic taxonomy in the field of neurosis. *Psychological Research Bulletin*, No.2, Monograph Series.

Hentschel, U., Ehlers, W. & Peter, R. (1993). The measurement of defense mechanisms by means of self-report questionnaires. In U. Hentschel, G. Smith, W. Ehlers & J. G. Draguns (Eds.), *The concept of defense in mechanisms in contemporary psychology* (pp. 53-86). New York: Springer.

Hentschel, U. & Hickel, U. (1977). German translation of the Defense Mechanism Inventory-DMI. University of Mainz, Unpublished.

Hentschel, U. & Kiessling, M. (1990). Are defense mechanisms valid predictors of performance on cognitive tasks? In G. van Heck, S. Hampson, J. Reykowski, & J. Zakrzewski (Eds.), *Personality psychology in Europe, Volume 3* (pp. 203-219). Amsterdam: Swets & Zeitlinger.

Hentschel, U., Kiessling, M., & Wiemers, M. (1998). *Fragebogen zu Konfliktbewältigungsstrategien-FKBS* (Confiict-solving strategies inventory-FKBS). Weinheim, Germany: Beltz.

Hentschel, U. & Klintman, H. (1974). A 28-variable semantic differential.*Psychological Research Bulletin, Lund University, 16,* No.4

Hentschel, U. & Schneider, U (1986). Psychodynamic personality correlates of creativity. In U. Hentschel, G. Smith, & J.G. Draguns (Eds.), *The roots of percption* (pp. 249-271). Amsterdam: North-Holland.

Hentschel, U. & Smith, G. (1980). Theoretische Grundannahmen und Zielsetzung des Buches (Theoretical frame of reference and aims of the book). In U. Hentschel & G. Smith (Eds.),.*Experimentelle Persönlichkeitspsychologie. Die Wahrnehmung als Zugang zu psychologischen Problemen* (pp. 15-29). Wiesbaden: Akademische Verlagsgesellschaft.

Hentschel, U. & Wigand, A. (1984). Einstellung zu Leben und Tod (Attitudes towards life and death). In J. Howe & R. Ochsmann (Eds.), *Tod, Sterben, Trauer* (Death, dying, mourning) (pp. 314-322). Frankfurt: Fachbuchhandlung für Psychologie.

Herrmann, T. (1980). Die Eigenschaftskonzeption als Heterostereotyp (The trait concept as hetero-stereotype) *Zeitschrift für Differentielle und Diagnostische Psychologie, 1*,7-16.

Hilliard, R., Mauch-Puhalak, I., & Wittman, L. (1988). The Speech Characterization Coding System (SCCS): A new tool for psychotherapy research. Paper Presented at the 19th Annual Meeting of Society for Psychotherapy Research, Santa Fé, NM.

Hoffmann, S.O. & Martius, B. (1987). Zur testdiagnostischen Erfassung des Abwehrstrukturen von Patienten mit Angstneurosen, paranoiden Syndromen und karzinomatösen Erkrankungen (On testing the defense structure of anxiety neurotic, paranoid, and cancer patients). *Psychotherapie, Psychosomatik, Psychosomatische Medizin, 37,* 97-104

Holmes, D. S. (1974). Investigations of represssion: Differential recall of material experimentally or naturally associated with ego threat. *Psychological Bulletin, 81,* 632-653.

Holmes, D. S. (1978). Projection as a defense mechanism. *Psychological Bulletin, 85,* 677-688.

Holmes, D. S. (1985). Defense mechanisms. In R.J. Corsini (Ed.), *Encyclopedia of psychology. Volume I* (pp. 341-350). New York: Wiley.

Holmes, D .S. (1990). The evidence for repression: An examination of sixty years of research. In J.L. Singer (Ed.), *Repression and dissociation: Implications for personality theory, psychopathology, and health* (pp. 85-103). Chicago: University of Chicago Press.

Holzman. P .S. (1960). Repression and cognitive style. In L. Postman & E.L. Hartley (Eds.), *Festschrift for Gardner Murphy* (pp. 330-343). New York: Harper.

Horowitz, M .J. (1986). *Stress response syndromes,* Northvale, NJ: J. Aronson.

Horowitz, M. J., Markman, H. C., Stinson, C. H., Fridhandler, B., & Ghannam, J.H. (1990). A classification theory of defense. In J.L.Singer (Ed.), *Repression and dissociation: Implications for personality theory, psychopathology, and health* (pp. 61-84). Chicago: University of Chicago Press

Jacobson, A. M., Beardslee, W., Hauser, S. T., Noam, G. G., Powers, S. I., Houlihan, J. & Rider, E. (1986). Evaluating ego defense mechanisms using clinical interviews: An empirical study of adolescent diabetic and psychiatric patients. *Journal of Adolescence, 9,* 303-319

Jones, E. (1911). The psychopathology of everyday life. *American Journal of Psychology, 22,* 477-527.

Johnson, N.L.; & Gold, S. (1995). The Defense Mechanism Profile: A sentence completion test. In H. Conte & R. Plutchik, (Eds.), *Ego defenses: Theory and measurement*(pp. 247-262). New York: Albert Einstein College of Medicine.

Juni, S. (1982). The composite measure of the Defense Mechanism Inventory, *Journal of Research in Personality, 16,* 193-200.

Juni, S. (1994). Measurement of defenses in special populations: Revision of the Defense Mechanism Inventory. *Journal of Research in Personality, 28,* 230-244.

Klein, G. S. (1954). Need and regulation. In M. R. Jones (Ed.), *Nebraska Symposium on Motivation: 1954* (pp. 224-274). Lincoln: University of Nebraska Press.

Klein, G. S. (1970). *Perception, motives, and personality.* New York: Knopf.

Kragh, U. (1985). *Defense Mechanism Test. DMT. Manual.* Stockholm: Persona.

Kragh, U. & Smith, G. (1970). *Percept-genetic analysis.* Lund, Sweden: Gleerup.

Kreitler, H. & Kreitler, S. (1972). The cognitive determinants of defensive behaviour., *British Journal of Social and Clinical Psychology, 11,* 359-372.

Kreitler, H. & Kreitler, S. (1976). *Cognitive orientation and behavior..* New York: Springer-Verlag..

Kreitler, H. & Kreitler, S. (1982). The theory of cognitive orientation: Widening the scope of behavior prediction. In B. Maher & W.B. Maher (Eds.), *Progress in Experimental Personality Research, Volume 11* (pp. 101-169). New York: Academic Press.

Kroeber, T.C. (1963). The coping functions of ego mechanisms. In R. White (Ed.), *The study of lives.* New York: Atherton.

Kubie, L. S. (1952). Problems and techniques of psychoanalytic validation and progress. In E. Pumpian-Mindlin (Eds.), *Psychoanalysis as science* (pp. 46-124). Stanford: Stanford University Press.

Laughlin, H. P. (1963). *Mental mechanisms.* Washington: Butterworth

Lazarus, R. S. (1993). Why we should think of stress as a subset of emotion. In L. Goldberger & S. Bresnitz (Eds.), *Handbook of stress. Theoretical and clinical aspects.* (2nd ed.) (pp. 21-39). New York: Free Press.

Lazarus, R. S. & Folkman, S. (1984). *Stress, appraisal, and coping.* New York: Springer-Verlag.

Lewis, H. B. (1990). Shame, repression, field dependence, and psychopathology. In J. L. Singer (Ed.), *Repression and dissociation: Implications for personality theory, psychopathology, and health* (pp. 233-257). Chicago: University of Chicago Press..

Little, K.B. & Fisher, J. (1958). Two new experimental scales of the MMPI. *Journal of Consulting Psychology, 22*,.305- 306

Luborsky, L.Crits-Christoph, P., & Alexander, K. J. (1990). Repressive style and relationship patterns-three samples inspected. In J.L. Singer (Ed.), *Repression and dissociation* (pp. 275-298). Chicago: University of Chicago Press.

MacKinnon, D.W. & Dukes, W.F. (1962). Repression. In L. Postman (Ed.), *Psy-*

chology in the making (pp. 662-744). New York: Knopf

Madison, P. (1961). *Freud's concept of repression and defense: Its theoretical and observational language.* Minneapolis: University of Minnesota Press.

Magnusson, D. & Endler, N.S. (1977).:*Personality at the crossroads: Current issues in interactional psychology*. Hillsdale, NJ: Erlbaum.

Maldavsky, D. (2003). Actualizacion del ADL: Instrumentos, confibialidad y validez (Theory, instruments, reliability, and validity). Buenos Aires: Universidad de Ciencias Sociales y Empresariales.

Maldavsky, D., Cusien, I.L., Roitman, C.R., & Tate de Stanley, C. (2003). Defenses in schizophrenics and in artists. Paper presented at the Annual Meeting of the Society for Psychotherapy Research, Weimar, Germany.

Massong, S.R., Dickson, A.I., Ritzler, B.A., & Layne, C.C. (1982). A correlation comparison of defense mechanism measures: The Defense Mechanism Inventory and the Blacky Defense Preference Inventory. *Journal of Personality Assessment, 46,* 477-480.

Matte-Blanco, I (1955). *Estudios de psicologia dinamica* (Studies of dynamic psychology). Santiago: Ediciones de la Universidad de Chile.

Messick, S. Style in the organization and defense of cognition. In S Messick, & J. M. Collis (Eds.), *Intelligence and personality: Bridging the gap in theory and measurement* (pp. 259-272). Mahwah, NJ: Lawrence Erlbaum.

Miceli, M. & Castelfranchi, C. (2001). Furhter distinctions between coping and defense mechanisms? *Journal of Personality, 69,* 285-296..

Milimet, C.R. (1970). Manifest anxiety-defensiveness scale: First factor of the MMPI revisited., *Psychological Reports, 27,* 603-616.

Mischel, W. (1968). *Personality assessment.* New York: Wiley.

Monson, T.C., Hesley, J.W., & Chernick, L. (1982). Specifying when personality traits can and cannot predict behavior: An alternative to abandoning the attempt to predict single-act criteria., *Journal of Personality and Social Psychology,43,* 385-399

Moore, B. E., & Rubinfine, D. L. 1969). The mechanism of denial. In B.D. Fine, E.D. Joseph, & H. F. Waldhorn.(Eds.), *The Kris Study Group of the New York Psychoanalytic Institute. Monograph III* (pp. 3-57). New York: International Universities Press.

Newman, L. S. (2001). Coping and defense: no clear distinction. *American Psychologist, 56,* 760-761.

Olff, M., Godaert, G., Brosschot, J.F., Weiss, K.E., & Ursin, H. (1991). The defense mechanism test and questionnaire methods for measurement of psychological defenses. In M. Olff, G. Godaert, & H. Ursin (Eds.), *Quantification of human defense mechanisms* (pp. 302-317). Berlin: Springer.

Olff, M., Godaert, G., & Ursin, H. (Eds.), *Quantification of human defense mechanisms*. Berlin: Springer-Verlag.

Ozolins, A. R. (1989). *Defence patterns and non-communicative body movements. An experimental study with the Defence Mechanism Test.* Stockholm: Almquist & Wiksell International.

Paulhus, D. L., Fridhandler, B., & Hayes, S. (1997). Psychological defense: Contemporary theory and research. In R. Hogan, J. Johnson, & S. Briggs (Eds.), *Handbook of personality* (pp. 544-580). New York: Academic Press.

Perry, J. C. (1990). *The Defense Mechanism Rating Scale manual.* (5th ed.). Cambridge, MA: Copyright by J.C. Perry, MD.

Perry, J. C. & F. F. Ianni (1998). Observer-rated measures of defense mechanisms. *Journal of Personality, 66,* 993-1024.

Plutchik, R. (1980). *Emotion. A psychoevolutionary synthesis.*. New York: Harper &Row.

Plutchik, R., Kellerman, H., & Conte, H.R. (1979). The structural theory of ego defenses and emotions. In C.E. Izard (Ed.), *Emotions in personality and psychopathology* (pp. 229-257). New York: Plenum.

Postman, L., Bruner, J.S., & McGinnies, E. (1948). Personal values as selective factors in perception. *Journal of Abnormal and Social Psychology, 43,* 142-154.

Raad, B. de (1992). The cross word-class replicability of the Big Five personality dimensions in the Dutch language. Paper presented at the Fifth Congress of the European Association for Personality Psychology, Rome,.

Rapaport, D. (1960). The structure of psychoanalytic theory. *Psychological Issues,* Monograph. 6. Madison, CT: International Universities Press.

Rapaport, D., Gill, M. & Shafer, R. (1945). *Diagnostic psychological testing Volume I* . Chicago: Yearbook.

Rimoldi, H.J.A., Insua, A.M., & Erdmann, J.B. (1975). Personality dimensions as assessed by projective and verbal instruments. *Journal of Clinical Psychology, 31*, 524-539.

Robin, E.D. (Ed.). (1979). Claude Bernard and the internal environment. A memorial symposium, New York: Marcel Dekker.

Rosenzweig, S. (1945). The picture-association method and its application in a study of reactions to frustration, *Journal of Personality, 14*, 3-23.

Rycroft, C. (1972). *A critical dictionary of psychoanalysis.* Hammondsworth, England: Penguin.

Sandler, J. (1960). The background of safety. *International Journal of Psychoanalysis, 41*, 352-356

Sandler, J. & Joffe, W G. (1969). Toward a basic psychoanalytic model. *International Journal of Psychoanalysis, 50,* 79-90..Sarason, I.G., Ganzer Y.J.,

& Singer, M. (1972). Effects of modeled self-disclosure on the verbal behavior of persons differing in defensiveness. *Journal of Consulting and Clinical Psychology, 39*, 483-490.

Schafer, R, (1954). *Psychoanalytic Interpretation in Rorschach testing.* New York: Grune & Stratton.

Shepard, R.N. (1978). The mental image *American Psychologist, 33*, 125-137

Sjöbäck, H. (1973). *The psychoanalytic theory of defensive processes.* Lund, Sweden: Gleerup.

Sjöbäck, H. (1991). Defence, defence and defence: How do we measure defence? In M. Olff, G. Godaert, & H. Ursin *Quantification of human defence mechanisms* (pp. 4-21). Berlin: Springer-Verlag.

Smith, G. J. W. (1957). Visual perception: An event over time. *Psychological Review, 64,* 306-313.

Smith, G .J .W. (1984). Stabilization and automatization of perceptual activity over time. In W.D. Fröhlich, G. J .W. Smith, J.G. Draguns, & U. Hentschel (Eds.), *Psychological Process in cognition and personality* (pp. 135-142). Washington, DC: Hemisphere.

Smith, G. J. W. (2001). *The process approach to personality: Perceptgeneses and kindred approaches in focus.* New York: Kluwer Academic.

Smith, G. J. W., Kragh, U., & Hentschel, U. PerzeptgenetischeVerfahren. Historische und methodologische Übersicht. In U. Hentschel & G. Smith (Eds.), *Experimentelle Persönlichkeitspsychologie. Die Wahrnehmung als Zugang zu psychologischen Problemen* (pp. 31-63). Wiesbaden: Akademische Verlagsgesellschaft.

SPSS (1990). *Categories, user's manual.* Chicago: SPSS Inc.

Stagner, R. (1977). On the reality and relevance of traits. *Journal of General Psychology, 96*, 185-207.

Stagner, R. (1988). *A history of psychological theories.* New York: Macmillan.

Suppes, P. & Warren, H. (1975). On the generation and classification of defense mechanisms. *International Journal of Psychoanalysis, 56* , 405-414

Ursin, H., Baade, E., & Levine, S. (Eds.). (1978). *Psychobiology of stress. A study of coping men.* New York: Academic Press.

Ursin, H., Vaernes, R. J., Conway, T. L., Ryman, D., Vickers, R. R., Jr., Blanshard, D. C., & Blanshard, R. (1991). The relation between defense and overt aggression. In M. Olff, G. Godaert, & H. Ursin (Eds.). *Quantification of human defence mechanisms* (pp. 222-237). Berlin: Springer-Verlag.

Vaernes, R. J. (1982). The Defense Mechanism Test predicts inadequate performance under stress. *Scandinavian Journal of Psychology, 23,* 37-43.

Vaillant, G.E. (1971). Theoretical hierarchy of adaptive ego mechanisms., *Archives of General Psychiatry, 24,* 107-118.

Vaillant, G.E. (1977). *Adaptation to life.* Boston: Little, Brown.

Vaillant, G. E. (Ed.). (1992). Ego mechanisms of defense: A guide for clinicians and researchers. Washington, DC: American Psychiatric Press.

Vaillant, G. E.. (1993). *The wisdom of the ego.* Cambridge, MA: Harvard University Press.

Van der Zee, M. (1992). *De invloed van defensie mechanismen en affectief-emotionele houdingen op psycho-fysiologische stress indikatoren* (On the effects of defense mechanisms and affective-emotional attitudes on psycho-physiological stress indicators). Leiden University, Unpublished Thesis.

Vasiliuk, F. K (1984). *Psikhologiya perezhivaniya.* Moscow: Izdatel'stvo Moskovskogo Universiteta.

Vickers, R.R. & Hervig, L.K. (1981). Comparison of three psychological defense mechanism questionnaires, *Journal of Personality Assessment, 24,* 630-638

von Auersperg, A. (1947). Das Schema des getasteten Gegenstandes (The schema of the touched object). *Festschrift O. Poetzl* (pp.82-97). Innsbruck: Wagner.

von Auersperg, A. (1963a). Grosshirnpathologische Syndrome als Zeitigungsstörung der Aktualgenese (Brain pathological syndromes as disturbances of timing during microgenesis). In G. Schaltenbrand (Ed.), *Zeit in nervenärztlicher Sicht* (pp. 19-31). Stuttgart: Enke.

von Auersperg, A. (1963b). *Schmerz und Schmerzhaftigkeit* (Pain and painfulness). Berlin: Springer-Verlag.

Walsh, W.B. & Betz, N.E. (199). *Tests and assessment* (2nd ed.). Englewood Cliffs, NJ: Prentice Hall.

Weizsäcker, V. von (1947). *Der Gestaltkreis* (The Gestalt region theory] (3rd ed.). Stuttgart: Thieme.

Westen, D. (1996). A model and a method for uncovering the nomothetic from the idiographic: an alternative to the five-factor model? *Journal of Research in Personality.*, 30, 400-413.

Westerlundh. B. (1983). The motives of defense: Percept-genetic studies: 1. Shame. *Psychological Research Bulletin, Lund University, 23,* (7), 1-13.

Wiggins, J. S. (1973). *Personality and prediction: Principles of personality assessment.* Reading, MA: Addison-Wesley.

Wiggins, J. S. (1982). Circumplex models of interpersonal behavior in clinical psychology. In P.C. Kendall & J.N. Butcher (Eds.), *Handbook of research methods in clinical psychology* (pp. 183-221). New York: Wiley.

Witkin, H.A., Dyk, R.B., Faterson, H. F., Goodenough, D. R., & Karp, S. A. (1962). *Psychological differentiation: Studies of development.* New York: Wiley.

Wittman, W.W. & Schmidt, J. (1983). Die Vorhersagbarkeit des Verhaltens aus Trait-Inventaren. Theoretische Grundlagen und empirische Ergebnisse mit dem Freiburger Persönlichkeitsinventar (FPI) [The predictability of behavior from trait inventories. Theoretical basis and empirical results with the Freiburg Personality Inventory (FPI)]. *Research report no.10.* Department of Psychology, University of Freiburg.

Defense Mechanisms
U. Hentschel, G. Smith, J.G. Draguns & W. Ehlers (Editors)

Chapter 2

A Critical Perspective on Defense Mechanisms

Paul Kline

In this chapter I shall describe the psychoanalytic notion of defense and show that as it has been elaborated and developed in psychology, it has undergone various changes such that what is now described as defenses or coping bears little resemblance to the original psychoanalytic propositions. These developments, it will be argued, are of considerably less psychological interest than the originals, since they have largely abandoned the unconscious aspects of defenses. However, it will be shown that it is possible to support a concept of defense that is in accord with the essence of psychoanalysis and with recent information theoretic accounts in psychology. The implications of this for the scientific study and measurement of defenses are also discussed.

Freudian Psychoanalytic Defense Mechanisms

Freud (1923) makes clear the nature of defense mechanisms. The neurotic conflict takes place between the ego and the id, the ego seeking to bar the expression of certain instinctual impulses by using defense mechanisms. In psychoanalysis these defense mechanisms have been carefully delineated and described, and Fenichel (1945) and Anna Freud (1946) contain excellent summaries of them. Before I briefly list the Freudian defense mechanisms, two further points should be made. These defenses are unconscious and can be categorized (Fenichel, 1945) as successful (where expression of the instinctual drive is allowed) and unsuccessful (where, because the instinct is not expressed, continuous repetition of the defense is required).

Sublimation

Sublimination refers to successful defenses and is not, in itself, a defense. Freud (1916), indeed, argued that sublimation consists in abandoning the sexual aim for another, which is no longer sexual. Indeed this deflection of aims is the most common definition of sublimation in psychoanalytic theory. There are various defenses within this category.

Reversal into Opposites (Freud, 1915). There are two processes involved in defense by reversal into opposites:

1. Change from active into passive: for example, sadism becomes masochism,
2. Reversal of content: for example, love becomes hate.

Turning Against Subject. Exhibitionism is voyeurism turned on the self.

Repression

Erdelyi (1990) has pointed out the ambiguity and diffuseness of Freud's terminology concerning repression and defense. He identifies in the writings of Freud 32 different phrases. However there is a general consensus, and I shall adopt here the definition in which Freud (1915) states that the essence of repression lies in the function of rejecting and keeping something out of consciousness. There are two types of repression.

1. Primal repression. This is the first phase of repression and refers to the denial of entry into consciousness of the mental presentation of the instinct.
2. Repression proper. This concerns the mental derivatives and associations of the repressed presentation, which are also denied entry into consciousness. The mental energy that belongs to repressed instincts is transformed into affects, especially anxiety, which renders repression an unsuccessful defense.

Denial

In denial the ego wards off by literally denying them some perceptions from the external world that would be painful. Freud (1925a) cites a patient who denied that a figure in his dream was his mother. Freud says that we amend it: it was his mother.

Projection

The attribution of one's own unacceptable impulses and ideas to others is called projection. This defense, together with reaction formation, is involved in the delusional persecutions of paranoia (Freud, 1911),

Reaction Formation

Reaction formation is a defense that results in the creation of an attitude opposite to the instinct that is defended against. Freud (1908) claims that the cleanliness of the anal character is a reaction formation against anal erotism.

Undoing is a defense characteristic of obsessional neurosis (Freud, 1909b). This is described as negative magic, which endeavors to "blow away" the consequences of some event and the event itself. Something is done that actually or magically is the opposite of something that actually or in the imagination was done (Fenichel, 1945).

Isolation

According to Freud (1925b), isolation is peculiar, to obsessional neurosis. Experiences are isolated from their associations and emotions. The isolation of sexuality from the rest of life, which allows men to express their sexuality without guilt, is an example of this defense (Fenichel, 1945).

Regression

Freud (1925b) argues that the process by which the ego regresses to an earlier stage can be used as a defense. Thus the obsessional frequently regresses to the anal-sadistic level.

These are the main defenses described in Freudian theory. As can be seen, they are all means of protecting the ego from pain, caused by instinctual impulses. However, in addition to defenses against instincts, the ego attempts to defend itself against affect. The same mechanisms are used, but there are a few other examples in psychoanalysis of defenses against affect.

Defenses Against Affect

Postponement of Affect. Freud (1918) cites a common example in which a man's grief at the death of a sister received no expression until he was inexplicably overwhelmed by grief at Pushkin's grave a few months later.

Displacement of Affect. Another example was a special case of displacement. Often there is displacement of object, as in fear of father displaced to animals (Freud, 1909a). Displacement can be seen when sexual excitement is displaced to irregularities of breathing or heart rhythm or indeed in the claim that anxiety is displaced sexual energy (Freud, 1906).

Identification with the Aggressor. Anna Freud (1946) regarded identification with the aggressor as the introjection of the object against which the affect was directed. The anti-Semitism of Jews is an example of this defense.

This brief description of the main defenses in psychoanalytic theory makes it clear that they are unconscious ego mechanisms aimed at preventing pain mainly from internal sources but also from the external world. Their psychological interest and importance springs from the fact that defenses help to explain and give insight into behaviors and feelings that otherwise would remain incomprehensible. The whole of human history suggests that we do not live in a rational world without defenses. It is also clear that the distinctions are to some extent arbitrary. Thus displacement and postponement of affects are hardly different, and reversal into opposites and turning against the subject are highly similar. Thus it would be expected that as the study of defenses continued, on a clinical and subjective basis, other new categories would be used. This is indeed the case and while, in a chapter of this length it is impossible to list them all, I shall briefly describe some of the more influential modern accounts.

The Work of Vaillant and Horowitz

Vaillant (e.g., 1977) has devoted considerable effort to the study of defenses, basing his work on that of Anna Freud. In his 50-year investigation of college men and in his studies of control groups, 18 defenses were assessed. These were classified according to developmental level, primitive to mature. Mature defenses were more adaptive and led to better mental health. In these studies the deliberate conscious effort to put out of mind unpleasant and insoluble problems was adaptive. Note the use of the words "conscious" and "deliberate". Vaillant's notion of defense is far more broad than that of Freud since it includes also conscious defenses. Vaillant defines the following defenses:

Primitive, pathological defenses: delusional projection, psychotic denial, and projection.
Immature defenses: projection, schizoid fantasy, hypochondriasis, passive-aggressive behavior, acting out.
Neurotic defenses: intellectualization, repression, reaction formation, and association.
Mature defenses: altruism, humor suppression, humor, anticipation, and sublimation.

I shall now list the defenses described in Horowitz (1989), a book that includes all the defenses of Vaillant and other classifications. It should again be noted that these defenses are in some cases very different from those of Freud, in that they are conscious and, rather than being mental mechanisms of any kind, are simply overt behaviors. This implies that the concept of defense, despite the use of the old psychoanalytic terminology, has changed. After the defenses have been defined, we discuss Horowitz's conceptualizations.

Acting out. Impulsive action, which may involve displacement, without thought of consequences (e.g., delinquent acts rather than expressing hostility directly to parents).

Altruism. Needs are met by fulfilling the needs of others rather than one's own.

Conversion of Passive to Active. Person becomes active as defense against weakness-identification with the aggressor.

Denial. Defined as in psychoanalysis.

Devaluation. Stress and conflicts are dealt with by attributing exaggerated negative qualities to self and others.

Disavowal. To avoid stress, person claims the matter is trivial or that emotions are not important. This is highly similar to denial.

Displacement. Defined as in psychoanalysis.

Dissociation. Conflicts and stress are dealt with by temporary failure of consciousness to integrate the dangerous material.

Distortion. Meanings of stressful topics are altered. Devaluation, disavowal, exaggeration, and minimization are forms of distortion.

Exaggeration. Certain meanings can be given exaggerated value-personal ability to argue can be overestimated to avoid fear during an oral examination.

Humor. Humor can be used to deal with problems, as Freud (1905) discusses in some detail.

Idealization. Exaggerated positive qualities are attributed to self or others. It is difficult to see how this defense differs from exaggeration.

Intellectualization. Emotional implications of a topic are avoided by treating it on a purely intellectual level. This chapter might be seen as an example of this defense.

Isolation. As in psychoanalytic theory.

Minimization. Topic is undervalued to avoid stress-highly similar to disavowal.

Omnipotent Control. For fear of being abandoned or failed by others, the person acts as if in total control of the object.

Passive Aggression. Stress and conflict are dealt with by indirectly expressing aggression toward others.

Projection. As in psychoanalytic theory.

Projective Identification. Hateful aspects of self are attributed to a person to whom one is close, thus enabling one to be angry with this other person and provoking hostility in him or her.

Rationalization. Finding good reasons for what one wants to do.

Reaction Formation. As defined in psychoanalytic theory.

Regression. As in psychoanalytic theory.

Repression. As in psychoanalytic theory.

Somatization. Conflicts and stress are dealt with by preoccupation with physical symptoms.

Splitting. Oneself and others are viewed as all good or all bad, there being no integration of positive and negative qualities.

Sublimation. As in psychoanalytic theory.

Suppression. Intentionally avoiding thinking about the source of pain.

Turning Against Self. Aggression, or any impulse is redirected to self.

Undoing. Defined by Horowitz somewhat differently from psychoanalysis: here it is the expression of an impulse followed almost immediately by its opposite.

From these definitions of defenses as they are used in the modern psychological literature, a number of points should be noted. The term is far more broad than the original psychoanalytic concept. Thus it embraces Freudian unconscious defenses, conscious acts such as suppression, and actions such as acting out. Similarly, altruism would not be seen as a defense in psychoanalytic theory but as the result of a defense-sublimation. Exaggeration and disavowal are entirely conscious and would seem to fit better the notion of coping mechanism as defined by Lazarus and his colleagues (Lazarus & Folkman, 1984). Thus the list groups together terms that are categorically different. The psychological significance of the original defenses was precisely that they were unconscious and thus influenced the behavior and feelings of the individual in ways that were inexplicable to him or her and by no means obvious to an observer. Conscious defenses, however, seem to have relatively less interest in affording insight into behavior simply because they are so obvious, at least to the observer and to the subject if pointed out. This is particularly true of the coping mechanisms, discussed by Lazarus and Folkman (1984). Folkman and Lazarus (1980, p. 233) define coping as "the cognitive and behavioral efforts made to master, tolerate or reduce, external and internal demands and conflicts among them. Such coping efforts serve two main functions: the management or alteration of the person-environment relationship that is the source of stress (problem-focused coping) and the regulation of stressful emotions (emotion-focused coping)." Furthermore, there are two aspects to coping that are intertwined: primary appraisal, in which the significance of an event or experience is evaluated in terms of the well-being of the subject, and secondary appraisal, in which the coping resources (behavior and responses designed to deal with the problems) are evaluated. This recent and influential viewpoint on coping is notable because coping has become such an umbrella term that it actually includes social behavior such as calling on friends or relatives for help. This conceptualization, although it includes psychoanalytic notions of defenses, is so broad as to become, in this writer's view, of little value. Thus if faced with conflict, whatever a person does is conceptualized as the individual's way of coping. In other words, if a conflict occurs, with this definition a person copes. This conceptualization of coping is an example of what Smedslund (1984) has referred to as a noncontingent proposition, and I shall not consider it further.

These linguistic difficulties surrounding the work of Lazarus and colleagues lead us on to the information theoretic approaches to the notion of defenses, which have been well expounded by Marcel (1983) and Erdelyi (1985, 1988). Thus, in discussing perceptual defense, which is an experimental analogue of repression (Kline, 1981), Erdelyi (1988) points out the linguistic confusion in some of the experimental psychological conceptualizations of the problem. For example, if perception is seen as an all-or-nothing event, perceptual defense is impossible, since for perceptual defense to take place it is necessary to perceive the stimulus, the event which the perceptual defense is supposed to prevent. However, if perception is reformulated in information theoretic terms this problem disappears. Thus it is a subset of computed perceptions that become conscious. Others remain below the level of awareness, although still affecting our conscious perceptions (Dixon, 1981). Similarly, as Erdelyi (1988) argues, if terms such as force, cathexis, and anticathexis, terms all implicated in the psychoanalytic concept of defenses, are conceived in the classical tradition of physics, that force = mass x acceleration, then Freudian theory is absurd. However, if the notion of forces is reformulated as interaction and counteractions (as is done by Fenichel, 1945), Erdelyi argues that there is little scientific or philosophical objection. Psychodynamic theory is no different from modern cognitive theories, although, of course, it is an empirical matter whether it is correct. Indeed Erdelyi (1990) is absolutely explicit on this point. He reanalyzes some of the early work on remembering by Bartlett (1932) to show that the Bartlettian descriptions of schemas have considerable overlap with the Freudian concepts of defenses and concludes that the only difference is that Freud's mechanisms are, rightly or wrongly, assumed to play a defensive role. Thus he suggests that the defense mechanisms provide the neglected defensive side of the pervasive operation of schemas in our lives. Clearly there is no antithesis between cognitive psychology and defenses, in this formulation.

I shall now examine the work of Horowitz, who has made extensive studies of defenses and attempted to synthesize cognition and defense (e.g., Horowitz, 1988, 1989). His work is neatly summarized in Horowitz, Markham, Stinson, Fridhandler, and Ghannam (1990). As these authors point out, Haan (1977) had attempted to link defenses to certain cognitive processes by arguing that these led to certain outcomes such as defenses or coping. However the problem with this work is that the cognitive processes discussed are idiosyncratic and not in accord with recent cognitive theory. Horowitz, however, has tried to avoid this pitfall. In his work (Horowitz et al., 1990), defense mechanisms are regarded as defensive outcomes of regulation, efforts that might, in different circumstances, also have outcomes that would be labeled either adaptive regulation or dysregulation, defined as succumbing to stress. In this account there are three kinds of regulatory process, whose aim is to control the conscious experience of emotions and ideas, although the former also affect the expression and communication of the latter. These are the regulation of mental set, the regulation of person schemas and role models, and the regulation of conscious representation and sequencing. It is as a result of the outcome of these processes that defenses occur. Some examples will clarify the point. Thus altering the schema of another person can result in projection while sequencing ideas by seeking information can result in intellectualization.

Although this work of Horowitz is a determined attempt to link cognition and defense I am not convinced of its success. The choice of cognitive processes is somewhat arbitrary and would not be undisputed in cognitive psychology. The classifications do not appear to be at all mutually exclusive. Consider the example, given earlier, of intellectualization. This is claimed to be the outcome of the regulatory control process, sequencing ideas by seeking information. However intellectualization is not the outcome of the this process. It is the process itself. Similarly rationalization is arranging information into decision trees rather than the outcome of it. The adaptive counterpart of rationalization, in this analysis, is problem solving. However the distinction between these two seems quite arbitrary. The notion of maladaptive and adaptive, which is surely cultural and subjective, is not useful in a truly scientific account. Since, however, there are undoubtedly cultural evaluative aspects of Freudian theory, the notion of defenses is not at risk. Thus problem solving would not necessarily be regarded as different from rationalization, or, indeed, intellectualization, with which it seems better juxtaposed. Certainly the brilliant work of some scientists could be seen as defensive, as indeed are the great literary creations of the world. This notion of adaptive and maladaptive stands no scrutiny, as a psychological phenomenon. However it is not my intention to subject the work of Horowitz to particular, detailed criticism. It is sufficient to see that it is an attempt to weld together cognition and defense, in a way that regards defenses as a maladaptive outcome of certain cognitive processes, even though, as was argued earlier in this discussion, this claim cannot always be maintained. However it suffers, compared to the work of Erdelyi, for example, from the choice of the cognitive processes based on the clinical research of Horowitz and his colleagues and would not fit easily into the experimental psychology, as described by Marcel (1983).

Conclusions

In 80 years there have been changes in the notion of defense, although, perhaps surprisingly, not as many as might have been expected-evidence that the concept, however difficult to formulate with precision, is still useful, in some guise or other, to understand emotional experiences. I think one clear conclusion may be drawn. Over these years the concept of defense has become far more broad. It began, in psychoanalytic theory, as a general term for an unconscious mechanism of ego protection. This became more precisely delineated into a number of unconscious defense mechanisms. These have been studied by clinical psychologists, and the concept of defenses has merged into a larger one of coping mechanisms, some unconscious, some conscious, and some actual behaviors designed to deal with stress. The term, indeed, embraces concepts that bear in some cases little psychological similarity. More recently attempts have been made to tie in the notion of defense to cognitive psychological concepts, thus bringing defenses into the orbit of experimental psychology. It appears from these studies that the original Freudian defense mechanisms, as unconscious processes to avoid pain, even if differently described, are still useful concepts in that they appear in most lists and descriptions. However one distinction seems essential-that between the defenses or coping mechanisms that are unconscious (the group in which the psychoanalytic defenses fall) and those that are not. This distinction is important because it profoundly affects the measurement of defenses, and precise valid measurement is critical for the scientific investigation of defenses. As has been argued (Kline, 1987), the measurement of unconscious processes by questionnaire is virtually impossible. This rules out many purported measures of defenses. What is needed, as the work in percept-genetics (Kragh and Smith, 1970) shows, as does research by Dixon (1981) and Erdelyi (1985) just for example, are subliminal stimuli. Silverman (1983), with his subliminal approach to the study of motivation and conflict, also supports this case.

In conclusion, therefore, it can be argued that the psychoanalytic notion of defense, even if it has to be conceptualized within a different framework, has stood the test of time. Care must be taken, in its objective investigation, that our measures are not so simplistic as to lose the essential unconscious nature of the concept, a danger particularly acute since the term "defense" has been widened to include a large variety of coping mechanisms.

References

Bartlett, F.C. (1932). *Remembering.* Cambridge: Cambridge University Press.

Dixon, N.F. (1981). *Preconscious processing.* Chichester: Wiley.

Erdelyi, M.H. (1985). *Psychoanalysis: Freud's cognitive psychology.* New York: Freeman.

Erdelyi, M.H. (1988). Some issues in the study of defense processes: Discussion of Horowitz's comments with some elaborations. In M.J. Horowitz (Ed.), *Psychodynamics and cognition.* Chicago: University of Chicago Press.

Erdelyi, M.H. (1990). Repression, reconstruction and defense: History and integration of the psychoanalytic and experimental frameworks. In J.L.

Singer (Ed.), *Repression and dissociation* (pp. 1-31). Chicago: University of Chicago Press.

Fenichel, O. (1945). *The psychoanalytic theory of neurosis.* New York: Norton.

Folkman, S. & Lazarus, R.S. (1980) An analysis of coping in a middle-aged community sample. *Journal of Health and Community Behavior, 21,* 219-230.

Freud, A. (1946). *The ego and the mechanisms of defence.* London: Hogarth Press and The Institute of Psychoanalysis.

Freud, S. (1966). *The standard edition of the complete psychological works of Sigmund Freud.* London: Hogarth Press and The Institute of Psychoanalysis.

Freud, S. (1905). *Jokes and their relation to the unconscious: Vol. 8.*

Freud, S. (1906). My *views on the part played by sexuality in the aetiology of the neuroses: Vol. 7, p.* 271.

Freud, S. (1908). *Character and anal erotism: Vol. 9, p.* 169.

Freud, S. (1909a). *Analysis of a phobia in a five-year-old boy: Vol. 10, p.* 3.

Freud, S. (1909b). *Notes upon a case of obsessional neurosis: Vol. 10, p.* 153.

Freud, S. (1911). *Psychoanalytic notes on an autobiographical account of a case of paranoia (dementia paranoides): Vol. 12, p.* 3.

Freud, S. (1915). *Repression: Vol. 14,* p. 143.

Freud, S. (1916). *Introductory lectures on psychoanalysis: Vol. 15.*

Freud, S. (1918). *From the history of an infantile neurosis: Vol. 17, p.* 3. Freud, S. (1923). *The ego and the id: Vol. 19, p.* 3.

Freud, S. (1925a). *Negation: Vol. 19, p.* 235.

Freud, S. (1925b). *Inhibition, symptoms and anxiety: Vol. 20, p.* 77.

Haan, N. (1977). *Coping and defending.* New York: Academic Press.

Horowitz, M.J. (Ed.) (1988). *Psychodynamics and cognition.* Chicago: University of Chicago Press.

Horowitz, M.J. (1989). *Introduction to psychodynamics.* London: Routledge.

Horowitz, M.J., Markman, H.C., Stinson, C.H., Fridhandler, B., & Ghannam, J.H. (1990). A classification theory of defense. In J.L. Singer (Ed.), *Repression and dissociation* (pp. 61-84). Chicago: University of Chicago Press.

Kline, P. (1981). *Fact and fantasy in Freudian theory* (2nd ed.). London: Methuen.

Kline, P. (1987). The scientific status of the DMT. *British Journal of Medical Psychology, 60,* 53-59.

Kragh, U. & Smith, G. (1970). *Percept-genetic analysis.* Lund: Gleerup.

Lazarus, R.S. & Folkman, S. (1984). *Stress, appraisal and coping.* New York: Springer.

Marcel, A.J. (1983). Conscious and unconscious perception: An approach to the relations between phenomenal experience and perceptual processes. *Cognitive Psychology, 15,* 238-300.

Silverman, L.H. (1983). The subliminal psychodynamic activation method: Overview and comprehensive listing of studies. In J. Masling (Ed.), *Empirical studies of psychoanalytic theories (pp.* 69-100). Hillsdale NJ: Analytic Press.

Smedslund, J. (1984). What is necessarily true in psychology. *Annals of Theoretical* Psychology, 2, 241-272.

Vaillant, G.E. (1977). *Adaptation to life.* Boston: Little, Brown.

Defense Mechanisms
U. Hentschel, G. Smith, J.G. Draguns & W. Ehlers (Editors)

Chapter 3

Defense Mechanisms in the Clinic, the Laboratory, and the Social World: Toward Closing the Gaps

Juris G. Draguns

Introduction: From Clinical Observation to Systematic Research

Defense mechanisms were discovered in the clinic, investigated under controlled conditions in experimental and other settings, and applied to the explanation of human behavior in its various contexts. As yet, the three strands of clinical observation, research investigation, and theoretical formulation have not merged into an integrated whole. Hence, the need for this volume. The contributors to it aspire to fill the gaps between the reference points of discovery, confirmation, and conceptualization. In the present chapter, an attempt will be made to provide, somewhat cursorily, a view of the current state of this three-pronged enterprise and of its future prospects, in order to help promote a continuous dialogue between clinicians, researchers, and theoreticians. The ambitious final objective, well beyond the reach at this time, is the description of a set of clinically observed and experimentally verified phenomena, linked by means of theoretically derived and empirically testable propositions. To this end, the present chapter will be organized around a number of topics and questions pertaining to the research based evidence on defense mechanisms. On the basis of this accumulation of findings, a number of unresolved research problems will be identified and avenues for future study will be proposed.

Defense Mechanisms: The Status of the Evidence

Early Studies

Do defense mechanisms exist? This is the basic question that stimulated interest in experimental studies of defense mechanisms as described in Freud's (1894/1964; 1896/ 1964) original two monographs. From the point of view of rigorous psychological experimenters, Freud's account of defense mechanisms was hearsay and his explanation of the phenomena he observed elicited skepticism. Yet, there was also the sense, shared by a great many contemporary observers, that something potentially significant was discovered. Combination of skepticism and curiosity often sparks research. Subject to the methods available at the time, studies were designed and initiated, and Freud's notions crossed the threshold from the clinic to the laboratory. In retrospect, it is readily apparent that the time was not ripe for crucial experiments on psychoanalytic propositions. The opportunities for investigating the replicas of clinical phenomena were just too limited and too crude, and perhaps the experimenters' ingenuity was not adequate to transcend the inherent limitations of time and intensity and make their investigations realistic. It is therefore not surprising that the reviewers of the early phase of this research effort (De Waele, 1961; Sears, 1941) documented a rather mixed bag of findings, some positive, some negative, and many inconclusive. Both of these reviewers refrained from any sweeping negative conclusions, but suggested the pursuit of systematic quantified research on psychoanalytic concepts by means of a greater variety of approaches.

Controversial Findings, Divergent Interpretations

Increasing sophistication of research in the ensuing decades has not yielded an unequivocal, generally acceptable answer to the fundamental question of whether the several classical defense mechanisms, as described by Anna Freud (1946), can be reproduced under controlled and replicable conditions of observation. The null hypothesis in regard to projection and repression is vigorously upheld by Holmes (1974, 1978. 1990, 1997) who maintains that sixty years of experimentation have produced no evidence for the selective forgetting of painful or traumatic events. Holmes does not deny selectivity in memory and perception, but proposes that these findings are more parsimoniously explained on the basis of voluntary or semivoluntary processes such as attention deployment instead of invoking the psychoanalytic concept of repression. In regard to projection, Holmes agrees that the research results extant provide a lot of support for the imputation of the person's own traits to other persons. However, he argues that these processes are neither unconscious nor automatic and are best conceptualized on the basis of social attribution rather than self-protective mechanisms of the ego. Perhaps as a result of these challenges, research that purports to demonstrate the operation of defense mechanisms under laboratory conditions has virtually ceased in the last two decades (cf. Cramer, 2000) while other types of controlled investigations pertaining to defense have continued and flourished.

Holmes' critiques have not gone unchallenged. In reference to repression, Erdelyi (1985) identified four experimentally substantiated findings: " (a) that there can be selective information rejection from awareness; (b) that aversive stimuli tend to be avoided; (c) that organisms strive to defend themselves against pain; and (d) that many psychological processes occur outside of awareness" (p.259). Erdelyi, however, emphasized that these four established facts do not imply or demonstrate a complete sequence of active banishment of threatening stimuli from awareness nor do they substantiate the subsequent recovery of such events.

This restriction is important to emphasize since a rash of claims of return of repressed memories, usually pertaining to sexual abuse in childhood, have swept through the United States and several other countries during recent years. These allegations have often been sympathetically accepted by segments of the public and in some cases charges of abuse have been pursued against the alleged perpetrators. Loftus (1993) has subjected these claims to searching scrutiny and has concluded that their veridicality cannot be demonstrated in the absence of other, independent corroborating evidence. Recall, as Loftus has shown in an extensive series of ingenious experiments, is susceptible to distortion through a variety of influences including suggestion. Although her experiments have recently come closer to the kinds of situations in which repression is claimed to occur in real life (Loftus, 2003), ethical considerations militate against inculcation of make believe memories of traumatic occurrences. Critics (e.g., Briere & Conte, 1993; Terr, 1994; Yapko, 1997) question whether Loftus' results are relevant to the actual traumatic memories that are allegedly recovered. In any case, caution is indicated for both researchers and clinicians before accepting the existence or veridicality of recovered memories in any specific case. On the other side of the ledger, the assertions that deny the very possibility of the return of traumatic memories are, at his point, unsupported by evidence. Karon and Widener (1997) have pointed to the well documented but forgotten store of data on the recovery of memories by large numbers of traumatized American veterans in World War II.

More recently, Baumeister, Dale, and Sommer (1998) reviewed recent research on seven classical defense mechanisms in normal populations. In warding off threats to self-esteem, denial, isolation, and reaction formation were shown to play an important role. Undoing was observed, but could not be tied to protecting self esteem. The role of projection was complicated; it emerged as a consequence, rather than an agent, of defense. Little evidence was produced pertaining to undoing, and virtually none relative to sublimation.

Vaillant's Contribution

A rich store of data pertaining to defenses was collected and sifted in the course of longitudinal research by Vaillant (1971, 1977, 1992, 1993, 1994). Working with two samples of normal men and one of normal women, Vaillant combined biographical and psychometric methods. Over a period of several decades, he was able to demonstrate that defenses are stable over time, largely independent of the person's environment, and associated with a host of meaningful social, personal, and biological characteristics. Moreover, defense mechanisms could be reliably measured and rated. On the basis of autobiographical questionnaires and other data, Vaillant expanded the original catalogue of ten defenses. He also established a hierarchy of defenses, demonstrated the very different sets of correlates for defenses at contrasting maturity levels, and proposed a set of 31 defense mechanisms which were incorporated into the current DSM-IV (American Psychiatric Association, 1994). Vaillant's research represents the most thorough and systematic investigation of defense mechanisms ever undertaken. In one of his books, he posed the question: "How can we prove that defenses exist?" (Vaillant, 1993, p. 118). In relation to the maturity of defense mechanisms, Vaillant (1993), he answered it as follows: "First, maturity of defenses can be rated reliably. Second, maturity of defenses is independent of social class but is affected by biology. In short, defense mechanisms are not just one more tenet of the psychoanalyst's religion. The study of the defense is a fit subject for social scientists" (p. 140). Vaillant's answer pertains to one dimension of defense mechanisms. It is not, however, a bold cognitive leap to extend it to other characteristics. Drews and Brecht (1971) described defenses as: "the core of the dynamic aspect of the psychoanalytic theory" (p. 128) and Vaillant (1977) characterized it as " perhaps ...Freud's most original contribution of man's understanding of man" (p. 77). Compared with many other Freudian notions, defense mechanisms are relatively easy to define operationally. As such, they were virtually destined to serve as the point of contact between the clinical enterprise of psychoanalysis and the increasingly research driven subdisciplines of psychology that deal with complex behavior: personality, abnormal, social, and developmental. Still, it should not be forgotten that defense mechanisms are constructs and not entities. As such, their value is determined by the extent to which defenses can be demonstrably related to antecedent, concurrent, and consequent variables. With this in mind, let us turn to the examination of the context in which defense mechanisms are experienced.

The Context of Defense Mechanisms

Defense Mechanisms and Their Antecedents: What Triggers Them?

Vaillant (1993) placed defense mechanisms between their four lodestars of conscience, people, desire, and reality. In classical psychoanalytic theory, conflict between any of these four points of reference provokes anxiety, and defense mechanisms are activated to reduce to reduce or eliminate this highly noxious state of arousal (Fenichel, 1945; Madison, 1961; Matte Blanco, 1955; Sjöbäck, 1973). Anxiety then prototypically precedes the imposition of defense mechanisms. This sequence, however, admits a number of modifications. First, even though psychoanalysis was clinically focused on internal threat and intrapsychic conflict, the fact that external dangers could trigger defense mechanisms was recognized, although not emphasized, by psychoanalysts. Second, anxiety may be the principal, but not the only, danger signal of the ego. Lewis (1990) in the United States and Westerlundh (1983) in Sweden have independently recognized and investigated shame as a motive for the mobilization of defense Shame may even play a more important role in activating defenses in cultures in which social evaluation is a principal regulator of conduct. Clinicians and researchers agree that guilt is reduced or warded off by a variety of defense mechanisms. Rejection by peers was shown by Sandstrom and Cramer (2003) to intensify reliance on defenses, especially when it occurred against the background of prior social neglect or rejection. Experience of failure had a similar effect in children (Cramer & Gaul, 1998). Other forms of distress may also serve as antecedents for enhanced use of defensive functioning. In particular, adolescents were found to be vulnerable to uncertainty and diffusion in their identity, and they attempted to lessen their discomfort by strong use of defenses (Cramer, 1995, 1998) Similarly, men whose personality organization was feminine and women whose personality organization was masculine tended to use more defenses than their peers with personality organization that was consonant with their gender (Cramer & Blatt, 1993). More subtly, Grzeglowska-Klarkowska and Zolnierzyk (1988. 1990) in Poland reported that the use of defense was increased when a personality characteristic was challenged that was central to the person's self-representation. These results are consonant with the dynamic model of self-deception (Paulhus & Suedfeld, 1988) that posits an increase in defensive self-deceptive strategies under conditions of increased threat to the self. Generically, a threat to the stability of a person in his or her world can be brought about by any kind of abrupt and unanticipated change, especially if it is pertinent to the self

Of course, it can be argued that in all of these instances anxiety is concurrently experienced and that it mediates the application of defenses. Such a possibility, however, needs to be empirically investigated. At this point, it is worth noting that the various threatening conditions experienced in the above studies were sufficient to elicit defenses. Moreover, the aggregate of these findings causes emphasis to shift from the ego as the person's executive adaptive agency to the self as the focus of his or her subjective experience. As a number of researchers have reported, it is not necessarily internal conflict that sets off defenses. Instead, dangers to one's sense of personhood as well as to its stability and uniqueness may be adequate to bring defenses into play. These new currents of thought are quite compatible with the changing notions of defense within the psychoanalytic framework, as described by Cooper (1998). The goal of defensive operations is construed as protecting the person's self esteem rather than shielding him or her from the awareness of unacceptable impulses.

A Russian psychologist, Vasiliuk (1984), identified the following four types of experience as antecedents for the imposition of defense: stress, frustration, conflict, and crisis. Often, several or all of these four conditions can occur together, but even one is sufficient to initiate defensive activity. Stress as antecedent of defense has been thoroughly described by Horowitz (1986).

A special case is that of illness, physical suffering, and pain, a topic that is represented in several chapters of this volume. There is no question that illness and its management are accompanied by defenses which may vary with the nature of disease, the patient's personality, his or her outlook, prognosis, and relationship with family and with the treatment of the disease. However, does the experience of illness lead to the activation of defenses, or are they the result of the person's negative anticipations of discomfort, pain, disability, and death? Beutel (1988) reviewed a number of German and American studies on the use of defense mechanisms in serious and life-threatening chronic illness. Denial was prominent in a number of conditions, sometimes accompanied by repression, reaction formation, projection, and regression.

It is clear than that defense mechanisms constitute an important component of a person's adaptation. The two central experiences in this regard are external stress and threat to the person's self. The focus on anxiety and on intrapsychic conflict is too narrow, although it is premature to dismiss anxiety as the active component in all conditions that produce defense.

Consequences of Defenses: What Do Defenses Predict?

It is a lot more difficult to study the consequences of defenses than their antecedents. Psychoanalytic theory posits that defenses either succeed in their primary objective, that of reducing anxiety and other modes of distress and discomfort, or they fail. There are no established ways of identifying defenses that would succeed or fail in a specific situation with a given individual. More recent classifications of defenses according to their maturity level (Vaillant, 1992, 1993) or developmental status (Cramer, 1991) make such predictions possible, and Vaillant's longitudinal methodology has permitted to put them to a test. In general, mature defenses, such as sublimation, suppression, altruism, and humor, predicted higher levels of marital adjustment, job satisfaction, and personal happiness (Vaillant, 1993). At the lowest level of functioning, even immature defenses contributed to maintaining minimal adaptation (Vaillant, 1994). Cramer (1999) reported that the denial and projection interacted with the IQ in predicting the level of ego functioning in young adults. At high IQ levels, use of denial was related to low ego functioning, and moderate level of projection was associated with high ego levels. At the low IQ level, however, both denial and projection predicted high ego functioning. Cramer in a longitudinal study (2002) also found that at the age of 23, both female and male respondents, who had used denial in earlier development exhibited numerous indicators of immaturity while women who predominantly used projection were sociable and free of excessive caution and of depression. By contrast, men who relied on projection were suspicious, hyperalert, anxious, and depressed. Identification, especially in women, was associated with socially competent mode of adjustment and absence of depression.

In clinical settings, immature defenses such as projection, acting out, and dissociation were found to predict poor interpersonal and global functioning (Cramer, Blatt, & Ford, 1988, Perry & Cooper, 1992; Vaillant & Vaillant, 1992). Hoglend and Perry (1998) reported that the initial assessment of defenses was a better predictor of outcome for depressive patients than the DSM-IV rating of global functioning.

Defense Mechanisms in the Present: A Variety of Clinically Relevant Results

Defense mechanisms based on observer ratings, projective techniques, and self report scales have been associated with psychiatric diagnoses, especially those of borderline disorder, affective disorder, and other DSM-IV diagnostic categories, as indicated in the recent review by Cramer (2000). Denial and other related mechanisms, prominently employed in various physical disorders (e.g., Katz,

Weiner, Gallagher, & Hellman, 1970; Oettingen, 1996), have emerged as something of a double edged sword. On the one hand, denial reduces the patients' anxiety and thereby improves their well-being and their quality of life. On the other hand, denial may also interfere with compliance with treatment and medication orders (Fulde, Junge, & Ahrens, 1995). In psychotherapy, immature defenses were found to decrease after prolonged and intensive psychotherapy (Cramer & Blatt, 1993) Changes in defense use also occurred as obsessive-compulsive and depressive symptoms declined in number (Akkerman, Carr, & Lewin, 1992; Albucher, Abelson, & Nesse, 1998; Hoglend & Perry, 1998). Thus, defense mechanisms are important to consider in the course of assessment, a development implicitly recognized by the incorporation of 31 defense mechanisms into the DSM-IV. In therapy, the findings extant corroborate the impressions and convictions of a great many practitioners; in the course of psychotherapy the client's defensive structure undergoes a change. Moreover, the limited research findings that have been reported suggest that change is experienced in the direction of greater maturity and appropriateness. Beutel (1988) has proposed additional criteria of defenses that could be incorporated into future process and outcome studies. They include flexibility versus rigidity, intensity and generality, duration, and balance, all of which remain to be converted into standardized ratings and other measures. Vaillant's (1977, 1993) biographical vignettes of participants in his research as well as of historical figures remain a source for other relevant, and sometimes subtle indicators which can potentially be tested for their applicability in assessment and intervention. Fascinating, but as yet unanswered, questions occur: Is change in defense mechanisms different and more pronounced in psychodynamic therapy as compared with behavioral and cognitive interventions? Do the extent and nature of change vary with the success of therapy? Does targeted change in defense mechanisms through counseling or psychotherapy accomplish its intended results (cf. Clark, 1998) ?

Beyond the Clinic: Extensions of Defense Mechanisms into Other Areas of Psychology

Defenses in Social Psychology: Theoretical Developments and Empirical Research

Over the past decade the concerns of social psychologists and those of the investigators of defense mechanisms have experienced considerable convergence. Social psychologists investigate self-deception, positive illusions, scapegoating, dissonance reduction, and social attributions. All of these concepts bear obvious resemblance to the defense mechanisms, a point vigorously propounded by Paulhus, Fridhandler, and Hayes (1997). Paradoxically, some of the critics of defense mechanisms (e.g., Holmes, 1990) have argued for replacing the psychodynamically derived concepts of defense with explanations based on contemporary social psychology. For example, projection in this argument can be more parsimoniously accounted for on the basis of attribution. In particular, in attempting to develop theories of irrational hatred, prejudice, discrimination, oppression, and other negative social phenomena, social psychologists increasingly invoke affective and cognitive processes that overlap, even if they do not coextend, with defense mechanisms as these terms are defined and understood by personality investigators and clinicians. On the basis of a long career as an investigator of defense mechanisms, Kline (2002) noted that, although the Freudian unconscious remains controversial and contentious, "What is not contentious, however, is the importance of these defense mechanisms in understanding human behavior and motives. For example, all studies of racism that ignore the defense of projection are likely to be doomed to failure. In this connection, the descriptions of despised races or outgroups are often remarkably similar, and in the case of Jews contradictory, suggesting their unconscious, nonrational basis" (p. 139-141).

Baumeister et al. (1998) reviewed a large number of studies by social psychologists who contributed observations and inferences on the operation of false consensus effect or projection, scapegoating or displacement, several self-protective tendencies in denial, and conversion of a socially or personally unacceptable impulse into its opposite in reaction formation It is remarkable that these findings have been obtained on the basis of the kinds of manipulations that are usually produced in social psychology experiments. Thus, no traumatic event nor major lifetime stress was required to produce these apparently defensive effects. The procedure and results of these studies shed little light on individual differences in producing the experimental effects nor do they provide information on the generality of these defensive operations across situation and time. Given the lack of consensus in defining defense mechanisms (Vaillant, 1998), the question remains whether the defense mechanisms observed in the social psychology laboratory are identical or only similar to the self-protective operations presented by individuals in psychotherapy, under real-life stress conditions, or in autobiographical accounts. To this end, incorporation of personality differences and/or degrees or diagnoses of psychological disorder, or lack thereof, would be a welcome next step in investigating defense mechanisms in the social arena.

Development of Defense Mechanisms: Results and Their Implications

Changes in the use and nature of defense mechanisms through childhood and beyond it have been systematically studied by Cramer (1991). Her research was focused on the defense mechanisms of denial, projection, and identification, which she studied by means of TAT stimuli scored according to a specially constructed manual. Validity and reliability of the scoring procedure were ascertained. In a series of studies of children differing in age, Cramer was able to substantiate her theoretically based expectations on the different developmental course of the three defenses. Denial, construed as a developmentally early defense, reached an early peak. Projection rose to its highest level in late childhood and preadolescence, and declined thereafter. The developmental progression for identification exhibited a progressive ascent all the way to late adolescence.

In part, these results corroborate the findings by Smith and Danielsson (1982) in Sweden, who studied defenses in children of various ages by percept-genetic methods. Denial was predominant in young children while projection peaked twice: first at approximately the age of five and then at puberty. Cramer's findings also converge with those of an earlier study by Dias (1976) in Switzerland, which also relied upon the TAT. Dias studied adolescents in a residential setting with a history of juvenile delinquency who were compared with their normal peers. Nondelinquent adolescents scored high in sublimation, introjection, and intellectualization. By contrast, prominent defenses in the delinquent group included denial, repression, and regression. The only mechanism that was used roughly to the same degree was projection. Even here, however, subtle differences were apparent. Normal respondents combined projection with temporal or spatial distancing while delinquent respondents evidenced loss of distance between the subject and the object.

Cramer and Brilliant (2001) discovered that the use of defense can be relatively easily modified by the understanding of its nature. They explicitly manipulated children's understanding of stories in which the use of defenses was featured. Understanding of the defense was in part mediated by age, but even the 7 to 8 year old children who understood denial were less likely to use that defense. At this point, it is not clear whether these findings generalize across tests, situations, and time.

Developmental trends have implications for the maturity and appropriateness of defenses beyond childhood. Early developmental defenses become maladaptive and ineffective when they are used later in life. Thus, denial is widely considered to be an immature and therefore primitive defense that copes poorly with the threats and stresses of adult living. However, this generalization is open to question. The widespread use of denial in serious illness has already been mentioned. It is probably indispensable and is likely to have adaptive value, at least temporarily, until the patient has been able to come to grips with the reality of his or her sickness. Similarly, Janoff-Bulman (1992) suggested that denial may buy the person time after a traumatic event, especially if its aftermath involves forced passivity. A sequence is envisaged from a blanket denial of the traumatic experience through accepting its reality, often in a piecemeal manner, while gradually coming to terms with the reality involved. It would therefore be a simplification to label a defense mechanism immature in a blanket fashion. Its appropriateness is primarily determined by its consequences. Has the defense worked for this person at a specific time or, more concretely, what effects has it produced? These are the questions that a clinician would seek to answer at a specific point in time, and the complexity of all the interacting relevant factors is notoriously difficult to incorporate into a research design.

Unfinished Tasks, Unanswered Questions

Recent Progress

The last two decades of the twentieth century have witnessed a great spurt in the acquisition of new knowledge about defense mechanisms. A whole array of standardized scales and other methods of inquiry has been developed and extensively applied. Chapter 1 provides an introduction to these various approaches. Moreover, several recent reviews are now available (Davidson & McGregor, 1998; Perry & Ianni, 1998; Smith, 2001). They document the range of choices that are now open to investigators of defense mechanisms. At the same time, a substantial body of information has accumulated on the manifestations of defenses, virtually through the life span. Their relationship to the adaptive and maladaptive aspects of functioning is by now a lot better appreciated, and the concept of defense has been considerably expanded. Discrete defenses have been grouped into meaningful categories. As a result, there is a lot more understanding of what a defense is and what it is not. Perhaps as a result of all of these developments, a listing of defense mechanisms is now featured in the current diagnostic manual, the DSM-IV. Meanwhile, the relevance of defense mechanisms has been recognized well beyond its traditional focus of convenience in psychopathology and personality. Social, developmental, and other psychologists are actively involved in research on defense mechanisms. The implications of defenses for adaptive functioning and indeed for creativity and innovation are a lot better understood than they were only a couple of decades ago. Defense mechanisms at this time are a vital and vibrant topic of inquiry, investigation, and implementation

Still, a host of questions remain answered, and with every new advance new points come up for future inquiry and exploration. In the remainder of this chapter, an attempt will be made to articulate these questions and to suggest avenues for seeking answers to them.

Methodology: Current Trends and Future Needs

Observing Defenses in Psychoanalysis. The term defense was coined by Freud (1894/1964; 1896/1964) on the basis of clinical observations of his analysands. At the time, he had nothing to go by but his observational acumen, inferential daring, and metaphorical talent. As a result, systematic investigation of defense mechanisms proceeded largely outside the psychoanalytic setting. Over a century later, opportunity is at hand for pursuing the task Freud had begun, in the context in which he made his seminal observations, but with the tools of modern technology at the current researcher's command. Over twenty five years ago, Liberman and Maldavsky (1975) in Buenos Aires developed a system for computerized "reading" of psychoanalytic transcripts. By means of the David Liberman Algorhythm (ADL) they were able to score automatically and objectively any psychoanalytic or other text and to investigate the relationship between of variables of their choice, provided they were based on the psychoanalytic record. Among other variables, Maldavsky and his coworkers (Maldavsky, 2003; Maldavsky, Cusien, Roitman, & Stanley de Tate, 2003) have initiated systematic study of defenses that can be related to any other information gleaned from the psychoanalytic record. The results of this effort are only now beginning to become apparent, and it is not yet known what ADL's limits are. Potentially, this development is a breakthrough, enabling researchers to study the interplay of defenses with other factors in psychoanalysis as it occurs. The tremendous complexity and probable cost of this system are concrete obstacles to be overcome before it can be effectively and innovatively utilized by interested psychoanalytic and other researchers.

ADL, however, is not the only approach for objectifying psychoanalysis and making it amenable to systematic study. Ehlers in this volume presents the account of several approaches that he has evolved for the quantitative study of the psychoanalytic process. As Ehlers demonstrated, these innovative methods can be applied in conjunction with the more conventional group-based research designs. Thus, conventional statistical analysis can be supplemented by objective within-individual information, and developments within psychoanalysis can be referred to the data on groups and populations.

Interrelating Measures of Defense. The advances in development, validation, and application of new and diverse measures of defenses have already been mentioned. However, their very multiplicity harbors a problem. Research runs the risk of being fragmented, and divergence of findings may make them incomparable and eventually uninterpretable within a broader frame of reference. The need at this point is not so much for new and better measures as it is for building bridges between findings already obtained, lest research become impossible to explain or interpret. Vaillant (1998) admonished: "In the future nobody should report a new test for defenses without providing its convergent validity with existing measures. Nobody should propose a terminology for defenses without reference to competing terminologies. Lastly, reliability must be continually striven for, even as the investigator reminds herself that validity is still more important" (pp. 1155).

Furthermore, factor analyses have usually been conducted on a specific test or on a small number of tests of the same format. What is needed is a set of more inclusive factor analyses in which observer ratings, self-report measures, percept-genetic procedures, and projective tests are included. It is highly unlikely that only test-specific factors will emerge. If they do, it will signify that for several decades psychologists have been studying unrelated constructs masquerading under the same name.

Psychophysiological Indicators, Not so long ago, reactions of participants in research on defensive operations were observed and recorded exclusively on the verbal and behavioral planes. As the final chapter in this book attests, the taboo against psychophysiological recording – if that is what it was – has been broken. Not only that, but a coherent and meaningful accumulation of data has come into being, which supplements in important ways the information hitherto available on the experience of defense mechanisms.

Methodological Flexibility and Pluralism. Alternation and combination of different tools and methods of investigation is a virtual imperative on a topic as multifaceted as that of defense mechanisms. De Waele (1961) and Vasiliuk (1984) independently suggested that naturalistic and clinical observation should go hand in hand with experimental manipulation. Vaillant's (1971, 1977. 1992,

1993) project, unique both in its continuity and in its methodological flexibility, provides a model for emulation. On a much smaller scale, it is always possible to incorporate collection of relevant biographical information into the pilot phases of even a tightly designed investigation. Interviewing and debriefing respondents on their cognitive and affective reactions may serve as a springboard for further exploration.

Studying the Process of Defense Emergence. The manifestations of defense mechanisms have usually been studied at a point in time or at a frozen moment. Percept-genetic researchers have made a major advance by initiating the study of the perceptual process during which threat elicits defense-like reactions (cf. Smith, 2001). The challenge is to open the entire sequence of threat, anxiety, defense, and its aftermath to empirical scrutiny. As yet, most of this progression remains hidden from view, even in percept-genetic experiments. How do we know that anxiety has, in fact, been experienced? What evidence do we have about the actual impact of supposedly anxiety arousing stimuli on a specific person? How does the person's reaction differ in a successful *versus* unsuccessful defense? The panoply of physiological indicators as well as some psychological ones can be considered for this purpose. Important technical problems, such as intrusiveness, distraction, and interruption of continuity of experience would need to resolved, and the objective of studying everything about the entire process of defense emergence is probably at this point unrealizable. However, small, sequential steps can be taken toward this ambitious, and perhaps grandiose, goal.

Breaking Down National Barriers. Finally, the divide between European and American research traditions has not yet been bridged. Percept-genetic investigation thrives in Europe, but is rarely undertaken in North America. More important, there is little evidence, that American researchers are informed or influenced by this yield of continuous research that has been pursued for more than fifty years. The study of defenses in somatic disorders appears to be a more prominent area of research in Germany and Switzerland than it is in North America. In a praiseworthy fashion, Perry and Ianni (1998) included percept-genetic procedures in their review of observer-rated measures of defense mechanisms. At the same time, the relatively new area of social psychology research on defense mechanisms is at this time concentrated in North America. It is urgent that the national isolation of researchers be broken, and the sooner the better.

Unfinished Tasks, New Topics

What remains to be done? From a multitude of possible tasks, here are three urgently needed topics.

From Explanation to Prediction. Although much progress has been made, the transition of defense mechanism from an explanatory concept to a predictive construct remains incomplete. Two objectives can be envisaged. On the basis of antecedent variables, it should be possible to predict the emergence of specific defense mechanisms under conditions of threat, conflict, and stress. Several approaches to this end have been initiated. The LSI, as described in Chapter 17 by Conte, Plutchik, and Draguns, makes such predictions possible. Percept-genetic researchers have used the Defense Mechanism Test and related techniques for predicting the emergence of specific defenses under stress (e.g., Torjussen & Vaernes, 1991; Vaernes, 1982) and in response to an experimentally provoked conflict (e.g., Westerlundh, 1976). These lines of research – and potentially many others- remain to be extended. Conversely, the appearance of a defense mechanism should be associated with predictable consequences in behavior. Do defense mechanisms in effect reduce anxiety? Are mature and complex defense mechanisms more effective in this respect than the less mature and more primitive ones? Empirically grounded answers to these questions are slowly emerging. Eventually, they may help place the activation of defense mechanisms within a functional sequence, which could be formulated on a theoretical basis. Pinpointing these links would involve taking seriously the basic Freudian view of defense mechanisms as intermediate points between the challenges of adaptation and responses to them

Linking Defenses to Personality Variables. When Freud introduced defense as a psychodynamic construct, personality psychology did not exist as a theory or as a research topic. In light of the developments in the course of the ensuing century, the question arises whether the use of various types of defenses is associated with the empirically and theoretically grounded dimensions of personality. Weinberger (1998) has proposed a typology based on self-restraint and high/low distress in which defense mechanisms are assigned a role. High self restraint is expected to be characterized by repression and intellectualization and low self-restraint by denial, acting out, and externalization. At the level of moderate restraint, the mature defenses of suppression, humor and sublimation are expected to be dominant. Without explicit, theoretically derived predictions, but on the basis of general plausibility, it would be worthwhile to explore the relationship between the Big Five personality dimensions (McCrea & Costa, 1993) and defenses as well as with other intensively investigated personality constructs.

Defenses and Culture. The last task that remains to be tackled pertains to the social context in which defense mechanisms are formed, applied, and modified. The enterprise of adaptation is inherently social and so are the challenges in which defense mechanisms are developed, as Bowlby (1979) has persuasively reminded us. As yet, information is sparse on the cultural variation or invariance of defense mechanisms, both in the multicultural milieus in North America and elsewhere, and across the various cultures of the world. Vaillant (1993) found negligible ethnic differences in his sample of Core City men, but this is only one finding at one point in time. Moreover, it is more likely that cultural differences will emerge in defense style rather than in defense maturity.

So far only fragmentary data are available. On the basis of his clinical experience in several African countries, Peltzer (1995) reported that identification, projection, denial, somatization, and dissociation were prominent among the patients in African mental health facilities. By contrast, isolation, reaction formation, undoing, and displacement were less frequently seen. In Europe, Blum (1956, 1964) found a few crossnational differences in defense mechanisms in students' responses to the Blacky Picture Test. The five factorial dimensions that have emerged from Hofstede's (2001) worldwide multicultural comparison may be used as a point of departure in exploring, of necessity on a much smaller scale, any association of defense variables with individualism-collectivism, power distance, uncertainty avoidance, masculinity-femininity, and short-range vs. long range time orientation.

References

Akkerman, K., Carr,V., & Lewin, R. (1992). Changes in ego defenses with recovery from depression. *Journal of Nervous and Mental Disease, 180,* 634-638.

Albacher, R. C., Abelson, J. L., & Nesse, R. M. (1998). Defense mechanism changes in successfully treated patients with obsessive-compulsive disorder. *American Journal of Psychiatry, 155,* 558-559.

American Psychiatric Association (1994). *Diagnostic and statistical manual of mental disorders* (4th ed.), Washington, DC: Author.

Baumeister, R. F., Dale, K., & Sommer, K. L. (1998). Freudian defense mechanisms and empirical findings in modern social psychology: Reaction formation, projection, displacement, undoing, isolation, sublimation, and denial. *Journal of Personality,66,* 1081-1124.

Beutel., M. (1988). *Bewältigungsprozesse bei chronischen Erkrankungen* (Coping processes in chronic illness): Munich: VCH.

Blum, G.S. (1956). Defense preferences in four countries. *Journal of Projective Techniques, 26,* 1-29.

Blum, G.S. (1964). Defense preferences among university students in Denmark, France, Germany, and Israel. *Journal of Projective Techniques and Personality Assessment, 28,* 13-19.

Bowlby, J. (1979). On knowing what you are not supposed to know and feeling what you are not supposed to feel. *Canadian Journal of Psychiatry, 24,* 403-408.

Briere, J. & Conte, J. (1993). Self-reported amnesia for abuse in adults molested as children. *Journal of Traumatic Stress, 6.* 21-31.

Clark. A. Jr. (1998). *Defense mechanisms in the counseling process.* Thousand Oaks, CA: Sage Publishers.

Cooper, S.H. (1998). Changing notions of defense within psychoanalytic theory. *Journal of Personality, 66,* 947-964.

Cramer, P. (1991). *The development of defense mechanisms: Theory, research and assessment.* New York: Springer-Verlag.

Cramer, P. (1995). Identity, narcissism, and defense mechanisms in late adolescence. *Journal of Research in Personality, 29,* 341-361..

Cramer, P. (1998). Threat to gender representation: Identity and identification. *Journal of Personality, 66, 895-918.*

Cramer, P. (1999). Ego functions and ego development: Defense mechanisms as predictors and intelligence as predictors of ego level. *Journal of Personality, 67,* 735-760.

Cramer, P. (2000). Defense mechanisms in psychology today. *American Psychologist,* 55, 637-646.

Cramer, P. (2002). Defense mechanisms, behavior, and affect, in young adulthood. *Journal of Personality, 7O,* 103-125.

Cramer, P. & Blatt, S.J. (1993). Change in defense mechanisms following intensive treatment, as related to personality organization and gender. In U. Hentschel, G. J. W. Smith, W. Ehlers, & J.G. Draguns (Eds.). *The concept of defense mechanisms in contemporary psychology* (pp. 310-320). New York: Springer-Verlag.

Cramer, P., Blatt, S.J., & Ford, R.Q. (1988). Defense mechanisms in the anaclictic and introjective personality configurations. *Journal of Consulting and Clinical Psychology, 56,* 610-616.

Cramer, P. & Brilliant, M. A. (2001). Defense use and defense understanding in children. *Journal of Personality, 69,* 297-312.

Cramer, P. & Gaul, R. (1988). The effects of success and failure on children's use of defense mechanisms. *Journal of Personality,56,* 729-742.

Davidson, K. & McGregor, M.W. (1998). A critical appraisal of self-report defense mechanism measures. *Journal of Personality, 66,* 965-992.

De Waele, J.P. (1961). Zur Frage der empirischen Bestätigung psychoanalytischer Grundannahmen. (On the problem of empirical confirmation of fundamental psychoanalytic tenets). *Zeitschrift für Psychologie, 165,* 900-134.

Dias, B. (1976). *Les mecanismes de défense dans la genese des normes de conduite. Etude experimentale basée sur le TAT* (Measurement of defense in the course of development of norms of conduct. An experimental study based on the TAT). Fribourg, Switzerland: Editions Universitaires.

Drews, S. & Brecht, K. (1975). *Psychoanalytische Ich-Psychologie* (Psychoanalytic ego Psychology). Frankfurt: Suhrkamp.

Erdelyi, M.H, (1985). *Psychoanalysis: Freud's cognitive psychology.* New York: Freeman.

Fenichel, O. (1945). *The psychoanalytic theory of neurosis.* New York: Norton.

Freud. A. (1946). *The ego and the mechanisms of defense.* New York: International Universities Press.

Freud, S. (1894/1964). The neuro-psychoses of defense *The complete psychological works of Sigmund Freud. Volume 3* (pp. 45-61). London: Hogarth Press.

Freud, S. (1896/1964).Further remarks on the neuro-psychoses of defense. *The complete psychological works of Sigmund Freud. Volume 3* (pp.161-185). London: Hogarth Press.

Fulde, R., Junge, A., & Ahrens, S. (1995). Coping strategies and defense mechanisms and their relevance for the recovery after discectomy. *Journal of Psychosomatic Research, 39, 819-826.*

Grzeglowska-Klarkowska, H. & Zolnierczyk, D, (1988). Defense of self-esteem, defense of self-consistency: A voice in an old controversy. *Journal o Social and Clinical Psychology, 6,* 171-179.

Grzeglowska-Klarkowska, H. & Zolniercczyk, D. (1990). Predictors of defense mechanisms under conditions of threat to the objective self: Empirical testing of a theoretical model. *Polish Psychological Bulletin, 21,* 129-155

Hofstede, G. (2001). *Culture's consequences: Comparing values, institutions and organizations across nations* (2nd ed.). Thousand Oaks, CA: Sage.

Hoglend, P. & Perry, J.C. (1998). Defensive functioning predicts improvement in major depressive episodes. *Journal of Nervous and Mental Disease, 186,* 238-243.

Holmes, D.S. (1974). Investigations of repression: Differential recall of material experimentally or naturally associated with ego-threat. *Psychological Bulletin, 81,* 632-653.

Holmes, D.S. (1978). Projection as a defense mechanism. *Psychological Bulletin, 85,* 677-688.

Holmes, D.S. (1990). The evidence for repression: An examination of sixty years of research. In J.L. Singer (Ed.), *Repression and dissociation: Implications for Personality theory, psychopathology, and health* (pp. 85-103). Chicago: University of Chicago Press.

Holmes, D.S. (1997). *Abnormal psychology* (3rd ed.). New York: Longman.

Horowitz, M.J. (1986). *Stress response syndromes.* (2nd ed.). New York: Aronson.

Janoff-Bullman, R. (1992). *Shattered assumptions: Toward a new psychology of trauma* New York: Free Press.

Karon, B. P. & Widener, A. J. (1997). Repressed memories and World War II: Lest we forget. *Professional Psychology: Research and Practice, 28,* 338-340.

Katz, J.L., Weiner, H. Gallagher, T,F., & Hellman, L (1970). Stress, distress, and ego defenses. *Archives of General Psychiatry, 23,* 131-142.

Kline, P.(2002). Defense mechanisms. In E. Erwin (Ed.), *The Freud encyclopedia: Theory, therapy, and culture* (pp. 139-141). New York: Routledge.

Lewis, H.B. (1990). Shame, repression, field dependence, and psychopathology. In J.L. Singer (Ed.), *Repression and dissociation: Implications for personality theory, psychopathology, ands health* (pp. 233-257). Chicago: University of Chicago Press.

Liberman, D., & Maldavsky, D. (1975) Psicoanalisis y semiotica [Psychoanalysis and semiotics]. Buenos Aires: Paidos.

Loftus, E. (1993). The reality of repressed memories. *American Psychologist, 48,* 518-537.

Loftus, E. (2003). Make-believe memories. Invited Address, American Psychological Association, August 2003.

Madison, P. (1961). *Freud's concept of repression and defense: Its theoretical and observational language.* Minneapolis: University of Minnesota Press

Maldavsky, D., & Cusien, I. L., (2003). Actualizacion del ADL: Instrumentos, congiabilidad y validez. (Bringing the ADL up to date: Instruments, reliability, validity). Buenos Aires: Universidad de Ciencias Sociales y Empresariales.

Maldawsky, D., Cusien, I. L., Roitman, C. R. & Stanley de Tate, C. (2003). Defenses in schizophrenics and in artists. Paper at the Society for Psychotherapy Research, Weimar, Germany.

Matte Blanco, I, (1955). *Estudios de psicologia dinamica.* (Studies of dynamic psychology). Santiago de Chile: Ediciones de la Universidad de Chile.
McCrea, R. R. & Costa, P. T., Jr. (1997). Personality trait structure as a human universal. *American Psychologist, 52,* 509-516.
Paulhus, D. L., Fridlander, B., & Hayes, S. (1997). Psychological defense: Contemporary theory and research. In R. Hogan, J. Johnson, & S. Briggs (Eds.), *Handbook of personality* (pp. 544-580). New York: Guilford Press.
Paulhus, D. L, & Suedfeld, P. (1988). Self-deception: A dynamic complexity model. In J.S. Lockard & D.L. Paulhus (Eds.). *Self-deception: An adaptive mechanism?* New York: Prentice-Hall.
Peltzer, K. (1995). *Psychology and health in African cultures. Examples of ethnopsychotherapeutic practice.* Frankfurt: IKO-Verlag.
Perry, J. C. & Ianni, F. F. (1998). Observer-rated measures of defense mechanisms. *Journal of Personality, 66,* 993-1024.
Sandstrom, M. J. & Cramer, P. (2003). Girls' use of defense mechanisms following peer rejection. *Journal of Personality, 71, 605*-627.
Sjöbäck, H. (1973). *The psychoanalytic theory of defensive processes.* Lund: Gleerups.
Smith, G. J. W. (2001). *The process approach to personality.* New York: Kluwer.
Smith, G. J. W., & Danielssson, A. (1982). *Anxiety and defensive strategies in childhood and adolescence.* New York: International Universities Press.
Terr, L. (1994). *Unchained memories.* New York: Basic Booms.
Terjussen, T. & Vaerness, R. (1991). The use of the Defence Mechanism Test in Norway for selection and stress research. In M. Olff, G. Godaert, & H. Ursin (Eds.), *Quantification of human defense mechanisms* (pp. 172-206). Berlin: Springer-Verlag.
Vaernes, R. J. (1982). The Defence Mechanism Test predicts inadequate performance under stress. *Scandinavian Journal of Psychology, 23,* 37-43.
Vaillant, G. E. (1971). Theoretical hierarchy of adaptive ego mechanisms. *Archives of General Psychiatry, 24,* 107-118.
Vaillant, G. E. (1977). *Adaptation to life.* Boston: Little, Brown.
Vaillant, G. E. (1992). *Ego mechanisms of defense.* Washington, Washington, DC: American Psychiatric Press.
Vaillant, G. E. (1993). *The wisdom of the ego.* Cambridge, MA: Harvard University Press.
Vaillant, G. E. (1994). Ego mechanisms of defense and personality psychopathology. *Journal of Abnormal Psychology, 103,* 44-50.
Vaillant, G. E. (1998). Where do we go from here? *Journal of Personality, 66,* 1147-1156.

Vaillant, G. E. & Vaillant, C. O. (1992). Empirical evidence that defensive styles are independent of environmental influence. In G.E. Vaillant (Ed.), *Ego mechanisms of defense.* (pp. 105-126). Washington, DC: American Psychiatric Press.

Vasiliuk, F. K. (1984). *Psikhologiya perezhivaniya* (Psychology of experience). Moscow: Izdatel'stvo Moskovskogo Universiteta.

Weinberger, D. A. (1998). Defenses, personality, structure and development: Integrating psychodynamic theory into a typological approach to personality. *Journal of Personality, 66,* 1061-1079.

Westerlundh, B. (1976). *Aggression, anxiety, and defense.* Lund: Gleerup.

Westerlundh, B. (1983). The motives of defense: Percept-genetic studies: I Shame. *Psychological Research Bulletin, Lund University,23,* (7), 1-13.

Yapko, M. (1997). The troublesome unknowns about trauma and recovered memories. In M. Conway (Ed.), *Recovered memories and false memories* (pp. 23-33) New York: Oxford University Press.

Defense Mechanisms
U. Hentschel, G. Smith, J.G. Draguns & W. Ehlers (Editors)

Chapter 4

What is a Mechanism of Defense?

Hans Sjöbäck

We are all agreed on this point: the theory of defense is a cornerstone of psychodynamic thinking. The analytical literature on various aspects of this theory is vast. Yet, there are few surveys of the theory as a whole (cf. Sjöbäck, 1973), and we find conspicuous confusion and salient dissent in the discussion of even its basic assumptions. Here are three instances of confusion and/or dissent.

1. Should the mechanisms of defense be described as "always pathogenic" (Freud's view, cf. Freud, 1937/1971, pp. 236-244), or perhaps labeled "pathologic" (cf. Sperling, 1958), or ought we to describe them as sometimes pathogenic, sometimes pathologic, and sometimes "normal" or adaptive, depending on the circumstances? (cf. A. Freud, 1970, pp. 177 -178; Hartmann, 1958; Loewenstein, 1967). The discussion of this question reveals a confusion as regards both the immediate and the longterm consequences of countercathectic defensive processes, a confusion that contrasts with the fairly clear conceptions of their causal chains, and also with the assumptions of the characteristics of the basic defensive processes.
2. There is also confusion and disagreement as regards the definition of the various mechanisms of defense, their specific characteristics, their delimitation from each other, etc. The proper definition of denial has troubled many analysts (cf. Dorpat, 1985; Jacobson, 1957; Moore & Rubinfine, 1969; Sjöbäck, 1973, pp 209-238). Today the definitions of splitting and projective identification seem to share the same fate (splitting: see Blum, 1983; Dorpat, 1979; Lustman, 1977; Pruyser, 1975, etc.; projective identification, see: Grotstein, 1981; Ogden, 1979; Sandler, 1988).
3. A third bone of contention, finally, is quite simply the question of the ontological status of the mechanisms of defense and the defensive processes. What type of entity is a defensive process? What kind of reality ought we to assign to it? (The unclarity reigning here is of course but one facet of the basic uncertainty about the nature of psychoanalytic theory, its concepts, and assumptions, from the point of view of the theory of science, and epistemology in general.)

One deplorable aspect of the analytical discussion of the nature of defense is actually a lack of clarity on a most basic point: a lack of delimitation between, on the one hand, the observed behaviors and reported experiences we wish to explain, and, on the other hand, the concepts and assumptions we use to transform the "explananda" (those behaviors, those experiences) we felt were insufficiently or inadequately explained by extant theories, into the empirical referents of the theory of defense. The basic rules of science teach us to proceed in this way: in the bewildering multitude of unexplained and unclassified phenomena, we single out some that we inspite, sometimes, of their superficial disparity- explain in terms of identical or similar causal chains, postulated common process characteristics, and identical consequences. In this way we single out and delimit a class of phenomena from the mass of phenomena, and delimit and explain this class in terms of "common fate". Doing this, we obey the principle of explanatory parsimony: we use as few concepts and assumptions as possible to construe the causal chain, and its variations. Regarding these variations, we attempt to create definitions of as few basic types as possible, in the interest of clarity, and, above all, of facility of survey.

If we do not observe this basic precept, of distinguishing between explanatory terms and their explananda, the result is a perturbing confusion because one important aim of explanatory endeavors (i.e., theory making) gets lost, namely: that of subsuming a great and (as to varying observable characteristics) bewildering number of phenomena under a few classifying definitions. In the analytical discussion of these matters, the terminology unfortunately invites this confusion, since the term "defense" is often used to refer both to explananda (empirical referents) and to explanatory constructs. The result will be that we get lost in an unmanageable, endless list of "defenses" (because practically all types of experience and behavior may, according to the basic assumptions of the theory of defense, have defensive aspects, certain conditions prevailing). A notorious illustration of this confusion is the list of "defenses" offered by Bibring, Dwyer, Huntington, and Valenstein (1961). Some theorists have attempted to counteract this muddled thinking by insisting (a) on the basic distinction between empirical referent and explanatory entity, and (b) on the nature of the entity referred to by the explanatory term: it is a discretionary explanatory construct, and nothing else. Gill (1963, p. 96) is a pioneer here, it seems: "To say that defense itself is unconscious cannot mean that the defense *mechanism* is unconscious, since a defense mechanism is a theoretical abstraction of a way of working of the mind which of course cannot become conscious." (Gill's italics) (Cf. Sjöbäck, 1973, pp. 29-33.)

A theorist who insistently has stressed these important points is Wallerstein (1967, 1983, and 1985). The core of his position seems to be as follows:

1. We must strictly observe the distinction between explananda, the empirical referents, on the one hand, and the propositions of the theory of defense, creating our explanatory constructs, on the other.
2. Explanatory constructs are not to be placed, ontologically, on a par with mental contents and events; rather, they are assumed to be discretionary patterns of contents ("structures," "defense mechanisms") or events ("processes," "defensive processes") created by the theorist to order and explain phenomena ("mental contents and events"). Thus, defense mechanisms and defensive processes are neither "conscious" nor "unconscious"; their ontological status as constructs, discretionary creations of the theorist, of course precludes the application of these terms to them.

This point of view is commendable and unobjectionable from the standpoint of the theory of science. It implies that the theorist creates hypothetical constructs as, above all, discretionary patterns of events, (a) to create primary regular sequences of events, "basic linear causal chains," (b) to construe patterns of complex interactions of mental contents and their ensuing transformations during and in the wake of the postulated interaction, the "mental process" as such, (c) to classify the events under scrutiny (the empirical referents) and separate them from other classes of events explainable by means of other hypothetical constructs, and (d) to create constructs describing subclasses of the basic process, thereby classifying the total class of empirical referents in subgroups (the empirical referents of the different mechanisms or processes). This position also has the advantage, not to say the unconditional precondition of good theory making, of directing, incessantly, the attention of the theorist to his aim, his sole task: of explaining observable, puzzling phenomena in as parsimonious a way as possible, and directing him away from the temptation to forget this in favor of theory making, as it were, for its own sake. These assumptions and observations are self-evident to every psychologist who has acquired a rudimentary understanding of the conditions of theory making, and the dangers of not taking them into account - dangers that become patent when we attempt to use theories whose construction has implied a neglect of these requisites. Yet, Wallerstein's views have, strangely enough, not gone uncontested in the recent analytical discussion.

The main aim of Gillett's article "Defense mechanisms versus defense contents" seems to be to question Wallerstein's view of the ontological status of defense mechanisms (defensive processes) and to propose another position which he deems better (Gillett, 1987). However, Gillett devotes a fair portion of his work to a discussion of the basic characteristics of the defensive processes their main causes, their functional characteristics, and their consequences. I shall scrutinize neither these deliberations nor Gillett's terminology but concentrate on his main target: the ontological status of defense mechanisms and defensive processes. Gillett offers a somewhat confused discussion of the question of the nature of abstractions used in theoretical discourse in general. Then he proceeds to acknowledge the fundamental distinction between what he calls "defensive contents" (the empirical referents) and the "defense mechanisms" (the explanatory entities). As to the basic characteristics of these entities, he says that they cannot be regarded to be just hypothetical constructs - they must be assumed to exist in some way. I guess that Gillett means they exist in the sense that the theorist's task is to observe or/and describe them in some way or another, not construe them. The main point of reasoning seems to be this: the observable behavior (reported experience) we label "defensive" must have causes. These causes must then be defense mechanisms.

It is clear that theoretical terms and concepts, if they exist at all, clearly exist in a form different from the working of the mind they refer to. However, it is hard for me to see how Wallerstein's definition of a defense mechanism is compatible with the usual way the term is used in the psychoanalytic literature. The activity of the defense mechanisms is triggered by signal anxiety and has effects on observable behavior. How is this possible if defense mechanisms don't exist? How is this possible if they are concepts or terms in a theoretical statement? It seems to me more plausible to regard defense mechanisms as part of the "working of the mind" rather than *denoting* a way of functioning of the mind. (Gillett, *1987, p 266;* Gillett's Italics) At other places in his article Gillett discusses the concept of causal chain, and the possible nature of causal chains, and it is obvious that the basic problem, as he sees it, is to construe (or to "find") the causal chain behind "defensive contents". "What I wish to stress is that there is no justification for claiming dogmatically that defense mechanisms do not exist, and on a commonsense level it is hard to see how they can have behavioral effects if they don't exist." (Gillett, *1987, p. 267).*

Now, first, as to Gillett's answer to the question of the links of the causal chain, that defense mechanisms ought to be regarded as some sort of "workings of the human mind," this conception unfortunately will involve him in innumerable difficulties. He evades them by not defining what he means by a "working of the human mind," but it appears that he thinks there are some "functions" or "processes" that exist as sorts of mental entities in their own right and in some way or other interact with "mental contents". Wallerstein has pointed out some of the difficulties this kind of conception will lead to (Wallerstein, *1985, pp. 208-211). 1* shall not discuss the further difficulties encountered by all conceptions of this kind, the most well known being that of "form" or "structure" as a type of empty entity filled by "contents", but instead first concentrate on the question by which Gillett starts, about the nature the causal chain behind experience and behavior said to he "defensive". Gillett repeats again and again, as if perplexed: What does cause them?

First we must do away with a confusion rampant in this context. Let us define mental content (conscious) as some experienced mental entity, which is described as static, a snapshot from the stream of conscious experience. Then a mental event (conscious) is a portion of the stream of conscious experience (stream of contents) that goes on uninterruptedly during our waking hours. The basic characteristic of a mental event is a change in the qualities of a mental content or some mental contents. Conscious mental contents and conscious mental events are the target of most psychological research, but, as we know, Freud said that these contents and events often appear to be (a) inexplicable, and (b) fragmented, disconnected, and to understand the confusing stream of conscious mental contents, we must postulate that many aspects of conscious mental events are caused by preconscious or unconscious contents or events. The ontological status of preconscious and unconscious mental contents and events is identical with that of conscious mental contents and events, but their epistemological status is different: they are postulated, but we postulate that they "exist" in the same way as conscious mental contents and events exist. (There are theorists, both inside and outside psychoanalysis, who would object here, saying that unconscious mental contents and events cannot be said to exist in the same way as conscious ones, but let us leave this objection so far.)

Before we proceed, another question must be touched on: the question of the two temporal categories, of "contents" versus "events." It is evident that psychologists in general, and also psychoanalysts, work with two classes of concepts, namely: content; structure/event; process. The first level, that of "contents and events," causes us no trouble, but the second level does. Defense mechanisms are mostly described as something in abeyance, a potentiality, a structured readiness to respond in a specific way. This readiness is released when some specific conditions arise. Then a defensive process takes place. Defense mechanisms are, from this point of view, sometimes also described as "structures of the mind" (I need not repeat here, e.g., Rapaport's (1960) discussion of the concept of structure), and again we encounter obscurities. Structure as a term is used, to denote, among other things, (a) a phenomenal pattern of contents (i.e., what we also call a gestalt), (b) a pattern of mental contents (conscious and/or unconscious, etc.) that is not an experiential entity, and (c) specifically, a motivational or functional entity that is activated under specific conditions; its specific quality, as structure, besides its organization, is resistance to change. These various definitions of structure have played roles in the discussion of "defense mechanisms" and confuse our issue, the issue of causality. A simple solution has two steps: (a) to regard the concept of defense mechanism as a dispositional concept, which entails that a defense mechanism in no type of theory can be regarded as a cause of anything but the defensive process whose potentiality it is, and (b) to avoid using the term "defense mechanism" except when we must have recourse to the dispositional concept, and on the whole, to avoid the "static" concepts. Thus, in the following, I shall use only "mental event" and "process"; this is quite enough for the pursuance of the discussion.

Now we return to Gillett and his Gretchenfrage about the causes of mental events. Insofar as we wish to point to the antecedent links of the causal chains of conscious mental events and the sometimes ensuing behavior, they of course consist of other mental events, and nothing else. The basic object of study is a stream of mental events, and nothing else. This stream has, according to analytical assumptions, conscious, preconscious, and unconscious sectors, and we study the latter two only indirectly. Here Gillett of course immediately ripostes: but this to me simplistic assumption of the nature of the causal chain does not explain why some mental events are assumed to be defensive! Quite so, but the point is of course that on this stream of mental events (portions of which we may observe, portions of which we postulate) we superimpose patterns of causal connections, above all patterns of more or less complex interactions of mental contents-during which these contents are transformed in various ways. It is like having a stream of dots on a paper, and superimposing on this stream another, translucent paper, with a proposal for a pattern of the dots. (This simple analogy cannot include the concept of interaction and transformation, unfortunately; it only illustrates a simple static concept of "pattern.") Such a pattern may make a more or less "good fit," but after all it is only an invention of the maker of the pattern. This conceptualization, which of course is nothing but a transcription in another (in my opinion, more manageable) temporal mode of the conceptions of Gill and Wallerstein, invites some further clarifying comments.

1. This conception implies that a great portion of the "sequences of regularity and interdependency" with which we operate in theoretical deliberations are created by theorists rather than "existing as phenomena." Gillett here takes

the opposite position. It seems to me reasonable that from all possible theories of the mind, some prove more useful in explaining and predicting the observable phenomena because they reflect sequences of regularities existing in the workings of the mind (Gillett, 1987, p. 267). Here, Gillett touches on some very difficult points of epistemology. How much order is inherent in the nature of things, and how much is a construct of the human theorist? More than two hundred years ago, David Hume attacked the position that we "experience" simple causal chains (those that refer to or are caused by, simple experiences of "before" and "after" in the world of material events) because they are "given" as "realities." Since the days of Hume, these problems have haunted philosophers and theorists of science; I shall not presume to pursue them; I only point out that Gillett's position seems to lead to a naive epistemological realism of the kind few philosophers (apart from convinced Marxists) would care to defend. In any event, even though we may provisionally postulate that simple causal chains (of the "before-after" type) in the world of things are real characteristics of the events of this world, the concept of complex causal interaction of mental contents (which are a trifle more elusive than billiard balls) is not thereby much clarified.

2. Gillett (1987, p. 267) attempts to bolster his assumption of the ontological status of the defensive process by referring to an analogy with nuclear and elementary particle physics: "Many physicists believe in the existence of atoms, electrons, and even quarks, which are all theoretical entities of physics, with the same logical status as defense mechanisms in psychoanalytic theory. Perhaps defense mechanisms and other theoretical entities of psychology refer to physical processes of the brain." Now, first, the term "physicists" is vague, but if it is used to refer to researchers within the field of elementary particle physics, Gillett's statement is lamentably uninformed. But here we have first to compare primarily the status of "atoms, electrons, and even quarks" and that of the constructs of analysts. That is, it is necessary, before we try to construe analogies, to analyze what kinds of entity the physicists in question operate with. First, we have assumptions of different kinds of "protomatter," such as electrons, protons, and neutrons. Then we have assumptions about their characteristics, of which mass and charge are basic (and then further, "charm," etc.). Then we have, based on the assumptions about the characteristics of particles, the hypotheses of interactions and their results. It is palpably clear that if we attempt to attain any reasonable analogy between psychology and elementary particle physics here, the assumptions of "protomatter" (something in some way analogous to "things" in the perceptible world), are analogous to assumptions of unconscious mental contents, and to nothing else. The assumptions of the characteristics

of elementary particles may be said to correspond to characteristics of mental contents, either in terms of protoexperience, such as "emotional charge," or in terms of a construct much more abstract, fetched from physics in a way, namely in terms of "cathexis," etc. As for the concept of defensive process, its only reasonable analogy is to "interaction of elementary particles, and their ensuing transformations."

3. With this question clarified, we might ask again, do many physicists really believe in the existence of elementary particles, as Gillett states? The term "physicist" delimits the class only in a vague way, but if we take it to refer to researchers within the field of elementary particle physics, Gillett is uninformed, to say the least. To be sure, in everyday talk, elementary particles are discussed as if really "existing" protomatter, but the researchers are of course well aware that even the particles, and the basic characteristics through which they are defined, are nothing but constructs. But, though constructs, are they thought to refer to some kind of reality? Here is one answer, and I think it represents a position that, for many reasons is unavoidable. In a recently published biography of Lord Rutherford, the author describes the physicist's attempts to build a model of the nucleus of the atom (consisting of positive and negative electrons). After describing Rutherford's endeavors, and his difficulties, the author concludes:

"But Rutherford was always honest and rarely, if ever, fudged an issue. He admitted here, for instance, that there was no evidence that negative electrons existed in any nucleus, but presumably they must be there for they were shot out as beta-rays in radioactive transformations which were certainly nuclear events. Here Rutherford shows that he was caught in a well-known philosophical trap: *it is not logically necessary that what comes out of something must have been inside it before it came out.* This fallacy was to lead Rutherford into a number of blind alleys in the years ahead, until the mathematics of quantum mechanics got him, and science in general, out of the impasse; and it remains true today that although electrons, as beta-rays, and helium nuclei, as alpha-rays emerge from the nucleus, we still have no evidence of their *independent existence as such within the nucleus."* (Wilson, 1983, p. 389. *Italics added.)*

These statements, which represent the views of sophisticated physicists of the "existence" of elementary particles, should warn us not to seek facile but deceiving analogies between psychology and physics. Let me add: if physicists one day were to be able, by means of refined "prostheses of the sense organs" to "look into" the interior of the atom (instead of being reduced to observing what comes out of the atoms when subjected to violent influence from without, as they are in today's experimental particle physics), something that appears impossible, for different reasons, but if it, although impossible, were to happen: this would not strengthen Gillett's position, for simultaneously the analogy would break down, there being no possibility of psychologists finding prostheses of the sensorium enabling them to "look deeper into the mind." Thus, sensible physicists know well that their models of what happens in the atoms are "models," discretionary constructs, to explain what is observable under certain conditions, namely scatters of elementary particles apparently expelled from the interior of the atoms and of which "pictures" can be caught. Physicists I have discussed the matter with stress that there is incessant competition among differing models, the criterion of a good model being the combination of "good fit" and parsimony. '

4. The foregoing quotation from Gillett ends with the suggestion that the theoretical entities of psychology refer to "physical processes in the brain." The comments on these cogitations of Gillett's need not be long: it is blatantly evident that Gillett confounds postulated ontological characteristics on the one hand, and levels of explanation, on the other (cf. Holt, 1975, esp. pp. 176 et seq., for an elementary exposition of this question).
5. Finally, what about the practical consequences of the two views ` discussed here, that of Gillett versus that of Gill, Wallerstein, and Sjöbäck? Gillett remarks, quite correctly (19$7, p. 261): "It has been shown historically in science that theoretical understanding can have very practical implications which are only apparent at a later time."

What are the very practical implications of the two positions competing here? Gill's position leads to a clear conception of the task of the theorist: it consists of construing a discretionary system of propositions designed to explain as parsimoniously and as free of contradictions as possible as large a portion of the explananda as possible. Gillett's position leads to a much more equivocal description of the theorist's task, as is quite clear from the history of psychoanalytic thinking. This theorist is of course also aware of the task of explaining some preliminarily delimited class of puzzling phenomena, but he evidently thinks that his task is also to spy into the dark, hidden reality of "the workings of the mind" (which comprises not only concrete mental contents and events, but also the "realities" of their interaction), and his attention is then split, vacillating between two directions, that of the empirical referents to be explained and the "hidden reality" to be discovered. As is well known, this stance which, unfortunately, is not rare among analysts, though seldom articulated with that frankness Gillett evinces-has led to dire results, that is, to a proliferation of concepts and assumptions that compete not on the basis of their explanatory range, their elegance, and parsimony, but on the basis of their alleged "truthfulness" as "descriptions" of a "hidden reality." Often enough, the empirical referents are almost neglected, or treated in a casual way, in discussions of assumptions of defense, because the author's interest is focused on the "exploration" of the "hidden reality." The quandary is of course that nobody is able to define this criterion of "truthfulness," since it is impossible to "demonstrate" (and no more possible to "prove") here, that is, to point to the "realities" as such or to point to empirical referents that logically and materially necessitate the existence of something not observable-or at least make the inference fairly compelling.

The muddle that we land in here is well illustrated by the contents of a recently published book, *Denial and Defense in the Therapeutic Situation* (Dorpat, 19$5). This work contains many astute observations and assumptions that appear to be highly useful as components of an encompassing theory of defense, but unfortunately the usefulness of the endeavor is marred by the position Dorpat takes on "the nature of defense" (and the nature of mental processes in general), which in essence corresponds to Gillett's: he assumes that the defensive processes are "realities," which he "describes." Within this framework Dorpat puts forward three basic propositions: (a) there is (exists) one basic defensive process; (b) this basic defensive process can be described in detail, at a microlevel of mental processes, as a process of "cognitive arrest"; and (c) this basic defensive process is denial. The reification to which Dorpat adheres prevents him from considering the following questions.

1. Would it in some instances, taking into account the characteristics of some groups of explananda, be useful -to postulate other basic defensive processes, or variants of the alleged basic process? This means, in other words: Does Dorpat's model of a defensive process "fit all instances" (of explananda), or does it not? In my opinion, his model cannot explain important aspects of some groups of explananda, for example, those connected with changes in reality feeling (cf. Freud, 193611971; Sarlin, 1962) and altered states of consciousness (cf. Dickes, 1965; Rohsco, 1967, etc.). From this point of view, Dorpat's picture of "the reality of the basic defensive process" appears to be a Procrustean bed for the explananda.
2. Throughout the history of psychoanalysis, from its inception in Freud's first analytical works until now, we find assumptions of a basic defensive process which, as is well known, Freud (and practically all analysts after him) called "repression." Dorpat now proposes that this basic process be called "denial." Why does he wish us to adopt this revision of analytical terminology, whose proposal alone causes confusion (not to speak of what would happen if it were adopted)? With regard to the basic differentiation of repression and de-

nial (which ought to form the basis for a decision as to what to call a presumed "basic defensive process"), Dorpat first states (1985, p. 94): "Writings on primal repression do not give clinical referents, and they do not state what is and what is not primal repression." Now, this is a somewhat astonishing statement at least from one point of view, that which refers to the connection of primal repression and fixation (no primal repression without fixation), but we proceed: Dorpat offers us a chapter on "primal repression and denial," and here he concludes (1985, pp. 104-105):

"I proposed that the clinical referents of these theories of the primordial defense are the same as the clinical referents of denial. The primitive defense that analysts have called primal repression is, in my opinion, the basic defense of denial. One argument for the equivalence of primal repression and denial is that they have the same consequences, namely: the primitive defense prevents the formation of verbal representations; the content of what is defended against is unrememberable, and when it is later repeated, it occurs in the form of enactive memory; and developmental defects are consequences of the defense.

New cases of primal repression are said to emerge in early childhood, in traumatic states, and in the psychoses and borderline conditions. Clinical evidence obtained from studies of young children, traumatic states, and the psychoses and borderline conditions indicates that denial, and not primal repression, is the basic defense on which developmentally later and higher-level defenses such as repression and reaction formation are developed."

Apart from the contradictions unveiled here, the main question is of course why-if there be a basic defensive process-this ought to be labeled denial. The term "denial" is connected with more confusion- and embarrassing contradictions than any other term in psychoanalytic thought (cf. Sjöbäck, 1973, pp. 209-238). Why choose it to designate the basic defensive process? Dorpat refers incessantly to "clinical referents" and "clinical evidence" which (a) are nonexistent as regards primal repression, (b) are the same for primal repression and for denial, and (c) demonstrate that denial, not primal repression, is the basic defense. When we search his text for these "clinical referents," we find only clinical vignettes from which no certain conclusions as to the specified characteristics of inferred or postulated defensive processes can be drawn. At no place in this work do we find enumeration and discussion of the differentiating clinical referents. This cavalier treatment of the question of the observations and the explananda the proposed theory should explain is explainable in only one way: Dorpat believes that there is an intrapsychic reality that he is able to describe; from this point of view, the empirical referents can be treated in a summary way. Only a deep commitment to reification of the sort Gillett recommends can cause a theorist to adopt a stance and a mode of processing like this.

What will be the consequences of such contributions as this on the development of analytical theorizing, here within the field of the theory of defense? Either Dorpat has demonstrated that his assumptions of the nature of the basic defense are "true" or so highly probable (as descriptions of "reality") that his colleagues (and all other psychologists interested in psychoanalysis) immediately are convinced, upon reading his work, or Dorpat has, in spite of his many valuable ideas, only added to the general confusion extant within the field of the theory of defense (and here especially within that portion of it associated with the term "denial"), because he can "convince" only a small number of friends, and other analysts who in advance happen to entertain ideas like his own, that he has created a "correct theory." Dorpat cannot demonstrate that his construct "exists"; this circumstance is so palpably evident that it demonstrates convincingly the untenability of Gillett's position. Instead of dividing their attention between the empirical referents and the attempt at spying into the "hidden dark reality" of mental events (and even "workings of the mind"), -with the dire consequences that this stance engenders analytical theorists ought to accept the much more reasonable position that assumptions about the workings of the mind are discretionary constructs and that such assumptions ought always to be developed in close contact with the explananda, and to be as elegant logically and as parsimonious as possible. At the same time, their range of application should encompass the whole field of explananda preliminarily delimited, and perhaps later extended in accordance with rules agreed upon.

This way of seeing theories and theory making may initially represent a threat to the self-esteem of analytical theorists who feel they are called upon and uniquely equipped to gaze down into the secret depths of the human mind-real depths. But in the long run the result of the rejection of reification will result in a much-improved psychoanalytic theory. This rejection will also bring to an end the ridicule that reification in theoretical matters calls forth in psychologists of all convictions outside psychoanalysis, a ridicule and a disdain that in an unfortunate way contribute to the isolation of psychoanalysts and their theories within the scientific community.

References

Bibring, G. L., Dwyer, T. F., Huntington, D. S., & Valenstein, A. F. (1961) A study of the psychological processes in pregnancy and of the earliest motherchild relationship. Appendix B. Glossary of defenses. *Psychoanalytic Study of the Child, 16,* 62-72.

Blum, H. P. (1983) Splitting of the ego and its relation to parental loss. *Journal of the American Psychoanalytic Association, Suppl., 31,* 301-324.

Dickes, R. (1965) The defensive function of an altered state of consciousness. *Journal of the American Psychoanalytic Association, 13,* 356-403.

Dorpat, T. L. (1979) Is splitting a defense? *International Review of Psychoanalysis, 6,* 105-113.

Dorpat, T. L. (1985) *Denial and defense in the therapeutic situation.* New York: Jason Aronson.

Freud, A. (1970) The symptomatology of childhood: A preliminary attempt at classification. In *The writings of Anna Freud: Vol. 7* (pp. 157-188). Madison, CT: International Universities Press.

Freud, S. (1971) A disturbance of memory on the Acropolis. In *The standard edition of the complete psychological works of Sigmund Freud: Vol. 22 (pp.* 239-250). London: Hogarth Press. (Original work published 1936).

Freud, S. (1971) Analysis, terminable and interminable. In *The standard edition of the complete psychological works of Sigmund Freud: Vol. 23 (pp.* 216-253). London: Hogarth Press. (Original work published 1937).

Gill, M. M. (1963) Topography and systems in psychoanalytic theory. *Psychological Issues, 3,* Monogr. 2.

Gillett, E. (1987) Defense mechanisms versus defense contents. *International Journal of Psychoanalysis, 68,* 261-269.

Grotstein, J. S. (1981) *Splitting and projective identification.* New York: Jason Aronson.

Hartmann, H. (1958) *Ego psychology and the problem of adaptation.* New York: International Universities Press.

Holt, R. R. (1975) Drive or wish? A reconsideration of the psychoanalytic theory of motivation. In M.M. Gill and P.S. Holzman (Eds.), *Psychology vs. metapsychology.* Psychoanalytic essays in honour of G.S. Klein. *Psychological Issues, 9,* Monogr. 36, pp. 158-197.

Jacobson, E. (1957) Denial and repression. *Journal of the American Psychoanalytic Association, 5,* 61-92.

Loewenstein, R. M. (1967) Defensive organization and autonomous ego functions. *Journal of the American Psychoanalytic Association, 15,* 795-809.

Lustman, J. (1977) On splitting. *Psychoanalytic Study of the Child, 32,* 119-154.

Moore, B. E. & Rubinfine, D.L. (1969) The mechanism of denial. *Monograph Series of the Kris Study Group of the New York Psychoanalytic Institute: Vol. 3,* pp. 3-57.

Ogden, T. H. (1979) On projective identification. *International Journal of Psychoanalysis, 60,* 357-373.
Pruyser, P. W. (1975) What splits in splitting? A scrutiny of the concept of splitting in psychoanalysis and psychiatry. *Bulletin of the Menninger Clinic, 39,* 1-46.
Rapaport, D. (1960) The structure of psychoanalyze theory: A systematizing attempt. *Psychological Issues, Monogr. 6.*. International Universities Press.
Rohsco, M. (1967) Perception, denial, and derealization. *Journal of the American Psychoanalytic Association, 15,* 243-260.
Sandler, J. (Ed.) (1988) *Projection, identification, projective identification.* London: Karnac Books.
Sarlin, C. N. (1962) Depersonalization and derealization. *Journal of the American Psychoanalytic Association, 10,* 784-804.
Sjöbäck, H. (1973) *The psychoanalytic theory of defensive processes.* New York: Wiley.
Sperling, S. J. (1958) On denial and the essential nature of defense. *International Journal of Psychoanalysis, 39,* 25-38.
Wallerstein, R. S. (1967) Development and metapsychology of the defensive organization of the ego. Panel report. *Journal of the American Psychoanalytic Association, 15,* 130-149.
Wallerstein, R. S. (1983) Self psychology and "classical" psychoanalytic psychology: The nature of their relationship. *Psychoanalysis and Contemporary Thought, 6,* 553-595.
Wallerstein, R. S. (1985) Defenses, defense mechanisms, and the structure of the mind. In H.P. Blum (Ed.), *Defense and resistance. Historical perspectives and current concepts (pp.* 201-225). Madison, CT: International Universities Press.
Wilson, D. (1983) *Rutherford: Simple genius.* London: Hodder and Stoughton.

Defense Mechanisms
U. Hentschel, G. Smith, J.G. Draguns & W. Ehlers (Editors)

Chapter 5

Percept-Genesis and the Study of Defensive Processes

Bert Westerlundh

Microgenesis, Percept-Genesis, and the Theory of Perception

"Percept-genesis" is a term introduced by Kragh and Smith (e.g. , 1970) and refers to the microdevelopment of percepts. The percept-genetic theory of perception is microgenetic. A general definition of microgenesis given by Hanlon and Brown (1989) reads: "Microgenesis refers to the structural development of a cognition (idea, percept, act) through qualitatively different stages. The temporal period of this development extends from the inception of the cognition to its final representation in consciousness or actualization (expression) in behavior."

Evidently, percept-genesis is a process theory of perception, which does not see the conscious percept as an immediate reflection of a given reality. Such theories were rare in psychology until the early 1960s. Thus, the "New Look" psychology of the 1940s and 1950s was very much oriented toward the study of nonveridical perception. But nonveridicality was explained as a secondary revision of an originally true copy of reality. This type of reflection theory was more or less supplanted in the 1960s by information processing models of perception, still very much with us. Typical such models (discussed by Marcel, 1983) can be said to be processual in the sense that they are sequential (proceeding in stages) and hierarchical (the stages become in some sense successively "higher" and more advanced). The process is generally thought to start with simple sensory information analysis and to end with perceptual meaning, the conscious end product.

This type of constructivist approach is radically different from that of microgenesis. Like most information processing models, microgenesis considers percept development to be a basically bottom-up, linear, sequential, and hierarchical process, and it states that all conscious percepts have such a prehistory. But the process is conceived of in quite a different way, where "primacy of meaning" and "biological development" are key concepts. Thus the perceptual process is thought to follow the basic regulatory principle of biological development, the orthogenetic principle (Werner & Kaplan, 1956): "Wherever development occurs, it proceeds from a state of relative lack of differentiation to a state of increasing differentiation, articulation and hierarchic integration." Furthermore, meaning is considered to be the subjective aspect of organismic adaptation, existing from the inception of a perceptual process. The most important characteristic of such a process is that it is a sequence of transformations of meaning. For microgenesis, the early stages of perception are characterized by lack of self- and object differentiation, lack of sensory modality differentiation, and diffuse meaning spreading over a global semiotic field. In the continuation of the process, subjective components reflecting important aspects of life experience are successively eliminated, until at last, at a stimulus proximal, conscious stage, the intersubjective meaning of the stimulus predominates.

At this point, it is possible to articulate the relationship of microgenesis to information processing models. Early such models (e.g., Haber, 1969) were conceived of in terms of hierarchical serial processing, leading up to perceptual meaning. Data from the fields of subliminal perception and automatization cast doubt on this type of conceptualization, and more recent models, such as that of Marcel (1983) tend to be different. They stress parallel processing and play down the idea of hierarchical organization. Parallel process theories are extremely common in present-day psychology, for instance in social cognition (Chaiken & Trope, 1999). Roughly, they state that social cognition has two typical forms, quick and dirty versus slow and reflective. A common feature is that the quick type of analysis preceeds the slow one. This is in line with the microgenetic model. If we were to express it in information processing terms, we would have to use both the concept of hierarchy and that of extensive parallel processing. But the biological and evolutionary orientation of microgenesis separates it from alternative conceptualizations. However, there is a similarity between Brown´s phylogenetically oriented microgenetic model and the combination of parallel processing and qualitatively different stages found in Klaus Scherer´s appraisal theory (Scherer, 1999; van Reekum & Scherer, 1997).

Schools and Research Paradigms of Microgenesis

Psychological theories tend to be associated with specific methods and procedures of investigation. This is true also for microgenesis, where two such research paradigms have been fundamental. Both are illustrated in a classical paper by Heinz Werner: in "Microgenesis and aphasia," Werner (1956) discusses the symptomatology of a specific type of aphasic patient who has difficulty in word finding. When presented with some object, the patient is unable to find the word denoting the object. However, he often answers with a word from the semantic sphere to which the object belongs -for instance, "smoke" for "cigar." Werner thinks that this type of report reflects a universal early and primitive processing stage, which becomes manifest in such patients as a result of the neurological injury. He reasoned that such reports could be obtained from normals if conscious access to intersubjective stimulus meaning were made impossible by information reduction. Thus he studied the reports of normal subjects to verbal stimuli presented tachistoscopically a number of times at successively prolonged presentation times. At short such times, some subjects indeed gave reports that were nonveridical but belonged to the semantic sphere of the stimulus.

In this way, microgenetically oriented researchers in psychiatry and neuropsychology have observed the symptoms of neurologically injured patients. In their frame of reference, such symptoms are considered to be real stages in the microgenetic sequence, but on a primitive level not ordinarily reaching consciousness and motility. Clinical observation is thus one major research paradigm of microgenesis, often oriented toward the study of thought processes (and actions). Microgenetically oriented general psychologists and psychologists interested in personality and psychopathology have instead concentrated their interest on perceptual processing, and they have used information reduction techniques, especially iterated tachistoscopic stimulus presentations at successively prolonged exposure times.

With this, the major orientations of microgenetic research have been mentioned. The German Aktualgenese school, initiated by Friedrich Sander (Sander & Volkelt, 1962) and represented today by for example, Werner Fröhlich (1978) has a cognitive and general psychological orientation. The percept-genetic school of Lund, headed by Ulf Kragh and Gudmund Smith (Kragh & Smith, 1970; Smith & Danielsson, 1982), is oriented toward personality and psychopathology. Psychiatrical and neurological researchers with a microgenetic frame of reference include Paul Schilder (1951, 1953). Jason Brown (1988) is a leading researcher in this tradition today.

The Perceptual Process

For percept-genesis, the stimulus initiating a perceptual process initially gives rise to a global cognitive/affective configuration within the mind. Through the process, this is successively differentiated and delimited, and the more subjective components are excluded in favor of the intersubjective meaning of the stimulus. This implies that perceptual microgeneses initiated by different stimuli are originally rather alike but become successively more specific and stimulus proximal. The earlier parts of the process reflect subjective "personality" functioning, the later show a greater influence of the stimulus. This ordering is accompanied by a diminution of affect. By studying a number of percept-geneses, it is possible to isolate hierarchical stages. In percept-genesis, it has been usual to speak of early, middle, and late levels of the process. From a theoretical point of view, the early level is characterized by extreme condensation of personal meaning and the use of primary process mechanisms. Its organization is influenced by drive functioning, and affect is not neutralized. The perceptual meaning configuration can take on a hallucinatory character. The middle level shows partly reduced affect. The differentiation between self and objects is greater, but not complete-objects are not completely objectified. The degree of condensation of meaning is lower. At this level, memory images with direct reference to significant life happenings are seen more often than in other parts of the process. The late level is more tied to the properties of the stimulus. Here, detailed analysis of fine form is possible. The differentiation of self and objects is complete. Affect is reduced, and the interpersonal meaning of the stimulus predominates.

Parallelisms

Microgenesis is conceived of as analogous to other processes of biological development and evolution. It has often been compared to two other such processes, namely phylogenesis and ontogenesis. As stated by Brown (1988), the physiological counterparts of the perceptual process are excitations starting at the upper brain stem and proceeding over limbic, temporal, and parietal areas to end in the visual cortex. This implies that there is a strict parallelism between the percept-genetic sequence and the phylogenetic acquisition of neural structure.

As regards the micro-ontogenetic parallelism, opinions are divided. The percept-genetic sequence shows a formal similarity over the levels to dream functioning, the functioning of small children and that of adults. Brown (1988) notices this but goes on to deny that it means that contents on different levels of the sequence belong to specific periods of life. He holds that position of a content in the sequence gives no information about its place in ontogenesis. In contrast, Kragh (Kragh & Smith, 1970, pp. 134-178) considers the percept-genetic sequence as the successive unfolding of personal history. The question is somewhat complicated. It is clear that the occurrence of reports in percept-geneses referring to important life experiences is not too uncommon. But on a priori considerations, the initial probability of Kragh's hypothesis seems low. However, a recent attempt at a small but reasonably strict test of this hypothesis came out in favor of it (Westerlundh & Terjestam, 1990). But even if it were to receive further empirical support, it is clear that this must be limited to "episodic" memories and signs of psychic structure formation, while "procedural" skills (to revive Tulving's 1972 distinction) become automatized and can be found at very early process levels. Thus, subliminally presented words can activate a "sphere of meaning," as shown already by Werner (1956).

Determinants of the Percept

There is a successive determination whereby earlier contents are transformed into later in the perceptual process. From a descriptive point of view, the process is characterized by cumulation, elimination, or emergence -respectively, the continued existence, loss, or new appearance of elements of the percept.

In percept-genesis, "stimulus" and "sensations" are regarded as hypothetical determinants that influence but do not create the contents of the perceptual process. Generally, microgenetic theory is congruent with a critical epistemology, such as that presented by neo-Kantian and symbolic construction philosophers like Paul Natorp, Ernst Cassirer, and Susanne Langer .

Processes of a motivational order, such as drives and strong situational needs, can influence the attribution of meaning and thus reduce subjective variability in a percept-genesis. Generally, a percept-genesis always interacts with other microgenetic processes of the individual that have just taken place or are taking place at the same time. Motivational factors press toward microgenesis, that is, toward psychic representation. Such microgeneses will interact with perceptual adaptation. In the same way, spontaneous or induced sets will influence percept-geneses.

Individual regulations of access to consciousness, cognitive styles, put their mark on the process and influence the final conscious product. When such cognitive strategies are used to avoid unpleasure, they are called defense mechanisms. This is a final determinant of the perceptual process systematically distinguished in percept-genesis. The percept-genetic approach to the study of defenses will be treated more fully later .

The Technique of Information Reduction

Only the end stage of a percept-genesis, the stimulus-proximal, intersubjectively equivalent, "correct" configuration and meaning, ordinarily reaches consciousness. Of course, this is a necessity for efficient adaptation. The quasi-instantaneous, objectified character of percepts explains the long rule of the theory of perception as an immediate reflection of reality.

To study the ordinarily preconscious stages preceding the conscious percept, percept-genesis makes use of the technique of information reduction. The same stimulus is presented repeatedly at successively longer exposure times by means of a tachistoscope. Each time, the subject reports what has been seen, verbally and perhaps with a simple drawing. The shortest time used may be of the order of 10 milliseconds (ms). Such trials are continued until the subject is able to give a report of stimulus contents at an intersubjective level. The longest times used in a percept-genetic serial are about 2500 ms. This way of protracting and fractioning the act of perception is in some ways not as unlike an ordinary perceptual act as might be imagined. Perception takes place in the "phenomenal now," a period of roughly a second. With stimuli depicting ordinary and unarousing objects, the sum total of tachistoscopic presentation times needed for correct recognition does not exceed this value.

Furthermore, the construction of a final, correct meaning and configuration from a number of discrete fixations, which is a feature of the fractioning technique, actually reflects the working of ordinary perception. As has been known for some decades, retinal stabilization of a stimulus input, which would in commonsense terms allow for a really "good look," actually leads to the breakdown of the percept (Pritchard, Heron, & Hebb, 1960). The phenomenal end product of a series of tachistoscopic presentations is in no way different from that of ordinary perception.

However, the instruction to verbalize experience sets up a micro-genetic context, and the successive verbalizations of experience create a fading series of microgeneses, which will serve as a background for later experiences. The thrust of this background will be in the direction of cumulation (i.e., reports of the same experience). This is one factor reducing the variability of percept-geneses. Instructions stressing the reporting of new features and change are very important here.

Many of the factors mentioned as determinants of the percept actually reduce the subjective variability of perceptual reports. A compulsive cognitive style, to report objects and their characteristics (perhaps with increasing clarity) while excluding all reference to action and emotional valence, is not uncommon. Here, what can become conscious is limited to the last, stimulus proximal stage. Percept-geneses, series of reports to successively prolonged exposures of the same stimulus, vary from such constricted protocols to protocols showing an extreme richness of subjective material, with most falling in between.

The percept-genetic group is perhaps best known for research in two areas. One of these is the study of individual consistencies in cognitive processing. The process of adaptation to a new, unknown situation shows a pattern that is characteristic for the individual. Studies of such regularities can use the tachistoscopic fractioning technique presented above, but also repeated encounters with other, new, situations, which are not within the scope of adaptation to an average expectable environment. These have included the serial presentation of the Stroop Color-Word Test (Smith, Nyman, & Hentschel, 1986) and the serial afterimage technique (e.g., Smith & Danielsson, 1982). The other area in which well-known contributions have been made by the Lund group is the study of psychological defenses in perception.

The Theory of Defense

In contrast to a number of present-day endeavors in the field, percept-genesis takes its starting point in the classical psychoanalytic formulations of the theory of defense. As is well known, Freud used the concept quite early, but it came into prominence with his second theory of anxiety (1926/1971) and Anna Freud's monograph on the mechanisms of defense (1936/1961).

Defenses are part of potentially pathogenic intrapsychic conflicts. In Freud's formulation, a forbidden impulse -a temptation- strives toward consciousness and motility. On its way through the psychic apparatus, it activates an associated representation of a danger situation. This releases an anxiety signal, which is the proximal cause of the activation of defense mechanisms. Anxiety signals can also be released by threats associated to the danger situation -for example, fantasies activated by castration threats (A. Freud, 1936/1961). The aim of the defenses is to avoid conscious unpleasure. This is done by keeping the anxiety signal and the impulse from reaching consciousness. Sometimes this strategy must be supplemented by others, which allow for some veiled and transformed conscious representation of the contents of the impulse. This theoretical account led to a list of defenses, with repression as the basic one, accompanied by others (isolation, undoing, etc.).

Modifications of the Classical Theory

Three modifications and emendations of the classical view are of importance here. The first concerns the nature of pathogenic, neurosis-producing conflict. That such conflicts involved drive fixation and regression (due to frustration) was part of the classical view. However, the defenses were not thought to be part of this regressive pattern. Actually, in the clinical situation almost anything can serve as a defense against almost anything else, and the only basis for classification of a behavior as defensive is functional (see Wallerstein, 1985). But a study of the major defenses of the classical neuroses led Sandler and Joffe (1965) to the conclusion that these defenses were indeed general cognitive strategies that were used defensively but were on a developmental level corresponding to the forbidden impulses. This made these authors enunciate a principle of correlative drive and defense fixations in neurosis. This is of importance here, since the type and level of a defensive report in a percept-genesis will give information about the experience of danger and the type of impulse involved in the conflict.

Second, the classical theory concerned the mental representatives of a drive and their vicissitudes. From a microgenetic point of view, the fantasy images evoked by the drive are incomplete percept-geneses, in principle not different from parts of the genesis of full-blown percepts. This way of looking at the influence on mental functioning of drive stimuli and outer stimuli has become common among psychoanalysts, especially those who find the topographical model fruitful (see Sandler & Joffe, 1969; Westerlundh & Smith, 1983). On this view, in principle all defenses that are used against the representatives of impulses can be used against psychic representations of outer stimuli. This is of obvious importance for percept-genesis, which relies on the tachistoscopic presentation of special types of stimuli. There are far-reaching correspondences between the topographical ("Jacksonian") model, with its distinctions between unconscious, preconscious, and conscious functioning, and microgenetic theory. Brown (1988) states that the former puts more stress on inhibition, the later more on transformation of meaning. However, the study of defense through perception has demonstrated the importance of inhibition within a microgenetic framework.

Finally, intrapsychic conflict was classically described in the rather abstract terms of the structural theory -id impulses, ego defenses, and so on. With the increasing importance of object relation conceptualizations, the nature of the mental contents that are drawn into conflict has received more attention. Sandler and Rosenblatt (1962) stressed the importance of dyadic images involving the interaction of self and significant others in their concept of the representational world. Such representations play an important part in regulating behavior, constitute the content of drive representations and danger situations, and are the targets of defense. Kernberg (1976) used the same ideas in his concept of introjection. For him, introjection is the reproduction and fixation of an interaction with the environment, involving images of the object and the self in interaction with it, together with affective valence. These conceptualizations inform us about how stimuli intended to evoke the typical defensive processes of a subject must be constructed. They ought to be dyadic, with one person intended as a self and another as an object representation. They should represent temptations or threats referring to the danger situations presented in the theory of anxiety.

Outside of psychoanalytic psychology, the phenomena referred to in the theory of defense have been conceptualized as emotion-focused coping (for instance, Smith & Lazarus, 1990). The focus here has been on person-situation interactions, with less stress on indivudual consistency or the person´s basic capacity to adapt to circumstances. However, recent years have seen a renewed interest in the theory of defense (Norem, 1998).

Percept-Genesis and the Study of Defensive Processes

The presentation of dyadic, interpersonal stimuli in the tachistoscopic information reduction research paradigm was introduced by Kragh. Already these early studies gave rise to conceptualizations in terms of defenses in the perceptual process (Kragh, 1955, 1959, 1960). Later, within the framework of a project for selecting aviation cadets by means of the percept-genetic technique, Kragh (1961) aimed at creating stimuli with a maximal relationship to the psychoanalytic theory of anxiety and defense. He devised two stimuli, structurally different but with the same content, for these young males. Both represented a scene with a neutral-looking, centrally placed young male (the self representation), and a peripheral, ugly and threatening older male person (the object representation). His idea was that stimuli of this type should activate signal anxiety, referring both to castration anxiety and to superego anxiety. Reports to them ought to reveal the defense mechanisms used by the subjects.

The Defense Mechanism Test

Kragh's early work was the starting point for one of the two reasonably standardized percept-genetic tests for the assessment of defenses, the Defense Mechanism Test (DMT: Kragh, 1985). This test is described in Chapter 7.

The Meta-Contrast Technique

Smith's Meta-Contrast Technique (MCT: Smith, Johnson, & Almgren, 1989) started as a way of studying how a stimulus is successively reported within the framework of an already stabilized perception. A coding system related to nosological entities and developmental levels was developed, and the instrument has been widely used in the clinical field. This test is also described in Chapter 7.

Validity of the Percept-Genetic Approach

The study of defensive processes has become increasingly popular in empirical psychology. Today, there are many such approaches. But it is reasonable to say that what is studied by most of them differs more or less radically from the original psychoanalytic formulations. This is probably most accentuated in the case of questionnaire approaches. What they study may be quite interesting from different points of view, but their relationship to the psychoanalytic theory of defense is tenuous. Naturally, this point is of importance practically. Quite conceivably, it would be possible to, for example, increase the power of the DMT as an instrument of selection by introducing scoring categories unrelated to conceptualizations of defense. The work of Cooper and Kline (1989) on an objectively scored version points in this direction. However, the question of the predictive and concurrent validity of the techniques concerns a body of research big enough to make separate treatment necessary.

What interests us in the present context is instead the relationship of the operationalizations to the theory of defense. The microgenetic and psychoanalytic formulations, and the basic methods of percept-genesis, have been presented above. It is of course suggested that the fit is better in this case than for the majority of other approaches. Certain aspects of the question of validity have been taken up by Cooper and Kline. In their evaluation of the Defense Mechanism Test, Cooper and Kline (1986) discuss the face validity of the percept-genetic scoring of defense. While most such categories do indeed look as they ought to according to the theory, there is a notable exception, namely repression. In psychoanalysis, repression refers to the exclusion of contents from conscious representation. In percept-genesis, repression is scored when one or both of the persons in the stimulus are seen as rigid or lifeless.

It could be argued that the empirical referents of psychoanalysis and percept-genesis are not the same, and that rigidity and lifelessness could be indications of repression on a perceptual level. To bolster such an argument, it would be necessary to show that the percept-genetic scores appear when the determining conditions are such that one would expect repression. Now, repression is a mechanism linked to the phallic stage of drive organization. It is primarily directed against infantile sexual impulses and is the typical defense of hysterical neurosis (Fenichel, 1946).

What is known about the percept-genetic sign is the following: it is abundantly reported by patients suffering from hysterical neurosis (Kragh, 1985; Smith, Johnson, & Almgren, 1989). Children's reports of the sign increase dramatically at puberty (Carlsson & Smith, 1987; Westerlundh & Johnson, 1989). In experiments using percept-geneses as dependent variables, more subjects report the sign at experimental operations intended as sexual threats and temptations than in other conditions (e.g., Westerlundh & Sjöbäck, 1986). Whatever it is, the sign certainly works as repression is supposed to work. Cooper and Kline's discussion of face validity is important because it points out that percept-genesis studies a perceptual level of functioning and that the principles of representation on this level must be studied in their own right if valid conclusions are to be drawn.

The repression example above is of course an instance of construct validation, where data from different areas concatenate to give support to specific interpretations. This is the way that must be followed and has been followed in clinical, developmental, and experimental research oriented toward the study of the validity of percept-genetic scoring categories. To state that a certain report is defensive is to infer the activity of a defense mechanism for the purpose of avoiding unpleasure. Such an interpretation is always probabilistic, but the more we learn about the conditions that produce such reports, the better our interpretations will be. Much work has been done in this area; much remains. A reasoned judgment at present would be that a big part of percept-genetic interpretations stands up to such scrutiny. There are other areas of doubtful validity, where more research must be performed before a final verdict can be made.

References

Brown, J. W. (1988) *The life of the mind: Selected papers.* Hillsdale, NJ: Erlbaum.

Carlsson, I. & Smith, G.J.W. (1987) Gender differences in defense mechanisms compared with creativity in a group of youngsters. *Psychological Research Bulletin, Lund University* , 27, 1.

Chaiken, S. & Trope, Y. (Eds.) (1999). *Dual process theories in social psychology.* NewYork: The Guilford Press.

Cooper, C. & Kline, P. (1986) An evaluation of the Defense Mechanism Test. *British Journal of Psychology,* 77, 19-31.

Cooper, C. & Kline, P. (1989) A new objectively scored version of the Defense Mechanism Test. *Scandinavian Journal of Psychology,* 30,228-238.

Fenichel, 0. (1946) *The psychoanalytic theory of neurosis.* London: Routledge and Kegan Paul.

Freud, A. (1961) *The ego and the mechanisms of defense.* London: Hogarth Press. (Originally work published in 1936)

Freud, S. (1971) Inhibitions, symptoms and anxiety. In James Strachey (Ed. and Transl.), *The standard edition of the complete psychological works of Sigmund Freud: Vol.* 20 (pp. 75-175). London: Hogarth Press. (Original work published 1926)

Fröhlich, W.D. (1978) Stress, anxiety, and the control of attention. In C.D. Spielberger & I.G. Sarason (Eds.), *Stress and anxiety: Vol.* 5. Washington, DC: Hemisphere.

Haber, R.N. (Ed.) (1969) *Information-processing approaches to visual perception.* New York: Holt, Rinehart and Winston.

Hanlon, R.E. & Brown, J .W .(1989) Microgenesis. Historical review and current studies. In A. Ardila & P. Ostrosky-Solis (Eds.), *Brain organization of language and cognitive processes* (pp. 3-15). New York: Plenum.

Kernberg, 0. (1976) *Object relations theory and clinical psychoanalysis.* New York: Jason Aronson.

Kragh, U. (1955) *The actual-genetic model of perception-personality.* Lund: Gleerup.

Kragh, U. (1959) Types of pre-cognitive defensive organization in a tachistoscopic experiment. *Journal of Projective Techniques,* 23, 315-322.

Kragh, U. (1960) Pathogenesis in dipsomania: An illustration of the actual-genetic model of perception-personality. *Acta Psychiatrica Neurologica Scandinavica,* 35,207-222,261-288,480-497.

Kragh, U. (1961) *DMT- Variabler som prediktorer för flygförarlämplighet* [DMT - Variables as predictors of pilot ability]. MPI rapport, 5.

Kragh, U. (1985) *Defense Mechanism Test. DMT manual.* Stockholm: Persona.

Kragh, U. & Smith, G.J.W. (1970) *Percept-genetic analysis.* Lund: Gleerup.

Marcel, A.J. (1983) Conscious and unconscious perception. *Cognitive Psychology,*15, 197-300.

Norem, J.K. (1998). Why should we lower our defenses about defense mechanisms? *Journal of Personality, 66,* 895-917.

Pritchard, R.M., Heron, W., & Bebb, D.O. (1960) Visual perception approached by the method of stabilized images. *Canadian Journal of Psychology,* 14, 67-77.

Sander, F. & Volkelt, B. (1962) *Ganzheitspsychologie.* Munich: Beck.

Sandler, J. & Joffe , W. (1965) Notes on obsessional manifestations in children. *Psychoanalytic Study of the Child,* 20, 425-438.

Sandler, J. & Joffe, W. (1969) Towards a basic psychoanalytic model. *International Journal of Psychoanalysis,* 50,79-91.

Scherer, K. R. (1999). Appraisal theories. In T. Dalgleish & M. Power (Eds.), *Handbook of cognition and emotion* (pp. 637-663). Chichester: Wiley.

Smith, C.A. & Lazarus, R.S. (1990). Emotion and adaptation. In L.A. Pervin (Ed.), *Handbook of personality* (1st ed., pp. 609-637). New York: The Guilford Press.
van Reekum, C.M. & Scherer, K.R. (1997). Levels of processing for emotion-antecedentappraisal. In G. Mathews (Ed.), *Cognitive science perspectives on personality and emotion* (pp. 259-300). Amsterdam: Elsevier Science.

Percept-Genetic, Projective, and Rating techniques for the Assessment of Defense Mechanisms

Defense Mechanisms
U. Hentschel, G. Smith, J.G. Draguns & W. Ehlers (Editors)

Chapter 6

Defense Mechanisms and Cognitive Styles in Projective Techniques and Other Diagnostic Instruments

Falk Leichsenring

Introduction

Defense mechanisms are regarded as means by which the ego protects itself against unpleasurable experiences, e.g. anxiety, depression, guilt or shame (cf. Freud, 1926; A. Freud, 1936; Fenichel, 1945). A symptom is regarded as a result of failure of defending the ego against instinctual drive derivatives (Freud, 1926). A certain constellation of defense mechanisms is regarded as more or less specific to the different types of neuroses (Freud, 1926; A. Freud, 1936). However, defense mechanisms are not regarded as pathogenic per se, but only when used in exaggeration (Freud, 1895, 1937) or in a rigid or overgeneralized way (Loewenstein, 1967). The adaptive functions of defense mechanisms were emphasized by A. Freud (1936), Hartmann (1939), and others. According to A. Freud (1936) each person chooses a limited number of defense mechanisms to protect against unpleasurable experiences. The constellation of defense mechanisms habitually used contributes to what is called a person's "character" (Reich, 1933; A. Freud, 1936; Hoffmann, 1984). According to Millon (1984, p. 460), a systematic assessment of defense mechanisms "is central to a comprehensive personality assessment."

A. Freud (1936) described ten defense mechanisms: repression, regression, reaction formation, isolation, undoing, projection, introjection, turning against the self, reversal and sublimation. However, an ever growing number of mechanisms has been proposed by more recent authors (e.g. Laughlin, 1970; Bibring, Dwyer, Huntington & Valenstein, 1961). In addition to intrapsychic defense mechanisms, interpersonal ones have been described (Richter, 1967; Willi, 1975; Heigl-Evers, 1972). In the glossary of the recent revision of the Diagnostic and Statistical Manual of Mental Disorders (DSM-IV, American Psychiatric Association, 1994), 28 defense mechanisms are included.

Various authors have tried to systematize the growing number of defense mechanisms (e.g. Vaillant, 1971, 1976; Plutchik, Kellermann & Conte, 1979). Kernberg (1977, 1984) differentiated two levels of defensive organization, neurotic versus. borderline or psychotic. The former is characterized by an advanced defensive constellation centered around repression and other advanced defensive operations (e.g. reaction formation, isolation and undoing). In contrast, borderline or psychotic defensive organization is characterized by a constellation of primitive defensive operations centered around the mechanism of splitting. Its subsidiary mechanisms include projective identification, primitive denial, devaluation, idealization, and fantasies of omnipotence. In Kernberg's definition splitting refers to the active keeping apart of the libidinally determined and the aggressively determined self and object representations. This mechanism serves to protect the core of the ego built around positive introjections. Thus, Kernberg emphasized the defensive function of splitting, whereas other authors regard splitting not as an active defense, but as passive fragmentation (e.g. Benedetti, 1977). Lichtenberg and Slap (1973) have provided a further discussion of splitting. According to Arlow and Brenner (1964), regression of particular ego functions in the service of defense against anxiety may lead to psychotic symptoms.

The Assessment of Defense Mechanisms

It is difficult to assess defense mechanisms empirically: These processes are conceptualized as unconscious. Furthermore, the presence of a defense mechanism has to be inferred from the absence or the distortion of certain drive derivatives or affects (Beutel, 1988). Self report instruments, ratings scales, content analytic methods, and projective techniques are usually employed for the assessment of defense mechanisms, each method being associated with specific methodological problems (Beutel, 1988).

In the present paper the assessment of defense mechanisms by projective techniques will be described and discussed. The focus will be on the so-called "primitive" defense mechanisms and their assessment by the Rorschach and the Holtzman Inkblot Technique (HIT, Holtzman, Thorpe, Swartz & Herron, 1961). The assessment of defense mechanisms by means of the Thematic Apperception Test (TAT) is described by Bellak (1975), Cramer (1987, Cramer & Blatt, 1990) and Rauchfleisch (1989).

Projective techniques are assumed to provide assessment in depth, thereby bringing to light the less conscious levels of psychological functioning. This expectation is embodied in the so called levels hypothesis (Murstein & Mathes,

1996; Leichsenring & Hiller, 2001). Thus, these methods appear to be especially appropriate for the assessment of defense mechanisms. For this purpose, it is necessary to specify test indicators that can be scored reliably and are valid for the defense mechanisms in question. As will be demonstrated below, sufficient interrater reliability has not been demonstrated for the Rorschach scores of all defense mechanisms Furthermore, a variable that is supposedly indicative of a specific defense mechanism may often be interpreted with regard to another hypothetical construct, thereby making validation more difficult. This aspect will be further discussed below. In my view, this ambiguity stems from the fact that it is not possible to pinpoint "pure" indicators of defense mechanisms: Variables that we use as indicators of "defense mechanisms" are complex products of several psychological functions. This view is consistent with Shapiro´s (1991) formulation of defenses as expressions of a person´s whole cognitive, affective, and behavioral style. Furthermore this position is concordant with Brenner's (1981) assertion that all psychological functions can serve as defense mechanisms.

The Assessment of Low-Level Defense Mechanisms by Means of the Rorschach and the Holtzman Inkblot Technique

Rorschach scoring systems for defense mechanisms were developed by Schafer (1954), Gardner et al. (1959), Baxter, Becker and Hooks (1963) and Bellak, Hurvich and Gediman (1973). In recent years several authors have tried to assess defense mechanisms considered to be characteristic of borderline patients by means of the Rorschach (Lerner & Lerner, 1980; Lerner, Sugarman and Gaughran, 1981; Lerner, Albert & Walsh, 1987). Lerner and collaboraters developed a content-based Rorschach scoring system focused on the human responses: Splitting is scored, for example, if two human figures are described, and the affective content of the description of one figure is clearly opposite to that of the other. Lerner et al. (1981, p. 710) provided this illustration: "Two figures, a man and a woman. He's mean and chanting at her. Being rather angelic, she's standing there and taking it." Devaluation is scored on a 5-point-scale. Low-level devaluation (scale value 5) is scored, if the humanness dimension is lost, for example, if figures are seen as robots, puppets or as humans with animal features. Denial is scored on a 3-point-scale. Low-level denial (scale value 3) is scored if something is added that is not there or an aspect that can be seen clearly is not taken into account. Incompatible descriptions are also noted,. as illustrated by Lerner et al. (1981, p. 711): "A person but instead of a mouth there is a bird's beak." Idealization is scored on a 5-point-scale. Low-level idealization (scale value 5) is scored if the humanness dimension is lost, but an enhancement of identity is implied, for example if statues of famous figures, giants or superheroes are described, as seen in the following response (Lerner et al. 1981, p. 710): "A bust of Queen Victoria." Projective Identification is scored for example, if confabulatory responses involving human figures are given in which the form level is weak or arbitrary (Lerner et al. 1981, p. 711), e.g." A huge man coming to get me. I can see his huge teeth. He's staring straight at me. His hands are up as if he will strike me." Details of the scoring rules were described by Lerner and Lerner (1980) and Lerner et al. (1981). According to their findings, sufficient interrater agreement was obtained in scoring these indicators (also Gacano, 1990).

Concerning the assessment of projective identification by means of projective techniques I see a fundamental problem: More recent definitions of projective identification provided by Kernberg (1977) and Ogden (1979, 1982) necessarily imply an interactional component by which the external object is influenced in a way that he or she feels, thinks or behaves as an externalized parts of the self. As inkblots cannot "react", the indicators proposed by Lerner and colleagues for projective identification can be construed to indicate projection rather projective identification (Leichsenring, 1991a,b).

With regard to validity, Lerner and Lerner (1980) found significantly more Rorschach indicators of splitting, projective identification, low-level devaluation and low-level denial in borderline patients than in patients with neurotic disorders. However, no differences were detected in indicators of idealization. Indicators of splitting and projective identification were found in the borderline group only. In another study, however, Lerner, Albert, and Walsh (1987) reported no differences between patients with neurotic disorders and borderline outpatients, except in projective identification. Borderline inpatients, however, had significantly more indicators of splitting, projective identification and omnipotence than patients with neurotic disorders. This result stands in contrast to the view, supported by some empirical findings, that the borderline personality disorder is an enduring state (Carr, 1987; Königsberg, 1982). Differences found between inpatients- and outpatients may have resulted from decompensation that had triggered hospitalization and may or may not have been connected with differences in defense mechanisms. Unfortunately, as Carr (1987) pointed out, the criteria used to classify neurotic and borderline outpatients were not specified by Lerner et al. (1987).

Lerner, Sugarman and Gaughran (1981) demonstrated that a mixed group of patients with schizotypal and borderline personality disorder (DSM-III, American Psychiatric Association, 1983) showed significantly more Rorschach indicators of splitting and projective identification and a significantly higher weighted sum for devaluation, idealization and denial than a group of schizophrenic patients. However, combining borderline and schizotypal patients is questionable, because these disorders are considered as quite different by authors of various theoretical orientations (Carr, 1987; Stone, 1980; Kernberg, 1984; Akiskal et al. 1985; McGlashan, 1983; Exner, 1986). Indicators of projective identification were found only in the borderline group (see also Lerner et al., 1987). As a weighted sum is used for devaluation, idealization and denial, it is not clear from the data presented by Lerner et al. (1981) whether the indicators of the "primitive" forms of these defense mechanisms differentiate significantly between the groups. The results obtained comparing borderline and schizophrenic patients are at variance with Kernberg's (1977, 1984) assertion that borderline patients and psychotics differ in reality testing, but not in primitive defense mechanisms. Even so, these mechanisms may serve a different purpose in psychosis, perhaps by helping prevent further disintegration of self-object-boundaries (Kernberg, 1977, 1984). Furthermore, the finding that projective identification was not found in schizophrenics stands in contrast to the position of several authors on that topic (Rosenfeld, 1954; Kernberg, 1977, 1984, Ogden, 1982). As Carr (1987) pointed out, the unexpected differences between borderline and schizophrenic patients may stem from schizophrenics giving fewer human and quasi-human responses, as Lerner et al. (1981) have found. It is on these variables that the Lerner scoring system is based.

In his 1990 review Lerner (1990, p. 35) spoke of "the general hypothesis that borderline patients exhibit a defensive structure significantly different from that of schizophrenics and neurotics." It is not clear to me from what kind of sources he drew that conclusion. Quite possibly, Lerner's principal basis for this statement was his own data on human responses. However, Lerner did not specify the defense structure he assumed schizophrenics to have. In a sample of borderline outpatients Hilsenroth et al. (1993) found significantly higher means for all Lerner indicators of defense mechanisms compared to a sample of out-patients with cluster C personality disorders, according to DSM-III-R (avoidant, dependent, obsessive-compulsive, passive-aggressive; American Psychiatric Association, 1987). These results are consistent with theoretical expectations (Kernberg, 1975). Borderline patients and outpatients with DSM-III-R narcissistic personality disorder did not differ in devaluation, idealization or denial. However, both groups differed significantly in Lerner's indicators of splitting and projective identification, borderline patients producing significantly higher means for both indicators (Hilsenroth et al., 1993). According to Kernberg (1975), however, no differences are to be expected between borderline patients and patients with narcissistic personality disorder in primitive defense mechanisms. It is not yet clear whether this result calls into question Kernberg's theory or Lerner's scoring method. Furthermore, the Lerner defense scores failed to discriminate between patients with narcissistic personality disorder and patients with cluster C personality disorders: Only in idealization was a significant mean difference found, with narcissistic patients producing higher means for idealization. These results are in contrast to the Kernberg's (1975) specification of the defensive structure of narcissistic personality disorder. Again, we do not know whether this result questions Kernberg's theory or the Lerner scoring method. Unfortunately, Hilsenroth et al. (1993) used weighted sums for devaluation, idealization and denial, a fact I already criticized above in relation to the study of Lerner et al. (1981). So it is not clear from the data presented by Hilsenroth et al. (1993) whether the indicators of "primitive" forms of these defense mechanisms differentiate between the groups.

The results of the studies by Lerner, Sugarman and Gaughran (1981) and Lerner, Albert and Walsh (1987) raise questions about the validity of the Lerner scoring system for primitive defense mechanisms, at least with borderline outpatients and schizophrenics. The results of the study of Hilsenroth et al. (1993) also open questions concerning the validity of the Lerner scoring system, especially for outpatients with narcissistic personality disorders. Furthermore, the data published by Lerner and collaborators and of Hilsenroth et al. (1993) are not sufficient to decide whether the differences found can be used for differential diagnosis of individual patients: Only means are reported, and no information is given about the percentages of patients with scores for the defense mechanism in question. Significant differences on a group basis are necessary but not sufficient for this purpose. This is true of some of the other studies using the Lerner system, e.g. by Gacono (1990), which did not even include a control group. In order to decide whether differential diagnosis of individual patients is possible, additional research is necessary classifying individual patients on the basis of indicators proposed by Lerner and collaborators.

Referring to object relation theory, Carr (1987) argues in favor of scoring not only human and quasi-human responses for defense mechanisms, but all responses, human and nonhuman, as well as all behavioral observations related to the testing situation.

In one of my own studies with borderline patients (Leichsenring, 1991a,b) I applied the Lerner scoring system to the responses of 30 borderline and 30 inpatients with neurotic disorders to the Holtzman Inkblot Technique (HIT). The patients had been classified on the basis of the Diagnostic Interview for Borderlines (DIB, Kolb & Gunderson, 1980). Sufficient interrater agreement with a blind rater was demonstrated both for the DIB and for the scoring of indicators of splitting, projective identification, low-level denial, and low-level devaluation (Leichsenring, 1991a,b). However, scoring of defensive operations was not restricted to human or quasi-human responses. Splitting was scored, for example, if the response "paradise, butterflies and birds in the sky" was followed by the response "a hangman, cutting off the head of man sentenced to death." Borderline patients showed significantly more indicators of the above defense mechanisms than patients with neurotic disorders. However, no difference in indicators of low-level idealization was found, a result supporting Lerner and Lerner's (1980) findings. Furthermore, no differences appeared in any other levels of idealization, devaluation or denial (Leichsenring, 1991a).

In reference to the defense mechanisms that significantly discriminated between the two groups, it was possible to classify individual patients with quite good results for sensitivity and specificity: By a criterion of at least one indicator of splitting, 80 percent (24/30) of the borderline patients and 70 percent (21/30) of the patients with neurotic disorders were correctly classified in sensitivity and specificity, respectively, in agreement with the DIB diagnoses. By a criterion of at least one indicator of projective identification, the corresponding percentages were 77 percent and 80 percent. Using low-level devaluation and denial as predictors, specificity was not sufficient for diagnostic classification (Leichsenring, 1991a). According to these data, the Lerner indicators of primitive defensive operations can be scored in the HIT with sufficient interrater agreement and high discriminative power. In another study, I compared borderline patients with acute and chronic schizophrenics diagnosed in accordance with DSM-IIIR, again using the HIT (Leichsenring, 1999a). There were no differences between borderline patients and acute schizophrenics in Lerner indicators of splitting and projection (Lerner´s "projective identification"). This result is in consistent with Kernberg's (1984) formulations. However, borderline patients used the Lerner indicators of primitive devaluation (scale value 5 according to Lerner) significantly more than acute schizophrenics. The results for chronic schizophrenics were heterogeneous: Some chronic schizophrenics produced Lerner indicators of splitting as frequently as borderline patients and acute schizophrenics while others did not produced them more frequently than patients with neurotic disorders. Indicators of splitting were found in 44 percent of the chronic schizophrenics compared to 76 percent of the acute schizophrenics. Chronic schizophrenics did not show more indicators of primitive devaluation or primitive denial than patients with neurotic disorders. However, indicators of projection (Lerner´s "projective identification") were significantly more frequent in chronic schizophrenics than in patients with neurotic disorders (Leichsenring, 1999a). Primitive idealization did not discriminate significantly between any groups. Thus, the level of defense mechanisms in chronic schizophrenics appears to vary considerably. This is consistent with clinical observations reported by Kernberg (1984). According to the results of factor analysis, borderline patients and acute schizophrenics differ on dimensions of primitive defense mechanisms measured by the Lerner criteria (Leichsenring, 1996): In borderline patients the Lerner scores of primitive denial (scale value 3) and projection (Lerner´s "projective identification") form one dimension. Splitting, primitive devaluation and primitive idealization (scale value 5) form a second dimension (see Table 6.1). In acute schizophrenics, however, splitting, projection, and primitive denial form one dimension while primitive devaluation and primitive idealization form a second dimension, as shown in Table 6.1. The same factor structure was also found in chronic schizophrenics. According to these results, splitting in borderline patients correlates with primitive idealization and devaluation of objects. In acute and chronic schizophrenics, however, splitting correlates with projection and primitive denial. These results are consistent with regarding splitting not as a single defense mechanism but as a complex process in which different mechanisms and processes play a role in separating "good" and "bad" self representations and object representations (Leichsenring, 1996; 1999b).

Table 6.1: *Results of a factor analysis of the Lerner scores in a sample of borderline patients (N=30) and in a sample of acute schizophrenics (N=25); rotated solution, varimax rotation*

	Borderline Patients		Acute Schizophrenics	
	Factor 1	Factor 2	Factor 1	Factor 2
Splitting	0.31	0.68	0.84	0.23
Projection	0.93	0.05	0.89	0.04
Devaluation 5	0.27	0.77	0.38	0.75
Denial 3	0.87	0.25	0.81	0.14

Note: Projection: "projective identification" according to Lerner

From the results of the factor analysis described above, for example, it can be concluded that primitive idealization and devaluation of objects play a constituent role in the process of splitting in borderline patients, while projection and primitive denial play a constituent role in the process of splitting in acute schizophrenics.

Nevertheless, the question remains whether the Lerner indicators measure primarily defense mechanisms: There is a considerable overlap between these indicators and several classical Rorschach and Holtzman variables: Indicators of low-level devaluation and of low-level denial both overlap with fabulized combinations and contaminations; indicators of projective identification overlap with confabulations, form level, and hostility and anxiety variables, as defined by Rapaport et al. (1950), Elizur (1949), Murstein, (1956) and Holtzman et al. (1961). Lerner indicators of low-level devaluation and low-level denial may not primarily measure these defense mechanisms, but may be closer to being indicators of such thought-related variables as fabulized combinations and contaminations. Similarly, indicators of projective identification may not primarily measure this defense mechanism, but may tap confabulations, form level, anxiety, and hostility. This problem is similar to the interpretation of fabulized combinations and contaminations as indicators of boundary disturbances (Blatt & Ritzler, 1974; Lerner, Sugarman & Barbour, 1985). In my own studies, significant and high correlations were demonstrated between thought-disordered responses like fabulized combinations and contaminations and the Lerner defense scores (Leichsenring, 1991b; 1999b). It is not clear whether these correlations can be attributed to the close connection between primitive defense mechanisms and primary process thinking assumed by Kernberg (1976) or whether these correlations simply stem from the overlap in scoring criteria. However, in contrast to the other Lerner scores, indicators of splitting do not overlap with any other Rorschach variable. However, according to results of my own studies, the Lerner scoring criteria for splitting do not form a homogeneous dimension (Leichsenring, 1999b): According to Lerner et al. (1981, p. 710) one variety of splitting refers to affective polarizations in two adjacent responses, which I have labeled splitting A. The second way of splitting refers to affective polarization within one figure, designated by me as splitting B. The third variant refers to affective polarizations within one response, named splitting C. A fourth way of splitting refers to the devaluation of an implicitly idealized figure or the enhancing of an implicitly devalued figure, or splitting D. I factor analyzed the data of 30 normals, 30 patients with neurotic disorders, 30 borderline patients, 25 acute schizophrenics and 25 chronic schizophrenics (Leichsenring, 1999b). The four Lerner scoring criteria for splitting were entered as variables; they made up two factors. Splitting A and D had high factor loadings on the first factor, while splitting B and C loaded on the second factor. Splitting B and C refer to either affective polarization within one figure or within one response (Leichsenring, 1999 b).

Furthermore, the different scoring criteria of splitting seem to have different meanings in different diagnostic groups: Splitting C, within one response, was significantly more frequent in borderline patients than in normals, patients with neurotic disorders, and schizophrenics (Leichsenring, 1999b). Thus, this variety of splitting appears to be characteristic of borderline patients. Splitting B, however, occurred very infrequently. Splitting A more frequently appeared in both acute and chronic schizophrenics, but the difference from the borderline patients was not significant. Moreover, in borderline patients splitting C correlated significantly with other indicators of psychopathology, such as primary process thinking, anxiety, hostility, impaired reality testing, disturbed object relations, and avoidance of ambiguity, whereas splitting A did not (Leichsenring, 1999b). In acute and chronic schizophrenics, however, both splitting A and splitting C showed significant correlations with the indicators of psychopathology listed above. In normals, there were no significant correlations with indicators of psychopathology for splitting A, B, or C (Leichsenring, 1999b). According to these results, splitting in one diagnostic group does not necessarily have the same meaning as it does in another diagnostic group. A phenomenon may be pathological in one diagnostic group and not pathological in another. This seems to be true at least as far as the Lerner indicators of splitting are concerned.

In future studies the four Lerner criteria for splitting should be treated separately, and special attention should be paid to splitting within one response in borderline patients and to splitting in a sequence of two adjacent responses in schizophrenics.

With regard to validity, it is necessary to determine whether the Lerner scores correlate with other measures of primitive defense mechanisms. In one of my own studies, patients were not only administered the HIT, but also the Borderline Syndrome Index (BSI, Conte, Plutchik, Karasu & Jarret, 1980) and the Borderline Personality Inventory (BPI), a self report instrument developed by me in order to assess borderline personality organization by means of the three structural criteria proposed by Kernberg (Leichsenring, 1999b, 1999c). The BPI scales assess identity diffusion, primitive defense mechanisms and object relations, and reality testing. According to the existing results, reliability and validity of the "Borderline Personality Inventory" appears to be adequate (Leichsenring, 1997; 1999c; Spitzer, Michels-Lucht, Siebel & Freyberger, 2002).

On the Borderline Syndrome Index, the Lerner indicators of projective identification and of low-level denial on the HIT yielded significant correlations with the BSI score in a sample of 30 borderline patients and 30 patients with neurotic disorders (r=0.37, 0.38). This was not true for indicators of splitting and low-level devaluation (r=0.13, 0.01). However, the BSI is not a measure of defense mechanisms and its differential diagnostic validity for classifying individual patients has as yet not been established (Leichsenring, 1992). On the Borderline Personality Inventory (BPI), the Lerner indicators of splitting, projective identification, low-level devaluation, and low-level denial showed significant correlations with the BPI scales of identity-diffusion, low-level defenses and impaired reality testing (Leichsenring, 1999a,b). For low-level idealization no such correlations were found. However, Lerner's global splitting indicator showed significant correlations with the BPI identity diffusion and reality testing scales, but, contrary to expectations, did nor correlate significantly with the BPI scale of low-level defenses. By contrast, Splitting C showed significant correlations with both the identity diffusion and the low level defense scales of the BPI (Leichsenring, 1999b).

According to Kernberg (1976), there is a genuine relationship between splitting, impaired reality testing, and primary process thinking. Thus, the correlations of the Lerner scores for projective identification, low-level denial and low-level denial with the BPI scale of low-level defense mechanisms or identity diffusion found by me (Leichsenring, 1999 a) do not necessarily imply that the corresponding Lerner scores tap primarily these defense mechanisms. These correlations may simply result from the aspects of primary process thinking included in the Lerner criteria.

Cognitive Style: Avoidance of Ambiguity

Various relationships have been demonstrated between certain defense mechanisms and cognitive styles (Klein & Schlesinger, 1949; Gardner, Holzman, Klein, Linton & Spence, 1959). Cognitive styles resemble character defenses in that they are ways of establishing and maintaining contact with reality (Klein & Schlesinger, 1949; Bellak, Hurvich & Gediman, 1973). According to Gardner et al. (1959, p. 128) cognitive styles may be "preconditions for the emergence of defensive structures". We have studied cognitive styles using the HIT. In one of my studies Ertel's (1972) DOTA-dictionary was applied to the responses of borderline and neurotic patients to the HIT(Leichsenring, Roth & Meyer, 1992). The DOTA-dictionary is a content analytic method, by which the relative number of the so called A-terms used in a text (e.g. "always", "all", "never", "total", "complete", "certain", "naturally", "only", "must", "must not") and the relative number of the so called B-terms (e.g. " sometimes", " some", "may", "partly", "hardly", "different") are assessed. A relatively frequent use of A-terms is interpreted as indicating cognitive dynamics characterized by the tendency to avoid cognitive ambiguity (Leichsenring et al., 1992).

In that study, borderline patients used significantly more A-terms than patients with neurotic disorders and could be distinguished quite well from the latter patients in sensitivity and specificity (Leichsenring et al., 1992). In another study, we showed that both acute and chronic schizophrenics also differed from patients with neurotic disorders by using A-terms significantly more frequently (Leichsenring and Meyer, 1992). The most frequent use of A-terms was found in paranoid and chronic schizophrenics. Avoidance of ambiguity also showed a significant correlation to the structural ambiguity of the HIT cards: The more ambiguous the cards, the more A-terms were used. Except for the chronic schizophrenics, this was true for all diagnostic groups studied, that is for normals, patients with neurotic disorders, borderline patients, and acute schizophrenics (Leichsenring and Meyer, 1994). These results are consistent with the interpretation that a relatively frequent use of A-terms is a defensive or coping mechanism which varies with both diagnostic and situational variables

Convergent results were obtained by means of a different method by Draguns (1963) who investigated the imposition of meaning upon pictures different in the degree of photographic blur Compared with normal controls, both acute and chronic schizophrenics avoided ambiguity by naming the objects depicted in these photographs prematurely and erroneously. However, there was a distinct trend toward bimodality, with a minority of schizophrenics lagging behind normals and imposing a label on the pictures belatedly. Cashdan (1966) confirmed and extended these results and related avoidance of ambiguity and search for certainty to delusional thinking in schizophrenia. Draguns (1991,p.297)) concluded that "information use in this disorder is disrupted, and efficient and realistic responding under conditions of uncertainty is impaired."

In the present context it is of interest that the Lerner indicators of splitting (within one response), "projective identification" (projection), and low-level denial on the HIT correlated significantly (r of 0.47, 0.34, and 0.36, respectively) with the A-terms of the DOTA-dictionary in borderline patients. According to these results, there seems to be a connection between low-level defense mechanisms as assessed by the modified Lerner criteria and cognitive dynamics of avoiding cognitive ambiguity as assessed by the DOTA-dictionary. These results are consistent with the general assumptions recapitulated above and with the findings of Klein, Gardner and colleagues.

In another study we examined the discriminative power of Kernberg's (1967) presumptive diagnostic elements of borderline disorder (Leichsenring & Ardjomandi, 1992). According to the data, 76 percent (19/25) of the borderline patients and 89 percent (17/19) of the patients with neurotic disorders were classified correctly using the criterion of at least three of Kernberg's presumptive diagnostic elements in diagnostic classification. In this sample, the Lerner indicators of splitting and low-level devaluation on the HIT correlated significantly with the following presumptive diagnostic elements: impulse neurosis and addictions (r=0.30, 0.33), suicidal attempts (r=0.38, 0.32), "mutilation of self or damaging others" (r=0.32, 0.51) and prepsychotic personality structure (r=0.32, 0.40). The Lerner indicators of low-level denial correlated significantly with suicidal attempts (r=0.40) and prepsychotic personality structure (r=0.48). Projective identification correlated significantly with prepsychotic personality structure" (r=0.53). The correlations are significant, but only moderate in size. These results indicate that the Lerner indicators of defense mechanisms are meaningfully associated with severe psychiatric symptoms that are regarded by Kernberg as presumptive diagnostic elements of a borderline disorder.

Summing up, the results of studies of the Lerner scores on the HIT point to the validity of the modified Lerner criteria, with the exception of primitive idealization. However, further research is necessary in order to determine whether these indicators measure primarily primitive defense mechanisms and whether these indicators are valid with regard to primitive defense mechanisms in outpatients with borderline and narcissistic personality disorder.

Cooper, Perry, and Arnow (1988) developed a Rorschach scoring system for 15 defense mechanisms which they grouped into three categories: neurotic (according to Fenichel, 1945, Schafer, 1954), borderline (according to Kernberg, 1967) and psychotic (according to Semrad, Grinspoon & Feinberg, 1973). Like the Lerner scores, Cooper et al.'s system relies primarily on content, but is not restricted to human responses. Its scoring criteria for neurotic defenses are strongly influenced by Schafer (1954), Holt (1960),, and Weiner (1966). In scoring borderline defenses, some of Lerner's criteria were utilized and others were developed by the authors. In line with Semrad, Grinspoon and Feinberg (1973), hypomanic and massive varieties of denial are scored as psychotic defense mechanisms that involve major distortions in perception or extreme affective or associative elaborations of perceptions. The criteria for scoring neurotic, borderline, and psychotic defense mechanisms have not been published by Cooper et al. (1988). However, in an earlier paper (Cooper & Arnow, 1986) scoring criteria for borderline defenses were presented, based on response content and comments about the examiner, the testing situation, and the self. Cooper et al. (1988) reported interrater agreements between 0.45 for rationalization and 0.80

for primitive idealization, with a median of 0.62. Interrater agreement for the three categories of neurotic, borderline and psychotic defense mechanisms was 0.71, 0.81 and 0.72, respectively. Only for primitive idealization did interrater agreement exceed 0.80; six defense mechanisms were scored with an interrater agreement of at least 0.70. Interrater agreement for repression as the central neurotic defense mechanism was only 0.58, for reaction formation it was 0.57. The validity of the Rorschach Defense Scales was tested by Cooper et al. (1988) in three samples of patients: borderline and antisocial personality disorder according to DSM-III, and bipolar Type II patients, according to the Research Diagnostic Criteria. Indicators of splitting, devaluation, projection and hypomanic denial were found to correlate significantly with external criteria of borderline personality disorder, Perry 's (1982) Borderline Personality Disorder Scale (BPD), and the sum of the positive DSM-III-criteria of the borderline personality disorder. These correlations, however, were only moderate (0.24 to 0.40). The indicators of projective identification did not correlate significantly with these external criteria. Contrary to expectations, hypomanic and massive denial did not correlate significantly with the bipolar criteria. The significant correlation of hypomanic denial with the borderline criteria makes the classification of this defense mechanism as psychotic questionable. Furthermore, none of the 15 defense mechanisms studied correlated significantly with the external criteria for antisocial personality disorder and bipolar Type II. Discriminant function analysis using the borderline defense indicators as predictors failed to discriminate the three diagnostic groups Cooper et al. (1988, p. 197) attributed this result to an assumed close relationship between "these three closely related disorders." However, the conceptual relationship between the bipolar Type II disorder and the other disorders is not yet clear.

Upon correlating the percentage of observed indicators of a defense mechanism relative to the total number of all defenses for each subject, the Rorschach splitting indicator exhibited significant coefficients with BPD subscales for splitting of the object (r=0.29) and splitting of the self image (r=0.31). However, the authors' conclusion (p. 200) that "bipolar Type II diagnosis showed a strong association with defense mechanisms of intellectualization and isolation of affect" seems to me a little bold: The correlation with isolation is significant, but amounts to only 0.23, and the one for intellectualization is not significant.

Summing up the findings about the Cooper scoring system, the reliability of scoring of specific defense mechanisms is not sufficiently high. For some of the defense mechanisms this may be due to the low base rates, as surmised by Cooper et al. (1988) In light their findings, the validity of the indicators of projective identification as a borderline defense mechanism and of massive and hypomanic denial as psychotic defense mechanisms is questionable. However, hypomanic denial appears to be associated with borderline pathology. The validity of neurotic defense mechanisms should be pursued through systematic research with neurotics. On the basis of the findings obtained so far, it is not possible to assess primitive defense mechanisms by the Cooper criteria in antisocial personalities, given Kernberg's (1975) assumption that antisocial personalities are a subgroup of borderline patients, which is supported by the findings of Pope, Jonas, Hudson, Cohen and Gunderson (1983).

Summing up, the findings presented here provide some evidence that primitive defense mechanisms can be assessed by Rorschach or HIT scores. However, I agree with Carr (1987, p. 353) that "convincing validation will have to come from evidence that shows that a Rorschach measure for a specific defense is correlated adequately with some clinical or behavioral evidence for that particular defense, rather than that a plethora of defenses differentiates large diagnostic groups that, on the basis on somebody's theory, presumably use these defenses".

Thus, further research is necessary in order to assess defense mechanisms by independent measures and to interrelate the findings to be obtained.

References

Akiskal, H. C., Chen, S. E., Davis, G. C., Puzantian, V. R., Kashgarian, M. & Bolinger, J.M. (1985). Borderline: An adjective in search of a noun. *Journal of Clinical Psychiatry, 46*, 41-48.

American Psychiatric Association (1987). *Diagnostic and Statistical Manual of Mental Disorders*, Third Edition, Revised (DSM-IIIR). Washington, DC: Author.

American Psychiatric Association (1994). *Diagnostic and Statistical Manual of Mental Disorders*, Fourth Edition (DSM-4). Washington, DC: Author

Arlow, J. & Brenner, C. (1964). *Psychoanalytic concepts and the structural theory*. New York: International Universities Press.

Baxter, J., Becker, J. & Hooks, W. (1963). Defensive style in the families of schizophrenics and controls. *Journal of Abnormal and Social Psychology, 5*, 512-518.

Bellak, L. (1975). *The TAT, CTA and SAT in clinical use*. New York: Grune & Stratton.

Bellak, L., Hurvich, M. & Gediman, H.K.(1973). *Ego functions in schizophrenics, neurotics and normals*. New York: Wiley.

Benedetti, G. (1977). Das Borderline-Syndrom. Ein kritischer Überblick zu neueren psychiatrischen und psychoanalytischen Auffassungen. (The borderline syndrome. A critical review of recent psychiatric and psychoanalytic concepts). *Der Nervenarzt, 48*, 641-650.

Beutel, M. (1988). *Bewältigungsprozesse bei chronischen Krankheiten*. (Coping mechanisms and chronic disease). Weinheim: VCH.

Bibring, G.L., Dwyer, T.M., Huntington, T.S., Valenstein, A.F. (1961). A study of psychological processes in pregnancy and the earliest mother-child-relationship. *Psychoanalytic study of the child, 16*, 25-72.

Blatt, S.J. & Ritzler, B.A.(1974). Thought disorder and boundary disturbances in psychosis. *Journal of Consulting and Clinical Psychology, 42*, 370-381.

Brenner, Ch. (1981). Defense and defense mechanisms. *Psychoanalytic Quarterly, 50*, 557-569.

Carr, A.C. (1987). Borderline defenses and Rorschach responses: A critique of Lerner, Albert and Walsh. *Journal of Personality Assessment, 51*, 349-354.

Cashdan, S. (1966). Delusional thinking and the induction process in schizophrenia. *Journal of Consulting Psychology, 30*, 207-212.

Conte, H.R., Plutchik, R., Karasu, T.B., Jerrett, I. (1980). A self-report borderline-scale. Discriminative Validity and preliminary norms. *Journal of Nervous and Mental Disease, 168*, 428-435.

Cooper, S.H. & Arnow, D. (1986). An object relations view of the borderline defenses: A Rorschach analysis. In: Kissen, M. (ed.), *Assessing object relations phenomena*. Madison, CT: International Universities Press.

Cooper, S.H., Perry, J.C. & Arnow, D. (1988). An empirical approach to the study of defense mechanisms: I. Reliability and preliminary validity of the Rorschach defense scales. *Journal of Personality Assessment, 52*, 187-203.

Cramer, P. & Blatt, S. (1990). Use of the TAT to measure change in defensive mechanisms following intensive psychotherapy. *Journal of Personality Assessment, 54*, 236-251.

Cramer, P. (1987). The development of defense mechanisms. *Journal of Personality, 55*, 597-614.

Cramer, P. (1999). Future directions for the Thematic Apperception Test. *Journal of Personality Assessment, 72*, 74-92.

Draguns, J.G. (1963). Responses to cognitive and perceptual ambiguity in chronic and acute schizophrenics. *Journal of Abnormal and Social Psychology, 66*, 24-30

Draguns, J.G. (1991). Microgenetic techniques in personality assessment. In R.E. Hanlon (Ed.), *Cognitive microgenesis: A neuropsychological perspective* (pp. 286-315). New York: Springer-Verlag.

Elizur, A.(1949). Content Analysis of the Rorschach with regard to anxiety and hostility. *Rorschach Research Exchange and Journal of Projective Techniques, 13*, 247-287.

Ertel, S (1981). Prägnanztendenzen in Wahrnehmung und Bewußtsein. (Tendencies toward Pragnanz in perception and consciousness). *Zeitschrift für Semiotik, 3*, 107-141.

Ertel, S. (1972). Erkenntnis und Dogmatismus. (Cognition and dogmatism). *Psychologische Rundschau, 23*, 241-269.

Exner, J. (1986). Some Rorschach data comparing borderline with schizophrenics and schizotypal personality disorder. *Journal of Personality Assessment, 50, 455-471.*

Fenichel, O. (1945). *The psychoanalytic theory of neurosis*. New York: Norton.

Freud, A. (1936). *Das Ich und die Abwehrmechanismen*. (The ego and the mechanisms of defense). Munich: Kindler, 1959.

Freud, S. (1895). *Studien über Hysterie*. (Studies on hysteria). GW, 75-312.

Freud, S. (1926). *Hemmung, Symptom und Angst*. (Inhibitions, Symptoms and Anxiety). GW XIV, 111-205.

Freud, S. (1937). *Die endliche und die unendliche Analyse*. (Analysis terminable and interminable). GW XVI, 57-99.

Gacano, C.B. (1990). An empirical study of object relations and defensive operations in antisocial personality disorder. *Journal of Personality Assessment, 54*, 589-600.

Gardner, R., Holzman, Ph.S., Klein, G.S., Linton, H., Spence, D.P. (1959). Cognitive control. A study of individual consistencies in cognitive behavior. *Psychological Issues, 4*.

Hartmann, H.(1939). *Ego psychology and the problem of adaptation*. New York: International Universities Press [Deutsch: Ich-Psychologie. Stuttgart, Klett, 1972].

Heigl-Evers, A. (1972). *Konzepte der analytischen Gruppenpsychotherapie*. (Concepts of the psychoanalytic group therapy). Vandenhoeck & Ruprecht, Göttingen.

Hilsenroth, M.J., Hibbard, S.R., Nash, M.R. & Handler, L. (1993). A Rorschach study of narcissism, defense and aggression in borderline, narcissistic, and cluster C personality disorders. *Journal of Personality Disorders, 60*, 346-361.

Hoffmann, S.O. (1984). *Charakter und Neurose*. (Character and neurosis). Frankfurt: Suhrkamp.

Holt, R. (1960). *Manual for scoring primary process on the Rorschach.* Unpublished Manuscript.

Holtzman, W.H., Thorpe, J.S., Swartz, J.D.& Herron, E.W. (1961). *Inkblot Perception and Personality*. Austin: University of Texas Press.

Kernberg, O.F. (1967). Borderline personality organization. *Journal of the American Psychoanalytic Association, 15,* 641- 685.

Kernberg, O.F. (1975). *Borderline conditions and pathological narcissism.* New York: Yason Aronson.

Kernberg, O.F. (1976). *Object relations theory and clinical psychoanalysis.* New York, Jason Aronson.

Kernberg, O.F. (1977). The structural diagnosis of borderline personality organization. In: P. Hartocollis (ed.), *Borderline personality disorders. The concept, the syndrome, the patient.* New York: International Universities Press.

Kernberg, O.F. (1984). *Severe personality disorders. Psychotherapeutic strategies.* New Haven, CT: Yale University Press.

Klein, G. & Schlesinger, H. (1949). Where is the perceiver in perceptual theory ? *Journal of Personality, 18*, 32-47.

Koenigsberg, W.H. (1982). A comparison if hospitalized and non-hospitalized borderline patients. *American Journal of Psychiatry, 139*, 1292-1297.

Kolb, J.E. & Gunderson, J. G. (1980). Diagnosing borderline patients with a semistructured interview. *Archives of General Psychiatry, 37*, 37-41.

Laughlin, H.P. (1970). *The ego and its defenses.* Appleton-Century-Crofts, New York.

Leichsenring, F. & Hiller, W. (2001). Projektive Verfahren. (Projective Techniques). In R.D. Stieglitz, U.Baumann, H.J. Freyberger, (Eds.), *Psychodiagnostik in Klinischer Psychologie, Psychiatrie, Psychotherapie* (pp. 183-191). (Second Edition). Stuttgart: Thieme.

Leichsenring, F. & Meyer, H.A. (1992). Kognitiver Stil bei Schizophrenen: Ambiguitäts-Reduktion und verminderte Abstraktheit. (Cognititive style in schizophrenics: reduction of ambiguity and reduced abstractness). *Zeitschrift für Klinische Psychologie, Psychopathologie und Psychotherapie, 40,* 136-147.

Leichsenring, F. & Meyer, H.A. (1994). Reduzierung von Ambiguität: sprachstatistische Untersuchungen an "Normalen", Neurotikern, Borderline-Patienten und Schizophrenen. (Reduction of ambiguity: content analytic studies in normals, neurotics, borderline patients and schizophrenics). *Zeitschrift für Klinische Psychologie, Psychopathologie und Psychotherapie, 42,* 355-372.

Leichsenring, F. (1991 a). "Frühe" Abwehrmechanismen bei Borderline- und neurotischen Patienten. ("Early" defense mechanisms in borderline and neurotic patients). *Zeitschrift für Klinische Psychologie, 20*, 75-91.

Leichsenring, F. (1991b). Primary process thinking, primitive defensive operations and object relationships in borderline and neurotic patients. *Psychopathology, 24*, 39-44.

Leichsenring, F. (1992). Zur differential-diagnostischen Validität des Borderline-Syndrom-Indexes. (On the differential diagnostic validity of the Borderline-Syndrom-Index). *Diagnostica, 38*, 155-159.

Leichsenring, F. (1996). *Borderline-Stile. Denken, Fühlen, Abwehrmechanismen und Objektbeziehungen bei Borderline-Patienten.* (Borderline styles. Thinking, emotions, defense mechanisms and object relations in borderline patients.). Huber, Bern.

Leichsenring, F. (1997). : *"Borderline-Persönlichkeits Inventar"* ("Borderline Personality Inventory"). Manual. Göttingen: Hogrefe.

Leichsenring, F. (1999a). Primitive defense mechanisms in schizophrenics and borderline patients. *The Journal of Nervous and Mental Disease, 187*, 229-236.

Leichsenring, F. (1999b). Splitting: An empirical study. *Bulletin of the Menninger Clinic, 63*, 520-537.

Leichsenring, F. (1999c). Development and first results of the Borderline Personality Inventory (BPI). A self-report instrument for assessing borderline personality organization. *Journal of Personality Assessment, 73*, 45-63.

Leichsenring, F. und Ardjomandi, M.E. (1992). Gibt es "borderline-verdächtige Symptome"? (Are there presumptive symptoms of a borderline disorder ?). *Gruppentherapie und Gruppendynamik, 28*, 29-39.

Leichsenring, F., Roth, T und Meyer, H.A. (1992). Kognitiver Stil bei Borderline-Patienten: Ambiguitäts-Vermeidung und verminderte Abstraktheit. (Cognitive style in borderline compared to neurotic patients: Avoidance of ambiguity and reduced abstractness). *Diagnostica, 38*, 52-65.

Lerner, H.D., Sugarman, A., Barbour, C.G. (1985). Patterns of ego boundary disturbance in neurotic, borderline and schizophrenic patients. *Psychoanalytic Psychology, 2*, 47-66.

Lerner, H.D., Sugarman, A., Gaughran, J. (1981). Borderline and schizophrenic patients. A comparative study of defensive structure. *The Journal of Nervous and Mental Disease*, 169, 705-711.

Lerner, P. M. (1990). Rorschach Assessment of primitive defenses: A review. *Journal of Personality Assessment, 54,* 30-46.

Lerner, H., Albert, C. & Walsh, M. (1987). The Rorschach assessment of borderline defenses: A concurrent validity study. *Journal of Personality Assessment, 51*, 334-348.

Lerner, R. & Lerner, H. (1980). Rorschach assessment of primitive defenses in borderline personality structure. In: J. Kwawer, Lerner, H., Lerner, P. & Sugarman, A. (Eds.), *Borderline phenomena and the Rorschach Test.* New York: International Universities Press.

Lichtenberg, J. & Slap, J. (1973). Notes on the concept of splitting and the defense mechanism of splitting of representations. *Journal of the American Psychoanalytic Association, 21*, 772-787.

Loewenstein, R. (1967). Defensive organization and autonomous ego functions. *Journal of the American Psychoanalytic Association, 15*, 795-809.

McGlashan, T.H. (1983). The borderline syndrome: Is it a variant of schizophrenia or affective disorder ? *Archives of General Psychiatry, 40*, 1319-1323.

Millon, T. (1984). On the renaissance of personality assessment and personality theory. *Journal of Personality Assessment,* 48, 450-466.

Murstein, B.I. & Mathes, S. (1996). Projection on projective techniques pathology: The problem that is not being addressed. *Journal of Personality Assessment, 66*, 337-349.

Murstein, B.I. (1956). *Handbook of projective techniques.* New York: Basic Books.

Noam, G.G. & Recklitis, C.J. (1990). The relationship between defenses and symptoms in adolescent psychopathology. *Journal of Personality Assessment, 54*, 311-327..

Ogden, Th.H. (1979). On projective identifikation. *International Journal of Psycho-Analysis, 60*, 357-373.

Ogden, Th.H. (1982). *Projective identification and psychotherapeutic technique.* New York: Jason Aronson.

Perry, C. (1982). *The borderline personality disorder scale: Reliability and validity.* Manuscript submitted for publication.

Plutchik, R., Kellermann, H. & Conte, H.R. (1979). A structural theory of ego defenses and emotions. In: C. Izard (ed.), *Emotions in personality and psychopathology*. Plenum: New York, 229-257.

Pope, H.G., Jonas, J.M., Hudson, J.I., Cohen, B.M., Gunderson, J.G. (1983). The validity of DSM-III borderline personality disorder. *Archives of General Psychiatry, 40*, 23-30.

Rapaport, D., Gill, M., Schafer, R. (1950). *Diagnostic psychological testing*, Vol.I & II. Chicago: Year Book Publishers.

Rauchfleisch, U. (1989). *Der Thematische Apperzeptionstest (TAT) in Diagnostik und Therapie.* (The Thematic Apperception Test (TAT) in diagnostics and therapy). Stuttgart: Enke.

Reich, W. (1933). *Charakteranalyse. Technik und Grundlagen.* (Character Analysis). Berlin: Selbstverlag.

Richter, H.E. (1967). *Eltern, Kind, Neurose.* (Parents, child, neurosis). Stuttgart: Klett.

Rosenfeld, H. (1954). Considerations regarding the psychoanalytic approach to acute and chronic schizophrenia. *International Journal of Psychoanalysis, 35*, 135-147.

Schafer, R. (1954). *Psychoanalytic interpretation in Rorschach testing. Theory and Application.* New York: Grune & Stratton.

Semrad, E., Grinspoon, L. & Feinberg, S. (1973). Development of an ego profile scale. *Archives of General Psychiatry, 28*, 70-77.

Shapiro. D. (1991). *Neurotische Stile.* (Neurotic styles). Göttingen: Vandenhoeck & Ruprecht.

Spitzer, C., Michels-Lucht, F., Siebel, U & Freyberger, H.J (2002). Zur Konstruktvalidität der Strukturachse der Operationalisierten Psychodynamischen Diagnostik (OPD) [On the validity of the axis "structure" of the Operationalized Psychodynamic Diagnostics]. *Z. Psychosom Med Psychother, 48,* 299-312.

Stone, M.H. (1980). *The borderline syndromes.* New York: McGraw- Hill.

Vaillant, G.E. (1971). Theoretical hierarchy of adaptive ego mechanisms. *Archives of General Psychiatry*, 24, 107-118.

Vaillant, G.E. (1976). Natural history of male psychological health. The relation of choice of ego mechanism of defense to adult adjustment. *Archives of General Psychiatry, 33*, 535-545.

Weiner, I.B. (1966). *Psychodiagnosis in schizophrenia.* New York: Wiley.

Willi, J. (1975). *Die Zweierbeziehung.* (The dyadic object relation) Reinbek: Rowohlt.

Defense Mechanisms
U. Hentschel, G. Smith, J.G. Draguns & W. Ehlers (Editors)

Chapter 7

Percept-Genetic Identification of Defense

Gudmund, J.W. Smith and Uwe Hentschel

Sigmund Freud's original idea about the operation of defense (repression) is illustrated by Figure 7.1. The percept-genetic tests described in this chapter are built on an analogous conception. Figure 7.2 shows that in these tests, a subliminal picture, eventually becoming supraliminal, is introduced as a threat to a hero figure, with whom the viewer is supposed to identify. How the viewer handles the subconscious anxiety generated by this situation, registered as bodily reactions, verbal reports, or drawings, forms the basis for the interpretation of these reactions as defensive.

Defenses are, of course, theoretical constructs: they cannot be seen or touched, either in clinical settings or in everyday life or experimental situations (cf. also the warnings by Hans Sjöbäck in Chapter 4 against reification of the construct). If you share your kitchen with a mouse you do not have to spot the animal itself, only such traces of it as black toppings or a gnawed flour bag are sufficient, to be convinced of its existence. In the case of defense mechanisms one *must* be content with the traces only. But these can be obvious enough, ranging from perceptual distortions to avoidance reactions. Moreover, they have a nonrandom distribution over situations and patients, manifesting themselves as severe symptoms, operating in one way in histrionics, in another in compulsives, differing between young and old, or remaining only latent possibilities. Freud himself vacillated in his view of defenses as purely pathogenic, finally settling for the pathogenic perspective. To some of his followers, the ego psychologists, the adaptive possibilities of defensive strategies were as interesting as the pathogenic ones. The introduction of defensive hierarchies with Gedo and Goldberg (1973) and Vaillant (1971) implied that some defenses, the mature ones, seen from the perspective of an adult way of functioning had to be considered to be less pathogenic than the immature ones. One of the methods presented below, the Meta-Contrast Technique (MCT), has been particularly adapted to a developmental perspective, because both behavioral and perceptual manifestations can be registered, the former being more typical of young children and considered to be prestages of the well-known adult mechanisms (Smith & Danielsson, 1982).

The MCT was introduced as a diagnostic tool in psychiatric settings but has lately also been applied in neuropsychology (cf. Hanlon, 1991). The Defense Mechanism Test (DMT) originally proved to be a useful instrument for the selection of stress-tolerant subjects but is now more and more adapted also to psychiatric problems.

impulse → conflict → defense → symptom

or :

impulse → conflict → defense → character

Figure 7.1: *The operation of defense in the psychoanalytic frame of references*

These applications should not be allowed to obscure the fact that defense manifestations are not only typical of the field of abnormal psychology but also appear in the protocols of so-called normals, perhaps in a more varied and flexible way than in psychiatric patients, cases of cerebral dysfunction, stress-intolerant people, etc. The scoring principles adopted for the DMT (Kragh, 1985) attest to this difference between adaptive and pathogenic uses of defenses. It thus seems obvious that defenses are employed not only to parry ominous anxiety signals but much more broadly to serve the maintenance of our general mental comfort. When using them we may feel better and less bothered by vague uneasiness, and we may be able more easily to concentrate on the task at hand, to be spared feelings of guilt for neglect of others, etc. It is instructive to learn that total absence of defenses in experiments with MCT (Smith & Danielsson, 1982) was most typical of children and youngsters who were unable to control their anxiety and were generally viewed by their therapists as having very bleak prospects. Also among patients who had attempted suicide, those who showed no signs of defense were, retrospectively evaluated, most at risk for a new fatal attempt

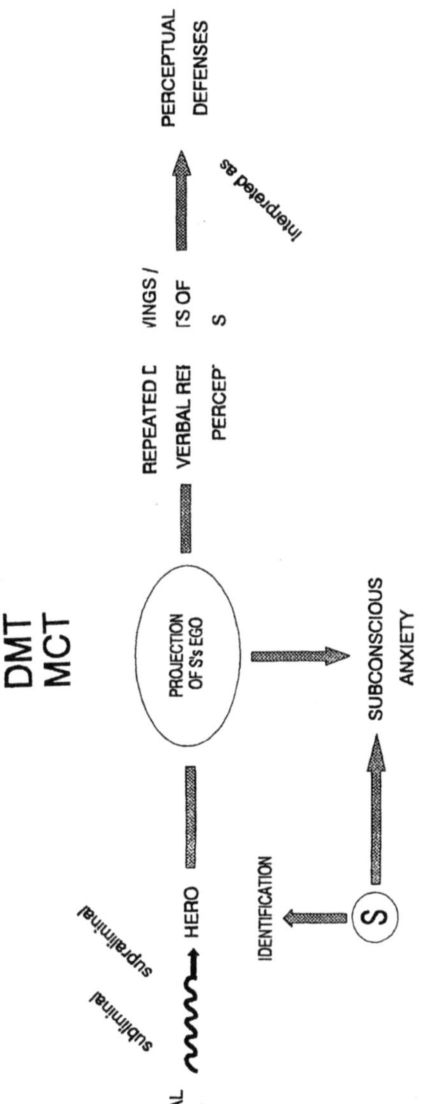

Figure 7.2: *The operation of defense in percept-genetic tests.*

(Berglund & Smith, 1988; Friberg et al. 1992). Perhaps defenses are also utilized for keeping at bay some of the subliminal influences constantly impinging on us, threatening to disturb our efficiency or equanimity. One aspect of defensive functioning that is often neglected is tolerance of anxiety. Signals of anxiety do not automatically trigger defensive reactions if the person can tolerate a certain level of discomfort. Studies in creativity (Smith & Carlsson, 1990) have shown that creative people are more tolerant of anxiety and less susceptible to subliminal influences of a negative, aggressive kind (Hentschel & Schneider, 1986), perhaps because they have the means to resolve conflicts in a productive way. Their defensive reactions tend toward the mature end of the continuum and seldom dominate their percept-geneses in a one-sided way.

One problem connected with the concept of defense is the tendency of defenses to multiply over the years in the writings on defenses. If we think of defenses as acting on different manifestations of our mental life-affects, ideas, percepts, motilities, it is a complex construct. Holland (1973) suggested that all defensive strategies are steered by a few or just one general operation in a quasi-algebraic way and proposed displacement as this general operator. He differentiated between displacement of direction (in the sense of a change in the self-nonself "localization": e.g., projection-introjection), displacement in time (e.g., regression), displacement in number (e.g., repression, denial), and displacement in similarity (e.g., sublimation, reaction formation). The idea of displacement as a central operation seems in a certain way similar to the central concept of reality distortion in percept-genetic techniques (cf. Chapters 13,18, 19). A schematic, parsimoni

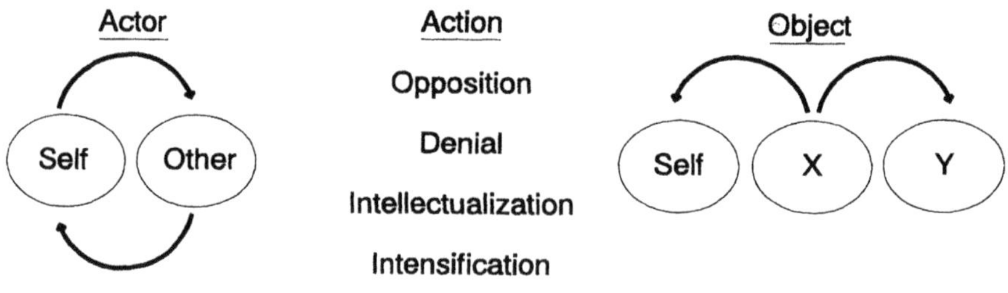

Figure 7.3: *Defenses as transformations on the actor, the action, and the object. (After Suppes and Warren, 1975)*

ous concept like this should not be used to rule out all specificity but rather as a help to explain the phenomena in their acknowledged variety. Holland has explicitly stated it in this way, and in percept-genesis the value that is given to the specific kind of reality distortion is already obvious from the scoring instructions of, for example, the DMT or MCT.

Suppes and Warren (1975) have made another attempt to provide a comprehensive classification of defense mechanisms. They use the basic idea that "transformations" are constituent for all defenses. They relate these transformations, however, not to physical or quasi-physical dimensions but to the "actor", the "action," and the "object" (cf. Fig. 7.3). Restricting their idea to the self as actor, and allowing also for the condition of no transformation, they can, on theoretical grounds, postulate a list of 29 different mechanisms of defense, which when identification as a basic principle is added, is extended to 44. An example for three transformations (on the actor, the action, and the object) would be, for example, the combination of projection plus reaction formation and turning against self which, in a verbalized form, could imply change from the nonacceptable unconscious proposition of "I love him" to the consciously acceptable one "He hates me."

From verbalizations given as examples, the transformations postulated by Suppes and Warren (1975) seem to be very sensible because they reflect the consequences of the whole defensive process. In reality an additional inference is needed because the unconscious proposition is not so easily available to the observer. Percept-genetic methods can help to uncover the unconscious proposition on the basis of a comparison of the subjectively perceived (and reported) content with the objectively presented stimulus. There are two inherent restrictions to this general statement. Whereas for example the object in the system of Suppes and Warren can be anybody ranging from mother, brother, or friend, to someone on the street, the application of a specific percept-genetic technique as a standardized test requires one stimulus or a restricted set of standardized stimuli, thus also limiting the range of potentially conflictual object representations. Restricting the object relation to the "Oedipal situation" as, for example, in the DMT and its modified version, DMTm (Andersson & Bengtsson, 1986) can, however, be defended with the argument that this is a very important and "prototypical situation" potentially influencing all other relations. The second restriction concerns the role of the actor, which in real life is the acting person, whereas in percept-genetic techniques, the identification of the responding subject with the hero must be postulated as an intermediate process to explain the transformations as defense mechanisms. Although an indirect proof for the feasibility of this latter assumption can be taken from all studies with results supporting the concurrent or predictive validity of percept-genetic tests, it could and should, as Martin Johnson (1986) has argued, be submitted to critical tests. Adding to Holland's (1973) remarks on the paradoxical thinking in psychoanalysis, the "paradox" in percept-genetic techniques lies in the need for the respondent first to have an idea of the objective stimulus before he or she can distort it, which however is an elementary process in all defense mechanisms. The effect or idea that is repressed or denied must necessarily have gained some representation before it is repressed or denied. The percept-genetic process in its beginnings thus necessarily comprises elements from subliminal perception, and the theoretical links between the two approaches have repeatedly been underlined (e.g., Dixon, Hentschel, & Smith, 1986; Hentschel, Smith, & Draguns, 1986).

The Defense Mechanism Test (DMT)

In 1955 Ulf Kragh started out to describe personality in its present functioning via perception in terms of perceptual construction and reconstruction processes. At the same time his intent was to overcome the restriction of a mere conscious conception of personality. After having experimented with different tachistoscopically presented TAT and TAT-like pictures, he published his DMT in 1969 (see also Kragh, 1960). From the beginning on, within the theoretical frame of references of perception-personality, the main aim of the DMT was the registration of defense mechanisms conceptualized in close relationship to the classical concept of defense (A. Freud, 1936/1946). Within the microgenetic tradition, the DMT can be characterized as a hologenetic procedure presenting repeatedly one and the same stimulus in a tachistoscopic device to the respondent starting with very short (subliminal) exposure times up to an exposure time of 2 seconds, at which a conscious representation is or at least should be possible.

The theoretical conception of perception-personality was worked out further by Kragh and Smith in 1970, and the first revision of the DMT was published in 1985 (Kragh, 1985). Thousands of subjects have been tested with the DMT, mainly with the purpose of selecting stress-resistant job applicants for jobs like jet pilot and frog man (Kragh, 1962). Ulf Kragh and others had also selected a number of case histories describing clinical cases (e.g., Kragh, 1970, 1980, 1984) and the DMT, although on a small scale, started to be used also for purposes of clinical diagnosis (Hentschel & Balint, 1974; Sharma, 1977). Today there are clinical research projects with the DMT going on in Sweden (Armelius & Sundbom, 1991), in the Netherlands (Godeart, Hagenaars, Olff, & Brosschot, 1991), in Italy (Rubino, Pezzarossa, & Grasso, 1991; cf. also Chapter 18), and in Germany (Gitzinger, 1988; and Hentschel et al.; cf. Chapter 19). Hentschel and Kiessling (1990) and Hentschel, Kiessling, and Hosemann (1991), have also used the DMT for the prediction of the performance in cognitive tasks and attention control (cf. also Chapter 14). Another important topic has become the relation of DMT categories to psychophysiological and endocrine variables, especially also in stress research (e.g., Ursin, Baade, & Levine, 1978; Endresen & Ursin, 1991). A bibliography edited by Sjöbäck and Bäckström (1990) lists more than 100 publications on the DMT, documenting the steadily increasing interest in the technique.

We refer to the DMT manual (Kragh, 1985) for most of the technical details of the testing procedure. The test is given in a darkened room (2.8 lux); the subject is told that he or she will see some pictures (this is explained with a demonstration slide) and is instructed to tell everything that is seen (including impressions) and to make a simple drawing of the exposed stimulus. There are strict rules for follow-up questions in which all kinds of suggestion are to be avoided. Each respondent is tested with two sex-specific test slides showing a male or female hero with an "instrument" and a threatening male or female figure peripheral to the hero. The answers of the respondent reflecting the subjective meaning of the stimulus are regarded as "phases" and registered as P1 (the first description with a meaningful structure), T1 a threshold phase in which for the first time a threat from the peripheral person is seen, and the C-phase, when the stimulus structure in all details is correctly represented in the subjective interpretation. The whole perceptual process reconstructed from the drawings and verbal answers from the respondent is subject of the DMT scoring procedure. The deviations from the objective content of the pictures shown are interpreted in terms of 10 main categories of defense mechanisms:

1. Repression, signified by the report of an inanimate hero or peripheral person.
2. Isolation, inferred from signs of separation of the hero and the peripheral person.
3. Denial, given on the basis of reports that deny or diminish the threat.
4. Reaction-formation, scored on the basis of answers turning the threat into its opposite.
5. Identification with the aggressor, standing for reports of an aggressive hero.
6. Turning against the self, scored when the hero or the instrument is hurt or worthless.
7. Introjection of the opposite sex, inferred from reports of the hero with another sex.

8. Introjection of another object, given in cases of duplication or multiplication of the hero.
9. Projection, interpreted on the basis of specific changes in the process of the hero perception during the P-phases.
10. Regression, scored in cases of breakdown of an earlier intaçt pictorial structure.

Within these main signs there are various numbers of other sign variants. Isolation has, for example, 14 variants, reaction formation has 4, turning against the self 2. Examples of the scoring of the subjects' drawings are given in Fig. 7.4. There are different models for the psychometric treatment of the signs. Kragh (1969) has worked with ratings for the severity of maladaptation, and Neuman (1978) has proposed a phase-related weighing model. The manual of the revised DMT (Kragh, 1985) mentions the possibility of partitioning the whole process into three sections (early, middle, and late phases), which is empirically applied in Chapter 19. In clinical applications comparisons between diagnostic groups are often also made on the basis of sign variants (Rubino et al., 1991). A phenomenological approach, basically without the need to use the psychodynamic theoretical frame of reference was chosen by Cooper (1991), who has tried to "construct" the basic variables by means of G-analysis (Holley & Guilford, 1964).

Reliability and Validity of the DMT

From the whole test procedure it is obvious that a simple retest within a short period of time is as inadequate as the calculation of a split-half coefficient. Reliability estimates thus can be made on interrater comparisons and retests using, for example, one test picture at the first instance and another for the retest. Interrater reliability has a range from .65 to .95, depending on the pretraining of the scorers. Stability over time for defensive signs estimated by parallel test results seems to be also very good (r = .81 after one year; cf. Kragh, 1985). Concerning validity, the 1985 manual lists 18 studies (16 with significant results) in which the group test version has been applied; this could be spplemented by other studies listed in the bibliography by Sjöbäck and Bäckström (1990) (cf. also the contributions in this volume using the DMT: Chapters 8, 18, 19). Concerning the selection of pilots especially, the incremental validity of the DMT is worth mentioning. The DMT has been used repeatedly in this context with highly preselected groups. Given very low correlations also to the other tests in the test battery used for selection, the resulting validity can be claimed almost exclusively for the DMT (cf. Kragh, 1985). The DMT results did not reach significance in a study with British Air Force pilots for the prediction of their success in flight training (Stoker, 1982).

Figure 7.4: *Examples for different DMT drawings and categorizations. (A) Identification with the aggressor: "A soldier with a gun. In winter dressing." (B) Turning against the self: "Maybe patient on the operation table during stomach operation. A male assistant and a female doctor?" (C) Repression and reaction formation: "A boy playing with a puppy." (D) Reaction formation: "A girl sitting at the other table, writing."*

The usefulness of the DMT has been tried again in a series of studies originating in Elisabet Sundbom's project group at Umeå, Sweden. They have been able to prove that perceptual defense patterns are different depending on the type of psychopathology: among adult psychiatric patients (Sundbom & Armelius, 1992); among teenagers in psychiatric care (Fransson & Sundbom, 1997), and among borderline personalities (Sundbom, 1992). Results from studies with various psychosomatic groups indicate that these can be differentiated along two independent dimensions: *defensive style* and *relational reciprocity* (Henningsson, 1999). The test has also been tried in transcultural comparisons (Sundbom et al., 2002).

Problems with the DMT

Olff (1991) has made an inquiry about the DMT procedures used by different researchers and has concluded that the procedures are far from standardized (differences in types of projector, illumination in the room and on the screen, distance to the screen, questions asked, etc.). Hans Sjöbäck (1991) has written a paper with the provocative title, "The Defence Mechanism Test: What pictures do you use?" also revealing an unexpected variety. Sjöbäck claims that many of these variants are unauthorized. The variance in the test material used and in the skill of the experimenters represents a serious problem for the accumulation of knowledge and impedes a conclusive judgment regarding the value of the test. However, for the selection of Scandinavian air force pilots, together with the studies by Sundbom et al. mentioned above, which provides the strongest support for the validity of the test, the test procedure is quite well standardized. Critical evaluations of the test from other psychological laboratories often concern the difficulty of learning the scoring system, unwillingness to accept the psychoanalytical frame of reference and, if the standards of the selecting institution so require (see Stoll, 1990), the difficult if not impossible task of explaining the test results to the testees.

Modifications of the DMT

In the DMT the defensive process in the respondent is stimulated according to the basic process as outlined in Fig. 7.2. The threat stems from a situation reminding one of the one-sided oedipal situation with the parental figure of the same sex as a punishing agent. In psychoanalysis the complete oedipal situation has been formulated with libidinal and aggressive impulses for both parents, thus also including the possibility of both parents as punishing agents. In line with this basic idea and the additional elaboration of a theoretical model based on Heinz Kohut's and Melanie Klein's psychoanalytical conceptions, combined with a developmental perspective, Alf Andersson (see Andersson & Bengtsson, 1986) has proposed a change of the test pictures confronting both males and females with a male and a female threat figure. Affect-defenses are described as a dialectical series represented in developmental order as reification, personification, and annihilation. These affect-defenses correspond to the following signs in the modified DMT version (DMTm): repression, introaggression, and isolation of affect. The three qualitatively different forms of handling the "evil" are directed by basic instrumental proficiencies. The main aim of Andersson (cf. Andersson & Bengtsson, 1986) is to demonstrate that it is not enough to name various forms of defense; one must also deepen the analysis of motives underlying the defensive activity bound to a verbal symbolic medium and thus protracted in relation to the original triggering situation. Most of the studies using the DMTm have not been published in English, but this test, with its elaborated theoretical frame of reference, seems to be useful in the clinical context when studying states of identity crises, neurotic and narcissistic problems, and psychotic states, yet not alleging, to have introduced a new test. DMT-like pictures without the claim that a new test has been constructed have been used among others by Westerlundh (e.g., Westerlundh and Sjöbäck, 1986; cf. also Chapter 13; Kline & Cooper, 1977). Gitzinger (1991) has changed the basic testing device by showing, compared to the DMT, slightly changed stimuli on a computer monitor and providing an interactive computer program for the scoring procedure that then follows. Brand, Olff, Hulsman, and Slagman (1991) have also experimented with digitized pictures for measuring defense. But their perceptual defense test (PD-test) does not pretend to replace the DMT. It is obvious that the new technical possibilities will stimulate other attempts to present DMT or DMT-like pictures on a computer screen or a video monitor. It should be kept in mind however that generating new stimuli is one thing and the introduction of a new "test" is another. This is, as every test author knows a very laborious task. The concept of defense in our view would profit more from a few well-standardized, reliable and valid test instruments than from a great number of experimental versions.

Percept-genetic Object-Relations Test (PORT)

Nilsson & Svensson (1999) have introduced a new set of pictures to study the micro-development of themes referring to child-parent relations. Among the themes used in the test those alluding to attachment or separation appear to be particularly potent. Studies of psychiatric groups are included in the manual and a study of children born preterm, referred to below. The test has also proved useful for descriptions of the effects of psychotherapy.

New Thematic Innovations Based on the DMT Device

The Mother-Child Picture Test (MCPT)

The MCPT utilizes the DMT presentation device. The stimulus is a picture of a woman feeding a child with a spoon. The child is sitting in a high chair. Both woman and child are seen in half profile. The feminine characteristics of the woman are quite obvious. Behind the woman, part of a half-open window is showing. Preliminary studies by S. Balint indicated that when respondents viewed this picture in a tachistoscope they often described it in such a way as to reveal their own very personal and deep-seated conflicts around mother-child relations. In the first systematic validation studies, the test was administered to 100 mothers and their children aged 7-8 years (Smith et al., 1980, 1981, and 1984). The scoring scheme partly referred to mothers and children together, partly to these groups separately. Only a selection of possible scoring categories is presented here.

Mother not reported even in the final phase (for children); the child in the picture reported to have disappeared from one phase to the next (for mothers and children).
The child is seen as a doll, an animal, an object, etc. (for mothers). The child is seen as naughty, dirty, unkempt, etc. (for mothers).
Picture reported as frightening, mother as aggressive, etc. (for children).

The first two of these groups of signs, in particular, could be classed as defensive; the latter two as more open expressions of disgust for the child or fright of the mother. These signs, together with signs not accounted for here, were arranged into strong, medium, and marginal categories. There was a high correlation between mothers and children in half of the groups ($p < .001$) and, still, in the other half when it was cross-validated ($p < .01$).

These scoring categories were also validated in a longitudinal study of children born preterm (Tideman et al., 2002). The MCT results obtained at the age of 9 showed that both the preterm children and their mothers differed significantly from a control group of full-terms. At the age of 19 these children again differed from controls in their reactions to the attachment and separation themes in the PORT. Both preterm children and mothers in the MCPT and young preterm adults in the PORT disclosed a special kind of emotional vulnerability hardly discernible at the surface of their everyday selves.

The Meta-Contrast Technique (MCT)

The original purpose of the MCT was to study the development of a new percept within the context of an old percept, stabilized beforehand, when the meaning of the new percept was at variance with or implied a threat against the old percept. The introduction of antagonistic material made the MCT a test of coping mechanisms concerned with mediation of conflict. These mechanisms, it has turned out, are the core of what we call defenses. As thus indicated, the MCT implies repeated tachistoscopic presentations of pairs of stimuli, one of them exposed immediately before the other. The second stimulus (B) in a pair is intended to offer a constant perceptual frame of reference to which the viewer has been adapted in advance. Within this frame the development of the first stimulus (A) is going to be followed step by step. A is either incongruent with B or represents a threat to a person depicted in B. To begin with, A is exposed very rapidly and does not manifest itself as a perceptual structure in its own right, but sometimes as changes in the B-percept. With subsequently prolonged exposure times, however, A gradually penetrates B, often in "disguise," to begin with. The test session is concluded when A+B have been correctly reported or when the longest exposure time has been reached. It would be unnecessary to dwell on the technical details (given in Smith, Johnson, Almgren, and Johanson, 2002). Let us just repeat the three basic phases of the test session:

1. Starting with .01 s (somewhat longer with the new computerized TV device), B is presented at gradually prolonged exposure times until it has been correctly reported.
2. Thereafter, B is exposed at a standardized level alone five times in a control series.
3. A is then introduced before B at .01 s (again somewhat longer with the new device). The time of B is held constant and that of A prolonged every second time (according to a geometric scale with a constant of the square root of 2).

There are presently eight stimulus pictures divided up into two tests that have proved to be parallel. Each test includes two tasks or two pairs of pictures (A+B). Each of the four pairs is assigned a number from 1 to 4. Stimulus B2 is a thoroughly revised version of card 1 in the Thematic Apperception Test. The other pictures are either original drawings or photomontages. The two picture pairs in the first test are Al = a car, B1 = interior of a room, A2 = apelike human, B2 = boy (hero) and background window. The original tachistoscopic contrivance allowed the second stimulus in a pair to be exposed on a semitransparent projection screen directly after the first one. Exposure times ranged from 10 ms upward (cf. Fig. 7.5). A new contrivance exploits a computer program and a swift TV screen. Stimuli are projected in front of the respondent, who describes what s/he has seen after each presentation. The experimenter not only records what the respondent says but also how s/he behaves (shutting the eyes, yawning, looking obviously panic-stricken, becoming restless, etc.).

Scoring

The scoring refers to changes in reports of B and interpretations of A and, not least important, the respondent's behavior. The sequential aspect is always in focus. What is scored late in a series is supposed to represent more manifest tendencies than what is reported early, the reason being that late phases are closer to the individual's habitual level of experiencing. There are two main groups of signs: signs of anxiety and signs of defense against anxiety and conflict. The former signs are ordered in a scale from open manifestations of panic to less severe forms of anxiety (internalized fear). The defensive signs range from primitive, behavioral forms to more advanced meaning transformations of A. They are grouped in the following categories: repressive strategies, isolation and negation strategies, projective strategies, depression, regressions, and self-referential sign variants.

In some instances the differentiation between various defenses, on the one hand, and cognitive style, on the other, can be difficult to ascertain.

1. The group of anxiety signs (mainly in the threat series). Signs of anxiety are organized in a hierarchy ranging from open fear or primary anxiety; via grave signs like broken structures, leaking (inefficient) defenses, zero-phases (without meaningful content); to moderate or mild signs like black structures reported late or early in the test series.

2. The group of defensive signs. Defensive activity in the individual is, of course, connected with fear and anxiety and a gradually progressing internalization during childhood. Still, at an age of 4-5 years and particularly in cognitively less mature children, external defenses dominate: it is the child itself who shuts its eyes, etc., later the hero as seen by the child. Behavioral defenses may, however, be registered even in normal adults, who often resort to them when more mature strategies prove inefficient. Primitive defenses are particularly common in psychologically disturbed people.

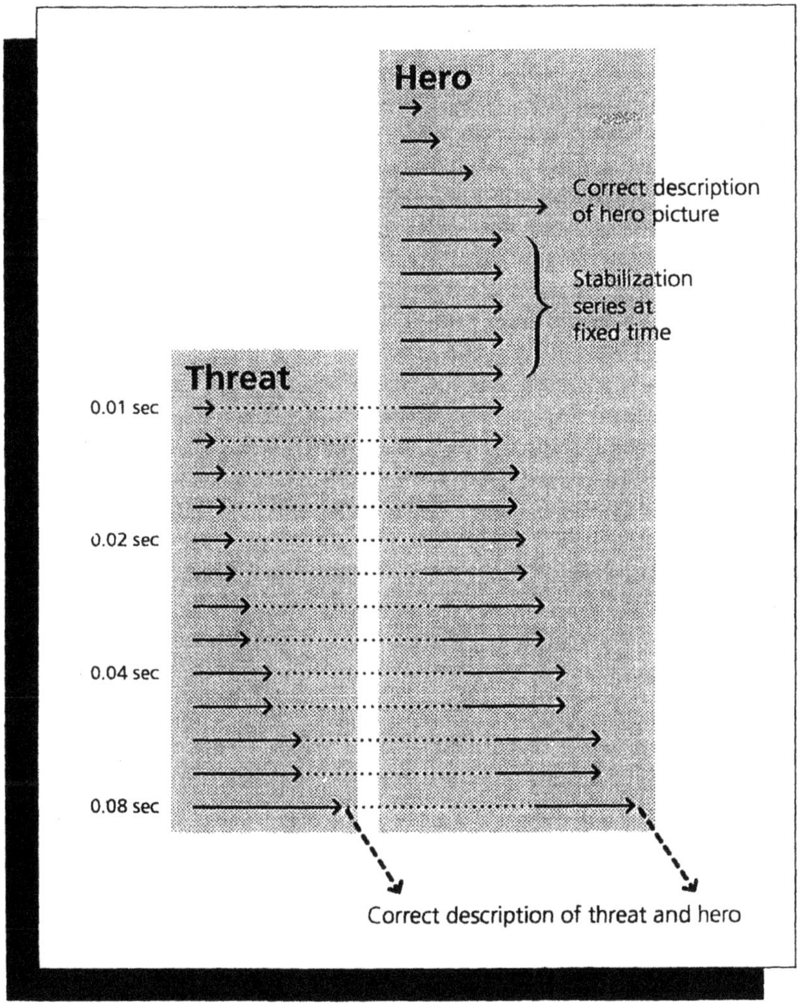

Figure 7.5: *The general design of the Meta-Contrast Technique (MCT)*

a) The group of repressive strategies (mainly in the threat series). The grouping presupposes that the adult strategy of repression originates in direct denial at the behavioral level in children of preschool age. Even more advanced and transformed signs imply a symbolic denial of danger. The signs range from direct denial like eye-shutting behavior; overinternalized but primitive strategies like eye-shutting reports; middle level strategies, when the threat becomes lifeless or is masked; to more transformed threats, like reports of a house, a tree, or a bike at the place of the threat.

b) The group of isolation and negation strategies (mainly in the threat series). This group of strategies does not attain full strength until late latency. The different strategies have an important characteristic in common: the separation of the hero from the threatening emotion. The most primitive isolation occurs when the subject isolates literally (hands on the screen, etc.). Spatial distortion and negation represent the next level. Genuine signs of isolation imply that the threat is whitened or covered. Empty geneses, where nothing happens, also belong in this group of signs.

c) The group of projective strategies (in both series). These strategies occur early in the development. The projectively functioning individual does not let a disturbing A become established as a structure in its own right, but interprets it via the habituated B-perception (which is affected more or less, e.g., by becoming almost unrecognizable or by just appearing in a new perspective-sensitive change). The subliminal influence of A on B often can be noted during the first exposures after the control series.

d) The group of depressive strategies (mainly in the threat series). Inhibition is the central, anxiety-dampening defense strategy in this group. In its massive variants it often indicates a psychotic "inhibition depression." Among the most common signs are stereotypies (i.e., reports at least five times in a row of an unchanged noninterpretation or wrong interpretation of A). Other severe signs of depression include reports of the threat as old, ill, etc. until the end.

e) The group of regressive strategies (in both series). All regressive reactions involve retreats from a habitual level to a more immature level. When a mature defense like genuine isolation fails (because anxiety is breaking through), the respondent may try a more primitive strategy like eye shutting. The depth of the regression may be defined as the difference between the baseline level and the final level. There are regressions to infantile ways of experiencing, discontinuities of a nonprojective type like zero-phases, leaking defenses (where the respondent may see a statue but still think that the statue is dangerous), and defensive regressions.

f) The group of self-referential signs or variants (in the threat series) where, for instance, the threat may be represented by a duplicate of the hero.

Standardization Data

The most recent manual (Smith, Johnson, Almgren, and Johanson, 2002) offers standardization data in detail. Let it just be said here that not only interrater but also test-retest correlations have been generally high, often close to the statistical ceiling. Validation data have been presented in more than 40 mutually independent studies, typical test criterion correlation coefficients ranging from .50 to .85. The first validation studies showed, for instance, that people with histrionic characters had more signs of what was called repression than other clinical groups, compulsive-obsessive subjects more signs of isolation-negation, psychotics more signs of regression, etc. The criterion groups were carefully selected. Later validations also refer to correlations with other tests, to change as a result of therapy, to differences between young children and older ones, etc. The MCT has also been applied in neuropsychological studies (e.g., in groups of demented people suffering from Alzheimer's or Pick's diseases, in brain tumor cases, and people suffering from exposure to organic solvents). The differentiating power of the test has proved to be surprisingly high (see Hanlon, 1991; Johanson et al., 1990; Lilja, Smith, & Salford, 1992). Studies of hemispheric laterality using a visual half-field technique when presenting the MCT pictures (Carlsson, 1989 a, b) could convincingly demonstrate that primitive defensive styles like regression and projection were more associated with the right hemisphere and the more mature repression and isolation with the left hemisphere (cf. also Chapter 27).

New Thematic Innovations Based on the MCT Device

A Test of Flight Phobia

In her attempts to analyze the problem of flight phobia Gunilla Amnér (Amnér, 1997) constructed special thematic pictures. "The B stimulus depicts the interior of a transportation vehicle, not necessarily a cabin, with four chairs, arranged in two rows of two chairs each, and with a person of indeterminate sex (hero), sitting in a front-row chair, next to a window. The window was drawn in relatively large size in order not to limit the possibilities of interpretation only to an airplane. Stimulus A depicts an airplane, seen from the outside, through the window." The stimuli were presented as in the ordinary MCT. All subjects in the criterion groups tested in the validation studies reported themselves to be severely afraid of flying. They were prepared to fly only if absolutely necessary and then with great discomfort, anxiety, and somatic symptoms before and during the flight. The following scoring dimensions were most effective in differentiating flight phobics and controls:

Grave anxiety, open fear, defined in accordance with the original MCT.

Primitive forms of repression, including avoidance behavior of the subject him- or herself or of the hero in the picture, and also reports of A reduced to only part of the aircraft.

Primitive forms of isolation. This category refers to magic behavior as described in the MCT, spatial distortions with changes of the distance between hero and threat, and denial of the threat.

Stereotypies. These are defined as in the original MCT.

Negative comments about the hero. Reports of hero as sad, lonely, bowed down, badly cut, curvy legs, etc.

Grave regression, as in the MCT.

Comforting strategies. All reports in which the subject seeks consolation or support: hero is strengthened, extra persons are seen in the cabin, the subject turns to the experimenter for support, the event does not take place in the air, not even in an aircraft.

There was generally more defensive activity in the flight phobia group than in the control group in the first study. By means of a general defense score, the investigator registered a highly significant difference ($p = .002$).

The Identity Test (IT)

Employing an MCT paradigm Smith and co-workers have developed a method where a subliminal A-stimulus is used to manipulate the test persons perception of the B-stimulus. The latter picture could be an indeterminate face and the A-stimulus such phrases as *I Bad* or *I Good.* If the B-picture includes two persons, one of them obviously being an aggresssor and the other his victim, the word *I* is used as the subliminal A-stimulus alternately projected on one or the other of these antagonists. The latter device has been particularly useful in studies of how, for instance, breast cancer patients handle aggressive impulses. These studies are summarized in Smith (2001).

DMT and MCT: A Comparison

The two tests may appear to be similar because both employ tachistoscopic techniques and anxiety-arousing stimulus pictures. But the different presentation devices make them obviously dissimilar. And even though both tests were developed from percept-genetic assumptions, the DMT was more clearly influenced by the psychoanalytic theory of defenses and the MCT by an interest in coping strategies for the mediation of conflict. After its implementation, the DMT was validated as a test of stress tolerance in groups of fighter pilots and frogmen. Systematic attempts at finical validation are relatively recent (see Armelius and Sundbom, 1991; Hentschel et al., Chapter 19; Sundbom, 1992, and above;).

The MCT was originally tried as a diagnostic instrument. It appears to be less differentiating than the DMT in normals and is particularly efficient in spotting regression, projection, psychotic dissociation, depressive inhibition, and cerebral dysfunction. Even if the DMT explicitly refers to e psychoanalytic model of defense as initiated by signal anxiety, signs of anxiety are not scored. In the MCT, anxiety is one of the main scoring dimensions. Many signs with identical labels are scored differently in the two tests (e.g., zero-phases and depression). A zero-phase in the MCT (i.e., the disappearance of an established B-percept) is obviously a more serious sign than in the DMT. Neurotic signs in the DMT may concern e threat as well as the hero and the hero's attribute. This has been particularly exploited in the modified DMT and most notably concerns repression. In the MCT, repression only pertains to the threatening A. The DMT in its original form misses the behavioral aspect. In the MCT behavioral defenses represent the most primitive level in the hierarchically organized defensive categories. The hierarchical organization is empirically based on the results of extensive developmental studies, from the age of 4 years upward (Smith & Danielsson, 1982).

To Sum Up the Differences

In the DMT the hero is alone with the evil from the very beginning, the question being where the evil is localized (inside me or outside me) and how it is handled. The MCT, rather, represents an inventory of the possible defensive strategies of a respondent who, via the picture material, is confronted with a contradiction or a threat insidiously creeping into his sheltered existence.

References

Amnér, G. (1997). *Fear of flying; A manifold phenomenon with various motivational roots.* Lund, Sweden: Dept. of Psychology.

Andersson, A.L. & Bengtsson, M. (1986). Percept-genetic defenses against anxiety and a threatened sense of self as seen in terms of the spiral aftereffect technique. In U. Hentschel, G. Smith, & J.G. Draguns (Eds.), *The roots of perception (pp.* 217-246). Amsterdam: North-Holland.

Armelius, B. & Sundbom, E. (1991). Hard and soft models for the assessment of personality organization by DMT. In M. Olff, G. Godaert, & H. Ursin (Eds.), *Quantification of human defense mechanisms (pp.* 138-148). Berlin: Springer.

Berglund, M. & Smith, G. (1988). Post-diction of suicide in a group of depressive patients. *Acta Psychiatrica Scandinavica 77,* 504-510.

Brand, N., Olff, M., Hulsman, R., & Slagman, C. (1991). Perceptual defense: The use of digitized pictures. In M. Olff, G. Godaert, & H. Ursin (Eds.), *Quantification of human defense mechanisms (pp.* 293-301). Berlin: Springer.

Carlsson, I. (1989a). Lateralization of defence mechanisms: Differing influences in perception with the left and right visual field presentation of anxiety-arousing stimulation. *European Journal of Psychology, 3,* 167-179.

Carlsson, I. (1989b). Lateralization of defense mechanisms in a visual half-field paradigm. *Scandinavian Journal of Psychology, 30,* 296-303.

Cooper, C. (1991). G-analysis of the DMT. In M. Olff, G. Godaert, & H. Ursin (Eds.), *Quantification of human defense mechanisms (pp.* 121-137). Berlin: Springer.

Dixon, N.F., Hentschel, U., & Smith, G.J.W. (1986). Subliminal perception and microgenesis in the context of personality research. In A. Angleitner, A. Furnham, & G. van Heck (Eds.), *Personality psychology in Europe: Vol. 2. Current trends and controversies (pp.* 239-255). Lisse, The Netherlands: Swets & Zeitlinger.

Endresen, I.M. & Ursin, H. (1991). The relationship between psychological defence, cortisol, immunoglobulins, and complements. In M. Olff, G. Godaext, & H. Ursin (Eds.), *Quantification of human defense mechanisms (pp.* 262-272). Berlin: Springer.

Fransson, P. & Sundbom, E. (1997). Defense Mechanism Test (DMT) and Kernberg´s theory of personality organization related to adolescents in psychiatric care. *Scandinavian Journal of Psychology, 38,* 95-102.

Freud, A. (1946). *The ego and the mechanism of defense.* Madison, CT: International Universities Press. (Original work published 1936).

Fribergh, H., Träskman-Bendz, L., Öjehagen, A., & Regnéll, G. (1992). The Meta-Contrast Technique: A projective test predicting suicide. *Acta Psychiatrica Scandinavica, 86,* 473-477.

Gedo, J.E. & Goldberg, A. (1973). *Models of the mind. A psychoanalytic theory.* Chicago: University of Chicago Press.

Gitzinger, I. (1988). *Operationalisierung von Abwehrmechanismen: Wahrnehmungsabwehr and Einstellungsmessung psychoanalytischer Abwehrkonzepte* [Operationalization of defense mechanisms: Perceptual defense and attitude measurement of psychoanalytical defense concepts. University of Freiburg, unpublished thesis.

Gitzinger, I. (1991). *DCT (Defense mechanisms computer test).* Unpublished manuscript, Center for Psychotherapy Research, Stuttgart.

Godaert, G., Hagenaars, J., Olff, M., & Brosschot, J.F. (1991). Defensiveness and cardiovascular reactions. In M. Olff, G. Godaert, & H. Ursin (Eds.), *Quantification of human defense mechanisms (pp.* 273-281). Berlin: Springer.

Hanlon, R.E. (Ed.) (1991). *Cognitive microgenesis: A neuropsychological perspective.* New York: Springer.

Henningsson, M. (1999). Defensive strategies in psychosomatic groups: A soft modelling approach to Defense Mechanism Test data. Umeå: Dept. of Psychology.

Hentschel, U. & Balint, A. (1974). Plausible diagnostic taxonomy in the field of neurosis. *Psychological Research Bulletin, Lund University, no. 2.* Monograph Series.

Hentschel, U. & Kiessling, M. (1990). Are defense mechanisms valid predictors of performance on cognitive tasks? In G. van Heck, S. Hampson, J. Reykowski, & J. Zakrzewski (Eds.), *Personality Psychology in Europe: Vol. 3. Foundations, models and inquiries (pp.* 203-219). Amsterdam: Swets & Zeitlinger.

Hentschel, U. & Schneider, U. (1986). Psychodynamic personality correlates of creativity. In U. Hentschel, G. Smith, & J.G. Draguns (Eds.), *The roots of perception (pp.* 249-271). Amsterdam: North-Holland.

Hentschel, U., Kiessling, M., & Hosemann, A. (1991). Anxiety, defense and attention control. In R.E. Hanlon (Ed.), *Cognitive microgenesis: A neuropsychological perspective (pp.* 262-285). New York: Springer,

Hentschel, U., Smith, G., & Draguns, J.G. (1986). Subliminal perception, microgenesis, and personality. In U. Hentschel, G. Smith, & J.G. Draguns (Eds.), *The roots of perception (pp.* 3-38). Amsterdam: North-Holland.

Holland, N.N. (1973). Defence, displacement and the ego's algebra. *International Journal of Psychoanalysis, 54,* 247-257.

Holley, J.W. & Guilford, J.P. (1964). A note on the G-index of agreement. *Educational and Psychological Measurement, 24,* 749-753.

Johanson, A., Gustafson, L., Smith, G.J.W., Risberg, J., Hagberg, B., & Nilsson, B. (1990). Adaptation in different types of dementia and in normal elderly subjects. *Dementia, 1,* 95-101.

Johnson, M. (1986). Percept-genesis and the "scientific method". In U. Hentschel, G. Smith, & J.G. Draguns (Eds.), *The roots of perception (pp.* 403-417). Amsterdam: North-Holland.

Kernberg, O.F. (1977). The structural diagnosis of borderline personality organization. In P. Hartocollis (Ed.), *Borderline personality disorders (pp.* 87-121). Madison, CT: International Universities Press.

Kline, P. & Cooper, C. (1977). A percept-genetic study of some defense mechanisms in the test PN. *Scandinavian Journal of Psychology, 18,* 148-152.

Kragh, U. & Smith, G. (Eds.) (1970). *Percept-genetic analysis.* Lund: Gleerup.

Kragh, U. (1955) *The actual-genetic model* of *perception-personality.* Lund: Gleerup.

Kragh, U. (1960). The Defense Mechanism Test: A new method for diagnosis and personnel selection. *Journal of Applied Psychology, 44,* 303-309.

Kragh, U. (1962). Prediction of success of Danish attack divers by the Defense Mechanism Test (DMT). *Perceptual and Motor Skills, 15,* 103-106.

Kragh, U. (1969) *Manual till DMT* [DMT Manual: Defense mechanism test]. Stockholm: Skandinaviska Testförlaget.

Kragh, U. (1970). Pathogenesis in dipsomania. In U. Kragh & G. Smith (Eds.), *Percept-genetic analysis (pp.* 160-178). Lund: Gleerup.

Kragh, U. (1980). Rekonstruktion verschiedener Aspekte einer Persönlichkeitsentwicklung mit dem Defense-Mechanism-Test: Eine Fallbeschreibung [Reconstruction of different aspects of a personality development with the Defense Mechanism Test: A case study]. In U. Hentschel & G. Smith (Eds.), *Experimentelle Persönlichkeitspsychologie* [Experimental personality psychology] (pp. 107-131). Wiesbaden: Akademische Verlagsgesellschaft.

Kragh, U. (1984). Studying effects of psychotherapy by the Defense Mechanism Test-Two case illustrations. In G.J.W. Smith, W.D. Fröhlich, & U. Hentschel (Eds.), *From private to public reality: Meaning and adaptation in perceptual processing (pp.* 73-84). Bonn: Bouvier.

Kragh, U. (1985). *Defense Mechanism Test-DMT Manual.* Stockholm: Persona.

Lilja, A., Smith, G.J.W., & Salford, L.G. (1992). Micro-processes in perception and personality. *Journal of Nervous and Mental Disease, 180,* 82-88.

Lindgren, M. (1992). Neuropsychological studies of patients with organic solvent induced chronic toxic encephalopathy. Lund: University of Lund.

Neuman, T, (1978) *Dimensionering och validering av perceptgenesens försvarsmekanismer. En hierarkisk analys mot pilotens stressbeteende* [Dimensions and validation of percept-genetic mechanisms. An hierarchical analysis of the stress behavior of pilots]. FOA rapport C 55020-H6, Stockholm: Försvarets Forskningsanstalt.

Nilsson, A. & Svensson, B. (1999).: *PORT: Percept-Genetic Object-Relation Test. Manual.* Lund: Dept. of Psychology.

Olff, M. (1991) The DMT method in Europe: State of the art. In M, Olff, G. Godaert, & H. Ursin (Eds.), *Quantification of human defense mechanisms* (pp. 148-171). Berlin: Springer.

Rubino, A., Pezzarossa, B., & Grasso, S. (1991). DMT defenses in neurotic and somatically ill patients. In M. Olff, G. Godaert, & H. Ursin (Eds.), *Quantification of human defense mechanisms (pp.* 207-221). Berlin: Springer.

Sharma, V.H.P. (1977). *Application of a percept-genetic test in a clinical setting.* Department of Psychology, Lund University (unpublished).

Sjöbäck, H. & Bäckström, M. (1990). *The Defence Mechanism Test. A bibliography.* Lund University, mimeographed.

Sjöbäck, H. (1991). *The Defence Mechanism Test. What pictures do you use?* Lund: Desmahago.

Smith, G.J.W. (2001). *The process approach to personality.* New York: Plenum.

Smith, G,J.W., Almgren, P.-E., Andersson, A.L., Englesson, I., Smith, M., & Uddenberg, G. (1980). The Mother-Child Picture Test: Presentation of a new method for the evaluation of mother-child relations. *International Journal of Behavioral Development, 3,* 365-380.

Smith, G.J.W., Almgren, P.-E., Andersson, A.L., Englesson, I., Smith, M., & Uddenberg, G, (1981). Mothers and their 7-8-year-old children: A follow-up study of mother-child relations. *Psychiatry and Social Science, 1,* 17-27.

Smith, G., Almgren, P. E., Andersson, A., Englesson, I., Smith, M., & Uddenberg, G. (1984). Der Einfluss negativer Einstellungen and Fehlanpassungen von Müttern auf das Verhalten ihrer sieben-bis achtjährigen Kinder [The effect of negative attitudes and maladaptation of the mothers on the behavior of their 7-8-year-old children]. In U. Hentschel & A. Wigand (Eds.), *Persönlichkeitsmerkmale and Familienstruktur* [Personality characteristics and family structure] (pp. 25-46). Munich: Weixler.

Smith, G.J.W. & Carlsson, I. (1990) The creative process. *Psychological Issues, Monogr. 57.* Madison, CT: International Universities Press.

Smith, G.J.W. & Danielsson, A. (1982). Anxiety and defensive strategies in childhood and adolescence. *Psychological Issues, Monogr. 52.* Madison, CT: International Universities Press.

Smith, G., Johnson, G., Almgren P.-E., & Johanson A. (2002). *MCT-The Meta-Contrast Technique.* Lund: Dept. of Psychology.

Stoker, P. (1982). An empirical investigation of the predictive validity of the Defence Mechanism Test in the screening of fast-jet pilots for the Royal Air Force. *Projective Psychology, 27,* 7-12.

Stoll, F. (1990). *Has the DMT passed the test?* Paper presented at the conference "Quantification of parameters for the study of breakdown in human adaptation: Psychological defense mechanisms." Copenhagen, April 1990.

Sundbom, E. & Armelius, B.-Å. (1992). Reactions to DMT as related to psychotic and borderline personality organization. *Scandinavian Journal of Psychology, 33,* 178-188.

Sundbom, E. (1992) *Borderline psychopathology and the Defense Mechanism Test.* University of Umeå, unpublished doctoral thesis.

Sundbom, E., Henningsson, M., Holm, U., Söderberg, S., & Evengård, B. (2002). The possible impact of defense and negative life events on patients with chronic fatigue syndrome. *Psychological Reports* (in press).

Suppes, P. & Warren, H. (1975). On the generation and classification of defense mechanisms. *International Journal of Psychoanalysis, 56,* 405-414.

Tideman, E., Nilsson, A., Smith, G., & Stjernqvist, K.A. (2002). Longitudinal follow-up of children born preterm: The mother-child relationship in a 19-year perspective. *Journal of Reproduction and Infant Psychology, 20,* 43-56.

Ursin, H., Baade, E., & Levine, S. (Eds.) (1978). *Psychobiology of stress. A study of coping men.* New York: Academic Press.

Vaillant, G. E. (1971). Theoretical hierarchy of adaptive ego mechanisms. *Archives of General Psychiatry, 24,* 107-118.

Westerlundh, B. & Sjöbäck, H. (1986). Activation of intrapsychic conflict and defense: The amauroscopic technique. In U. Hentschel, G. Smith, & J.G. Draguns (Eds.), *The roots of perception (pp.* 161-215). Amsterdam: North-Holland.

Defense Mechanisms
U. Hentschel, G. Smith, J.G. Draguns & W. Ehlers (Editors)

Chapter 8

Contributions to the Construct Validity of the Defense Mechanism Test

Barbara E. Saitner

There has been an upsurge of interest in the Defense Mechanism Test (DMT) following the publication of reports of its success in predicting personally characteristic patterns of coping with stress (e.g. Kragh & Smith, 1970). However, some unresolved : questions remain concerning the construct validity of the DMT, and serious disagreement persists about how perceptual distortions observed on the DMT are to be interpreted (Bäckström, 1994; Cooper, 1998; Cooper & Kline 1989, Kragh, 1998, 2001; Meier-Civelli, 1989; Zuber & Ekehammar, 1997, 1999). So far Cooper and Kline (1986) and Olff, Broschot, Godaert, Weis, & Ursin, (1991) have chosen to investigate construct validity of the DMT by comparing it with other established psychological tests. Cooper and Kline were able to confirm some of the relationships they had predicted, even though the pattern of their results was far from clear-cut. Olff et al., however, did not find any significant correlations. In studies with psychiatric patients, correlations were reported between certain personality disorders and their corresponding patterns of defense (Sundbom 1992, Rubino et al. 1992, Zanna et al. 1997). This chapter pursues the investigation of the construct validity of the DMT by comparing responses to it with the data from a battery of established psychological tests. This research is different from Cooper and Kline's study in that the sample is made up of male individuals with personality disorders who were apprehended for driving under the influence of alcohol. The predicitive validity of the DMT for this purpose was established in an earlier study (Saitner, 1991). Hypotheses were derived from the DMT literature (e.g., Kragh, 1985), studies of drunken driving (Kunkel, 1977; Müller, 1976; Richman, 1985), and psychoanalytic theory (e.g., Fenichel, 1945; Hartmann, 1958). The following relationships between the DMT data and the variables assessed by means of the several measures within the test battery were predicted:

Repression will be associated with lowered self-consciousness, lower excitability, and higher composure on the Freiburg Personality Inventory (FPI);

Isolation is expected to be correlated with carefulness and accuracy on the concentration test d2 by Brickenkamp (1966) and on the Vienna Determination Apparatus (Wiener Determinationsgerät [WDG]).

Denial will be positively associated with the choices of "gray," scored for denial on the Color Pyramid Test (CPT), and "purple," scored for tension on the same test; a negative relationship is expected between denial and openness and emotional stability, both measured by means of FPI) as well as denial and aggressiveness, as assessed by means of the FPI and the Swedish Personality Questionnaire (SPQ).

Reaction formation is expected to yield a negative relationship with aggressiveness, as assessed by means both of the FPI and SPQ.

Introaggression is expected to be associated with depression on the FPI.

Identification with a female role, or introjection of the opposite sex, is expected to be associated with high scores for "purple" on the CPT, emotional instability on the FPI, and low scores for masculinity on the FPI.

Polymorphous identification is predicted to be associated with depression on the FPI.

Projection is expected to be related to high sensitivity scores on the SPQ.

Regression will be associated with the choice of "orange", as scored on the FPI and marked by the choice of "purple" on the CPT. No hypotheses were formulated for identification with the aggressor because of the low rate of occurence of manifestation for this mechanism.

Method

For a detailed description of the procedure, the interested reader is referred to Saitner (1990, 1991). Briefly, members of a random sample of male individuals with several severe traffic offenses, mostly drunken driving, were assessed by means of a test battery for the purpose of determining the probability of future transgressions. The DMT was administered in accordance with ist original manual (Kragh, 1969). The DMT scores were weighed: scores for the middle and late phases were multiplied by 2 and 3, respectively. The total scores were then computed by adding the weighted scores for all phases and series.

In addition the following tests were administered.

1. The d2 measure (Brickenkamp, 1966), a derivative of the concentration test developed by Lauer (1955): it measures attention to detail.
2. A choice reaction test of sensorimotor and perceptual tasks, the WDG. Participants are required to respond to visual and auditory stimuli of different kinds with specific hand and foot movements. Constancy, speed, and accuracy of performance are measured.
3. The German version of the Wechsler-Bellevue Adult Intelligence Scale (HAWIE: Wechsler, 1964) This test comprises 11 subtests, grouped into Verbal (Information, Digit Span, Vocabulary, Arithmetic, Comprehension, Similarities) and Peformance (Picture Completion, Picture Arrangement, Block Design, Object Assembly, Digit Symbol) measures. With respect to scales, factor analytic techniques have sorted out three factors: Verbal Comprehension and Similarities; Perceptual Organization with large weights on Block Design and Object Assembly, and Freedom from Distractibility, with loadings in Digit Span, Arithmetic, and Digit Symbol.
4. The Freiburg Personality Inventory (FPI: Fahrenberg & Selg, 1970). It is scored for the following 12 dimensions: nervousness, aggressiveness, depression, excitability, sociability, composure. dominance, self-consciousness, openness, extraversion, emotional instability, and masculinity.
5. The German version of the Swedish Personality Questionnaire. It comprises introversion, sensitivity, and aggressiveness scales.
6. The Color Pyramid Test (Schaie & Heiss, 1964), a color preference measure. Particpants are asked to pick out colored papers, in 14 different colors, and place them within a pyramid design. They are asked to construct three "pretty" pyramids and then are instructed to build three more pyramids and to make them "as ugly as possible". Response to color is thought to relate to the sphere of affect and emotion, which are construed as basic aspects of personality. The "pretty" series is associated with the more overt part of personality while the "ugly" series is designed to tap its more hidden and subconscious emotional sphere.

Research Design

Two extreme groups were formed, based on the frequency of defensive reactions on nine of the ten DMT scales; scale 5 (identification with the aggressor) was excluded because incidence of this sign was low in the sample. On each of these nine scales, the sample was divided, with subjects who had no scores on the scale in question and those whose scores on that scale were high. Comparisons were then carried out with the scores of these two contrasting groups of subjects on the several tests described above (the d2 measure, the WDG, the HAWIE, the FPI, the SPQ, and the CPT). The percentage of the subjects varied because of the distribution of frequencies on the several DMT scales (see tables). Group comparisons were performed by means of t-tests..

Results and Discussion

Similar to the results by Cooper and Kline, the number of significant correlations was found to be low. Of the hypotheses pertaining to repression, only the predicition concerning low self-consciousness (FPI) was confirmed. Additionally, high scores on the repression scale were found to be associated with self-representation characterized by sociability on the FPI, stability in the sphere of affects and emotions (CPT), and high capacity to withstand stress (d2). These results appear to indicate that the repressors possess stable and „normal", well-adapted personalities. However, this impression is contradicted by the comparatively high record of traffic offenses of drivers who tend toward repression (Saitner, 1990). On the other hand, Bell and Byrne (1977) found the repressive defense style to be correlated with emotional stability in self-representation, and also with greater aggressiveness and lower sensitivity in social contacts. Table 8.1 provides the summary of quantitative findings pertaining to repression. No support for the hypotheses concerning isolation was found (Table 8.2). On the other hand, a significant correlation between carefulness on the WDG and isolation emerged for the entire sample, as reported elsewhere (Saitner, 1990).

Table 8.1: *Difference in personality measures as a function of occurrence of repression as defense style*

	Repression = 0 (*N*=34)		Repression>/= 7 (*N*=34)		
	X	*sd*	*X*	*sd*	*p*
d2 total of details	376.91	80.24	420. 41	86.96	<.05
FPI sociability	6.88	3.49	9.04	2.67	<.05
FPI Self-consciousness	3.73	2.07	2.45	1.88	<.05
CPT/difference	42.08	10.64	36.76	8.98	<.05

A surprising finding was the lower performance of respondents with a distinct isolating and intellectualizating defense style on the Wechsler Performance Scale and the Picture Arrangement, Picture Completion, and Block Design subtests.

These subjects seem to have a cognitive style that seems to make it difficult for them to form complete gestalten and to perform effectively in practical contexts.

Table 8.2: *Difference in personality measures as a function of occurence of isolation as a defense style*

	Isolation </=2 (*N*=21)		Isolation >/=10 (*N*=29)		
	X	*sd*	*X*	*sd*	*p*
Wechsler					
Performance scale	106.47	9.91	100.05	9.92	<.01
Picture arrangement	10.28	2.63	9.00	2.01	<.05
Picture completion	11.28	1.70	9.77	2.61	<.05
Block design	10.47	2.48	8.88	1.99	<.05
FPI/dominance	2.08	0.90	3.03	1.71	<.05
CPT/pretty series,purple	3.04	3.78	1.02	1.92	<.05

Table 8.3: *Difference in personality measures as a function of occurrence of denial as defense style*

	Denial = 00 (*N*=78)		Denial >/=1 (*N*=30)		
	X	*sd*	*X*	*sd*	*p*
d2/vacillating of attention	12.06	4.12	15.00	8.03	<.05
FPI Aggression	2.29	2.08	1.34	1.22	<.05
FPI Openness	8.81	2.95	6.60	1.97	<.05

Moreover, subjects with a high isolation score tend to be dominant and rigid, as measured on the FPI, which may shield them from emotional excitability, as assessed on the CPT. These results support the psychoanalytic view of the link between isolation as a defense style and compulsive personality traits. (See Table 8.2 for the details of these results.) In keeping with the hypothesis, denial was associated with low scores in openness and aggressiveness on the FPI . There was, however, no emotional instability found, as indexed on the FPI, for subjects characterized by reliance on denial, nor did the high-denial groups make significantly more choices of the color gray on the CPT. The Pearson correlation coefficient between the choice of gray and denial was significant, as reported by Saitner (1990). The relationship of denial to vacillating attention on the d2 measure may be indicative of distractibility and, by implication, emotional instability. Table 8.3 presents these findings in greater detail. No support was obtained for the hypothesis pertaining to reaction formation. Specifically, subjects with high scores for this defense mechanism did not produce lower scores in agggression either on the FPI or the SPQ. They tended, however, toward passive adaptation and are inclined to deny their conflicts, as expressed in their choice of gray on CPT, regardless of situational aspects. In contrast to subjects whose scores in reaction formation were zero, this pattern remained stable and was. resistant to change, which may be indicative of the rigidity that is frequently imputed to people who tend toward reaction formation (e.g., Fenichel, 1946). resistant to change, which may be indicative of the rigidity that is frequently imputed to people who tend toward reaction formation (e.g., Fenichel, 1946).

Table 8.4: *Difference in personality measures as a function of occurence of reaction formation as defense style.*

	Reaction formation=0 (*N*=32)		Reaction formation>/=8 (*N*=37)		
	X	*sd*	*X*	*sd*	*p*
CPT					
gray/pretty series	0.40	1.13	2.18	4.12	<.05
gray/ugly series	7.90	9.40	3.24	3.42	<.05
FPI					
Excitability	3.04	2.21	1.92	1.57	<.05
Openness	9.00	2.96	7.23	2.94	<.05

Table 8.5: *Difference in personality measures as a function of occurrence of introaggression as defense style*

	Introaggression = 0 (*N*=73)		Introaggression >/= 1 (*N*=29)		
	X	*sd*	*X*	*sd*	*p*
Wechlser					
Digit span	10.55	2.76	12.75	2.38	<.01
Comprehension	10.47	3.08	12.25	1.94	<.01
CPT/ugly series, black	10.64	7.43	7.50	7.15	<.05

On the basis of their self-description, respondents in the reaction formation group experience themselves as basically calm and "unaffected". These findings are presented in Table 8.4. There was no correlation between the FPI manifestations of depression and introaggressive defense style, as shown in Table 8.5. Respondents with an introaggressive defense style tended, however, toward less intense and less abrupt attenuation of affect, as exemplified by the use of black on the CPT. Thus, the superior performance of these respondents on some of the Wechsler subtests might be connected with their less inhibited use of energy. Andersson and Ryhammar (1998) found that respondents with an introaggressive defense style displayed higher creativity by comparison with their counterparts with other defense styles.

The hypothesis concerning the relationship between the masculinity scale on the FPI and the DMT scale for the identification with a female role received no support. However, as hypothesized, respondents who scored high on this scale experienced excitability and emotional instability, as indicated by their choice of "purple" on CPT, and were sensitive in

Table 8.6: *Difference in personality measures as a function of occurrence of identification with a female role as defense style*

	Identification with a female role = 0 (*N*=63)		Identification with a female role >/= 1 (*N*=45)		
	X	*sd*	*X*	*sd*	*p*
SPQ:Sensitivity	10.74	5.50	13.37	6.15	<.05
CPT/pretty series,purple	0.98	1.83	2.08	3.35	<.05

Table 8.7: *Difference in personality measures as a function of occurrence of polymorphous identification as defense style*

	Polymorphous Identification=0 (*N*=73)		Polymorphous Identification >/=14 (*N*=38)		
	X	*sd*	*X*	*sd*	*p*
Wechsler:Information	11.47	2.22	9.68	2.62	<.05
CPT/ugly series, white	1.44	2.94	3.42	4.69	<.05

light of their SPQ scores. Thus, their personality can be described as soft and pliable. In this respect they tend toward a traditionally female self-attribution. Table 8.6 provides the particulars of these results. In reference to the hypothesized relationship between polymorphous identification and depression on the FPI, the results were negative. High scores on this scale were associated with lower intellectual performance (Information and Similarity on the HAWIE), which could be interpreted as depressive inhibition of intellectual functions and lack of flexibility. Low scores on Information suggest withdrawal from the environment. There was also a relationship between polymorphous identification as defense style and the tendency toward latent aggression, as shown by the use of „white“ on the CPT. These findings lend support to the relationship between suppressed anger and depression. All of these results are contained in Table 8.7. Analyses pertaining to projection were entirely inconclusive and shed no light on the characteristic personality variables of individuals who rely on this defense. Regression was not associated with emotional instability in light of either FPI or CPT, nor with the regressive sign of "orange“ on the CPT. However, there was a significant relationship between the choice of "orange“ and the DMT regression scale in previous analyses (Saitner, 1990). In this sample, subjects with a regressive defense style tended toward less introversion on the SPQ and were not very excitable, as shown by the choice of "red 1“ on the CPT. They relied less on denial, as marked by the lower use of "gray“ on the CPT, were less. achievement oriented, as indicated

Table 8.8: *Difference in personality measures as a function of occurrence of regression as defense style*

	Regression = 0 (N=84)		Regression>/=1 (N=24)		
	X	*sd*	*X*	*sd*	*p*
SPQ:Introversion	11.83	4.78	9.28	4.88	<.05
CPT/pretty series, red1	2.21	2.92	1.13	1.91	<.05
CPT/pretty series, gray	1.51	3.08	0.47	1.08	<.05
CPT/ugly series,yellow	2.01	2.78	1.04	1.18	<.05
CPT/ugly series, blue4	3.28	5.36	1.69	2.24	<.05

by the choice of "yellow“ on the CPT, and possessed less control over the expression of affect, as expressed by the use of "blue“ on the CPT. Their defense mechanisms were incompletely developed, and their selection of environmental stimuli tended to be poorly differentiated. Thus they were easily disoriented when stress occurred and were then not able to control their reactions adequately. These results were summarized in Table 8.8

Conclusion

The number of significant findings obtained is small. Some defenses have not been elucidated at all by the analyses performed. Projection is a case in point. For some scales, such as denial, however, support for construct validity was found. As in earlier studies, the overlap between the personality variables and the DMT scales was low. However, there was sufficient confirmation of several of the hypotheses to support the conclusion that the defense style is intertwined with structural personality traits. Moreover, the connection between defense and cognitive style, as revealed, for example, for the scales of isolation and polymorphous identification, indicates that the personality as a whole is expressed through the manner in which defensive reactions are structured. In this respect, the DMT method may be more valuable for research than the self-report defense mechanism measures (Davidson & MacGregor, 1998).

To make the DMT an effective diagnostic tool, further research on this topic is needed. Examination of correlations between the DMT data and variables from other tests should be carried out with a large-scale heterogeneous sample, and the significance of correlations should be tested by means of Dunn's multiple comparison procedure.

References

Andersson, A.L.; Ryhammar, L. (1998) Psychoanalytic models of the mind, Creative functioning, and percept-genetic reconstruction. *Psychoanalysis and ContemporaryThought.16,* (4), 359-382.

Bäckström, M. (1994) The Defense Mechanism Test at a turning point. Department of Psychology, University of Lund, Sweden.

Bell, P.A. & Byrne, D. (1977) Repression-sensitization. In H. London & J.E. Exner (Eds.), *Dimensions of personality* (pp.449-485). New York: Wiley.

Brickenkamp, R. (1966) *Aofmerksamkeits-Belastungs-Test (d2)* (The Attention Stress Test d2) (2nd edition). Göttingen: Hogrefe.

Cooper, C. (1998) The scientific status of the Defense Mechanism Test. *British Journal of Medical Psychology, 61.* 381-384.

Cooper, C. & Kline, P.(1986) An evaluation of the Defence Mechanism Test *British Journal of Psychology, 77,* 19-31.

Cooper, C. & Kline, P. (1989) A new objevtively scored version of the Defence Mechanism Test , *Scandinavian Journal of Psychology, 30,* 228-238.

Davidson, K, & MacGregor, M. W. (1998) A Critical Appraisal of Self-Report Defense Mechanism Measures, *Journal of Personality, 66.* 965-992.

Fahrenberg, J. & Selg, H. (1970) *FreiburgerPersonlichkeitsinventar (FPI)* (Freiburg Personality Inventory (FPI)). Göttingen: Hogrefe.

Fenichel, O. (1946) *Psychoanalytic theory of neurosis.* London: Routledge Kegan Paul.

Häkkinen, S. (1958). *Traffic incidents and driver characteristics.* Helsinki: Suomalaisen Kirjalisuuden Kirjapaino.

Hartmann, H. (1958) *Ego psychology and the problem of adaptation.* Madison, CT, International Universities Press.

Kragh, U. (1985) *Defense MechanismTest. DMT Manual.* Stockholm: Persona

Kragh, U. (1998) In defence of the Defence Mechanism Test (DMT) - a reply. *Scandinavian Journal of Psychology, 39,* 123-124.

Kragh, U. (2201) DMT interminable. A re-reply to I.Zuber and B.Ekehammar. *Scandinavian Journal of Psychology, 42,* 135-136.

Kragh, U. & Smith, G.J.W.(1970) *Percept-Genetic Analysis.* Lund: Gleerup

Kunkel, E. (1977) *Biographische Daten und Rückfallsprognose bei Trunkheitstatern im Strassenverkehr* (Biographic data and relapse prognosis for drunk offenders in vehicular traffic) Cologne: TÜV Rheinland.

Lauer, A.R. (1955) Comparison of group paper-and-pencil tests for measuring driving aptitude of army personnel. *Journal of Applied Psychology, 39,* 318.

Meier-Civelli, U. (1989). Der Defense Mechanism Test (DMT). Eine Evaluationsstudie aufgrund publizierter Untersuchungen (The DMT. An evaluative study based on published investigations) *Bericht der Abteilung für angewandte Psychologie.Universität Zurich. No.26*

Müller, A. (1976) *Der Trunkheitstäter im Strassenverkehr der BRD* (The drunk offender on the roads of the Federal Republic of Germany). Frankfurt: Lang.

Olff, M. Brosschot, J.F.; Godaert, G.; Weiss, K.W. & Ursin, H. (1991) The Defence Mechanism Test related to questionnnaire methods for measurement of psychological defence. In M.Olff , G. Godaert & H.Ursin (Eds.) *Quantification of human defence mechanisms* (pp. 302-320). Berlin: Springer.

Richman, A. (1985) Human risk factors in alcohol-related crashes. North American Conference on Alcohol and Highway Safety.*Journal of Studies on Alcohol,10,* 21-23.

Rubino, I.A., Savino, M.L. & Pezzarossa, B. (1992): Types of percept-genetic defenses in self-defeating personality disorder. *Perceptual and Motor Skills* , *75*, 1219-1224.

Saitner, B. (1990) Die Leistungsfähigkeit des Defense Mechanism Test (DMT) für die Vorhersage der Verkehrsbewährung von Kraftfahrern. (The efficiency of the DMT for the prediction of performance of car drivers in traffic) Unpublished doctoral dissertation, University of Cologne, Germany

Saitner, B. (1991) Application of the DMT for assessing serious drinking and driving offenders. In M.Olff, G. Godaert & H. Ursin (Eds.), *Quantification of human defence mechanisms* (pp.238-251). Berlin: .Springer

Schaie, K. W. & Heiss, R. (1964) *Color and personality.* Bern: Huber.

Sundbom, E. (1992) Borderline psychopathology and the Defense Mechanism Test. Doctoral Dissertation, Department of Applied Psychology, Umea, Sweden.

Wechsler, D. (1964 *Die Messung der Intellgenz Erwachsener* (Measurement of adult intelligence) Bern, Huber.

Zanna, V.; Fedeli, B.; Belsanti, S. Percept-genetic defenses and personality disorders: preliminary correlational data. *Psichiatria.e psicoterapia analitica, 16,* , 359-363.

Zuber, I,. & Ekehammar, B. (1997) An Empirical Look at the Defense Mechanism Test , *Scandinavian Journal of Psychology, 38,*, 85-94.

Defense Mechanisms
U. Hentschel, G. Smith, J.G. Draguns & W. Ehlers (Editors)

Chapter 9

Studying Defense Mechanisms in Psychotherapy using the Defense Mechanism Rating Scales

J. Christopher Perry and Melissa Henry

Introduction

The Defense Mechanism Rating Scales (DMRS), fifth edition, is a system for guiding clinical inference in the identification of specific defense mechanisms (Perry 1990a). The author, created the first version in 1981 and revised it based on subsequent studies. The most recent, fifth edition incorporated editorial suggestions by other members of the Subcommittee on Defense Mechanisms (reporting to the Multiaxial Committee of the Task Force for DSM-IV of the American Psychiatric Association), including Drs. Michael Bond, Steven H. Cooper, Marianne E. Kardos, and George E. Valliant. The DMRS has benefited from the perspective and consensus of these researchers on definitions, functions and examples of individual defenses. This chapter reviews issues pertinent to studying defenses in both process and outcome research in psychotherapy. It describes the DMRS rating procedures and reliability, an optimal program for selecting and training raters, then discusses the implications of using different data sources. After reviewing some examples of recent or ongoing research on psychotherapy, the chapter ends with a brief discussion of potential issues and hypotheses for studying defenses in psychotherapy. A bibliography of the DMRS is included in the reference section.

Description of the Defense Mechanism Rating Scales

The DMRS manual describes how to identify 28 individual defense mechanisms. The introduction includes general directions for the qualitative and quantitative identification of defenses, along with suggestions about handling problems presented by different data sources. Additional directions for quantitative scoring are available separately from the author (Perry 2000). The body of the manual consists of directions for identifying 28 individual defenses, recently expanded to 30 on the current rating form. Specifically the defense devaluation was subdivided into devaluation of others, and devaluation of self, while idealization was similarly subdivided into idealization of others, and idealization of self. The manual includes a definition of each defense, a description of how the defense functions, a section on how to discriminate each defense from near-neighbor defenses (e.g. suppression v. repression v. denial), and a three-point scale. Each scale is anchored with specific examples of (1) the probable use and (2) the definite use of the defense. The examples provide prototypical instances of the defense thereby providing some ostensive definition to complement the formal definitions. Unfortunately, because defenses are open-textured constructs, that is, there is no absolute criterion demarcating the boundaries of each defense, an exhaustive catalogue of all instances of each defense is impossible. Some degree of inference in rating defenses will always be required, a task which is more difficult at the conceptually "fuzzy" boundaries of each construct. In practical terms, classical examples of a defense that approximate the center of the construct are more easily identifiable, while those close to the boundary of the definition are harder to identify and rate reliably.

In the DMRS system there are seven defense levels which are arranged hierarchically based on the average correlation of each defense within each level with some measure of overall adaptiveness. The defense levels are as follows : High Adaptive Level (sometimes called "Mature"), Obsessional, Other Neurotic (including Hysterical and Other Neurotic), Minor Image-distorting (sometimes called "Narcissistic"), Disavowal, Major-Image-distorting (sometimes called "Borderline") and Action. Not included in the manual but included in an appendix, still under revision, are the so-called psychotic defenses considered at the Level of Defensive Dysregulation. This ordering is based on a series of empirical studies (reviewed in Perry 1993) which utilized both the DMRS (Perry & Cooper 1989; Perry 1990b) as well as other methods. The defense levels and their individual defenses are shown in Table 9.1.

Identifying when a Defense occurs in the Interview/Text

The defenses defined and described in the DMRS are compatible with the definition of a defense mechanism as noted in DSM-IV Appendix B (APA 1994, p. 787).

"Defense mechanisms are the automatic psychological processes that mediate the individual's reaction to emotional conflicts and internal or external stressors".

A defense causes some anomaly or unexpected event in the course of what the subject is saying or doing. It produces an anomaly in the interview, similar to a disturbance on an otherwise calm surface. The anomalies include, but are not limited to, those aspects of cognition, speech, affect, and behavior noted in Table 9.2. Whenever the observer detects any anomaly, the next question is whether a defensive function is present, or whether it is merely an idiosyncracy of the subject's way of expressing him or herself that is non-defensive. Finally, the observer should try to ascertain where the defensive activity starts, and where it stops, bracketing the text in-between which aids the next task of identifying the specific defense used.

Table 9.1: *The DMRS hierarchy of adaptation: Defense levels and individual defenses*

7 High Adaptive (Mature)	affiliation, altruism, anticipation, humor, self-assertion, self-observation, sublimation, suppression
6 Obsessional:	isolation of affect, intellectualization, undoing
5 Neurotic: a.hysterical b.other	repression, dissociation, reaction formation, displacement
4 Minor Image-distorting (Narcissistic):	devaluation*, idealization*, omnipotence
3 Disavowal:	denial, projection, rationalization, autistic fantasy**
2 Major Image-distorting (Borderline):	splitting of other's images, splitting of self-images, projective identification
1 Action:	acting out, help-rejecting complaining, passive-aggression

* For most purposes, devaluation and idealization are divided into two defenses each, like splitting: e.g., devaluation of self images, and devaluation of other's images.

** Although not a disavowal defense, autistic fantasy is scored at this level.

When beginning to rate an interview, it is often hardest to identify defensive activity at the outset, say in the first few pages of text. Partly this is due to needing time to get acquainted with the subject, and partly because the beginning of interviews often involve introductory chit-chat or relating some historical story without eliciting enough material to rate defenses. When it is hard to get started, it is best to read on until one begins to notice several defenses. At that point, one can stop and return to the beginning then review and rate the text. Then it is easier to see where the defenses are.

Table 9.2: *Anomalies or signs that defensive activity may be occurring*

- showing an unexpected affect
- a sudden change in tone of voice
- showing an affect that is not compatible with the ideas in the text
- the absence of affect, when it is expected
- showing an affect but not being able to talk about it accurately or directly
- gross disturbance in the prosody or flow of speech, e.g., undue hesitation
- expressing an idea that is highly unlikely to be true
- a clear contradiction between two or more ideas without resolution
- unexpected statements about the interviewer
- sudden, loud or uncontrolled speech or behavior
- an unexpected change in topic or the object of conversation
- talking which appears to avoid the immediate topic
- talking about a topic in an emotionally charged and excessive way
- taking offence, when there seems little reason to see any actual offense
- descriptions of the self or others that appear distorted, unrealistic or excessively good or bad
- the meaning is obscured
- reasons are given that appear to cover up or distort the truth

Qualitative Scoring

The DMRS was originally devised for rating the qualitative presence of a defense in a 50- minute dynamically oriented interview. This qualitative scoring can be employed when one only has access to live or recorded interviews without transcripts. Qualitative assessment yields information for the current time period, answering the categorical question: "Does the subject use this defense?" Information like this can be used for a "defense diagnosis" informing clinical work, but does not yield data on the actual frequency of usage of individual mechanisms. The first edition of the DMRS combined rating the presence of a defense as well as its frequency or importance. This procedure proved less reliable than rating the presence alone, apparently because the error variances in each judgement were additive. Thus, subsequent editions have kept to the 3-point qualitative rating of absence, probably present or definitely present. Data relevant for rating include events occurring in the interview itself, such as dialogue, actions by the patient, silences, slips of the tongue, etc, or vignettes reported on from outside the interview. In the latter case, data are only included for rating if they have occurred within the past two years [the "two-year rule"], unless there is additional supportive evidence that the defense is still probably present. This arbitrary rule decreases the problem of rating defenses as current when they were delimited to a subject's distant past. When teaching the DMRS for the first time, the author has found that the original qualitative method is more accessible. As for its use in empirical research, qualitative scoring does not yield estimates as precise as the quantitative method does, because of the restricted range of scores (0 to 2). These do not adequately reflect the greater differences found among defenses within an interview or over time between interviews using the quantitative method.

Quantitative Scoring

The DMRS can be used for quantitative assessment when interview recordings and transcripts are available. Using this scoring method, the rater identifies each use of the defense as it occurs, bracketing that part of the text over which it operates. The distinction between probable and definite usage is ignored, and all examples are treated as equal. Similarly the time-frame of the defense (distant or recent past or currently occurring in the interview] is ignored, and all examples are included for scoring. After the completion of the ratings, the number of times each defense was identified in the text is divided by the total instances of all defenses to yield a proportion or percentage score. The resulting profile is the percentage of defensive functioning due to each defense. The proportional score is also calculated for groups of related defenses called defense levels (e.g., Action defenses 12%, Obsessional defenses 18%, etc.). Rationale and statistical use of these scores are described below. A computer program in SAS is available from the author to make the quantitative calculations from raw scores, as well as additional summary scales described below.

The Importance of Consensus Ratings

Because defenses are rated on the basis of inference from observations, there is room for disagreement. While a strict logical positivist might be unhappy with this, one need consider that a subject is under no obligation to give sufficient detail for correct identification in every case where a defense is probably operating whether in a psychotherapy session, a dynamic interview or elsewhere in life. Instead, the rating system has to handle limitations in the data without throwing out the less detailed sections of the interview. To restrict rating only to sections with complete data would yield a biased, less representative assessment of the individual. The defense definitions and scales provide guides for justifying a rating, but not firm inference rules, which are not possible in any case. The process of having two raters score the interview independently, then discuss their ratings and form a consensus, therefore provides several advantages. First, using two raters rather than a single one improves the likelihood of identifying more defensive phenomena, as any single rater will miss some. Second, whenever transcripts are not available or imperfect, occasionally factual questions about what occurred may arise, and one rater may have a more vivid recollection than another, thereby providing a check on the veridicality of observation. Third, the rater must justify any identified defense to the other rater by describing how the defensive function in the relevant text matches the relevant function defined in the manual. This justification process, going back and forth from observational data to the defense construct, diminishes insupportable speculation. When the raters must agree about both the observations and the basis for the defense rating, only stronger inferences are supported, thereby improving validity. This process also effectively calibrates the raters and improves reliability, as they develop a consensual interpretation of how to use the manual in rating less prototypical examples. Participating in consensus ratings is valuable even for experienced raters. The author still find that "two heads are better than one", even when one rater is less experienced.

A previous study using the DMRS, third version, estimated the gain in reliability when comparing the ratings of individuals against those of a consensus process (Perry & Cooper 1989). Two groups of three baccalaureate level raters independently viewed 46 videotaped 50-minute initial dynamic interviews. Each rater made independent ratings blind to others' ratings, using the qualitative method. Then three raters met in each of the two consensus groups, discussed their ratings and formed consensus ratings. The median intraclass R reliability for the six individual raters was .36, whereas for the two consensus group ratings it was .57, accounting for 58% more variance attributable to the subject. When the scores of empirically and conceptually related defenses were summed (e.g. intellectualization + isolation + undoing = obsessional defenses), the median reliability of the resulting defense summary scores rose to .53 for the individual raters, and .74 for the consensus ratings, a gain of 40% more variance for the consensus ratings. Whether individual defenses or the combined defense level scores were used, consensus ratings were consistently more reliable than individual ratings.

The Selection of Raters

Certain characteristics associated with rater proficiency are worth noting. First, a certain intellectual skill is desirable, that is, the ability to scan clinical material for dynamically meaningful data, then articulate it to discern patterns connecting motivationally related data. While this requires one or two levels of inference below the raw data, the rater must be restrained from deep theorizing. This potential problem is clearly evident whenever a rater justifies a defense rating by describing how it fits in to an overall formulation of the patient's dynamics. In such situations, the author gently commends the rater's ability to make an extensive clinical hypothesis that *may* be correct, but suggests that it is too deep to be reliable in the present instance. The opposite problem occurs in the individual who avoids looking for underlying patterns, often evident by remarks such as: "The patient just said that; it doesn't mean anything." If this is due to clinical inexperience, the rater will probably discard this attitude as training proceeds. If it is defensive in nature, for instance, reflecting denial or devaluation of dynamic data, then the rater may appreciate being counselled out of the training process. It is important to acknowledge that raters *also* present a certain defensive style that could bias their ratings or be detrimental to the subsequent consensus process. An old saw suggests that a particular defense that one never sees whenever present, or often sees even though it is not present, is likely to be a prominent defense in one's own defensive repertoire. Careful selection of "mature" raters is desirable, as raters who use self-observation, self-assertion and affiliation can facilitate the process of validly identifying defenses. Passive-aggressive individuals should be counselled out of serving as raters.

A second desirable characteristic in potential raters is having had some clinical experience. Training will be prolonged if raters need to be trained to observe and think dynamically in general, while simultaneously engaging in the harder task of learning to look for specific patterns of defense and related motives.

A third characteristic is having an open mind toward defenses along with the ability to think in new ways. Potential raters with extensive preconceptions about defenses, whether based on previous training or on a preference for another psychological model, have more difficulty modifying previous learned constructs in order to rate according to the manual. A worst case example of this is the rater who agrees with the manual during training but reverts to previous conceptions during subsequent ratings. This can usually be ascertained by noting diminishing inter-rater reliability after training is completed. Notable here is the need to offer raters continued supervisory sessions with an experienced rater throughout their period of rating. This will help prevent the abovementioned problems (deep theorizing, avoidance of underlying patterns, reverting to previous conceptions about defenses, etc.). We recommend a minimum of two hours of rater group supervision per month when raters have just finished training, or one hour of supervision per month for experienced raters.

A fourth characteristic, work style, also affects the consensus process. Raters who form judgments quickly, closing their minds to additional disconfirming evidence or to articulating the data in different ways, are difficult to work with. They prove especially difficult under rushed conditions. This defensive approach may particularly be present in novice raters, as the initial learning period is associated with insecurities that can influence raters to adopt a more rigid attitude. Usually, this stance diminishes with time and experience, giving way to more confidence and flexibility in raters. An attitude of open-mindedness, cooperation, and give-and-take is necessary in the absence of an absolute criterion of valid assessment.

Raters must strike compromises whenever a situation is somewhat ambiguous, with the rater who has the least evidence conceding. In irreconcilable disputes, raters often engage in horse-trading, with the rater who feels most strongly winning, while implicitly agreeing to a future concession in the other's favor. While this may appear unscientific, it does tend to work, because raters usually argue over near neighbor defenses, both of which may at times be used by the subject. As successive give-and-take consensus judgments are added, the ratings increasingly approximate the subject's true defensive profile. Nonetheless, these conflicts are best resolved by an expert when brought to an ongoing rater supervision group.

Rater Training

Formal Training Sessions

The following procedures optimize rater training. Prior to training, the rater should read the DMRS manual concentrating on the definition and function sections. One shouldn't try to learn everything at once, because the manual is better learned through repetitive use, as a reference.

Second, one can initially employ the qualitative rating method, because it requires more global judgments, and is easier to succeed at. The quantitative method requires many more judgements and is more discouraging to the novice.

Third, in training with clinical material, it is best to begin with videotapes and transcripts. Transcripts alone are hard to learn from because novice raters find the auditory and visual cues, which are missing, very helpful.

Fourth, raters watch a videotaped interview, make notes, preferably on an accompanying transcript, if available, and rate. They learn the scales and other manual material as they frequently refer to them. During qualitative rating training, the rater should justify each rating by reference to the appropriate defense scale items (e.g. 1b, or 2c & d, etc.). However, the author has moved away from qualitative approaches generally focussing on quantitative training. For these initial training tapes, the author has prepared transcripts with the text demarcated in sequence where each defense is present, but leaving blank which defense is present at each point. This simplifies the rater's task to focus on learning how to match the individual defenses with the function of the unknown defense in the marked text. During quantitative rating training, the rater should justify each defense by describing its function at that point in the text. Every discussion of which defense choice is correct should refer to the function of a candidate defense as described in the manual. Raters can also refer to the text immediately preceding or following the defensive text as supporting data for the justification process, because in real interview time what just happened and what is unfolding are intimately related to the defense at hand temporally and motivationally.

Fifth, it is best to have expert ratings available for practice sessions as a gold standard, against which raters can compare and discuss their ratings.

Sixth, teaching is better in small groups than in one-to-one settings. Hearing a variety of comments observing the justification process by others benefits learning. Two to four is an optimal number. Larger training groups present some difficulties. Most individuals don't get enough opportunity to talk and therefore to learn actively, and an excessive amount of time is required to finish one transcript. In large groups the author keeps up the pace by limiting the number of comments per defense under question to three individuals.

To complete the training, raters usually need to rate about five practice tapes and discuss them in group training sessions. This should be followed by five to ten more tapes in which the rater makes individual ratings followed by a consensus discussion with another rater, or receives expert corrective feedback. At this point most raters are quite reliable, although increasing experience results leads to increments in validity.

Supervision and Calibration of Trained Raters.

After training is complete the author usually runs supervisory calibration sessions. In these, raters bring in sessions in which rater pairs have completed consensus ratings. The inter-rater-reliability of the various scores is reviewed for systematic differences between raters [see number of defenses identified, number identified in each defense level, and ODF below]. As an example new raters often have biases in the differential identification of defenses with overlapping functions. Common examples include intellectualization v. rationalization, or self-assertion v. passive-aggression. Identifying and correcting the bases of these repetitive disagreements is very important for improving reliability and validity.

The second function of the calibration sessions is to allow raters to bring in examples from text where they were uncertain of their consensus. The relevant section of the text is read and discussed with the expert leading to a discussion of the function and final decision as to the correct defense. The consensus rating used for data analysis may then be amended based on the final decision. These sessions are invaluable for promoting raters to the highest levels of reliability and validity. In research projects, they also aid motivation by preventing raters from going stale without intellectual stimulation in the face of rating a large number of sessions.

Methods of Comparing DMRS Defense Scores

It is possible to make cross-sectional comparisons of study groups using either the qualitative or quantitative scoring methods. However, for detecting change over time within subjects or groups, only the quantitative scoring method is recommended because it is much more sensitive than the qualitative method. The three descriptive scores described below are all capable of detecting change.

1. Individual Defense Score. Table 9.1 displays the 30 individual defenses divided among the seven Defense Levels [q.v. below]. Subjects or groups can be compared by the score of any individual defense. When quantitative ratings are used, the proportional individual defense score should be used, that is, the raw count of each defense divided by the total raw count of all defenses scored in the session, e.g. four instances of repression among 50 instances for all defenses or 4/50 = .08) An example of a diagnostic comparison might be a test of the following hypothesis about the dynamics of obsessive-compulsive symptoms: "Do patients with obsessive-compulsive disorder score higher than those with major depressive disorder on the proportion of isolation of affect, reaction formation and displacement?" Another example might be to use individual defenses at intake to predict some occurrence in a subsequent psychotherapy such as: "Does extensive use of passive-aggression or denial predict premature termination?"

2. Defense Level Scores. The defense levels are derived from the hierarchy of defenses, in which those defenses with related functions are grouped together. Comparison of subjects or groups by the defense level scores is statistically more powerful because summing scores from three or four defenses produces longer scales with higher reliability and greater sensitivity to detect group differences. Using quantitative ratings, the related individual proportional scores are simply added together to produce the summary scores. For example, the sum of isolation plus intellectualization plus undoing = Obsessional Level defense score, e.g. .01 + .08 +.04 =.13. The initial study that used these summary of Defense Level scores demonstrated that 1) borderline psychopathology correlated with action and major image-distorting (formerly borderline level) defenses; 2) antisocial psychopathology correlated with disavowal and minor image-distorting (formerly narcissistic) defenses; while 3) bipolar type II affective disorder correlated with obsessional defenses (Perry & Cooper 1986).

In the DMRS system there are seven levels arranged hierarchically based on the average correlation of the defenses within each level with some measures of overall adaptiveness. This ordering is based on a series of empirical studies (reviewed in Perry 1993) using other methods as well as the DMRS. The defense levels and their individual defenses are shown in Table 9.1.

Psychotic defenses, those at the Level of *Defensive Dysregulation,* as described in the Defensive Functioning Scale in DSM-IV (Appendix B), were not included in the DMRS, Fifth edition. This was largely because the DMRS was developed on on non-psychotic populations. As a result, the author has since added four defenses at the *Defensive Dysregulation Level* which reflect psychotic defensive functioning. These include delusional distortion, delusional projection, psychotic denial, and psychotic dissociation. Except for delusional distortion, the other defenses have related non-psychotic defenses with overlapping names and functions.

3. Overall Defensive Functioning (ODF) and the Hierarchy of Adaptation. All of the defense scores can be summarized by an Overall Defensive Functioning (ODF) score (previously called Overall Defense Maturity). This is calculated by multiplying each defense by a weight according to its place in the overall 7-point hierarchy of defenses (see Table 9.1) and taking the weighted average of all the defenses rated in the session. The weight for each defense is the same as the rank order designating the defense level containing the defense. Although the theoretical limits of the ODF score are 1 to 7, in clinical samples based on whole interviews, scores usually range between 2.5 and 6.5 using either qualitative or quantitative scoring methods. Approximate reference scores for ODF are as follows: 1. Scores below 5.0 are associated with personality disorders or acute depression; 2. Scores between 5.0 and about 5.5 are associated with neurotic character and symptom disorders; 3.) scores from 5.5 to 6.0 are associated with average healthy neurotic functioning, while 4.) scores above 6.0 are associated with superior healthy-neurotic functioning

Important Considerations Regarding Different Data Sources

Experience in rating defenses has shown that differences in the source and type of data to be rated may affect the identification of certain defenses. The following describes six of these source conditions and their apparent biassing effects, moving from most to least optimal. For optimal reliability and validity, rating recorded data is better than rating clinical interviews in real time, for reasons stated below.

1. Videotaped Interview plus Transcript

This condition provides the best data source. In observing a videotaped interview, having a remote control makes it easier to stop and review parts of the session, whereas without it, one is less likely to take the time to revisit difficult sections. The major advantage of the videotaped playback of the interview is the relative completeness of the data. The rater can see the affects, behaviors, body language, and the interaction between the patient and interviewer, in addition to hearing what is spoken. Silences are more interpretable if one can fully perceive the immediate context. An example is the patient who appears anxious or irritable, then takes one minute to light a cigarette [an unlikely event in North American offices these days!]. Seeing the behavior in real time makes it easier to determine whether it clearly represents displacement from the topic at hand to the ritual of lighting a cigarette. Certain behaviors might be missed altogether. In one example a transcript only displayed the therapist's remark: "May I sit down?" whereas the videotape showed the patient beginning the session by putting her feet up on the therapist's chair before he sat down, which was clearly scorable as acting out and passive-aggression.

Tone of voice which is captured on audiotape may need further interpretation supplied by seeing the facial expression. This may help in identifying isolation of affect in individuals without a very expressive voice. Furthermore, behavior showing changes in concentration (facial features, body attitude) may punctuate changes in topics and defenses, which are harder to discern without the visual record.

The availability of an interview transcript allows the rater to concentrate more fully on the interview at hand. Otherwise, having to record verbatim speech or other observations distracts from the tasks of observing and identifying defenses. This is especially true considering that experience has shown that a range of approximately 15 to 75 defensive acts can be identified in single interviews. Fewer defenses are missed when transcripts are available. The lack of a transcript increases the error among raters especially in making quantitative ratings. The identification of certain defenses is improved by an accurate transcript. For instance, when considering displacement, one may need to review material earlier or later in the interview in order to identify the conflictual person or issue away from whom affect is being directed. Finally, a transcript may allow one to examine defenses in relationship to other therapeutic processes. Examples include rating the therapist's interventions as to which defenses they address, including the accuracy of defense interpretation, or examining the patient's defensive response to the therapist's interventions (e.g., did the intervention lead the patient to use defenses from higher levels). This is essential for quantitative process research in psychotherapy.

We therefore recommend that raters initially observe the videotaped session, taking note of important anomalies, after which they score the defenses by reviewing the transcript. With time and experience, raters might become successful in rating the transcripts while they listen to the videotaped sessions.

2. Audiotape plus Transcript

While missing the visual information, an audiorecording allows one to hear many non-lexical aspects of speech, including intonation, pauses in speech, prolonged silences, and fidgeting in the chair. Given a transcript, the information loss moving from video to audio recording appears less deleterious than if transcripts are used alone. However, it is important that the transcription include reference to pauses (e.g., short pause, long pause) and affective cues (e.g., sobbing, cries quietly, laughs, raises voice, shouts, whispers). Table 9.3 displays some difficulties attending the absence of the audiorecorded portion.

3. Videotape or Audiotape alone
Without a transcript, too much of the rater's attention is diverted into note taking. This slows down the rating process and inevitably results in loss of data. While using multiple raters mitigates the information loss somewhat, raters don't end up with highly comparable verbatim transcripts. As a consequence they then rate somewhat different interviews. In particular, defenses more likely to be missed are those which are better discerned by juxtaposing disparate parts of the session, something readily done when reviewing a transcript. Examples of this are splitting (e.g. describing an "all good" self image at one point, then an "all bad" object image later) and reaction formation (e.g. expressing the wish for a girlfriend at one point but later claiming to want nothing to do with women). The ability to review the transcript protects against getting caught up in the momentary story at the expense of missing the immediate or larger context. Whenever transcripts are not available, there is a slight advantage to rating videotapes over audiotapes because of the visual cues.

4. Transcript alone
The disadvantages of this condition have greatest effect on defenses which are better identified with their affective and behavioral cues intact. This problem can be partly mitigated if the transcription designates obvious affective cues in parentheses, as noted above. If a transcript contains sporadic instances of humor, isolation, help-rejecting complaining, and the like, the lower sensitivity of a text-only data source may result in missing them altogether. However, this source will still capture some instances of those defenses if they occur at higher prevalence.

5. Interviewer alone
When the individual doing the interviewing subsequently also rates the session without the aid of a transcript or recording, information loss and bias is potentially most serious. In this case, the interviewer-rater's attention is divided initially into the tasks of interviewing and observing and later into the tasks of reconstructing the session and rating the defenses. However, if provided with either a transcript or audio recording, the interviewer can subsequently rate as efficiently as in any condition, using the aids to reconstruct the interview more fully.

It is important to mention the possible influence of the interviewer-subject relationship on ratings. For example, counter-transference issues can foster a bias in some instances, creating a tendency in an interviewer-rater towards reactive inferences, based on subjective experience more than objective observation. This can skew ratings toward either lower or higher level defenses, depending on the valence of counter-transference. We therefore recommend that the roles of interviewer and rater be separated whenever possible, in order to limit the occurrence of such bias.

Table 9.3: *Effects of rating defenses from a transcript without hearing an audio-recording*

Humor. Hearing the delivery helps in discerning the meaning. Reading a joke is not the same as hearing one told. For instance, the combined cues may help differentiate whether one is devaluing someone or oneself to dismiss a threat or disappointment, or laughing at one's or someone's foibles to diffuse a conflict.

Isolation of affect. One may hear evidence of feelings while the transcript is devoid of emotionally laden words. Alternately, without listening to the audio portion, one may incorrectly infer the presence of affect whenever the subject uses words with emotional meaning, whereas the audio recording might show an absence of expressed feeling.

Undoing. Repeated expressions, such as "I don't know," can be difficult to interpret without the voice quality which would indicate whether it was meant to negate the previous statement, or whether it is used as filler like "ummh..." Similarly, hearing doubt in someone's voice helps underline that an apparent qualification may actually be a negation of a previous assertion.

Repression v. Denial. Non-lexical aspects of speech help in determining whether the person is searching for an idea which cannot be found or whether the person is convinced that the idea is not present, as evidenced by a vehement tone of voice and dismissal.

Dissociation. The onset of dissociation is often accompanied by a change in tone of voice, such as a wispy, quiet or distant tone of voice or change in pitch.

Reaction formation. Tone of voice helps in discerning whether an affect has really been turned into its opposite.

Devaluation. The tone of voice helps differentiate whether certain common phrases are meant to disparage or merely to punctuate speech in a colorful way.

Idealization. Idealization may be missed if the text contains few superlatives, whereas it is highlighted by an overly enthusiastic tone of voice.

Rationalization. A conning or histrionic tone of voice can be very helpful in discerning an attempt to disguise a motive. If it sounds bogus, the subject may be somewhat uncomfortable with the motive offered as an explanation.

Passive aggression. In response to a therapist's question or comment, whenever a patient says "no" or ignores something said, the tone of voice and manner of speaking indicates whether anger is indirectly conveyed by a begrudging attitude.

Help-rejecting complaining (hypochondriasis). A whining tone may help underline the defensive expression of covert aggression alongside helplessness.

6. *Using Multiple Data Sources*
Overall, ratings from different data sources are not strictly comparable, because loss of information will bias the sensitivity with which raters can identify individual defenses. While this is qualitatively clear, the exact amount of bias is yet to be determined for each defense for each data source.

Reliability and Stability of Defense Ratings

Inter-rater reliability of defense ratings has been determined as part of a number of studies. In most studies, two raters listened to an audiotaped interview or session and followed a written transcript, blind to subject identity and session number. Sessions were presented in random order to prevent a bias (e.g., rating earlier sessions with more lower level defenses than later sessions). Raters independently marked each defense on the transcript, and tallied each occurrence for each defense to yield a quantitative profile of defenses. Raters subsequently discussed and arrived at consensus ratings for each session, although the consensus rating did not contribute to the determination of reliability.

Table 9.4 displays the inter-rater reliabilities obtained in six studies, two early ones using qualitative ratings, and four more recent ones using quantitative ratings. In a field trial using many different clinicians (Perry et al., 1998), the inter-rater reliability of ODF was as good as that of the commonly used Global Assessment of Functioning (current GAF or Axis V), while the stability was actually higher for ODF than GAF at one and six months. This probably reflects that the more trait-like aspect of defensive functioning makes ODF more resistant than GAF to fluctuations which coincide with episodes of psychiatric disorders.

The quantitative reliabilities for the number of defenses rated in a session (No.) and for ODF are generally above intraclass R >.80 (respective median figures from Table 9.4, 0.83 and 0.84). The median reliabilities for the defense levels are also close (median 0.795). Figures for the 28 or so individual defenses would undoubtedly be lower, although these were usually not reported. The reliability of any individual defense varies much more widely, with those occurring at very low base rates in a given case being the most problematic. Studies which use a small consistent group of trained raters, and which have good variability in subject defensive functioning will generally obtain the higher median reliability figures.

The stabilities of defense ratings were examined in two studies (see Table 9.3). Using qualitative ratings, Perry et al. (1998) obtained a one-month stability for

Table 9.4: *Interrater reliability and stability of defenses rated by the DMRS*

	Inter-rater reliability			Stability		
	No.	ODF	Defense Levels Med. (range)	No.	ODF	Levels Med. (range)
Qualitative ratings						
Perry&Cooper, 1989			.53/.74			
Perry et al., 1998		.68			.75/.51**	
Quantitative Ratings						
Lingiardi et al., 1999	.83	.87	.87 (.67-.95)			
Despland et al., 2001		.80	.80			
Perry, 2001	.83	.85	.625 (.52-.80)	.14	.48***	.47 (.08-.73)
Herzoug, 2002		.83				
Drapeau et al., 2003			.79			

* Figures are for inter-rater reliability/reliability of two consensus ratings.
** Stabilities are one-month/six-month.
*** Stability figure is session to session over five weekly sessions.

ODF of 0.75. However when quantitative ratings are used, which are more sensitive to change, Perry (2001) found a lower figure, 0.48, for ODF, examining week to week variability in five consecutive psychotherapy sessions from a personality and depressive disorder sample, whereas there was virtually no stability for the number of defenses per session. Drapeau et al. (2003) found that over a 4-session Brief Psychodynamic Investigation, the number of defenses decreased significantly from session to session, as the level of distress decreased. The range of stability coefficients for the number of defenses, as well as for the defense levels appears to indicate that certain of these are more sensitive to state effects, but that on average close to 50% of the variance reflects a stable defense repertoire. This figure rises to 57% if corrected for measurement error (Perry 2001). Interestingly, the high adaptive level defenses showed the lowest stability, suggesting that among those with depressive and personality disorders, these defenses are the most sensitive to disruption by state effects, such as mood or stress. This further suggests that with improvement, increased psychological resilience might be accompanied by an increase in both the proportion and the stability of high adaptive defenses across time.

Recent and Ongoing Research Relevant to Psychotherapy

Defenses and Depression

A recent naturalistic study of subjects seeking treatment for major depression examined the predictive value of clinicians' ratings of defenses at intake (Hoglend & Perry, 1998). Eight lower level defenses previously associated with depression (Perry & Cooper 1986; Block et al. 1993) were compared to the remaining six other lower level defenses, thereby controlling for the general level of adaptiveness of the defenses. The eight defenses included passive aggression, acting out, help-rejecting complaining, splitting of self-images, splitting of others' images, projective identification, projection, and devaluation. Patients were treated as usual which generally included antidepressants and psychotherapy, and then reassessed at six months. A greater prevalence of the eight defenses linked to depression predicted worse outcome at six months, even after controlling for the presence of an Axis II disorder. The comparison group of six other lower level defenses (e.g. denial, rationalization) did not predict a worse outcome. The findings suggest that these eight defenses have an effect on depression apart from their overall level of adaptiveness, and strengthens the case that they are contributing factors to the course of depression. If further study indicates that they contribute to the overall vulnerability to depression (e.g. episode onset, duration, treatment resistance, recurrence), then a dynamic therapy could be refined for depression by specifying how to focus on improving these specific defenses.

Furthermore, the proportion of all defensive functioning attributable to this group of defenses could serve as an indicator of the degree of risk for depression.

Studying Improvement in Defensive Functioning in Psychotherapy

Table 9.5 displays the results from four studies that have examined change in ODF over the course of evaluations and psychotherapies of different durations. The changes in ODF are converted to within-condition effect sizes (ES) for more direct comparison. Perry, Hoglend et al., (Perry & Hoglend et al. 1997; Hoglend & Perry, 1998) examined change in defensive functioning in a heterogeneous sample of outpatients. Most received supportive psychotherapy and two-thirds of those with major depression also received medication. ODF improved a small amount by one-month (0.25 ES), and somewhat more by six-months (0.42 ES). Perry (2001) examined a sample with personality disorders and/or depression entering long-term psychotherapy. At one year, the sample had improved slightly (0.16 ES). The same study reported on one patient who had 4 years of psychotherapy and a follow-up at ten years. The patient regressed before finally improving substantially by termination (ODF at intake and termination: 4.63 and 4.93, change 0.89 ES). Furthermore, by the 10 year follow-up, the individual had continued to improve, with a final ODF in the healthy-neurotic range of 5.80, equivalent to a 10-year ES of 2.60. Herzoug et al. (2002) examined a heterogeneous sub-group from the Norwegian Multi-Center Psychotherapy Study receiving 40 session Brief Dynamic Psychotherapy. They found virtually no change in ODF at one-month, but a large amount at one year (0.82 ES). Drapeau et al. (2003) reported on a heterogenous sample of 61 individuals who received a 4-session Brief Dynamic Investigation, over one month or less. A moderate amount of change occurred (0.49 ES), which the authors attributed as most likely a return to the status quo before the crisis, facilitated by the therapeutic sessions.

These samples are heterogeneous as to patient and treatment characteristics thus hazarding generalization. In all cases improvement was a function of time both in and following treatment. In the short-term (one-month) change is either negligible or small, with the difference likely affected by whether the individuals present in a crisis (yielding more change) or closer to their usual level of functioning (yielding less change). By 6-months to one year improvement was either small, in samples having a high proportion of PDs, or moderate in size in more heterogeneous, treated samples. However, none of the samples attained a healthy-neurotic mean level of functioning in the one year time frames of most studies. The one exception was the single long-term case reported (Perry, 2001). Thus all studies indicated that significant personality and affective psychopathology are likely to require treatments of greater than one year to attain a healthy-neurotic level of defensive functioning.

Attention to patterns of change among defensive levels may inform upon the process of improvement (Perry, 2001). First are the overall patterns of change in defensive functioning. For individuals with significant, chronic or recurrent disorders, such as those with a personality disorder or multiple Axis I disorders, stable change may not be evident in a short time-frame. In fact, defensive functioning often appeared to improve for a short time in the early sessions. However, this was generally followed by a return to the usual level of defensive functioning. This "honeymoon effect" probably reflects the initial but temporary response to the non-specific factors of therapy, including relief, decrease in depressive/anxiety symptoms, and a resurgence of hope, rather than stable change. For some patients stable change was evident by one year, but for the majority it was not evident until the second or third year. In fact, several patients demonstrated some regression in defensive functioning in the first several years. This appeared to be most evident in patients using major and minor image-distorting defenses (borderline and narcissistic), suggesting that issues arising from both self-protection and self-esteem regulation may have been related to regression. The sample was too small to refine this idea further.

Table 9.5: *Change in overall defensive functioning with psychotherapy.*

	Perry et al.1998	Perry 2001	Herzoug et al. 2002	Dapreau et al. 2003
N	37	15	39	61
Major Diagnosis				
Dysthymia	20%	40%		62% all mood disord.
MDE	49%	40%	16%	" "
PD	62%	80%	65%	38%
GAF	52	56	55	
GSI	1.38		1.38	0.90
ODF mean (SD)	4.68 (1.05)	4.27 (0.45)	4.40 (0.51)	4.37 (0.57)
1-month*	4.94 (0.25)		4.41 (0.02)	4.65^{+} (0.49)
6-month*	5.11 (0.41)		4.82 (0.82)	
12-month*		4.34 (0.16)		

* mean and within-condition effect size. $^{+}$Improvement by the 4th session.studies.

The amount of change over time in treatment was variable. Those patients who made it past two years of treatment showed the greatest amount of change, generally greater than one effect size (i.e. more than one standard deviation of the sample's mean ODF score at intake). The amount of change was clearly a function of time. However, change was not linear initially, but became increasingly so over a longer time frame. This was principally because of periods of regression in defensive function which occurred in the first one to three years. This study did not include healthier patients who might be suitable for short-term treatment. It is possible that somewhat healthier patients may demonstrate changes over shorter time frames, as found by Herzoug et al. (2002). This issue will require further study.

Table 9.6: *Subject A: Changes in defenses over 180 sessions (five years)*

	Rate of change* (Proportional score/session)	% Variance explained by session	*p*-value
7 high adaptive level	.000018	< 1%	*ns*
Neurotic Levels			
6 obsessional	-.00032	-5%	*ns*
5 a. hysterical	.00050	27%	
b. displacement/ reaction formation	.0010	44%	
Immature Levels			
4 minor image-distorting	-.00057	-33%	.002
3 disavowal	.00015	1%	*ns*
2 major image-distorting	--	--	--
1 action	-.00045	-20%	.02

* expressed as change per session in the proportion of defenses at each level. For example, reaction formation/displacement rate of .001 indicates an increase of 0.1%of total defensive functioning attributed to these defenses each session, or 1% each 10 sessions, etc.).

The second pattern is that change in the seven levels of defensive functioning appeared to proceed following the hierarchy of adaptation. This finding is exemplified by the case noted above (Perry, 2001), who was treated in weekly dynamic psychotherapy for four years. Five therapy sessions from each year were rated as noted above. The ODF score and the proportional score for each of the seven defense levels were examined as a function of session number by linear regression analysis. Over 180 sessions, this individual showed an improvement in ODF score of 0.45 points, as noted above. The lowest defense levels that were highly prevalent (action and minor image-distorting) demonstrated significant and marked decrease as a percentage of overall defensive functioning. Interestingly, the minor image-distorting defenses increased slightly in the early years before tapering rapidly in years four and five. Table 9.6 displays changes in all seven defense levels. Defenses in the middle of the hierarchy (repression/dissociation and reaction-formation/displacement) actually increased over the same period of time, while obsessional defenses, which were initially highly prevalent remained about the same. Finally, significant increases in the high adaptive level defenses did not occur during these four years, but did increase over the following six year follow-up. This overall pattern suggests that improvement in ODF initially involved trading off the lowest level defenses in favor of relying more on mid-level, neurotic defenses which the individual already employed in his defense repertoire to some extent. Insofar as lower level defenses reflect resistance to change, while high adaptive level defenses represent flexibility in adapting, it appears that, for those who use a high proportion of lower level defenses, there is no way to circumvent becoming "more neurotic" prior to becoming "more mature". This hierarchical hypothesis about change in defenses suggests an interesting implication. Therapies which try early in the course of therapy to teach skills that require high level defenses to enable learning may not achieve their aims well. These observations will require further replication to refine this hypothesis about hierarchical pathways to improvement.

Potential Directions for Studying Defenses in Psychotherapy

An intriguing consequence of studying defenses as basic psychological mechanisms is that they can be viewed either as outcome or as process phenomena in psychotherapy. Defenses can be assessed at the outset of therapy and periodically reassessed as a measure of dynamic functioning to-date. Because of the empirical support for the hierarchy of adaptation (Perry 1993), improvement in the Overall Defensive Functioning score or the constituent defense levels or individual defenses represents improvement in dynamic functioning. However, from a microanalytic perspective, the individual use of a defense can be examined as an appropriate unit of psychological functioning to elucidate the process of change in psychotherapy. The following are several suggested areas to pursue.

1. A common complaint about descriptive diagnosis is that it does not offer very much for considerations of treatment selection and focus. By contrast, defense mechanisms potentially offer a meaningful component of a dynamic diagnosis relevant for treatment (Skodol & Perry 1994). Studies that examine defenses at the outset of therapy may determine what defenses predict in the subsequent treatment course. For instance, a high prevalence of the least adaptive defenses, e.g. action and major image-distorting, should predict regressive and impulsive phenomena which require very different therapeutic interventions than those appropriate whenever obsessional or repressive-dissociative defenses predominate. Perry (2001) found evidence that lower level defenses were associated with attrition in long-term treatment. By contrast, Herzoug et al. (2002) found that the level of defensive functioning did not predict the amount of change with Brief Dynamic Psychotherapy. Both Herzoug et al. (2002) and Despland et al. (2001) found that ODF did not predict the development of the alliance, However, Despland et al. (2001) did

find an apparent interaction between defense levels and types of therapist interventions: patients developed positive alliances when the therapists level of supportive v exploratory interventions were better matched to the initial ODF score. These predictive relationships should be systematically studied to inform the selection of treatment approaches.

2. More data are needed to elucidate the lawful relationships between external stressors, salient motives (wishes and fears), affects, and specific patterns of defensive functioning. Defenses are easier to identify than the underlying motives and meanings which the individual attributes to events. Defenses thereby serve as clincial signposts. Their occurence suggests that the observer should look for certain underlying dynamics. For instance, whenever repression and dissociation predominate, there may be an association with both past sexual trauma and current stressful experiences. Certain current experiences may trigger conflicts because of their meaning to the individual, in which both sexual wishes and counterbalancing motives (e.g. fear of harm, guilt, blame) are subjectively threatening. Given that patients may be unaware of the connection between such past and current experiences, general knowledge about such relationships to these defenses would help the therapist find a salient focus.
3. Process research can also describe the relationships between patients' defensive responses and the preceding and subsequent interventions by the therapist. Given that defenses reflect the patient's immediate adaptive ability in action, one can test dynamic hypotheses about the utility of specific interventions. A successful intervention, or series of them, should lead to improved defensive functioning within the session, i.e. moving up the hierarchy. Summed across sessions these should lead to long-term stable improvement. By contrast, unsuccessful interventions would leave defensive functioning unchanged or regressed. Two specific aspects of this are worthy of study.

A. Focus on defense or on motive, conflict or relationship pattern? One dynamic hypothesis suggests that therapists should focus their interventions on defensive operations as a precursor to addressing the conflictual content or interpersonal situations that trigger defenses. This hypothesis is readily accessible to testing. After identifying the patient's defensive responses, the therapist's interventions should be categorized as to whether they address the predominating defenses accurately, or whether they address something else, such as an affective response, an underlying conflict, or another person's response to the subject. When a series of these observations is examined (defense – intervention type – defense), the efficacy of the different types of interventions can be judged by the probability of subsequent improvements or decrements in the patient's overall defensive functioning either inside or outside the session.

B. Support versus Exploration. Some ongoing studies are already examining defensive functioning and the type of therapist interventions used to highlight why some interventions backfire at times, leading to problems in the alliance and worsening of the patient's symptoms. For instance, whenever a patient is using predominantly lower level defenses, highly change-oriented interventions, such as interpretation or cognitive restructuring, which are stressful themselves, may result in negative therapeutic reactions and a diminution in the therapeutic alliance. By contrast, the temporary use of more supportive interventions, which are far less threatening, may allow the individual to move his or her defensive set-point further up the hierarchy, thereby permitting the re-introduction of some change-oriented interventions later. Despland et al. (2001) found preliminary evidence supporting this hypothesis over a 4-session Brief Dynamic Investigation.

C. Certain lower defense levels should predict trouble tolerating and staying in psychotherapy. In particular the action defenses are well known for exacerbating difficulty in level of cooperation, tolerance for distressing affects, acceptance of limits etc. Major-image-distorting (borderline) defenses correlate with periods of regression and volatile ruptures in the therapeutic alliance. Disavowal defenses are associated with discomfort at acknowledging subjective distress, guilt, inadequacy, powerlessness. Minor-image-distorting defenses relate to difficulties regulating self-esteem in the face of disappointment, shame and criticism.

    i.) Thus, it is reasonable to hypothesize that these four lower defense levels would predict drop-out in psychotherapy in general.

    ii.) In particular, action and disavowal defenses might predict early attrition from therapy, since they reflect the least degree of tolerance for subjective distress. Evidence for this was noted above (Perry, 2001).

    iii.) Once therapy has been established, image-distorting defenses might predict subsequent stalemate, associated with troubled or brittle alliance formation.

    iv.) Similarly both major and minor image-distorting defenses may predict late course attrition.

If the above are demonstrated to be true, then it will be possible to test whether a given therapeutic approach (e.g. high support, low confrontation, moderate exploration) might improve retention in treatment for those groups of patients at risk for attrition. Subsequent improvement in these lower defense levels should then correlate with the ability to tolerate a deeper process, including greater exploration and use of interpretation.

4. Some day we should be able to describe the effects of specific treatments on defensive functioning for specific groups of patients. The following question applies to two examples. For specific treatment types, such as dynamic psychotherapy or CBT, what treatment durations (e.g. 25th, 50th, 75th percentiles of number of sessions) are associated with

A. Patients with borderline personality disorder no longer using splitting or other major image-distorting defenses, and showing a predominance of neurotic defenses?

   i) patients with chronic or recurrent depression no longer using the eight defenses associated with risk for continued depressive symptoms, and therefore demonstrating significantly lower risk for recurrence?

With knowledge of the above, one could further predict that such patients have attained psychological protection from the stressors which previously triggered the problematic defenses and precipitated regressive behaviors or depression.

5. The psychotherapy manuals of the future will be increasingly based on a firm empirical explication of the individual patient's psychopathology. Defense mechanisms are ideal candidates for treatment manuals designed both for general patient samples and for those with specific disorders, because of the intimate role defenses serve in adaptation to stress and conflict. The manuals will address identifying these mechanisms as they occur, choosing which defenses to focus on, and then suggest ways to address them. The dynamic manuals will include case examples that specify interventions varying from the supportive to the exploratory and interpretive, depending on the specific defenses or patient's overall defensive state at the time. To use a common analogy, these manuals will not resemble the traditional cookbook approach, with a series of recipes to be followed as written session by session. Instead, they will begin with a list of ingredients, the patients' defenses, and then consider therapists' interventions. The manuals will teach how to combine them to the betterment of the patients' adaptation. Taking this viewpoint, therapy consists of an ongoing series of examples provided by the patient in which the therapist's task is to facilitate the patient's defensive functioning toward successively higher level defenses which are within his or her grasp.

Conclusion

Defenses can be viewed both as process phenomena (psychological mechanisms in action) and as a measure of adaptive outcome, when aggregated across sessions and time. This gives the study of defenses great potential clinical relevance. To develop and test predictive hypotheses about treatment will make the study of defenses very relevant to daily clinical work, and both scientifically promising and exciting.

References

Bader M., Perry J. C. (2001). Mécanismes de défense et épisodes relationnels lors de deux psychothérapies brèves mère-enfant. (Eng trans. Defense mechanisms and relationship episodes among two brief mother-infant psychotherapies). *Psychothérapies; 21*: 123-131.

Bloch A. L., Shear M. K., Markowitz J. C., Leon A. C., Perry J.C. (1993). An empirical study of defense mechanisms in dysthymia. *Am J Psychiatry*; *150*: 1194-1198.

Bond M., Perry J. C., Gautier M., Goldenberg M., Oppenheimer J., Simand J. (1989). Validating the self-report of defense styles. *J Personality Disorders 3*: 101-112.

Despars J., Kiely M. C., Perry J.C. (2001). Le développement de l'alliance thérapeutique: influence des interventions du thérapeute et des défenses du patient. (Eng. trans., The development of the therapeutic alliance: influence of therapist interventions and the defenses of the patient.) *Psychothérapies*; *21*:141-152.

Despland, J. -N., Despars, J., de Roten, Y., Stiglar, M., Perry, J. C. (2001). Contribution of patient defense mechanisms and therapist interventions to the development of early therapeutic alliance in a Brief Psychodynamic Investigation *J Psychother Pract Res* 10: 155-164.

Drapeau, M., de Roten, Y., Perry, J. C., & Despland, J. N. (in press 2003). A study of stability and change in defense mechanisms during a Brief Psychodynamic Investigation. *J Nerv & Ment Dis.*

Guldberg, C, Hogelend, P, Perry, J. C.(1993). Scientific Assessment of Defense Mechanisms. *Nordic Journal of Psychiatry*; 47:435-446.

Herzoug, A. G., Sexton, H. C., Hoglend, P. A.(2002) Contribution of defensive functioning to the quality of working alliance and psychotherapy outcome. *Am J Psychotherapy, 56*:539-554.

Hoglend, P, Perry, J. C. (1998). Defensive functioning predicts improvement in major depressive episodes. *Journal of Nervous and Mental Disease 186,* (4):1-7.

Horowitz, M. J., Cooper, S. H., Fridhandler, B., Perry, J. C., Bond, M., Vaillant, G.E. (1992). Control Processes and defense mechanisms: a theory to phenomena linkage. *J Psychotherapy Research and Practice, 1,* 325-336.

Lingiardi, V, Lonati, C, DeLucchi, F, Fossati, A, Vanzulli, L, Maffei, C. (1999) Defense mechanisms and personality disorders. *J Nerv Ment Dis 187,* 224-228.

Perry, J. C. (1988). A prospective study of life stress, defenses, psychotic symptoms and depression in borderline and antisocial personality disorders and bipolar type II affective disorder. *J Personality Disorders 2*:49-59.

Perry, J. C. (1990a). *The Defense Mechanism Rating Scales Manual,* fifth edition. Copyright by J.C. Perry, M.D., Cambridge, Massachusetts.

Perry, J. C. (1990b). Psychological defense mechanisms in the study of affective and anxiety disorders. In, Maser J, Cloninger CR, eds., *Co-morbidity in Anxiety and Mood Disorders,* pp 545-562. Washington, D,C., American Psychiatric Press, Inc.

Perry, J. C. The study of defense mechanisms and their effects. (1993). In Miller N, Luborsky L, Barber J, Docherty J, eds. *Psychodynamic Treatment Research: A Handbook for Clinical Practice,* pp. 276-308. New York, Basic Books.

Perry, J. C.(1994). Scala di Valutazione dei Meccanismi di Difesa. In, Lingiardi V, Madeddu F. *I Meccanismi di defesa: Teoria clinica e ricerca empirica.* Raffaello Cortina Editore, Milano, appendix pp 117-198. [The Defense Mechanism Rating Scales, Italian version translated by Susanna Brambilla, published as an appendix in the above book.]

Perry, J. C. (1996). Defense mechanisms in impulsive versus obsessive-compulsive disorders. In: Oldham J, Skodol A.E., eds., *Impulsive Versus Obsessive-compulsive Disorders,* pp 195-230. Washington DC: American Psychiatric Press Inc.

Perry, J. C. (2000). *Guidelines for the Quantitative Identification of Defenses,* manual available from the author, Montreal, Canada.

Perry, J. C. (2001) A pilot study of defenses in psychotherapy of personality disorders entering psychotherapy. *J Nerv & Ment Dis.; 189,* 651-660.

Perry, J. C, Cooper, S. H (1986): A Preliminary Report on Defenses and Conflicts Associated with Borderline Personality Disorder, *J Am Psychoanal Assoc 34,* 865-895.

Perry, J. C., Cooper, S. H. (1987): Empirical studies of psychological defense mechanisms. In: Michels R., Cavenar J.O., (eds.), *Psychiatry, Vol I,* pp 1-19.. New York: J.B. Lippincott, and Basic Books.

Perry, J. C. & Cooper, S. H. (1989). An empirical study of defense mechanisms: I. Clinical interview and life vignette ratings. *Arch Gen Psychiatry 46,* 444-452.

Perry, J. C., Kardos, M. E. (1994). A review of research using the Defense Mechanism Rating Scales. In Conte H, Plutchik R, eds., *Ego Defenses: Theory and Practice*, Chap 13, pp 283-299. New York: John Wiley & Sons.

Perry, J. C., Hoglend, P., Shear, K., Vaillant, G. E., Horowitz, M. J., Kardos, M. E., Bille, H., Kagan, D. (1998). Field Trial of a diagnostic Axis for defense mechanisms for DSM-IV. *J Pers Dis 12,*1-13, 1998.

Perry, J. C., Ianni, F. (1998). Observer-rated measures of defense mechanisms. *Journal of Personality 66,* 993-1024, 1998.

Perry, J. C., Hoglend, P. (1998). Convergent and discriminant validity of overall defensive functioning. *Journal of Nervous & Mental Disease 186,* 529-535.

Saltzstein, B. J., Wyshak, G., Hubbach, J. T., Perry, J. C. (1998). A naturalistic study of chronic fatigue syndrome among women in primary care. *General Hospital Psychiatry 20,* 307-316.

Skodol, A., Perry, J. C., (1993). Should an Axis for Defense Mechanisms be included in DSM-IV? *Compr Psychiatry, 34,* 108-119.

Defense Mechanisms in Differential and Applied Psychology

Defense Mechanisms
U. Hentschel, G. Smith, J.G. Draguns & W. Ehlers (Editors)

Chapter 10

The Motivational and Cognitive Determinants of Defense Mechanisms

Shulamith Kreitler and Hans Kreitler

Introduction

Defense mechanisms (DMs) are a unique set of mental operations, first described by Freud, 1923/1961, 1896/1962, 1933/1964a), elaborated by Anna Freud (1966), and further developed in recent decades (e.g., Conti & Plutchik, 1995; Cramer, 1988; Schafer, 1987; Singer, 1990). Yet, despite their popularity, little has been learned about their acquisition, their selection, cognitive roots, impact on overt behavior and relation to personality traits.

This chapter is designed to fill in some of these gaps. We start by clarifying the close relations of DMs to cognitive strategies. We then proceed to discuss, in the framework of the cognitive orientation theory, the role of DMs in the input-output chain. This will lead to a new conceptualization of DMs and will uncover some of the motivational determinants of DMs and their relation to belief systems. The theoretical presentation will be followed by the description of four studies predicting the occurrence of specific DMs on the basis of belief measures. Next we focus on clarifying, in the the framework of the meaning system, the cognitive determinants of the dynamic-operational aspect of DMs and their relation to personality traits. A study describing the prediction of DMs on the basis of both beliefs and meaning variables is then presented. The next section deals with modifying DMs and describes a study in which DMs were changed by changing beliefs and meaning variables. Finally, the motivational and cognitive determinants of DMs are integrated within the framework of a blueprint for a cognitive approach to DMs.

The Function of DMs

A few dozen DMs have been identified by different investigators. Though they differ in their particular dynamics and outcomes, they share their basic underlying function. In most general terms, DMs are strategies for the resolution of conflicts, which in psychoanalytic terms may be characterized as conflicts between the strivings of the id and the demands of the ego or the superego. These strategies are not specific to a particular type of conflict, which implies that a conflict such as between a homosexual wish and the ego's striving to comply with the moral and social rules against it, may be dealt with by projection, sublimation, or modified by regression into child-like submission to a father figure. The intrapsychic function of DMs, emphasized by psychoanalytic approaches, serves a variety of specific purposes: to resolve the original conflict in some form, to provide at least partial discharge to the involved tensions, to prevent the emergence of the threatening drives or wishes into consciousness (in the form of ideas or emotions) (Freud, 1915/1957; 1936), to control unacceptable id impulses, to avoid the pain of constant conflict (Munroe, 1956, p. 243), to keep emotions within tolerable limits, to restore equilibrium disrupted by sudden increases in drives, to gain time for mastering changes in 'life image' that cannot be easily integrated, and to deal with unresolved conflicts with important figures in one's life from whom one cannot take leave (Vaillant, 1983, p. 344). In short, the major function of DMs is to defend the ego against internal dangers (Freud, 1937/1964b, p. 237), which may be triggered by internal or external events.

DMs as Cognitive Strategies

Progress in the understanding of DMs requires a conception of how DMs accomplish their ego-protective function. An important observation that provides a clue for an answer is that beyond their application for resolving intrapsychic conflicts, DMs are widely used in everyday life as strategies for the successful performance of simple or complex cognitive tasks. Most DMs are likely to remind us of highly similar procedures occurring in contexts that are unrelated to ego defense. Thus, some DMs resemble strategies applied by children before they are assumed to have an ego that may stand in need of defense, for example, ignoring and immediately forgetting a parental restriction (i.e., repression), or assuming that a beloved doll is hungry and trying to feed it (i.e., projection). Indeed, projection remains for a long time an important means for understanding of engines and other appliances (e.g, "Look, the fireplace must be very hungry, it eats the wood so fast"). It is however complemented by introjection that also figures often in children's attempts to comprehend how things work. A famous example was provided by Piaget (1951) who described how a child understood the mechanism of the matchbox only after it opened and closed its mouth a few times.

Most impressive are examples demonstrating the frequent use of defense-like strategies in different domains, notably problem solving, geometry, logic and regular daily functioning. For example, methods for solving mathematical problems include decomposing the complex problem into its constituent parts and working on isolated parts one at a time (i.e., isolation), or focusing first on a simpler problem (i.e., regression or displacement) (Polya, 1954, 1957; Wickelgren, 1974). Also in working on non-mathematical problems it is often necessary "to repress" habitual strategies so as to overcome functional fixedness; "to isolate" strategies previously applied for solving problems of another kind and "to project" them onto the presently given situation; "to regress" to an earlier stage, perhaps "undoing" something of what has already been done; raise the problem onto a more theoretical, hence higher level, thus exercising sublimation; and even to engage in reversal by trying the contrary of that which has previously been attempted. In the domain of logic we encounter the procedures of disproving a thesis by driving it ad absurdum (i.e., exaggeration) or by showing that reversing it ends up in a contradiction (i.e., reversal). In the domain of geometry we deal with projection into other dimensions (i.e. projection), reversals (e.g., of symmetry) and rotations (i.e., displacement).

More familiar examples concern everyday life. Thus, we naturally expect others to know what we know (Nickerson, 2001) and behave as we do (i.e., projection). Or, we may have become so proficient at ignoring disturbing stimuli that we no longer hear the usual traffic noise (i.e., repression). Again, if irritated by the recurrent misunderstanding of journal editors, we may decide to write a book (i.e., reaction formation). Or, when Beethoven lost some coins he wrote the piece "Die Wut ueber den verlorenen Groschen" (The anger over the lost nickel) that exemplifies sublimation, and perhaps acting out too.

These examples indicate that DMs are essentially basic and often applied cognitive strategies. Yet there are evident differences between the use of these strategies as DMs and in general. The most important difference is that as DMs they are much less amenable to conscious control, and hence are also far less flexible and less situation-relevant. Accordingly, we suggest that DMs are cognitive strategies that have undergone a transformation as a result of their specialized use. Thus, they become DMs under three major interrelated conditions: (a) when their function is limited primarily to serving intrapsychic needs in general or to resolving conflicts, such as those between the superego or ego and the id in particular; (b) when they are used without conscious control; and (c) when they have undergone schematization resulting in reduced flexibility and variation.

Thus, DMs may be defined as cognitively-based schemata functioning mainly in the intrapsychic sphere, especially in conflict resolution. Yet, the definition of DMs as cognitive strategies does not limit their manifestations only to the cognitive domain. DMs may affect perceptions (Shervin, 1995), emotions (Kwon, 2002), verbal behavior (Barett, Williams, & Fong, 2002), interpersonal behaviors (Cramer, 2002) and physiological responses (Derakshan & Eysenck, 2001) no less than cognitions (Borton, 2002). Any theory of DMs would need to account for the broad psychological impact of DMs.

The Motivational Determinants of Defense Mechanisms

DMs in the Input-Output Chain

There is evidence about the effect of DMs on perception, such as distorted input identification (Kragh, 1984), as well as on output behavior, such as addictions (Winegar, Stephens, & Varney, 1987). As a result of their theoretical concern with a particular set of internal processes and their use of psychotherapeutic rather than experimental methods, psychoanalysts failed to clarify the position and role of DMs in the chain of events intervening between perceptual input and behavioral output. Neither have there been other systematic attempts to specify the role of DMs in the various stages of behavior evocation and formation. Attempts of this kind, which fill in the gap between defensively distorted inputs and outputs, are important for understanding the evocation, operation and selection of DMs as well as the broad range of domains in which their impact may be manifested. We have tried to fill the gap by applying to the issue of DMs the cognitive orientation (CO) theory (Kreitler & Kreitler, 1976, 1982, 2002).

The CO Theory

The CO theory was developed originally for the prediction and modification of human overt behavior. It was later extended to further domains, mainly cognition, emotions, psychopathology and physical disease or health (e.g., Kreitler & Kreitler, 1991), so that CO came to denote the general theory underlying a series of models referring each to one of the specific domains. In this context we will present briefly the model referring to overt behavior.

The major thesis of the CO theory is that human behavior is the product of a motivational disposition, that shapes the directionality of behavior, and a behavioral program, that shapes the performance of behavior. Cognition contributes to both the directionality and performance though differently. The directionality is produced by cognitive contents and processes - meanings, beliefs and attitudes. Contrary to other cognitive models of behavior (e.g., Ajzen & Fishbein, 1980) CO does not confound cognition with rationality and voluntary control: rather than assuming that behavior is the product of rational decision or carefully reasoned weighting of benefits and losses, it specifies the underlying cognitive dynamics and shows how behavior proceeds from meanings and clustered orientative beliefs. It has been applied successfully to predicting in different samples (adults, children, adolescents, psychiatric patients, retarded persons and physically ill individuals) a great variety of overt behaviors, such as coming on time, achievement, reactions to success and failure, exploration, smoking, quitting smoking, planning, coping with danger, self-disclosure and undergoing examinations for the early detection of breast cancer (Breier, 1980; Kreitler & Kreitler, 1976, 1982, 1987, 1988a, 1994; Kreitler, Schwartz & Kreitler, 1987; Tipton & Riebsame, 1987; Westhoff & Halbach-Suarez, 1989). Further support for the assumption of a causal impact of beliefs on behaviors was obtained by demonstrating that modifying beliefs leads to predicted changes in behavior, for example, in regard to changing pain tolerance, raising the level of curiosity in children, and reducing impulsiveness as well as rigidity behaviors (Kreitler & Kreitler, 1976, chap. 9, 1988a; Zakay, Bar-El, & Kreitler, 1984).

The CO theory seemed to provide an adequate framework for examining the nature of DMs and especially their role in the different stages of behavior evocation, first because it is a comprehensive and empirically-grounded theory whose major tenets were validated by research; and second, because it enabled uncovering the role of cognitions in regard to behavioral and physiological phenomena often assumed to be affected by DMs, such as sexual dysfunctions, menstrual disorders, genital infections, eating problems, chronic pain and medical symptoms (Drechsler, Brunner & Kreitler, 1987; Kreitler & Chemerinski, 1988; Kreitler & Kreitler, 1990c, 1991, 1994; Kreitler, Kreitler & Carasso, 1987; Kreitler, Kreitler & Schwartz, 1991).

The detailed descriptions the theory provides of the processes intervening between input and output (Kreitler & Kreitler, 1976, 1982) can be grouped into four stages, each characterized by metaphorical questions and answers. The first stage is initiated by an external or internal input and is focused on the question "What is it?" It consists in assigning meaning to the input ("initial meaning") and may result in identifying the input (a) as a signal for defensive, adaptive or conditioned response, (b) as a signal for molar action, (c) as irrelevant in the present situation, or (d) as new or particularly significant and hence as a signal for an orienting response.

The second stage is focused on the question "What does it mean to me and for me?" It is initiated when the input has not been identified sufficiently to inhibit the orienting response, by a meaning signalling the need to consider molar action, or by feedback indicating failure of the conditioned or unconditioned responses to cope with the situation. By means of enriched elaboration of meanings ("meaning generation"), it leads to a specification of whether action is required or not.

A positive answer initiates the third stage which is focused on the question "What will I do?" The answer is sought by means of relevant beliefs of four types: (a) Beliefs about goals, expressing actions or states desired or undesired by the individual, e.g., "I want to know everything people think about me"; (b) Beliefs about rules and norms, expressing ethical, esthetic, social and other rules and standards, e.g., "One should trust no one"; (c) Beliefs about self, expressing information about oneself, such as one's habits, actions, feelings, abilities, etc., e.g., "I often get very excited","As a child I was often punished by my parents"; and (d) General beliefs expressing information concerning others and the environment, e.g., "Most people try to get the better of you". The four belief types refer to relevant beliefs, namely, beliefs reflecting deeper personal meanings evoked by the behavior in question.

The directionality of behavior is determined by means of meaning elaboration which involves matchings and interactions between beliefs ("belief clustering"), based on clarifying the orientativeness of the beliefs (namely, the extent to which they support or do not support the indicated course of action). If the majority of beliefs of a certain type support the action, that belief type is considered as positively oriented in regard to that action. Alternately, a belief type may have negative or no orientativeness. If all four belief types point in the direction of the same behavior, or when three belief types support it whereas the fourth is neutral, a cluster of beliefs ("CO cluster") orienting toward a particular act will result. Thus, a unified tendency orienting toward the performance of the action is formed. It is called behavioral intent and answers the question "What will I do?" In other cases, when two belief types point in one direction and two in another, there may be conflict reflected in the formation of two CO clusters and two corresponding behavioral intents. There are further alternatives to the formation of a full-fledged CO cluster: the retrieval of an almost complete CO cluster that has been formed in the past in a series of similar recurrent situations (e.g., a CO cluster orienting toward achievement) and has merely to be completed and slightly adapted to a current situation; the emergence of an incomplete CO cluster due, for example, to the paucity of beliefs in one of the belief types; or the formation of an inoperable cluster due, for example, to the inclusion of 'as if' beliefs in one or more belief types so that the cluster may orient toward daydreaming.

The fourth stage is focused on the question "How will I do it?" The answer is in the form of a program, which is a hierachically structured sequence of instructions governing the performance of some act. It may often be analyzed profitably in terms of two levels: the level of the more general instructions or strategy ("program scheme") and the level of the more specific instructions or tactics ("operational program"). Different programs are involved in executing an overt molar act (performance programs), an act of fantasy, conflict resolution, etc. It is convenient to classify programs into four kinds in line with their origin: (a) *innately determined programs*, such as those controlling reflexes or tropisms; (b) *programs determined both in-*

nately and through learning, such as those controlling instinctive sequences or linguistic behaviors; (c) *programs determined only through learning*, such as those controlling culturally shaped behaviors (e.g., running political elections) and personally formed habits (e.g., modes of preparing for an exam, taking revenge or relaxing); and (d) *programs that have been constructed by the individual ad hoc in view of the requirements of a specific situation.* Implementing a behavioral intent by a program requires selecting a program, retrieving it, and often adapting it to prevailing circumstances before it can be set into operation. Sometimes the need arises to resolve a program conflict, when two different programs appear to be equally adequate for implementing the same behavioral intent or when a present program cannot be set in operation so long as another program is being enacted.

The brief account of the CO theory indicates that the major constructs to be considered in studies of predicting and changing behavior are the meaning assigned by the individual to the situation, the CO cluster concerning the particular act, and the availability of an adequate program for performing the act. Since in many cases the meaning likely to be assigned to the situation and the availability of the program can be assumed with high probability, one may predict that an individual will show the expected behavior if there are enough relevant beliefs orienting toward that behavior in all four belief types or at least three if the fourth does not point in a contrary direction. Beliefs are identified as relevant for a certain behavior if they represent important aspects of the meaning of that behavior, as identified by means of a standard procedure generated by the CO theory (Kreitler & Kreitler, 1982).

Defense Mechanisms as a Specific Kind of Programs

Within the framework of the CO theory DMs may be readily identified as programs. DMs are however stored programs of a specific kind. They have a special function, which is to resolve conflicts between two CO clusters, at least one of which is barred from consciousness. Such conflicts often correspond to conflicts between the id and ego or superego, in psychoanalytic terminology, and their occurrence engenders anxiety. The defensive program resolves the conflict by producing a new behavioral intent. This intent differs from those that constituted the original conflicting intents, but it is related to them, in a form specific to each DM (e.g., through displacement, reversal, sublimation). Moreover, it does not impair the unconsciousness of one or both of the original conflicting behavioral intents. Further, the application of the DM itself is not conscious. The new behavioral intent may become conscious, though not necessarily so. It elicits a behavioral program that may be manifested in any domain, such as motor, emotional, verbal, perceptual or cognitive behavior. Strictly speaking, these manifestations are products of the application of the DM but are not an actual part of it. Hence, we may call them defense-based responses. It is evident that the defense-based responses may take many forms and be manifest in a great variety of domains.

The claim that at least one of the conflicting behavioral intents is not conscious needs elaboration. Behavioral intents in general are not conscious but may become so, for example, when awareness of the intent serves a special function, such as providing the individual orientation for the future, guaranteeing the implementation of intents involving delayed action (e.g., the intent is "to go to China next year") or actions spreading over longer periods of time and hence subject to interruptions and interferences (e.g., the intent is "to go to graduate school and get a doctorate"). To repeat, consciousness is not a necessary condition for the formation of behavioral intents but many or even most intents may become conscious for shorter or longer periods of time. Yet some intents are barred from consciousness. In psychoanalytic terms, this happens because the intents are repressed. In terms of the CO theory, this may happen when the intents are threatening, that is, they oppose the majority of the individual's *basic* beliefs about self and/or beliefs about rules and norms and/or beliefs about goals and/or general beliefs. Examples of basic beliefs include the following: I want to live, There exists a world outside me, Human beings are essentially good (or evil), I am capable of loving, etc. Basic beliefs are permanently stored beliefs that constitute the individual's orientative core in the external and internal environments and provide the raw materials out of which other and often more transient beliefs are formed. Because of its great importance for the individual's well-being, the core of basic beliefs is defended when endangered (Grzegolowska-Klarkowska & Zolnierczyk, 1988, showed DMs' role in defending, e.g., self esteem).

Let us illustrate the processes described above. The chain of events starts with an input identified (in stage 1) by the observer (a man) as "a young man". Meaning generation (stage 2) leads to the evocation of the goal belief "I want to have sex with him". The emergence of "having sex with him" as a possible course of action initiates the third stage, in which it is subjected to meaning elaboration in terms of further beliefs, that include representatives of all four belief types. Some of the beliefs support "having sex"; others do not. A strong set of opposing beliefs may be grouped around the focus of norm beliefs of the kind "One should not have a homosexual relation". Each of the two sets includes many beliefs and beliefs of the four types. Thus, two CO clusters are formed, generating two opposing behavioral intents, say, "to have sex with the young man" and "to avoid having sex with the young man". Let us assume that the intent "to have sex with the young man" is barred from consciousness because it has been repressed or because it opposes most of the individual's basic beliefs about self. Thus, we have the situation that triggers the application of a DM as a conflict-resolving program. If "reaction formation" is applied, it may generate the behavioral intent "to reject or alienate the young man", which may be implemented by behavioral programs, such as humiliating the young man, or offending him; if "sublimation" is applied, it may generate the behavioral intent "to help young people", which may be implemented by behavioral programs, such as becoming a volunteer worker helping young male drug addicts or donating money to schools.

To emphasize the special character of DMs, it may be useful to distinguish between them and two apparently similar kinds of programs. One type consists of different *resolution modes of cognitive inconsistencies* that have been studied primarily in the domain of cognitive dissonance, and include mechanisms, such as denial, distortion, derogation of source, restructuring, changing one of the two clashing cognitions, rationalization, transcendence, and compartmentalization (Abelson, 1968; Kelman & Baron, 1968). According to the original investigators of these mechanisms, the resolution modes are designed to deal with inconsistencies, dissonances and clashes between single cognitions, mostly two. In terms of the CO theory it seems likely that these mechanisms are designed to deal with inconsistencies, dissonances and clashes between beliefs in the stage of CO clustering (the third stage), in an attempt to avoid the formation of two CO clusters that engender a conflict. Hence, these mechanisms resemble DMs in being applied internally, for cognitive manipulations and transformations. But they differ from DMs in two points: (a) they deal with clashes between different beliefs and not between behavioral intents, (b) they are designed to prevent the formation of a conflict between behavioral intents rather than resolving it after it has been formed.

The other set of mechanisms is usually known as *coping strategies*. They have been studied primarily in the domains of stress, disease, and trauma, and they include strategies such as avoidance, repression, denial, humor, problem solving, displacement, and resigned acceptance. The common definitions of coping strategies emphasize that they are designed to deal with threat, stress, life demands and goals, debilitating or chronic sickness, life threat, "very difficult conditions", "external life strains", or demands that are appraised as exceeding the person's resources (Caplan, 1981; Lazarus & Folkman, 1984; Moos, 1984; Pearlin & Schooler, 1978; Watson & Greer, 1998). The major functions of coping are usually identified as managing the problem causing the distress by eliminating or modifying the conditions giving rise to it, altering the meaning of the distressing conditions so as to neutralize their impact, and regulating the emotional distress (Pearlin & Schooler, 1978). In terms of the CO theory, it is evident that coping strategies are programs. They differ from DMs in four points: (a) they are performance programs rather than conflict resolution programs, (b) they may be, and often are, enacted overtly rather than internally, (c) they may be applied consciously, and (d) they deal with major defined threat or stress that endangers the individual's physical or psychological survival or both.

Since coping strategies are behavioral programs they may be expected to be amenable to prediction on the basis of CO scores as other behaviors proved to be. An interesting example is provided by Breier's (1980) study which showed that CO scores predicted significantly which coping strategy a person adopted under conditions of physical danger: the one designed to cope with the external source of danger (danger control), or the one designed to cope with one's internal reaction of fear (fear control).

Notably, all three sets of programs – DMs, dissonance resolution modes and coping strategies - share a large group of apparently similar mechanisms, such as denial, displacement, or rationalization. As noted above, the same principles underlie an even broader range of programs (of thinking, interpersonal relations, etc.) than those included in mechanisms of defense, dissonance resolution, and coping. Hence, it is justified to assume that the three sets of mechanisms utilize several principles that are very basic and common in human action. Since they recur in different domains (e.g., behavioral, cognitive), we may conclude that in regard to programs they constitute the level of the overall strategy (designated in the CO theory as "program scheme") rather than the level of detailed instructions controlling the performance and operation of the program (designated as "operational program"). Hence, in terms of the CO theory, DMs correspond to program schemes, each of which may elicit or be implemented by a variety of operational programs that may be manifested in different domains. The overt manifestation is called a defense-based response. It is likely that in some cases – probably in young children, or psychiatric cases - the program scheme and the operational program form one rigid unit. But in most cases the relation seems to be flexible, so that a great variety of operational programs may implement the same program scheme. This is in accord with the growing flexibility of behavior in line with evolutionary and ontological development (Kreitler, 2001). Further, this may also subserve the function of DMs since it renders their detection more difficult. Thus, while the number of DMs is relatively small, the number of operational programs and defense-based responses may be assumed to be very large, in principle limited only by the individual's potentialities.

Predicting the Application of DMs

The conception of DMs as a special set of programs gave rise to the idea that elicitation of a DM depends on the activation of specific beliefs of four types forming a CO cluster. Hence, we expected that the CO theory would enable predicting the application of DMs just as was done in regard to other behaviors which are program-dependent responses. Testing this expectation empirically was of particular interest in view of the paucity of theoretical and empirical material about the determinants of selecting specific DMs. Success in the prediction would lend support to our conception about DMs. Four studies examined the relation of belief constellations to DMs.

The first study (Kreitler & Kreitler, 1969, Study 1) was devoted to constructing a CO Questionnaire of DMs and validating it. We focused on rationalization, denial, and projection because they represent DMs differing in manifestations and elaboration, are manifested in the different domains of interpersonal, personal and general behavior (Colby & Gilbert, 1964; DeNike & Tiber, 1968), are highly common, and may be assumed to be readily elicited under experimental conditions. After pretesting and item analyses, the constructed CO questionnaire included beliefs of the four types referring to themes, such as control over actions and impulses, accuracy in perception, the role of adopting an ideology or the implications of violating common morality. Thus, the beliefs did not refer directly or indirectly to the DMs to be predicted or to their manifestations (in line with clinical judgments) but to contents that were assumed to orient toward the adoption of one or another of the DMs.

The CO Questionnaire of DMs included four parts, one for each type of belief. The items were of the multiple-choice kind and included two or three response alternatives (orienting toward different DMs), of which the participant was to check only one. For example, "A person should guide his or her behavior according to logical rules that can be justified" (norm belief; rationalization), "I usually try to maintain internal calm and do not let small things upset it" (belief about self; denial). Beliefs orienting toward denial included, for example, emphasis on preserving one's peace of mind, concentrating on one's own well-being, rising above the trivialities of everyday life, disregarding small details, and cultivating optimism and hope. Beliefs orienting toward rationalization included, for example, emphasis on promoting the public well-being, improving others, developing one's rationality and clarity of thinking, depending only on oneself, and striving for self control. Finally, beliefs orienting toward projection included, for example, emphasis on attending to the smallest details in any event and especially in the behavior of others, preserving one's safety, getting one's due, and behaving to others as they behave to you. Each part of the questionnaire included an equal number of responses relevant to the three DMs. The participant got scores for the four belief types in regard to each of the three DMs. The four belief scores were transformed into CO scores (i.e., index scores representing the four belief types) assessing the degree of support of the belief types for each of the three DMs.

A sample of 45 participants was administered the CO questionnaire as well as two scales assessing aggression and hostility: The Buss-Durkee Inventory and the authors' scale of Personal Aggression assessing readiness to admit anger in highly frustrating situations. The results showed that the scores of the four belief types had satisfactory reliability, were not interrelated significantly with one another, but each was significantly related to the overall CO score. Further, the questionnaire's validity was confirmed by findings on the aggression scales. As expected, on the Buss-Durkee inventory highest aggression scores characterized participants with the pattern of CO scores Projection > Rationalization > Denial, and the lowest those with the pattern Denial > Rationalization > Projection. Similarly, on the Personal Aggression scale, participants with CO scores supporting Projection more than Rationalization admitted the highest degrees of anger.

The second study (Kreitler & Kreitler, 1972) was devoted to predicting on the basis of the CO Questionnaire of DMs which defensive response a participant would preferentially manifest: rationalization, denial or projection. The participants (24 undergraduates of both genders) participated in two independent sessions, four to six weeks apart, in one of which they were administered the CO questionnaire of DMs and in the other they were exposed individually to a series of frustrating incidents designed to evoke anger or aggression under conditions that do not promote direct emotional expression. The most frustrating aspect of the situation was that the participants, who were led to believe that their clinical intuition and sensitivity were being tested, had to cooperate with another participant (an accomplice) who contributed very little in the cooperation but presented to the experimenter the products of the cooperation as if they were his or her alone. The participants' DMs (the dependent variables) were assessed by their evaluation of the accomplice, responses to pictures portraying aggression and violence, and responses to a questionnaire assessing DMs (DM Questionnaire). All three measures were based on precoded response alternatives and provided for each participant scores representing the relative frequency with which the participant used each of the three DMs in each measure as well as in all together (=weighted behavior index).

The results showed that the ranking of beliefs orienting toward rationalization, denial and projection according to CO scores is related positively and significantly to the ranking of the behavioral manifestations of these DMs according to each of the dependent measures separately and together. In line with the theory, all four belief types or at least three were involved in the relation of the CO measure with the behaviors. The validity of the results is further increased by the fact that the matching was equally good for each of the three ranks and for each of the three DMs; indeed, in many participants it was perfect.

Also *the third study* (Zemet, 1976) dealt with predicting defense-based responses on the basis of CO scores, but it extended the scope of the former study in several respects: first, the sample included schizophrenics in addition to normals; second, a broader range of eliciting conflict situations was used; third, a broader range of response types was assessed; and fourth, the responses were assessed by a different method. Hospitalized schizophrenics (N=30) and normal individuals (N=34) of both genders were administered a modified version of the CO Questionnaire for DMs (shortened and extended to include items referring to two further common responses: coping and doing nothing). The questionnaire provided CO scores (index scores representing the four belief types) concerning each of the five responses: denial, rationalization, projection, coping and doing nothing. The reactions to conflict were assessed by the participants' role playing in 14 predetermined scenes, each of which included some problem as its major theme (e.g., faithfulness and obligation toward one's parents versus the desire to be independent in a scene dealing with leaving the home of one's parents in order to live on one's own). In line with the procedure developed in the Psychodramatic Role Test (Kreitler & Kreitler, 1964, 1968), the participants enacted both the role of themselves as well as of the other "persons" in the scenes. All behavioral and verbal responses were recorded and classified into one of the five categories (i.e., denial, rationalization, etc.), in accordance with predetermined criteria.

The results showed that in both schizophrenics and normals CO scores were related significantly and in the expected direction to four of the five response categories. For example, high scorers on the CO of denial used denial significantly more often in their responses to the conflicts than low scorers. The only deviations from the expected were (a) concerning "projection" in the group of the normals (the responses were in the expected direction but the difference between high and low scorers was nonsignificant, probably due to the very low frequency of these responses in the group of normals) and (b) concerning "coping" in schizophrenics (the relation was significant but reversed, probably because for schizophrenics the program bound to coping is projection!).

In *the fourth study* (Eldar, 1976) the original CO Questionnaire of DMs was applied for predicting the responses of participants in a situation presenting incongruities between messages conveyed concurrently through different communication channels. Clarifying the determinants of selectivity in such situations is important because incongruous communications and play a role in interpersonal relations in general and psychopathology in particular (e.g., Bugenthal, 1974; Watzlawik, Beavin, & Jackson, 1967). The hypotheses were that high scorers on CO of rationalization would focus on the verbally conveyed content of the communications (because they seem more "rational" and definite), disregarding the nonverbal communications; high scorers on the CO of projection would focus on the nonverbally conveyed communications (because they are more indirect and fuzzy), disregarding the verbally expressed content; whereas high scorers on the CO of denial would focus on the positive aspects of the communications, regardless of channel, disregarding the negative aspects.

The 51 participants (27 men, 24 women) were selected from a sample of 197 tested individuals according to their scores on the CO questionnaire and belonged to one of three subgroups: (a) participants scoring high on the CO of denial and low on the CO of rationalization and projection; (b) participants scoring high on the CO of rationalization and low on the CO of denial and projection; and (c) participants scoring high on the CO of projection and low on the CO of denial and rationalization. They were exposed to evaluative communications (positive or negative) of one person to another that were conveyed simultaneously through 3 channels: verbal, visual and auditory. The communications were structured so that the evaluative aspects conveyed through the different channels were contradictory: for example, the verbal content "You have done an absolutely wonderful job" was conveyed by a person with a rejecting facial expression and in a rejecting tone of voice. All combinations of evaluations in the three channels were used (after extensive pretesting of the credibility and intensity of effects in each channel). Half of the communications were presented by men and half by women (all professional actors). The participants were exposed to the communications, which were presented as videotaped excerpts of conversations between students, and were asked to consider each as if it had been addressed to them personally. Their task was to evaluate the degree of positiveness or negativeness of each communication on a 9-point scale. The results confirmed the three hypotheses in the sample of men, and the hypothesis about projection in the sample of women too. There were however unexpected results in the women's sample: the high scorers on the CO of rationalization focused more than the others on all channels rather than on the verbal alone (perhaps because rationalization necessitated considering as much information as was available); and the high scorers on the CO of denial focused on the positive contents but especially if it was conveyed nonverbally. In sum, even though we are at present unable to account for the different patterns of results in the two genders, the point to emphasize is that individuals with different CO scores on the CO Questionnaire of DMs respond differentially to incongruous inputs.

Motivational Determinants of DMs: Interim Summary

Our basic assumption was that DMs are programs of a special kind, designed to subserve the intrapsychic function of resolving a conflict between two behavioral intents, at least one of which is sufficiently threatening to be barred from consciousness. A DM's application results in forming a new behavioral intent that differs from the conflicting intents but is related to them and is manifested in some defense-based response, for example, in the perceptual, emotional or behavioral field. In line with the CO theory, it seemed likely that DMs would depend on motivational determinants and that these determinants would be manifested in the form of belief clusters. Hence we applied to the prediction of DMs the usual procedure based on the CO theory. Four studies demonstrated that it is indeed possible to predict which specific DM an individual would apply in a specific situation. The prediction was based on beliefs of four types (about self, goals, norms and general) concerning themes orienting toward a particular DM. The beliefs formed a kind of vector or motivational disposition orienting toward the DM.

Cognitive Determinants of Defense Mechanisms

In Search for the Determinants of Defense-Implementing Programs

According to the CO theory, the occurrence of defense-based responses depends on (a) a sufficiently high number of beliefs in the four types, relevant for a specific DM, to enable the formation of a behavioral intent orienting toward that DM, and (b) a program implementing the behavioral intent. The last section dealt with the first condition; the present section focuses on the second. How do individuals acquire the specific conflict-resolution programs we call DMs? Why do some individuals adopt consistently the program we call projection and others programs we call denial or rationalization? Anna Freud (1966, p. 62) is of no help in this respect mainly because she claimed that DMs are "as old as the instincts ...or at least... as the conflict between instinctual impulses and any hindrance". So far, little is known about the determinants of the actual programs. The dynamic approaches, including psychoanalysis, would tend to emphasize identification with the preferred parent as the source of an individual's beliefs. Yet, there is no empirical data supporting this claim by showing, for instance, congruence in the DMs preferred by parents and offspring (e.g., Cermak & Rosenfeld, 1987). The learning approaches would emphasize the impact of learning from adults and peers, in formal and informal contexts, whereas the social approaches would emphasize the sociocultural impacts on program acquisition and application (e.g., Gibbs, 1987; Sahoo, Sia & Panda, 1987). Yet so far there are only few data supporting these approaches. Furthermore, they do not account for individual differences in the availability of programs.

In the present context we will present evidence about the role of cognitive determinants in accounting for individual differences in DMs. The determinants we discuss can be considered to constitute the micro level of cognitive functioning, for they deal with units and processes underlying larger units, such as beliefs or programs, constituting the macro level. They consist of meanings and meaning properties as outlined in the framework of the theory of meaning (Kreitler & Kreitler, 1990a). Our concept of meaning differs markedly from that adopted in the framework of the information processing model of cognition, according to which meaning consists of inactive content items that are to be inserted, for example, into the empty slots of grammatical structures. The narrow limits of this approach to meaning become evident through Chomsky's (1972) example of a grammatically perfect but nonetheless completely meaningless sentence, such as "colorless green ideas sleep furiously". In contrast to this approach which distinguishes sharply between meaning and cognition, we define cognition as the meaning processing system whose functioning is codetermined by meaning characteristics in general as well as by the meanings it is currently processing. Hence, cognition and meaning are complementary terms in the sense that one cannot be exhaustively defined and understood without the other. Each meaning operation is a cognitive act, whereas each cognitive function has aspects that can be understood satisfactorily only by considering meaning characteristics. Nonetheless cognition is the more comprehensive term because often it operates on levels and produces units that can be described more efficiently without invoking the meaning system. Constructs such as beliefs, programs, and DMs depend on cognitive processes that may best be described in terms of the meaning system, but it would be cumbersome and misleading to describe the major processes of the CO theory in terms of meaning variables. Such an attempt would produce results as adequate as describing whisky in terms of molecules and atoms or, even worse, in terms of subatomic particles. Thus, to examine the processes underlying the operation of specific DMs, it would be necessary first to describe the meaning system.

The Meaning System

The system of meaning was developed for characterizing and assessing human meanings of different kinds (e.g., Kreitler & Kreitler, 1982, 1986, 1988b,c, 1990a,b). It was designed to be broader in coverage and to have higher validity than the available measures of meaning (Kreitler & Kreitler, 1976, Chap. 2). In the present context we will present only those aspects of the system necessary for describing the studies about the meaning-anchored determinants of DMs.

The major assumptions underlying the system of meaning are that meaning is a complex phenomenon with a multiplicity of aspects, that it is essentially communicable, that it may be expressed through verbal and different nonverbal means, and that it comes in two varieties - the lexical interpersonally-shared meaning and the subjective-personal one. These assumptions have enabled collecting and coding a great amount of empirical data in regard to a rich variety of inputs, from thousands of individuals differing in age, education, gender, and cultural background.

On the basis of this material, we define meaning as a *referent-centered pattern of content items*. The referent denotes the representation of the input to which meaning is assigned, for example, a word, an image, an object, or a situation. The content items, called meaning values, denote particular cognitive contents, expressed verbally or nonverbally (e.g., red, dangerous, made of wood), which are assigned to the referent and express or communicate its meaning. The referent and the meaning value together form the meaning unit. Four kinds of meaning variables are used for characterizing the meaning values and their relations to referents: (a) *Meaning Dimensions*, that characterize the contents of the meaning values in terms of general kinds of information they provide about the referent (e.g., Sensory Qualities, Material, or Structure); (b) *Types of Relation*, that characterize the relations of the meaning value to the referent in terms of its immediacy or directness (e.g., attributive or metaphoric-symbolic); (c) *Forms of Relation*, that characterize the relation of the meaning values to the referent in formal-logical terms (e.g., positive or conjunctive); and (d) *Referent Shifts*, that characterize the sequential shifts in the referent in the course of meaning assignment (e.g., a modified or associated referent). (see Table 10.1). Our concept of meaning is double-faced in that, on the one hand – in the static application - it serves for coding, characterizing, quantifying and evaluating cognitive contents or the results of cognitive performance, and, on the other hand – in the dynamic application – it serves as a set of strategies that explain major aspects of cognitive functioning.

Table 10.1: *Variables of the system of meaning*

1. Meaning Dimensions			
1	Contextual allocation	13	Size and dimensionality
2	Range of inclusion: a. Subclasses; b. Parts	14	Quantity and number
		15	Locational qualities
3	Function, purpose and role	16	Temporal qualities
4	Actions and potentialities for action: a. By referent; b. To/with referent	17	Possession: a. By referent ; b. Of referent (belongingness)
5	Manner of occurrence and operation	18	Development
6	Antecedents and causes	19	Sensory qualities[e]: a. Of referent; b. Perceived by referent
7	Consequences and results		
8	Domain of application: a. Referent as subject; b. Referent as object	20	Feelings and emotions: a. Evoked by referent; b. Experienced by referent
9	Material	21	Judgments and evaluations: a. About referent; b. Of referent
10	Structure		
11	State and changes in state	22	Cognitive qualities: a. Evoked by referent; b. Of referent
12	Weight and mass		
Types of Relation[a] (TR)			
1	Attributive: a. Qualities to substance; b. Actions to agent	3	Exemplifying-Illustrative: a. Instance; b. Situation; c. Scene
2	Comparative: a. Similar; b.Different; c. Complementary; d. Relational	4	Metaphoric-Symbolic: a. Interpretation; b. Conventional metaphor; c. Original metaphor; d. Symbol
Forms of Relation[b] (FR)			
1	Propositional	5	Disjunctive
2	Partial	6	Normative (obligatory)
3	Universal	7	Questioning
4	Conjunctive	8	Desired
Shifts of Referent[c] (SR)			
1	Identical	8	Linguistic label
2	Opposite	9	Grammatical variation
3	Partial	10	Former meaning values combined
4	Input + addition	11	Superordinate
5	Former meaning value	12	Synonym a. Original language; b. Translated; c. Other medium
6	Associated on same level		
7	Unrelated	13	Former implicit meaning value
Forms of Expression[d] (FE)			
1	verbal	4	Auditory
2	Graphic	5	Object or situation
3	Motor		

The assessment of meaning is done by coding in terms of the meaning variables units of contents in the cognitive product (e.g., a dialogue, a text, a solution to a problem, jokes, questions or the meaning communications of individuals). The individual's meaning assignment tendencies are assessed by the Meaning Test. This test requires the participants to communicate to an imaginary other person the meaning (general and/or personal) of a standard set of 11 stimuli. Coding the responses consists of assigning to each response unit four scores, one of each type of meaning variable (i.e., one meaning dimension, one type of relation, etc.). Thus, the response "blue" to the stimulus "ocean" is coded in terms of the meaning dimension Sensory Qualities, the attributive type of relation, the propositional positive form of relation, referent identical to input (no referent shift) and verbal form of expression. Summing these scores across all response units yields the individual's *meaning profile*, namely, the distribution of the individual's frequencies of responses in each meaning variable. These frequencies were found to be characteristic of the individual; hence we call them meaning assignment tendencies. Various studies showed that the meaning assignment tendencies are related to different cognitive activities, such as planning, memory, analogical thinking, or conceptualizations (Arnon & Kreitler, 1984; Kreitler & Kreitler, 1986, 1987, 1988b, 1990b). For example, high scorers on the meaning dimension Locational Qualities perform better than low scorers on problems requiring consideration of spatial properties such as mazes. Findings of this kind demonstrate the cognitive function of meaning assignment tendencies. These tendencies also play a role in personality, because it was shown that each of over 100 common personality traits corresponds to a unique pattern of meaning assignment tendencies (Kreitler & Kreitler, 1990a).

Patterns of Meaning Variables and Defense Mechanisms

The study (Kreitler & Kreitler, 1990a) was devoted to exploring the interrelations between meaning variables and DMs. We expected such an interrelation because we conceive of DMs as essentially basic means of cognitive manipulations and transformations (see *DMs as Cognitive Strategies*). As such, they are to be expected

←

[a] Modes of meaning: Lexical mode: TR1+TR2; Personal mode: TR3+TR4

[b] Each of the FRs has two forms: a. Positive; b. Negative

[c] Close SR: 1+9+12 Medium SR: 3+4+5+6+10+11Distant SR: 2+7+8+13

[d] Each of the FEs has three forms: a. Direct; b. Described; c. By means of available materials. The studies described in this chapter did not make use of FEs.

[e] This meaning dimension includes a listing of subcategories of the different senses/sensations that may also be grouped into "external" and "internal".

Table 10.2a: *Meaning variables correlated significantly with the three defense mechanisms: Denial*

Meaning Dimensions		Types of Relation		Referent Shifts	
Contextual allocation	.28**	Comparative: difference	.31***	Sticking to presented referent (identical)	-.25**
Range of inclusion (subclasses)	.36***	Metaphoric-symbolic: original metaphor	.40***	Shift to former meaning value	.38***
Consequences and results	.29**			Shift to referent associated on same level	-.27**
Structure	-.25**			Shift to grammatical variation of referent	-.26**
Size and dimensionality	.37***			Close shifts	.35***
Quantity and number	.31***				
Sensory qualities (perceived by referent, internal)	-.42***				
Feelings and emotions (by referent)	-.27**				
Judgments and evaluations (by referent)	-.42***				
Cognitive qualities (evoked by referent)	-.37***				

$^{**}p < .01$. $^{***}p < .001$.

to depend on processes of meaning, which constitute the basic dynamic core of cognition.

The participants were 129 undergraduates of both genders who were administered in random order in two group sessions, six to eight weeks apart, the standard Meaning Test and the CO Questionnaire of DMs (see *Predicting the Application of DMs*). The Meaning Test was designed to provide information about the participant's meaning assignment tendencies (viz. the meaning profile), the CO Questionnaire about his or her predispositions (viz., behavioral intents) toward rationalization, denial and projection. Assessing the predispositions seemed to us to provide more reliable and stable measures of DMs than assessing specific manifestations of these DMs in one or another domain. The significant intercorrelations presented in Table 10.2a demonstrate that each DM is correlated with a specific set of meaning variables. Analyzing the meaning variables in the sets corresponding to the three DMs shows that each set consists of the kind of cognitive processes that enable implementing the performance of the DM.

Let us illustrate the latter conclusion. For example, *high scorers on the CO of denial* (Table 10.2a) tend to refer to the size, quantity and possessions of inputs, and to their superordinate and subordinate classes, but do not refer to emotions, internal sensations, judgements and evaluations and cognitive qualities (see positive and negative correlations with meaning dimensions, respectively). Notably, those aspects to which they refer are relatively "objective" whereas those they disregard are "subjective" and potentially emotionally loaded. Furthermore, the deniers tend to shift away from the presented inputs, but not too far away (see positive correlation with shifts to near referents and negative with shits to distant referents) and usually focus on aspects of the referent that they themselves have brought up, a tendency that would enable dwelling preferentially on the "safe" aspects. In case a threatening aspect does emerge, the deniers can still rely on their tendency to emphasize differences and thus explain away the apparent similarity to a threat; or alternately they may apply their tendency toward metaphorization and grasp the input in a metaphorical way, which diminishes the threat. Many of these processes were confirmed by observations on denial in cancer patients (Kreitler, 1999). Further, *high scorers on the CO of rationalization* (Table 10.2b) have a rich store of cognitive tendencies: they tend to refer to actions, how actions occur, who or what are involved in an event or situation, to functions, structures, evaluations and cognitive properties, while they disregard aspects such as quantity, belongingness and results. They tend to grasp relations either in a straightforward way (i.e., attributive) or metaphorically, present examples but do not dwell on similarities. They use preferentially negations or modulated connections (e.g., 'sometimes') and tend to shift away from the presented inputs, mostly to distant referents. Notably, they have a rich stock of referent-modulating mechanisms and of contents (meaning values) that enables them to present an issue to themselves and others in an acceptable "rational" form (compare with the finding about the richness of information acquired by women, high scorers on rationalization in study 4, above, Eldar, 1976).

Finally, *high scorers on the CO of projection* (Table 10.2c) tend not to refer to the causes of inputs, their constituent parts, their state, size, location, belongingness and development, as well as emotional and evaluative aspects, while they do refer to structure, and who or what is involved in the situation. It is likely that disregarding so many aspects of inputs may subserve the tendency of these individuals to replace the perceived with the conceived or desired. This tendency may be further subserved by the disregard for interpersonally-shared reality (see negative correlation with the attributive type of relation), and preferences for subjective interpretations as well as shifting away from the presented inputs to distant referents. Notably, the concern with structure and with whole referents (see negative correlation with shifting to partial referents) could contribute to implementing the potential for paranoia that is sometimes related to projection.

The examples given above illustrate how the cognitive processes and contents assessed by the meaning variables may implement the operation of DMs. If one assumes that meaning dimensions reflect to a greater extent a focus on contents whereas the other kinds of meaning variables reflect rather a focus on cognitive processes, it is possible to examine whether the patterns of meaning variables corresponding to DMs are biased more in the direction of contents or rather of processes. As programs they may be expected to be fairly content free. However, comparing the distribution of meaning variables in the patterns (dimensions vs other kinds) with that expected in view of the structure of the meaning system, shows that in no case were the deviations significant (the chi-square values for Denial, Rationalization and Projection were .215, .0002, and .005, respectively). Hence, it seems that DMs rely on both cognitive contents and processes.

The relatively large number of meaning variables in the patterns should not be surprising. Previous studies (Kreitler & Kreitler, 1990a) showed that the patterns provide a variety of means for implementing the overall strategy of the program. These means are alternatives that may be applied selectively according to the demand characteristics of the situation or the problem at hand, one at a time, or several in a sequence in case previous attempts at resolving the conflict have failed. Thus, denial may be implemented by referring to aspects of the input, such as size and quantity that do not suggest emotions, or by dwelling on the general superordinate category suggested by the input (e.g., if the input is painful, focusing on human suffering in general), or by metaphorization which enables changing the meaning of the perceived. The variety of means guarantees the flexibility and hence the pervasiveness of a DM once it has been adopted by an individual.

As may be expected, each of the patterns of meaning variables corresponding to the three DMs has unique characteristics. The richest pattern is the one corresponding to rationalization, perhaps because it is so common in a normal population and emphasizes its cognitively acceptable façade. The highest number of negative constituents is found in the pattern corresponding to projection (76%) as compared with 40% in rationalization and 25% in denial (the percentage for projection differs significantly from those for rationalization, $z = 3.802$, $p < .001$, and for denial, $z = 2.466$, $p < .01$). Previous studies (Kreitler & Kreitler, 1990a) showed that negative correlations are indicative of active disregard for the cognitive operation or content domain represented by that meaning variable. Accordingly, the frequencies of negative elements in the patterns correspond to the prevalent psychoanalytic conception that projection involves the highest degree of repression and cognitive transformation, and denial the least (A. Freud, 1966).

Comparing the three patterns shows that they share only five meaning variables: the meaning dimensions results, belongingness and evaluations, and the types of relation exemplifying instance and metaphor. This is a relatively narrow common core. Moreover, the direction of the correlations across patterns is not the same for any of the variables. Hence, the data for the three defenses does not support the hypothesis of a general tendency for defensiveness that transcends the specific DMs (e.g., Weinberger, Schwartz, & Davidson, 1979).

DM's Patterns of Meaning Variables and the Individual

The finding that each DM corresponds to a specific pattern of meaning variables has important implications concerning the selection of DMs and individual differences in DMs. As noted, both the DM's pattern of meaning variables and the individual's meaning profile consist of the same kind of meaning variables. Hence, it is justified to conclude that the selection of DMs is a function of the individual's meaning assignment tendencies. Both the selection and the meaning assignment tendencies, reflected in the individual's meaning profile, are not conscious. Our claim is that an individual adopts preferentially that DM which matches most closely his or her characteristic meaning assignment tendencies. By examining how many of the meaning variables corresponding to a DM are represented in the individual's meaning profile (in comparable strength and direction), it is possible to assign the individual's a score for that DM and predict how likely that individual is to adopt that DM when the opportunity arises. This procedure was applied in regard to paranoid individuals and led to the conclusion that their relatively strongest tendency is to apply projection, followed by rationalization (Kreitler & Kreitler, 1997). These findings are in accord with the theory of paranoia and demonstrate the validity of the described procedure.

Since an individual's meaning profile may include meaning variables corresponding to more than one DM, it is likely that individuals may be able to respond in terms of several DMs. Further, the richer and more variegated an individual's meaning profile, the larger the number of different DMs that the individual would be able to adopt. Hence, individuals differ both in the kind of DMs and in the number of DMs they are able to adopt. Finally, it may be of interest to mention the possibility of determining to what extent the individual's meaning profile include meaning variables inhibiting or antagonistic to those included in the pattern corresponding to a particular DM. This would provide a measure of the degree of resistance an individual would have for adopting a specific DM ('anti-DM' tendencies comparable to the 'anti-trait' tendencies, Kreitler & Kreitler, 1990a)

DMs and Personality Traits and Types

As noted above, each personality trait corresponds to a pattern of meaning variables, as was shown by correlations between over 200 traits and sets of meaning variables. These patterns were found to be characterized by specific features, e.g., specific number of meaning variables (Kreitler & Kreitler, 1990a). Is it justified to consider the three DMs as personality traits? To answer this question it is necessary to examine if the patterns of meaning variables corresponding to the DMs resemble those corresponding to personality traits in terms of five major empirically-based criteria (see Table 10.3). Table 10.3 shows that the patterns for denial and rationalization do not deviate from those of personality traits in more than one of the criteria. This degree of deviation is considered acceptable, so that the patterns corresponding to these two DMs fall within the boundaries of variation of personality traits. Hence, denial and rationalization can be considered as personality traits. In contrast, projection cannot be considered as a personality trait (the pattern of meaning variables corresponding to it deviates from personality traits according to three criteria). Denial and rationalization resemble traits perhaps because they are common in a normal population, or at least more common than projection, which reflects to a greater extent psychopathological tendencies. Be it as it may, the findings in regard to denial and rationalization support the psychoanalytic claim that DMs may affect character so that character itself turns into a DM (Munroe, 1956, pp. 264-266).The patterns of meaning variables corresponding to each of the three DMs can be used also in order to examine to which extent each of the DMs plays a role or constitues a component within the framework of other well-defined personality traits. One example is provided by the study of authortarianism and dogmatism. Comparing the pattterns of meaning variables coresponding to the DMs with the patterns corresponding to these two traits showed that 62% of the meaning variables of projection occurred in the pattern of authoritarinism and none in that of dogmatism, whereas 60% of the meaning variables of denial occurred in the pattern corresponding to dogmatism and none in that of authoritarianism (Kreitler & Kreitler, 1990a, Study 13). This finding helps to better characterize and differentiate the two complementary traits.

Table 10.2b: *Meaning variables correlated significantly with the three defense mechanisms: Rationalization*

Meaning Dimensions		Types of Relation		Forms of Relation		Referent Shifts	
Function, purpose and role	.31**	Attributive: qualities to substance	.26**	Propositional negative	.41***	Sticking to presented referent (identical)	.26**
Actions (by referent)	.26**	Attributive: actions to agent	.31***	Partial positive	.40***	Shift to former meaning value	-.38***
Actions (to/with referent)	.28**	Attributive: qualities and actions	.32***	Conjunctive negative	.40***	Shift to referent associated on same level	.42***
Manner of occurrence or operation	.39***	Comparative: similarity	-.37***			Shift to linguistic label	-.38***
Domain of application (referent as object)	.37***	Comparative: complementariness	.33***			Close shifts	-.45***
Consequences and results	-.46***	Exemplifying-illustrative: exemplifying instance	.38***			Distant shifts	.41***
Structure	.37***	Metaphoric-symbolic: interpretation	-.27**			Number of different shifts	.35***
Quantity and number	-.27**	Metaphoric-symbolic: original metaphor	.34**				
Possession (belongingness)	-.25**						
Judgments and evaluations (about referent)	.36***						
Judgments and evaluations (about and of referent)	.42***						
Cognitive qualities (evoked by and of referent)	.49***						

$^{**}p < .01$. $^{***}p < .001$

Table 10.2c: *Meaning variables correlated significantly with the three defense mechanisms: Projection*

Meaning Dimensions		Types of Relation		Forms of Relation		Referent Shifts	
Range of inclusion	-.33***	Attributive: qualities and actions	-.52***	Propositional positive	-.33***	Shift to partial	-.41***
Antecedents and causes	-.48***	Exemplifying-illustrative: exemplifying instance	.37***	Conjunctive positive	-.42***	Shift to linguistic label	-.36***
Consequences and results	-.54***	Metaphoric-symbolic: interpretation	.52***	Disjunctive negative	-.26**	Distant shifts	.55***
Domain of application (referent as subject and as object)	.51***	Metaphoric-symbolic: all subtypes	-.28**	Normative (obligatory)	-.30***		
Structure	.48***						
State	-.39***						
Locational qualities	-.31***						
Possession (belongingness)	-.42***						
Development	-.36***						
Feelings and emotions (evoked by and experienced by referent)	-.35***						
Judgments and evaluations (about and by referent)	-.32***						

$^{**}p < .01$. $^{***}p < .001$

Table 10.3: *Comparing the patterns of meaning variables corresponding to the three defense mechanisms with the patterns corresponding to personality traits*

Criteria of comparison		Rationalization	Denial	Projection
1. Number of different kinds of meaning variables in pattern [3 or 4]		4 [no dev.]	3 [no dev.]	4 [no dev.]
2. Proportion of different kinds of meaning variables in pattern:				
Meaning Dimensions	[54.75%]	45.16%	55.00%	52.00%
Types of Relation	[25.75%]	25.80%	20.00%	20.00%
Forms of relation	[5.90%]	9.38%	0.00%	16.00%
Referent Shifts	[12.57%]	19.35%	5.00%	12.00%
Chi^2 of differences		7.76 [no dev.]	19.48*** [no dev.]	18.74*** [dev.]
3. Proportion of negative correlations [.38]		.26 $z = 1.30$ [no dev.]	.40 $z = .35$ [no dev.]	.76 $z = 3.45$*** [dev.]
4. Number of meaning variables in pattern [range 7-20]		31 [dev.]	20 [no dev.]	25 [dev.]
5. Proportion of general to specific meaning variables in pattern [.44]		.41 $z = .37$ [no dev.]	.40 $z = .40$ [no dev.]	.61 $z = .90$ [no dev.]
Total number of deviations		1	1	3

Note: The standard values of the criteria are presented in brackets in the first column. For a more complete presentation and illustration of the procedure for checking the similarity to personality traits, see Kreitler & Kreitler (1990a, pp. 303-310). dev. = deviation from the pattern of personality traits.
*** $p < .001$.

A similar procedure was applied for comparing samples of hospitalized paranoids and normals on the three DMs in terms of scores based on the patterns of meaning variables corresponding to each DM. As noted above, the comparison showed that paranoids score significantly higher than normals on both projection and rationalization but do not differ from them in denial (Kreitler & Kreitler, 1997). These findings confirm psychopathological approaches to paranoia.

Cognitive Determinants of DMs: Interim Summary

DMs were defined as programs of a special kind: their function is to resolve intrapsychic conflicts; they operate without consciousness; and they consist of general strategies of problem solving. The latter implies first, that they occur in the framework of different responses which are not necessarily DMs and second, that they represent the general level of behavioral programs rather than the level of specific operational tactics, so that the actually enacted responses are defense-based and not the actual DMs. Examining the interrelations of DMs to the individuals' meaning profiles enabled identifying sets of meaning variables corresponding to each DM. The set for each of the examined DMs was unique. The sets provided insights about the manner of operation of the DM. Each set includes a variety of means for implementing the DM. The means were shown to be partly complementing one another and partly alternative and possibly even replacing each other. Further, it was shown that the selection of DMs is a function of the availability of the meaning variables corresponding to the DM in the individual's meaning profile. The individual is able to adopt those DMs whose meaning variables are represented in his or her meaning profile to a sufficient extent. Comparing the patterns of meaning variables corresponding to DMs with those of personality traits showed that some DMs resemble traits (viz. rationalization, denial), whereas others differ from traits (viz. projection). It was also shown that some DMs may constitute elements within the framework of personality traits (viz. denial in dogmatism).

Beliefs and Meaning Variables as Predictors of Defense Mechanisms

In view of the evidence that belief constellations predict which of three DMs an individual would adopt (see *Predicting the Application of Defense Mechanisms*) whereas meaning variables clarify the underlying cognitive dynamics of the operation of the defenses (see *Patterns of Meaning Variables and Defense Mechanisms*), it is likely that combining CO scores and meaning variables would provide for a better prediction than either CO or meaning variables separately. This expectation, which was confirmed in other fields of study (e.g., planning and curiosity: Kreitler & Kreitler, 1987, 1994), was examined in regard to DMs (Kreitler, in press). In a group of 159 participants of both genders (85 high school students, 17 to 18.2 years old, and 74 undergraduates, 22 to 31 years old) we assessed the CO for each of the three DMs (by the CO Questionnaire of DMs, see Zemet, 1976), the meaning profile (by the Meaning Test), and two kinds of defense-based responses: The DMs Questionnaire (Kreitler & Kreitler, 1972) and a slightly modified version of the Hopkins Symptom Checklist (Derogatis, Lipman, Rickels, Uhlenhuth & Covi, 1974) which requested rating on a 4-point scale the degree of distress caused by 72 items and provided a measure of neurotic symptoms. The questionnaires were administered in two group sessions in random order. The questionnaires were administered in two group sessions in random order. Each participant got (a) three CO scores, one for each DM, indicating the number of belief types supporting the DM (range 0 to 4); (b) three meaning variables indices, one for each DM, that summarized the number of meaning variables in the participant's meaning profile that matched those in the pattern corresponding to the DM (matching was defined as a frequency of a variable above the group's mean when the variable in the pattern has a positive sign, and a frequency below the group's mean when the variable has a negative sign); (c) three scores, one for each DM, on the basis of responses in frustrating situations (DMs Questionnaire); and (d) one score reflecting the overall self-reported distress of neurotic symptoms. Scores a and b served as predictors, whereas scores c and d served as dependent variables.

Table 10.4 shows that the CO scores and meaning variable indices predicted significantly the defense-based responses obtained on the DMs Questionnaire. Together they accounted on the average for 39.1% of the variance in the responses, ranging from 33.64% for rationalization to 47.61% for projection. The prediction for projection was significantly highest (it differed from that for denial, $CR = 2.10$, and for rationalization, $CR = 2.53$, $p < .01$). In one case CO scores were entered first into the prediction equation, in two cases they were entered second (the same order was obtained for neurotic symptoms). The mean amount of improvement in the prediction due to the addition of the second predictor was 13.58% (ranging from 6.84% for denial to 17.64% for rationalization).

The extent of prediction was lower in regard to the neurotic symptoms (a mean of 14.13% of variance accounted for as compared with 39.1% in the case of the DMs Questionnaire, $CR = 5.03$, $p < .001$). This was to be expected, first, because DMs are only one of the determinants of neurotic symptoms, possibly not even the major one; and second, because the predictors were not adapted specifically for the prediction of the dependent variable. The highest rate of variance was accounted for when the predictors were the CO and meaning index of denial (29.16% of the variance was accounted for) but it was low when the predictors were the CO and meaning index of rationalization (8.41%) or projection (4.84%). These findings are in accord with the psychoanalytic claim that neurotic symptoms are based on repression and denial more than on the other two assessed DMs (Fenichel, 1945).

Table 10.4: *Results of multiple stepwise regression analyses with co scores and indices of meaning variables as predictors and responses on the defense mechanisms questionnaire and neurotic symptoms as dependent variables*

	Multiple correlation coefficients	
Predictors	DM Questionnaire	Neurotic symptoms
CO of Rationalization	.40***	.18*
CO of Rationalization + Meaning Index of Rationalization	.58***	.29**
Meaning Index of Denial	.54***	.35**
Meaning Index of Denial + CO of Denial	.60***	.54***
Meaning Index of Projection	.56***	.17*
Meaning Index of Projection + CO of Projection	.69***	.22*

Note. In the column headed DM Questionnaire, the dependent variable in the first two rows is Rationalization, in the next two rows it is Denial, in the last two rows it is Projection. The predictors are listed in the order in which they were entered into the prediction equation.
*$p < .05$. **$p < .01$. ***$p < .001$.

Modifying Defense Mechanisms

Modifying Defenses in the Framework of Psychoanalysis

The goal of psychoanalytic treatment has often been defined to eliminate or at least to modify DMs, because of their pathogenic nature and effects. The major means applied for this purpose are (a) providing insight into the harmful DMs and (b) transference-supported suggestions for a more realistic and healthier approach to one's internal processes. These means are more often than not frustrated by the patients' resistance or, in the best case, require years of therapeutic work. The resistance may become so intense that Freud (1937/1964c) doubted whether the venture can at all be successful. The main difficulty encountered by psychoanalysts derives from their attempt to combat the consciousness-distorting defenses by rendering their functioning conscious. It would be advisable to circumvent this vicious circle by modifying the conscious processes and entities that underlie DMs, namely, modifying the beliefs conducive to DMs and the meaning assignment tendencies that implement them. Both beliefs and meaning variables have been modified successfully in previous research.

Modifying CO Clusters and Meaning Variables

Modifying CO clusters has been done successfully in an experimental framework in different domains, e.g. impulsive behavior in children, rigidity, pain tolerance, curiosity, and eating disorders (Bachar, Latzer, Kreitler et al., 1999; Kreitler & Kreitler, 1976, 1988a; 1994; Zakay, Bar-El, & Kreitler, 1984). For example, increasing in children the number of beliefs of the four types, relevant for curiosity, brought about an increase in the children's exploratory behavior in different contexts. The basic methods for modifying beliefs consist in working systematically through each of the aspects of the belief's meaning, proceeding from one belief type to another until all four are covered. The techniques of change use means, such as exposing inconsistencies between beliefs or between beliefs and behavior, changing the meaning of the major terms of the belief, or narrowing down the meaning of the belief (Kreitler & Kreitler, 1990d). The major thrust of the effort is directed at mobilizing sufficient support of relevant beliefs for the desired course of operation, without however dealing with the action itself by way of persuasion, training, reinforcement, etc. Our results show that providing for the formation of the adequate CO cluster produces the motivationally-supported disposition for the specific course of action.

A large body of reseach shows that also the individual's meaning variables can be modified, as shown by successful attempts in the domains of anxiety, creativity, problem solving and cognitive enrichment (Arnon & Kreitler, 1984; Kreitler & Kreitler, 1988c, 1990a,d). A variety of techniques have been developed for increasing or decreasing the frequency with which an individual uses particular meaning variables (e.g., Kreitler & Kreitler, 1990d). For example, a study of special interest in the present context showed that modifying specific sets of meaning variables changed the Rorschach responses of schizophrenics in the direction of normality and of normals in the direction of pathology (Kreitler, Kreitler, & Wanounou, 1987-1988). Since we were dealing with psychopathological responses, the training was brief and focused, designed to produce only transitory effects.

Modifying DMs by Changing Beliefs and Meaning Variables

Similar considerations inspired the study on modifying DMs (Kreitler, in press). The goals were to demonstrate that it is possible to modify DMs in a desired direction by means of focused modification of relevant beliefs and meaning variables. In view of the role of DMs in psychological adaptation and functioning, we took special precautions in these studies: we focused only on denial and rationalization which are relatively common in a normal population; we applied modification procedures designed to be brief and attain only transitory effects; we applied the modification of beliefs and meaning variables separately so as to keep the effects at low intensity; and we chose participants screened for absence of pathology.

The study had two parts, one devoted to denial and one to rationalization. In each part there were four groups of participants: those who got the training of beliefs and a control group, those who got the training of meaning variables and a control group. In the denial study there were 15 in each (total n=60), in the rationalization study 18 in each (total n=72). The participants were undergraduates (in the age range of 21 to 26) of both genders, who had undergone brief screening on the basis of the CDI criteria and were found to have no pathological tendencies. Each participant was administered the DMs questionnaire (Kreitler & Kreitler, 1972, second study, above), which provided the dependent measure, and the CO Questionnaire of DMs and the Meaning Test, which provided the measures of relevant beliefs and meaning variables, respectively. The assignment into experimental and control groups was random. All the questionnaires were administered twice: first about a week prior to the training, and again the day following the training. The training consisted in subjecting the participants individually, in groups of 3-4, to the manipulation which was designed to be either experimental (change of beliefs or of meaning variables) or control. For changing beliefs, about a third of the themes relevant for the particular DM (denial or rationalization) were chosen randomly and phrased in a reversed direction so that they did not support the DM. The participants got a list of each of these themes in the form of beliefs of the four types, and were asked to note down at least three different arguments to support each belief. For changing meaning variables, we made a list of meaning variables that were related negatively to the DMs (Tables 10.2a, 10.2b), namely, five of the 17 in the pattern corresponding to denial (all negatively correlated except Structure) (35.3%) and 10 of the 30 in the pattern corresponding to rationalization (all negatively correlated plus the positive and absolute forms of relation that negate the two forms of relation in the pattern) (33%). The participants were asked to note down at least three different examples for each of the presented meaning variables. It will be noted that in all cases the training consisted in strengthening specific tendencies rather than weakening, which was expected to be attended by less damage, if any. The participants in the control groups were presented random phrases from the daily newspaper (the same number as in the groups trained for beliefs or meanings) and were asked to write for each at least three arguments or examples. The training lasted about 30 minutes.

The changes on the scores of the CO Questionnaire of DMs and the Meaning Profile were in the expected directions but minimal, as expected. However, the changes in the Questionnaire of DMs were remarkable. Table 10.5 shows that following the training of beliefs there was a 33% decrease in denial and of 22% in rationalization responses; following the training in meaning variables, there was a decrease of 19.8% in denial and of 13.2% in rationalization. The comparable decreases in the control groups that did not undergo the experimental training were much smaller. In each case the DM scores of the experimental participants differed significantly from the control ones in the post session, though not in the pre session. Table 10.6 shows that the main effects due to the manipulation and to the repeated assessments (pre-post) were mostly significant but of major interest are the significant interaction effects of the two factors which demonstrates the impact of the training on the DM responses. Notably, the effect on denial seems to be larger than on rationalization, either because of differences in the training or because rationalization may be more deeply entrenched in a normal population.

Following the experiment, the participants were invited for a debriefing session which was concluded with their responding again to the DMs questionnaire. The results showed that all participants reverted back to their initial scores on the investigated DMs. The results of the modification study demonstrate that it is possible to modify DMs by using the adequate psychological tools. Our demonstration referred to transitory effects. It is likely that under adequate conditions, the effects may be enhanced and made more durable. Further, our demonstration referred to weakening of two DMs. It is still an open issue whether weakening DMs is always beneficial psychologically. Other options are to be considered, for example, by chyanging beliefs and meaning variables it may be possible to strengthen specific DMs which would replace or inhibit the use of other more pathological or less desirable DMs; or, making a large array of different medium-strength DMs available to the individual for selection in line with situational demands and possibilities. Moreover, there seem to be further options for affecting defense-based responses in addition to changing beliefs and meaning variables involved in the DM. For example, it is possible to try to resolve the conflict underlying the use of a DM by modifying the CO clusters which gave rise to the two clashing behavioral intents. Finally, the CO conception of DMs as special programs of conflict resolution raises the posibility that many individuals may have at their disposal too few means for coping with problems, mainly those that arise due to clashes between the desired and the morally permissible, common reality and norms, the existing and the fantasied.

Table 10.5: *Mean changes in defense mechanism scores following changes in beliefs (co) and meaning variables*

Defense Mechanism	Exp. Manip.	Pre		Post		Difference (%)		Sig. of Differences (*t*-test)	
		Exp. (a)	Control (b)	Exp. (c)	Control (d)	Exp.	Control		
Denial	Beliefs	10.3	9.7	6.9	9.1	-33.01	-6.18	(a)-(c)	6.75**
		2.3	2.1	1.4	1.9			(c)-(d)	3.61**
	Meaning	10.1	10.3	8.1	9.9	-19.80	-3.88	(a)-(c)	2.68*
		2.4	2.1	1.9	2.1			(c)-(d)	2.46*
Rationalization	Beliefs	10.9	11.2	8.5	10.5	-22.02	-6.25	(a)-(c)	3.98**
		2.1	2.7	1.9	2.3			(c)-(d)	2.89**
	Meaning	10.6	11.6	9.2	10.9	-13.21	-6.03	(a)-(c)	2.17*
		2.3	2.9	1.8	2.5			(c)-(d)	2.39*

Note. In each cell the first number denotes the mean and the number below it the SD. The range of the scores on the Questionnaire of DMs is 1-15. The significance of the differences for groups (c) & (d) is based on t-tests for independent samples, and for groups (a) & (b) on t-tests for dependent (correlated) samples. CO = Cognitive orientation.

Table 10.6: *Results of repeated measures analyses of variance with two factors:Experimental manipulation (experimental and control) and pre-manipulation versus post-manipulation scores in defense mechanisms*

Manipulated Variable	Defense Mechanism	Source of Variation	*df*	*MS*	*F*
Beliefs (CO)	Denial	Between subjects effects			
		Within cells	28	6.71	
		Manipulation	1	29.32	4.37*
		Within subjects effects			
		Within cells	28	5.12	
		Pre-post	1	21.85	4.27*
		Manipulation X pre-post	1	32.96	6.44*
Meaning		Between subjects effects			
		Within cells	28	5.25	
		Manipulation	1	24.52	4.67*
		Within subjects effects			
		Within cells	28	5.87	
		Pre-post	1	24.18	4.12
		Manipulation X pre-post	1	24.99	4.76*
Beliefs (CO)	Rationalization	Between subjects effects			
		Within cells	34	7.85	
		Manipulation	1	32.73	4.17*
		Within subjects effects			
		Within cells	34	8.54	
		Pre-post	1	38.60	4.52*
		Manipulation X pre-post	1	40.91	4.79*
Meaning		Between subjects effects			
		Within cells	34	8.63	
		Manipulation	1	36.68	4.25*
		Within subjects effects			
		Within cells	34	7.98	
		Pre-post	1	33.59	4.21*
		Manipulation X pre-post	1	35.75	4.48*

Note. The analysis was done by applying the BMDP Model 2V (Dixon, Brown, Engelman and Jennrich, 1990). CO= Cognitive orientation.
$^*p < 0.05$.

The need for relying on DMs may be greatly weakened by alerting the individuals to the conflicts and helping them acquire new ways of resolving them.

Summing up and afterthoughts: The Blueprint for a Cognitive Theory of DMs

DMs appear to be a special kind of program, designed to serve internal conflict resolution so as to render action possible. Though they function internally, they may have multiple and varied manifestations in different domains – perceptual, emotional, cognitive, behavioral, and physiological by means of what may be called defense-based responses. They represent general strategic principles of conflict resolution that have undergone schematization and functional specialization. Their application is dependent on motivational factors, which were examined in the framework of the cognitive orientation theory. The motivational determinants are DM-specific and differ from the motivation for the particular actions or behavioral intents that have necessitated the use of the DM. The motivational difference is in contents but not in form and structure. Hence, the motivational determinants of DMs consist of specific constellations of beliefs of four types (about self, norms, goals, and general) that refer to themes orienting toward the adoption of a particular DM. The constellation of beliefs gives rise to a vectorial motivational disposition for a specific DM. Four studies demonstrated the identification of the particular belief constellations and how they enable predicting which DM the individual would adopt.

Further, the cognitive determinants of DMs were examined in the framework of the theory of meaning. Each DM was found to correspond to a unique set of meaning variables which provide the means for implementing the DM. Each set includes several diferent means, which may account for the possibility of applying the DM in various situations. Some of the DMs were found to resemble personality traits, but others not. Moreover, some DMs may form part of personality traits. Selection of DMs was shown to depend on the extent to which the individual's meaning profile contains the meaning variables corresponding to the specific DM. Individuals differ in the degree to which their meaning profile contains the constituents of different DMs.

Theoretically a comprehensive understanding of DMs requires considering both the motivational and cognitive determinants. In actual practice, an empirical study showed that the joint application of the motivational and the cognitive determinants provided a better prediction than the application of either set of determinants alone.

Another important support for the presented conception of DMs is the empirical evidence that our theoretical approach enables modifying DMs by changing beliefs or meaning variables. This confirmation has theoretical as well as clinical implications.

The proposed conception of DMs is an integrative one. It is based on considering interactively and conjointedly the motivational and the cognitive determinants of DMs. It proceeds simultaneously on the theoretical and the empirical levels. It combines the experimental-scientific approach with the clinical-psychotherapeutic one. Last, but not least, it brings together the personal and social viewpoints, by highlighting the contribution of society to identifying or rendering certain themes or issues as sufficiently threatening so as to require DMs and by specifying the individual's contribution to the shaping and selection of DMs to deal with these issues.

The last remarks serve to raise the question, that may seem disconcerting to some extent, whether and for how long will DMs still be necessary in a society or culture that has already broken down so many taboos and is intent upon breaking them all down. This question may seem topical to those who assume that psychoanalysis has been so successful in destroying taboos, that soon there will not remain many targets for DMs to defend. This conclusion would be justified only if one assumes that the objects of defense are limited to superego-banned wishes and drives. From the point of view of a cognitively-based theory of personality, objects worthy of defense would include basic beliefs about oneself, basic rules and norms, basic wishes and goals, and basic beliefs about the world and others that form the core of orientation in the internal and external environments. These beliefs address issues such as: What kind of person am I? Does life in general and my life in particular make sense, and if yes, what sense? Is there justice in the world? Are people basically good or evil? and Should I behave in a moral way? Also from the viewpoint of a more emotionally and motivationally based theory of personality, there are enough issues that may provoke anxieties sufficiently serious for triggering DMs. These include the morbidity and loneliness of old age, the progressive loss of wishes due to their fulfillment, the certainty of unavoidable uncertainty, and last but not least, the need for limitations and restrictions and the unconquerable wish to cross them (Snyder, 1988).

To be faced with problems of this kind is not a cause for shame, and hence is not likely to promote repression. Denying them and still maintaining a workable contact with common reality would be almost impossible. Yet denying their immediate and personal relevance by projecting them into the post-personal future is already fairly common. So is partial regression that is often referred to as 'learned helplessness'

(Seligman, 1975). Rationalization adorned by sublimated presentation is the preferred answer of many existentialist and humanistic therapists and philosophers, while the denial of the future may be practiced only as long as one is not hit by the harsh confrontation with the present. In sum, it seems likely that DMs are used and will continue to be used beyond the realm of superego-banned contents and domains. They seem to contribute to quality of life, but it remains unclear whether human beings would be happier if they are helped to live without any DMs and whether this is at all possible and desirable.

References

Abelson, R. P. (1968). A summary of hypotheses on modes of resolution. In R. P. Abelson, E. Aronson, W. J. McGuire, T. M. Newcomb, M. J. Rosenberg, & P. H. Tannenbaum (Eds.), *Theories of cognitive consistency: A sourcebook* (pp. 716-720). Chicago, IL: Rand McNally.

Ajzen, I., & Fishbein, M. (1980). *Understanding attitudes and predicting social behavior*. Englewood Cliffs, NJ: Prentice Hall.

Arnon, R., & Kreitler, S. (1984). Effects of meaning training on overcoming functional fixedness. *Current Psychological Research and Review, 3*, 11-24.

Bachar, E., Latzer, Y., Kreitler, S., & Berry, E. M. (1999). Emprical comparison of two psychological therapies: Self psychology and cognitive orientation in the treatment of anorexia and bulemia *Journal of Psychotherapy Practice and Research, 8,* 115-128.

Barrett, L. F., William, N. L., & Fong, G. T. (2002). Defensive verbal behaior assessment. *Personality and Social Psychology Bulletin, 28,* 776-788.

Borton, J. L. S. (2002). The suppression of negative self-referent thoughts. *Anxiety, Stress and Coping, 15,* 31-44.

Breier, G. (1980). *Effects of cognitive orientation on behavior under threat.* Master's thesis, Department of Psychology, Tel Aviv University (summarized in Kreitler & Kreitler, 1982, pp. 137-140).

Bugenthal, D. E. (1974). Interpretation of naturally occurring discrepancies between words and intonation: Modes of inconsistency resolution. *Journal of Personality and Social Psychology, 30,* 125-133.

Caplan, G. (1981). Mastery of stress. *American Journal of Psychiatry, 138*, 413-420.

Cermak, T. L., & Rosenfeld, A. A. (1987). Thherapeutic considerations with adult children of alcoholics. *Advances in Alcoholism and Substance Abuse, 6*, 17-32.

Chomsky, N. (1972). *Language and mind* (enlarged ed.). New York: Harcourt, Brace.

Colby, K. M., & Gilbert, J. P. (1964). Programming a computer model of neurosis.

Journal of Mathematical Psychology, 1, 405-417.

Conte, H. R., & Plutchik, R. (1995). *Ego defenses: Theory and measurement.* New York: Wiley.

Cramer, P. (1988).The Defense Mechanism Inventory: A review of research and discussion of the scales. *Journal of Personality Assessment, 52*, 142-164.

Cramer, P. (2002). Defense mechanisms, behavior, and affect in young adulthood. *Journal of Personality, 70*, 103-126. .

DeNike, L. D., & Tiber, N. (1968). Neurotic behavior. In P. London & D. Rosenhan (Eds.), *Foundations of abnormal psychology*. New York: Holt, Rinehart & Winston.

Derakshan, N., & Eysenck, M. W. (201). Effects of focus of attention on physiological, behavioral, and reported state anxiety in repressors, low-anxious, high-anxious, and defensive high-anxious individuals. *Anxiety, Stress and Coping, 14*, 285-299.

Derogatis, L. R., Lipman, R. S., Rickels, K., Ulenhuth, E. H., & Covi, L. (1974). The Hopkins Symptom Checklist (HSCL): A measure of primary symptom dimensions. In P. Pichot (Ed.), *Psychological measurements in psychopharmacology: Modern problems in pharmacopsychiatry* (Vol. 7, pp. 79-110). Basel, Switzerland: Karger.

Drechsler, I., Kreitler, S., & Brunner, D. (1987). Cognitive antecedents of coronary heart disease. *Social Science and Medicine, 24*, 581-588.

Eldar, S. (1976). *Cognitive orientation and the perception of incongruent communication.* Master's thesis, Department of Psychology, Tel Aviv University.

Fenichel, O. (1945). *The psychoanalytic theory of neurosis* . New York: W. W. Norton.

Freud, A. (1966). *The ego and the mechanisms of defense.* (rev. ed). New York: International Universities Press.

Freud, S. (1936). *The problem of anxiety*. New York: W. W. Norton.

Freud, S. (1957). Repression. In In J. Strachey (Ed.), *The standard edition of the complete psychological works of S. Freud* (Vol. 14, pp. 141-158). London: Hogarth Press (originally published in 1915).

Freud, S. (1961). The ego and the id. In In J. Strachey (Ed.), *The standard edition of the complete psychological works of S. Freud* (Vol. 19, pp. 3-66). London: Hogarth Press (originally published in 1923).

Freud, S. (1962). Further remarks on the neuro-psychoses of defense. In In J. Strachey (Ed.), *The standard edition of the complete psychological works of S. Freud* (Vol. 3, pp. 162-185). London: The Hogarth Press (originally published in 1896).

Freud, S. (1964a). New introductory lectures on psychoanalysis. In J. Strachey (Ed.), *The standard edition of the complete psychological works of S. Freud*

(Vol. 22, pp. 3-182). London: Hogarth Press (originally published in 1933).

Freud, S. (1964b). Analysis terminable and interminable. In J. Strachey (Ed.), *The standard edition of the complete psychological works of S. Freud* (Vol. 23, pp. 211-253). London: Hogarth Press (originally published in 1937).

Freud, S. (1964c). Constructions in analysis. In J. Strachey (Ed.), *The standard edition of the complete psychological works of S. Freud* (Vol. 23, pp. 257-269). London: Hogarth Press (originally published in 1937).

Gibbs, J. T. (1987). Identity and marginality issues in the treatment of biracial adolescents. *American Journal of Orthopsychiatry, 57*, 265-278.

Grzegolowska-Klarkowska, H., & Zolnierczyk, D. (1988). Defense of self-esteem, defense of self-consistency: A new voice in an old controversy. *Journal of Social and Clinical Psychology, 6,* 171-179.

Horney, K. (1945). *Our inner conflicts*. New York: W.W. Norton.

Kelman, H. C., & Baron, R. M. (1968). Determinants of modes of resolving inconsistenciey dilemmas: A functional analysis. In R. P. Abelson, E. Aronson, W. J. McGuire, T. M. Newcomb, M. J. Rosenberg, & P. H. Tannenbaum (Eds.), *Theories of cognitive consistency: A sourcebook* (pp. 670-683). Chicago, IL: Rand McNally.

Kwon, P. (202). Hpe, defense mechanisms, and adjustment: Implications fir false hope and defense hopelessness. *Journal of Personality, 70*, 207-231.

Kragh, U. (1984). Defense mechanisms manifested in perceptgenesis. In W. D. Froehlich, G. Smith, J. G. Draguns, & U. Hentschel (Eds.), *Psychological processes in cognition and personality* (pp. 165-170). Washington, DC: Hemisphere Publishing.

Kreitler, S. (1999). Denial in cancer patients. *Cancer Investigation, 17,* 514-534.

Kreitler, S. (2001). An evolutionary perspective on cognitive orientation. *Evolution and Cognition, 7,* 81-97.

Kreitler, S. (2002). The cognitive guidance of behavior. In E. Jost et al. (Eds.), *The Yin and Yang of social cognition: Perspectives on the social psychology of thought systems.* Washington, DC: American Psychological Association.

Kreitler, S. (in press). Cognitive perspectives on personality. *European Journal of Personality.*

Kreitler, S., & Chemerinski, A. (1988). The cognitive orientation of obesity. *International Journal of Obesity, 12,* 403-412.

Kreitler, H., & Kreitler, S. (1964). Modes of action in the psychodramatic role test. *International Journal of Sociometry and Sociatry, 4,* 10-15.

Kreitler, H., & Kreitler, S. (1968). The validation of psychodramatic behavior against behavior in life. *British Journal of Medical Psychology, 41*, 185-192.

Kreitler, H., & Kreitler, S. (1969). *Cognitive orientation and defense mechanisms.* Research Bulletin (RB-69-23), Princeton, NJ: Educational Testing Service.

Kreitler, H., & Kreitler, S. (1972). The cognitive determinants of defensive behaviour. *British Journal of Social and Clinical Psychology, 11*, 359-372.

Kreitler, H., & Kreitler, S. (1976). *Cognitive orientation and behavior.* New York: Springer.

Kreitler, H., & Kreitler, S. (1982). The theory of cognitive orientation: Widening the scope of behavior prediction. In B. Maher & W. B. Maher (Eds.), *Progress in experimental personality research* (Vol. 11. pp. 101-169). New York: Academic Press.

Kreitler, S., & Kreitler, H. (1986). Types of curiosity behaviors and their cognitive determinants. *Archives of Psychology, 138*, 233-251.

Kreitler, S., & Kreitler, H. (1987). The motivational and cognitive determinants of individual planning. *Genetic, Social and General Psychology Monographs, 113*, 81-107.

Kreitler, S., & Kreitler, H. (1988a). The cognitive approach to motivation in retarded individuals. In N. W. Bray (Ed.), *International review of research in mental retardation* (Vol. 15, pp. 81-123). San Diego, CA: Academic Press.

Kreitler, S., & Kreitler, H. (1988b). Horizontal decalage: A problem and its resolution. *Cognitive Development, 4,* 89-119.

Kreitler, S., & Kreitler, H. (1988c). Trauma and anxiety: The cognitive approach. *Journal of Traumatic Stress, 1,* 35-56.

Kreitler, S., & Kreitler, H. (1990a). *The cognitive foundations of personality traits.* New York: Plenum.

Kreitler, H., & Kreitler, S. (1990b). Psychosemantic foundations of creativity. In K. J. Gilhooly, M. Keane, R. Logie & G. Erdos (Eds.), *Lines of thought: Reflections on the psychology of thinking* (Vol. 1, pp. 15-28). Chichester, England: Wiley. Kreitler, S., & Kreitler, H. (1990c). Cognitive orientation and sexual dysfunctions in women. *Annals of Sex Research, 3,* 75-104.

Kreitler, H., & Kreitler, S. (1990d). Cognitive primacy, cognitive behavior guidance, and their implications for cognitive therapy. *Journal of Cognitive Psychotherapy, 4*, 151-169.

Kreitler, S., & Kreitler, H. (1991). Cognitive orientation and physical disease or health. *European Journal of Personality, 5*, 109-129.

Kreitler, S., & Kreitler, H. (1994). Motivational and cognitive determinants of exploration. In H. Keller & K. Schneider (Eds.), *Curiosity and exploration: Theoretical perspectives, research fields and applications* (pp. 259-284). New York: Springer Verlag.

Kreitler, S., & Kreitler, H. (1997). The paranoid person: Cognitive motivations and personality traits. *European Journal of Personality, 11*, 101-132.

Kreitler, S., Kreitler, H., Carasso, R. (1987) Cognitive orientation as predictor of pain relief following acupuncture. *Pain, 28*, 323-341.

Kreitler, S., Kreitler, H., & Schwartz, R. (1991). Cognitive orientation and genital infections in young women. *Women and Health, 17*, 49-85.

Kreitler, S., Kreitler, H., & Wanounou, V. (1987-1988). Cognitive modification of test performance in schizophrenics and normals. *Imagination, Cognition, and Personality, 7*, 227-249.

Kreitler, S. Schwartz, R., & Kreitler, H. (1987). The cognitive orientation of expressive communicability in schizophrenics and normals. *Journal of Communication Disorders, 24*, 73-91

Lazarus, R. S., & Folkman, S. (1984). *Stress, appraisal, and coping*. New York: Springer Publishing.

Moos, R. H. (Ed). (1984). *Coping with physical illness: New perspectives* (Vol. 2). NY: Plenum.

Munroe, R. L. (1956). *Schools of psychoanalytic thought* (3rd printing). New York: Dryden Press.

Nickerson, R. S. (2001). The projective way of knowing: A useful heuristic that sometimes misleads. *Current Directions in Psychological Science, 10*, 168-172.

Pearlin, L. I., & Schooler, C. (1978). The structure of coping. *Journal of Health and Social Behavior, 19*, 2-21.

Piaget, J. (1951). *Play, dreams, and imitation in childhood.* New York: W. W. Norton.

Polya, G. (1954). *Induction and analogy in mathematics* (Vol. 1). Princeton, NJ: Princeton University Press

Polya, G. (1957). *How to solve it.* Garden City, NY: Doubleday.

Sahoo, F. M., Sia, N., & Panada, E. (1987). Individualism, collectivism and coping styles. *Journal of Psychological Researches, 31*, 77-81.

Schafer, R. (1987). Self-deception, defense, and narration. *Psychoanalysis and Contemporary Thought, 10*, 319-346.

Seligman, M. (1975). *Helplessness.* San Francisco, CA: Freeman. Singer, J. L. (Ed.), *Repression and dissociation.* Chicago, IL: University of Chicago Press.

Shervin, H. (1995). Subliminal perception and repression. In J. L. Singer (Ed.), *Repression and dissociation: Implications for personality theory, psychopathology, and health.* (pp. 103-119). Chicago, IL: Chicago University Press.

Singer, J. L. (Ed.), (1990). *Repression and dissociation.* Chicago: University of Chicago Press.

Snyder, C. R. (1988). From defenses to self-protection: An evolutionary perspective. *Journal of Social and Clinical Psychology, 6*, 155-158.

Tipton, R. M., & Riebsame, W. E. (1987). Beliefs about smoking and health: Their measurement and relationship to smoking behavior. *Addictive Behaviors, 12*, 217-223.

Vaillant, G. E. (1983). Childhood environment and maturity of defense mechanisms. In D. Magnusson & V. L. Allen (Eds.), *Human development: An interactional perspective* (pp. 343-352). San Diego, CA: Academic Press.
Watson, M., & Greer, M. (1998). Personality and coping. In J. C. Holland (Ed.), *Psycho-oncology* (pp. 91-98). New York: Oxford University Press.
Watzlawick, P., Beavin, J. H., & Jackson, D. D. (1967). *Pragmatics of human communication*. Palo Alto, CA: Norton.
Weinberger, D. A., Schwartz, G. E., & Davidson, R. J. (1979). Low anxious, high anxious, and repressive coping styles: Psychometric patterns and behavioral and physiological responses to stress. *Journal of Abnormal Psychology, 88*, 369-380.
Westhoff, K., & Halbach-Suarez, C. (1989). Cognitive orientation and the prediction of decisions in a medical examination context. *European Journal of Personality, 3*, 61-71.
Wickelgren, W. A. (1974). *How to solve problems*. San Francisco, CA: W. H. Freeman.
Winegar, N., Stephens, T. A., & Varney, E. D. (1987). Alcoholics Anonymous and the alcoholic defense structure. *Social Case Work, 68*, 223-228.
Zakay, D., Bar-El, Z., & Kreitler, S. (1984). Cognitive orientation and changing the impulsivity of children. *British Journal of Educational Psychology, 54*, 40-50.
Zemet, R. (1976). *Cognitive orientation theory and patterns of behavior in conflictual situations in schizophrenic and normal subjects.* Master's thesis, Department of Psychology, Tel Aviv University (summarized in Kreitler & Kreitler, 1982, pp. 150-153).

Author Note
Hans Kreitler died on January 9, 1993. He is listed as co-author of the present chapter because he co-authored the previous version and some of the material in the present chapter is based on work in which he had participated.

Defense Mechanisms
U. Hentschel, G. Smith, J.G. Draguns & W. Ehlers (Editors)

Chapter 11

Repressive Coping Style and the Significance of Verbal-Autonomic Response Dissociations

Andreas Schwerdtfeger and Carl-Walter Kohlmann

Since the early work by Lazarus (1966), repressive coping style has frequently been associated with discrepancies between subjective reports of anxiety and physiological responses to stress. This divergence has been referred to as verbal-autonomic response dissociation. In this chapter we shall focus on the relationship between this response pattern and repressive coping in more detail. In order to familiarize the reader with the repressive coping style, we shall first present an overview of the development of the repression construct and its various ways of operationalizing it. We shall then introduce the discrepancy hypothesis and report several, classical as well as recent, studies that were aimed at relating the repressive coping style to verbal-autonomic response dissociations. Following that, we shall subsume studies that used skin conductance and cardiovascular responses as separate autonomic measures. We shall then offer a theoretical framework for explaining discrepancies by utilizing Gray's (1991) theory of behavioral inhibition / activation. Finally, we shall conclude the chapter with a discussion of possible pathological influences of verbal-autonomic response dissociations.

The Repression Construct

Research on the construct of repression has developed from the fusion of two traditions, one perception oriented and the other clinical (Erdelyi, 1990; Krohne, 1996). The perception-oriented line of development has its origins in Brunswik's functionalistic interpretation of behavior (Brunswik, 1947) and has served as the basis for the person-oriented approach in perception research (Bruner, 1951; Bruner & Postman, 1947; Frenkel-Brunswik, 1949; Klein & Schlesinger, 1949). The clinical approach is represented by psychoanalytical approaches to defense mechanisms against anxiety (Freud, 1936).

The expectancy or hypothesis theory of perception (Bruner, 1951), developed for dealing with both laboratory experiments on perception and observations by clinicians, forms the foundation for the merger of these two traditions. According to this theory, both progress and product of perceptual operations are predominantly determined by the hypotheses an individual brings to the perceptual situation. The nature and the strength of these hypotheses may be determined by person-specific needs (e.g., the need for safety and order or for control over instinctive impulses). In their classical experiment on perceptual defense inspired by Jung's word association studies (1906/1909), Bruner and Postman (1947) discovered two ways of responding to emotionally significant stimuli. Individuals with a defensive orientation attempted to avoid the perception of the critical stimulus for as long as possible. By contrast, the so-called sensitizing orientation was characterized by intensified vigilance in the face of emotionally significant stimuli (for overviews, methodological criticisms, and various updates see Blum, 1955; Dixon, 1971, 1981; Erdelyi, 1974, 1990; Goldiamond, 1958; Hentschel & Smith, 1980; Holmes, 1974, 1990; Krohne, 1978, 1996; and Shevrin, 1990).

Eriksen (1951) proposed dividing defense mechanisms into two basically antagonistic categories, in terms of their mode of anxiety reduction, either by avoiding danger-related stimuli or by intensified attention and sensitization to them. Lazarus, Eriksen, & Fonda (1951) identified these two response tendencies in a classical auditory recognition experiment. The type of mechanism a person preferably employs to cope with anxiety-arousing circumstances in perception can be mediated by personality variables. Gordon (1957) introduced the term repression-sensitization to describe this one-dimensional bipolar personality characteristic. To investigate this trait empirically, a number of projective methods as well as scale combinations, based mostly on the MMPI, have been employed (Byrne, 1964). Byrne's Repression-Sensitization scale (R-S scale: Byrne, 1961; also Byrne, Barry & Nelson, 1963; Epstein & Fenz, 1967; Krohne, 1974), compiled from MMPI items, is probably the most extensively used measure of this construct.

In a great many studies on repression-sensitization (for overviews, see Bell & Byrne, 1978; Byrne, 1964; Krohne, 1996; Krohne & Rogner, 1982; Singer, 1990; Tucker, 1970), associations, albeit often weak, were established between repression-sensitization and various theoretically relevant behavioral indicators. Halperin (1986), for example, examined the relationship between repression-sensitization, assessed by the revised R-S scale (Byrne et al., 1963), and visual focusing of attention when viewing pleasant or unpleasant emotionally arousing slides, and Haley (1974) conducted a similar study using films. While the subjects were looking at neutral (i.e., landscape), sexually arousing (i.e., men and women at different stages of undress), or disgusting (i.e., open wounds caused by injury) slides, the areas examined for the longest amount of time were registered by means of an eye movement camera. In pilot studies, key areas of the sexual and disgusting slides that were particularly effective in inducing emotion, as well as the more interesting parts of the neutral ones, were determined. The hypothesis that sensitizers direct their attention longer than repressors only to the key areas of unpleasant slides was not completely confirmed. When confronted with slides that induced emotion, disgusting or sexual, sensitizers generally examined the central areas longer (injury theme, 41 percent of viewing time; sexual theme, 37 percent) than the medium group, whose R-S scores were in the middle of the distribution (28 and 22 percent, respectively), and the repressors (27 percent and 22 percent, respectively). The groups did not differ when viewing the areas of the neutral slides judged to be interesting.

Halperin (1986) believes that these results fundamentally confirm the construct validity of the R-S scale. However, he also doubts the linearity of the scale, since there was no difference between the medium group and the repressors. . Moreover, Halperin suggests that the criterion range of the approach-avoidance construct should be extended from stimuli or situations that arouse unpleasant emotions to the entire category of emotionally arousing stimuli. From both information-theory and percept-genetic perspectives on repression-sensitization (Erdelyi, 1974; Krohne, 1978; see also Fröhlich, 1984), it would be interesting to establish whether repressors, when viewing slides that induce emotion, already focus on and register the emotionally relevant areas at a very early phase of the perceptual process and then turn away from them in a relatively permanent manner. Halperin's data, however, have not yet been analyzed from these points of view.

Regarding the operationalization of repression-sensitization, two sets of objections have been formulated (cf. Krohne, 1996):

1. The R-S scale correlates with anxiety scales at the level of good reliability coefficients (Abbott, 1972; Bell & Byrne, 1978; Boucsein & Freye, 1974; Krohne, 1974; Watson & Clark, 1984). The relationship between these two characteristics suggests, that both constructs are associated with a common emotionality factor which Watson and Clark (1984) called "negative affec-

tivity." Another possibility is that the R-S scale is merely appropriate for recording self-reported emotional and psychopathological symptoms (Budd & Clopton, 1985; Lefcourt, 1966). The second problem, just about to be presented, is directly related to this criticism

2. A linear relationship exists between the R-S scale and different indicators of emotional adaptation, which contradicts the conceptualization of extreme high or low repression-sensitization scores as indicators of rigid, and thereby frequently maladaptive, forms of coping.

A curvilinear relationship would have met these expectations better (Bell & Byrne, 1978). Moreover, the homogeneity of the group of individuals in the middle section of the distribution of scores for the R-S scale is controversial in regard to their coping behavior (Chabot, 1973). It is however not surprising that the answers to questions on the R-S scale regarding, for example, bodily symptoms, health, and depression, as indirect indicators of defensive style, correlate with reports and observations of the same factors, as direct indicators of emotional adaptation (Angleitner, 1980; Watson & Pennebaker, 1989). The disregard of item overlap in operationalizing predictors and criteria in life-event research has also led to an initial, methodologically contingent, overestimation of the strength of the relationship between critical life events and the appearance of impairment to the psychic and physical well-being (Schroeder & Costa, 1984).

Later developments in the theoretical and operational determination of repression-sensitization pursue the optimization of several focal points. The multiple variable approaches, which are based on the simultaneous application of anxiety and defensiveness scales, attempt to overcome the confounding of anxiety and repression-sensitization and suggest, in particular, separating the truly low-anxious individuals from repressors. The intersection of high anxiety and sensitization appears, in contrast, to be less problematic. Several authors (e.g., Beck & Clark, 1988; Carver & Scheier, 1988; Eysenck, 1997) determine anxiety on the basis of cognitive indicators assumed to be characteristic of sensitization (e.g., selective perception and processing of threatening stimuli, anticipation of negative events). In more recent, person-oriented approaches, preferences for certain coping behaviors are not inferred, as is still done in multiple variable approaches Instead, persons are explicitly asked about their preferred coping reactions and actions in imaginary stressful situations.

Multiple Variable Approaches with Traditional Instruments

Since both repression-sensitization and anxiety are conceptualized as one-dimensional personality characteristics, separation of high anxiety from sensitization, as well as of low anxiety from repression, is not possible due to the strong correlations between anxiety tests and the R-S scale. To overcome this difficulty, many authors (Hill & Sarason, 1966; Holroyd, 1972; Kogan & Wallach, 1964; Krohne & Rogner, 1985; Lefcourt, 1969; Weinberger, Schwartz & Davidson, 1979) have suggested multiple variable approaches (Krohne & Rogner, 1985) with the simultaneous application of tests for anxiety (e.g., the Manifest Anxiety Scale, MAS, J.A. Taylor, 1953), defensiveness, and anxiety denial (e.g., scales for the "social desirability tendency," Crowne & Marlowe, 1960; Edwards, 1957). Weinberger (1999) and Weinberger and Schwartz (1990) proposed defining coping strategies within a broader view of social emotional adjustment. Their typology is based on the intersection of two supraordinate dimensions: self-control, conceptualized as suppression of egoistic desires, and affective reaction, formulated as subjective experience of distress. Repressors, for example, are defined as individuals who report low distress but high levels of self-restraint.

Anxiety tests should help determine the degree of person's readiness to recognize potential threats. By contrast, scales of defensiveness should assess variations in avoiding threat and in recognizing possibly aversive situations and in denying contingently evoked anxiety. Since the empirical indicators for both of these tendencies are in general only weakly correlated, the division at the median for these distributions of scores results in four approximately equal large groups of individuals, which are characterized by distinctive patterns of anxiety and defensiveness.

Individuals who exhibit comparatively low scores on both tests are designated nondefensive or truly low-anxious (Krohne & Rogner, 1985; Weinberger et al., 1979). They should evaluate comparatively few situations as threatening and have little motivation to deny anxiety. Similarly, low anxiety scores in combination with comparatively higher defensiveness characterize individuals who typically deny environmental threats as well as their own emotional and cognitive anxiety reactions. This group constitutes the repressors. The interpretation of the other two patterns is debatable. Weinberger et al. (1979), for example, who are centrally concerned with the differentiation of truly low-anxious individuals from repressors, designate the pattern of high anxiety and low defensiveness as high-anxious and that of high anxiety and high defensiveness as defensively high-anxious. The distinctions proposed by Weinberger et al. are accepted by other researchers including Asendorpf and Scherer (1983), Davis (19870), Davis and Schwartz (1987), Hansen and Hansen (1988), and Tremayne and Barry (1988).

Krohne and Rogner (1985), however, have suggested considering the pattern of high anxiety / high defensiveness as an indicator of unsuccessful coping, (equivalent to high anxiety. Since these individuals admit their anxiety in spite of a general tendency to block negative emotions (also Hill, 1971), they should, according to Krohne and Rogner, experience anxiety particularly frequently and intensely. Krohne and Rogner label the configuration of comparatively high anxiety and low defensiveness as sensitization, since persons in this group do not block their anxiety, although they rate many situations as threatening.

If the defensiveness scale is, however, interpreted in line with Crowne and Marlowe (1964) as "search for social acceptance," the defensiveness interpretation favored by Weinberger et al. (1979) should not be dismissed. Intensified anxiety would then be instrumentally reported in the sense of an excuse for inadequate performance (Laux & Glanzmann, 1987). Wieland, Eckelmann, & Bosel, 1987) have offered a similar functional interpretation of the lowering of the aspiration level. The difference in the interpretation of the desirability scale, either in the direction of defense (Krohne & Rogner) or of search for social acceptance (Weinberger et al.), appears particularly to underlie the different designations of the coping groups. While defensively high-anxious individuals, according to Weinberger et al., report their anxiety because of their craving for social acceptance, the high-anxious persons, as conceptualized by Krohne and Rogner, report their intensified anxiety in spite of their increased defensiveness.

Recently, Mendolia (2002) has criticized the shortcomings of the categorical approach for classifying repressors, low-anxious, high-anxious and defensive high-anxious individuals because of artificial boundaries between these groups. As an alternative, she proposes a dimensional approach to repression by introducing an index of self-regulation of emotion (ISE). The ISE is calculated as the difference between anxiety (MAS) and defensiveness (SDS). On the basis of this index, high-anxious individuals and repressors can be separated, whereas both defensive high-anxious subjects and truly low-anxious subjects are placed in the middle of the scale. Although this approach takes advantage of using the whole subject sample without establishing artificial boundaries, it is accompanied by loss of information. More research is needed to further evaluate the usefulness of this index.

Person-Oriented Approaches

Attempts to classify coping dispositions with the instruments just described pay little attention to how people evaluate stressful situations. At best, they only indirectly allude to the fact that persons have preferences for distinct coping behaviors. Thus, very little is learned about the strategies preferred by a specific person in a given situation. To overcome these problems, the Miller Behavioral Style Scale (MBSS: Miller, 1987), the Mainz Coping Inventory (MCI: Egloff & Krohne, 1998; Krohne, Egloff, Varner, Burns, Weidner & Ellis, 2000), and the Multidimensional Coping Scale (MCS: Cook, 1985) have been developed to assess preferred coping strategies at the dispositional level.

Taking the lead from stimulus-response inventories in anxiety research (Endler, Hunt & Rosenstein, 1962), these instruments present several fictitious situations, followed by a number of statements representing vigilant or avoidant ways of dealing with the situation, with which respondents either agree or disagree. Because these instruments require subjects to report their use of coping strategies rather than their awareness of specific symptoms, they assess cognitive and behavioral referents of vigilance and avoidance more directly. In particular, the MBSS scale for monitoring, the MCI scale for vigilance, and the MCS scale for approach represent coping preferences for approach, whereas the MBSS scale for blunting, the MCI scale of cognitive avoidance, and the MCS avoidance scale represent avoidant coping preferences. Beside the theoretical similarities especially to the approaches developed by Miller (1987) and Krohne (1986, 1989), these scales also overlap empirically . In a study, applying the MBSS (Miller, 1987; German adaptation by Schumacher, 1990) to assess monitoring and blunting and the MCI (Krohne, Rösch & Kürsten, 1989) to assess vigilance and cognitive avoidance, associations between the corresponding scales were demonstrated. After correlations had been computed between the four coping scales using the data on 72 male and female undergraduates (Kohlmann, 1990), only two significant coefficients between the four coping variables emerged: while cognitive avoidance was positively associated with blunting only ($r = .46$), vigilance correlated only with monitoring ($r = .47$). Applying a principal component analysis to the four coping scores resulted in a clear two-factor solution, with vigilance and monitoring as the first factor and cognitive avoidance and blunting as the second factor.

Differentiation of the two kinds of "intolerance" responsible for approachlike and avoidant coping preferences, respectively, has been introduced by Krohne and his coworkers (Kohlmann, 1990; Krohne, 1989; Krohne & Fuchs, 1991) and has been extended to the dimensions of vigilance and cognitive avoidance. Moreover, this distinction can be applied across a variety of instruments, provided that the approach and avoidance preferences are operationally defined as independent of each other (Kohlmann, 1990). Basic to this view is the idea of intolerance of uncertainty underlying vigilant coping preferences, and intolerance of emotional arousal underlying avoidant preferences. In a similar way, Rothbart and Mellinger (1972) identified motivation to avoid harm and ability to tolerate short-term fear arousal as the two central factors affecting coping behavior (see also Frenkel-Brunswik, 1949). They proposed that repressors differ from sensitizers on both of these variables. The model of coping modes (Krohne, 1989) also assumes fundamental differences between repressors and sensitizers on the two dimensions. However, repression and sensitization are not the only modes of coping considered. Because of the independence of both dimensions of habitualized coping, four configurations of coping patterns, in part related to those introduced by Weinberger et al., 1979, can be distinguished:

1. Vigilant mode: persons with high vigilance and low avoidance are called sensitizers. They should primarily be susceptible to stress by experiencing uncertainty in a situation of threat, hence they should exhibit an increased tendency in a variety of threatening situations to seek out information about the stressor in order to construct a mental picture of the anticipated confrontation. Without taking into account coping-relevant characteristics of the stress situation, these persons should try to obtain information about the situation.

2. Avoidant mode: persons with high avoidance and low vigilance are labeled repressors. For these subjects, the emotional arousal triggered by cues prior to a confrontation with an aversive event probably constitutes a major threat. Therefore, they would generally tend to pay little attention to threat-relevant characteristics of situations.

3. Situation-related use of coping strategies: persons with the combination of

vigilance and low avoidance are called nondefensive or flexible copers. In a threatening situation , they are expected to be able to tolerate uncertainty, negative surprise, and prospects of emotional arousal. This mode of flexible use of coping strategies is assumed to be characterized by a pronounced orientation toward whatever situational requirements may prevail at a given time. For example, a flexible coper would monitor a dentist‘s warning signal (e.g., raising a hand before the drill comes close to a nerve) if it reliably predicts painful drilling. However, if the dentist‘s behavior proved to be unreliable in predicting painful interventions, the flexible coper would no longer monitor the unreliable signal but instead would engage in distracting thoughts.

4. Inconsistent, unsuccessful coping mode: persons with the pattern of high vigilance and high avoidance are called anxious persons or unsuccessful copers. They are susceptible to stress as a result of both the uncertainty in aversive situations and the emotional arousal triggered by cues. These conditions tend to elicit fluctuating coping behavior. While attempting to reduce the uncertainty that they experience as stressful by increased preoccupation with the stressor, they may simultaneously increase their emotional arousal beyond the level that they can tolerate. However, when turning away from the stressor in order to reduce anxiety, their uncertainty is likely to increase together with the stress resulting from it. In a dentist's chair, for example, the inconsistent coper, like the flexible coper, should not exhibit any rigid pattersns of coping behavior. However, variations in actual coping behavior are not expected to result in a fit between situational demands (e.g., the reliability of the dentist's signals) and actual coping efforts.

Thus, according to the model outlined above, employment of a specific coping strategy is, of course, dependent in part on situational characteristics. There is, for example, generally more vigilance in predictable situations, and cognitive avoidance prevails in unpredictable situations (Krohne & Rogner, 1982; Miller, 1981). At the same time, there is also strong dependence on dispositional antecedents in the use of coping . This is obviously implied in the definitions of the vigilant and avoidant coping modes preferred by sensitizers and repressors, respectively. But even in the case of persons who vary their coping strategies across situations, coping behavior may be traceable to personality dispositions: for example, to the competence in analyzing situations appropriately and in choosing the optimal strategy in one's coping repertoire for specific situational demands, as Mischel (1984) has pointed out. Kohlmann (1993a).has extended Mischel's model and has provided a critical empirical test of some of its aspects.

Within the model of coping modes, several results have emerged pertaining to the cognitive aspects of emotion regulation. Egloff and Krohne (1996), for example, examined the relationship between coping dispositions and emotional responses after failure in an anagram task. They observed that repressors (low vigilance, high avoidance) roughly reported the same amount of guilt as sensitizers (high vigilance, low avoidance). However, repressors reported lower levels of fear, sadness, and hostility. Positive emotions, on the other hand, were not significantly affected by the coping dispositions. This finding suggests that repressors contrary to sensitizers exhibit a comparatively low degree of elaboration when processing threat-related stimuli.

In order to test the expectation that vigilant individuals construct a detailed schema of the expected encounter, especially with regard to its potentially harmful aspects, Hock, Krohne and Kaiser (1996) applied an ambiguous sentence task. They investigated whether vigilant persons would tend to interpret ambiguous event descriptions in a threatening fashion. Moreover, vigilant individuals are also expected to be better able to later remember their threat-related as opposed to their nonthreatening implications. By comparing reaction times to and unpleasantness ratings of the sentences, Hock et al. observed that vigilant individuals, especially sensitizers, often imposed threatening interpretations on ambiguous event descriptions. Moreover, vigilant persons more easily recognized threatening rather than nonthreatening variants of ambiguous stimuli as having been presented previously.

Both of these studies demonstrate that vigilance and avoidance are related to differences in the cognitive processing of threat-related stimuli. Avoidance seems to be associated with an impoverished representation of the stimulus material or situation and vigilance, with more elaborate processing of stimuli in ambiguous situations.

Applying the MBSS (Miller, 1987) and the MCI (Krohne et al., 1989), important findings regarding health-related behavior have also been documented. For health-related research applying the multiple variable approach introduced by Weinberger et al. (1979), see Schwartz (1990) for an overview and Jensen (1987) for an impressive study.

Miller, Brody, and Summerton (1988) studied patients visiting a primary care setting for acute medical problems. Monitors (i.e., high monitoring and low blunting scores) and blunters (i.e., low monitoring and high blunting scores) differed in the level of seriousness of their actual medical problem. Evaluations by physicians showed that monitors actually had less severe medical problems than blunters. Miller (1990) concluded that monitors may have a lower threshold of scanning for internal bodily cues. This would make them more inclined to detect new or changing physical symptoms (for studies on the role of vigilant and avoidant coping preferences in interoception, see Hodapp & Knoll, 1993; Kohlmann, 1993b). Recently, Kohlmann, Ring, Carroll, Mohiyeddini and Bennett (2001) found that individuals scoring high in cardiac vigilance appear not to be good detectors of their heartbeats. However, they are inclinced to attach importance to heart symptoms in real life, thus resulting in health-protecting behavior.

The Discrepancy Hypothesis

The discrepancy hypothesis is based on the idea formulated by Lazarus (1966) that the patterns of coping reactions on the subjective-affective, physiological-biochemical, and behavioral-expressive levels can be interpreted as indicators for the employment of intrapsychic coping behavior. The following quotations represent his central premise:

"The point is that we should not necessarily expect all classes of response to agree with each other. It is their combined pattern that yields the best information about the psychological processes we wish to understand. Thus, when a person says he does not feel anxious or disturbed but shows a marked physiological-stress reaction, we learn something different about the ongoing psychological processes (assuming physical demands have been ruled out) than if he reports marked anxiety along with concordant physiological responses. In the former instance, we might speak of social pressures or defensive efforts; in the latter, these are evidently not operating. The answer, therefore, is that no one of these classes of response must be considered *the* indicator of threat processes by itself. A more dependable and complete analysis can be accomplished using combinations of indicators and examining their patterning.... different ways of coping with threat are associated with different autonomic as well as behavioral patterns of reaction". (Lazarus, 1966, pp. 387-388, 390).

Although Lazarus argues that discrepancies are indicators of actual coping behavior (defensive efforts), the overwhelming majority of the studies on the discrepancy hypothesis do not directly analyze the relationship between actual coping behavior and patterns of subjective and objective stress reactions (for exceptions, see Houston & Hodges, 1970; Kohlmann, Singer & Krohne, 1989). Most of the studies follow a more indirect path. Proceeding from the assumption that coping dispositions determine actual coping behavior and that this behavior leads to certain reaction patterns, they primarily attempt to predict the pattern of stress reactions by using their knowledge of certain coping dispositions. Conventionally, discrepancies are computed by calculating reactivity scores (task value minus baseline value) for subjective and physiological variables. These reactivities are then transformed into z-scores and the difference between them is computed.

The first studies that were conducted in connection with the discrepancy hypothesis were derived from the one-dimensional operationalization of repression-sensitization.

The One-Dimensional Operationalization of Repression-Sensitization and the Discrepancy Hypothesis

The initial research impetus was provided by a study performed by Weinstein, Averill, Opton, and Lazarus (1968). Using a reanalysis of several empirical studies conducted by Lazarus' research group, the authors investigated the hypothesis that low anxiety is reported by repressors when they respond with comparatively high physiological arousal, while sensitizers report high anxiety despite exhibiting low physiological anxiety. For each of the dependent variables (i.e., mean heart rate, skin conductance, and verbal anxiety reports), z-scores were calculated and integrated into their respective activation indices. Individual discrepancy scores were then calculated by subtracting the activation indices (physiological minus subjective index). According to expectations, repressors verbally admitted less anxiety than they manifested physiologically while sensitizers reacted in the opposite manner (for a replication Otto & Bösel, 1978; for a further experimental study, see Scarpetti, 1973; for a clinical study, see Shipley, Butt, Horwitz & Farbry, 1978). Weinstein et al. (1968) explicitly point out, however, that the differences between the groups were found only for the verbal anxiety report. Repressors and sensitizers did not differ in heart rate or skin conductance.

Parsons, Fulgenzi, and Edelberg (1969) conduct a comparison of repressors, sensitizers, and an R-S middle group. In group discussions, repressors rated themselves as unaggressive and dominant (experiments 1 and 2) while an observer judged them as especially aggressive (experiment 1). In addition, repressors reacted with more frequent changes in skin conductance than the other two groups (experiment 2). The observed or genuine discrepancies between the self-description and the observer's description as well as the physiological activation supported the discrepancy hypothesis. However, contradictory results were reported, for example, in a study by Stein (1971), in which the R-S middle group reacted more strongly during sentence association tasks than the extreme groups. In a study by Boucsein and Frye (1974), repressors manifested stronger subjective than physiological reactions to criticism while sensitizers displayed the opposite reaction pattern. This effect is diametrically contradictory to the theoretical expectations.

Thayer (1971, experiment 2) determined the discrepancy score for the difference between physiological and subjective measures of activation changes and correlated the discrepancy measure with, among other factors, repression-sensitization. It is not surprising that no relationship was found, since only sleepiness, which is not anxiety related, was used as a negative subjective indicator of arousal.

Asendorpf, Wallbott and Scherer (1983) traced the equivocal and partly contradictory results especially to the variations in selecting extreme groups. The necessity of separating repressors from the truly low-anxious individuals was a major concern by Asendorpf et al. The comparison of R-S extreme groups with a middle group, whose status is unclear with regard to the preferred coping behavior (Chabot, 1973), is not conducive to solving this problem.

Multiple Variable Approaches and Person-Oriented Approaches and the Discrepancy Hypothesis

As previously described, the single variable approaches to repression-sensitization have been criticized because of their substantial overlap with anxiety tests. In contrast, multiple variable approaches or person oriented approaches have succeeded in overcoming this problem and have been instrumental in establishing more valid indicators of coping style. Empirical analyses of the discrepancy hypothesis based on the two-dimensional operationalization of coping styles mainly focus on the prediction of different reactions manifested by low-anxious individuals (i.e., low anxiety / low defensiveness) and repressors (i.e., low anxiety / high defensiveness).

Weinberger et al. (1979) introduced the designations repressor, low-anxious, high-anxious, and defensively high-anxious for the four coping groups differentiated on the basis of anxiety and defensiveness. In their investigation, however, they studied only three groups: repressors (i.e., anxiety < median; defensiveness > 75% ranking), low-anxious (i.e., anxiety < median; defensiveness < 75%), and moderately high-anxious individuals (i.e., anxiety > median, defensiveness < 75%). While free associating to sentences with neutral, sexual, and aggressive content, these three groups were compared using different parameters. Repressors reacted, in contrast to the low-anxious, with higher increases in heart rate and greater number of spontaneous changes in skin resistance and in frontal muscular tension, in reference to their respective baselines. Moreover, they manifested longer reaction times when confronted with aggressive and sexual content. In transcribed statements, higher indices for avoidance of the affective content in the presented sentences were registered for repressors. It is worth mentioning that the reaction times of the moderately high-anxious group lay between those for the low-anxious individuals and the repressors. They resembled repressors with regard to increases in heart rate, while their changes in skin resistance were similar to those of low-anxious individuals. Subjective stress reactions were not recorded. Information about subjective stress reactions were only available in the form of two applications of a shortened form of the MAS (Bendig, 1956), one 7 weeks before the investigation and the other immediately following it. While the moderately high-anxious participants reacted with an increase in anxiety, the low-anxious showed no changes and the repressors even showed a decrease in anxiety.

In the meantime, several studies have been conducted on the relationship between repressive coping and verbal-autonomic response dissociation. These studies, however, are quite heterogeneous in methodology. For example, different stressors have been applied (e.g. active vs. passive coping tasks) and different autonomic (skin conductance, heart rate, blood pressure, cortisol) and subjective variables have been recorded. Only few studies recorded more than one physiological variable (e.g. Asendorpf & Scherer, 1983; Barger, Kircher & Croyle, 1997; Houtveen, Rietveld, Schoutrop, Spiering & Brosschot, 2001, Rohrmann, Hennig & Netter, 2002). Moreover, some of the studies investigated differences in dissociation between low-anxious, high-anxious, repressors, and defensive high-anxious, whereas others focused exclusively on the comparison between repressors and the combined group of non-repressors. In the ensuing sections, we shall briefly review the results of these studies, under the headings of skin conductance and cardiovascular studies, respectively. At the end of the section we shall attempt to integrate these results and thereby provide a theoretical framework for the interpretation of discrepancy scores.

Skin Conductance Studies

Gudjonsson (1981) was the first and so far the only researcher who reversed the dependent and independent measures in research on coping and response dissociation. Instead of classifying subjects into each of the four coping groups by questionnaire, as the conventional multivariate approach suggests, he identified repressors and sensitizers by comparing their autonomic and subjective stress responses. Subjects were asked questions with neutral themes (e.g., "Are you wearing black shoes?") and lie-questions (e.g., "Have you ever lied?"), which had to be answered by "yes" or "no." For each question, the skin conductance responses (SCRs), the number of nonspecific skin conductance responses (NSSCRs), and the subjective arousal ratings were recorded and then summarized for all questions, without, however, being separated by theme. Distributions for SCRs, NSSCRs, and subjective arousal were divided at the median. It was then ascertained whether the subjective and objective data for a person lay in the same or the different half of the distribution. Individuals who were under the median for the subjective variable and above it for the objective variable were designated repressors. The group with the opposite configuration made up the sensitizers, while subjects with both the subjective and objective arousal above or below the median, respectively, were placed into a middle group. These three groups were compared in their scores on neuroticism, extraversion, and lie scale of the Eysenck Personality Inventory (EPI: Eysenck & Eysenck, 1964) as well as the SDS. Repressors manifested significantly lower neuroticism scores and higher lie and SDS scores than either of the other two groups.

Another skin conductance study was conducted by Barger et al.(1997). They classified repressors and non-repressors on the basis of anxiety and defensiveness questionnaires, in keeping with the traditional multivariate approach. Barger et al. were interested in examining the effects of social context on the relationship between repressive coping and verbal-autonomic response dissociation.

Therefore, a speech task was presented in either an anonymous (private instruction without a plugged camera) or a public context (social instruction and camera plugged on). Repressors were found to exhibit stronger electrodermal activation (as measured by NSSCRs) compared with the combined group of non-repressors. This result was obtained irrespective of context. Repressors' discrepancy scores, however, were not significantly different from zero. Furthermore, heart rate and negative affect did not discriminate between groups.

Two further studies recorded electrodermal activity and subjective arousal to passive stressors. Brosschot and Janssen (1998) observed higher tonic skin conductance compared with self-reported tenseness in repressors during emotional film clips. Participants continuously rated their perceived tenseness by means of a mechanical lever while their skin conductance level was being recorded. Repressors, defined on the basis of high scores on Marlowe and Crowne's social desirability scale and low scores on trait anxiety, showed significant negative associations between verbal and autonomic tenseness, indicative of dissociation between verbal and autonomic responses. Non-repressors, who were not broken down into more specific subgroups, showed only marginal associations between the two measures. Differences between coping groups were restricted to psychologically, as opposed to physically, threatening film clips. A recent study (Houtveen et al., 2001) presented affective pictures from the International Affective Picture System (IAPS; Lang, Bradley & Cuthbert, 1995) as stressors. In addition to skin conductance, heart rate and facial muscle activity (musculus zygomaticus, corrugator supercilii) were recorded. However, repressors did not differ significantly from non-repressors on any of the above variables, although subjective data indicated emotional involvement during the task. The authors interpreted their failure to find differences on the basis of the affective pictures not representing a threat to the self.

In summary, most skin conductance studies have revealed significant differences in verbal-autonomic response dissociation between repressors and non-repressors. Such effects, however, have been principally observed with self-threatening stressors.

Cardiovascular Studies

Several studies on verbal-autonomic response dissociation recorded cardiovascular variables, like heart rate or blood pressure in order to obtain an index of autonomic stress response.

Asendorpf and Scherer (1983) adopted the method introduced by Weinstein et al. (1979). In addition to the low-anxious and repressor groups, two additional groups determined by extreme scores on the MAS and SDS were taken into consideration: a high-anxious group, based on high MAS and low SDS scores, and a defensively high-anxious anxious group, based on high MAS and high SDS scores. Not only heart rate, but also finger pulse volume, and behavioral ratings of anxiety, based on facial expressions, were recorded. During a sentence association task with neutral, sexual or aggresive content, subjects with high MAS scores (i.e., high-anxious and defensively high-anxious) reported more anxiety than subjects with low MAS scores (i.e., low-anxious and repressors). With regard to the objective stress indicators (i.e., heart rate adjusted to a baseline, amplitude of the finger pulse volume, mimic anxiety), only the repressors, characterized by the conjunction of low MAS score and high SDS score, manifested higher responses than the low-anxious subjects, with low MAS and low SDS scores. The authors interpreted their result as pointing to dissociation between objective and subjective anxiety in repressors.

Newton and Contrada (1992) aimed at investigating the dependence of verbal-autonomic response dissociations on context. Therefore, they incorporated a speech task in either a social or a private condition. They instructed their subjects first to prepare and then to deliver a speech about their most undesirable trait, while either one person, in the private condition, or three people, in the public condition, watched via closed-circuit television. Blood pressure and heart rate were monitored during a baseline period, the 3-minute preparation, and the 3-minute speech. Heart rate elevations were greatest for repressors (i.e., low in anxiety and high in defensiveness) in the public condition during speech delivery. Significantly lower heart rate elevations were observed in the same subjects during speech preparation. Moreover, repressors showed a substantial discrepancy between their high autonomic activity and their low self-report of negative affect, but only while delivering a self-disclosing speech to three observers. Such a discrepancy was not in evidence while they self-disclosed to a single individual. High-anxious subjects, with high anxiety and low defensiveness, in both conditions showed a reverse discrepancy, i.e. their negative affect was stronger as compared to their heart rate, whereas low-anxious subjects, low both in anxiety and in defensiveness, did not exhibit such a a discrepancy. Newton and Contrada suggested that the repressive coping style may be activated by conditions likely to evoke social evaluative concerns.

Barger et al. (1997) were unable to replicate Newton and Contrada's results. They investigated differences in discrepancies between repressors and non-repressors in private and public contexts. Similar to the several investigators whose results were presented in the preceding section., they found significant differences between repressors and non-repressors in skin conductance throughout both contexts. However, no significant differences were observed in heart rate, either under the private or under the social condition. In interpreting this result one has to consider that the authors did not give an explicit evaluative instruction in their public condition. Accordingly, mean heart rate changes from baseline to speech delivery were quite moderate for the total sample (around 9 beats per minute). The omission of an evaluative instruction might have prevented repressors from showing stronger heart rate responses compared with non-repressors.

Similarly, Kohlmann, Weidner, and Messina (1996) did not report differences in verbal-cardiovascular response dissociation between repressive and non-repressive individuals. In contrast to the majority of the studies, they used a different measure of repressive coping. Instead of referring to specific coping dispositions rather indirectly as favored by the traditional multivariate approach, Kohlmann and colleagues applied the avoidant coping subscale of the MCI (Krohne, 1989), in line with the person-oriented approach. Avoidant coping is assumed to constitute a major dimension of repression (Krohne, 1989). Participants were instructed to imagine that they had applied for a job as television news announcers. As part of the interview, they had to present a difficult newspaper article. Kohlmann et al. found that high-avoiders exhibited higher systolic blood pressure increases throughout all experimental phases (preparation, delivery, and recovery[1]) compared with low-avoiders. Their self-reported anxiety,

---

[1] A resurgence of interest in cardiovascular recovery from stress has been observed (Linden, Gerin & Davidson, 2003). In addition to cardiovascular reactivity, sustained cardio-

however, did not differ significantly from non-avoiders, leading to a significant difference in discrepancies between high- and low-avoiders. Interestingly, the authors also recorded their subjects' estimated blood pressure reactivity in order to obtain an index of perceived autonomic arousal. No significant difference was found between high- and low-avoiders when this measure was entered as the verbal part of the verbal-autonomic response dissociation index. This result suggests that subjects with an avoidant coping disposition do not underestimate their perceived autonomic arousal; instead they probably underestimate their anxiety.

Derakshan and Eysenck (1997a) obtained measures of self-reported anxiety, other-rated anxiety, and heart rate, and interpretations of heart rate increases from their subjects during videotaped and public speech tasks, in front of an audience. Repressors showed diminished reactivity in self-reported anxiety compared with anxiety as rated by others. For high-anxious individuals the opposite pattern was found. Moreover, the low-anxious group exhibited significantly lower heart rate increases compared with the other groups. Repressors did not differ significantly from high-anxious and defensive high-anxious groups in heart rate. However, they did differ significantly from the other participants in their interpretations of heart rate reactivity. They agreed significantly less with the statements that their heart rate substantially increased during the speech task and that their heart rate increases were due to the stressful – threatening nature of their talk. In contrast, they endorsed more frequently than the other groups the statement that their heart rate increases were primarily due to their talk being exciting and challenging. These results favor the view that repressors have an opposite interpretive bias for their own behavior. In contrast to high-anxious individuals they underestimate how anxious their behavior is (for an overview of the cognitive perspective on repression see Derakshan & Eysenck, 1997b). In a recent study, Derakshan and Eysenck (2001) replicated their finding on differences in verbal-autonomic response dissociation between repressors and the other groups. Although repressors were again found not to differ from non-repressors in heart rate reactivity per se, they showed a pronounced verbal-autonomic response dissociation. Moreover, in a social-evaluative context they additionally exhibited higher behavioral anxiety compared with self-reported anxiety. For

---

vascular arousal and recovery patterns may be mediating variables in the process of acute stress leading to chronic maladaptation (Schwartz et al., 2003).

high-anxious individuals the opposite pattern was found; they dispayed higher subjective than behavioral anxiety.

In summary, several studies have found dissociations between subjective indicators of emotionality and cardiovascular responses between repressors and non-repressors (e.g. Asendorpf & Scherer, 1983; Derakshan & Eysenck, 1997a, 2001; Kohlmann et al., 1996; Newton & Contrada, 1992). It is noteworthy that all of these studies were conducted using beta-adrenergic stressors that were mostly applied in social-evaluative contexts. In some studies discrepancies were due to the elevated cardiovascular responsiveness in repressors (e.g. Kohlmann et al., 1996; Newton & Contrada, 1992), whereas other researchers found discrepancies to be mainly due to the underreporting of negative emotions in repressors (e.g. Derakshan & Eysenck, 1997a, 2001).[2]

Conclusions: What Do the Discrepancies Indicate?

In the foregoing sections we have reviewed several studies that report significant differences between repressors and non-repressors in discrepancies between subjective and autonomic stress responses. Some studies found significant effects for skin conductance while others found differences in cardiovascular variables.. Studies that recorded more than one autonomic variable are rare and have yielded inconsistent results (e.g. Barger et al., 1997).

Since the early work of Lazarus (1966) discrepancies have generally been interpreted in terms of divergent responses between the subjective and the objective components of anxiety in repressors (e.g. Asendorpf & Scherer, 1983; Derakshan & Eysenck, 1997a). It may be tempting to conclude that the research reviewed suggests increased levels of objective anxiety in repressors compared with their experience of subjective anxiety. Such an interpretation, however, would imply that both autonomic measures, skin conductance and cardiovascular variables, are indicators of the same construct of anxiety. Psychophysiological studies have

---

[2] According to Walschburger (1981), discrepancies should be affected by both attenuated negative emotionality *and* enhanced autonomic arousal. This is regarded necessary in order to obtain incremental information on the combined index compared with each measure alone. Otherwise the dissociation score merely represents the significant correlation between a personality measure and self-reported negative affect. Furthermore, Walshburger points out that repression should be accompanied by an enhanced consumption of energy as indicated by increased physiological responding.

thrown serious doubts on this assumption. Large-scale studies have shown that autonomic variables which refer to different physiological subsystems are only weakly interrelated and that they often respond differently to the same stressor. Fahrenberg and Foerster (1982) referred to this lack of correspondance in psychophysiological systems as the covariation problem (see also Fahrenberg, Walschburger, Foerster, Myrtek, & Müller, 1979).

Furthermore, autonomic variables are not only weakly interrelated, but they also respond differentially to a variety of motivational states and external task demands (Fowles, 1988). Therefore, caution is indicated in interpreting differences between repressors and non-repressors in various autonomic parameters as differences in objective anxiety. This recognition led Krohne (2003) to recommend that research on verbal-autonomic response dissociation should pay much more attention to the specific autonomic variable which is most likely to be influenced by the regulatory processes related to coping.

Barger et al. (1997) were the first to offer a theoretical framework for the selection of sensitive autonomic variables in repressive coping research. They refer to Gray's (1982, 1990, 1991) two-process theory of learning, which introduces three major motivational systems: the behavioral inhibition system (BIS), the behavioral approach or activation system (BAS), and the fight-flight system. The BIS is supposed to be a substrate of anxiety and is neurobiologically based on the septo-hippocampal system. It is considered to be sensitive to signals of punishment, nonreward, and novelty. The BAS, on the other hand, is located at dopaminergic regions (caudatus, putamen, medial forebrain bundle) and the nucleus accumbens. It is thought to trigger approach-oriented behavior and should be sensitive to reward and escape from punishment. Barger et al. argue that repressive copers inhibit their emotional responses (as indicated by attenuated self-reports of anxiety) and thus should be prone to heightened BIS-reactivity. In line with Fowles (1980, 1983, 1988) who proposed a relationship between skin conductance and the BIS, they favor the use of electrodermal measures in repressive coping research. Although the correspondance between electrodermal activity and BIS-activation has been challenged by some studies (Andresen, 1987; Naveteur & Roy, 1990; Pecchinenda & Smith, 1996), Fowles' approach continues to have heuristic value.

There are several studies that report differences between repressors and non-repressors in cardiovascular reactivity. According to Fowles (1988), heart rate is presumably not an indicator of anxiety but rather an indicator of an appetitive motivational state; thus, it should be concordant with BAS-reactivity. Therefore, heart rate or blood pressure should respond whenever signals for reward are registered and approach toward a situation or stimulus ensues. In line with this reasoning, several authors have linked cardiovascular reactivity to incentive conditions of the experimental situation or to the engagement / involvement by the subject (e.g. Gendolla & Kruesken, 2002; Smith, 1989; Smith, Nealey, Kircher & Limon, 1997; Tomaka, Blascovich, Kibler & Ernst, 1997; Tomaka & Palacios-Esquivel, 1997; Waldstein, Bachen & Manuck, 1997; Wright & Kirby, 2001). Moreover, a number of studies have related the mere presence of social-evaluative cues (e.g. an audience) to enhanced cardiovascular responsivity (Blascovich, Mendes, Hunter & Salomon, 1999; Wright, Killebrew & Pimpalapure, 2002; Wright & Kirby, 2001; Wright, Tunstall, Williams, Goodwin & Harmon-Jones, 1995). Again, audience may exert its influence via enhanced effort mobilization, which in turn should lead to stronger cardiac responses (Blascovich et al., 1999).

Correspondingly, those studies that report enhanced cardiovascular responsiveness of repressors compared with non-repressors might be interpreted in terms of stronger effort mobilization in repressors (cf. Kohlmann, 1997). This interpretation is substantiated by the methodology applied in these experiments. Indeed, all of these studies employed active coping tasks, typically in social-evaluative situations, for example, in front of a camera or of a significant other in combination with evaluative instructions. Observed in a private condition, repressors are less likely to differ from other individuals (e.g. Newton & Contrada, 1992). Following this line of reasoning, it appears that differences in cardiovascular reactivity between high and low repressive subjects may not be attributed to differences in objective anxiety, but rather to differences in motivational state when social-evaluative standards are salient. The enhanced behavioral activation in repressors might be triggered by their need to present themselves in a favorable light in front of significant others (e.g. Kohlmann, 1997; Newton, Haviland & Contrada, 1996). Accordingly, Schulz (1982) demonstrated that subjects who strive for social acceptance, in line with Crowne and Marlowe's original interpretation of SDS, invest an extremely high amount of time and energy in solving tasks. Correspondingly, they show greater increases in heart rate compared with subjects who do not acknowledge a striving for social acceptance. Similarly, Schwerdtfeger (2001) observed that subjects with high scores on a recently constructed social desirability scale (SDS-17R; Stoeber, 2001) exhibited enhanced heart rate responses to an evaluative speech task (relative to baseline and recovery period) compared with subjects scoring low on this questionnaire.

The relationship between task engagement and autonomic responding poses a challenge for the interpretation of dissociation scores when multiple variables are applied for the assessment of coping styles (MAS and SDS). Increased trait anxiety (MAS) may lead to reports of higher state anxiety, and increased social desirability (SDS) may lead to an intensified engagement which is accompanied by increased cardiovascular reactivity. From this perspective, it is possible to ely dispense completely with the R-S concept as an explanation of the discrepancies between subjective and objective indicators of arousal. Such discrepancies then are simply regarded as the manifestations of two main effects on two different classes of variables (cf. Kohlmann, 1990).

Taken together, cardiovascular variables may be more strongly affected by differences in task engagement than by anxiety. Skin conductance variables, on the other hand, may represent more valid indicators of negative emotionality. Recently, Schwerdtfeger (in press) experimented with a mental arithmetic task in private versus social contexts, i.e. with the experimenter present or absent. Subjects underwent both conditions consecutively. High cognitive avoiders compared with low avoiders (cf. Krohne et al., 2000) showed stronger increases in heart rate from the private to the social condition. Their skin conductance responses (NSSCRs), however, remained elevated throughout both conditions. This result demonstrates how different autonomic variables can be utilized in the same study within the framework of the BIS / BAS theory: While high avoiders presumably showed enhanced objective anxiety compared with low avoiders throughout both conditions, as indicated by skin conductance, their heart rate responses suggest that they were especially challenged by the social-evaluative task. It was our intention to show that differentially derived dissociation scores are not directly comparable across studies. Recorded in the same study, however, they have the potential of providing interesting insights. Obviously, more studies are needed that directly compare discrepancies derived from skin conductance and heart rate, respectively, in order to explore the leads we have proposed.

Verbal-Autonomic Response Dissociation and Health

Researchers have tried to identify links between verbal-autonomic response dissociations in repressors and negative health outcome. Health may be affected via two pathways: First, the discrepancy between emotional discomfort and autonomic responses to stress may deprive repressors of the emotional cues necessary to engage in preventive health behaviors, and thus may place them at an increased risk for disease (Kohlmann, 2003; Weidner & Collins, 1993; for a study on avoidant coping style and health behaviors, see Kohlmann, Weidner, Dotzauer & Burns, 1997). The second pathway involves a link between enhanced cardiovascular reactivity of repressors (e.g. Asendorpf & Scherer, 1983; Newton & Contrada, 1992; Kohlmann et al., 1996) and cardiovascular disease in later life. This formulation is closely linked with the so-called reactivity hypothesis.

Within the first pathway, repressors are postulated to display discrepancies between subjective and autonomic responses habitually, throughout different situations and with sufficient stability in order to influence health. However, there are nearly no studies available that demonstrate transsituational consistency or long term stability (retest reliability) of this measure. Bonanno, Keltner, Holen and Horowitz (1995) are so far the only investigators who have tested long–term stability of the discrepancy score. They conducted two stressful interviews on the same topic, described in detail in the following section, separated by 8 months. Discrepancies between heart rate and negative emotionality were recorded. A significant correlation was obtained between the discrepancies in the first and the second interview ($r = .63$ ($p < .001$; $n = 20$). Thus, there is some evidence for a moderate long-term stability of dissociation scores, at least for heart rate recordings. Furthermore, there is support for the expectation that repressors habitually attenuate the perception or impact of bodily symptoms. In line with this reasoning, Drinkman and Hauer (1995) could observe that silent ischemias, i.e.,ischemias without the angina pectoris pain, are most prominent among individuals with an repressive coping style. These data suggest that the attenuated perception of bodily symptoms may prevent repressors from seeking medical treatment or compliance for medical procedures, leading eventually to more severe illnesses.

The second pathway can influence health more directly. Enhanced cardiovascular stress responses have been identifed as a potential risk factor for later hypertension development or cardiovascular disorders, such as stroke or heart attack (Linden et al, 2003; Pickering & Gerin, 1990; Schwartz, Gerin, Davidson, Pickering, Brosschot, Thayer, Christenfeld & Linden, 2003). Although prospective studies suggest a rather small impact of cardiovascular reactivity by itself on hypertension development, elevated responses may constitute a potential risk for hypertension when combined with other risk factors (Light, 2001). Several studies that report elevated cardiovascular reactivity in repressors were presented earlier in the present chapter (Asendorpf & Scherer, 1983; Newton & Contrada, 1992; Kohlmann et al., 1996). Moreover, there is additional evidence for cardiovascular hyperreactivity to social-evaluative stress in repressors. Shedler, Mayman, and Manis (1993) tried to separate mentally healthy individuals from illusory mentally healthy individuals or repressors. In addition to self-reported mental health, they obtained ratings by others relevant to the adequacy of functioning and freedom from distress and disability. Subjects whose mental health ratings were high across both methods were identified as genuinely mentally healthy, whereas those subjects who reported mental health but were rated as non-healthy were classified as illusorily mentally healthy. Interestingly, the subjects with the discrepant pattern, i.e. repressors exhibited elevated cardiovascular responses throughout various active coping tasks compared with the subjects who were concordant on both kinds of indicators.

King, Taylor, Albright and Haskell (1990) presented a mental arithmetic task consisting of serial subtractions to four groups of subjects constituted on the basis of median splits on measures of anxiety and defensiveness. These groups were designated as repressors, low-anxious, moderately anxious, and defensive-moderately anxious. Data on blood pressure reactivity were collected. Subjects were informed of their wrong answers. King et al. reported stronger systolic blood pressure reactivity in repressors as compared with the other groups. Furthermore, repressors displayed higher resting systolic blood pressure than the other groups. This finding is especially significant. Unlike most studies on verbal-autonomic response dissociation, subjects in King et al.'s study were substantially older than the students who are usually recruited for research. In fact, the average age of King et al.'s subjects approximated 50 years. Nykli •ek, Vingerhoets, van Heck and Limpt (1998) also reported heightened systolic blood pressure levels of subjects who were around 47 years of age and were defensive / repressive copers. Similarly, a meta-analysis on personality and elevated blood pressure (Jorgensen, Johnson, Kolodziej & Schreer, 1996) identified a moderate effect size (d = .37) between defensiveness and systolic blood pressure. These studies provide substantial support for a relationship between repression and risk for cardiovascular diseases. Given the possibility that repressors or defensive individuals in all these studies also tended to underreport negative emotions, it can be speculated that enhanced baseline blood pressure levels are -at least partially-caused by verbal-autonomic response dissociations early in life.

Thus, there appears to be a good reason for expecting a significant negative impact of discrepancies on health. Contrary to this expectation, however, an impressive longitudinal study found evidence for a positive health outcome in individuals with stronger autonomic than subjective stress responses (Bonanno et al., 1995). Bonanno and colleagues investigated verbal and autonomic responses to a stressful narrative interview. Participants were conjugal bereaved individuals. The interview was conducted six months after the loss of the partner. The topics of the interview referred to the deceased person and to the most important person currently in the participant's life. Individuals whose heart rate was higher than their subjective responses to the interview were designated avoidant copers. They were found to display fewer grief symptoms eight months later than subjects with the opposite response pattern, i.e. whose subjective responses were higher than their heart rate. In a more recent follow-up at 25 months after loss, Bonanno, Znoj, Siddique and Horowitz (1999) noted and that a verbal-autonomic response dissociation was still significantly associated with a mild grief course and with no evidence of delayed grief. The authors conclude that avoidance of unpleasant emotions as indicated by verbal-autonomic response dissociation, is associated with better adaptation to conjugal bereavement. The n importance of this study lies in demonstrating that avoidant coping can be associated with better health outcome in the long run. This finding is consistent with the discussion of the relative efficacy of avoidant and nonavoidant coping strategies by Suls and Fletcher (1985). Obviously, more research is needed on this topic. It may be necessary to distinguish between cardiovascular health and other psychological and behavioral symptoms related to grief when evaluating possible health outcomes in repressive copers.

Concluding Remarks

The association of the repressive coping style with specific physiological responses to stress has received support in several studies. These findings can be generalized for avoidant coping preferences within Ruth and Cohen's (1986) broad theoretical framework as assessed by the R-S scale (Byrne, 1961), a combination of anxiety and defensiveness scores (e.g., Weinberger et al., 1979), and several coping inventories (e.g., Krohne et al., 2001; Miller, 1987). In future research regarding the prediction of discrepancies between subjective and physiological stress reactions, more attention should be paid to the physiological variables investigated and the context within which they are observed. Many of the studies in this field used different physiological indicators of arousal and the selection of those variables seemed to be mainly motivated by the availability of the measure rather than by more fundamental theoretical considerations. We have proposed a theoretical framework for interpreting dissociations derived from either cardiovascular or electrodermal measures by utilizing Gray's theory of behavioral inhibition / activation. Nonetheless, more work is needed to examine the mechanisms that are involved in the "etiology" of verbal-autonomic discrepancy scores. Therefore, we would strongly recommend recording additional behavioral indices of anxiety and task engagement in future studies and to relate them to autonomic responding. Such a course of action may – or may not – validate our interpretations.

References

Abbott, R. D. (1972). On confounding of the repression-sensitization and manifest anxiety scales. *Psychological Reports, 30,* 392-394.

Andresen, B. (1987). *Differentielle Psychophysiologie valenzkonträrer Aktivierungsdimensionen* [Differential psychophysiology of activation dimensions contrary to valence]. Frankfurt: Lang.

Angleitner, A. (1980). *Einführung in die Persönlichkeitspsychologie. Band 1: Nichtfaktorielle Ansätze* [Introduction to personality: Nonfactorial approaches]. Bern: Huber.

Asendorpf, J. B., & Scherer, K. R. (1983). The discrepant repressor: Differentiation between low anxiety, high anxiety, and repression of anxiety by autonomic- facial-verbal patterns of behavior. *Journal of Personality and Social Psychology, 45,* 1334-1346.

Asendorpf, J. B., Wallbott, H. G., & Scherer, K. R. (1983). Der verflixte Represser: Ein empirisch begründeter Vorschlag zu einer zweidimensionalen Operationalisierung von Repression-Sensitization [The confounded repressor: An empincally based suggestion for a two-dimensional operationalization of repression-sensitization]. *Zeitschrift für Differentielle und Diagnostische Psychologie,* 4, 113-128.

Barger, S. D., Kircher, J. C., & Croyle, R. T. (1997). The effects of social context and defensiveness on the physiological responses of repressive copers. *Journal of Personality and Social Psychology, 73,* 1118-1128.

Beck, A. T., & Clark, D. A. (1988). Anxiety and depression: An information processing perspective. *Anxiety Research, 1,* 23-36.

Bell, P. A., & Byrne, D. (1978). Repression-sensitization. In H. London & J. E. Exner (Eds.), *Dimensions of personality* (pp. *449-485).* New York: Wiley.

Bendig, A. W. (1956). The development of a short form of the Manifest Anxiety

Scale. *Journal of Consulting Psychology, 20,* 384.

Blascovich, J., Mendes, W. B., Hunter, S. B., & Salomon, K. (1999). Social "facilitation" as challenge and threat. *Journal of Personality and Social Psychology, 77,* 68-77.

Blum, G. S. (1955). Perceptual defense revisited. *Journal of Abnormal and Social Psychology, 51,* 24-29.

Bonanno, G. A., Keltner, D., Holen, A., & Horowitz, M. J. (1995). When avoiding unpleasant emotions might not be such a bad thing: Verbal-autonomic response dissociation and midlife conjugal bereavement. *Journal of Personality and Social Psychology, 69,* 975-989.

Bonanno, G. A., Znoj, H., Siddique, H. I., & Horowitz, M. J. (1999). Verbal-autonomic dissociation and adaptation to midlife conjugal loss: A follow-up at 25 months. *Cognitive Therapy and Research, 23,* 605-624.

Boucsein, W., & Frye, M. (1974). Physiologische und psychische Wirkungen von Mißerfolgsstress unter Berücksichtigung des Merkmals Repression-Sensitization [Physiological and psychological consequences of negative feedback with reference to the repression-sensitization dimension]. *Zeitschrift* für *experimentelle und angewandte Psychologie, 21,* 339-366.

Brosschot, J. F., & Janssen, E. (1998). Continuous monitoring of affective-autonomic response dissociation in repressors during negative emotional stimulation. *Personality and Individual Differences, 25,* 69-84.

Bruner, J. S. (1951). Personality dynamics and the process of perceiving. In R. R. Blake & G. V. Ramsey (Eds.), *Perception: An approach to personality* (pp. 121-147). New York: Ronald.

Bruner, J. S., & Postman, L. (1947). Emotional selectivity in perception and reaction. *Journal of Personality, 16,* 69-77.

Brunswik, E. (1947). *Systematic and representative design of psychological experiments: With results in physical and social perception.* Berkeley: University of California Press.

Budd, E. C., & Clopton, J. M. (1985). Meaning of the Repression-Sensitization scale: Defensive style or self-report of symptoms of psychopathology. *Journal of Clinical Psychology, 41,* 63-68.

Byrne, D. (1961). The Repression-Sensitization scale: Rationale, reliability, and validity. *Journal of Personalily, 29,* 334-349.

Byrne, D. (1964). Repression-sensitization as a dimension of personality. In B.A. Maher (Ed.), *Progress in experimental personality research: Vol. 1* (pp. 169-220). New York: Academic Press.

Byrne, D., Barry, J., & Nelson, D. (1963). Relation of the revised Repression-

Sensitization scale to measures of self-description. *Psychological Reports, 13,* 323-334.

Carver, C. S., & Scheier, M. F. (1988). A control-process perspective on anxiety. *Anxiety Research, 1,* 17-22.

Chabot, J. A. (1973). Repression-sensitization: A critique of some neglected variables in the literature. *Psychological Bulletin, 80,* 375-389.

Cook, J. (1985). Repression-sensitization and approach-avoidance as predictors of response to a laboratory stressor. *Journal of Personality and Social Psychology, 49,* 759-773.

Crowne, D. P., & Marlowe, D. (1960). A new scale of social desirability independent of psychopathology. *Journal of Consulting Psychology, 24,* 349-354.

Crowne, D., & Marlowe, D. (1964). *The approval motive.* New York: Wiley.

Davis, P. (1987). Repression and the inaccessibility of affective memories. *Journal of Personality and Social Psychology, 53,* 585-593.

Davis, P., & Schwartz, G. E. (1987). Repression and the inaccessibility of affective memories. *Journal of Personality and Social Psychology, 52,* 155-162.

Derakshan, N., & Eysenck, M. W. (2001). Effects of focus of attention on physiological, behavioral, and reported state anxiety in repressors, low-anxious, high-anxious, and defensive high-anxious individuals. *Anxiety, Stress, and Coping. An International Journal, 14,* 285-299.

Derakshan, N., & Eysenck, M. W. (1997a). Interpretive biases for one's one behavior and physiology in high-trait-anxious individuals and repressors. *Journal of Personality and Social Psychology, 73,* 816-825.

Derakshan, N., & Eysenck, M. W. (1997b). Repression and repressors: Theoretical and experimental approaches. *European Psychologist, 2,* 235-246.

Dixon, N. F. (1971). *Subliminal perception: The nature of a controversy.* London: McGraw-Hill.

Dixon, N. F. (1981). *Preconscious processing.* New York: Wiley.

Drinkman, A., & Hauer, K. (1995). Selbstaufmerksamkeit und Angstabwehr als Bedingungen der Schmerzverarbeitung bei koronar-bedingten Herzbeschwerden: Zum Problem der „stummen Ischämien“ [Self-awareness and repression-sensitization as factors influencing pain management in coronary heart disease. The case of silent ischemia]. *Zeitschrift für Gesundheitspsychologie, 3,* 24-38.

Edwards, A. L. (1957). *The social desirability variable in personality assessment and research.* New York: Dryden.

Egloff, B., & Krohne, H. W. (1998). Die Messung von Vigilanz und kognitiver Vermeidung: Untersuchungen mit dem Angstbewältigungs-Inventar (ABI).[Measurement of vigilance and cognitive avoidance: Investigatrions with the Anxiety Coping Inventory (ABI)] *Diagnostica, 44*, 189-200.

Egloff, B., & Krohne, H. W. (1996). Repressive emotional discreteness after failure. *Journal of Personality and Social Psychology, 70*, 1318-1326.

Endler, N. S., Hunt, J. McV., & Rosenstein, A. J. (1962). An S-R inventory of anxiousness. *Psychological Monographs, 76,* 17, whole no. 536.

Epstein, S., & Fenz, W. D. (1967). The detection of areas of emotional stress through variations in perceptual threshold and physiological arousal. *Journal of Experimental Research in Personality, 2,* 191-199.

Erdelyi, M. H. (1974). A new look at the New Look: Perceptual defense and vigilance. *Psychological Review, 81,* 1-25.

Erdelyi, M. H. (1990). Repression, reconstruction, and defense: History and integration of the psychoanalytical and experimental frameworks. In J. L. Singer (Ed.), *Repression and dissociation: Implications for personality theory, psychopathology, and health* (pp. 1-31). Chicago: University of Chicago Press.

Eriksen, C. W. (1951). Some implications for TAT interpretation arising from need and perception experiments. *Journal of Personality, 19*, 282-288.

Eysenck, H. J., & Eysenck, S. B. G. (1964). *Manual of the Eysenck Personality Inventory.* London: Hodder & Stoughton.

Eysenck, M. W. (1997). *Anxiety and cognition: A unified theory.* Hove, UK: Psychology Press.

Fahrenberg, J., & Foerster, F. (1982). Covariation and consistency of activation parameters. *Biological Psychology, 15*, 151-169.

Fahrenberg, J., Walschburger, P., Foerster, F., Myrtek, M., & Müller, W. (1979). *Psychophysiologische Aktivierungsforschung* [Psychophysiological research on activation]. München: Minerva.

Fowles, D. C. (1988). Psychophysiology and psychopathology: A motivational approach. *Psychophysiology, 25*, 373-391.

Fowles, D. C. (1983). Motivational effects on heart rate and electrodermal activity: Implications for research on personality and psychopathology. *Journal of Research in Personality, 17*, 48-71.

Fowles, D. C. (1980). The three arousal model: Implications of Gray's two-factor learning theory for heart rate, electrodermal activity, and psychopathy. *Psychophysiology, 17*, 87-104.

Frenkel-Brunswik, E. (1949). Intolerance of ambiguity as an emotional and perceptual personality variable. *Journal of Personality, 18,* 108-143.

Freud, A. (1936). *Das Ich und die Abwehrmechanismen* [Ego and the mechanisms of defense]. Vienna: Internationaler Psychoanalytischer Verlag.

Fröhlich, W. D. (1984). Microgenesis as a functional approach to information processing through search. In W. D. Fröhlich, G. Smith, J. G. Draguns & U. Hentschel (Eds.), *Psychological processes in cognition and personality* (pp. 19-52). Washington, DC: Hemisphere.

Gendolla, G. H. E., & Krüsken, J. (2002). The joint effect of informational mood impact and performance-contingent consequences on effort-related cardiovascular response. *Journal of Personality and Social Psychology, 83,* 271-283.

Goldiamond, I. (1958). Indicators of perception: 1. Subliminal perception, subception, unconscious perception: An analysis in terms of psychophysical indicator methodology. *Psychological Bulletin, 55,* 373-411.

Gordon, J. E. (1957). Interpersonal predictions of repressors and sensitizers. *Journal of Personality, 25,* 686-698.

Gray, J. A. (1982). *The neuropsychology of anxiety: An enquiry into the functions of the septo-hyppocampal system.* Oxford: Oxford University Press.

Gray, J. A. (1990). Brain systems that mediate both emotion and cognition. *Cognition and Emotion, 4,* 269-288.

Gray, J. A. (1991). The neuropsychology of temperament. In J. Strelau & A. Angleitner (Eds.), *Explorations in temperament: International perspectives on theory and measurement. Perspectives on individual differences* (pp. 105-128). New York: Plenum Press.

Gudjonsson, G. H. (1981). Self-reported emotional disturbance and its relation to electrodermal reactivity, defensiveness and trait anxiety. *Personality and Individual Differences, 2,* 47-52.

Haley, G. A. (1974). Eye movement responses of repressors and sensitizers to a stressful film. *Journal of Research in Personality, 8,* 88-94.

Halperin, J. M. (1986). Defensive style and direction of gaze. *Journal of Research in Personality, 20,* 327-337.

Hansen, R. D., & Hansen, C. H. (1988). Repression of emotionally tagged memories: The architecture of less complex emotions. *Journal of Personality and Social Psychology, 55,* 811-818.

Hentschel, U., & Smith, G. (Eds.) (1980). *Experimentelle Persönlichkeitspsychologie: Die Wahrnehmung als Zugang zu diagnostischen Problemen*

[Experimental personality psychology: Perception as a tool for diagnostic problems]. Wiesbaden: Akademische Verlagsgesellschaft.

Hill, K. T. (1971). Anxiety in the evaluative context. *Young Children, 27,* 97-118.

Hill, K. T., & Sarason, S. B. (1966). The relation of test anxiety and defensiveness to test and school performance over the elementary school years: A further longitudinal study. *Monographs of the Society for Research in Child Development, 31* (2, serial no. 104).

Hock, M., Krohne, H. W., & Kaiser, J. (1996). Coping dispositions and the processing of ambiguous stimuli. *Journal of Personality and Social Psychology, 70,* 1052-1066.

Hodapp, V., & Knoll, J. F. (1993). Heartbeat perception, coping, and emotion. In H.W. Krohne (Ed.), *Attention and avoidance: Strategies in coping with aversiveness* (pp. 191-211). Seattle: Hogrefe & Huber.

Holmes, D. S. (1974). Investigation of repression: Differential recall of material experimentally or naturally associated with ego threat. *Psychological Bulletin, 81,* 632-653.

Holmes, D. S. (1990). The evidence for repression: An examination of sixty years of research. In J. L. Singer (Ed.), *Repression and dissociation: Implications for personality theory, psychopathology, and health* (pp. 85-102). Chicago: University of Chicago Press.

Holroyd, K. (1972). Repression-sensitization, Marlowe-Crowne defensiveness, and perceptual defense. *Proceedings of the 80th Annual Convention of the American Psychological Association, 7,* 401-402.

Houston, B. K., & Hodges, W. F. (1970). Situational denial and performance under stress. *Journal of Personality and Social Psychology, 16,* 726-730.

Houtveen, J. H., Rietveld, S., Schoutrop, M., Spiering, M., & Brosschot, J. F. (2001). A repressive coping style and affective, facial and physiological responses to looking at emotional pictures. *International Journal of Psychophysiology, 42,* 265-277.

Jorgensen, R. S., Johnson, B. T., Kolodziej, M. E., & Schreer, G. E. (1996). Elevated blood pressure and personality: A meta-analytic review. *Psychologcal Bulletin, 120,* 293-320.

Jung, C. G. (Ed.) (1906/1909). *Diagnostische Assoziationsstudien. Beiträge zur experimentellen Psychopathologie* (2 vols.) [Diagnostic studies on association: Contributions to experimental psychopathology]. Leipzig: Barth.

Jensen, M. R. (1987). Psychobiological factors predicting the course of breast cancer. *Journal of Personality, 55,* 317-342.

King, A. C., Taylor, C. B., Albright, C. A., & Haskell, W. L. (1990). The relationship between repressive and defensive coping styles and blood pressure responses in healthy, middle-aged men and women. *Journal of Psychosomatic Research, 34,* 461-471.

Klein, G. S., & Schlesinger, H. J. (1949). Where is the perceiver in perceptual theory? *Journal of Personality, 18,* 32-47.

Kogan, N., & Wallach, M. A. (1964). *Risk taking: A study in cognition and personality.* New York: Holt, Rinehart and Winston.

Kohlmann, C.-W. (1990). *Streßbewältigung und Persönlichkeit* [Personality and coping with stress]. Bern: Huber.

Kohlmann, C.-W. (1993a). Rigid and flexible modes of coping: Related to coping style? *Anxiety, Stress, and Coping, 6,* 107-123.

Kohlmann, C.-W. (1993b). Strategies in blood pressure estimation: The role of vigilance, cognitive avoidance, and gender. In H. W. Krohne (Ed.), *Attention and avoidance: Strategies in coping with aversiveness* (pp. 213-238). Seattle: Hogrefe & Huber.

Kohlmann, C.-W. (1997). *Persönlichkeit und Emotionsregulation. Defensive Bewältigung von Angst und Stress [Personality and the regulation of emotions: Defensive coping with anxiety and stress].* Göttingen: Huber.

Kohlmann, C.-W. (2003). Gesundheitsrelevante Persönlichkeitsmerkmale [Health-related personality variables]. In M. Jerusalem & H. Weber (Eds.), *Psychologische Gesundheitsförderung: Diagnostik und Prävention* (pp. 39-55). Göttingen: Hogrefe.

Kohlmann, C.-W., Ring, C., Carroll, D., Mohiyeddini, C., & Bennett, P. (2001). Cardiac coping style, heartbeat detection, and the interpretation of cardiac events. *British Journal of Health Psychology, 6,* 285-301.

Kohlmann, C.-W., Singer, P., & Krohne, H. W. (1989). Coping dispositions, actual coping, and the discrepancy between subjective and physiological stress reactions. In P. Lovibond & P. Wilson (Eds.), *Clinical and abnormal psychology* (pp. 67-78). Amsterdam: North-Holland.

Kohlmann, C.-W., Weidner, G., & Messina, C. (1996). Avoidant coping style and verbal-cardiovascular response dissociation. *Psychology and Health, 11,* 371-384.

Kohlmann, C.-W., Weidner, G., Dotzauer, G., & Burns, L. R. (1997). Gender differences in health behaviors: The role of avoidant coping. *European Review of Applied Psychology, 47,* 115-120.

Krohne, H. W. (1974). Untersuchungen mit einer deutschen Form der Repression-Sensitization-Skala [Investigations of a German version of the Repression-Sensitization scale]. *Zeitschrift für Klinische Psychologie, 3,* 238-260.

Krohne, H. W. (1978). Individual differences in coping with stress and anxiety. In C. D. Spielberger & I. G. Sarason (Eds.), *Stress and anxiety: Vol. 5* (pp. 233-260). Washington, DC: Hemisphere.

Krohne, H. W. (1986). Coping with stress: Dispositions, strategies, and the problem of measurement. In M. H. Appley & R. Trumbull (Eds.), *Dynamics of stress* (pp. 209-234). New York: Plenum.

Krohne, H. W. (1989). The concept of coping modes: Relating cognitive person variables to actual coping behavior. *Advances in Behavior Research and Therapy, 11,* 235-248.

Krohne, H. W. (1996). Repression-Sensitization [Repression-sensitization]. In M. Amelang (Ed.), *Enzyklopädie der Psychologie. Serie Differentielle Psychologie und Persönlichkeitsforschung: Band 3. Temperaments- und Persönlichkeitsunterschiede* (pp. 153-184). Göttingen: Hogrefe.

Krohne, H. W. (2003). Individual differences in emotional reactions and coping. In R. J. Davidson, K. R. Scherer & H. H. Goldsmith (Eds.), *Handbook of affective sciences* (pp. 698-725). New York: Oxford University Press.

Krohne, H. W., Egloff, B., Varner, L. J., Burns, L. R., Weidner, G., & Ellis, H. C. (2000). The assessment of dispositional vigilance and cognitive avoidance: Factorial structure, psychometric properties, and validity of the Mainz Coping Inventory. *Cognitive Therapy and Research, 24,* 297-311.

Krohne, H. W., & Fuchs, J. (1991). The influence of coping dispositions and danger-related information on emotional and coping reactions of individuals anticipating an aversive event. In C. D. Spielberger, I. G. Sarason, J. Strelau & J. M. T. Brebner (Eds.), *Stress and anxiety: Vol. 13* (pp. 131-155). Washington, DC: Hemisphere.

Krohne, H. W., & Rogner, J. (1982). Repression-sensitization as a central construct in coping research. In H. W. Krohne & L. Laux (Eds.), *Achievement, stress, and anxiety* (pp. 167-193). Washington, DC: Hemisphere.

Krohne, H. W., & Rogner, J. (1985). Mehrvariablen-Diagnostik in der Bewältigungsforschung [Multivariable diagnosis in coping research]. In H. W. Krohne (Ed.), *Angstbewältigung in Leistungssituationen* (pp. 45-62). Weinheim: Edition Psychologie.

Krohne, H. W., Rösch, W., & Kürsten, F. (1989). Die Erfassung von Angstbewältigung in physisch bedrohlichen Situationen [The assessment of coping in physical threat situations]. *Zeitschrift für Klinische Psychologie, 18,* 230-242.

Lang, P. J., Bradley, M. M., & Cuthbert, B. N. (1995). *International Affective Picture System (IAPS): Technical manual and affective ratings.* The Center for Research in Psychophysiology, University of Florida, Gainesville, FL.

Laux, L., & Glanzmann, P. (1987). A self-presentational view of test anxiety. In R. Schwarzer, H. M. van der Ploeg & C. D. Spielberger (Eds.), *Advances in test anxiety research: Vol. 5* (pp. 31-37). Lisse, Netherlands: Swets & Zeitlinger.

Lazarus, R. S. (1966). *Psychological stress and the coping process.* New York: McGraw-Hill.

Lazarus, R. S., Eriksen, C. W., & Fonda, C. P. (1951). Personality dynamics and auditory perceptual recognition. *Journal of Personality, 19,* 471-482.

Lefcourt, H. M. (1966). Repression-sensitization: A measure of the evaluation of emotional expression. *Journal of Consulting Psychology, 30,* 444-449.

Lefcourt, H. M. (1969). Need for approval and threatened negative evaluation as detenninants of expressiveness in a projective test. *Journal of Consulting and Clinical Psychology, 33,* 96-102.

Linden, W., Gerin, W., & Davidson, K. (2003). Cardiovascular reactivity: Status quo and a research agenda for the new millennium. *Psychosomatic Medicine, 65*, 5-8.

Light, K. (2001). Hypertension and the reactivity hypothesis: The next generation. *Psychosomatic Medicine, 63*, 744-746.

Mendolia, M. (2002). An index of self-regulation of emotion and the study of repression in social contexts that threaten or do not threaten self-concept. *Emotion, 2*, 215-232.

Miller, S. M. (1981). Predictability and human stress: Toward a clarification of evidence and theory. In L. Berkowitz (Ed.), *Advances in experimental social psychology: Vol. 14* (pp. 203-256). New York: Academic Press.

Miller, S. M. (1987). Monitoring and blunting: Validation of a questionnaire to assess styles of information seeking under threat. *Journal of Personality and Social Psychology, 52,* 345-353.

Miller, S. M. (1990). To see or not to see: Cognitive informational styles in the coping process. In M. Rosenbaum (Ed.), *Learned resourcefulness: On coping skills, self-regulation, and adaptive behavior* (pp. 95-126). New York: Springer.

Miller, S. M., Brody, D. S., & Summerton, J. (1988). Styles of coping with threat: Implications for health. *Journal of Personality and Social Psychology, 54,* 142- 148.

Mischel, W. (1984). Convergences and challenges in the search for consistency. *American Psychologist, 39,* 351-364.

Naveteur, J., & Roy, J.-C. (1990). Electrodermal activity of low and high trait anxiety subjects during a frustrative video game. *Journal of Psychophysiology, 4,* 221-227.

Newton, T. L., & Contrada, R. J. (1992). Repressive coping and verbal-autonomic response dissociation: The influence of social context. *Journal of Personality and Social Psychology, 62,* 159-167.

Newton, T. L., Haviland, J. M., & Contrada, R. J. (1996). The face of repressive coping: Social context and the display of hostile expressions and social smiles. *Journal of Nonverbal Behavior, 20,* 3-22.

Nykli •ek, I., Vingerhoets, A. J. J. M., & van Heck, G. L. (1998). The under-reporting tendency of hypertensives: An analysis of potential psychological and physiological mechanisms. *Psychology and Health, 13,* 1-21.

Otto, J., & Bösel, R. (1978). Angstverarbeitung und die Diskrepanz zwischen Selfreport und physiologischem Streßindikator: Eine gelungene Replikation der Weinstein-Analyse [Coping with anxiety and the discrepancy between subjective and physiological stress reactions: A positive replication of the Weinstein analysis]. *Schweizerische Zeitschrift für Psychologie, 37,* 321-330.

Parsons, O. A., Fulgenzi, L. B., & Edelberg, R. (1969). Aggressiveness and psychophysiological responsivity in groups of repressors and sensitizers. *Journal of Personality and Social Psychology, 12,* 235-244.

Pecchinenda, A., & Smith, C. A. (1996). The affective significance of skin conductance activity during a difficult problem-solving task. *Cognition and Emotion, 10,* 481-503.

Pickering, T. G., & Gerin, W. (1990). Cardiovascular reactivity in the laboratory and the role of behavioral factors in hypertension: A critical review. *Annals of Behavioral Medicine, 12,* 3-16.

Rohrmann, S., Hennig, J., & Netter, P. (2002). Manipulation of physiological and emotional responses to stress in repressors and sensitizers. *Psychology and Health, 17,* 583-596.

Roth, S., & Cohen, L. J. (1986). Approach, avoidance, and coping with stress. *American Psychologist, 41,* 813-819.

Rothbart, M., & Mellinger, M. (1972). Attention and responsivity to remote dangers: A laboratory simulation for assessing reactions to threatening events. *Journal of Personality und Social Psychology, 24,* 132-142.

Scarpetti, W. (1973). The repression-sensitization dimension in relation to impending painful stimulation. *Journal of Consulting und Clinical Psychology, 40,* 377-382.

Schroeder, D. H., & Costa, P. T. (1984). Influence of life event stress on physical illness: Substantive effects or methodological flaws? *Journal of Personality and Social Psychology, 46,* 853-863.

Schulz, P. (1982). Person-Unwelt-Interaktion und Streß [Person-environment interaction and stress]. In H. W. Hoefert (Ed.), *Person und Situation* (pp. 44-66). Göttingen: Hogrefe.

Schumacher, A. (1990). Die "Miller Behavioral Style Scale" (MBSS): Erste Überprüfung einer deutschen Fassung [The "Miller Behavioral Style Scale": First investigation of a German adaptation]. *Zeitschrift für Differentielle und Diagnostische Psychologie, 11,* 243-250.

Schwartz, A. R., Gerin, W., Davidson, K. W., Pickering, T. G., Brosschot, J. F., Thayer, J. F., Christenfeld, N., & Linden, W. (2003). Toward a causal model of cardiovascular responses to stress and the development of cardiovascular disease. *Psychosomatic Medicine, 65,* 22-35.

Schwartz, G. E. (1990). Psychobiology of repression and health: A Systems approach. In J. L. Singer (Ed.), *Repression und dissociation: Implications for personality theory, psychopathology, and health* (pp. 405-434). Chicago: University of Chicago Press.

Schwerdtfeger, A. (in press). Effects of social context on psychophysiological indicators of behavioral inhibition / activation in cognitive avoiders. *Journal of Psychophysiology* (Abstract).

Schwerdtfeger, A. (2001). Zum Einfluß von Fremdtäuschung und vermeidendem Bewältigungsstil auf die verbal-kardiovaskuläre Reaktionsdissoziation. [Impression management, defensive coping and verbal-cardiovascular response dissociation]. In B. B. Seiwald, J. Guthke, H. Petermann, J. F. Beckmann, M. Roth (Hrsg.). *6. Arbeitstagung der Fachgruppe für Differentielle Psychologie, Persönlichkeitspsychologie und Psychologische Diagnostik der Deutschen Gesellschaft für Psychologie* (p. 138). Leipzig: Leipziger Universitätsverlag GmbH.

Shedler, J., Mayman, M., & Manis, M. (1993). The illusion of mental health. *American Psychologist, 48,* 1117-1131.

Shevrin, H. (1990). Subliminal perception and repression. In J. L. Singer (Ed.), *Repression and dissociation: Implications for personality theory, psycho pathology, und health* (pp. 103-119). Chicago: University of Chicago Press.

Shipley, R. H., Butt, J. H., Horwitz, B., & Farbry, J. E. (1978). Preparation for a stressful medical procedure: Effect of amount of stimulus preexposure and coping style. *Journal of Consulting und Clinical Psychology, 46,* 499-507.

Singer, J. L. (Ed.) (1990). *Repression und dissociation: Implications for personality theory, psychopathology, and health.* Chicago: University of Chicago Press.

Smith, C. A. (1989). Dimensions of appraisal and physiological response in emotion. *Journal of Personality and Social Psychology, 56*, 339-353.

Smith, T. W., Nealey, J. B., Kircher, J. C., & Limon, J. P. (1997). Social determinants of cardiovascular reactivity: Effects of incentive to exert influence and evaluative threat. *Psychophysiology, 34*, 65-73.

Stein, S. H. (1971). Arousal level in repressors and sensitizers as a function of response context. *Journal of Consulting und Clinical Psychology, 36,* 386-394.

Stoeber, J. (2001). The Social Desirability Scale-17 (SDS-17): Convergent validity, discriminant validity, and relationship with age. *European Journal of Psychological Assessment, 17*, 222-232.

Suls, J., & Fletcher, B. (1985). The relative efficacy of avoidant and nonavoidant coping stratgies: A meta-analysis. *Health Psychology, 4*, 249-288.

Taylor, J. A. (1953). A personality scale of manifest anxiety. *Journal ofAbnormal und Social Psychology, 48,* 285-290.

Thayer, R. E. (1971). Personality and discrepancies between verbal reports and physiological measures of private emotional experiences. *Journal of Personality, 39,* 57-69.

Tomaka, J., Blascovich, J., Kibler, J., & Ernst, J. M. (1997). Cognitive and physiological antecedents of threat and challenge appraisal. *Journal of Personality and Social Psychology, 73*, 63-72.

Tomaka, J., & Palacios-Esquivel, R. L. (1997). Motivational systems and stress-related cardiovascular reactivity. *Motivation and Emotion, 21*, 275-296.

Tremayne, P., & Barry, R. J. (1988). An application of psychophysiology in sports psychology: Heart rate responses to relevant and irrelevant stimuli as a function of anxiety and defensiveness in elite gymnasts. *International Journal of Psychophysiology, 6,* 1-8.

Tucker, I. F. (1970). *Adjustment: Models and mechanisms.* New York: Academic Press.

Waldstein, S. R., Bachen, E. A., & Manuck, S. B. (1997). Active coping and cardiovascular reactivity: A multiplicity of influences. *Psychosomatic Medicine, 59*, 620-625.

Walschburger, P. (1981). Die Diskrepanz zwischen subjektiven und physiologischen Belastungsreaktionen: Ein informativer Indikator des individuellen Bewältigungsstils? [The discrepancy between subjective and physiological stress responses: An informative indicator of habitual coping style?] *Schweizerische Zeitschrift für Psychologie, 40*, 55-67.

Watson, D., & Clark, L. A. (1984). Negative affectivity: The disposition to experience aversive emotional states. *Psychological Bulletin, 96,* 465-490.

Watson, D., & Pennebaker, J. W. (1989). Health complaints, stress, and distress: Exploring the central role of negative affectivity. *Psychological Review, 96,* 234-254.

Weidner, G., & Collins, R. L. (1993). Gender, coping, and health. In H. W. Krohne (Ed.), *Attention and avoidance: Strategies in coping with aversiveness* (pp. 241-265). Seattle: Hogrefe & Huber.

Weinberger, D. A. (1990). The construct validity of the repressive coping style. In J. L. Singer (Ed.), *Repression und dissociation: Implications for personality theory, psychopathology, and health* (pp. 337-386). Chicago: University of Chicago Press.

Weinberger, D. A., & Schwartz, G. E. (1990). Distress and restraint as superordinate dimensions of self-reported adjustment: A typological perspective. *Journal of Personality, 58,* 381-417.

Weinberger, D. A., Schwartz, G. E., & Davidson, R. J. (1979). Low-anxious, high-anxious, and repressive coping-styles: Psychometric patterns and behavioral and physiological responses to stress. *Journal of Abnormal Psychology, 88,* 369-380.

Weinstein, J., Averill, J. R., Opton, E. M., & Lazarus, R. S. (1968). Defensive style and discrepancy between self-report and physiological indexes of stress. *Journal of Personality und Social Psychology, 10,* 406-413.

Wieland-Eckelmann, R., & Bösel, R. (1987). Konstruktion eines Verfahrens zur Erfassung von dispositionellen Angstbewältigungsstilen im Leistungsbereich [Development of a procedure for the assessment of coping-styles in achievement situations]. *Zeitschrift für Differentielle und Diagnostische Psychologie, 8,* 39-56.

Wright, R. A., Killebrew, K., & Pimpalapure, D. (2002). Cardiovascular incentive effects where a challenge is unfixed: Demonstrations involving social evaluation, evaluator status, and monetary reward. *Psychophysiology, 39*, 188-197.

Wright, R. A., & Kirby, L. D. (2001). Effort determination of cardiovascular response: An integrative analysis with applications in social psychology. In M. P. Zanna (Ed.), *Advances in experimental social psychology* (Vol. 33, pp. 255-307). New York: Academic Press.

Wright, R. A., Tunstall, A. M., Williams, B. J., Goodwin, J. S., & Harmon-Jones, E. (1995). Social evaluation and cardiovascular response: An active coping approach. *Journal of Personality and Social Psychology, 69*, 530-543.

Defense Mechanisms
U. Hentschel, G. Smith, J.G. Draguns & W. Ehlers (Editors)

Chapter 12

Perceptual and Emotional Aspects of Psychophysiological Individuality

Fernando Lolas

Most theories of personality and temperament include statements about spontaneous and elicited behavior. We may refer to them as activity and reactivity statements, respectively. Personality theories are abstracted systems of dispositional traits that predict behavior on a qualitative or quantitative basis. The type of prediction and the nature of the data base vary across theories. Some do not include statements regarding physiological indicators while others neglect social factors.

A psychophysiological theory considers from its inception data about observable behavior, subjective experience, and physiological reactions (Lolas, 1996). A trait is defined not only on the basis of its persistence over time but also on the basis of concordance of the three types of responses (Lolas, 1996). However, the inclusion of information of these different types does not imply that they are isomorphic or redundant. The "psychophysiological triad" is an expression of the methodological pluralism needed in behavioral science, not a prediction for a correlation matrix. A basic tenet underlying our research is that homeostatic regulation can be achieved either physiologically (short loop regulation, internal homeostasis) or behaviorally (long loop regulation, external homeostasis). Thus, a comprehensive homeostatic formulation posits that each person possesses a distinctive style of homeostatic awareness and concomitant behavior. Psychophysiological stability is then achieved by the joint action of defense mechanisms and cognitive styles

Classic Notions of Augmenting/Reducing

The notion that individuals respond differently to stimulation and emotion goes back at least to the humoral theories of temperament and constitutes the basis of theories proposed by writers as diverse as Pavlov, Freud, and Sherrington. In a modern version of the theory, known as stimulus intensity modulation theory, three assumptions are made. The first is that individuals differ from each other in the magnitude of their response to sensory stimulation. "Reducers" and "augmenters" differ both in the level of preferred stimulation and in overt behavioral manifestations. The second assumption is that there is some optimal level of internal or endogenous stimulation (or arousal) that is pleasurable and is sought out. The third assumption, not explicitly stated by all the authors, is that the level of stimulation perceived as optimal tends to be similar across individuals. This is a point that deserves emphasis, since it defines the personality characteristic not by differences in subjective perception but by differences in the amount of objective stimulation necessary to achieve and maintain a certain level of functioning.

Conceptualizations of the Activity/Reactivity Typology

Although classical work on the augmenter/reducer typology emphasized perceptual reactivity, it is obvious that the underlying construct need not be restricted to perception and cognition and can encompass emotional and motivational aspects as well (Larsen & Zarate, 1991). It is in these latter aspects that augmenting/reducing overlaps with the psychodynamic concept of defense. The system for stimulus modulation or regulation is assumed to be programmed and reprogrammed throughout life. The idea here is that the program is read out recursively: Genetic factors determine certain forms of behavior that influence the environment, which in turn poses certain demands. It cannot be ascertained whether a given outcome is cause or effect, or antecedent or consequent, unless context, time, and developmental factors are taken into account.

Dating back to humoral theory, statements regarding spontaneous and reactive behavior have referred to *quality* and *intensity*. While psychodynamic theories base predictions on the quality of behavior or affect that is predominant or can be aroused by environmental demands, most physiological theories emphasize intensity and explain diversity on the basis of quantitative differentiation along the continua of physiological activation. Intensity regulation can be effected by both internal and external mechanisms. In relation to behavior, writers as diverse as Pavlov, Sherrington, and Freud suggested mechanisms for controlling overstimulation: transmarginal inhibition, stimulus barrier, and central inhibitory state (see Silverman, 1972; Lolas, 1998). The Freudian notion of complementary series, referring to intensity aspects of organism-environment transactions, is a forerunner to later stress theories (von Knorring, Jacobsson, Perris, & Perris, 1980). The pioneering work of Petrie (1960) kindled an interest in the biological foundations of individual differences that later developed into a growing body of research on the augmenting/reducing construct. The original studies were based on the Kinesthetic Figural Aftereffect (KFA). In one of its forms of application, this procedure is based on the subjective judgment of the width of a bar before and after kinesthetic stimulation. Subjects who judge the magnitude of the stimulus as larger after a distracting stimulus are termed augmenters; reducers judge the standard as markedly reduced following distraction. In ensuing years, questions were posed about the relationship of this categorization to established psychometric knowledge regarding the validity and reliability of this procedure. KFA is a complex task involving joint spatial and tactile stimulation that may be influenced by dexterity, experience, and sequence effects, Like other difference measures, it shows poor test-retest reliability. This state of affairs has led researchers to search for alternative ways of evaluating augmenting/reducing (A/R). Brain electrical potentials evoked by sensory stimulation constitute the second most important source of data regarding the A/R construct (see Buchsbaum, Haier, & Johnson, 1983). In this procedure, a subject is termed an augmenter if the slope of the amplitude-intensity function is positive, that is, greater than zero, and a person is considered a reducer if a paradoxical reduction in amplitude ensues with increased stimulation intensity or if comparatively, slopes are lower for a given group of subjects. It should be noted that what is measured with this procedure is not a behavioral aftereffect but response to stimulation.

In clinical or research applications, an important issue is measurement. Recently, Beaudurcel, Debener, Brocke, and Kayser (2000) have addressed The long neglected issue of reliability of A/R measures, specifically in reference to auditory stimulation. Beaudurcel et al. have determined that a minimum of five to six intensity levels are necessary for reliable measures to be obtained The augmenting/reducing construct is a descriptive label that can be applied to behavioral or physiological data. It may overlap with other descriptive labels, such as strength of the nervous system, extraversion-introversion, repression-sensitization, and defense style, and it shows differences depending on the assessment procedure. Findings by Brocke, Beaudurcel, John, Debener, and Heilemann (2000), Schwerdtfeger and Baltissen (2002), and Zuckerman and Kuhlman (2000) converge in substantiating a positive relationship between sensation seeking and reducing. Generally, sensation seeking has emerged as one of the more predictable correlates of A/R. Moreover, Zuckerman and Kuhlman have succeeded in identifying several potentially useful biological markers for A/R. In relation to drug abuse, Compton (2000) ventured the prediction that perceptual reducers would prefer mind expanding drugs, exemplified by cocaine and amphetamines, while augmenters would opt for sensory restricting drugs, such as opioids and sedative hypnotics. These predictions were confirmed, but only for the subgroup of participants high in electrodermal reactivity.

Regarding the nature of the underlying process, augmenting and reducing may constitute a characteristic feature across all sensory systems, as a general property of the central nervous system. On the other hand, predictions may be valid only within a given sensory modality (Lolas, Collin, Camposano, Etcheberrigaray, & Rees 1989). One may hypothesize, for example, that auditory augmenters need not be visual augmenters and that a further differentiation in terms of the preferred modality for augmenting or reducing would introduce a more specific, individual factor (Lolas, 1987). Lolas, Camposano, & Etcheberrigaray (1989) explored differences in perceptual predispositions, as posited by personality theorists. They proceeded from the expectation that not all people employ identical perceptual defenses in regulation within a specific modality. A/R as a general property of the CNS may be differently expressed depending on the modality and the recording site. This stipulation does not necessarily contradict A/R being construed as a nonspecific mode of reactivity. Instead, more specific perceptual reactivities for each sensory or motivational system are envisaged. Defense systems may vary across sensory contexts. "Sensoriostasis," an appropriate name for sensory and informational homeostasis, is expected not only to interact with bodily homeostasis but also provide clues to physiological dysfunction and its symptomatic expression (Lolas, 1991). In this regard, the search for appropriate markers of central nervous system activity and reactivity may produce information relevant to psychodynamic theory building in the field of defense mechanisms.

The correlates of sensoriastasis in emotional perception and expression need to be sought by means of other methods. In studies related to the expression of emotions, we have made extensive use of the content analysis of verbal behavior, in the form proposed by Gottschalk, Lolas, and Viney (1986). Reactivity to certain stimuli can be assessed concurrently by means of physiological data and interview information. In this manner, a more complete data set is provided for the analysis of the ways in which physiological, perceptual, and emotional dimensions interact. One of the fundamental assumptions of much of the current theorizing is that quality of life and psychological well being depend upon a balance or equilibrium between the several interacting psychophysiological domains. Stimulus intensity modulation provides clues for ascertaining whether balance is equivalent to equilibrium, Health holds different meanings for different individuals, and information about the exact position of any given person along the continua of perceptual reactance, physiological activation, and emotion perception and expression is central to any theory which purports to account for individual differences account.

References

Beaudurcel, A., Debener, S., Brocke, B., & Kayser, J. (2000). On the reliability of augmenting/reducing: Peak amplitudes and principal component analysis of auditory evoked potentials. Journal of Psychophysioology, 14. 226-240.

Brocke, B., Beaudurcel, A., John, R., Debener, S., & Heilemann, H. (2000). Sensation seeking and affective disorders: characteristics in the intensity dependence of acoustic evoked potentials. Neurophysiology, 41, 24-30.

Buchsbaum M., Haier, R., & Johnson, J. (1983). Augmenting and reducing Individual differences in evoked potentials. In A. Gale & J.A. Edwards (Eds.), *Physiological correlates of human behavior* (pp. 117-138). London: Academic Press.

Compton, P. (2000). Perceptual reactance, drug preference, and electrodermal activity. In treatment seeking substance abusers. Issues in Mental Health Nursing, 21, 109-125.

Gleser, G. C. & Ililevich, D. (1986). *Defense mechanisms: Their classification correlates and measurement with the Defense Mechanisms Inventory, Owosso*, MI: DMI Associates.

Gottschalk, L. A., Lolas, F. & Viney, L. (1986). *Content Analysis of Verbal havior. Significance in clinical medicine and psychiatry.* Heidelberg: Springer Verlag.

Larsen, R. J. & Zarate, M. A. (1991). Extending reducer/augmenter theory in the emotion domain: The role of affect in regulating stimulation level. *Personality and Individual Differences*, 12, 713-723.

Lolas, F. (1987). Aumento/reducci6n: La investigaci6n electrofisiologicá de la reactividad sensorial (Augmenting/Reducing: Electrophysiological investigation of sensory reactivity). *Anales de Salud Mental*, 2, 45-53.

Lolas, F. (1991). Attention, meaning and somatization: A psychophysiological view, *Psychopathology*, 24, 147-150

Lolas, F. (1996). La investigacion psicofisiologica de personalidad: hacia una definicion multidimencional de rasgos (Psychophysiological investigation of personality: Toward a multidimensional definition of characteristics) Actas Luso-Espanoles de Neurologia, Psiquiatria y Ciencias Afines, 24, 129-134.

Lolas, F. (1998). *Psicofisiología de la personalidad.* (Psychophysiology of personality). Santiago de Chile: Bravo & Allende

Lolas, F., Camposano, S., & Etcheberrigaray, R. (1989). Augmenting/ reducing and personality: A psychometric an evoked potential study in a Chilean sample, *Personality and Individual Differences*. 10, 1173-1176.

Lolas, F., Collin, C.,, Camposano, S., Etcheberrigaray, R., & Rees, R. (1989). Hemispheric asymmetry of augmenting/reducing in visual and auditory evoked potencial (VEP reducing: A vertex feature of late components. Research *Comunications in Psychology, Psychiatry and Behavior*, 14, 173-176.

Petrie, A. (1960). Some psychological aspects of pain and the relief of suffering. *Annals of the New York Academy of Sciences*, 86, 13-27.

Schwerdtfeger, A. & Baltissen, R. (2002). Accenting-reducing paradox lost? A Test of Davis et al.'s (1983). hypothesis. Personality and Individual Differences, 32, 257-271.

Silverman, J. (1972). Stimulus intensity modulation and psychological disease.*Psychopharmacologica*, 24, 42-80.

Von Knorring, L., Jacobsson, L., Perris, C., & Perris, H. (1980). Reactivity to incoming stimuli and the experience of life-events. *Neuropsychobiology,* 6, 297-203.

Zuckerman, M. & Kuhlman, D. M. (2000). Personality and risk taking: Common biosocial factors. Journal of Personality, 68, 999-1029.

Defense Mechanisms
U. Hentschel, G. Smith, J.G. Draguns & W. Ehlers (Editors)

Chapter 13

A Psychodynamic Activation Study of Female Oedipal Fantasies Using Subliminal and Percept-Genetic Techniques

Bert Westerlundh

This chapter presents an experimental study of conflict and defense originating in the female Oedipus complex, using subliminal stimulation and a tachistoscopic percept-genetic technique. This is related to Kragh's (1985) Defense Mechanism Test (DMT) and consists of successively prolonged presentations of interpersonal stimuli, to which subjects report, verbally and with a drawing. In the experiment, factors were varied within and between subjects. All subjects saw and reported to two percept-geneses. For one of these, all percept-genetic presentations were preceded by a neutral subliminal verbal message, the words "Taking a walk". For the other, the presentations were preceded by a provoking subliminal message, "Fuck daddy". These messages were the same for all subjects. For half of the subjects, the two percept-genetic stimuli showed a girl (central figure, technically "hero") and a man, for the other half a girl and a woman. The only difference between the sets of stimuli was in the sex of the grown-up "peripheral person" (pp.). The presentation order for the subliminal and the percept-genetic stimuli was balanced, and the subjects randomly assigned to the different combinations. The design was thus of a mixed type.

In classical psychoanalytic theory (e.g., Bonaparte, 1953; Fenichel, 1946; Freud, 1925/1961; Nagera, 1975), the oedipal period is the time when the difference between the sexes begins to have psychological consequences. The boy directs his phallic sexual love toward his mother, feelings that are ultimately renounced under the influence of castration fear. The boy's Oedipus complex is terminated by the castration complex. The story for the girl is different. She starts with the same phallic longings, but upon her recognition of the difference between the sexes she experiences a crucial disappointment-she has not got what it takes, her mother has let her down. Under the influence of this disappointment and maturational changes, she turns from the mother as a love object toward the father. Her sexual aim changes from phallic/active (clitoral) to a more passive mode, based on earlier (oral and anal) incorporative modes. She feels jealous rivalry toward the mother and tender sexual impulses toward the father, together with a wish to have a child by him. For the girl, the castration complex antedates and leads up to the Oedipus complex. In contrast to the anxiety-laden and abrupt end of the boy's oedipal strivings, the girl's Oedipus complex dissolves gradually, with time giving place to other forms of object choice.

As has been demonstrated by, among others, Silverman (1983, Silverman & Geisler, 1986), oedipal strivings and conflicts are common in normal adults and can be studied experimentally. In the present investigation, female students served as subjects. It is expected that a sizeable proportion will show observable reactions indicating conflict and defense, in accordance with the hypotheses of psychoanalytic theory.

Hypotheses

Henceforth, the girl-man percept-genetic stimuli will be called the "Man" and the girl-woman the "Woman" stimuli. The sexually provocative subliminal message, "Fuck daddy", will be abbreviated fd, and the neutral message, "Taking a walk" will be referred to as tw. The combinations of factors (e.g., girl-man percept-genetic stimulus preceded by the fd message) will be called Man fd, etc.

The first group of predictions concerns general indications of psycho- logical conflict. As will soon be evident, the load of provocation in the different conditions can be conceived of in the following way (where "+" stands for provocation):

	Man	Woman
fd	++	+
tw	+	0

There are three general indications of conflict. The *later* percept-genetic signs of anxiety and defense are scored in the series, the greater the conflict. Thus, if significantly more subjects have late signs in one condition in comparison to another, the former condition has activated more conflict. The *greater* the number of such signs scored, the greater the conflict. Many subjects with many signs are an indicator of conflict. Finally, *many different scored variants* of percept-genetic signs in a protocol point to problems of adaptation. Different numbers of subjects with many different variants in separate conditions indicate more conflict activation in the condition with the greater number .

The second group of predictions concerns specific signs of impulse, anxiety, and defense. They will be discussed for the different conditions under separate headings.

Man Conditions

For women, an oedipal, erotic interpretation of the Man stimuli should be close at hand. It is not known whether the Man and fd/tw factors interact additively or whether one of the provoking factors is enough to produce the expected results in regard to the Man stimuli. Thus, no differential predictions are given for the Man fd and Man tw conditions.

Impulse

The wishes supposed to be activated by the girl-man stimuli and the fd message are oedipal sexual ones, fantasies about having sexual inter- course with the father. Such wishes are of course strongly prohibited by the incest taboo, and impulsive reports of this type are not expected.

Anxiety

The reverse of the erotic wish is the basic feminine genital anxiety of being sexually assaulted and tom, mangled, and castrated by the father in the intercourse. This type of anxiety may determine, for example, female hypochondria, mania for surgery, and certain developments of penis envy. Homey, for instance, discussed it in a number of classical papers, later collected in a book (Homey, 1973). This leads to the following predictions regarding signs of anxiety: more subjects should give reports of perceived aggression and introaggression (damage, injury , and anxiety: stimulus inadequate black parts) to the Man than to the Woman stimuli. (The basic situation is one of aggression from pp toward a damaged hero, but the location of aggression and damage may sometimes vary as a result of superimposed layers of projective and introjective mechanisms.) Both Man fd and Woman fd are provoking conditions, and no differences are expected here with regard to reports of anxiety and fear, but more subjects should give such reports in the Man tw than in the Woman tw condition.

Defense

The mechanism of choice against activated oedipal sexual impulses is repression, and that against the threat of aggression is isolation (Fenichel, 1946, pp. 522-524, and in an experimental context, e.g. , Westerlundh & Sjöbäck, 1986). Thus, in comparison to the Woman stimuli, the Man stimuli should produce reports of repression and isolation in more subjects.

Woman Conditions

In contrast to the Man, there is no strongly compelling interpretation of the Woman stimuli. The subliminal messages should steer the interpretation of them and give differential conflict activation.

Impulse

The Woman fd condition should, in comparison to Woman tw, produce reports related to oedipal rivalry. More subjects in Woman fd are expected to activate aggressive impulses directed toward the mother. But more dramatic or violent signs of this activation are not expected. Presumably, these reports will concern specifically female forms of aggression. However, at this stage, this is speculative. Three such types of report- that perceived persons leave each other, that one of them is beautiful while the other is not, and that their affective communication is negative or strangulated-will be explored.

Anxiety

More subjects should give reports of anxiety and fear in the provoked Woman fd than in the Woman tw condition.

Defense

The type of report primarily seen in percept-genetic tests as a defense against one's own aggressive impulses is reaction formation against aggression. Such reports were early supposed to be related to inhibition of aggression (Kragh, 1969), an idea that was later experimentally verified (Westerlundh, 1976).

Thus more subjects are expected to give such reports of reaction formation in the Woman fd than in the Woman tw condition (actually, compared to any other condition). This rather anti- commonsensical statement is the central prediction concerning defense activation with regard to these comparisons.

In addition to these questions, the effect of presentation order will be studied. In the experiment, fd and tw are equally often associated with the first and the second percept-genetic series. Some design-threatening order effects are possible.

1. Reports to a percept-genesis administered after another series with the same thematic content may show contraction as a consequence of perceptual automatization. Then fewer scorable signs of anxiety and defense will be

found. In that case, fd after tw should be a less efficient provocation than fd before, and half of the protocols will be contaminated.

2. The provoking fd shown before the presentations of the first percept- genesis may initiate mental processes that reverberate into-and perhaps through-the second series. In that case, reports to tw after fd may well reflect this provocation, and the other half of the protocols will be contaminated. In both cases, the probability of finding predicted results will decrease.

Method

Subjects

Eighty female university students, volunteers who were paid for their participation, served as subjects. They were randomly assigned to the eight subgroups of the experiment (Man/Woman percept-genetic stimuli x percept-genetic stimulus A first/B first x subliminal fd first/tw first), with 10 in each. The mean age for those who saw the Man stimuli was 22.5 years, with a standard deviation of 1.5 and a range of 20-25 years. Corresponding values for those who saw the Woman stimuli were 22.4, 1.6, and 20-25 years.

Stimuli

Half the subjects saw two percept-genetic stimuli depicting a girl and a man (Man stimuli). One pair was shown in a landscape (stimulus *A),* the other in a townscape (stimulus B). The other half saw two such stimuli, in all respects equivalent to the Man stimuli, but with the man exchanged for a woman (Woman stimuli). Before the percept-genetic presentations, one of two subliminal stimuli were shown. These were verbal messages, printed on one line and consisting of two words:

Stimulus (Swedish/English)	Horizontal visual angle (degrees)
KNULLA PAPPA / fd	9.34
PÅ PROMENAD / tw	8.56

The messages had irregular black frames to avoid easily recognized right angles, and were presented centrally on the area of the screen where the percept-genetic pictures were seen.

Apparatus

The components of the experimental arrangement were two projectors, one with a timer and a rheostat for subliminal presentations, the other with a camera shutter for tachistoscopic ones. Both projectors were standard, with 220 V input and a 24 V, 150 W lamp. The projector for subliminal presentations was always fed 34 v. There were 14 tachistoscopic presentations. The presentation times (ms) were: exposure 1,20; 2-4,40; 5-7, 100; 8-10, 200; 11-14, 500. Placed at one end of a table, the projectors were arranged vertically to project on the same area of a screen. This screen, made from plastic-coated white linen, measuring 50 cm high x 61 cm wide was placed on the table. The projected picture was 15.0cm *high* x 22.5cm *wide. The picture area was indicated* by four small *black* points *at* its corners. The subject sat *at the* end of *the* table, facing the screen. When looking at it, the subject's head was fixed by a support. The screen was 65 cm from the eyes. The only source of light in the room during the experiment was a lamp, mounted behind the screen together with the projectors, and directed at the table. It gave an illuminance at the screen of 50 lux, as measured at the subject's side of the table. This value was not affected by subliminal presentations, but rose to 63 lux when a tachistoscopic picture was shown (with the tachistoscope in "constant on" position). These values were constant for all conditions.

Presentation Mode

The testing was individual. The session started with instructions to the subject to report what she saw on the screen, verbally and with a drawing. Reporting format followed the DMT standard (Kragh, 1985; Westerlundh, 1976). A trial consisted of a 7-second presentation of one of the subliminal stimuli. This was immediately followed by a tachistoscopic stimulus presentation. After this presentation, the subject reported what she had seen. Fourteen trials, with the same stimuli and increasing exposure times, were run in a row. These constitute a percept-genetic series.

A control for subliminality was performed after testing (see below). During the instructions at the beginning of the session, the DMT demonstration picture was shown at 200 ms. Before and after the experiment, the DMT distractor picture was shown once at 40 ms. Between the two series, two such presentations were given.

Blindness of Tester and Scorer

Both tester and scorer knew the design and the conditions of the experiment. The tester knew the percept-genetic stimuli each subject saw, and the order in which they were shown. The tester also knew that each percept-genetic stimulus presentation was paired with a subliminal one, but not which subliminal stimulus was used. The subliminal stimuli were always placed in the projector magazine in such a way that a number at their back, but nothing else, could be seen. The tester had to feed the appropriate stimulus into the projector in accordance with a randomization list, and was instructed never to handle them in any other way. Before each testing, the tester controlled the focusing of the subliminal projector by increasing its voltage and looking at a blank stimulus, consisting only of an irregular black frame. Then she immediately reduced the voltage to 34 V for the experiment. The scorer did not know at all what condition any experimental subject belonged to. The identification pages of the precept-genetic protocols were removed by the tester, who marked them, as well as the protocols, with a number from 1 to 80 chosen by her. The identification pages were filed out of reach from the scorer until the scoring was completed.

Subliminality

After testing, the subliminality of the verbal stimuli was investigated. The subject was (a) told that a very weak picture had been shown before each I short one and (b) asked if she had seen any of them. No subject in any condition reported having seen anything structured. Then, the subject was shown the two subliminal stimuli in the same way as subliminal presentations in the experiment. She was told that these two stimuli would be shown in this way 10 times in all and was asked to guess which one it was each time. This is a variant of Silverman's (1966) discrimination task. Subjects with eight or more correct identifications were excluded from the study and immediately replaced. The number of subjects that had to be replaced was five, to be compared to a chance expectation of 4.4. This shows that the verbal stimuli fulfill criteria for subliminality.

Percept-Genetic Scoring

The reports to the tachistoscopic presentations were scored with a scoring scheme related to that of Kragh's (1985) DMT. A more extended presentation, with definitions of the separate variants, can be found, for ex- ample, in Westerlundh and Sjöbäck (1986).

The main scoring classes were as follows

1. Repression: all reports where hero or the peripheral person (pp) is made rigid or lifeless.
2. Isolation: combines categories 21 and 22.

2:1. Barrier isolation: hero and pp are separated by a barrier, referred to different levels of reality, or separated by a distance.

2:2. Deficient reconstruction: depicted persons are not perceived, or earlier perceived person disappears, partially or completely.

3. Denial of aggression: aggression is explicitly denied with regard to hero, pp, or the situation in its totality.
4. Reaction formation: hero acts positively toward pp, pp toward hero, they have a positive relationship, or the mood in the picture is said to be positive.
5:1. Aggression: reports of aggression from hero toward pp, from pp toward hero, or emanating from the field.
5:2. Fear: hero or pp is afraid, the situation is said to be dangerous.
6. Introaggression: hero, pp, or an object in the field is either damaged, hurt, dead, or worthless, or stimulus inadequately blackened.
7. Faulty sex ascriptions: hero or pp either is ascribed incorrect sex or changes sex from correct to undecided or incorrect.
8. Multiplications: more than two persons are said to be in the picture
8:92. Pp young: pp is seen as a child or teenager, under 20 years of age.
9. Affect reports: positive or negative affect reported, with regard to hero or pp. (Relating to affects not otherwise scored.).

Results

General Signs of Conflict Activation

Only significant results are given in Table 13.1. For last scored sign and number of signs, the data refer to the number of subjects showing the characteristic (late last scored sign, great number of signs) in the different groups, but for subjects/variant the data refer to the number of variants, where one group is represented by more subjects than another in the comparisons. The total number of variants scored (excepting affect and "pp young" reports) was 44.

More subjects show late last scored percept-genetic sign in the fd than in the tw condition. The difference is caused by the Man fd subjects. These have significantly later last sign than both the Man tw and the Woman fd subjects. Regarding the number of signs scored in the series, there is one significant difference: Man tw subjects have more signs than Woman tw ones.

Table 13.1: *General signs of conflict activation: X2, sign, and binomial tests; one- tailed tests: 18 comparisons*

	+	–	z	$p \leq$
Last scored sign				
fd (+)/tw (-)	42	25	1.96	.025
Man fd (+)/Man tw (-)	23	10	2.09	.02
	Median	Subjects/total	X^2	$p \leq$
Man fd/Woman fd	13.0	22/12	4.14	.025
Number of signs				
Man tw/Woman tw	7.0	24/15	3.20	.05
	+	–	z	$p \leq$
Subjects/variant				
Man (+) Woman (-)	27	11	2.43	.007
Man tw (+) Woman tw (-)	27	10	2.63	.004

Finally, more subjects have many different variants of percept-genetic signs in the Man as compared to the Woman condition. Here, the contrast between the Man tw and the Woman tw subgroups is especially strong.

Specific Signs

Tables 13.2 and 13.3 give information about specific signs of anxiety and defense. The only sign that shows significant differences between conditions in the fd/tw (with subgroups) comparisons is reaction formation. This sign is reported by more subjects in Woman fd than in any other condition. Calculated significant differences are found in the fd/tw, Woman fd/Woman tw, Man/Woman, and Man fd/Woman fd comparisons. Table 13.3 shows that the variants of reaction formation-one perceived person behaves positively toward the other, the mood in the picture is said to be positive-contribute equally to the results. Further predictions of fd/tw differences concerned a greater number of subjects with reports of fear/anxiety and female aggression in the Woman fd than in the Woman tw condition. Reports of fear/anxiety are generally few in these conditions, and no differences are found between them. Of the reports presumably showing female forms of aggression, the beautiful/ugly category was discarded, since it was difficult to score reliably. The separation and affect categories did not give any significant fd/tw contrasts but were instead of interest in Man/Woman comparisons. There is a tendency for separation reports to be given by more of those who saw the Woman as compared the Man stimuli. The Woman fd and Woman tw subgroups contribute equally to this result. The same statements are true for two types of affect report: no positive hero affect is ever mentioned and no hero affect at all is ever mentioned. Here, the results are much stronger and generally reach significance level.

With regard to the Man-Woman comparisons, the predicted greater number of subjects reporting repression and isolation in Man is found in the Man/Woman and Man fd/Woman fd comparisons. The result for repression is weak in the Man tw/Woman tw comparison, but the result for isolation reaches tendency level. Table 13.2 shows that it is not the sign subclass barrier isolation but the subclass deficient reconstruction that determines the result. Here all contrasts are significant. Table 13.3 further shows that both subgroups of deficient reconstruction, total or partial loss of earlier perceived person and no pp seen initially for one-third of the series, contribute, but that the contrasts are stronger for the latter subgroup.

The predicted greater number of subjects reporting direct aggression in Man as compared to Woman is found in all comparisons. Furthermore, denials of aggression show a tendency in the same direction in Man/Woman and Man tw/Woman tw. Fear reports show the expected Man dominance in Man tw/Woman tw, and introaggression the same expected significance, except for the Man fd/Woman fd comparison. Of the two subclasses of introaggression, damage and blackening, significances are limited to damage reports for the Man/Woman and Man tw/Woman tw comparisons.

There are two unpredicted significances. Faulty sex ascriptions are reported by more subjects in the Woman than in to the Man condition. Table 13.3 reveals that this result concerns only the peripheral person. The trend is the same in all conditions, and significances reached in Man/Woman and Man fd/Woman fd. Furthermore, more subjects report a young peripheral person in Woman than in Man. The result is significant in all comparisons. These two categories correlated positively, with a significance in the Woman tw condition ($p < .01$).

Table 14.2: *Sign classes: fd/tw and Man/Woman comparisons; χ^2, Fisher and (for fd/tw) McNemar changes tests*

Sign class	fd/tw						Man fd/Man tw						Woman fd/Woman tw					
	A +–	B ++	C ––	D –+	χ^2	$p <$	A +–	B ++	C ––	D –+	χ^2	$p <$	A +–	B ++	C ––	D –+	χ^2	$p <$
4: Reaction formation	27	27	14	12	5.03	.05	12	10	11	7	.84	–	15	17	3	5	4.05	.025*

Sign class	Man	Woman	χ^2	$p <$	Man fd	Woman fd	χ^2	$p <$	Man tw	Woman tw	χ^2	$p <$
1: Repression	21	12	3.30	.05*	15	6	4.13	.025*	9	6	.33	–*
2: Isolation	38	30	4.80	.025*	29	20	3.37	.05*	31	24	2.09	.10*
2:1 Barrier Isolation.	30	28	.06	–*	23	19	.45	–*	22	22	.05	–*
2:2 Deficient reconstruction	25	11	8.54	.005*	16	6	5.08	.025*	17	6	6.10	.01*00
3: Denial	13	5	3.51	.10	7	3	1.03	–	8	2	2.86	.10
4: Reaction Formation	29	37	4.24	.05	22	32	4.62	.025*	17	22	.80	–
5:1 Aggression	20	6	9.63	.005*	12	2	7.01	.005*	13	4	4.78	.025*
5:2 Fear	18	6	7.20	.01	10	3	3.31	.10	12	3	5.25	.025*
6: Introaggression	19	7	6.89	.005*	7	6	0	–*	13	2	8.21	.005*
7:1 Incorrect gender	24	33	3.91	.05	15	23	2.46	–	14	21	1.83	–
7:4 Gender changes	10	13	.24	–	4	6	.11	–	7	8	0	–
8: Multiplications	17	16	0	–	11	11	.06	–	10	6	.70	–

Note: * = predicted contrasts, one-tailed tests.

Table 13.3: *Results for subclasses and further results: Man/Woman comparisons; χ^2 and Fisher tests; two tailed*

Subclasses of	Man	Woman	χ^2	$p <$	Man fd	Woman fd	χ^2	$p <$	Man tw	Woman tw	χ^2	$p <$
2:2 Deficient reconstruction												
2:20-2:32 Within the series	21	11	4.21	.05	16	6	5.08	.05	12	6	1.79	–
2:42b No pp seen initially	15	0	16.08	.001	8	0		.01	8	0		.01
4: Reaction formation												
4:1 Activity	15	20	.81	–	11	16	.89	–	8	11	.28	–
4:2 Affect	25	31	1.49	–	16	23	1.80	.–	16	19	.20	–
6: Introaggression												
6:1 Damage	13	4	4.78	.05	5	3		–	9	1	5.6	.02
6:2 Blackening	8	4	.88	–	3	3		–	5	1		–
7:1 Incorrect gender	24	33	3.91	.05	15	23	2.46	–	14	21	1.83	–
7:10-7:11 Both or hero	12	11	0	–	8	5	.37	–	7	8	0	–
7:12 Pp only	14	31	13.00	.001	7	18	5.82	.02	8	15	2.20	–
Further results												
2:10 Separation	9	17	2.79	.10	5	9		–	6	11		–
8:92. Pp child or youthful	6	22	12.36	.001	3	12	5.25	.05	3	14	7.47	.01
9:31 No possitive hero affect	9	25	11.52	.001	23	31	2.79	.10	20	31	5.41	.02
9:41 Negative hero affect	15	10		–	8	3		–	8	7		–
9:51 No hero affect	2	20	18.12	.001	16	28	6.11	.02	15	26	5.00	.05

Order Effects

The only significant presentation order differences were found for sign 7, faulty sex ascriptions. The general trend of the results is in the direction of fewer subjects attributing wrong or undecided sex to the perceived persons in the second series.

Discussion

The use of subliminal stimuli raises a number of questions. The use of verbal subliminal stimuli was discussed by Spence in a path-breaking paper (Spence, Klein, & Fernandez, 1986). His conclusions, while complex, were quite negative for the subliminal psychodynamic activation paradigm. My own studies (Westerlundh, 1986) show that Spence is partly correct. Subliminal sentences are not read syntactically, or are read so only under special circumstances. However, there seems to be a highly emotional unconscious appraisal of the individual words presented, and the outcome of this may result in complex psychodynamic activation effects on the dependent variables. However, the simple messages presented in this study should not be problematical. Each of the two provoking subliminal words, "fd," individually or in any combination, should result in a steering of the interpretation of the tachistoscopic stimuli in the intended direction.

There seems to be some agreement on an operational definition of strict subliminality: the subject's inability to discriminate the experimental from a control stimulus at the time of the experiment. The usual method of assessing this is a forced-choice guessing task. This is of course the strategy that, following the lead olf Silverman (1966) has been implemented in this experiment. This inability to guess correctly corresponds to the objective recognition threshold of Cheesman and Merikle (1986), in contrast to the subjective threshold of not being able to report a perceptual experience. Methods used in the field of subliminal perception vary, and give different results. Today, main research paradigms include that of Greenwald (Greenwald, Draine, & Abrams, 1996) which produces short lived non-spreading semantic activation, and that of Bargh (Bargh, Chaiken, Govender & Pratto, 1992), which in contrast is used as a priming procedure to activate social knowledge. The method used in this study is different from these tachistoscopic techniques. It is based on relatively long, quite weak presentations. It always seemed to me that this is a more ecologically valid approach, since the realm in nature where we find subliminal stimuli is the night.

In attempts to experimentally provoke intrapsychic conflict-such as in the present study-not all predictions have the same theoretical status. A simple diagram of the hypothetical process would involve the following components: experimental provocation- (activated impulse)- threat/danger-anxiety signal-defense-eventual outcome, possibly iterated in a number of loops before a conscious representation is achieved and re-ported in the dependent measure. This is a statement within the directional topographic model of psychoanalysis, a type of model I with Reyher (Moses & Reyher, 1985) hold to be indispensable in the conceptual understanding of the type of process studied here. Its consequences are that while, ceteris paribus, valid experimental and control conditions give rise to different reported spectra of defense, it is probable but not necessary that they will produce differences in reports of danger, fear, and anxiety, and of the "defensive struggle," what has here been called general indications of psychological conflict. A specific danger may be countered by an efficient defense, inhibiting conscious unpleasure and different in form from defensive reports in the baseline condition, but not in, for example, number or place in the series of reports. A number of content and intensity factors will determine the outcome. This is seen in, for example, a series of studies on experimentally manipulated superego functioning in men and women (Westerlundh & Terjestam, 1987). In these, the general indications sometimes show, sometimes fail to show condition differences.

What then are the results of the present study? The design is not invalidated by sequence effects. The only significant differences of this type are found for incorrect sex attributions, which are reported by fewer subjects in the second series. This type of result has been reported for the DMT (Sjöbäck, 1972; Westerlundh, 1976). In the DMT context, this finding has generally been attributed to stimulus differences. Here, an explanation in terms of set, induced by the perception of the first series, is nearer at hand. All three types of general indication show significant results in predicted directions. One-third of the comparisons give such results.

Of the fd/tw predictions, the important one concerning a defense mechanism, reaction formation dominance in Woman fd, is verified. The one concerning fear and anxiety does not receive support. This type of prediction was discussed above. The reports studied as signs of female aggression give interesting results-they seem to be related to girl-woman rather than girl-man interactions, and thus to be topical to the area of interest. On the other hand, they do not differentiate between Woman fd and Woman tw. Possibly, even without subliminal steering the oedipal interpretation of the Girl-Woman stimuli is so close at hand that a number of subjects have given the reports in the control condition.

The predictions for the Man/Woman comparisons concerning the use of repression and isolation by and large receive support. The same is true for the other predictions (aggression, introaggression, fear) with regard to these comparisons. For instance, reports of aggression are much more frequent in both Man fd and Man tw as compared to the Woman conditions. Reactions to percept-genetic stimuli with a pp who really is aggressive and threatening (as in the DMT) are of interest in this context. Interindividual differences do not come to an end when the aggressive content is perceived. Male subjects who see boy-aggressive man stimuli often give reports of the type "Man beats boy." Female subjects who see girl-aggressive woman stimuli hardly ever report "Woman beats girl." Instead, if physical violence is reported by women in this situation, it is with the pp transformed to a man, even though exposure times are quite long. Direct violence belongs to a sphere of male activity. There is a middle ground where the sexes meet: "Man gives boy a rating" and "Woman gives girl a rating" are rather common reports for respective sex. Finally, there is a typically female form of report to this type of stimulus: "She (pp) is so angry and sorry because the girl will not eat what she has served her," etc. Male subjects may report pp as angry and completely mad, or as angry and physically hurt, but the angry-and-sad combination is a distinct female mode of aggression.

Some results were not predicted. Denials of aggression show the same pattern as reports of aggression. This is generally found, but so few subjects use denial that predictions for the category as a rule are not given. Faulty sex ascriptions and reports of a young pp are fairly common in the Woman group, and especially in the neutral condition, Woman tw, they tend to be associated. The subjects report neutral but pleasant scenes with a girl and a boy together. To quote Kragh (1985), "this is not a genuine defense mechanism but rather a sign of object relations.

Thus, this study gives experimental support to aspects of the psycho-analytic theory of the female Oedipus complex and its precipitates in later mental functioning. Of especial importance is the verification of predictions concerning differential use of defense mechanisms (repression, isolation, and reactionformation) in contrasting conditions. Of course, what has been studied here relates to the dynamic propositions of psychoanalysis- those concerning unconscious anxieties, wishes, defenses, and fantasies motivating behavior in the "here-and now" (Silverman, 1983). General propositions concerning the nature of mental conflict and specific propositions about types of content frequently involved in such conflict receive support. On the other hand, genetic propositions-those that link present functioning to earlier experiences and events-cannot, in the nature of things, be directly investigated by laboratory techniques. Such propositions serve as connecting frameworks, pointing to probable regularities in the present (in this case with success).

Much can be said about psychoanalytic theory. Its highly colorful and mythographic appearance may make it hard for it to gain adherents among those used to the machine analogies of academic psychology. But-in contrast to the latter-its predictions are not trivial. They concern central aspects of human functioning and development. (For a full and spirited statement of this position, see Kline, 1988.) Many of these predictions are empirically testable if the proper methods-for instance, percept-genetic ones-are used.

References

Bargh, J. A., Chaiken, S., Govender, R., & Pratto, F. (1992). The generality of the automatic attitude activation effect. *Journal of Personality Psychology*, 62, 893-912.

Bonaparte, M. (1953). *Female sexuality.* London: Imago.

Chessman, J. & Merikle, P. M. (1986). Distinguishing conscious from unconscious perceptual processes, *Canadian Journal of Psychology*, 40 343-367.

Fenichel, 0. (1946). *The psychoanalytic theory of neurosis.* London: Routledge and Kegan Paul.

Freud, S. (1961). Some psychical consequences of the anatomical distinction between the sexes. In *The standard edition of the complete psychological works of Sigmund Freud: Vol.* 19. London: Hogarth Press (Original work published 1925)

Greenwald, A. G., Draine, S. C. & Abrams, R. L. (1996). Three cognitive markers of unconscious semantic activation. *Science,* 273, 1699-1702.

Homey, K. (1973). *Feminine psychology.* New York: Norton.

Kline, P. (1988). *Psychology exposed: Or, the emperor's new clothes.* London: Routledge.

Kragh, U. (1969). *Manual till DMT. Defense Mechanism Test.* [Manual of the DMT]. Stockholm: Skandinaviska Testforlaget.

Kragh, U. (1985). *DMT manual.* Stockholm: Persona.

Moses, I. & Reyher, J. (1985). Spontaneous and directed visual imagery: Image failure and image substitution. *Journal of Personality and Social Psychology,* 48, 233-242.

Nagera, H. (1975). *Female sexuality and the Oedipus complex.* New York: Jason Aronson.

Silverman, L. H. (1966). A technique for the study of psychodynamic relationships: The effects of subliminally presented aggressive stimuli on the production of pathological thinking in a schizophrenic population. *Journal of Consulting Psychology,* 30,103-111.

Silverman, L. H. (1983). The subliminal psychodynamic activation method: Over- view and comprehensive listing of studies. In I. Masling (Ed.), *Empirical studies of psychoanalytic theory: Vol.* 1 (pp. 69-100). Hillsdale, N.I.: Erlbaum.

Silverman, L. H. & Geisler, C.I. (1986). The subliminal psychodynamic activation method: Comprehensive listing update, individual differences, and other considerations. In U. Hentschel, G.I.W. Smith, & I. Draguns (Eds.), *The roots of perception* (pp. 49- 74). Amsterdam: North-Holland.

Sjöbäck, H. (1972). *Apparatkonstruktion, bildkonstruktion och grundliiggande bildprovningsforsok med defense mechanism test.* [The construction of the apparatus, the layout and basic testing of the pictures for the Defense Mechanism Test]. Mimeographed, Department of Psychology, Lund University.

Spence, D. P., Klein, L., & Fernandez, R. I. (1986). Size and shape of the subliminal window. In U. Hentschel, G.J.W. Smith, & I. Draguns, *The roots of perception* (pp. 103-142). Amsterdam: North-Holland.

Westerlundh, B. (1976). *Aggression, anxiety, and defense.* Lund: Gleerup.

Westerlundh, B. (1986). On reading subliminal sentences: A psychodynamic activation study. *Psychological Research Bulletin, Lund University,* 26, 10.

Westerlundh, B. & Sjöbäck, H. (1986). Activation of intrapsychic conflict and defense: The amauroscopic technique. In U. Hentschel, G.I.W. Smith, & J. Draguns (Eds.), *The roots of perception* (pp. 161-216). Amsterdam: North- Holland.

Westerlundh, B. & Terjestam, Y. (1987). Psychodynamic effects of subliminal verbal messages on tachistoscopically presented interpersonal stimuli. *Psycho- logical Research Bulletin, Lund University,* 27, 3.

Defense Mechanisms
U. Hentschel, G. Smith, J.G. Draguns & W. Ehlers (Editors)

Chapter 14

Adaptation to Boredom and Stress: The Effects of Defense Mechanisms and Concept Formation on Attentional Performance in Situations with Inadequate Stimulation

Uwe Hentschel, Manfred Kiessling and Arn Hosemann

Introduction

The present chapter describes part of a project that was aimed at providing information about what personality characteristics are best suited to predict attentional deficits under boredom and stress. It can be placed in the broader context of man-machine interaction and was planned as a computer simulation task for the attention-related activity of driving a car. Man-machine interactions usually do not attract much interest as long as everything runs smoothly. In the case of obvious problems or disturbances of the system, an analysis is required from which in the best case something can be learned about the optimal functioning of the system. These analyses usually have either a stronger technical impact, directed at the functioning of the machine, or a stronger psychological impact, directed at the user and his or her interaction with the existing technical solutions. The relevance of man-machine interactions for differential or personality psychology is to be found in those examples where personality characteristics have or may have an influence on the reaction to the machine.

A rather famous example is provided by the driver of a tank truck who in spite of a slightly defective transmission decided to drive down a steep hill in Herborn, a small town in Germany. He could not change into a lower gear, the brakes did not hold the extra load put on them, and the truck crashed into an ice-cream parlor and exploded. Five people were killed and a number of neighboring houses completely destroyed. In this case different technical prevention measures would have been possible, ranging from better technical control of trucks in general to forbidding heavy trucks to use that specific road (later pronounced by the local government). But it is also legitimate to ask whether another driver could not have come to a decision better adapted to this situation, which generally would suggest the attempt at better selection and/or training of drivers, to which another question has to follow: selection (and training) on the basis of which criteria?

The contribution of psychology to traffic studies was for a long time dominated by the search for the accident-prone type of driver. On the whole this attempt was not very successful. The majority of accidents are caused by normal drivers, not belonging to this special group (see, e.g., Forbes, 1972). For the study of accident risks it seems generally better (a) to favor a probabilistic approach and (b) try to find a possible link between accident proneness and certain types of situation. The second part of this assumption is based on the idea that the probability for making a mistake changes with different situations, which in turn are related to personal characteristics (cf. McGuire, 1976) and such inner states as, for example, vigilance, which is, as far as external preconditions are concerned, among the variables influenced by noise and vibration (Floru, Damongeot, & di Renzo, 1988). Being tired or being bored has direct consequences for the task of driving. It increases the chance of reacting inadequately, especially in case of an unexpected new situation. There are also interindividual differences in getting bored while, for example, driving on a straight highway with almost no traffic. Experiencing stress with internal or external factors as potential sources can also lead to inadequate reaction. The driver's activity, basically comparable with many other man-machine interactions, can be summarized as a complex input-output process with a continuous feedback loop (cf. Rockwell, 1972). The input is the attention-related registration and evaluation of changing scenes. The output are motor reactions (reactions fitted to fulfill the intentions of accelerating, braking, changing the direction of the car, etc.). With experience, the motor reactions become highly automatized, so that the psychologically more interesting questions seem to be connected with the input side: the observation and evaluation of constantly changing stimulus patterns.

Whether both observation and evaluation of the incoming stimuli can be subsumed under attention control depends on which definition of attention is used. More complex definitions recognize its multidimensional features (e.g., Froehlich, 1978), consider a potentially unconscious part of it (Dixon, 1981; Dixon, Hentschel, & Smith, 1986), regard attention as an organized set of procedures (Glass, Holyoak, & Santa, 1979), or focus on its contribution to resources of ability (Cooper and Regan, 1982; Hunt, 1980). Seen from a broader perspective, including observation and evaluation, attention is part of a reaction to a complex social environment (Chance, 1976), an aspect of attention that is certainly relevant for the activity of driving a car as well as for many other types of man-machine interaction. Within the aims of this research project, we intended to study the effect of three basic situations: understimulation, overstimulation, and a normal input level, with two variants for each of the inadequate stimulation conditions: monotony and satiation for the condition of understimulation and two levels of information overload (stress1 and stress2) for the overstimulation condition.

Monotony, satiation, and stress are terms related to subjective experience, but through their operationalization there is, of course, a relationship with physical characteristics too. It should be noted, however, that no complete congruence is possible. The experience of monotony or stress is ultimately a subjective one (cf. Chapter 27). With that characterization, a mere physical description of the stimuli is clearly abandoned, but a potential goal that we also tried to reach in the present study is to create situations that at least for most of the respondents, if not all, are boring, stressful, etc. (i.e., the attempt to create situations prototypical in that respect). Our general research question can be formulated in everyday language as follows: What kind of people lose their composure to a greater extent in conditions of inadequate stimulations and what kind of people can manage these situations better? We wanted to control the differential effect of being able to cope with these different conditions with the basic hypothesis of an interaction of defense mechanisms and cognition. With these prerequisites in mind, we thus had to select the set of variables to be used from the whole test battery. From the cognitive tests we wanted to include a test requiring logical thinking. The most difficult in the battery was a concept formation test, called Symbol Maze Test (SMT: Hentschel & Kiessling, 1983). We knew from previous analyses of the project data (Hentschel, Kiessling, & Hosemann, 1989, 1991) that the perceptual defense mechanisms of the Defense Mechanism Test (DMT: see Chapter 7) interact with anxiety on attentional performance. The hypothesis of an interaction of DMT defenses and concept formation, however, did not find support. From previous studies and from the project data, we knew also that the defense mechanisms registered by the FKBS (Fragenbogen zu Konfliktbewältigungsstrategien [Inventory for Conflict Resolution Strategies]) and by the DMT did not reveal any substantial correlations (see Chapter 1). The cognition-defense interaction hypothesis thus could get another chance by using the FKBS self-report measures of defense. The computer simulation task for the measurement of attentional performance is described in greater detail in the method section. Based on studies using the FKBS (e.g., Hentschel & Schneider, 1986) and in contrast to the DMT defenses, we did not expect that all the FKBS defense mechanisms would hamper the attention performance. A higher score of Turning Against Object (TAO, see below) seems to be a rather positive sign in many situations. We thus kept the hypothesis for TAO as a favorable sign and excluded PRO from the predictions. For the other clusters of defense, the general hypothesis was that higher defense scores in interaction with a poor concept formation ability are related to more errors in the understimulation and overstimulation conditions of the attention task.

Method

The Construction of the Experimental Conditions and the Attentional Performance Measure

The main dimension in the construction of the dependent variable in the experiment, taken from the analogy of driving a car, is the variation of information load. This dimension was to be introduced into the psychological conditions of understimulation (monotony and satiation), normal, and overstimulation (stress1 and stress2, which should give a higher level of stress in comparison to stress1).

Monotony, provoking a state of lower vigilance with the feeling of being bored, usually comes about by repetition, lack of interaction and minmal variation in the surrounding (cf. Conrad, 1999). One possible way to introduce it into an attention control task is to use a low frequency of the events to be controlled. Kurt Lewin (1935) and his coworkers made the first experiment on the effects of repetition by introducing a so-called satiation task. Karsten (1928) asked her subjects to make strokes in a certain rhythm until they did not want to continue any longer even upon slight pressure from the experimenter. She described in detail how subjects became bored, tired, and inattentive and tried to introduce minor variations until finally they could not be persuaded to go on. The main characterization for satiation is repetition. It is less easy to trace it in the activity of driving a car, although a longer stop-and-go condition might provoke it, especially in cars that do not have automatic transmissions. In our experiment we tried to operationalize it through the requirement of repetitive motor reactions (pressing the keys of the keyboard in a certain ordered sequence in reaction to visual stimuli). From the deviations of a normal information load, as hitherto mentioned, the normal conditions can be delineated: Events to be controlled should have a higher frequency, they should be nonrepetitive, and presented at a manageable speed.

Conditions featuring an overload of information usually can be characterized by the speed of presentation of the stimuli to which reactions are required and/or the simultaneous presentation of different stimuli (all or only some of relevance) comprising the necessity of quick decisions and reactions. The stress1 and stress2 conditions were both of the latter kind, and it was impossible to react to the relevant stimulus without making errors, although there was enough space

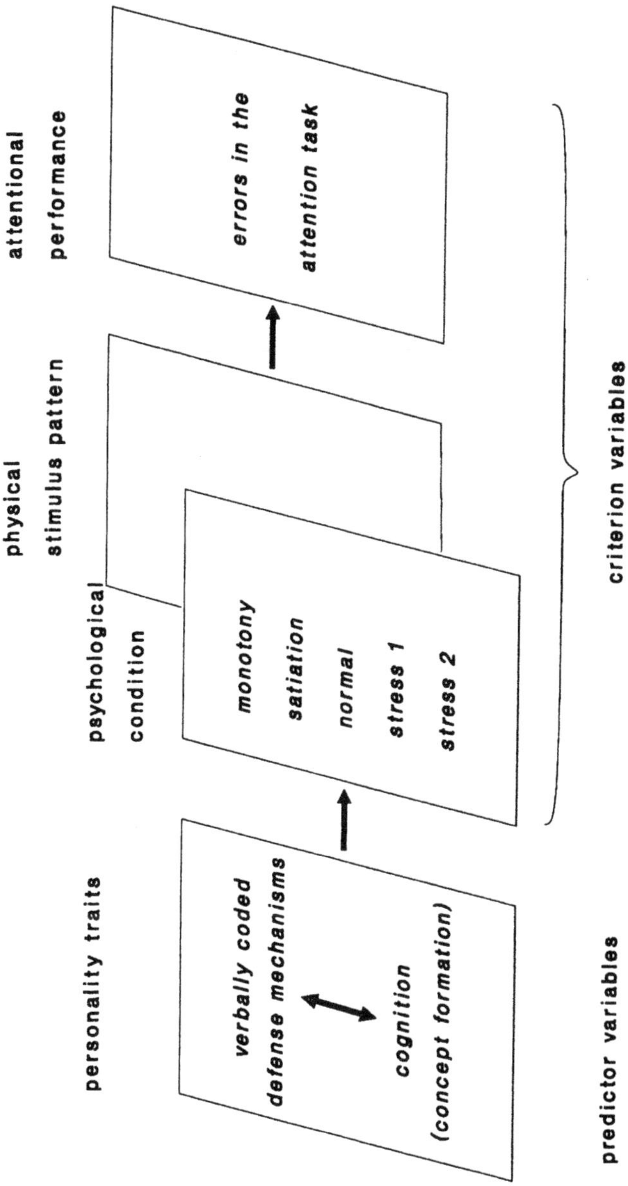

Figure 14.1: *Schematic overview of the design of the study.*

for interindividual differences with regard to correctness. A schematic overview of the design of the study is given in Figure 14.1. The stress situations were planned to provoke feelings of being ill at ease, of nervous tension, and of hyperactivity.

The order of the different conditions as presented to the respondents was monotony, stress1, normal, satiation, and stress2. The subjects were seated in front of a computer monitor and had to give their reactions on the keyboard. In each of the conditions, reactions were required to either on specific relevant symbol or up to three. The basic setting is graphically presented in Figure14.2. A more detailed description of the different conditions is given in Table 14.1. For the condition of satiation, the appearance of the symbols was restricted to the four upper left fields corresponding to the key numbers 4, 5, 7 and 8, which for correct reactions had to be pressed as a repeated series in the following order, 7, 8, 4, 5, 7, 5. Errors in reaction were registered automatically; errors were scored when subjects pressed the wrong key, missed the reaction, or did not respond within the given time limit, which varied for the different conditions. An adequate measure for interindividual comparisons of the performance is the error rate (i.e., the percentage of the maximally possible errors in each of the conditions). This measure was used as dependent variable in all group comparisons to follow.

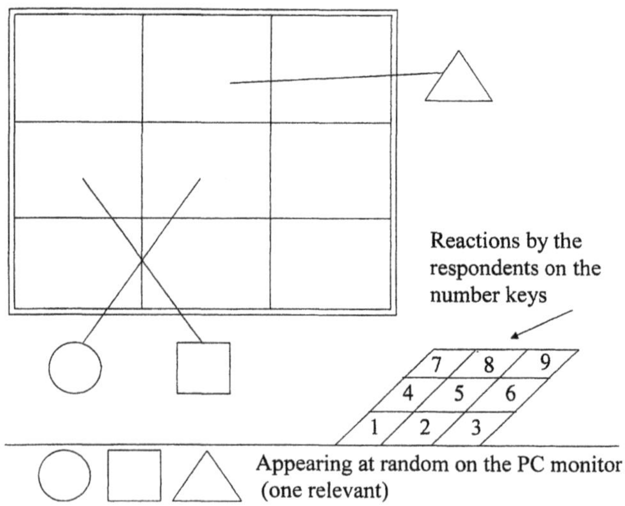

Figure 14.2: *The task of the respondents: react at the relevant symbol(s) on the PC monitor with corresponding reactions on the number keys*

Table 14.1: *Parameters of the experimental conditions*

	Monotony	Satiation	Normal	Stress1	Stress2
Relevant symbol	Square	Circle	Triangle	Circle	Circle
Presented in color	Green	Yellow	Green	Changing	Changing
Background color	Black	Black	Blue	Black	Changing
Number of symbols	1	1	Max. 3	Max. 3	Max. 3
Number of trials	25	594	200	250	300
Error feedback	No	No	Yes	Yes	Yes
Minimum time between two trials (0.1s)	300	10	10	5	3
Acceleration factor	1	1	15	50	50
Exposure time (0.1 s)	7	5	8	4	4

The Predictor Variables

FKBS

The FKBS registers defense mechanisms as self-reported reactions to frustrating events. Like the DMI (Gleser & Ihilevich, 1969) it has some similarity to Rosenzweig's (1945/1946) Picture Frustration Test, but unlike the DMI it asks only for two kinds of reactions, i.e. feeling and doing, to be given on a 5-point

Likert scale. The scores for these two reactions can also be summarized into an overall score. Also comparable to the DMI five scales are discerned in the FKBS. They can be used separately for the levels of feeling and doing or as an overall score for a specific defense scale. With regard to reliabilities and the content of the scales, i.e. a summary of the specific goals to which the items were scale-specifically formulated, Table 14.2 provides an overview. In the present study the overall scores (combining the answers for the feeling and behavior level) were used.

Table 14.2: *Description of the FKBS scales and their reliabilities*

Scale	Theoretical concept		Reliability	
		Content	Cronbach's Alpha	r_{tt} (8 week interval)
Abbreviation	Full name			
TAO	Turning against Object	Substitutive reactions of aggression against an extemaJ object	0.90	0.78
TAS	Tuming against self	Coping with the conflict is attempted by seeing oneself as the reason for the frustration	0.86	0.77
REV	Reversal	Positive or neutral intentions are attributed to the person seen as the source of frustration	0.80	0.84
INT	Intellectualization	Splitting off affects by intellectualization and rationalization	0.78	0.79
PRO	Projection	Negative intentions or characteristics are attributed to the person seen as the source of frustration	0.72	0.71

SMT

To measure concept formation, we have developed a new test, the Symbol Maze Test (SMT; Hentschel & Kiessling, 1983; Hentschel & Kiessling, in preparation), the validity of which has been studied in different experiments (cf. Hentschel, 1997, Hentschel & Kiessling, 1986; Hentschel, Kiessling, & Ternes, 1984). The SMT is a computer-controlled experimental task. It is presented to the respondents in form of a mental maze in which the "right way" has to be found. Getting at the right way implies the necessity to find a symbol (i.e., a correct combination of signs indicating this way). There are no real blind alleys as in other mental mazes, but when the subject enters a forbidden way (i.e., a way with a combination of signs other than the correct one), he or she receives an error feedback in form of a low tone. On the way through the maze there are 25 decision points, which allow the respondent to learn the concept asked for in that specific maze. When the solution is found, the further way through the maze can be made without any errors. An example is given in Figure 14.3. From earlier studies, the characteristics that make a maze more or less difficult were known. The difficulty depends on the redundancy of symbols in a specific maze and the kind of combination rule: that is, how often the subject encounters the same combination of signs in a maze and what the required rule of combination is ("and"; "or"; "and plus or": e.g. , a red square and a blue triangle; a red square or a blue square; a red square and a blue triangle or a blue square and a red triangle). Subjects are confronted with a series of eight mazes (two with houses, three with abstract figures, and three with faces). The score is the weighted sum of errors in a particular maze, which can be summed up to the whole series or separately for subseries of difficult and easy mazes. The task is process-oriented and within the tradition of microgenesis (cf. Hentschel, 1984) has been labeled "schematogenetic" (Hentschel & Kiessling, 1983). According to the hitherto available results, concept formation has an intermediate position between intelligence tests and more complex problem-solving tasks (Hentschel & Kiessling, 1986).

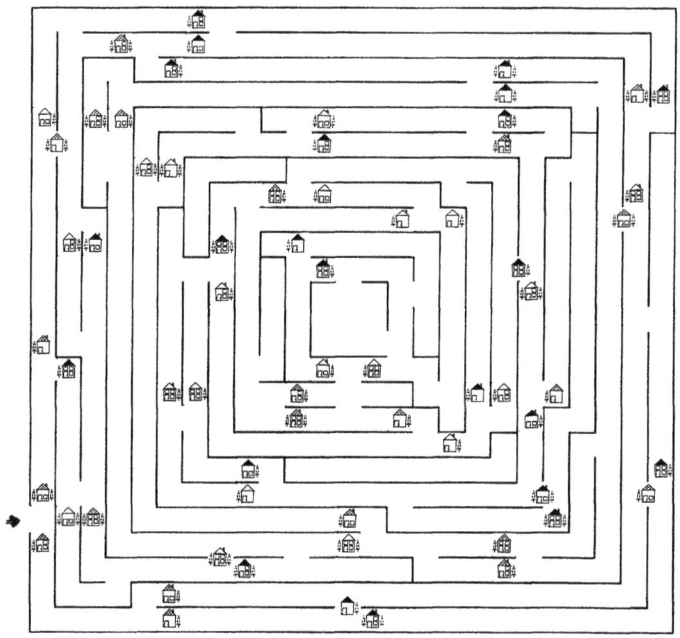

Figure 14.3: *An example for the SMT (solution: one window $_v$ with chimney)*

Sample

One hundred respondents (48 males, 52 females, mean age 34 years) voluntarily took part in the experiment; they were tested individually and received renumeration. They had to have a driving license. It was necessary to exclude from the sample 24 respondents in the condition of understimulation and 23 respondents in the condition of overstimulation because of data missing from either the SMT and/or the attention task.

Results

On the Differentiation of the Situations of Inadequate Stimulation

The results of a pilot study (N = 5) gave a first indication that the construction of the different psychological conditions had been successful. With the main sample (N = 77 resp. 76), for the 10 nonredundant possibilities of comparison between the five different conditions, *t*-tests were calculated which were all significant ($p < 0.005$). The stress2 condition following the stress1 situation resulted, however, in a lower number of errors. Moreover, the two stress conditions were highly correlated ($r = .83$).

The Effect of Defense Mechanisms and Concept Formation on Attention Control Under the Conditions of Inadequate Stimulation

To study the differences within the conditions of understimulation and overstimulation, the different situations were compared in groups of three (understimulation: monotony, normal, satiation; overstimulation: stress1, normal, stress2), using the normal stimulation for both conditions as a control. The effects of defense mechanisms and concept formation were controlled by using separate median splittings for all five defense scores and the error score in the concept formation task.

Understimulation

Results for the condition of understimulation are presented in Table 14.3, which shows significant effects for concept formation, for TAS and the sequence, an interaction effect for concept formation and the sequence, and for concept formation, TAS and the sequence. The results are graphically presented in Figures 14.4 and 14.5. Figure 14.4 gives the attention task results for the groups with good versus bad concept formation. Figure 14.5 shows the interaction between TAS and concept formation over the different conditions of understimulation. A higher score of TAS combined with a higher error score in the concept formation task results in higher error scores in the attention task under both conditions of understimulation.

Table 14.3: *Analysis of variance: TAS by concept formation by understimulation*

Source of variation	*df*	*F*	*p*
TAS	1	3.93	<.05
Concept formation	1	15.93	<.001
TAS by concept formation	1	2.11	.15
Within cells	72		
Understimulation	2	17.60	<.001
TAS by understimulation	2	2.31	.10
Concept formation by understimulation	2	4.89	<.009
TAS by concept formation by understimulation	2	3.04	<.05
Within cells	14		
	4		

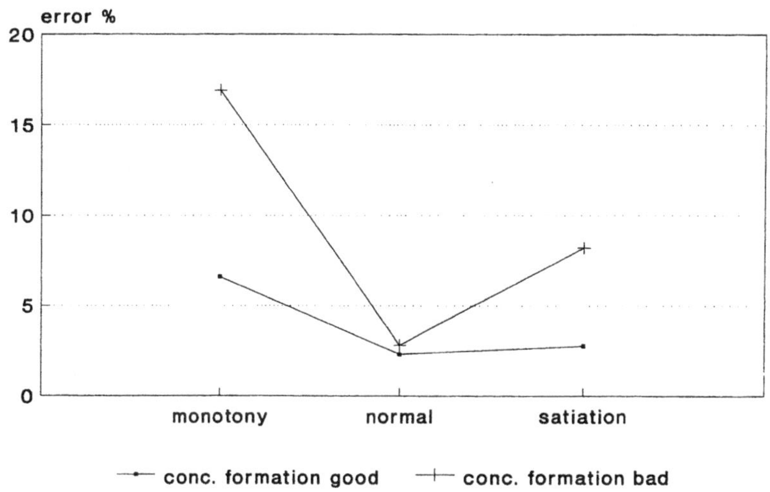

Figure 14.4: *Performance in the concept formation task and errors in the attention task under the condition of understimulation.*

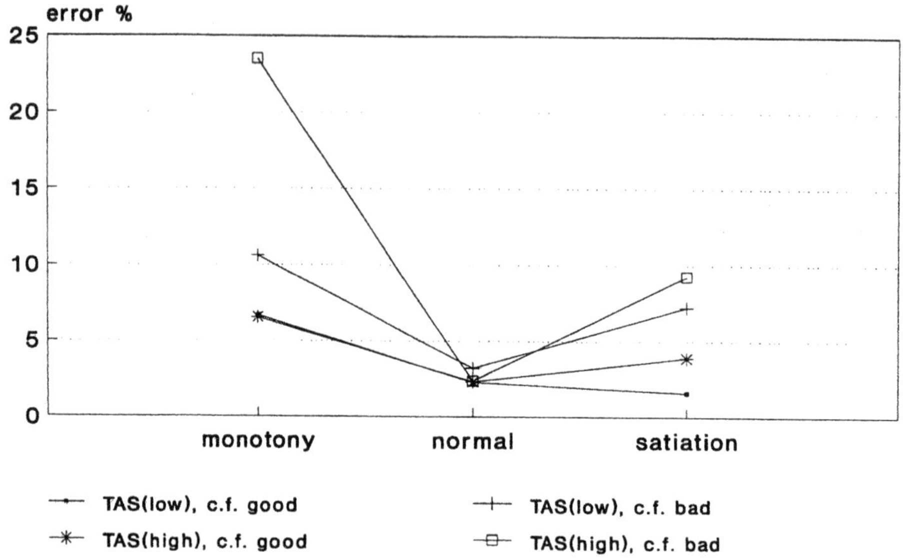

Figure 14.5: *Performance in the concept formation task, high versus low TAS scores, and errors in the attention task under the condition of understimulation.*

Overstimulation

In Table 14.4 results are presented for the overstimulation condition. Concept formation, TAS and TAO show main effects. TAS, TAO and REV have interactions with the sequence. No interaction is given, however between concept formation and the defense mechanisms. The results are graphically presented in Figs. 14.6 and 14.7.

Respondents with good results in the concept formation task make less errors in the attention control task under both stress conditions. Also the group with higher TAO scores makes fewer errors in the attention task and there seems to be a learning effect for the group with lower TAO scores from stress1 to stress2. The group with higher TAS scores makes more errors under both stress conditions and for REV there is a significant difference for the stress2 situation, indicating, fewer errors for the group with lower REV scores. This group shows also a significant learning effect from stress1 to stress2.

Table 14.4: *Analysis of variance: TAO, TAS, REV by concept formation by overstimulation*

TAO by concept formation			
Source of variation	*df*	*F*	*p*
TAO	1	7.01	<.01
Concept formation	1	5.10	<.03
TAO by concept formation	1	.14	.71
Within cells	72		
Overstimulation	2	517.34	<.001
TAO by overstimulation	2	5.30	<.006
Concept formation by overstimulation	2	3.48	<.03
TAO by concept formation by overstimulation	2	.24	.78
Within cells	144		
TAS by concept formation by overstimulation			
Source of variation	*df*	*F*	*p*
TAS	1	5.56	<.02
Concept formation	1	8.20	<.005
TAS by concept formation	1	.82	.37
Within cells	72		
Overstimulation	2	531.40	<.001
TAS by overstimulation	2	4.67	<.01
Concept formation by overstimulation	2	5.70	<.004
TAS by concept formation by overstimulation	2	1.19	.31
Within cells	144		
REV by concept formation by overstimulation			
Source of variation	*df*	*F*	*p*
REV	1	3.12	<.08
Concept formation	1	4.88	<.03
REV by concept formation	1	.56	<.46
Within cells	72		
Overstimulation	2	485.13	<.001
REV by overstimulation	2	3.31	<.04
Concept formation by overstimulation	2	3.13	<.05
REV by concept formation by overstimulation	2	.43	.65
Within cells	144		

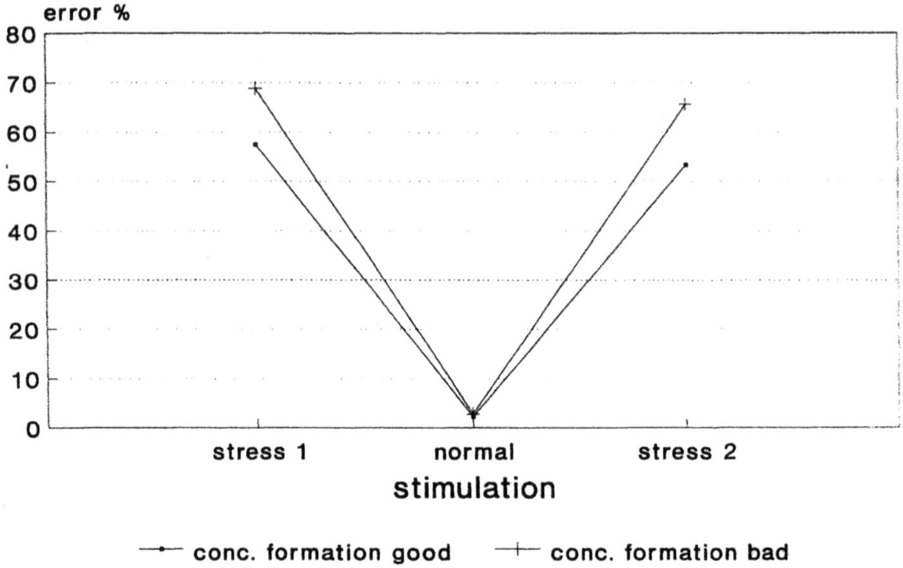

Figure 14.6: *Performance in the concept formation task and errors in the attention task under the condition of overstimulation.*

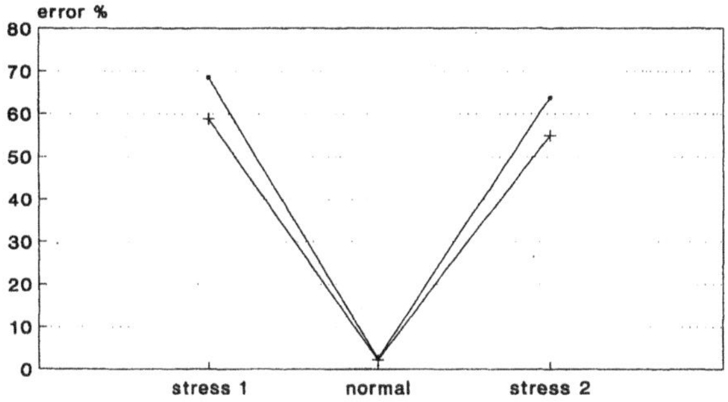

A

TAO(low) TAO(high)

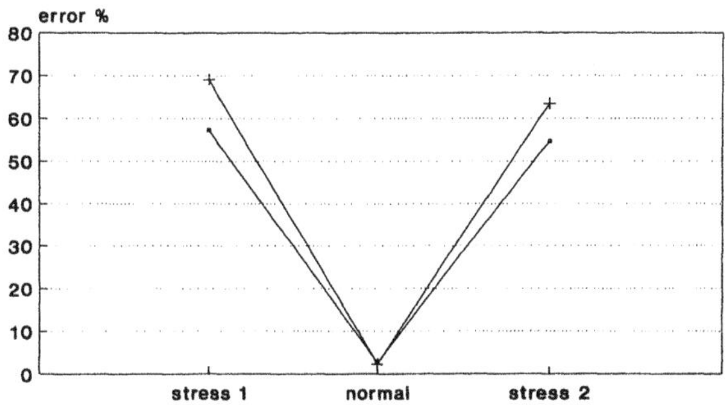

B

TAS(low) TAS(high)

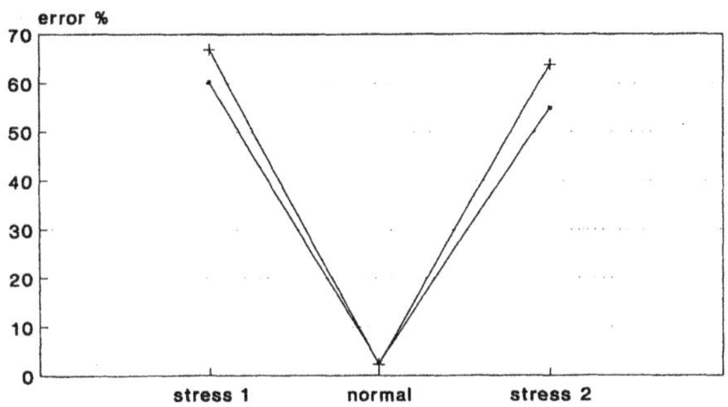

C

REV(low) REV(high)

Figure 14.7: *High versus low defense scores and performance in the attention task under the condition of overstimulation (A) TAO, (B) TAS, and (C) REV*

Discussion

The results give some support for the general working hypothesis that defense mechanisms, concept formation, and attentional performance are related to each other. The relation of the SMT to the attention task might to a certain degree be influenced by an overlap of the requirements in the predictor and the criterion task. Attention is also important for the microgenetic concept formation task. The results nevertheless remain interesting especially if it were possible to show a close relationship between the computer simulation task of attention control and real car driving. This would give the SMT an extra value as a real-life task predictor, so far no experiments could be performed to this end, however.

In formulating our hypothesis for this study we were more interested in the potential effects of the FKBS defense mechanisms and, especially, in the interaction between defense mechanisms and concept formation with regard to the criterion, i.e. the performance on the attention task. With regard to the hypothesized interaction effect, one result appeared for the condition of understimulation, namely for the combination of TAS and concept formation, especially salient in the monotony situation. A lower concept formation ability combined with a tendency to ascribe in frustrating situations the faults to oneself hampers attentional performance under the condition of understimulation. Formulated as a probabilistic statement, this would mean that given the condition of understimulation, the risk of making a mistake is greater for people showing this combination of personality characteristics (25% of the sample).

Concept formation also shows a main effect for the condition of overstimulation, but no interaction with defense mechanisms is found here. Among the defense mechanisms, TAS, REV, and (with an opposite direction) TAO give significant effects as presented in Fig. 14.7.

In summarizing the FKBS results for both conditions of inadequate stimulation (understimulation and overstimulation), one could say that attributing faults to oneself (TAS) results in a decrease of performance in both conditions. REV hampers learning, and a higher TAO score seems to have a favorable influence on managing the attention task under stress.

From earlier research with the FKBS it can be concluded that these results are partly in congruence with others. TAO, for example, has shown a positive influence on creativity under very different experimental conditions (Hentschel &

Schneider, 1986), TAS a negative effect on cognitive performance (Hentschel & Kiessling, 1990), and REV significantly lower learning effects in a complex sorting task (Udenhout & Bekker, 1990). We did not expect an effect to come fromPRO under the given conditions, our basic hypothesis did, however, cover INT, which actually showed no effects. When we try to come to a conclusion based on the results available thus far from our research on attention control, which was focused on the predictor side on defense mechanisms (measured by a self-report inventory and the percept-genetic DMT), anxiety (measured by a questionnaire), and concept formation (measured by the SMT), a clear method effect regarding the measurement of defenses appears, leading to predictive validities that are method-specific for different defense mechanisms and different interactions. With regard to the results comprising defense mechanisms it thus seems very difficult to use one theoretical umbrella. The problem of method specificity has been discussed to a greater extent in a theoretical context in two chapters of this book (cf. Chapters 1 and 7), but it remains a concrete obstacle in empirical research too. We do not share the opinion of Lazarus and Folkman (1984) that persisting with one method and ignoring others is a good way out of the dilemma. An intermediate solution could be to look for an optimalization of the predictors, to this end cross-validating the set of predictor variables used in this study would be a necessary step.

The state of affairs as far as defense mechanisms are concerned is thus unsatisfying mainly from a theoretical point of view and provides better perspectives in regard to practical applications. Drivers of tank trucks as well as pilots, flight controllers, railway operators, or captains of ships should have a certain tolerance for inadequate stimulation (some unexpected stress seems to be as unavoidable in these jobs as well as certain forms of understimulation). Understimulation is a somewhat neglected topic in traffic research, but it constitutes a real safety problem (cf. Coblentz, Mollard, & Cabon, 1989; McDonald, 1984). Personnel selection on the basis of defense mechanisms could reduce the probability of errors under these circumstances of inadequate stimulation. Whereas the validity of the DMT regarding the prediction of performance under stress in real-life situations has been shown in many studies, for the FKBS, the generalizability of the results reported here remains to be proved. Some of the FKBS scales seem to exert a filter function with respect to attention control: TAS and REV in a negative, TAO in a positive direction. The application of the FKBS in combination with the microgenetic SMT seems to be also very promising.

The requirements in attention control are rather complex, and it could be that perceptually and verbally coded defense mechanisms predict different aspects of this complex task. One could try to reduce the complexity of attention control and use instead of a measure for an overall performance the performance on basic cognitive dimensions (e.g. focusing and scanning; Gardner, Holzman, Klein, Linton, & Spence, 1959; Hentschel, 1980). Wachtel (1967) has compared the difference between these dimensions to a torch directed at a dark object, where you can distinguish between the size of the circle of the light and its movements over the object. But in our task there was a double matching of the symbols shown on the screen, with their specific location and the reaction on the number keyboard in a disjunctive reaction sequence. Validity estimates for some elements, if they could be achieved, thus would not necessarily end up in the prediction of the complex task. A reduction of the complex attention requirements to their hypothetical components thus would have been of doubtful value.

A criterion-related optimization of the predictors seems to be more promising. Especially interesting in this respect are interactions of defenses with emotional and cognitive variables (cf. Messick, 2001). One major aim to which the present study also was devoted to, would be to enlarge the mere correlational proof of the interrelatedness of defenses with these variables by experimental evidence. Another important aspect would be to submit the results found here to a reality test of actual driving, where neurocognitive tests seem to provide relevant results when the category of accidents is sufficiently specified (De Raedt & Ponjaert-Kristoffersen, 2001). Possible conclusions to be expected from this research are not only in regard to person-related decisions but also to other variables in the system that can be used for the individual prevention of negative consequences of inadequate stimulation.

Acknowledgment. This study has received financial support by Daimler-Chrysler, Stuttgart, Germany.

References

Chance, R. M. A. (1976). Social attention: Society and mentality. In .R.M.A. Chance & R.A. Larsen (Eds.), *The social structure of attention* (pp. 315-333). London: Wiley.

Coblentz, A., Mollard, R., & Cabon, P. (1989). Vigilance and performance of human operators in transport operations. Applications to railway and air transport. *Proceedings of the ESTEC-Workshop: A task-oriented approach to human factors engineering.* November 21-23. Noordwijk: ESA.

Conrad, P. (1999). It's boring: Notes on the meaning of boredom in everyday life. In B. Glassner, & R. Hertz (Eds.), *Qualitative sociology as everyday life* (pp123-133). London: Sage.

Cooper, L. A. & Regan, D. T. (1982). Attention, perception and intelligence. In R.J. Stemberg (Ed.), *Handbook of human intelligence* (pp. 123-169). Cambridge: Cambridge University Press.

De Raedt, R., & Ponjaert-Kristoffersen, I. (2001). Predicting at-fault car accidents of older drivers. *Accident Analysis and Prevention, 33*, 809-819.

Dixon, N. F. (1981). *Preconscious processing.* Chichester, England: Wiley.

Dixon, N. F., Hentschel, U., & Smith, G.J.W. (1986). Subliminal perception and microgenesis in the context of personality research. In A. Angleitner, A. Fumham, & G. van Heck (Eds.), *Personality psychology in Europe: Vol. 2. Current trends and controversies* (pp. 239-255). Lisse, The Netherlands: Swets & Zeitlinger .

Floru, R, Damongeot, A., & Di Renzo, N. (1988). Vigilance et nuisances physiques. 2. Effets de l'association du bruit et des vibrations sur la vigilance du conducteur. Etude experimentale [Combined effects of noise and vibrations on vigilance during driving. Experimental investigation]. *1NRS, Cahiers de notes documentaires,* 130, ND 1661.

Forbes, T. W. (1972). Introduction. In T. W. Forbes (Ed.), *Human factors in highway traffic safety research* (pp. 1-22). New York: Wiley.

Froehlich, W. D. (1978). Stress, anxiety and the control of attention. In C.D. Spielberger & I.G. Sarason (Eds.), *Stress and anxiety: Vol. 5* (pp. 99-130). Washington, DC: Hemisphere.

Gardner, R. W., Holzman, P.S., Klein, G.S., Linton, H., & Spence, D.P. (1959). Cognitive control: A study of individual consistencies in cognitive behavior. Psychological Issues, 1, No.4.

Glass, A. L., Holyoak, K.J., & Santa, J.L. (1979). *Cognition.* Reading, MA: Addison-Wesley.

Gleser, G. C. & Ihilevich, D. (1969). An objective instrument for measuring defense mechanisms. *Journal of Consulting and Clinical Psychology, 33*,51-60.

Hentschel, U. (1984). Microgenesis and process description. In W.D. Froehlich, G. Smith, J.G. Draguns, & U. Hentschel (Eds.), *Psychological Processes in cognition and personality* (pp. 59-70). Washington, DC: Hemisphere.

Hentschel, U. (1980). Kognitive Kontrollprinzipien und Neuroseformen [Cognitive styles and forms of neuroses]. In U. Hentschel & G. Smith (Eds.), *Experimentelle Persönlichkeitspsychologie* [Experimental personality psychology] (pp. 227-321). Wiesbaden: Akademische Verlagsgesellschaft.

Hentschel, U. (1997). Konzeptbildung als ein zentrales Konstrukt für Informationsverarbeitung und Handeln [Concept formation as a central construct for information processing and action]. In H. Mandl (Ed.), *Bericht über den 40. Kongreß der Deutschen Gesellschaft für Psychologie in München 1996* (pp.661-667). Göttingen: Hogrefe.

Hentschel, U., & Draguns, J. G. (in preparation). Percept-genetic techniques in the study of cognitive styles and defense mechanisms: From assessment toward psychotherapy. In G. Smith & U, Kragh (Eds.), Constructing personality: Actualization of the personal world by means of perceptgenetic/microgenetic techniques.

Hentschel, U. & Kiessling, M. (1983). On the predictability of performance in a serial problem-solving task: First results with the Symbol Maze Test. *Archives of Psychology, 135*, 85-101.

Hentschel, U. & Kiessling, M. (1986). Über die Beziehung von Inlelligenz-Konzeptbildungs- und Problemlöseleistung. Eine theoretische Skizze und einige empirische Ergebnisse [On the relation of intelligence, concept formation and problem-solving performance. A short theoretical outline and some empirical results] *Archives of Psychology, 138,* 287-294

Hentschel, U. & Kiessling, M. (1990). Are defense mechanisms valid predictors of performance on cognitive tasks? In G. van Heck, S. Hampson, J. Reykowsky, & J. Zakrzewski (Eds.), *Personality psychology in Europe Vol.* 3 *Foundations, models, and inquiries* (pp. 203-223). Lisse: Swets & Zeitlinger.

Hentschel, U., & Kiessling, M. (in preparation). *Manual for the Symbol Maze Test (SMT)*

Hentschel, U., Kiessling, M., & Hosemann, A. (1989). The effect of cognitive and affective personality variables on attention control. *Proceedings of the ESTEC-Workshop A task-oriented approach to human factors engineering* November 21-23, Noordwijk: ESA.

Hentschel U., Kiessling, M., & Hosemann, A. (1991). Anxiety, defense and attention control In R. E. Hanlon (Ed.), *Cognitive microgenesis. A neuropsychological perspective* (pp. 262-285). New York: Springer.

Hentschel U., Kiessling, M., & Ternes, G. (1984). *Kognitive Aspekte des Problemlösens bei Konzeptbildungsaufgaben* [Cognitive aspects of problem-solving in concept formation tasks]. Mainz: Arbeitsbericht aus dem DFG-Forschungsprojekt "Symbol-Labyrinthe" [Working report from the DFG research project "Symbol Mazes"]

Hentschel U., & Schneider, U. (1986). Psychodynamic personality correlates of creativity. In U. Hentschel, G.J.W. Smith, & J. G. Draguns (Eds.), *The roots of perception* (pp 249-275). Amsterdam: North-Holland.

Hunt, E. (1980). Intelligence as an information processing concept. *Journal of British Psychology, 71*, 449-474.

Karsten, A. (1928). Psychische Sättigung [Psychic satiation]. *Psychologische Forschung, 10*, 142-254.

Lazarus, R.S., & Folkman, S. (1984). *Stress, appraisal and coping.* New York: Springer.

Lewin, K. (1935). *A dynamic theory of personalit. Selected papers.* New York: McGraw-Hill.

McDonald, N. (1984). *Fatigue, safety and the truck driver.* London: Taylor & Francis.

McGuire, F.L. (1976). Personality factors in highway accidents. *Human Factors, 18*, 433-442.

Messick, S. (2001). Style in the organization and defense of cognition. In J. M. Collis, & S. Messick (Eds.), *Intelligence and personality: Bridging the gap in theory and measurement* (pp. 259-272). Hillsdale: Erlbaum.

Rockwell, T. (1972). Skills, judgment and information acquisition in driving. In T.W. Forbes (Ed.), *Human factors in highway traffic safety research* (pp 133-164). New York: Wiley.

Udenhout, M.Y., & Bekker, F.J.B. (1990). *Defensiemechanismen, een barriere voor het feedbackproces?* [Are defense mechanisms hampering the feedback process?] Leiden University (mimeographed).

Wachtel, P. (1967). Conceptions of broad and narrow attention. *Psychological Bulletin, 68*, 417-429.

Defense Mechanisms
U. Hentschel, G. Smith, J.G. Draguns & W. Ehlers (Editors)

Chapter 15

Stress, Autonomic Nervous System Reactivity, and Defense Mechanisms

Phebe Cramer

Defense Mechanisms and Physiological Reactivity to Stress

The defense mechanism has been one of the most elusive concepts in psychology. Its definition as an unconscious process removes it from being directly observable, while its very functioning may distort the individual's ability to report on its consequences. Recently, psychologists have again begun to focus on the importance of defense mechanisms for understanding psychological functioning (see Cramer & Davidson, 1998). However, since defense mechanisms function outside of awareness, there may be an inherent inconsistency in asking people to self-report on a process of which they are unaware. Various approaches to defense assessment have confronted this problem, by relying on observers' judgements of defense use or by using ratings based on projective techniques. (For a summary of these approaches, see Cramer and Davidson, 1998).

Another source of difficulty in studying this area has been an occasional confusion between the terms 'defense mechanism' and 'defensiveness'. The term 'defense mechanism' is a theoretical construct that describes a cognitive operation which occurs on an unconscious level, the function of which is to modify the conscious experience of thought or affect. Specific defense mechanisms are defined by the specific cognitive operations that bring about this modification, as discussed below. 'Defensiveness' is a more general term, and refers to behaviors that protect the individual from anxiety, loss of self-esteem, or other disrupting emotions. Defensiveness may thus be served by defense mechanisms, but there are other mechanisms that support defensiveness, such as the conscious decision to act differently than one feels, or to suppress a disturbing idea. A critical distinction between the concept of defense mechanism and defensive behavior is that the former is always unconscious, while the latter may be consciously rec-

---

Portions of this paper have appeared in the *Journal of Personality*, 71 (2), 2003

ognized by the individual. Thus defensiveness is the broader category, including both defense mechanisms as well as other behaviors that are designed to reduce anxiety. (For further discussion of this issue, see Cramer, 1991a).

Both defensiveness and the use of defense mechanisms have been shown to distort people's self-report of their emotional state. For example, defensive individuals often under-report their own level of anxiety or psychological maladjustment (Shedler, Mayman & Manis, 1993; Weinberger, 1990); likewise, college students, who experienced an experimental threat to their identity, indicated they were not upset, although their use of defense mechanisms increased (Cramer, 1998). Findings such as these create further interpretive problems for understanding the relation of defensiveness to outcome behaviors. When individuals who are assessed as being defensive then report that they are happier (healthier, less anxious) than others, how is this to be understood? There are two possibilities: either the defensive individuals are truly better off, or their self-assessment is influenced by their defensiveness, which results in an illusive self-presentation not supported by independent judgements. These alternative explanations of the consequence of defensiveness have been discussed at some length by Taylor (Taylor & Brown, 1994) and Block (Colvin & Block, 1994), and by Cramer (1998), Cramer and Davidson (1998), and Davidson (1996).

One way to tease apart the question of true mental health from illusory, or defensive mental health is to note discrepancies in self-report, or discrepancies between self-report and observers' report. Weinberger (1990) has used the discrepancy between two self-report measures to assess the "repressor" personality, a style of defensiveness rather than the defense mechanism of repression. Shedler et al (1993) have used the discrepancy between self- and observer-report to assess illusory mental health. In both cases, the discrepancy measure of defensiveness was related to subsequently assessed physiological reactions to stress, as seen in greater autonomic reactivity among the discrepant individuals.

The use of autonomic nervous system measures to assess stress has the advantage that it is a response system not normally under the conscious control of the individual, and so may be free of possible self-report biases. This feature suggests that autonomic reactions might be related to another type of stress response that is out of the conscious control of the individual - namely, the defense mechanism. According to theory, psychological stress will activate the use of defense mechanisms; the greater the stress, the greater the need for defense. Since stress also activates the autonomic nervous system, an increased use of defenses should be related to heightened physiological arousal. The use of defenses then protects the individual from the conscious experience of anxiety, although arousal on the physiological level continues. Indeed, it was this formulation in an early paper by Alexander (1939) that was used to explain certain psychosomatic illnesses – namely, that defenses against the expression of negative emotions could be a cause of physical illness. More recently, work by Pennebaker, Barger and Thiebout (1989) has supported a similar thesis. Thus, to demonstrate a clear relation between stress-induced autonomic reactivity and the use of defenses would provide validity support for the defense mechanism construct.

The Assessment of Defense Mechanisms

Dissatisfied with the use of self-report defense measures, Cramer has carried out a series of studies in which the measure of defense is based on narrative material, coded for the use of three defenses (Cramer, 1991a). These defenses - denial, projection and identification - were selected because they differ in cognitive complexity and thus might be expected to relate to different developmental levels. Denial, a cognitively simple defense, involves a single operation, which may be characterized as inhibition. Denial may produce inhibition of the perceptual system through the withdrawal of attention from a stimulus: "I don't see anything;" "It's not there." Denial inhibits thought or emotion by the attachment of a negative marker to the idea or affect: "It didn't happen;" "I'm not afraid".

Projection is a defense of somewhat greater complexity, involving at least three steps: differentiating between internal and external, comparing the thought or feeling with internal standards, and attributing unacceptable thoughts/feelings to an external source. Further, rather than inhibiting the thought or affect, projection functions by displacing unacceptable thoughts and feelings from the self onto someone else, thereby avoiding shame or guilt.[1]

Identification is the most complex of the three, requiring the capacity to differentiate self from others, to differentiate among others, to form inner representations of others, and to adopt some qualities of important persons (while rejecting others) in the process of identification. Again, thoughts and feelings are not inhibited, but rather are taken over from others and incorporated into the self, thereby providing both security through the 'presence' of the other, and protection of the self through affiliation.

This approach to defense assessment has demonstrated the existence of a developmental hierarchy of defense use (Cramer, 1991a; Cramer & Gaul, 1988; Porcerelli, Thomas, Hibbard & Cogan, 1998) and has confirmed theoretical expectations regarding the relation between defense mechanisms and other facets of personality (e.g., Cramer, 1999a,b; Hibbard, Farmer, Wells et al, 1994). Most important for the present paper, this measure has been shown to be sensitive to increases in psychological stress, such that stressed individuals demonstrate an increase in defense use (Cramer, 1991b, 1998; Cramer & Gaul, 1988).

Based on the previous discussion, these latter findings suggest that stress-induced use of the three defense mechanisms should be accompanied by increases in autonomic nervous system reactivity. Such a relation would add further support to the assumption that defense mechanisms occur in response to psychological stress, even though the individual may be unaware of the functioning of either of these response systems.

Defensive Behavior and Autonomic Reaction to Stress: Skin Conductance Level

There is considerable evidence indicating that individuals who are disposed to use defensive emotion inhibiting strategies show increased electrodermal reactivity when faced with stress, while those who are less disposed to defensive inhibition show less reactivity. Thus, those who score high on the Repression end of Byrne's (1961) Repression-Sensitization (R-S) scale (Cook, 1985; Hare, 1966), high on Marlowe-Crowne defensiveness (Gudjonsson, 1981;Tomaka, Blascovich & Kelsey, 1992), high on Weinberger's measure of repressive coping (Weinberger, Schwartz & Davidson, 1979), who use avoidance or denial (e.g., Assor, Aronoff, & Messe, 1986; Dozier & Kobak, 1992; Lazarus & Alfert, 1964), who engage in thought suppression (e.g., Wegner, Short, Blake et al, 1990) and who do not disclose feelings (e.g., Hughes, Uhlmann & Pennebaker, 1994; Pennebaker & Chew, 1985) have all been found to show greater electrodermal reactivity than their less inhibiting counterparts.

This greater autonomic reactivity of inhibitors, however, is often at odds with their self-report of subjective experience of stress. Summarizing early work in this area, Weinstein, Averill, Opton and Lazarus (1968) demonstrated that Repressors (as assessed by Byrne's R-S scale or by MMPI Denial) showed greater autonomic arousal than self-report stress reactions to threat. More recently, the discrepancy between Marlowe-Crowne defensiveness and self-reported anxiety has been used by Weinberger (1990) to identify Repressors – individuals who are high on defensiveness but low on self-reported anxiety. This group is found to show higher electrodermal reactivity in response to stress than individuals who are low on defensiveness (Barger, Kircher & Croyle, 1997; Weinberger,

Schwartz & Davidson, 1979). Barger et al (1997) further suggest that emotional inhibition involves the same physiological process -- i.e., increased skin conductance level (SCL) -regardless of whether it is used automatically, as in the case of an unconscious defense, or used on demand, as a result of instructions. Again, research supports this assumption. Individuals who are instructed to suppress or withhold a response show an increased SCL (e.g, Gross & Levenson, 1997; Pennebeker & Chew, 1985; Wegner, Broome & Blumberg, 1997). Even more interesting are findings that instructions to use *specific* defenses may differentially affect SCL. Some 40 years ago, Lazarus and colleagues demonstrated that instructing, or encouraging participants to consciously use the mature defense of intellectualization was more effective in reducing SCL than was encouragement to use the immature defense of denial (Lazarus & Alfert, 1964; Speisman, Lazarus, Mordkoff & Davison, 1964). Thus, while defensiveness involving inhibition may increase SCL, other types of defensiveness may be effective in reducing SCL.

Defensive Behavior and Autonomic Reaction to Stress: CV Reactivity

It is generally believed that stress conditions that are responded to with active behavioral or cognitive coping are associated with an increase in both systolic blood pressure (SBP) and diastolic blood pressure (DBP) (Fowles, 1980; Gray, 1975; Lacey, 1967; Obrist, 1981). While research bears this out (e.g., Lovallo, Wilson, Pincomb, Edwards, Tompkins & Brackett, 1985; Middleton, Sharma, Agouzoul, Sahakian, & Robbins, 1999; Steptoe, 1983), it has also been demonstrated that both active *and* passive coping demands result in increased SBP and DBP, but for different hemodynamic reasons (Sherwood, Dolan & Light, 1990).

Individual differences in psychological dispositions, including defensiveness, are also likely to contribute to CV reactivity. Thus, individuals characterized by dispositional defensiveness involving suppression, distancing, emotional inhibition, repressiveness and denial have all been found to show a greater increase in BP (both SBP and DBP) in reaction to stress situations than that found in their less defensive counterparts (Bongard, al'Aabsi & Lovallo, 1998; Davidson, 1993, 1996; Fontana & McLaughlin, 1998; Jamner, Shapiro, Goldstein & Hug, 1991; King, Taylor, Albright & Haskell, 1990; Weinberger, 1990). Further, as with SCL, the use of different defense mechanisms may have differential CV consequences, as hypothesized by Schwartz (1990); while all defenses involve a common process of repression, "defenses will vary in their levels of complexity and therefore vary in the levels of consequence for the person" (Schwartz, 1990, p. 425).

Since both skin conductance and cardiovascular reactivity have been associated with defensive response patterns, one might expect a positive relation between these two physiological measures in response to stress (Kelsey, 1991). However, contrary to this expectation, evidence shows that CV and SC reactions are not necessarily correlated. One reason is that both sympathetic and parasympathetic systems modulate the heart, whereas the sweat glands are activated by sympathetic innervation alone (Kelsey, 1991). Low correlations may also reflect individual response stereotypy, as described by Dawson, Schell and Filion (1990), whereby some individuals show increased SCL arousal but minimal CV change, while others show the reverse pattern. Thus research on the relation between cardiac reactivity and electrodermal response to stress has yielded inconsistent results, often showing that the two response systems are independent or can even produce opposite effects (e.g., Barger et al, 1997; Hughes, Uhlmann, & Pennebaker, 1994; Lacey, 1969; Speisman et al, 1964; Wegner et al, 1990). On a psychological level, this is consistent with the idea that increases in CV reactivity reflect behavioral activity, including cognitive work, whereas SCL increase reflects behavioral inhibition (Fowles, 1980; Gray, 1975; Lacey, 1956).

Paradigm to Study Defense and Physiological Reactivity

The large majority of studies that have investigated the relation between defensiveness and physiological reactivity have assessed the two variables at different points in time.[2] Defensiveness typically is assessed prior to the stress task, and participants are divided into high and low defensive groups on the basis of these self-report tests. Subsequently, their physiological reaction to stressful conditions is determined. This procedure assumes a correspondence between trait and state defensiveness, such that those who are higher on trait defensiveness will continue to be higher on state defensiveness. However, the relation between defensiveness and physiological response would be more clear if the defense assessment could be made during the time that the stress is occurring.

Data collected in a previous study make this possible. Shedler et al (1993) investigated the physiological ramifications of 'illusory mental health,' based on the discrepancy between the participant's self-report score of health/distress on the Beck Depression Inventory (BDI) and an experienced clinician's rating of each participant on one Q-sort item: "Has a brittle ego-defense system; would be disorganized under stress." Participants who self-reported little distress (low BDI score) but were given a high rating by the clinician were judged as showing illusory mental health; those who self-reported little distress and were given a low rating by the clinician were judged to have genuine mental health. When these two groups were presented with ten different stress tasks, the illusory mental health group showed significantly greater cardiac reactivity, including higher DBP, than the genuinely healthy group. The authors interpreted their findings to mean that the CV reactivity was due to the "defensive denial of distress" (p. 1117), although the use of the defense mechanism of denial was not directly assessed.

The present study investigates this same group of individuals in greater depth, focusing on the relation between their use of defense mechanisms and their physiological reactions to stress. In particular, autonomic reactions indicative of cognitive activity (DBP) and of inhibition (SCL) are studied. Since all ego defense mechanisms require cognitive activity, they should all be related to an increase in DBP. However, those defenses of greater complexity should require greater activity, which in turn should be reflected in a larger increase in DBP. In contrast, only some defenses, such as denial, are characterized by the inhibition of thought or affect ("I don't think/feel that"). Others do not inhibit so much as displace or transform the manifestation of the emotion. For example, projection attributes the personally upsetting emotion to someone else, while identification involves taking on the emotion of the other as one's own. For these reasons, denial should be associated with an increase in SCL, since inhibiting strategies, such as suppression or avoidance, have previously been demonstrated to be associated with SCL increase (see above); this increase is expected regardless of whether the inhibition is used as a conscious strategy, as in the case of suppression, or whether it occurs automatically, as in the case of a defense (Barger et al, 1997). In contrast, since the use of projection and identification involves the acknowledgement of emotion, rather than its inhibition, the use of these latter two defenses might be expected to be associated with lower SCL.

Based on the preceding discussion, the following hypotheses were investigated:
1. Psychological stress will increase autonomic nervous system reactivity, as seen in increased DBP and increased SCL.
2. Because increased DBP is associated with cognitive activity, and because the use of defenses involves cognitive activity, the use of defenses in response to psychological stress will be associated with increased DBP. This should be especially true when the defense mechanism is more cognitively complex, as in the case of Identification.

3. Because both SCL and denial are associated with emotion inhibition, participants who respond to stress with an increased use of denial will show a greater increase in SCL than will those who use projection and identification, which involve less emotion inhibition.

Method

Participants

The participants in this investigation are part of the Block and Block longitudinal study of personality and cognitive development. (See J.H. Block & J. Block, 1980, for a full description of the study). These men and women were initially recruited into the study at age 3, while attending either a university-run or parent cooperative nursery school; they reside primarily in urban areas and are heterogeneous with respect to parental social class and education. Approximately two-thirds of the participants are Caucasian, one-fourth are African-American, and one-twentieth are Asian-American. In the most recent assessment at age 23, 104 persons (of the original 128) participated. Data for the defense and physiology measures were available for 84 participants, and were collected by J. Shedler and J. Block, neither of whom had knowledge of the defense coding method at the time of data collection. Due to occasional recording difficulties, there were 76 participants (40 men, 36 women) for whom DBP measures on all 10 tasks were available, and 78 participants (41 men, 37 women) for whom SCL measures on all 10 tasks were available. These participants are included in the present study.

Apparatus

Diastolic blood pressure (DBP) was measured with an Ohmeda Model 2350 Finapress blood pressure monitor, which uses a pressurized finger cuff attached to the middle finger of the non-dominant hand. Diastolic blood pressure was continuously monitored, with readings updated at each heart beat. Skin conductance level (SCL) was measured using a J & J IG-3 GSR preamp and a J & J model T-68 monitor. Electrodes were attached to the middle pads of the index and third fingers of the non-dominant hand, as suggested by Venables and Christie (1980). The DBP and SCL data were fed to a J & J I-330 digitized physiological recording and display system, from which data values were sampled at 3-second intervals. The DBP and SCL values used for subsequent analyses represent the mean values obtained during the baseline and during periods when each of ten stress tasks was being performed. Further details are described in Shedler, Mayman and Manis (1993).

Procedure

On arrival at the laboratory, participants were asked to sit quietly and relax for 10 minutes. Baseline measures for DBP and SCL were taken during the final minute of this adaptation period. Physiological monitoring continued during 10 stressful tasks; these included one mental arithmetic task, three sentence association tasks, and six stories created in response to TAT cards. Although the particulars of each task are described below, it should be noted that for the purpose of the present study we are not interested in the effect of any particular stress task on autonomic nervous system reactivity or on defense use. Rather, the study is concerned with the question of whether autonomic nervous system reactivity is related to defense use, regardless of the source of the reactivity – i.e., regardless of the stress task used.

Stress Tasks

Mental Arithmetic

This task required participants to count backwards by 13s from 609 for a one minute period. Described as a test of mental ability, speed and accuracy were stressed. Participants were asked to make their maximum effort. Regardless of performance, after 30 seconds they were asked to count faster.

Sentence Association

In this procedure, three blocks of 5 sentences each were presented to each participant. Participants were instructed: "I am going to show you some cards, and each card has a sentence printed on it. Please read each sentence aloud, loud and clear, then tell me the first thing that comes to mind after reading the sentence" (Shedler et al, 1993, p. 1126).

Following these three sentence tasks, there was a 2-minute rest period.

Thematic Apperception Test (TAT)

Using standard instructions for the TAT (Murray, 1943), Cards 18GF, 8GF, 8BM, 10, 15, and 2 were presented, one at a time. Participants told stories to each card; the stories were tape-recorded and subsequently transcribed.

Physiological reactivity

Baseline measures of DBP and SCL were computed by averaging the observations recorded during the last minute of the initial 10-minute rest period. Subsequently, measures of DBP and SCL during each stress task were computed by averaging all 3-second samples obtained during that task.

Measuring Defense Mechanisms

The Defense Mechanism Manual (DMM: Cramer, 1991a) was employed to assess the use of defense mechanisms in TAT stories. Without knowledge of the subject's gender or other information, each of the transcribed 468 (6 x 78) stories was scored by a trained coder for the presence of three defense mechanisms -- Denial, Projection, and Identification -- according to the DMM.

For each defense, there are seven categories representing different aspects of the defense; each category is scored as many times as it occurs in each story. The scores for each defense were then summed over the six stories, yielding a total score for Denial, for Projection, and for Identification.

The categories for each defense are as follows:
Denial: (1) Omission of major characters or objects; (2) Misperception; (3) Reversal; (4) Statements of negation; (5) Denial of reality; (6) Overly maximizing the positive or minimizing the negative; (7) Unexpected goodness, optimism, positiveness, or gentleness.

Projection: (1) Attribution of hostile feelings or intentions, or other normatively unusual feelings or intentions, to a character; (2) Additions of ominous people, animals, objects, or qualities; (3) Magical or autistic thinking; (4) Concern for protection from external threat; (5) Apprehension of death, injury or assault; (6) Themes of pursuit, entrapment and escape; (7) Bizarre story or theme.

Identification: (1) Emulation of skills; (2) Emulation of characteristics, qualities, or attitudes; (3) Regulation of motives or behavior; (4) Self-esteem through affiliation; (5) Work; delay of gratification; (6) Role differentiation; and (7) Moralism.

A more complete description of these categories, with detailed rules for scoring, is presented in Cramer (1991a).

These measures of defense mechanisms have been demonstrated in previous studies to have adequate inter-rater reliability, with children, adolescents and adults (Cramer, 1991a, 1995, 1998; Cramer & Block, 1998; Cramer & Gaul, 1988; Luciano, 1999; Porcerelli, Thomas, Hibbard & Cogan, 1998). In the present study, a second coder independently scored a random selection of 100 of the stories.* The agreement between coders, based on Pearson's *r*, was .80 for Denial, .85 for Projection, and .78 for Identification, indicating adequate inter-rater reliability.

The validity of the coding approach has been demonstrated both through observational studies, in which defense mechanism scores differentiated between age groups or were related to personality in ways predicted by theory (e.g., Cramer, 1991a, 1999a,b; Hibbard, Farmer, Wells, Difillipo, Barry, Korman, & Sloan, 1994; Porcerrelli et al, 1998) and through experimental investigations in which a stress manipulation produced predicted changes in defense use (Cramer, 1991b, 1998; Cramer & Gaul, 1988).

Results

Descriptive Statistics

Defenses

A Defense (3) x Gender(2) MANOVA was carried out. The results indicated a main effect for Defense, F (2,152) = 37.43, $p < .001$. T-tests indicated a higher score for Projection (M = 10.37, *S.D.* = 7.12) than Denial (M = 5.63, *S.D.* = 4.59), $t(78) = 6.19$, $p < .001$, and than Identification, (M = 4.65, *S.D.* = 2.87), $t(78) = 7.40$, $p < .001$. Neither the main effect for Gender, nor the Defense x Gender interaction was significant, *ps* > .50. The intercorrelations among the three defense measures were : Denial with Projection, $r = .23$; Denial with Identification, $r = .11$; Projection with Identification, $r = .04$.

Evidence for Physiological Reactivity to Stress.

The DBP and SCL raw score means for Baseline and Stress tasks are presented in Table 15.1. In order to demonstrate that the stress tasks did increase autonomic reactivity, a series of MANOVAs comparing each stress task with the baseline measure, including Gender as a factor, were conducted.

DBP

A DBP Baseline/Stress Task (2) by Gender (2) MANOVA was carried out for each stress Task. For all 10 of the DBP comparisons, the DBP levels during the

* Appreciation is expressed to Jennifer Whitfield for her assistance in the scoring process.

stress tasks were significantly higher than the pre-stressor baseline reading, *ps* < .001. (See Table 15.1). In no case was Gender, or the Gender by Task interaction significant.

Table 15.1: *Comparison of Mean (and SD) Baseline and Task Physiological Levels: Raw Scores*

TASK	DBP	SCL
Baseline	68.74 (10.67)	4.63 (3.53)
Math	81.24 (11.12)***	10.16 (5.59)***
Sentence 1	83.06 (11.26)***	11.22 (6.25)***
Sentence 2	84.32 (11.50)***	11.14 (6.22)***
Sentence 3	83.98 (11.76)***	11.18 (6.32)***
TAT 1	80.25 (11.63)***	11.66 (6.67)***
TAT 2	84.78 (12.27)***	11.68 (6.52)***
TAT 3	84.30 (12.24)***	11.64 (6.72)***
TAT 4	84.89 (12.23)***	11.99 (6.75)***
TAT 5	84.31 (12.02)***	12.10 (7.11)***
TAT 6	84.15 (12.35)***	12.04 (6.97)***

Also noteworthy is the drop in DBP reactivity following the 2-minute rest period between Sentence Association and TAT story-telling (see Table 15.1), consistent with the assumption that the Sentence Association task was stressful. The subsequent increase in DBP reactivity following the introduction of the TAT task is consistent with the assumption that the TAT task was stressful.

SCL

A SCL Baseline/Task (2) by Gender (2) MANOVA was carried out for each stress Task. For all 10 of the SCL comparisons, the SCL levels during the stress tasks were significantly higher than during the pre-stressor baseline reading (*ps* < .001). (See Table 15.1.). In no case was Gender, or the Gender by Task interaction significant.

Physiological Reactivity as a Function of Defense Use

Because there were no significant gender effects for Defense, DBP or SCL, the data were collapsed across gender. On the basis of a median split, participants were divided into High and Low defense groups, for each of the three defenses. To test the relation of defense use to physiological reactivity, High and Low defense groups were compared for DBP and SCL on each stress task.

DBP

An initial comparison of the baseline DBP for High and Low defense groups indicated no difference for High and Low Identification, t (79) = .91, $p > .36$, or for High and Low Projection, t (79) = .35, $p > .73$. Baseline DBP was higher in the Low Denial group than in the High Denial group, t (79) = 2.11, $p < .04$. In addition, Baseline DBP was found to correlate significantly with DBP change (Actual DBP minus Baseline DBP) for 6 of the 10 stress tasks, *ps* = .001 to .06. When the baseline measure correlates with change scores, it is necessary to adjust for the baseline measure. Otherwise, the subsequent differences between High and Low defense groups could be due to baseline differences, not to stress reaction. Thus, the initial baseline level was subtracted from each of the stress task mean DBP levels, yielding 10 separate DBP change scores for each participant. These DBP change scores were used for all subsequent analyses.

To analyze these data, an analysis of covariance (MANCOVA) was used, with Baseline DBP as the covariate and DBP change as the dependent variable (Manuck, Kasprowicz & Muldoon, 1990; see also Davidson, 1996). In order to use MANCOVA, two assumptions must be met. First, there must be a significant linear relation between the dependent variable (DBP change) and the covariate (Baseline DBP). Second, the slope of the regression line must be the same in each defense group (High, Low). The first assumption was met for the analyses of all three defenses. The second assumption was met for Denial and Identification, but not for Projection, where the interaction between Baseline DBP and Projection group was significant. Further analyses of the relation between DBP change and Projection indicated that the High and Low Projection groups did not differ in DBP change for any of the 10 stress tasks, *ts* (76 - 79) = -.47 to 1.11, *ps* > .27.

Using DBP Baseline as the covariate, the Task (10) x Hi/Lo Identification (2) MANCOVA yielded a main effect for Identification, F (10,64) = 1.96, $p < .05$. As predicted, univariate F-tests indicated that for every stress task, the High Identification group showed greater DBP change than did the Low Identification group, F (1,73) = 4.27 to 12.11, *ps* = .04 to .001 (see Figure 15.1). Figure 15.1 also shows the drop in DBP reactivity following the 2-minute rest period.

Again using DBP Baseline as the covariate, the Task (10) x Hi/Lo Denial (2) MANCOVA did not show a significant main effect for Denial, F (10,64) = .92, $p > .50$. However, t-tests indicated that for the first two stress tasks, DBP change was greater in the High Denial than in the Low Denial group, *t*s (78 and 79) = 1.95 to 2.30, *ps* < .05 and .02.

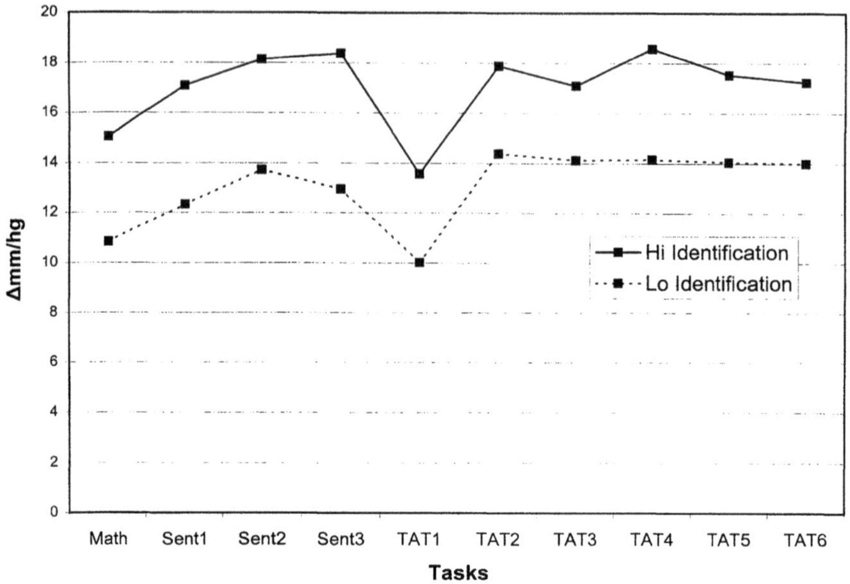

Figure 15.1: *Diastolic blood pressure change and Idenfication*

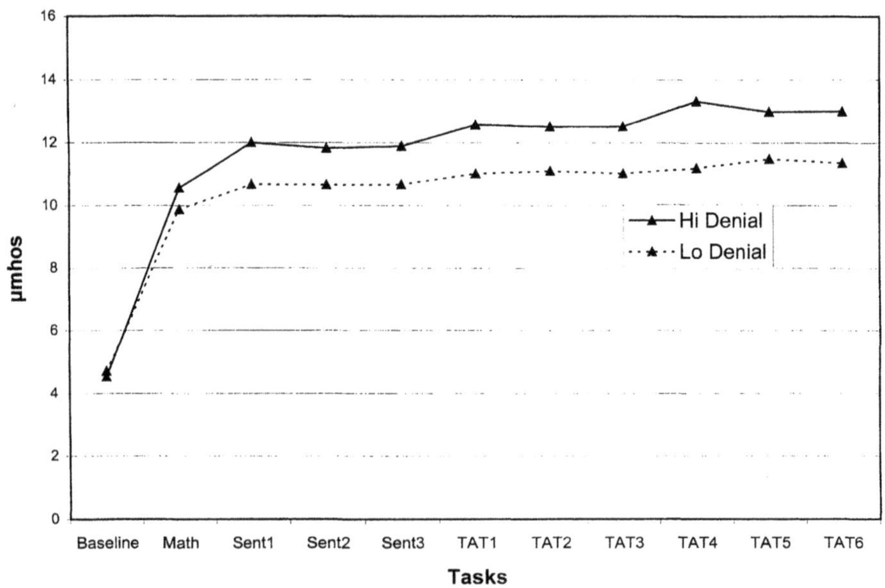

Figure 15.2: *Skin conductance level and Denial*

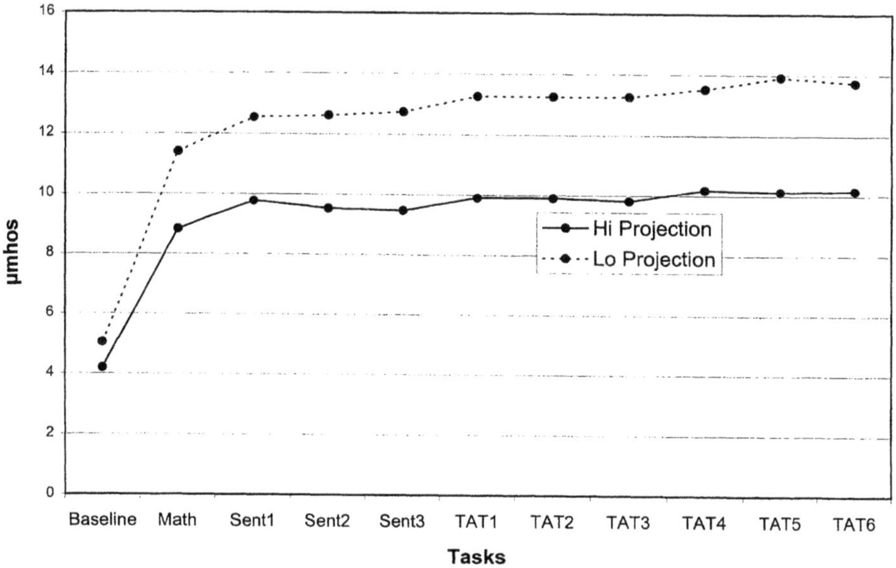

Figure 15.3: *Skin conductance level and Projection*

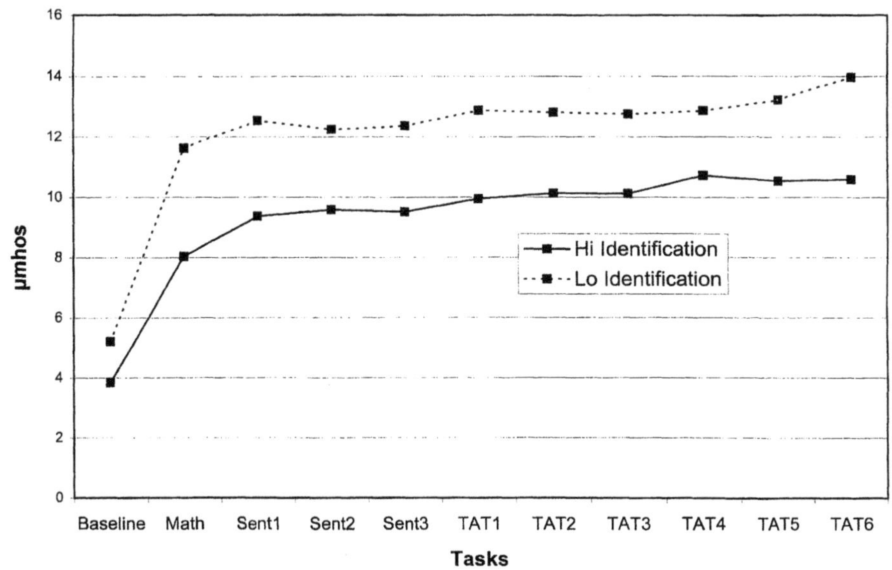

Figure 15.4: *Skin conductance level and Identification*

SCL

A comparison of the High and Low defense groups for Baseline SCL indicated no significant differences for any defense. Further, there was no correlation between Baseline SCL and any of the SCL change scores (*r*s = -.05 to .03, *p*s > .63). As indicated by Lykken (1968), these findings allow for the use of raw, rather than change scores as dependent measures, to assess the relation of SCL to defense use, for each of the 10 stress tasks. It was predicted that the defense involving inhibition – Denial – would be associated with a greater increase in SCL than the defenses not involving inhibition (Projection and Identification). However, for the Task (10) x Hi/Lo Denial (2) MANOVA, neither the main effect for Denial $F(1,76) = 1.23$, n.s., nor the interaction was significant. Nevertheless, as may be seen in Figure 15.2, for every stress task, the High Denial group was characterized by a higher SCL.

A Task (10) x Hi/Lo Projection (2) MANOVA yielded a main effect for Projection, $F(1,76) = 5.46$, $p < .02$. The interaction was not significant. Further t-tests indicated that the High and Low Projection groups differed significantly on every task, *t*s (78 to 82) = 2.10 to 2.51, *p*s < .04 to .01. For each task, the High Projection group showed a lower SCL (see Figure 15.3).

A Task (10) x Hi/Lo Identification (2) MANOVA yielded a main effect for Identification, $F(1,76) = 2.75$, $p < .10$ of borderline significance. The Task x Identification interaction was significant, $F(9,68) = 2.24$, $p < .03$ (see Figure 15.4). T-tests indicated that the High and Low Identification groups differed significantly on 7 of the 10 tasks: Math, Sentences 1, 2, and 3, and TATs 1, 2, and 3, *t*s (81 and 82) = 1.93 to 3.22, *p*s < .057 to .002. In addition, the difference between the High and Low Identification groups was of borderline significance for TAT5 and TAT6, *t*s (79 and 80) = 1.83 and 1.73, *p*s < .07 and .08. In each case, the High Identification group showed a lower SC (see Figure 15.4).

In a further test of the hypothesis that the use of Denial would be associated with higher SC levels than the use of Identification or Projection, additional analyses were carried out. First, the High Denial group was compared with the High Identification group. The results indicated significantly higher SCL scores on every stress task among those who used Denial, *t*s (49-50) = 2.12 to 3.07, *p*s < .04 - .004. An additional comparison of the High Denial group with the High Projection group indicated significantly higher SCL scores on every stress task among those who used Denial, *t*s (48-52) = 3.26 to 3.82, *p*s < .002 to .001.[3]

Discussion

With but a few exceptions (e.g., Davidson, 1996) the majority of previous studies of defense and autonomic nervous system reactivity have focused on the self-reported defensive reactions of denial or suppression, which were assessed either *before* or *after* the stress experience. An even stronger demonstration is to show that defense use occurs *concurrently* with changes in physiological markers of stress, indicating that there are physiological concomitants to the use of defense mechanisms. In the present study, three defenses of differing levels of complexity were assessed, using a non-self-report measure. The defense assessment was made concurrently with measures of autonomic nervous system reactivity in response to a series of stress tasks. These tasks were shown to increase autonomic reactivity, producing higher diastolic blood pressure and skin conductance levels, as compared to a non-stressed baseline.

As predicted, defense mechanisms were related to autonomic reactivity. Even more striking, different defense mechanisms were shown to be associated with different patterns of autonomic response. Because CV reactivity is associated with behavioral activity, including cognitive work (Fowles, 1980; Gray, 1975; Lacey, 1956), it was predicted that an increase in DBP would be associated with the use of the defense of identification, a defense that is cognitively complex and thus requires cognitive work to carry out. This prediction was confirmed. DBP level, over and above that obtained at baseline, was predicted by high use of identification. Those participants with high identification scores showed a greater DBP increase than those with low Identification scores. In contrast, cognitively simpler defenses – projection and denial – did not show a reliable association with DBP reactivity. Level of projection use was unrelated, while an initial association with denial became non-significant after the first two stress tasks, likely reflecting the minimal amount of cognitive work involved in the continuing use of the defense.

Because SC reactivity is associated with behavioral inhibition (Fowles, 1980; Gray, 1975; Lacey, 1956) it was further predicted that an increase in SCL would be associated with the use of denial, a defense that involves the inhibition of sensory and cognitive functioning. Although high denial users showed higher SC levels than low denial users on every stress task, the differences were not statistically significant. However, when high denial users were compared with those who were high users of projection or identification, those who used denial showed significantly higher SC levels. Further, those who relied on projection and identification – more mature defenses that do not rely on inhibition – showed significantly lower SCL than those who made less use of these defenses. These results are consistent with the earlier findings of Lazarus and colleagues (Lazarus & Alfert, 1964; Lazarus et al, 1965; Speisman et al, 1964), which demonstrated that encouraging the use of intellectualization, a relatively mature defense, was more effective in reducing SCL than was encouraging the defense of denial.

These findings may cast light on the problem of inconsistent or contradictory results from earlier studies that related autonomic nervous system reactivity to stress. Previous studies have demonstrated that stress-induced change in SCL may or may not be accompanied by changes in BP (Kelsey, 1991). One way of understanding these discrepant results has been to suggest that there are individual differences in physiological response to stress -the idea of individual response stereotypy (cf. Dawson et al, 1990). The present results are consistent with this explanation, and go further to identify the psychological concomitants of these individual differences, based on the individual's proclivity for using different defense mechanisms. Individuals who favor the use of identification show both lower SCL and higher DBP; the use of projection is associated only with lower SCL, and denial is associated primarily with an increase in SCL but only a transitory increase in DBP. Thus, what might look like inconsistent or inconclusive relations between stress and autonomic reactivity becomes more distinctive once the effect of differential defense use is considered.

The present study was not concerned with autonomic reactivity as related to type of task, but rather with the relation between reactivity (regardless of the task producing the reactivity) and defense use. Of the three types of stress tasks, mental arithmetic, with the demand to count faster, was likely the most stressful. The sentence completion and TAT tasks may be considered mildly stressful because, in the presence of an unknown experimenter, the individual is asked to provide personally revealing information (sentence completion) or to create imaginative stories to ambiguous stimulus pictures (TAT). Evidence for the stressful nature of these tasks is seen in the fact that the autonomic measures remained high during the sentence completion tasks, but decreased (DBP) during the rest period between sentence completion and TAT, only to increase again, once the TAT began. The increase in reactivity after the rest period indicates that the autonomic response to the TAT was not simply a "carryover" effect from the earlier tasks, but rather reflected stress associated with the demand to tell imaginative stories.

The history of the concept of the defense mechanism has followed a rocky road in academic psychology. After an initial flurry of interest and experimentation from 1930 to 1960, the defense mechanism was dismissed from serious consideration, often with negative connotations. Among the reasons for this dismissal were the origins of the concept in psychoanalysis – a theory largely rejected by academic psychology – and the status of the defense as an unconscious process – an assumption contradictory to the tenets of behaviorism (cf. Cramer, 2000; Lazarus, 1998; Paulhus, Fridhandler & Hayes, 1997). In reaction, attempts were made to assess defensive functioning using paper and pencil tasks (e.g., Byrne, 1961). By relying on self-report and objective scoring keys for operationally defined constructs, these measures avoided the criticisms associated with psychoanalysis and unconscious processes.

Over the past decade, there has been increasing concern about the use of self-report measures to assess psychological adjustment and reaction to stress. A number of investigators have suggested that the lack of correspondence between verbal report and physiological measures of affective arousal to stress may be explained by dynamic factors, such as defensive distortion (e.g., Cramer, 2000; Shedler et al, 1993), as had been suggested earlier by Lazarus and Alfert (1964) and by Mordkoff (1964). This idea has again been presented by Schwebel and Suls (1999), who indicated that the denial of distress, rather than the self-report of negative emotions, might be the effective predictor of physiological hyperreactivity. The present study provides evidence that defense mechanisms do, in fact, moderate the relation between stress and physiological response.

On a final note, although the present findings clearly demonstrate a relation between defenses and autonomic reactivity, they leave open the question of the direction of this relation. Do changes in the autonomic nervous system elicit the use of defenses? Or, does the defense use provoke autonomic reactivity? Further inquiry into the possible causal relation between defenses and autonomic reactivity may clarify the role that defenses play in a person's physical, as well as mental well-being.

Acknowledgements. The data for this paper come from the longitudinal study supported by NIMH Grant MH 16080 to Jack and Jeanne H. Block. Jonathan Shedler and Jack Block have generously made these data available. Appreciation is expressed to Andrew B. Crider for his helpful comments in writing this paper.

References

Alexander, F. (1939). Emotional factors in essential hypertension: Presentation of a tentative hypothesis. *Psychosomatic Medicine*, *1*, 173 – 179.

Assor, A., Aronoff, J., & Messe, L.A. (1986). An experimental test of defensive processes in impression formation. *Journal of Personality and Social Psychology, 50*, 644 – 650.

Barger, S.D., Kircher, J.C., & Croyle, R.T. (1997). The effects of social context and defensiveness on the responses of repressive copers. *Journal of Personality and Social Psychology, 73*, 1118 – 1128.

Block, J., & Block, J.H. (1980). The role of ego-control and ego-resiliency in the organization of behavior. In W.A. Collins (Ed.), *Development of cognition, affect and social relations: Minnesota Symposia on Child Psychology* (Pp. 39 – 101). Hillsdale, NJ: Erlbaum.

Bongard, S., al'Absi, M., & Lovallo, W.R. (1998). Interactive effects of trait hostility and anger expression on cardiovascular reactivity in young men. *International Journal of Psychophysiology, 28*, 181 – 191.

Byrne, D. (1961). The Repression-Sensitization scale: Rationale, reliability, and validity. *Journal of Personality, 29*, 334 – 349.

Cacioppo, J.T., & Tassinary, L. G. (Eds.) (1990) *Principles of psychophysiology.* New York: Cambridge University Press.

Chandler, M.J., Paget, K.F, & Koch, D.A. (1978). The child's demystification of psychological defense mechanisms: A structural developmental analysis. *Developmental Psychology, 14*, 197 – 205.

Cook, J. R., (1985). Repression –sensitization and approach-avoidance as predictors of response to a laboratory stressor. *Journal of Personality and Social Psychology,49*, 759 – 773.

Cramer, P. (1991a) *The development of defense mechanisms: Theory, research and assessment.* New York: Springer-Verlag.

Cramer, P. (1991b). Anger and the use of defense mechanisms in college students. *Journal of Personality, 59*, 39 – 55.

Cramer, P. (1998) Threat to gender representation: Identity and identification. *Journal of Personality, 66*, 335 - 357.

Cramer, P. (1999a). Personality, personality disorders, and defense mechanisms. *Journal of Personality, 67*, 535 – 554.

Cramer, P. (1999b). Ego functions and ego development: Defense mechanisms and intelligence as predictors of ego level. *Journal of Personality*, 735 – 760.

Cramer, P. (2000). Defense mechanisms in psychology today: Further processes for adaptation. *American Psychologist, 55*, 637 – 646.

Cramer, P., & Gaul, R. (1988). The effects of success and failure on children's use of defense mechanisms. *Journal of Personality, 56*, 729 – 742.

Cramer, P., & Davidson, K. (Eds.) (1998). Defense mechanisms in contemporary personality research [Special issue]. *Journal of Personality, 66*(6).

Dandoy, A.C., & Goldstein, A.G. (1990). The use of cognitive appraisal to reduce stress reactions: A replication. *Journal of Social Behavior and Personality, 5*, 275 – 285.

Davidson, K. (1993). Suppression and repression in discrepant self-other ratings: Relations with thought control and cardiovascular reactivity. *Journal of Personality, 61*, 669 – 691.

Davidson, K. (1996). Self- and expert-reported emotion inhibition: On the utility of both data sources. *Journal of Research in Personality, 30*, 535 – 549.

Davidson, K., Hall, P. & MacGregor, M. (1996). Gender differences in the relation between interview-derived hostility scores and resting blood pressure. *Journal of Behavioral Medicine, 19*, 185 – 201.

Davidson, K., & MacGregor, M. (1998). A critical appraisal of self-report defense mechanisms measures. *Journal of Personality,66*, 965 – 992.

Davis, M.C., Matthews, K.A., & McGrath, C.E. (2000). Hostile attitudes predict vascular resistance during interpersonal stress in men and women. *Psychosomatic Medicine, 62*, 17 – 25.

Dawson, M.E., Schell, A.M. & Filion, D.L. (1990). The electrodermal system. In J.T. Cacioppo & L.G. Tassinary (Eds.) *Principles of psychophysiology*. Mew Hprl: Cambridge University Press.

Dozier, M., & Kobak, R.R. (1992). Psychophysiology in attachment interviews: Converging evidence for deactivating strategies. *Child Development, 63*, 1473 – 1480.

Drummond, P.D. (1999). Facial flushing during provocation in women. *Psychophysiology, 36*, 325 – 332.

Fichera, L.V., & Andreassi, J.L. (1998). Stress and personality as factors in women's cardiovascular reactivity. *International Journal of Psychophysiology, 28*, 143 – 155.

Fontana, A., & McLaughlin, M. (1998). Coping and appraisal of daily stressors predict heart rate and blood pressure levels in young women. *Behavioral Medicine, 24*, 5 – 16.

Fowles, D.C. (1980). The three arousal model: Implication of Gray's two-factor learning theory for heart rate, electrodermal activity and psychopathy. *Psychophysiology, 17*, 87 – 104.

Gray, J.A. (1975). *Elements of a two-process theory of learning* New York: Academic Press.

Gross, J.J., & Levenson, R.W. (1997). Hiding feelings: The acute effects of inhibiting negative and positive emotion. *Journal of Abnormal Psychology, 106*, 95 – 103.

Gudjonsson, G.H. (1981). Self-reported emotional disturbance and its relation to electrodermal reactivity, defensiveness and trait anxiety. *Personality and*

Individual Differences, *2*, 47 – 52.
Hare, R.D. (1966). Denial of threat and emotional response to impending painful stimulation. *Journal of Consulting Psychology*, *30*, 359 – 361.
Hibbard, S., Farmer, L., Wells, C., Difillipo, E., Barry, W. Korman, R., & Sloan, P. (1994). Validation of Cramer's Defense Mechanism Manual for the TAT. *Journal of Personality Assessment*, *63*, 197 – 210.
Holmes, D.S., & Houston, B.K. (1974). Effectiveness of situation redefinition and affective isolation in coping with stress. *Journal of Personality and Social Psychology*, *29*, 212 – 218.
Hughes, C.F., Uhlmann, C., & Pennebaker, J.W. (1994). The body's response to processing emotional trauma: Linking verbal text with autonomic activity. *Journal of Personality*, *62*, 565 – 585.
Jamner, L.D., Shapiro, D., Goldstein, I.B., & Hug, Rozanne. (1991). Ambulatory blood pressure and heart rate in paramedics: Effects of cynical hostility and defensiveness. *Psychosomatic Medicine*, *53*, 393 – 406.
Kelsey, R.M. (1991). Electrodermal lability and myocardial reactivity to stress. *Psychophysiology*, *28*, 619 – 631.
King, A.C., Taylor, C.B., Albright, C.A., & Haskell, W.L. (1990). The relationship between repressive and defensive coping styles and blood pressure responses in healthy, middle-aged men and women. *Journal of Psychosomatic Research*, *34*, 461 – 471.
Lacey, J.I. (1967). Somatic response patterning and stress: some revisions of activation theory. In M.H. Appley & R. Trumbull (Eds.), *Psychological stress*. New York: Appleton-Century-Crofts. Pp. 14 – 42.
Lazarus, R.S. (1998). *Fifty years of the research and theory of R.s. Lazarus: An analysis of historical and perennial issues.* Mahwah, NJ: Lawrence Erlbaum Asssociates.
Lazarus, R.S., & Alfert, E. (1964). Short-circuiting of threat by experimentally altering cognitive appraisal. *Journal of Abnormal and Social Psychology*, *69*, 195 – 205.
Lovallo, W.R., Wilson, M.F., Pincomb, G.A., Edwards, G.L., Tompkins, P., & Brackett, D.J. (1985). Activation patterns to aversive stimulation in man: passive exposure versus effort to control. *Psychophysiology*, *22*, 283 – 367.
Lykken, D.T. (1968). Neuropsychology and psychophysiology in personality research. In E.F. Borgatta & W.W. Lambert (Eds.). *Handbook or personality theory and research*. Chicago: Rand McNally. Pp. 413 – 509.
Manuck, S.B., Kasprowicz, A.L., & Muldoon, M.F. (1990). Behaviorally-evoked cardiovascular reactivity and hypertension: Conceptual issues and potential associations. *Annals of Behavioral Medicine*, *12*, 17 – 29.

Mente, A., & Helmer, K.F. (1999). Defensive hostility and cardiovascular response to stress in young men. *Personality and Individual Differences, 27*, 683 – 694.

Mordkoff, A.M. (1964). The relationship between psychological and physiological response to stress. *Psychosomatic Medicine, 26*, 135 – 150.

Murray, H.A. (1943). *Thematic apperception test.* Cambridge: Harvard University Press.

Newtown, T.L., Bane, C.M., Flores, A., & Greenfield, J. (1999). Dominance, gender, and cardiovascular reactivity during social interaction. *Psychophysiology, 36*, 245 – 252.

Obrist, P.A. (1981). *Cardiovascular psychophysiology: A perspective.* New York: Plenum Press.

Paulhus, D.L., Fridhandler, B. & Hayes, S. (1997). Psychological defense: Contemporary theory and research. In R. Hogan, J. Johnson & S. Briggs (Eds.), *Handbook of Personality Psychology*, New York: Academic Press.

Pennebaker, J.W., Barger, S.D., & Tiebout, J. (1989). Disclosure of traumas and health among Holocaust survivors. *Psychosomatic Medicine, 51*, 577 – 589.

Pennebaker, J.W., & Chew, C.H. (1985). Behavioral inhibition and electrodermal activity during deception. *Journal of Personality and Social Psychology, 49*, 1427 – 1433.

Porcerelli, J.H., Thomas, S., Hibbard, S., & Cogan, R. (1998) Defense mechanisms development in children, adolescents, and late adolescents. *Journal of Personality Assessment, 71*, 411 – 420.

Raikkonen, K, Matthews, K.A., Flory, J.D., Owens, J.F., & Gump, B.B. (1999). Effects of optimism, pessimism, and trait anxiety on ambulatory blood pressure and mood during everyday life. *Journal of Personality and Social Psychology, 76*, 104 – 113.

Richards, J.M., & Gross, J.J. (1999). Composure at any cost? The cognitive consequences of emotion suppression. *Personality and Social Psychology Bulletin, 25*, 1033 – 1044.

Schwartz, G.E. (1990). Psychobiology of repression and health: A systems approach. In J.L. Singer (Ed.) *Repression and dissociation.* Chicago: University of Chicago Press. Pp. 405 – 434.

Schwebel, D.C., & Suls, J. (1999). Cardiovascular reactivity and neuroticism: Results from a laboratory and controlled ambulatory stress protocol. *Journal of Personality, 67*, 67 – 92.

Shedler, J., Mayman, M., & Manis, M. (1993). The *illusion* of mental health. *American Psychologist, 48*, 1117 – 1131.

Sherwood, A., Dolan, C.A., & Light, K.C. (1990). Hemodynamics of blood pressure responses during active and passive coping. *Psychophysiology, 27,* 656 –668.

Smith, T.W., & Gallo, L.C. (1999). Hostility and cardiovascular reactivity suring marital interaction. *Psychosomatic Medicine, 61,* 436 – 445.

Speisman, J.C., Lazarus, R.S., Mordkoff, & Davison, L. (1964). Experimental reduction of stress based on ego-defense theory. *Journal of Abnormal and Social Psychology, 68,* 367 – 380.

Steptoe, A. (1983). Stress, helplessness and control: The implications of laboratory studies. *Journal of Psychosomatic Research, 27,* 361 – 367.

Tomaka, J., Blascovich, J., & Kelsey, R.M. (1992). Effects of self-deception, social desirability, and repressive coping on psychophysiological reactivity to stress. *Personality and Social Psychology Bulletin, 18,* 616 – 624.

Venables, P.H., & Christic, M.J. (1980). Electrodermal activity. In I. Martin & P.H. Venables (Eds.), *Techniques in psychophysiology.* New York: Wiley. Pp. 4 – 7.

Wegner, D.M., Broome, A., & Blumberg, S.J. (1997). Ironic effects of trying to relax under stress. *Behavior Research Therapy, 35,* 11 – 21.

Wegner, D.M., Shortt, J. W., Blake, A.W., & Page, Michelle S. (1990). The suppression of exciting thoughts. *Journal of Personality and Social Psychology, 58,* 409 – 418.

Weinberger, D.A. (1990). The construct validity of the repressive coping style. In J.L. Singer (Ed.) *Repression and dissociation.* Chicago: University of Chicago Press. Pp. 337 –386.

Weinberger, D.A., Schwartz, G.E., & Davidson, R.J. (1979). Low-anxious, high-anxious, and repressive coping styles: Psychometric patterns and behavioral and physiological responses to stress. *Journal of Abnormal Psychology, 88,* 369 - 380.

Weinstein, J., Averill, J.R., Opton, E.M., & Lazarus, R.S. (1968). Defensive style and discrepancy between self-report and `physiological indexes of stress. *Journal of Personality and Social Psychology, 10,* 406 – 413.

---

[1] Chandler, Paget & Koch (1978) have provided a somewhat different analysis of the cognitive operations involved in denial and projection, with a similar conclusion that projection is a defense of greater cognitive complexity than denial.

[2] Exceptions to this are studies by Davidson (1996), Pennebaker, Barger & Tiebout (1989) and by Hughes, Uhlmann & Pennebaker (1994).

[3] Similar results were obtained using the more stringent comparison of participants who were High on Denial and Low on Identification (or Projection) versus those who were Low on Denial and High on Identification (or Projection).

Defence Mechanisms in Psychotherapy and Clinical Research

Defense Mechanisms
U. Hentschel, G. Smith, J.G. Draguns & W. Ehlers (Editors)

Chapter 16

Clinical Evaluation of Structure and Process of Defense Mechanisms Before and During Psychoanalytic Treatment

Wolfram Ehlers

Introduction

Freud (1917d) regarded the psyche as a hierarchy of superordinate and subordinate formations, comprising a multitude of drives and links with the external world. Very often there are divergent and incompatible relations among these diverse components. Freud attributed the defense process and the object of id, containing that which is defended against, to separate systems according to their diverging function and conceptual meaning. The defense process is activated in the ego (A. Freud, 1936) whereas the targets of defense are generated in the id and superego. For conscious observation of defense mechanisms, the ego is the medium through which images of the two other structures are apprehended. The ego senses oncoming urges, increased tensions with concomitant feelings of displeasure, and, finally, the resolution of the tension through a gratifying experience of pleasure. These structures can be observed through their effects on images, affects, and social relations.

In contemporary psychoanalysis this structural theory of the psyche remains highly controversial because of the complex and ambiguous implications of its metapsychological concepts for clinical thinking. Thus, one of the prominent representatives of American ego psychology concluded: "It is anything but agreeable to have to realize that one has dedicated most of one's career to a worthless theory as which metapsychology has itself proven" (Holt, 1989, p.327). On the other hand, Arlow and Brenner (1988) have devoted their efforts to construct and elaborate ego psychology, which they consider clinically useful and theoretically essential. Many psychoanalysts (e.g. Edelson, 1988) regard research as the only possible way out of the unresolved dilemmas of structural theory. This chapter is based on three empirical clinical studies of the application of defense mechanisms in the diagnostic phase of inpatient psychoanalytic treatment of severely disturbed patients and on two case studies of outpatient treatment with analytical psychotherapy.

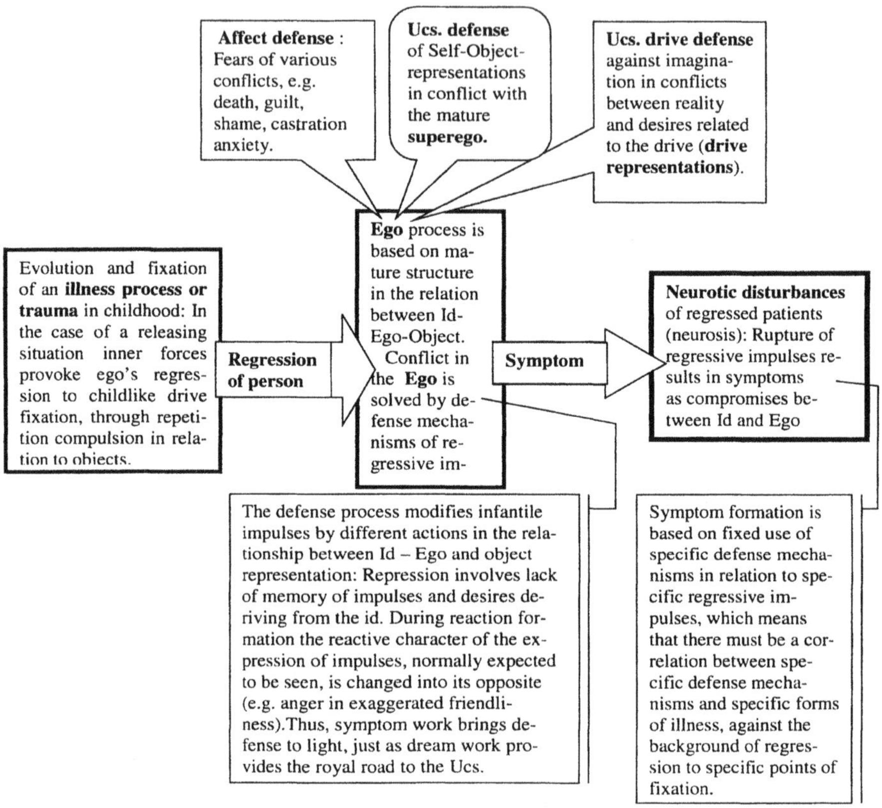

Hypotheses:

1. Defense structures can be extracted by means of factor analysis from 16 defense mechanisms. This structure resembles A. Freud's model. The model of affect defense in the case of greater regression in patients with an immature structure (e.g. severe regression) and the model of drive repression and superego defense in the case of lesser regression are indicative of symptom formation and illness. Both the differentiation of structure and the defense mechanisms within this distinctive model of affect defense, drive defense, and superego defense are mutually interactive. The principal symptoms of compulsive, hysterical, and depressive illness correlate with these defense factors.
2. Symptom formation in various forms of illness (depressive, hysterical, compulsive) is associated in each case with different models of defense mechanisms across the extracted defense factors.

Figure 16.1: *Psychoanalytic model of defense processes in symptom formation through the repetition compulsion of conflicts (based on A. Freud, 1936)*

The diagnostic data were gathered by psychoanalysts at a residential clinic in Stuttgart, Germany, a facility for approximately 120 patients with neurotic and personality disorders, many of them borderline. Many of the patients exhibited some psychotic symptoms. For research on the psychoanalytic process, the author selected two patients from among his outpatients in analytic psychotherapy and rated their defense mechanisms by himself after each therapy session.

The aim of these studies is to attempt to identify through clinical exploration those structures of defense mechanisms which can be described by quantitative methods and to compare with these instruments the two proposed metapsychologies which underlie defense mechanisms.

The Defense Model of Ego Psychology

The classical psychoanalytical conceptualisation of defense developed by Anna Freud (1936) describes the defense process as a self-protective activity of the ego. In this formulation, the ego was construed and described in line with Freud's (1923b) structural theory. Whenever conflicts arise between the ego, id, and superego, defense mechanisms act to enable the ego to banish unconscious desires and affects from consciousness (see Figure 16.1). In a discussion with a group of members of the British Psychoanalytic Association in London (Sandler & A. Freud, 1989), Anna Freud shared a revised explanation of her model of defense.

Psychoanalysis sets itself the task of acquiring as much knowledge as possible about the structural model of a given patient's personality. In this model, the ego serves as a medium for observing the effects of the id and superego upon a patient's experience and behavior. The ego never impinges upon behavior through subordinate id emotions, such as drive wishes. Invariably, its effects stem from the defense activities of the ego. In treatment, the psychoanalyst must disentangle the ego, id, and possibly superego components frequently merged in the process of pathological compromise formation. In this task, psychoanalyst's familiarity with specific arousing situations that are typically encountered in the process of transference is indispensable for the recognition of deviant ego activities. The characteristic modes of ego activity associated with the various mechanisms of defense provide useful descriptive and classificatory information on these mechanisms, as illustrated below:

1. In repression, memory of impulses and desires derived from the id is lacking. The resulting gaps, i.e. the unavailability of the expected attitudes and emotions, point to the specific defense mechanism of repression.
2. The striking feature of reaction formation is the encounter with the exact opposite of one's expectations. In most cases, compulsive exaggerations of

> specific behaviors point to the reactive character of the expression of impulses, which is usually evidenced through drive activation. Only through the work on defense in the analytic process is the person enabled to discover, if only for a fleeting moment, the drive derivatives as they enter consciousness because, at that point, they are experienced in the ego together with their opposites, for example, in the form of simultaneous rage and exaggerated friendliness.

A.Freud distinguished between drive defense and affect defense, (Sandler & A. Freud, 1989, p. 68)on the basis of the object of defense activity. The child's ego is focused on the defense against affect whereas in the adult ego, defensive activities tend to be concentrated on the effects of drive desires on imagination. Typically, an adult has learned to bring his or her affects under ego control early in life. Consequently, defense against drive presupposes the ability to experience the content and representation of imagination on the basis of drive desires. Thus, in adults a relatively weak defense against drive is indicative of a lower stage of intrapsychic maturity, or it may point to the extent of regression to the infantile modalities of ego activity. As drive desires in adults are observable through imagination, free association and dream reports provide excellent opportunities for observing ego defense activity. If this defense activity acquires a degree of autonomy, it becomes part of what Sandler and A. Freud (1989, p. 70) called a person's style. They proposed, in Hartmann's terminology, the existence of secondary autonomy of symptoms and characteristic traits. Opinions differ on the extent to which these symptoms and traits are modifiable during transference. Thus, A. Freud denied the possibility of analyzing character here and now because that would force a patient directly into transference.

Activation of a defense is triggered by an anxiety signal. The ego must have access to the unconscious process of the other structures. Thus, the goal of defense is to prevent the reactivation of traumatic situations (Moser, 1965)or their appearance in a less severe form. If repression fails as the main defense, other mechanisms assume the task of making the repressed acceptable to consciousness. Symptoms and character traits can be interpreted as the results of this defense process (Freud, 1908b).

Earlier dynamic conceptions of defense focused on their functional aspects. The psychodynamic conception of defense is based on repression. If a new situation is similar to the former events during which repression was experienced, repressed and unconscious mechanisms may exercise a permanent and pathogenic influence. Thus, suppressed impulses develop links to other memory traces and subsequently attempt to gain access to consciousness through less threatening pathways. This dynamic concept has served as a model for the regulation of impulses and affects as embodied in the cognitive interpretation of defense mechanism by Moser, von Zeppelin, and Schneider (1968). The conflict model of defense has been modified by Moser, von Zeppelin, and Schneider(1981) on the basis of recognizing the limitations of ego's information processing capacity.

It is therefore necessary to modify the classical structure theory by incorporating aspects of the regulation model. The logical structure of the controlling devices of the defense models holds implications for the clinical description of defense mechanisms. For a graphic representation of this classical structural model of defense in neurotic illness, see Figure 16.1.

The Defense Model in Melanie Klein's Object Relations Theory

Klein's structural model is focused on the accumulation of inner objects (Hinshelwood, 1993). This inner world of object representations acquires its structure by assimilating external objects into the representational structure of the ego. At a given moment, in order to recognize the external world appropriately and realistically, the individual identifies with his or her self or ego through its respective inner objects (cf. Figure 16.2).

Upon her discovery of preoedipal conflicts in the course of analyzing children, Melanie Klein intensively investigated the consequences of the defense by splitting for ego structure. She distinguished between a depressive structure and a paranoid-schizoid structure. In 1930, she divided defense mechanisms into neurotic and psychotic defenses based upon their origin, and concentrated her efforts between 1930 and 1935 upon the psychotic defense directed against aggression. Subsequently, between 1935 and 1946, she described the specific defense mechanisms of the depressive position, and followed it up with the description of those of the paranoid-schizoid position after 1946.These mechanisms were found to revolve around the relation between projective identification and the anxiety of annihilation, and the defenses against envy, upon which Klein concentrated after 1957. In contrast to Anna Freud, Melanie Klein was less interested in defense mechanisms during therapy than she was in the content of anxious fantasies which defense had prevented from arising, because they could be more easily modified through direct interpretation at the moment of maximal fear through direct interpretations.

Normally, the progression from the paranoid-schizoid position to the depressive position establishes reasonably stable constellations of object relations, which consist of different structures of personality characterized by their respective typ-

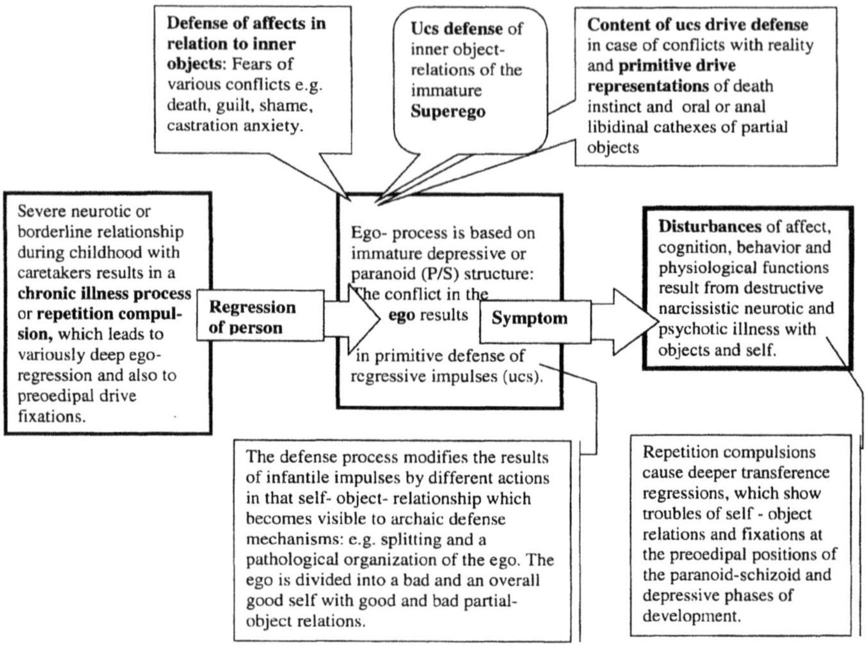

Hypotheses for empirical research:

1. Primitive defense structures can be extracted by means of factor analysis from 23 defense mechanisms. It is further hypothesized that the models of affect defense in the case of deep regression' of drive displacement in the case of lesser regression, and of superego defense together with narcissistic defense structure in the more regressive processes may correspond to the factors of defense structure. Both the factors and the defense mechanisms corresponding to these several models are characterized by distinctive affect defenses, drive defenses, superego defenses, and narcissistic defenses in various types of illness.
2. Results of process analysis for a less regressed patient point to a smaller number of process factors of defense than for a patient who in her illness regressed to a deeper fixation point. The structure and number of process factors of defense change during the psychoanalytic treatment process.

Figure 16.2: *Defense of the object relation disorders in the case of neurotic and borderline regression during inpatient psychotherapy and the psychoanalytic process (model of Melanie Klein, 1975)*

ical impulses, anxieties, and defense mechanisms. A. Freud's model needed to be expanded in order to accommodate the explicit diversification of superego analysis on the basis of the specific disturbances of object and self representations. Research on the pathological organization of various aspects of death instinct (Segal, 1972; Steiner, 1982; Brenman, 1985), especially in borderline personalities (Kernberg, 1984) and in psychosis (Rosenfeld, 1978), revealed pathological structures of the ego, dominated by the impulses of death instinct ("bad self") which attempted to defeat the "good ego" by means of intimidation and seduction.

Idealization of the "bad" parts of the self seduces the affectionate, constructive, and more realistic parts of personality (Rosenfeld, 1971) to give up its goals. A cruel superego supports the revenge seeking destructive aspects of personality and thereby assures their continued existence (Brenman, 1985). Connected with it, perceptual constriction and narrow mindedness combine to obliterate interpersonal understanding and to promote the glorification of omnipotence, experienced as though it was superior to human love and forgiveness. These mechanisms are placed at the service of defense against depression and worship of rancor and revenge. Identification of the self with a sense of omnipotence brings about predominance of destructiveness. As a consequence, the person devalues the idealized object and makes it into an appendage of his or her self.

This omnipotent self, which has split off from its needy and dependent portion, has appropriated for itself all the good qualities of the idealized object and regards itself as the ego in its entirety. Weaker parts of the self are disregarded while the rest of the inner world is subordinated and the existence of a separate external world is denied (Sohn, 1985). It is as though the omnipotent self had penetrated the object and had subjected it to its control. Inner emptiness of the ego is experienced as a symptom, because the external object has become worthless and the ego has been weakened by the divisions among internal objects. The omnipotent self often attempts to change its objects in order to stabilize its defenses in the form of splitting, projection, control, and omnipotence. Compulsive mechanisms such as undoing, isolation, and compulsive rituals serve to camouflage an underlying paranoia which spawns the defense mechanisms of projection and introjection.

The splitting of personality into psychotic and nonpsychotic parts (Bion, 1957) brings into being a pathological organization of the ego, typically characterized by the arrest of development at a point between the paranoid-schizoid position and the depressive position, which in stressful and difficult situations may precipitate malignant regression (Balint, 1970). Envy and death drives dominate affects. The "bad ego" dominates the "good ego". A person can only overcome the paranoid situation with the support of a narcissistic organization (Rosenfeld, 1964). The illusory defense system (Segal, 1972)involves the fixation on certain object relations that serve to satisfy perverse desires (Steiner, 1982, 1987).

These developments help generate a defense structure in which relationships between self and object representations come to the foreground. These primitive defense mechanisms (Hinshelwood, 1991) are directed against anxieties, usually of the paranoid or depressive variety, that are brought about by the activity of the death instinct. Instead of the compulsive defense against sadism and destructiveness favored by neurotic patients, the psychotic ego attempts to resist death instinct impulses by massive omnipotent projection, through the annihilation and ejection of its persecutors. These primitive and psychotic defenses contain denial and splitting as well as excessive forms of projection, through the expulsion of the bad object, and of introjection, through the incorporation of the good object.

In the paranoid-schizoid developmental position, fear of annihilation is the primary form of anxiety. More specifically, this fear involves the death instinct working from within to annihilate the self or ego and its objects. Its origin goes back to the baby's failure to deflect the death instinct to an external object. The destructiveness of the self results in the fear of an internal persecutor working to bring about the death of the subject from within. The subsequent projection of this inner persecutor unto the external world constitutes the foundation of all defensive activity in the paranoid-schizoid position. If this defense fails, disturbances of the self result in a multitude of bodily symptoms which refer to a lethal object inside, for example in cancer phobia, or in a variety of experiences of "falling apart". In Klein's (1946) words, "the early ego splits the object and the relation to it in an active way, and this may imply some active splitting of the ego itself. Thus one consequence is the experience of the ego being fragmented and in pieces" (p.5). This vertical splitting of the ego and objects result into dividing the self and the object into "good" or "bad" parts. The good parts of objects are idealized and the bad are omnipotently denied, ejected, and annihilated. The defense mechanisms of projective identification, idealization of the good objects, and expulsion of the bad objects are important for this narcissistic stage of development. In psychotic repression in illness or in transference we can see the early defense pattern of object relations, in the striving to survive the experienced or fantazied persecutory activity of the internal part objects.

In the depressive position the self aims to preserve its good and reliable internal object. This results in specific anxieties of loss and separation. The anxiety of losing the internal love object may provoke paranoid defenses against depressive anxiety, manic defenses, or the quest for restitution. The paranoid defense against the depressive position is the result of a retreat from the depressive position, when depressive anxieties become too strong. Paranoid defenses differ from the corresponding mechanisms of the earlier periods because the activity is linked to the duration of anxiety. Manic defenses are attempts to evade the extreme pain of guilt in the early depressive position. The cluster of manic defenses includes denial of psychic reality, contemptuous devaluation of love objects in order to minimize the impact of their loss, and a triumphant and omnipotent striving for restitution.

Restitution as a defense mechanism is derived from the obsessional defense of undoing, in which there is an attempt to annul a destructive action by retracing its steps. It has the same aim of adaptation to society as the Freudian concept of sublimation.

These depressive defenses are normal mechanisms of development, just as introjection and projection are, and it is important to differentiate them from pathological mechanisms in the transference-relation. Bion (1959) illustrated this distinction at length for the mechanism of projective identification. Its pathological character is highlighted by the prominence of hostility and destructiveness.

Research Methodology and Logical Definitions of Defense Mechanisms

The empirical investigation of the above models of defense introduced by Anna Freud and Melanie Klein, respectively, requires some methodological considerations. It should, however, be made clear from the very start that there is no intention of evaluating or comparing the seminal contributions of these two major psychoanalytic figures (King & Steiner, 2000). The present objective is limited to the ezamination of their respective models of ego psychology and object relations theory as they pertain to defense mechanisms. On the one hand, these models are the result of conceptual analysis (Dreher,1998) which should be a prerequisite for all empirical research. On the other hand, clinical classification requires a clear definition of each individual defense mechanism in the analytic sense of the term, whereby the logical structure of the various categories of defense is determined. With such defense algorithms in mind, a clinical rater is enabled to carry out a logical consistency check of various concepts.

I therefore followed the suggestion of Suppes and Warren (1975) and defined defense mechanisms as a logical link between the behaving subject and the object toward which the action of the subject is directed. In a generalized way such a sentence can be defined as follows: a subject (S) only partly activates, modifies or erases a drive impulse (D) or an affect (A) with respect to an object (O) into his consciousness or behavior. By replacing subject (S), drive-impulse (D) affect (A),or object (O) with concrete meanings, and by inserting the correct verb into the defense action, this highly abstract sentence makes it possible to formulate specific definitions of any and all defense mechanisms.

This abstract definition provides the psychoanalytic evaluator with the logical structure of the algorithm enabling him or her to solve the more complex problems of identifying drive and affect in the behaving subject and object in communication with the patient (Ehlers, 1993).

Dahl (1991) prefers the concept of affect to the concept of drive in his definition of defense mechanisms. In his formulation, the concept of defense is divested from its association with instinct psychology. To apply this more general definition of defense mechanism to our algorithm, we need only to exclude the instinct model (D), and we can work on the surface of the linguistic material proceeding from the expression of affect in the transcript. These mechanisms are the major regulatory tools of self and object relations (Steffens, & Kächele, 1988) in libidinally and aggressively determined representations. The specific algorithm for concrete clinical ratings and the description of specific empirical research methodology are presented in Table 16.1.

The empirical methodology for the statistical testing of the clinical hypotheses about the structure of defense is based on factor analysis. This method factors a correlation matrix of each items from all defense mechanisms. Each item was rated on a five-point scale by the analytic psychotherapists for their patients. The output of this analysis is made up of dimensions or factors, on which defense mechanisms have high or low loadings. Each dimension can explain a portion of the variance of the data. In the extreme case, if there is no dimensional structure of the defense concept, no item has a significant loading on any dimension. If the output of factor analysis yields a general factor, each defense mechanism is considered to be a subunit of the same dimension. The dimensions are labeled for the defense with the highest loading.

To investigate the structure of personality dispositions (Ehlers & Czogalik, 1984a), within Anna Freud ego-psychological model of defense, 11 analytic psychotherapists applied a diagnostic classification using a list of 16 defense mechanisms and four symptoms (CADM, Clinical Assessment of Defense Mechanisms; German: KBAM) to their 147 patients before beginning inpatient

Table 16.1: *Dimensions of defense: Abstract definitions of defense mechanisms (S = subject, D = drive/impulse, O = object)*

Factor 1	*Turning against self*	*Introjection*	*Delayed affect expression*	*Undoing (compulsive rituals)*	*Reaction formation*
Superego defense/affect defense	S turns aggression (D) against himself or herself (O).	S unites himself with the whole object (O), which represents the repressed impulse (D).	S delays affect expression to avoid connection between impulse (D) and object(O).	S takes back a prohibited impulse (D) in regard to an object (O).	S shows toward object (O) oppositional attitude and behaviors, other than what would be expected from the repressed.
Factor 2	*Rationalization*	*Denial*	*Repression*	*Reversal into the opposite*	*Primitive denial*
Impulse defense	S disguises existence of impulses (D) toward object (O) through logical and morally accepted explanations.	S denies existence of threatening perception or action concerning impulse (D) with regard to self or to external object (O).	S excludes images, memories, and thoughts of threatening impulse (D).	S shows controversial impulse toward the object (O), other than what would be expected from the stimulus situation.	S is aware of emotional significance of denied impulse (D). Yet S de-nies existence of threatening perception of thought or emotion toward self or object O.
Factor 3	*Dominance of affect equivalence*	*Identification*	*Conversion*	*Isolation*	
Consequences of affect defense	S is not aware of the affective significance of physical reaction usually accompanying the affect.	S unites himself with parts of the object (O) that represent impulse (D).	S shows expression of impulse (D) through bodily reaction.	S divides related associations or actions as well as images and affects to avoid contact between repressed impulse (D) and self (O).	
Factor 4	*Regression*	*Displacement of aggression*	*Displacement of libido*	*Projection*	
Libido displacement	S condemns oedipal impulse (D_{oe}) and retreats to pregenital impulse (D_R).	S cathects an image toward a neutral object (O) with destruction(D).	S cathexes a less threatening thought or behavior toward an object (O) with libido D	S displaces the repressed impulse (D) onto the object.	
Factor 5	*Primitive idealization*	*Mechanisms of splitting*	*Projective identification*	*Devaluation of external object*	*Fantasies of omnipotence*
Narcissistic defense	S idealizes an object (O), which is to protect him from own aggressive impulses (D^-) and from negative external objects (O^-)	S feels negative (D^-) and positive (D^+) impulses or expresses negative (O^-) and positive (O^+) object images concerning the same object (O), which have a character of exclusiveness, and acts accordingly. S is not affected by contrast of his emotions and imaginations.	S displaces own defended impulse (D) onto object (O) and at the same time feels linked empathically with object (O) in anxious empathy, because of knowledge about own aggressive impulse.	S devalues (dropping, shifting, denigrating) external object (O) because of feelings of revenge for being frustrated and feeling defenseless.	S clings to "magically" overrated object or develops overrated self, claiming special privileges or the devotion of objects (O) in regard to the subject (S).

treatment. Patients' diagnoses were distributed as follows: hysterical neurosis (N = 16, mean age = 31); neurotic depression (N = 70, mean age = 40); borderline personality disturbance (N = 22, mean age = 31); and compulsive neurosis (N = 9, mean age = 33). Thirty cases remained unclassified. For the clinical assessment of each defense mechanism, a five point scale was devised. Defense mechanisms could be rated on it from their highly probable to highly improbable presence.

Results of the Structure of Diagnostic Evaluation of Defense Mechanisms (Part 1)

Test of the Model of Ego-Psychology

In a previous factor analytic research project (Ehlers & Czagolik, 1984a), we were able to construct defense dimensions (see Table 16.2 for the ranking of factor-loadings from these 16 defense mechanisms). Quantitative evaluations were factored to obtain a numerical assessment of similarity between defense mechanisms. On the basis of a principal component analysis (SPSS-program), we found a total of 5 dimensions, which explained 41,1 percent of variance.

Table 16.2: *Results of factor analysis of 17 defense algorithms (CADM) and 3 symptoms (Ehlers & Czogalik, 1983a): N= 147 neurotic patients at a psychotherapeutic clinic in Stuttgart (Germany) evaluated by 11 analytic psychotherapists (Freudian or Jungian training). The + mark indicates replicated item structure*

Factor description/ Ranking	Superego defense	Defense of Impulse	Affect-defense	Consequences affect-defense	Displacement of impulse
of factor loadings	Factor 1 = 21,3%	Factor2 = 7,0%	Factor 3 = 5,2%	Factor 4 = 3,9%	Factor 5 = 3,7%
1	+Turning against self	Undoing	+Isolation	+Dominance of affect-equivalence	+Displacement of libido
2	+Introjection	Reaction formation	Inhibited affect expression	+Conversion	+Displacement of aggression
3	Identification	+Reversion			Denial
4	Regression	+Rationalisation			
5	Projection	+Repression			
6 Symptoms	Self-pity-Resignation	Obsession-Compulsion	Avoiding social contacts		

Table 16.3: *Results (Ehlers, 1993) of factor analysis of 23 defense algorithms (CADM 2): N= 284 neurotic and borderline patients of a psychotherapeutic clinic in Stuttgart (Germany) evaluated by 11 analytic psychotherapists (Freudian or Jungian training)*

Factor description/ Ranking of factor loadings	Superego defense	Defense of Impulse	Consequences affect-defense	Displacement of impulse	Narcissistic defense
	Factor 1 = 9,7%	Factor 2 = 6,1%	Factor 3 = 8,8%	Factor 4 = 7,4%	Factor 5 = 17,9%
1	Turning against self	Rationalisation	Dominance of affect-equivalence	Regression	Primitive idealiszation
2	Introjection	Denial	Identification	Displacement of aggression	Mechanisms of splitting
3	Inhibited affect expression	Repression	Conversion	Displacement of libido	Projective identification
4	Undoing	Reversion into the opposite	Isolation	Projection	Devaluation of external objects
5	Reaction formation	Primitive denial			Fantasies of omnipotence

They were named on the basis of a characteristic shared by the high ranking defense mechanisms, as follows:
Factor 1: superego defense (turning against self, introjection, identification, regression, projection);
Factor 2: impulse defense (undoing, reaction-formation, reversal);
Factor 3: affect defense(isolation, inhibited affect expression);
Factor 4: consequences of affect defense (equivalents of affect, conversion);
Factor 5: displacement of impulses (displacement of libido or aggression, denial).

Four symptoms corresponded to the following dimensions: self-pity and resignation (superego defense); compulsion (impulse defense); avoiding social contacts (affect defense) affect equivalent (consequences of affect defense). These results can be compared with the findings of the more recent study in Table 16.2.

Results and Discussion

In a subsequent study (Ehlers, 1993), I analyzed 284 evaluations of patients by 11 analytical psychotherapists. Nosological and age distributions of the patients were quite similar to those in our earlier research on defense mechanisms (Ehlers & Czogalik,1984), and data were analyzed in the same manner. Our objective was to study the factorial structure of classical defense mechanisms in a new data set with 17 or 23 items.

Factor analysis of the defense items on the CADM was carried out by means of computating an R-similarity matrix of correlations on 17 or 23 item defense scales for 284 patients. Upon the application of scree-test criteria, we found five dimensions for the structure of the defense system. Four of the five dimensions identified in the earlier publication (Ehlers & Czogalik, 1984a) were replicated in this larger sample. Only the order of the extracted factors changed, as well as the factor loadings of some defense mechanisms. Factor 3 and 4 of the former study (Ehlers & Czogalik,1984) gave a new factor, which is named "consequences of affect defense".

Anna Freud (1936) developed a procedure for the evaluation of discrete defense mechanisms. As a result, she was able to provide a relatively differentiated description of ego functions. French (1938) argued that these isolated descriptions produce a distorted and fragmentary image of the synthetic ego activity. He therefore recommended combining isolated defense mechanisms in a defense pattern. This idea was taken up by Suppes and Warren (1975) in their macrodefinition of defense mechanisms. In both of our studies we demonstrated empirically that there is a structure of defense that is based on the interaction or combination of specific defense mechanisms. This structure can now be empirically defined proceeding from the dimensions that have emerged from the research on psychoanalytic data. Statistical methods of correlation analysis and subsequent principal component analysis of these correlations have enabled us to extract independent dimensions or factors with varying contributions by the several discrete defense mechanisms. We found five factors (see Table 16.2) which largely correspond to the conceptual classification of defense by Anna Freud (1936) who made the distinction between drive rejection, affect rejection, and symptom formation as enduring defense phenomena in character traits and resistance.

Test of the Model of M. Klein's and O. Kernberg's Object Relations Theory

In this section I shall extend the empirical study of defense structure to the aspects of defense in object relations and narcissistic development. This extension of the conceptualization of defense is based on Kernberg's (1977, 1984) differentiation of neurotic and borderline levels of defensive organization. Kernberg's formulation has points of contact with the British theory of object relations (Hinshelwood, 1993) that differentiates neurotic and psychotic defense structures. The neurotic level is centered on the more mature defenses such as repression and reaction formation. A crucial component of this model is the horizontal defense of repression, which differentiates between conscious and unconscious representation of conflict, anxiety, and drive. The more primitive defensive operations on the borderline level are centered on the mechanisms of splitting and devaluation and are termed vertical defenses. In the present study we expanded the list of defense mechanism to aspects of object-relation and narcissistic development. On the basis of Kernberg's (1977) description, abstract definitions of primitive idealization, splitting, projective identification, devaluation of the external object, fantasies of omnipotence, and primitive denial (see Table 16.1) have been formulated.

Results and Discussion

The results of the factor analysis of 23 scales (CADM 2), which include the newly defined narcisssistic defense variables, yielded a five factor solution, which explained 49,9 % of the variance in the data.

The first dimension of the classical model of defense encompassed the third dimension of the earlier model so that the items of superego defense and of affect defense loaded on the same dimension (see Tables 16.2 and 16.3). The 2., 3. and 4. factor are the replicated factors of the former study.

The new dimension in this factor solution explains the most variance (17,9 %)and was characterized by the highest loadings on the defense mechanisms relevant to object relation and narcissistic development, such as primitive idealization, splitting, projective identification, fantasies of omnipotence, devaluation of the external object, and primitive denial. Therefore, this new dimension was termed "narcissistic defense". This dimension in earlier research was embedded in the former classical model of defense, because in the earlier factor analysis there were no relevant items of narcissistic defense. Thus, there was no opportunity for psychoanalytic ratings of object relations to appear in the factorial results.

In conclusion, it can be said that the factorial structure of previous research was replicated in this new study. Moreover, the results indicate the need for an additional defense dimension if the concept of defense is to be expanded to the domains of narcissistic development and object relations.

This quantitative description of the structure in defense evaluation demonstrates that clinicians' ideas of defense styles generate a profile of defense mechanisms similar to that developed in contemporary psychoanalytic theory (Gedo & Goldberg, 1973; Sandler & A. Freud, 1985). Anna Freud's (1936) structural concept of impulse defense, affect defense, and formation of symptoms was reconstructed empirically. It can be safely assumed that the eleven analytical psychotherapists were not aware of these correlations among the discrete defense mechanism. However, the narcissistic defense concept derived from object relations theory (Hinshelwood, 1993) can be possibly identified by clinicians in the diagnostic classification of their patients if they are given the chance to rate defenses within the object relations model.

I would conclude that the classical working model of defense should be expanded to incorporate the dimensions of narcissistic defense variables. Definitions of these specific narcissistic defenses show that the concepts of splitting and of archaic self-object relationship are empirically important in differentiating the concept of defense within the new structural model of object relation theory. The test of the expanded model with patients presenting severe structural deficits in a residential clinic shows that these patients with high levels of self object disturbances can be described within the framework of their specific defense structure. For a more explicit differentiation of the two clinical working models, I shall somewhat later in part 2 extend the instruments for diagnosing patients' personal styles of defense (CADM 1 and 2) to the evaluation of the process of psychotherapy with the same patient across sessions.

Defense Structure as a Determinant of Personality Diagnosis

There are two determinants of diagnosis of personality structure. On the one hand, psychoanalysts diagnose a person's fixation at a specific level of development, e.g. "oral fixation combined with depressive personality structure." On the other hand, they diagnose the person's defense pattern, as described earlier. The latter diagnosis refers to the adaptive and psychopathological modification of personality. Clinical personality theory within psychoanalysis postulates high correlations between developmental fixations and defenses (Ehlers & Czogalik,1984b). For depressive personality structure a distortion of superego-development is posited, which results in the dominance of a defense pattern with high values on introjection, projection, and turning against self. The compulsive personality structure, by contrast, features major defense mechanisms such as reaction formation and isolation, because drive generating fixation appears later in development. These defense mechanisms work on behalf of drive defense whereby the drive impulse, contrary to the mechanism of repression, can be detected in compulsive behavior. Hysterical disorder exhibits sypmtomatology that is based on the mechanisms of conversion and displacement, and in phobic patients symptoms are linked to repression. These clinical hypotheses should be tested by means of objective personality diagnosis derived from standardized questionnaires. For clinical evaluation of defense (CADM, Clinical Assessment of Defense Mechanisms; German: KBAM, (Ehlers & Czogalik, 1984a)), differences between hysterical, compulsive, and depressive character structures should be tested empirically.

Results and Discussion

The method for objective personality diagnosis is based on the semantic arrangement of various questionnaire scales for the three predominant conceptions of depressive, compulsive, and hysterical personality structure. Upon factor analysis of psychometric scales, three characteristic profiles were found for depressive, compulsive and hysterical subgroups, respectively. The stability of this classification was ascertained through the replication of the taxonomy in a new clinical sample by means of discriminant analysis (Ehlers & Czogalik, 1984b). For the new sample an average hit rate of 75 percent was established with the classification function of discriminant analysis (SPSS-program). This classification function was the basis for the selection of three subgroups, which were evaluated with the 20 item version of CADM. The automatic classification of patients by discriminant function guarantees a maximum of objectivity for testing the psychoanalytic hypothesis about the relationship between personality structure and defense.

The factorial scores of the five dimensions from the 20 item version of defense mechanisms (CADM) were computed for the three subgroups, depressive, compulsive, and hysterical. Analysis of variance for the mean values for each dimension between these subgroups was used for testing the hypothesized differences in personality structure.

Figure 16.3 displays the results of these analyses. The depressive subgroup is characterized by significantly higher superego defense in comparison to the hysterical subgroup. The higher level of superego defense is apparently traceable to the interaction of turning against object, introjection and inhibited affect expression. The compulsive subgroup is significantly higher in the dimension of impulse defense in comparison to the hysterical and the depressive subgroup. Compulsive patients then exhibit predilection for such defense mechanisms as isolation, rationalization, denial, reaction formation, and repression. For the hysterical subgroup, there were no significant differences in libido displacement. Thus, the predicted relationship between personality structure and defense could be demonstrated for depressive and compulsive subgroups, but not for the hysterical subgroup. Nevertheless, it remains plausible that hysterical patients at a residential clinic exhibit a more immature personality structure. It is recommended that the search for such differentiation be pursued with CADM 2, which more adequately taps the dimension of narcissistic defense. Indeed, Sandler and A. Freud (1989, p. 70) foresaw the likelihood that the relationship between defense in personality and in symptoms would vary across personality structures.

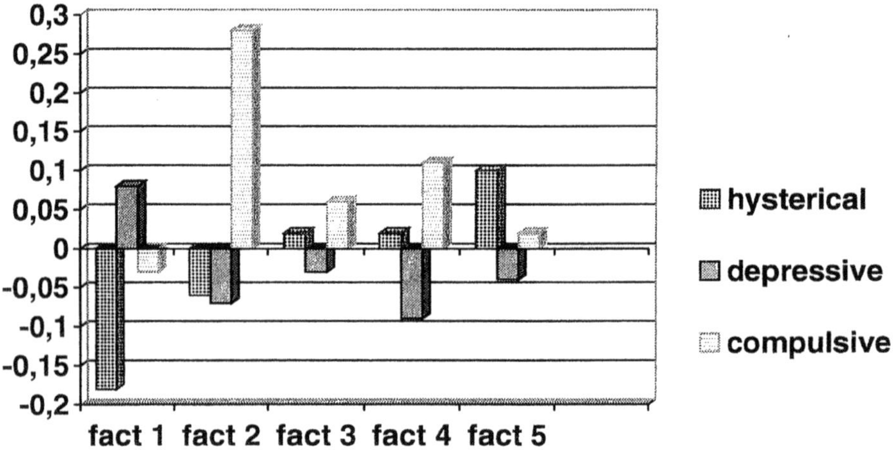

Figure 16.3: *Mean factor scores for three ego-structure or character types (n = 70 husterical-, n = 56 compulsive-, n = 150 depressive) with significant differences (< 5%) on fact 1 and 2. Fact 1 = superego defense (turning against self, introjection), fact 2 = defense of impulse (undoing, reaction formation), fact 3 = defense of affect (delayed affect expression, reaction formation) fact 4 = consequences of defense of affect (dominance of affect equivalence, conversion reaction) fact 5 = libido displacement (displacement of libido or aggression) (Ehlers, 1993).*

The Process of Defense in Psychoanalytic Treatment (Part 2)

Introduction

The justification for the discussion of the relationship between structure and process in psychoanalysis is based on the genetic perspective. In early development, parts of the contents of the id are absorbed by the ego and transferred into the subconscious. Other portions remain in the Id as the unconscious. As the ego continues to evolve, defenses against conflict-related psychological impressions and events cause some of the ego's contents to be excluded from consciousness. These contents are described as being repressed.

British object relation theory (Hinshelwood, 1993) in its classical model of defense posits a horizontal defense within the framework of the topical model of psychoanalysis which originates with the separation of self-awareness into the unconscious (ucs), preconscious (pcs), and conscious (cs) levels of the ego. More important for the British Kleinian object relation theory is vertical defense, which results from vertical splitting in the ego. Vertical splitting precedes the oedipal conflict, which is explicitly described in the topical model. This vertical splitting in the early phases of development provides the foundation for primitive defenses. Ego's splitting into personality fragments then leads to a state of disintegration for the Ego. This more extreme defense divides the mind into two parts, with portions of object, relationship, and self located in either part. The bad and good partial object and self relationships not only coexist side by side, but are destructive of the integrity of the ego. They remain as interrelated elements in the ego (part-object-relationships) and return in case of regression to former genetic points of fixation with archaic self-object relationships(see Figure 16.2).

Analytic work on repression has evolved on the basis of making use of normal regression of ego functions which enables the analyst to enter into an alliance with the ego, thereby extending self-awareness and making lost contents once again accessible to consciousness. These developments are facilitated by the interpretation of patients' memories and by the numerous nonverbal interactions which, together with interpretation, decisively co-determine transference and can lead to deepening regression. With increased depth of regression, less mature defense mechanisms are employed which provides greater scope for verbal expression of emotional control. By intensifying regression, the ego reverts to earlier modes of defense. For the examination of this thesis, a comparison of development of the defense process should be made between two female patients, one,

G, with a hysterical personality structure and another, S, with a borderline depressive personality structure.

Because of her more mature personality structure, Patient G is expected to employ fewer immature defense mechanisms. During the analytic process, less intense ego-regression should be observed, which should be expressed in content through the dominance of oedipal themes.

On the basis of the model formulated within object relations psychology, Patient S with borderline personality and with depressive symptoms is expected to exhibit a primitive defense structure, built around former fixation points, with a predominantly destructive narcissistic structure of unconscious fantasies and correspondingly serious problems in adapting to reality. By contrast, Anna Freud's (1936, 1989) model of ego-psychology is more readily applicable to patient G with her more mature defense structure.

Theory and Method of Process Analysis

There are several specialized empirical research strategies in psychoanalytic clinical investigation which were thoroughly discussed by Dahl, Kächele and Thomä (1988). These authors emphasized, and reflected upon the distinctive features of research on psychoanalysis. The crux of the problem lies in the conjunction of being cured and observed by the same person, that of the psychoanalyst. Freud defined the psychoanalyst as both a healer and a scientific observer. This merger of cure and observation has given rise to very different opinions about the nature of the data generated in the psychoanalytic process, discussed by Dreher (1998). Dreher insists on the indispensibility of original data, especially for basic conceptual psychoanalytic research. Ethical and practical considerations exclude the participation of any third parties. Of necessity, original data are only produced by the patient and the psychoanalyst. Secondary data are partial sets of original data reported by the analyst or prepared by means of technical aids. External clinical data include information gathered outside of the analytic situation, by means of a variety of methods and measures. Dreher objects to the more inclusive view by Moser (1991) who strove both to spell out the difference and to narrow the gap between contemporary empirical psychotherapy investigation and Freud's conjunctive model of psychoanalytic research.

Because the author of this chapter is both the psychoanalyst of the two patients and the observer and evaluator of their defense mechanisms after each session, the resulting data are based on original psychoanalytic observations. This circumstance exercises an influence on the results of secondary data included in the present investigation. These are the data that have been processed with the help of external procedures and techniques, as in factor analysis, yet they pertain to the time of the treatment process. Proceeding from the standard of objectivity or intersubjective verifiability, numerous criticisms can be voiced which we would like to counter by pointing to the approach represented in the first part of this investigation. The knowledge transfer from the first part to the clinical investigation of an individual case can of course only take place in the analytic situation, which highlights once again the problem of original data. Methodologically, it is exceedingly important for process research to include the comparison of single cases with data from the same instruments or measure between patients (Strupp, Schacht, & Henry, 1988).

On the basis of this rationale, both the selection of the two individual cases for process analysis and the choice of the setting of data extraction, by the same rating scale at the end of an analytic session, presented in the second part of this report, should assure comparability. Thus, it should be possible to test the statistical hypotheses pertaining to the conceptual distinction between the two models of defense, represented by ego psychology and object relations theory, respectively. The methodological details of external data processing need not concern us further at this point. Information about these procedures is contained in an earlier report by Ehlers (1993). Suffice it to say that the data in Figures 16.4 and 16.5 (A to D) were the result of factor analysis of CADM ratings gathered at specific points in time during the analytic sessions. Consequently, they represent model ratings of defense by the psychoanalyst who was treating the patients.

In process analysis, the topics of theory, experience, and therapy stand in an interactive relationship. The philosopher Hampe (2001) has represented these mutual relationships in a hierarchical model of convictions in the communications between the psychoanalyst and the analysand (see Figure 16.4). The psychoanalyst and the analysand search for understanding through communication. In this quest they are to a great extent guided by their respective implicit subjective theories about the Other (C) and about the self (D). Theoretical assumptions underlying the subjective theory of the psychoanalyst about the defense of the analysand (A,B) stem at a specific point in time in the psychoanalytic process from the more or less objectifiable everyday communicative understanding. This understanding provides the foundation for the provisional subjective theories about the analysand's drive/defense structure and repressed experiences. In conceptual terms, these formulations are couched in terms of ego psychology and object relations theory, respectively Unlike the patient, the analyst must include in his or her cognitive processes not only the patient but also himself or herself; otherwise it would not be therapy. The patient cannot test his or her subjective theories about the analyst explicitly because the analytic setting is designed to reduce such opportunities to a minimum. For the patient, these complex influences at the beginning of the therapeutic process are neither conscious nor can they be recognized nor steered. The patient is subject to a regressive staging through transference which should be resolved by the end of the analytic process. For the understanding and interpretation of the patient's utterances, the analyst has at his or her disposal subjective theories about himself or herself as well as about the patient. The specific terms of the explanation may vary, depending, for example, on the analyst's predilection for meta psychology or for defense theory. The empirical study to be presented here aims at observing and reconstructing the patients' implicit defense constructs in the process of therapy and to docu ment them at the completion of each session. This external research process should clarify areas of agreement, if any, between the data and the explicit hypothetical constructs of ego psychology and/or of object relations theory in the course of two psychoanalyses.

Assessment was carried out by means of CADM or CADM 2, consisting of 17 and 23 items, respectively.

Selection of therapy segments, which were then described with regard to content quality, was carried out by means of visual inspection and on the basis of the comparison of the time series for each defense factor. The criteria were the presence of detectable differences between the two or four factors, which were extracted for both patients.

The presentation of process development with regard to quality was produced by structured content analysis. Using the protocol of the session as a base, a paraphrase of the central conflict or transference and/or resistance was recorded. This information was then incorporated in summary form into the account of therapy segments. As a result of this qualitative assessment, written descriptions were obtained of each segment in the two psychoanalytic therapies. These data were utilized in our interpretation of results.

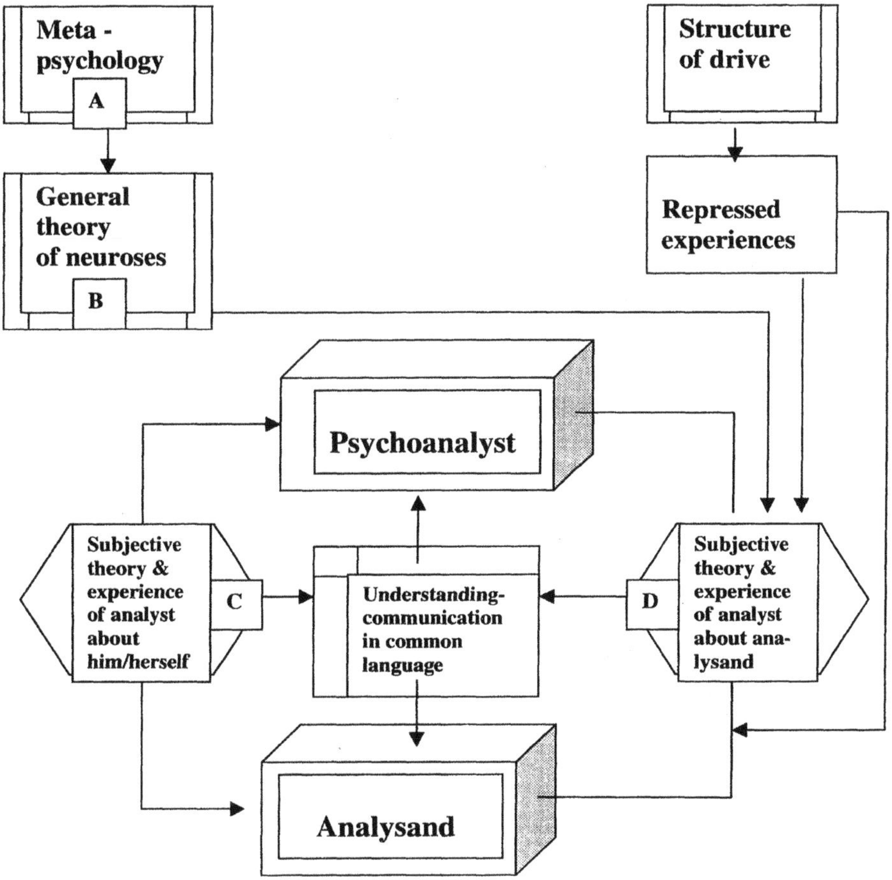

Figure 16.4: *Hierarchical model of factors influencing understanding and communication between Psychanalyst and Analysand (Hampe, 2001)*

Clinical Process Description of the Two Selected Patients

Symptomatically, Patient G was part of a large group of patients who experience recurrent headaches against the background of conversion neurosis. Her somewhat vague description of tension headaches (Beyme, 1966) does not necessarily imply a neurotic diagnosis. Her headaches could be attributed to muscular contractions in connection with tension, depression, and fear. Specific trigger situations, mostly connected with ambition, jealousy, and envy, were explored. Psychoanalytic therapy, in a lying position, was conducted at the rate of three times a week; it lasted for 160 sessions over a period of two years.

Patient S presented major depression. She was apathetic, lacked drive, and was slowed down in her psychomotor functions. Mood changes were not fixed at specific times of day. Feelings of guilt and need for punishment were pronounced. S experienced extreme fear of failure and dreaded being unable to shoulder her professional responsibilities. In her household she was incapable of performing work satisfactorily. Her sleep was disrupted by waking up early. Her depressed mood, fear of failure, and feelings of inferiority went back to puberty. There were recurrent depressive episodes to explore. Analytic psychotherapy, first on the couch (until session 175), and then after a phase of inpatient psychotherapy in a sitting position, was carried out twice to three times a week. There was a total of 370 sessions over a period of five and a half years, with an interruption for one year. In the present report, information is only included up to Session 305, which was the point at which the patient was faced with assuming responsibility for fees because the insurance company discontinued payments.

Results and Discussion

Process Development and Identification of Segments for Patient G

Quantitative process analysis of psychoanalytic psychotherapy for Patient G revealed two factors, which were produced by the P-factor analysis of the 17 defense mechanisms on the CADM; they accounted for 9.8 and 9.1 percent of total variance, respectively.

Factor A, which refers to the structural analysis of development, contains immature defense mechanisms related to the superego, such as turning against self, introjection, regression, and predominance of affect equivalents, with respective loadings of 0.53, 0.49, 0.47, and 0.59. Factor B is characterized by mature defense mechanisms and can be designated as related to impulse defense. Loadings for rationalization, isolation, and repression amounted to 0.65, 0.61, 0.47. and 0.58, respectively.

Only through changes in Factor B, which is the mature dimension in this therapy, was it possible to distinguish individual therapy segments (see B in Figure 16.5) After a decrease in mature defenses from Session 1 to 20 in Segment 1, there is change from Session 21 to 34 to a relatively stable high defense level in Segment 2, which between Sessions 34 and 68 gives way to increased fluctuation in Segment 3. From Session 69 to 99 a relatively stable high level of defense is again in evidence in Segment 4. Segment 5 is marked by major fluctuation in Factor 2 while Factor 1 remains largely constant across segments. An inverse relationship has emer between Factors 1 and 2. When the values for Factor 1, indicative of immature defense, are highest, those for Factor 2, on which mature defenses are loaded, are low, and vice versa.

Qualitative Process Analysis of the Therapy Segments for Patient G (High Structural Level)

Therapy Segment 1: Development of an incestuous oedipal conflict situation in the relationship with a married man was brought up. Ms. G. has sought his presence so that he could free her from the slur of bein a silly little girl. She is torn between the wish for a proper marriage and the romance with an already married lover. If it became known that she is in love with a married man, she would be open to strong moral condemnation. Because of painful cramps in her back and lower abdomen she has to take pain killing tablets all day. She has again lived with her lover for several days, although she had already parted from him. Manifest dream content expresses her destructive desire: G breaks into the house of a couple who are her friends and wrecks their living room. She must hide from her parents that she is still keeping up this relationship.

Therapy Segment 2: The guilt ridden aspect of her rivalry with her lover's wife and with her parents moves to the foreground. In transference, resistance increases to opening herself in the therapy process, because she fears the contempt she had experienced from her maternal grandfather. At the same time, outside of therapy,she builds a new stress free relationship from which nothing is allowed to filter into the therapy process. Even in dreams, this extratherapy relationship is veiled and only implied.

Therapy Segment 3: Ambivalence develops concerning her desires for the new vs. old lover. A dominant theme of the sessions is fighting against the pressing demands of her old lover and against being treated like a child by her mother and her boss. The necessity of moving out of her parents' house in order to detach herself from her parents causes her much pain. After Ms.G.informed her old lover of her new relationship she experienced increasingly intense courting by him. The incestuous relationship to her father is so strongly activated that it is experienced in dreams as being sexually oppressive. Consuming feelings change to a playful state of being in love, as between two children. In this way, feelings can be expressed with the new lover. The identification with women's strengths and assets let her experience the powers of a mature woman in regard to her old lover. With her new lover, this identification awakens her wish for children.

By assigning her analyst the role of protecting her from seduction by the old lover, she was free to experience being in love and her new relationship could develop freely; eventually, she received a marriage proposal. She then canceled her flight to America with her old lover – and decided to continue with therapy.

Therapy Segment 4: Dealing with intrapsychic conflicts moves to the foreground. She now tries to involve herself more in the analysis of her personal development and no longer sees herself as just bein pushed and pulled by men. Rivalry with and distrust of other women make her conceal her marriage plans. She struggles against the analysis of her new relationship. Instead, she brings up the themes of rivalry with her mother, her affection for her father when she was a child, and the alliance with her father against her mother and brother. Her mother's acute illness makes it clear to her that she will personally have to make preparations for her wedding. In the therapy process, work on repression resistance during the detailed examination of mature defense mechanisms is significant, whereby a thorough study of her incestuous desire is made possible.

→

Figure 16.5: *CADM factor scores (P-technique) for 160 therapy sessions of patient G. A. Factor 1: Turning against self/introjection/regression dominance of affect equivalence. B. Factor 2: Rationalization/isolation/repression*

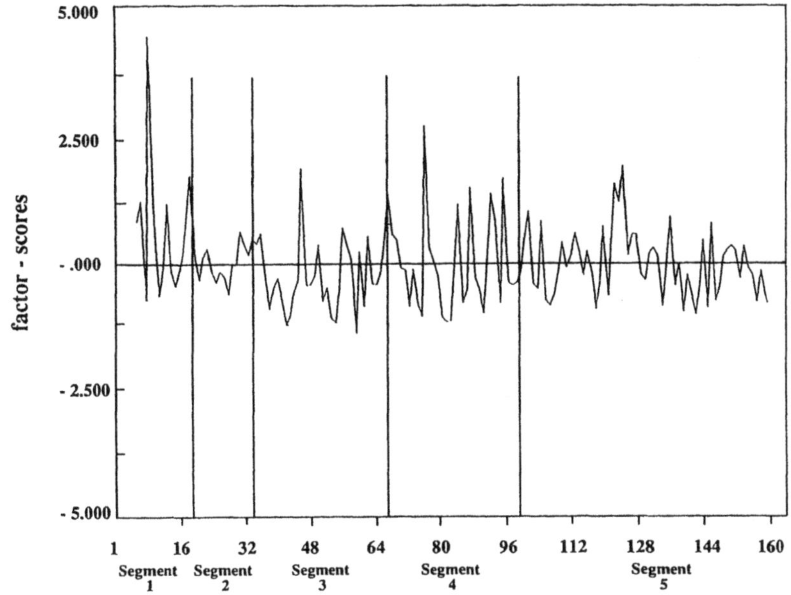

A Number of session

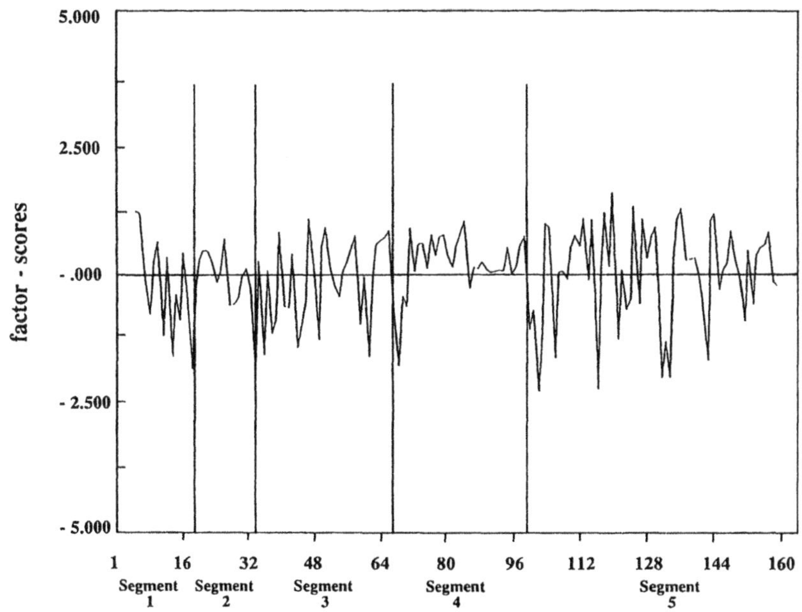

B Number of session

Therapy Segment 5: The wedding takes place after the bridegroom has passed the test of not deceiving her with other women, which she had repeatedly experienced with her old lover and her father. In a dream, she experiences her honeymoon as a sensual mountain climb during which she is always accompanied by her envious mother. She has more frequent discussions and arguments with her "archaic" mother who wants to prevent her from having children. She must conceal from her husband her jealousy of his earlier companion, although she is constantly confronted with reminders of her in their apartment. In the marriage bed she has to take the responsibility for contraception, as both of them have not yet finished their education. She fears being unable to have children. After she has finally made up her mind to terminate her analysis, she sets up a home with her husband, as she happily reports in her last therapy session.

In a catamnestic interview one and a half years later she proudly reports her motherhood and her new role as a doctor's wife following her husband`s certification as a specialist in internal medicine.

Process Segments of Patient S (low structural level)

The expansion of the spectrum of therapeutic application of psychoanalysis has necessitated modifications in technique so as to make it possible to psychoanalyze patients with narcissistic problems of character structure. These modifications pertain in particular to the early interpretation of transference and countertransference patterns in superego-analysis of psychotic patients (Rosenfeld, 1990).These modifications were introduced into child analysis by Melanie Klein (Hinshelwood, 1993) in opposition to Anna Freud. They are based on the expansion of Freud's defense concept of horizontal defense structure. The interpretation of the negative aspects of children's imagination at the moment of maximum fear was observed to reduce negative transference thereby changing oppositional feelings against the analyst into positive transference. The increase in sensitivity to negative transference with children allowed Melanie Klein's successors to extend the interpretation of the hidden aspects of transference to adult patients thereby also generating new ideas for interpreting adults' defenses (Hinshelwood, 1993). These interpretations concentrated on the mechanisms of projective identification, splitting, and archaic idealization, as well as on manic and paranoid defense mechanisms. The interpretation of transference of the analytic relationship here and now leads to the externalization of unconscious fantasies because analysts provoke conflictual feelings as well as annoyance, fear, distrust, and gratitude in the patient through their interpretive activity.

The structural analysis of the development (P-factor analysis) of the 23 defense mechanisms on the CADM 2 produced four factors that accounted for 9.8 percent and 9.1 percent of the total variance. On the basis of their principal loadings in defense mechanisms, these four factors can be described as follows: Factor A (super-ego) is characterized by the superego defenses of self-pity, turning against self, and introjection. Factor B (paranoid defense) is marked by such typical immature defense mechanisms in coping with archaic aggression as primitive denial, devaluation of external objects, and splitting. Factor C (depressiv defense) is also considered to be an immature defense mechanism related to narcissistic defenses, such as primitive idealization and fantasies of omnipotence. Factor D (defense as undoing) is viewed as a more mature defense, characterized by such mechanisms as reversal into the opposite and undoing(see Factors A-D in Figure 16.6).

For the segmentation of the development of these four factors the interaction of the first 2 factors appears highly suitable for the presentation of the segments. In this process the qualitative description must summarize larger units, because the process lasts twice as long. It appeared meaningful due to the greater complexity of the interplay of the factors that immediately after each formal segment description the qualitative description follows.

Therapy Segment 1 extends from Session 1 to Session 60 and is distinguished by contrasting progressions of Factors A (turning against self) and B (primitive denial and splitting). Over the same period, the mature Factor D (undoing) decreases progressively up to Session 23 and then levels off. The simultaneous decrease of the mature defenses in Factor D and of the paranoid defenses of denial, splitting, and devaluation as well as the increase of the typical depressive superego defenses of self-pity, turning against self, and introjection coincide in content with the inner struggle for oral supplies by the simultaneous renunciation of erotic activity, expressed through fascination with the fairy tale about Sleeping Beauty. The devaluation of her own marriage stands in contrast to her high expectations focused on the analyst who she expects would free her from her contaminated relationship. The analyst`s neutrality, however, leads to a massive disappointment which expresses itself in an increasing paralysis. She wants to stop teaching school, to give up, and to appear awkward and incompetent to her pupils. She intently watches other couples argue. She avoids resolving disagreements in her own relationships. She cannot explain her dissatisfaction with her husband and wishes for deliverance by the analyst. When her headmaster tries to get her to go back to teaching, from which she is on sick leave, she refuses. When sleeping with her husband, she "acts dead." She is only active in transference, especially in dreams. Analyst's absence during the Easter break causes everything to break down again. After the school principal presses her for transfer after the summer holiday, she experiences intense fear of the future. Her first experiences in the new school after the summer holiday give rise to strong disappointment in the school's principal who she claims made her false promises.

Segment 2 describes developments between the Sessions 61 and 175. While the paranoid defense of Factor 2 (splitting) progressively increases, a similar trend for Factor 1 does not appear until Session 117. With Factor 3 (depressive defense), increase begins with Session 103 whereupon it is interspersed with a succession of steep increases and declines.

The increase of archaic paranoid defense in Factor 2 is paralleled in content by the increasing experience of slights, which trigger regressive withdrawal into passivity, inactivity, and resistance through refusal.

Her husband's waning interest in her leads to her hypersensitivity to slights in analysis. She wants to prove to me that she can cope with the children at school. However, time and again she has only failures to report. Consequently, she must come to terms with the shame she feels before me. Her fear of the principal, who has observed her lessons twice and who also advises her, has increased tremendously. She is appalled by her supposed failure, increasingly devalues her self, and sinks ever more deeply into regression, which is expressed through silences in analysis of more than 20 minutes in duration. The analyst can only maintain contact with her through his utmost sensitivity to her unspoken thoughts and feelings. After suicidal ideas appear, antidepressive medication therapy is initiated in collaboration with a psychiatrist, and it takes effect. After the husband clearly states his plans for separation, she wants to break off her outpatient therapy and be cared for passively as an inpatient in psychotherapy, like a baby. By refusing food she forces her husband to feed her, just as the analyst, after long silences, administered emotional nourishment to her by speaking to her about her possible feelings. With Session 159 her first stay in the clinic begins while therapy is continued. After the separation from her husband, resistance to therapy becomes so strong that termination is the one solution she can fantasize. She arranges admission into a clinic for psychotherapeutic treatment in another city and ends up fantasizing that she is accompanying the analyst, who symbolizes an idealized object, on holiday sitting in the back seat of his car, just as she did as a child when she traveled alone with her father. Her separation is never mentioned. Decreases in archaic defense from session 174 on are explained by her private decision to break off therapy and thereby to terminate her negative therapeutic transference.

Segment 3 stretches from Session 176 to Session 305. It is marked by a comparatively low level of defense in Factors A (superego) and B (paranoid). After

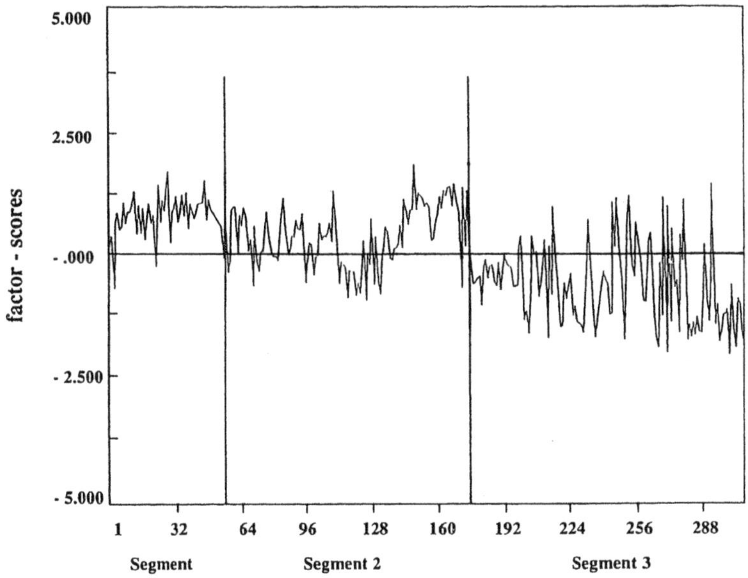

A Number of session

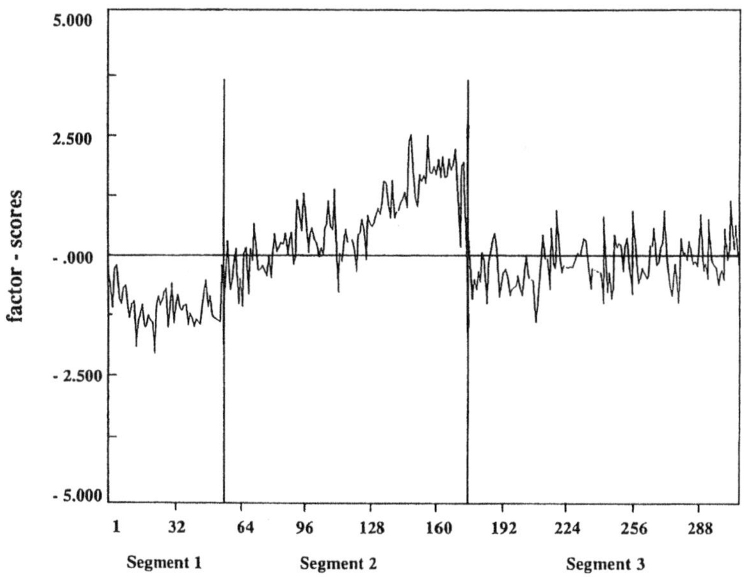

B Number of session

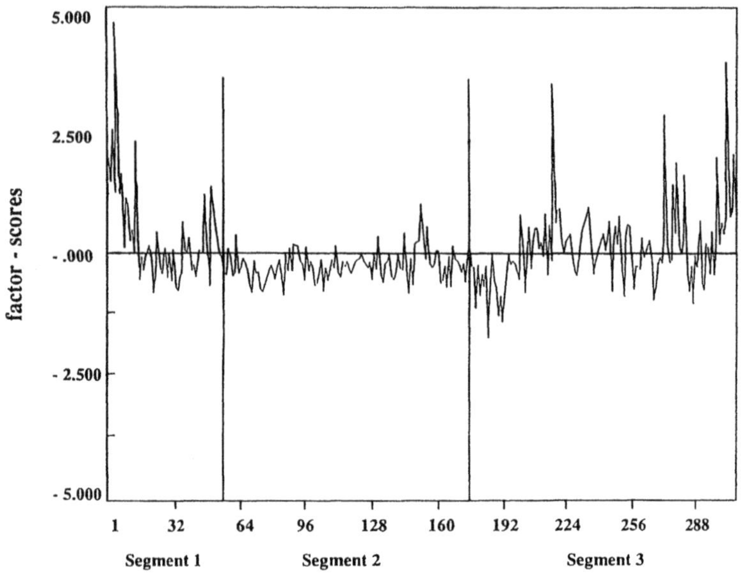

C Number of session

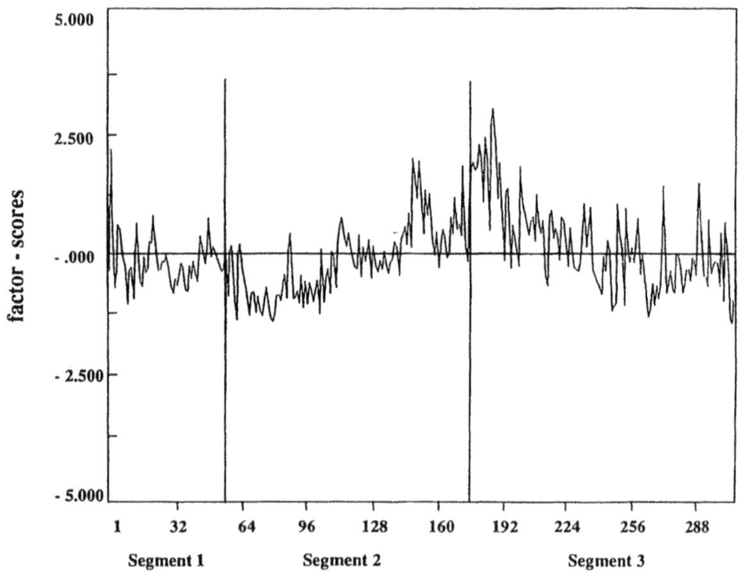

D Number of session

continuation of therapy after one year (from Session 184), narcissistic defense (depressive position) in Factor C (primitive idealization and fantasies of omnipotence) reaches its maximum, but does not maintain it consistently. During some periods, Factor D, characterized by relatively mature defenses, appears in greater intensity and frequency. Toward the end of the process, this variety of defense, from Session 282 onward, increases continuously. The content of this therapy segment is marked by a more realistic working alliance that makes it possible for therapeutic work to continue, despite a marked decrease in the idealization of the analyst. One year after discontinuing therapeutic contact, she wants to resume outpatient psychotherapy. Analysis in a sitting position is resumed with two sessions per week. After idealization of the analyst was made an object of the analysis, work on the present relationship with the analyst is made possible. Work on this topic facilitates verbalizing her own tendencies toward regressive withdrawal in critical situations of narcissistic vulnerability in her relationships.

Working through of libidinal transference in the last segment was the main theme after the 305th session. Work on her sadomasochistic relationship patterns in therapy became increasingly possible. In her struggle between the wishes for passive care and aggressive self-fulfilment in the transference relationship she faced up to the realities in her professional life after passing the Second State Examination. Only after this development did identification with her wishes for feminine bodily potency become possible. In a central dream, she crept out of her narrow cave, baring her breasts and seducing a shy man sitting in front of the cave. She also asserted her bodily expression through an upright gait.

←

Figure 16.6: *CADM factor scores (P-technique) for 305 therapy sessions of patient S. A. Factor 1: Self-pity/turning against self/introjection. B. Factor 2: Primitive denial/devaluation of external objects/mechanism of splitting. C. Factor 3: Primitive idealization/fantasies of omnipotence. D. Factor 4: Reversal into opposite/undoing*

The Process of Defense for Patients G and S in Constructing Distinctive Defense Models During the Therapy Process

The romance of Patient G with a married lover reflected her unacceptable drive representations, which resulted from the regression to her unconscious wishes for object-representations of her father. Her recurrent headaches were a symptomatic compromise of this oedipal conflict. Her real father and the psychoanalyst evoked her cramplike pains, which she could only externalize by "pain killing tablets". The affect defense of her unconscious fantasy of killing her persecuting object, which through transference could sometimes refer to the psychoanalyst, was the background for working through in Segment 2. Patient G demonstrated in the same segment stronger resistance against transference, which apparently led to the stabilization of mature defense mechanisms (Factor 2) in opposing more severe regression during transference. In Segment 4, intensive work on intrapsychic conflicts led to an increase of repressive resistance which stabilized over a period of 31 sessions. In the other three therapy segments, fluctuations in mature defenses were so pronounced that no uniform defense level could be pinpointed. Therapy results endured to be evident at the point of catamnestic information. The higher level of ego structure ushered in a psychoanalytic process with predominantly mature, presumably oedipal, defenses. The result of the psychoanalytic process evidenced the resolution of the patient's oedipal problem, which was prominent before marriage.

Patient S embarked upon Segment 1 with high depressive defense after separation from a very restrictive partnership with her husband in Africa and ended up again with high depressive defense in Segment 3 after her insurance company denied further payments. In Segment 1 mature (D,undoing) and paranoid (B) defenses were reduced. The idealization of the psychoanalyst and the devaluation of the husband paralleled the triggering of separation anxiety during analyst's absences on weekends and holidays. Acting out of this anxiety with her husband and with her headmaster could not be stopped by the analyst's interpretations. Presumably, her anxiety persisted because the splitting between the inner and outer worlds of objects. It enabled her to reunite with the good inner objects evoked in the idealized transference relation to the analyst and to exclude the bad objects projected on her husband und her headmaster. In Segment 2, paranoid defense (B) increased sharply, as a sign of the threatening fragmentation of the self. Only by retreating into passivity and leaving the psychoanalytic setting could she free herself from the negative therapeutic transference, which she did by becoming an inpatient in a psychosomatic clinic. In Segment 3, she returned to analytic psychotherapy with an increased mature defense (undoing). There were some short periods of increase of depressive defense (C), as a sign of working through of the depressive position by disillusionment with the idealized analytical object. At the end of this process an upsurge of the same defense occurred, related to the insurance company's refusal of further payments. In the last segment, after her discharge from the residential clinic, the patient no longer showed the extreme paranoid defense (Factor B). The process of analytic psychotherapy for patient S followed the defense-structure within the object relations model.

Conclusions

Psychoanalytic treatment brings about the revival of repressed conscious contents that are represented in object relations with the analyst. Resistance towards this transference relationship presents itself in the form of interrelated defense structures; the nature of their relationship can be established empirically. In the course of treating patients with oedipal or neurotic and pre-oedipal narcissistic disturbances, these defense structures differ in symptomatic levels and in personality organization.

Patient G with hysterical symptoms and phallic hysterical personality structure developed a relatively mature defense structure within the framework of resistance by means of repression. Her romance with a married man reflects her unacceptable drive representations (see Figure 16.1), which was analyzed in the transference relationship with the psychoanalyst, who interpreted her unconscious (ucs) wishes in relation to the object representations of her father. Her recurrent headaches were a symptomatic compromise of this ucs oedipal conflict. The psychoanalytic process reduced these attacks. The affect defense was expressed in the ucs fantasy of killing the persecuting object. Debt anxiety was observed in the guilt-ridden aspects of her rivalry with her lover's wife and with her own mother in Segment 2 of the psychoanalytic process. Libidinal transference increased in Segment 3. Analysis of the repression resistance lowered her mature defense in Segment 4, which increased again in Segment 5, thereby giving Patient G the chance to separate from the psychoanalyst and to organize her wedding with a physician. The model of ego-psychology appears to provide an adequate explanation of this therapy process.

In contrast to Patient G, Patient S with depressive symptoms and a lower structural level of personality presented a less mature defense structure. It was marked by archaic defense mechanisms of primitive denial and splitting so that the transference resistance led to a temporary interruption of therapy. The activation of narcissistic defenses (primitive idealization and omnipotence fantasies) and the successful working through of this defense after the resumption of therapy represented an important secondary condition for the overcoming of the immature defense structure in the transference relationship.

The division of the process into segments was based on the placement of discrete defense mechanisms in their corresponding, mature or immature, defense patterns. For the patient with a mature defense structure the model of ego psychology was adequate for the explanation of the therapy process. For the patient whose defense structure was immature the object relations theory was better suited for the understanding of the more complex interaction of defenses. The empirical data about the defense mechanisms outside of therapy were also compared with the two metapsychological models of the defense process: A. Freud's model of ego psychology and the Kleinian model of object relations theory.

References

Arlow, J. A.& Brenner, C. (1988). The future of psychoanalysis. *Psychoanalitic Quarterly, 57,* 1-14.

Balint, M. (19700. *Therapeutische Aspekte der Regression. Die Theorie der Grundstörung.* E. Klett Verlag: Stuttgart. Original (1968): The Basic Fault. Therapeutic Aspects of Regression. London: Tavistock Publications.

Beyme, F. (1966). Der Verlauf der Migräne mit und ohne Psychotherapie (The process of migraine with and without psychotherapy). *Psychotherapie und Psychosomatik, 14,* 90-96.

Brenman, E. (1985). Cruelty and narrow-mindedness. *International Journal of Psycho-Analysis, 66,* 273-281.

Bion, W. R. (1957). Differentiation of the psychotic from the non-psychotic personalities. *International Journal of Psycho-Analysis, 38,* 266-275.

Bion, W. R. (1959). Attacks on linking. *International Journal of Psycho-Analysis, 40,* 308-315.

Dahl, H. (1991). The key to understanding change: Emotions as appetitive wishes and beliefs about their fulfillment. In J. G. Safran L (Ed.), *Emotion, psychotherapy, and change* (pp. 130-165). New York: Guilford Press.

Dahl, H., Kächele, H., & Thomä, H. (Eds.) *Psychoanalytic process research strategies.* Berlin: Springer Verlag.

Dreher, A. U. (1998). *Empirie ohne Konzept? Einführung in die psychoanalytische Konzeptforschung.* (Empiricism without conceptualization? Introduction to conceptual research in psychoanalysis) Stuttgart: Verlag für Internationale Psychoanalyse.

Ebel, R. L. (1951). Estimation of the reliability of ratings. *Psychometrica, 16,* 4-12.

Edelson, M. (1988). *A theory in crisis*. Chicago: University of Chicago Press.

Ehlers, W. (1993). The structure and process of defense in diagnosis of personality and in psychoanalytic treatment. In U. Hentschel, G. Smith, W. Ehlers, & J.G. Draguns (Eds.), *The concept of defense mechanisms in contemporary psychology. Theoretical, research, and clinical perspectives* (pp. 253-274). New York: Springer-Verlag.

Ehlers, W., & Czogalik, C. (1984a). Dimensionen der klinischen Beurteilung von Abwehrmechanismen (Dimensions of clinical ratings of defense mechanisms). Praxis, *Psychotherapie, Psychosomatik, 29,* 129-138.

Ehlers, W., & Czogalik, D. (1984b). Taxonomic aspects of clinical character typology in psychotherapy. *Psychotherapy and Psychosomatics, 42,* 156-163.

French, T. M. (1938). Defense and synthesis in the function of the ego. *Psychoanalitic Quarterly,7*, 537-553.

Freud A. (1936). *Das Ich und die Abwehrmechanismen* (The ego and the mechanims of defense). Vienna: Internationaler Psychoanalitischer Verlag.

Freud, S. (1908b). Charakter und Analerotik (Character and anal eroticism). *The standard edition of the complete psychological works of Sigmund Freud (Vol. 9,* pp. 169-175). London: Hogarth Press.

Freud, S. (1917d). Metapsychologische Ergänzungen zur Traumlehre (Metapsychological additions to the dream theory*). The standard edition of the complete psychological works of Sigmund Freud (Vol. 14,* pp. 222-235). London: Hogarth Press.

Freud, S. (1923b). Das Ich und das Es (The ego and the id) *.The standard edition of the complete psychological works of Sigmund Freud (Vol. 19,* pp. 19-27). London: Hogarth Press.

Gedo, J. E., & Goldberg, A. (1973). *Models of the mind*. Chicago: University of Chicago Press.

Hampe, M. (2001). Theorie, Erfahrung, Therapie. Anmerkungen zur Beurteilung psychoanalytischer Prozesse (Theory, experience,therapy. Remarks on the evaluation of psychoanalytic processes). *Psyche, 55,* 328-336.

Hinshelwood, R.D. (1993). *Wörterbuch der kleinianischen Psychoanalyse.* Stuttgart: Internationaler Verlag fur Psychoanalyse. Orig. (1991). A dictionary of Kleinian thought. London: Free Association Books.

Holt, R. R. (1989) *Freud reappraised. A fresh look at psychoanalytic theory.* New York: Guilford Press.

Kernberg, O. F. (1977). The structural diagnosis of borderline personality organization. In P. Hartocollis (Ed.), *Borderline personality disorders* (pp. 87-121). New York: International Universities Press.

Kernberg, O. F. (1984). *Severe personality disorders. Psychotherapeutic strategies*. New Haven, CT: Yale University Press.

King, P. & Steiner, R. (2000). *Die Freud/Klein-Kontroversen. 1941-1945* (The Freud/Klein contraversies 1941-1945) Volumes 1 &,2. Stuttgart: Klett-Cotta.

Moser, U. (1965). Zur Abwehrlehre (On the theory of defense). *Jahrbuch für Psychoanalyse, 4*, 56-85.

Moser, U. (1991). Vom Umgang mit Labyrinthen. Praxis und Forschung in der Psychoanalyse – eine Bilanz (About dealing with mazes. Practice and research in psychoanalysis – an appraisal). *Psyche, 45*, 315-334.

Moser, U.,von Zeppelin, I., & Schneider, H. (1981). *Wunsch, Selbst, Objektbeziehung. Entwurf eines Regulierunsmodells kognitiv-affektiver Prozesse* (Wish, self, and object relations. Sketch of a regulation model of cognitive-affective processes). Berichte aus der interdisziplinären Konfliktforschungsstelle. 9.unveröffentlichter Bericht. Zürich: University of Zürich.

Moser, U., von Zeppelin, I., & Schneider, W. (1968). *Computersimulation eines Modells neurotischer Abwehrmechanismen. Ein Versuch zur Formalisierung der psychoanalytischen Theorie* (Computer simulation of a model of neurotic defense mechanisms. An attempt at formalizing psychoanalytic theory) Bulletin 2. Zürich: Psychologisches Institut der Universität Zürich.

Rosenfeld, H. (1978). Notes on the psychopathology and psychoanalytic treatment of some borderline patients. *International Journal of Psycho-Analysis, 59*, 215-221.

Rosenfeld, H. (1990). Bemerkungen zur Psychoanalyse des Über-Ich-Konfliktes bei einem akut schizophrenen Patienten (Remarks on the psychoanalysis of a superego conflict in an acute schizophrenic patient). In E. B. Spilius (Ed.). *Melanie Klein heute. Entwicklungen in Theorie und Praxis.* Stuttgart: Verlag Internationale Psychoanalyse. Original (1988): Melanie Klein today. Developments in theory and practice. Tavistock Publications: London.

Sandler, J., & Rosenblatt, B. (1962). The concept of the representational world. *Psychoanalytic Study of the Child, 17*, 128-145.

Sandler, J & Freud, A. (1989). *Die Analyse der Abwehr* (The analysis of defense). Stuttgart: E. Klett Verlag. Original (1985): The analysis of defence. New York: International Universities Press.

Segal, H. (1972). A delusional system as a defence against re-emergence of a catastrophic situation. *International Journal of Psycho-Analysis, 53*, 393-403.

Sohn, L. (1985). Narcissistic organization, projective identification and the formation of the identificate. *International Journal of Psycho-Analysis, 66,* 201-213.

Steffens, W., & Kächele, H. (1988). Abwehr und Bewältigung - Vorschläge zu einer integrativen Sichtweise (Defense and coping – Proposals for an inegrative perspective) *Psychotherapie, Medizinische Psychologie, 38,* 3-7.

Steiner, J. (1982). Perverse relationships between parts of the self: A clinical illustration. *International Journal of Psycho-Analysis,* 63, 241-252.

Steiner, J. (1987). Interplay between pathological organization and the paranoid-schizoid and depressive positions. *International Journal of Psycho-Analysis, 68,* 69-80.

Strupp, H. H., Schacht, T. E., & Henry, W. P. (1988). Problem-treatment-outcome congruence: A principle whose time has come. In H. Dahl, H. Kächele, & H. Thomä (Eds.) *Psychoanalytic process research strategies* (pp. 1-14). Berlin: Springer Verlag.

Suppes, P., & Warren, H. (1975). On the generation and classification of defense mechanisms. *International Journal of Psycho-Analysis, 56,* 405-414.

Defense Mechanisms
U. Hentschel, G. Smith, J.G. Draguns & W. Ehlers (Editors)

Chapter 17

The Measurement of Ego Defenses in Clinical Research

Hope R. Conte, Robert Plutchik and Juris G. Draguns

Among the more important contributions of psychoanalysis to personality theory and to the theory of psychological adaptation is the concept of ego defenses. The term "defense mechanism" first appeared in Anna Freud's *The Ego and the Mechanisms of Defense* (1936). She described 10 methods of functioning used by the ego to ward off dangerous drives or wishes that would lead to painful feelings of anxiety, depression, or shame. Since that time, there has been general agreement that defenses may be triggered by both internal and external stressors: that is, by internalized prohibitions on the one hand and external reality on the other. There has also been substantial agreement on a number of aspects or facets of defense mechanisms: (a) they are the major means that the ego uses to manage instinct and affect and forestall potential conflict; (b) they are unconscious; (c) although a patient may be characterized by his or her most dominant defense, each patient uses several defenses; (d) the defenses are dynamic and reversible; and (e) they may be adaptive as well as pathological (Freud, 1936; Perry & Vaillant, 1990).

Variations in the Concept of Ego Defenses

However, there is considerably less agreement among psychoanalysts and other clinicians on just how many defenses there are and over what should or should not be considered a defense mechanism (Brenner, 1973; Moore & Fine, 1990; Plutchik, Kellerman, & Conte, 1979; Vaillant, 1977; Wong, 1989). While Anna Freud (1936) originally described 10 defenses, Vaillant's (1971) glossary defines 8 and Brenner's (1973) textbook lists 11, and the current DSM-IV (American Psychiatric Association, 1994) includes 31 defenses.

These schemata identifying differing numbers of defenses exist partly as a result of the differing theories on which they are based. They are, however, also a function of the extensive overlap of meanings. There are, for example, no distinct boundaries differentiating one defense from another. Noyes and Kolb (1963) point out that projection is, in many respects, a form of identification, while Arieti (1974) notes that isolation and splitting are merely two names for the same concept.

Regarding what should be included as an ego defense, Brenner (1973), for example, does not list "suppression" as a defense mechanism, considering it rather to be a conscious activity (i.e., the familiar decision to forget about something and think no more about it). It is also not included by Plutchik et al. (1979) in their Life Style Index or by Perry and Cooper (1989) in the Defense Mechanism Rating Scales. In contrast, Andrews, Pollock, and Stewart (1989), Bond (1983), Meissner, Mack, and Semrad (1975), and Vaillant (1985) do include suppression as a defense mechanism. They also include "humor." It appears that the decision to include suppression, humor, and other mechanisms such as altruism and anticipation depends to a great extent on an investigator's willingness to admit the more conscious mechanisms as defenses.

This issue leads directly to that of the classification of the ego defenses. Here, too, there is disagreement. They can be classified developmentally, whereby they are categorized according to the libidinal phase in which they are presumed to arise. Denial and projection would thus be assigned to the oral stage. But some defenses, such as regression, cannot be classified in this manner. They may also be divided hierarchically into narcissistic, immature, neurotic, and mature categories (see Wong, 1989, pp. 375-376).

The point to be made is that an investigator's choice of classification depends largely on that investigator's theoretical model. For example, some investigators include in their models, in addition to the more unconscious regressive aspects of defenses, the more conscious, adaptive aspects of an individual's functioning. For these authors, empathy, substitution, suppression, humor, altruism, and asceticism are all part of defensive functioning (Bond, Gardner, Christian, & Sigal, 1983; Haan, Stroud, & Holstein, 1973; Meissner et al., 1975; Semrad, Grinspoon, & Feinberg, 1973; Vaillant, Bond, & Vaillant, 1986). Others, like the present authors, remain closer to the original Freudian notion of defenses as unconscious mechanisms, preferring rather to label the more conscious, adaptive processes as a separate category, that is, as coping styles (Plutchik & Conte, 1989). The present chapter is not concerned with processes in the latter category.

One final area in which there exists little agreement concerns the issue of how to measure, reliably and validly, the presence and extent of defensive functioning in an individual. Over the past several decades a modest, but growing, literature has evolved that is concerned with this problem. The oldest of the measures explicitly developed for the assessment of defenses is Kragh's (1969) Defense Mechanism Test, embedded in the process-oriented percept-genetic framework. In this volume, several chapters are devoted to current and recent research with this instrument. Other techniques require the judgment of an interviewer (e.g., Ablon, Carson, & Goodwin, 1974; Hackett & Cassem, 1974), while still others depend on self-reports (e.g., Gleser & Ihilevich, 1969; Kreitler & Kreitler, 1972; Marshall, 1982; Sarason, Ganzer, & Singer, 1972). Quite often, these scales are focused on a small number of defense mechanisms rather than on the entire range of defensive operations. Moreover, an issue which, as yet, has been rarely addressed in a systematic manner is the nature of the relationship between defenses and related constructs.

In 1979, Plutchik, Kellerman, and Conte described a new self-report instrument, the Life Style Index for the measurement of ego defenses, that does provide such a theoretical framework. This framework is based on Plutchik's general theory of affect, which has been fully described elsewhere (Plutchik, 1962, 1980). Basically, this model provides a rationale for the choice of defenses to be measured, and at the same time, it helps to define the relations among those defenses. The model assumes that a circumflex or circular structure is most appropriate for the relations among the ego defenses. The circumflex indicates the relative similarity of the different defenses and ensures that an adequate sample of this hypothetical domain is obtained by making certain that every sector of the circle is sampled. The rationale for the proposed relations among the ego defenses and between the ego defenses and diagnostic constructs is presented more fully elsewhere (Plutchik et al., 1979).

In the following sections, we present a description of the Life Style Index, examples of its use in clinical research, and suggestions for its use in future research projects.

The Life Style Index

Originally, the Life Style Index (LSI) consisted of 224 items designed to represent 16 defense mechanisms. These 16 were selected on the basis of a review of a large number of psychoanalytic, psychiatric, and psychological sources. A series of studies designed to determine the psychometric properties of the test was then conducted. In the course of these studies, the number of items was systematically reduced to 97, and some of the items were reworded. In addition, as the result of an analysis of an intercorrelation matrix that indicated considerable overlap among the defenses and a factor analysis of the matrix, it was concluded that 16 defenses were too many. Thus, on the basis of these empirical data as well as psychoanalytic theory, which holds that anxiety is at the core of the development of any defense, the items were regrouped into eight scales: compensation (including identification and fantasy), denial, displacement, intellectualization (including sublimation, undoing, and rationalization), projection, reaction formation, regression (including acting out), and repression (including isolation and introjection). These defenses are listed in Table 17.1, along with their definitions.

Each scale contains between 10 and 14 items. Coefficient alphas were computed on two samples of subjects, 60 inpatients on the psychiatric wards of a municipal hospital and 75 Midwestern college students. Table 17.2 presents these coefficients, along with the items ranking highest on relevance for each of the eight ego defense scales as rated by 17 experienced clinicians with an average of 13 years of experience (Plutchik et al., 1979). As is evident from the table, these coefficients show considerable variation, both within a sample of subjects and between the two samples, but in all instances internal consistency is higher for the patients. The median alpha for the patients is .62, with a range from .54 to .86. For the students, the median is .54, with coefficients ranging from .30 to. 75.

It is likely that the alphas for the patient sample are higher than those for the students because for each of the scales, the patients' scale variance was higher, and greater variability influences the magnitude of the correlation. It is a more difficult task to explain the considerable variation in internal consistency among the scales themselves. Defense mechanisms are difficult, abstract concepts about which there is much difference of opinion, even among the experts. Some defenses, however, appear to be clearer than others. Projection, for example, may be one of the concepts whose components are more readily agreed upon and one that is therefore more easily operationalized in statements about behavior. Inspection of Table 17.2 suggests that when one combines several abstract concepts into a single, relatively short scale, even when there are both empirical and theoretical reasons for doing so, one is bound to sacrifice a certain amount of internal consistency for that scale. The scale combining intellectualization, sublimation, undoing, and rationalization is a case in point.

Table 17.1: *Synthesized definitions of eight ego defense scales.*

Compensation, identification, fantasy	Intense attempt to correct or find a suitable substitute for a real or imagined physical or psychological inadequacy; unconscious modeling of attitudes and behaviors after another person as a way of increasing feelings of self-worth or coping with possible separation or loss; retreat into imagination to escape realistic problems or to avoid conflicts.
Denial	Lack of awareness of certain events, experiences, or feelings that would be painful to acknowledge.
Displacement	Discharge of pent-up emotions, usually of anger, on objects, animals, or people perceived as less dangerous than those that originally aroused the emotions.
Intellectualization, sublimation, undoing, rationalization	Unconscious control of emotions and impulses by excessive dependence on rational interpretations of situations; gratification undoing, of a repressed instinct or unacceptable feeling, particularly sexual or aggressive, by socially acceptable alternatives; behavior or thoughts designed to cancel out an act or thought that has much anxiety or guilt attached to it; use of plausible reasons to justify actions caused by repressed, unacceptable feelings.
Projection	Unconscious rejection of one's emotionally unacceptable thoughts, traits, or wishes, and the attribution of them to other people.
Reaction formation	Prevention of the expression of unacceptable desires, particularly sexual or aggressive, by developing or exaggerating opposite attitudes and behaviors.
Regression, acting out	Retreat under stress to earlier or more immature patterns of behavior and gratification; reduction of the anxiety aroused by forbidden impulses by permitting their direct or indirect expression, without the development of guilt.
Repression, isolation, introjection	Exclusion from consciousness of an idea and its associated emotions, or an experience and its associated emotions; recollection of emotionally traumatic experiences or situations, without the anxiety originally associated with them; incorporation of values, standards, or traits of other people in order to prevent conflicts with, or threats from, these people.

A study comparing the use of ego defenses by 29 schizophrenic patients in a state hospital and 70 college students provides some evidence of the discriminant validity of the LSI. The schizophrenic patients scored significantly higher than the students did on seven of the eight defenses (Plutchik et al., 1979). These findings are consistent with a comparison of the mean scale scores for the 60 inpatients and 75 students whose test data served as the basis for the computation of LS1's internal consistency. For all scales, the patients' means were greater than the students'. In general, it could be said that increasing psychiatric symptomatology leads to increasing anxiety, which in turn stimulates a greater use of ego defenses.

Table 17.2: *Coefficient alphas and items ranking highest on relevance for the eight ego defense scales*

	Scale coefficient alpha	
	Inpatients (N=60)	Students (N=75)
Compensation, identification, fantasy		
In my daydreams I'm always the center of attention.	.59	.43
Denial		
I am free of prejudice	.54	.52
Displacement		
If someone bothers me, I don't tell it to him, but I tend to complain to someone else.	.69	.62
Intellectualization, sublimation, undoing, rationalization		
I am more comfortable discussing my thoughts than my feelings.	.58	.30
Projection		
I believe people will take advantage of you if you are not careful.	.86	.75
Reaction formation		
Pornography is disgusting	.73	.63
Regression		
I get irritable when I don't get attention	.65	.56
Repression, isolation, introjection		
I rarely remember my dreams	.55	.38

A degree of construct validity for the scales of the LSI was obtained when it was found that all but one of the scales correlated positively with the Taylor Manifest Anxiety Scale (Bendig, 1956) and that there were negative correlations between five of the eight defenses and total score on a test of self-esteem based on the Tennessee Self-Concept Scale (Fitts, 1965).

The Life Style Index and Clinical Research

Since the publication of the original description of the LSI (Plutchik et al., 1979), normative data, derived from test data of 147 normal adults (no history of psychiatric difficulties), have been constructed. They are available both as percentiles and as *T* -scores. In addition; the LSI has been used in a number of studies relating the use of ego defenses to outcome data and to the clinical variables of risk of suicide and risk of violence.

Ego Defenses and Outcome for Hospitalized Schizophrenics

As part of an attempt to examine the possible relations between psychodynamic variables assessed at admission to the hospital and outcome after discharge, 30 schizophrenics, 15 male and 15 female, on an inpatient ward of a large municipal hospital were asked to complete the LSI (Conte, Plutchik, Schwartz, & Wild, 1983). The profile presented in Fig. 18.1 represents their percentile scores based on the normative group of 147 adults. The outcome measure was readmission to the hospital.

Patients were followed for 2 years after their index admission. It was found that 16 of the 30 were not rehospitalized during either the first or second year subsequent to their discharge. Point-biserial correlations were computed that related scores on each of the eight ego defenses obtained at the time of admission to whether the patients had been readmitted to the hospital during the 2-year follow-up.

In general, variables reflecting patients' psychodynamics proved to be less predictive of whether a schizophrenic patient would be rehospitalized than did more traditionally used predictors such as reduction of overall symptomatology. However, significant positive correlations were found between the use of the ego defenses of repression ($r = .40, p < .03$), displacement ($r = .36, p < .05$), and denial ($r = .35, p < .05$) and the likelihood of readmission. It is interesting to note that repression and denial have been considered to be primitive or immature defenses (Bond et al., 1983; Plutchik et al., 1979; Wong, 1989), and displacement has at best been termed "intermediate" or "neurotic" (Vaillant, 1985; Wong, 1989).

Thus, while there are undoubtedly multiple causal factors that determine rehospitalization, it appears that patients high in the use of these relatively immature defense mechanisms are more likely candidates than those who report lower levels of their usage.

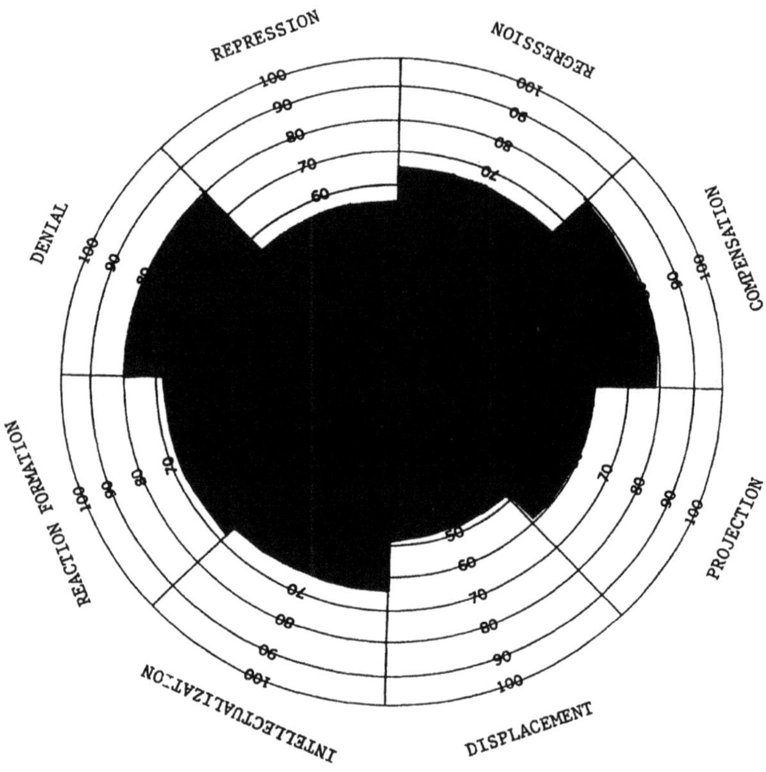

Figure 17.1: *Life Style Index: Ego defense profile based on 30 schizophrenics*

These findings were extended by Offer, Lavie, Gothelf, and Apter (2000) who compared adolescent schizophrenic inpatients with their depressive and obsessive compulsive counterparts as well as with normal controls. LSI was found to contribute to the diagnostic differentiation of schizophrenics from the other clinical and nonclinical groups. There were also significant relationships between defenses and negative emotional states, notably between projection, as scored on the LSI, and anger. A study done in Poland with a translated version of the LSI (Jakubik, Kuzma, Moczulska, & Rozskowska, 1991) investigated paranoid schizophrenics and nonclinical volunteers. The results pointed to the greater reliance on rationalization and denial by the paranoid schizophrenics. On the basis of the composite results of several self-report scales, paranoid schizophrenics were found to be more egocentric than normal controls.

Ego Defenses and Outcome of Long-Term Psychotherapy

The Life Style Index has also been used in a study of variables that might predict the outcome of psychotherapy (Buckley, Conte, Plutchik, Wild, & Karasu, 1984). In this study, 21 medical students were seen in psychotherapy, averaging 42 sessions. At intake, each student completed a battery of self-report tests that included the LSI. Outcome was evaluated by psychiatrists' ratings on a termination form that consisted of 13 items, each rated on a four-point scale ranging from "got worse" to "markedly improved." The items included such symptoms as depression and suicidal impulses, paranoid ideation, sexual problems, and difficulties with academic work.

Of the statistically significant pretreatment predictors of outcome, two, reaction formation and projection, were self-report assessments of ego defenses as measured by the LSI. The first of these, reaction formation, characterizes a person who substitutes socially acceptable behavior, thoughts, or feelings for his or her diametrically opposed unacceptable ones. This implies at least an openness to change that would enable the individual to benefit from psychotherapy.

The use of projection as a predictor of good outcome is somewhat surprising, since projection is regarded as a low-level defense, more typical of serious pathology. However, a comparison of the percentile scores obtained for the patients who were rated most improved by the psychiatrists with those rated least improved sheds some light on this finding. Those rated most improved (N = 11) were at the 31st percentile on the norms based on normal adults, the majority of whom fall at approximately the 50th percentile, whereas those rated least improved (N = 10) fell at the 4th percentile. This suggests that projection may reflect a capacity for emotional engagement, albeit distorted, a certain amount of which is necessary for therapeutic change. This raises the possibility that the use of either too little or too much of any defense may be maladaptive.

Defense Mechanisms in Relation to Risk of Suicide and Risk of Violence

Psychodynamic theorists have addressed the role of defense mechanisms in relation to suicide. Freud (1957), for example, assumed that suicidal behavior may result as an individual turns toward himself or herself the originally repressed anger felt against another person who has been lost. Yet there have been few attempts to use empirical methods in the study of the defense mechanisms of suicidal or outwardly violent patients.

Apter and his colleagues, using the LSI to assess defenses, did conduct such a study (Apter, Plutchik, Sevy, Korn, Brown, & van Praag, 1989). Shortly after admission, 60 patients on the psychiatric inpatient wards of a municipal hospital center were administered a Suicide Risk scale (SR), a Past Feelings and Acts of Violence scale (PFAV), and the LSI as part of a battery of tests designed to identify correlates of suicide and violence risk in psychiatric patients. It should be mentioned that the SR and PFAV scales are not meant to predict future suicides or acts of violence, but, rather, the probability that an individual will make a suicide attempt or perform a violent act. No attempt was made to select any particular diagnostic category of patients, but 30 were selected because they had been admitted subsequent to a suicide attempt. These were matched according to sex, age, and diagnosis with non-suicidal control patients. Of the group of 30 suicidal patients, 20 had to be secluded or restrained for assaulting a staff member or fellow patient. These constituted the violent group and were compared with the other 40 patients.

Risk of suicide and risk of violence were highly correlated ($r = .62$) with one another. For this reason, partial correlations were computed between each of the defenses and risk of suicide or violence. Application of the Bonferroni correction indicated that correlations greater than .32 were significant. It was found that repression, denial, and displacement were significantly correlated with risk of suicide after risk of violence was partialed out ($r = .47$, -. 51; $p < .001$; and $r = .34$, $p < .01$, respectively). When the risk of suicide was partialed out, risk of violence correlated .46 ($p < .001$) with projection and .32 ($p < .01$) with denial. The remaining correlations were not significant. Thus, patients who scored high on repression had a relatively high probability of making a future suicide attempt, whereas the risk for suicidal behavior of those scoring high on denial was relatively low. However, their risk for violent behavior was high.

Interpretation of why an individual who scored high on displacement would be considered to be at risk for suicide is somewhat less obvious. It is, however, possible that these individuals turn the anger that low scorers on displacement would normally express toward those who rejected or frustrated them back on themselves. In so doing, they would increase their risk for self-destructive behavior. High scorers on the use of projection as a defense also were at significant risk for violence, but were at little risk of suicidal behavior. These findings are in accord with what one would predict from psychoanalytic theory and provide a degree of validity to the scales.

Suicidal patients were also compared with nonsuicidal patients and violent patients with nonviolent ones. Suicidal patients scored significantly higher on regression ($I = 2.61$, df = 58, $p < .01$) than did the nonsuicidal patients. Comparing the violent with the nonviolent patients, two significant differences were found. The violent group scored significantly higher on displacement ($I = 2.96$, df = 58, $p < .01$) and lower on reaction formation ($I = 2.64$, df = 58, $p < .01$).

That use of regression was significantly greater in the suicidal patients than in the nonsuicidal ones is consistent with the clinical observation that suicidal patients have greater potential for severe infantile, impulsive acting out behavior in the face of intolerable life stress than do non-suicidal patients. The finding that displacement was more marked in the violent than in the nonviolent patients also provides support for clinical impressions and expectations from psychodynamic theory. Many acts of violence appear to represent displacement of aggression from primary objects onto symbolic representations of or substitutes for those objects. That the violent patients should score lower on the use of reaction formation is also consistent with both theory and what is noted in clinical practice. Individuals prone to violence have little tendency to adopt attitudes or behavior opposite to their feelings. Their aggressiveness is more often expressed directly.

The relationship between the risk of violence and of suicide was further investigated by means of the LSI in a group of hospitalized alcoholics by Greenwald, Reznikoff and Plutchik (1994). By means of stepwise multiple regression it was established that displacement contributed to the prediction of both violence and suicidality. Displacement in combination with regression predicted suicidal risk. In Israel Apter, Gothelf, Offer, Ratzoni, Orbach, Tyano, and Pfeffer (1997) applied the Hebrew version of the LSI in an investigation of the relationship of suicidal potential and defense mechanisms. Fifty-five adolescents admitted to a psychiatric hospital after a suicide attempt were compared with 87 hospitalized but nonsuicidal peers and 81 normal controls. Again, suicidal adolescents obtained higher LSI scores in displacement as well as in denial, repression, and total defense.

Less directly relevant to the issue at hand is a large-scale study at a treatment facility for juvenile delinquents in Thailand by Tori and Emawardhana (1998). In this research the Thai translation of LSI was administered to 300 juvenile delinquent boys and 100 girls who were matched with 400 nondelinquent controls. Male delinquents exceeded nondelinquents in regression, projection, repression, and denial; girls were described as being more sexually repressed, guarded, and inecure than their nondelinquent peers. No comparisons, however, were undertaken with the type of offense; thus, the relationship between LSI and violence in this sample remains unknown.

On the basis of these research findings, it can be concluded that ego defenses, as assessed by means of the LSI, play an integral role in determining the probability that a person will engage in suicidal or violent behavior. The ability to actually quantify the role of the defense in this regard may have important implications for the management and treatment of patients.

Defense Mechanisms and Psychophysiology

A surprising finding that emerged in the course of validating Dutch and Norwegian versions of the LSI pertain to psychological stress factors and levels of immunoglobulins (Endresen, 1991). In two studies, complex relationships were established between defense scores on the LSI and immunological parameters in air force pilots and nurses that involved health state, psychological stress levels, and defensive and adaptive strategies. These results remain to be replicated and extended, especially in light of the burgeoning interest in bridging the gap between defense mechanisms and physiological responsiveness, as exemplified by the final chapter in this volume by Hentschel, Smith, and Draguns.

Another approach to the same problem is illustrated by Raudino (1993), who investigated the Italian version of LSI in relation to intermittent photic stimulation in patients suffering from migraine and tension headaches. Although the results obtained were inconclusive, relating defenses to psychophysiological responses continues to be a promising research objective.

Clinicians' Conceptions of Ego Defenses in Relation to Psychotherapy Outcome

Clinicians have implicit beliefs about characteristics that make some patients more likely to benefit from psychotherapy than others. As one way of looking at this issue, 20 clinicians, 15 psychiatrists, 4 social workers, and a psychologist with an average of 12 years of post-training experience, were asked to respond to the 97 items of the Life Style Index in the following way. They were to assume that a patient had answered "yes" to each item, indicating that the item described him or her. They were then asked to indicate whether a "yes" response to each of the items was indicative of a probable "good" or "poor" prognosis in psychodynamic psychotherapy, or whether they believed that this description was "irrelevant" to outcome. Table 17.3 presents a brief summary of the data obtained.

Included under the heading of "good prognosis" are items to which 70% or more of the clinicians responded that an individual who fit these descriptions would do well in psychotherapy. Top candidates for a good prognosis would be those who use the defenses of intellectualization and compensation. There was almost total agreement that an individual who is willing to listen to all sides of an argument would do well. Slightly less predictive of good outcome, but still endorsed by 70% of the clinicians, was the item describing an individual who describes him or herself as being logical in arguments. Two items from the compensation scale were endorsed by 80% of the clinicians as predicting good prognosis. The first, "There has always been a person whom I wished I were like" suggests that a patient who responds "yes" would readily develop a positive transference. The second, descriptive of someone who is willing to work hard to realize a gain, suggests that the person is persistent and not easily discouraged, characteristics that are an asset in making progress in therapy.

Table 17.3: *Defense mechanisms as prognostic indicators of psychotherapy outcome as rated by clinicians (N = 20).*

	Clinicans' response (%)
Good prognosis	
Intellectualization	
I am always willing to listen to all sides of an argument.	95
In arguments, I'm usually more logical than the other person.	70
Compensation	
There has always been a person whom I wished I were like.	80
I work harder than most people to be good at what I like.	80
Poor prognosis	
Regression	
I lie a lot.	90
I "fly off the handle" easily.	80
When I'm upset, I often get drunk.	75
I can't seem to finish anything I start.	70
Projection	
Most people are obnoxious.	80
I am irritated because people can't be trusted.	70
Most people annoy me because they are too selfish.	70
Displacement	
When I've been rejected, I've sometimes felt suicidal.	85
Sometimes I wish an atom bomb would destroy the world.	70
Repression	
When I read or hear about a tragedy, it never seems to affect me.	70

The clinicians rated considerably more items of the LSI as reflective of poor prognosis. Consistent with the notion that patients who utilize relatively immature defenses are not likely to have a good outcome is the finding that these poor prognosis items represent the ego defenses of regression, projection, displacement, and repression. As illustrated in Table 17.3, a large percentage of the rating clinicians (70-90%) indicated their belief that patients who regress under stress to immature patterns of behavior or gratification would have a poor prognosis for psychotherapy. In addition, 70-80% responded that patients who attribute their own unacceptable characteristics to others would not do well. Similarly, 70-85% of the clinicians considered the prognosis to be poor of patients who do not deal directly with their pent-up emotions or whose emotional responses have become blunted.

Further research is necessary to determine the accuracy of these clinicians' predictions about who would and who would not do well in therapy. It would be interesting, for example, to administer the Life Style Index to a sample of patients before they enter treatment and to follow them over the course of therapy to determine which patients, in fact, had a good or a poor outcome. Nevertheless, it is unlikely that the raters were merely responding to stereotypes. They were asked to make predictions 1 about specific items, not to the use of a given defense per se. What is J likely is that the items they endorsed as good prognosticators described 1 individuals with whom they believed they could work well. That in itself 1 might make for a good prognosis

Translations and Adaptations: International Extensions of the LSI

Perhaps more than other related measures, LSI has been translated, investigated, and adapted in a number of languages. Usually, the procedure involved a three-stage sequence of translating the instrument, independently back translating it into English, and resolving any discrepancies in the two versions in conference between the translators. This is usually followed by a systematic effort to obtain validational data

Conte and Apter (1995) reported on the early stages of translating LSI into Russian at the Moscow State Pedagogical University, in the course of which the psychometric properties of the new version were established, norms and percentiles were developed, and information was obtained on the differences and similarities between the LSI scores of delinquents and addicts ands normal controls.

The development and validation of Dutch and Norwegian versions of the LSI has been described by Endresen (1991) and Olff and Endresen (1991). Both in The Netherlands and in Norway, validation was primarily based on large numbers of available normal adult respondents, mostly associated with higher education, health-related professions, and the military, although a group of Dutch outpatients was also included. Data obtained pointed to a relationship between the experience of stress and LSI scales. The results showed a greater similarity on the LSI between the two linguistically and culturally related countries of Northwestern Europe than with the original American validation sample (Plutchik et al., 1979). Suggestively, this result may reflect the greater cultural divide between North America and Norway and The Netherlands. Correlational and factorial analyses were conducted for both sets of data, and certain psychometric imperfections of the LSI in its translated versions were identified. Endresen (1991) commented: "The correlation analyses showed that most of the subscales of LSI ere significantly associated with each other, indicating overlap between the scales. In addition, the internal consistency of the specific scales was low; all had an Alpha below O.70" (p. 111). As Endresen proceeded to say, these findings do not necessarily represent a psychometric deficiency. Instead, the various scales may measure both specific defense mechanisms and the generic aspects of psychological defense.

The validation of the Hebrew translation of the LSI in Israel was initiated with the comparison of adolescent psychiatric inpatients with high school students (Apter et al., 1997). The obtained data were thoroughly analyzed in relation to the structured diagnostic interview, K-SADS, Beck Depression Inventory, and suicidal versus nonsuicidal status at the time of admission. The results conformed to the theoretically based expectations regarding the nature of defenses utilized and their rank order across the several groups of respondents.

The validation of the LSI in Thailand (Tori & Emavardhana, 1998) was based on the responses of a total of 2535 participants from all parts of the country. The factor structure of the Thai version of the LSI differed somewhat from the original American one. Consequently, the test was scored for the following six defense mechanisms: regressive emotionality, reaction formation, projection, repression, denial, and compensation.

Use of the LSI translations has also been reported in Italy (Raudino, 1983) and Poland (Jakubik et al., 1991). However, we lack detailed information on the psychometric properties of these versions of the LSI.

Although data on the several translations of the LSI are fragmentary, complex, and ambiguous, there is no reason to suspect that the LSI measures fundamentally different constructs in other language communities and cultures. That is why we have incorporated the results obtained across political, linguistic, and cultural barriers into our account of LSI research, but have always indicated the country in which the data were gathered.

Conclusions and Directions for Future Research

We believe that the LSI is a reasonable test for measuring some important ego defenses. Among its salient characteristics, the LSI has a self-report format and is thus easy to administer and to score. It is of special significance that the selection of defenses to be measured was based on a general theory of affect (Plutchik, 1980, 1990, 2000). This theory assumes that ego defenses are basic adaptive mechanisms that function to deal with specific emotional conflicts. Displacement, for example, functions to handle conflicts involving anger or aggression. Projection handles conflicts over issues of acceptance of self or others, while repression deals with conflicts produced by intolerable anxiety.

While the connections between emotions, ego defenses, and diagnoses are at this stage hypothetical, the theory also assumes that individuals with particular personality disorders such as borderline, schizoid, or antisocial, are likely to emphasize the use of specific ego defenses. In the case of these three disorders, they might be regression, fantasy, and projection, respectively. In addition, the theory postulates a systematic structuring of the ego defenses that closely approximates a circumplicial, or circular, order that reflects the degree of similarity among the defenses. The Life Style Index is thus based on a theory that permits systematic inferences to be made about the relations among the ego defenses themselves and about their relation to other clinical domains

The relation between defense mechanisms and psychiatric diagnoses is an area that is in need of clarification. Before the advent of DSM-IV, no standardized classification system existed for the ego defenses. This is not really surprising. Vaillant and Drake put it well when they state: "Defenses are, after all, metaphors; they are a shorthand way of describing different cognitive styles and modes of rearranging inner and outer realities" (1985, p. 601). As such, they reflect integrated processes that are both difficult to identify and to define. The incorporation of the description of 31 defense mechanisms into the current DSM-IV is a harbinger of a new and potentially significant trend. Implicitly, mental health professionals are now encouraged to systematically take note of defense mechanisms and to incorporate them into their diagnostic formulations

It is our belief that the Life Style Index represents a comprehensive and relatively well agreed upon selection of defense mechanisms when they are defined as unconscious mental processes. It might prove productive, therefore, to test the notion of Laplanche and Pontalis (1973) that the type of illness a patient has in large measure determines which defense mechanisms will predominate. Vaillant and Drake (1985) related Axis II of the DSM-III to patients' dominant choice of ego defenses and found that two-thirds of the men with personality disorders used primarily immature defense mechanisms. Bond and Vaillant (1986) compared patients' defense styles with their diagnoses on Axes I, II, and IV of DSM-III and found that a significant relationship existed between defense style and only one diagnosis, major affective disorder.

Further investigations of this sort would help to provide a clearer picture of the extent to which defense mechanisms relate to an aspect of human functioning that is distinct from that encompassed in diagnoses or whether the use of particular defenses is an integral part of a given diagnostic status. In addition to investigating the relations between defense mechanisms and diagnoses, future research should address the relation- ship between ego defenses and general level of adjustment in varying psychiatric populations. Beyond psychopathology, it is worth exploring individual differences on LSI in relation to personality constructs and dimensions. For example, it may be interesting to ascertain any differences in defense preferences across the factorially based Big Five personality dimensions (McCrea & Costa, 1997) and to investigate the distribution of defenses in relation to Hofstede's (2001) five cultural axes.

Research in the area of psychotherapy has been concerned with such issues as predictors of outcome, factors influencing process, matching of therapist and patient, and identification and training of good psychotherapists. We believe that measures of ego defenses are important parameters for investigations in these areas. Furthermore, their use should enrich the findings in these investigations by adding psychodynamic insights to the more traditional demographic, symptom, and personality-oriented variables.

References

Ablon, S. L., Carlson, G. A., & Goodwin, F. K. (1974). Ego defense patterns in manic-depressive illness. *American Journal of Psychiatry,* 131, 803- 807.

American Psychiatric Association (1994). *Diagnostic and Statistical Manual of Mental Disorders* (4th ed.). Washington, DC: American Psychiatric Association.

Andrews, G., Pollock, C., & Stewart, G. (1989). The determination of defense style by questionnaire. *Archives of General Psychiatry,* 46,455-460.

Apter, A., Gothelf, D., Offer, R., Ratzoni, G., Orbach, I., Tyano, S. & Pfeffer, C. R. (1997). Suicidal adolescents and ego defense mechanisms. *Journal of the American Academy of Child and Adolescent Psychiatry, 36,* 1520-1527.

Apter, A., Plutchik, R., Sevy, S., Kom, M., Brown S., & van Praag, H. (1989). Defense mechanisms in risk of suicide and risk of violence. *American Journal of Psychiatry,* 146, 1027-1031.

Arieti, S. (Ed.) (1974) *American handbook of psychiatry.* New York: Basic Books.

Bendig, A. W. (1956). The development of a short form of the Manifest Anxiety Scale. *Journal of Consulting Psychology,* 20,384-387.

Bond, M. (1986) Defense Style Questionnaire. In G.E. Vaillant (Ed.), *Empirical studies of ego mechanisms of defense* (pp. 146-152). Washington, DC: American Psychiatric Press.

Bond, M., Gardner, S. T., Christian, I., & Sigal, 1. 1. (1983) Empirical study of self-rated defense styles. *Archives of General Psychiatry,* 40, 333-338.

Bond, M. P. & Vaillant, I. S. (1986). An empirical study of the relationship between diagnosis and defense style. *Archives of General Psychiatry,* 43,285-288.

Brenner, C. (1973). *An elementary textbook of psychoanalysis.* Madison, CT: International Universities Press.

Buckley, P., Conte, H. R., Plutchik, R., Wild, K. V., & Karasu, T. B. (1984). Psychodynamic variables as predictors of psychotherapy outcome. *American Journal of Psychiatry,* 141, 742- 748.

Conte, H. R. & Apter, A. (1995). The Life Style Index: A self-report measure of ego defenses. In H.R. Conte & R. Plutchik (Eds.) *Ego defenses: Theory and measurement* (pp. 179-201). New York: Wiley.

Conte, H. R., Plutchik, R., Schwartz, B., & Wild, K. (1983). *Psychodynamic variables related to outcome in hospitalized schizophrenics.* Paper presented at the Convention of the American Psychological Association, Anaheim, CA.

Endresen, I. M. (1991) A Norwegian translation of the Plutchik questionnaire for psychological defense. *Scandinavian Journal of Psychology, 32,* 105-113.

Fitts, W. H. (1965) *The Tennessee Self-Concept Scale.* Nashville: Counselor Recordings & Tests.

Freud, A. (1936) *The ego and the mechanisms of defense.* Madison, CT: International Universities Press.

Freud, S. (1957) Mourning and melancholia. In *The standard edition of the complete psychological works of Sigmund Freud: Vol.* 14. London: Hogarth Press.

Gleser, G. C. & Ihilevich, D. (1969) An objective instrument for measuring defense mechanisms. *Journal of Consulting and Clinical Psychology,* 33, 51-60.

Greenwald, D. J., Reznikoff, M., & Plutchik, R. (1994). Suicide risk and violence risk in alcoholics. Predictors of aggressive risk. *Journal of Nervous and Mental Disease, 182,* 3-8.

Haan, N. A., Stroud, I., & Holstein, C. (1973). Moral and ego stages in relationship to ego processes: A study of "hippies." *Journal of Personality,* 41, 596-612.

Hackett, T. P. & Cassem, N. H. (1974). Development of a quantitative rating scale to assess denial. *Journal of Psychosomatic Research,* 18,93-100.

Hofstede, G. (2001). *Culture's consequences: Comparing values, institutions and organizations across cultures* (2nd ed.) Thousand Oaks, CA: Sage.

Jakubik, A., Kuzma, A., Moczulska, E. & Roszkowska, J (1991). Mechanizmy obronne w schizofrenii paraoidalnej (Defense mechanisms in paranoid schizophrenia). *Psychiatria Polska, 25,* 1-5.

Kragh, U. (1969). *The Defense Mechanism Test.* Stockholm: Testfoerlaget.

Kreitler, H. & Kreitler, S. (1972). The cognitive determinants of defensive behavior. *British Journal of Social and Clinical Psychology,* 11, 359-373. Laplanche, *I.* & Pontalis, *I.B.* (1973) *The language of psychoanalysis.* London: Hogarth Press.

Marshall, I. B. (1982). *Psychometric and validational studies of an objective test of Freudian defense mechanisms.* Unpublished doctoral dissertation, University of North Carolina at Chapel Hill, NC.

McCrea, R. R. & Costa, P. T, Jr. (1997). Personality trait structure as a human universal. *American Psychologist,* 52, 509-516.

Meissner, W. W., Mack, I. E., & Semrad, E. V. (1975). Theories of personality and psychopathology: Classical psychoanalysis. In A.M. Freedman & H.I. Kaplan (Eds.), *Comprehensive textbook of psychiatry: Vol.* 11 (pp. 535-536). Baltimore: Williams & Wilkins.

Moore, B. & Fine, B. D. (Eds.) (1990). *Psychoanalytic terms and concepts.* New York and New Haven, CT: American Psychoanalytic Association and Yale University Press.

Noyes, A. P. & Kolb, L. C. (1963). *Modern clinical psychiatry.* Philadelphia: Saunders.

Olff, M. & Endresen, I. M. (1991). The Dutch and the Norwegian translations of the Plutchik questionnaire for psychological defence. In M. Olff, G. Godaert, & H. Ursin (Eds.) *Quantification of human defence mechanisms.* (pp. 59-71). Berlin: Springer Verlag

Offer, R, Lavie, R., Gothelf, D, & Apter, A. (2000). Defense mechanisms, negative emotions, and psychopathology in adolescent inpatients. *Comprehensive Psychiatry, 41,* 35-41.

Perry , I. C. & Cooper, S. H. (1989). An empirical study of defense mechanisms. I. Clinical interview and life vignette ratings. *Archives of General Psychiatry,* 46, 444-452.

Perry, J. C. & Vaillant, G. E. (1990) Personality disorder. In H.I. Kapalan & B.J. Sadock (Eds.) *Comprehensive textbook o psychiatry. Vol. 2* (5th ed.) (pp. 1352-1395). New York: Plenum.

Plutchik, R. (1962). *The emotions: Facts, theories, and a new model.* New York: Random House.

Plutchik, R. (1980). *Emotion: A psycho-evolutionary synthesis.* New York: Harper & Row.

Plutchik, R. (1990). Emotions and psychotherapy. A psycho-evolutionary perspective. In R. Plutchik & H. Kellerman (Eds.) *Emotions: Theory, research, and experience. Vol.5* (pp. 3-41). New York: Academic Press.

Plutchik, R. (2000). *Emotions in the practice of psychotherapy.* Washington, DC: American Psychological Association.

Plutchik, R. & Conte, H. R (1989). Measuring emotions and their derivatives: Personality traits, ego defenses, and coping styles. In S. Wetzler & M.M. Katz (Eds.) *Contemporary approaches to personality assessment* (pp. 239-269). New York: Brunner/Mazel.

Plutchik, R., Kellerman, H.,& Conte, H. R. (1979). A structural theory of ego defenses and emotions. In C.E. Izard (Ed.) *Emotions in personality and psychopathology* (pp. 229-257). New York: Plenum.

Raudino, F. (1983). Cefalea e risposta alla stimolazione luminosa intermittente (Headache and response to intermittent photic stimulation). *Rivista di Neurologia, 53,* 280-283.

Sarason., I. G., Ganzer, N. J., & Singer, M. (1972). Effects of modeled self-disclosure on the verbal behavior of persons differing in defensiveness. *Journal of Consulting and Clinical Psychology, 39,* 483-490.

Semrad, E. V., Grinspoon, L., & Feinberg, S. E. (1973). Development of an ego profile scale. *Archives of General Psychiatry, 28,* 70-77.

Tori, C. D. & Emavardhana, T. (1998). The psychology of Thai delinquent youth: A study of self-perception, ego-defenses, and personality traits. *International Journal of Offender Therapy and Comparative Criminology,42,* 305-318.

Vaillant, G. E. (1971). Theoretical hierarchy of adaptive ego mechanisms: A 30-year follow-up of 30 men selected for psychological health .*Archives of General Psychiatry, 24,* 107-118.

Vaillant, G. E. (1977). *Adaptation to life.* Boston: Little Brown.

Vaillant, G. E. (1985). An empirically derived hierarchy of adaptive mechanims and its usefulness as a potential diagnostic axis *Acta Psychiatrica Scandinavica, 71,* (suppl.319), 171-180.

Vaillant, G. E., Bond, M., & Vaillant, G. O. (1986). An empirically validated hierarchy of defense mechanisms. *Archives of General Psychiatry, 43,* 786-794.

Vaillant, G. E. & Drake, R. E. (1985). Maturity of ego defenses in relation to DSM-III, Axis II personality disorder. *Archives of General Psychiatry, 42,* 597-601.

Wong. N. (1989). Theory of personality and psychopathology. In H.I. Kaplan & B.J.Sadock (Eds.) *Comprehensive textbook of psychiatry: Vol. 1* (5th ed.) (pp. 356-410). Baltimore: Williams & Wilkins.

Defense Mechanisms
U. Hentschel, G. Smith, J.G. Draguns & W. Ehlers (Editors)

Chapter 18

Patterns of Adaptation and Percept-Genetic Defenses

I. Alex Rubino and Alberto Siracusano

Introduction

The framework of the present study rests on three premises advanced fifty years ago by Smith and Klein (1953): (a) The concept of defense represents "a stabilized coping mechanism concerned with mediation of conflict" (p. 188); (b) Preferred styles of cognitive organization, which are expressed in the course of adaptation to various types of conflicting situations, constitute fundamental components of personality; and (c) These patterns of adaptation or regulatory styles are "especially evident in serials (i.e., in the manner in which response unfolds in a situation)" (p. 188). Consequently, the focus of research to be reported in this chapter is upon the temporal patterning of responses and not upon the average achievement level scores.

The instrument chosen by Smith and Klein to assess patterns of adaptation was a serial version of the Color-Word Test (Stroop, 1935), currently known as the Serial Color-Word Test (S-CWT). The manual by Smith, Nyman, Hentschel, and Rubino (2001) contains a detailed review of validity studies, mainly in the field of clinical psychology, but also in applied fields, e.g. in traffic studies and studies on physical symptoms. The Stroop task activates in the respondent two conflicting response tendencies: reading the printed hue or naming the name of a number of color words printed in an incongruent color. The respondent is instructed to name the color, thereby resisting the interference effect. A table with ten lines of incongruent color words is presented five times or in five subtests, with a one-minute pause between presentations; reading times are registered for every two lines. Instead of measuring the overall interference effect, in line with the standard neuropsychological use of the Stroop task, attention is focused upon the relationship between naming times. The two fundamental measures of the S-CWT are linear regression (R) and residual variability (V), both within and across subtests. Table 18.1 provides the main definitions and formulas.

Table 18.1: *Serial Color-Word Test: Essential Glossary and Main Formulas*
Subtest –the task of naming the color of one table of 100 incongruent color-words. The test is comprised of five subtests t_1, t_2, t_3, t_4, t_5 - Naming times of each of the five pairs of lines (20 words) of each subtest t_I, t_{II}, t_{III}, t_{IV}, t_V - Naming times pertaining, respectively, to the first, second, third, fourth, and fifth subtest, e.g., $t_{III\,2}$ is the naming time of the second pair of lines of the third subtest

R - Linear change $2\,t_5 + t_4 - t_2 - 2t_1$

V - Nonlinear change $\sqrt{\Sigma\, t^2 - (\Sigma\, t)^2 /5 - R^2 /10}$

Stabilized pattern – a pattern characterized by low R and low V

Cumulative pattern –a pattern characterized by high R and low V

Dissociative pattern –a pattern characterized by low R and high V

Cumulative-Dissociative pattern – a pattern characterized by high R and high V

R_I, R_{II}, R_{III}, R_{IV}, R_V - Linear change of the first subtest, of the second subtest, etc.

V_I, V_{II}, V_{III}, V_{IV}, V_V - Nonlinear change of the first subtest, of the second subtest, etc.

R_R - Linear change of linear changes $2R_V + R_{IV} - R_{II} - 2R_I$

V_R - Nonlinear change of linear changes $\sqrt{\Sigma\, R^2 - (\Sigma\, R)^2 / 5 - R_R^2 / 10}$

R_V - Linear change of nonlinear changes $2V_V + V_{IV} - V_{II} - 2V_I$

V_V - Nonlinear change of nonlinear changes $\sqrt{\Sigma\, V^2 - (\Sigma\, V)^2 / 5 - R_V^2 / 10}$

IT_A - Initial Type A $(t_{I\,1} : t_{II\,1}) : [t_{II\,1} : (t_{III\,1} \vee t_{IV\,1} \vee t_{V\,1})_{min}]$

IT_B - Initial Type B $(t_{I\,1} : t_{I\,2}) : [t_{I\,2} : (t_{I\,3} \vee t_{I\,4} \vee t_{I\,5})_{min}]$

R_{AD} - Adaptation Index $2 \log t_{I\,1} + \log t_{II\,1} - \log t_{IV\,1} - 2 \log t_V$

Note.- $(t_{III\,1} \vee t_{IV\,1} \vee t_{V\,1})_{min}$ means: the lowest value among the first couple of lines of the last three subtests. The corresponding expression for IT_B regards the last three couple of lines of the first subtest.

The most systematic published attempt to relate S-CWT patterns to defenses (Almgren, 1980) employed the Meta-Contrast Technique (MCT: Smith, Johnson, & Almgren, 1989), a well validated tachistoscopic method which provides information on anxiety and defenses. Persons with high nonlinear change of naming times on the three first S-CWT subtests, exhibiting the dissociative style, presented more signs of repression and fewer signs of isolation by comparison with nondissociative participants. Moreover, more instances of isolation and fewer of repression were found among persons characterized by high initial times followed by a series of stable and much lower times. These sequences were found among the so called Initial Types (IT). The latter finding confirmed high positive correlations between IT and isolation that had been reported earlier, in a paper devoted more to the clinical significance of S-CWT and MCT than to the relationship between these two measures (Smith, Nilsson & Johnson, 964).

Subsequently, Westerlundh (1983) studied the relationship between the S-CWT and the defenses reported by subjects who were administered the stimuli of the other major percept-genetic method designed to assess defensive organization, the Defense Mechanism Test (DMT; Kragh, 1985). However, the anxiety-arousing pictures on the DMT were not administered tachistoscopically, which is their usual mode of presentation, but by limiting perception to peripheral vision by means of Sander's ambient focal technique. In agreement with Almgren's (1980) findings, the dissociative style was significantly correlated with indicators of several variants of repression, albeit at a rather low level of significance. A number of clinical investigations employed both the S-CWT and the MCT, often to compare combinations of adaptive patterns and codings of defense with symptom constellations and outcome criteria (see e.g., Kragh & Smith, 1970, pp. 286-318). However, in the present context these studies are only marginally relevant.

A different line of research compared defenses on the DMT with patterns of adaptation on the Spiral Aftereffect Technique (SAT: Andersson, Nilsson, Ruuth, & Smith, 1972). The principal significant results juxtaposed repression to introaggression. Repression, except for the repetition of repression variant, correlated with the diminishing duration of the aftereffect over the 10 massed SAT trials while introaggression directed against the central figure varied with linearly increasing duration (Andersson & Weikert, 1974; Andersson & Bengtsson, 1985). In line with his interpretation of SAT variables, Andersson and his coworkers argued that repression and introaggression show, respectively, with regard to their reflection of anxiety an orientation toward nonself and toward self. Furthermore, also the strongest variant of isolation, the so-called barrier isolation, was found to be linked to the extraceptive (nonself) orientation. It may be added that no simple relationship was established between SAT and S-CWT patterns. Rising curves of aftereffect duration, for example, were not significantly associated with rising curves for naming times (Andersson, 1967). The present investigation into the relationships between regulatory styles and types of defense was originally envisaged as an endeavour with four instruments (MCT, DMT, CWT, and SAT). Unfortunately, technical problems permitted the administration of the MCT and SAT to only a small proportion of the sample.

Therefore, only the hypotheses and findings relative to DMT and S-CWT are reported here.

Proceeding from the assumption of a close similarity between defense scores on MCT and DMT, the following major hypotheses about the relationships between S-CWT and DMT were advanced: (a) there should be a positive correlation between the dissociative style and repression, or some varieties of repression, and (b) a positive correlation should be obtained between IT and the strongest isolation indicators. Beyond these two predictions, our research pursued exploratory objectives in taking note of any additional significant findings, even though we refrained from formulating specific theoretically based expectations.

Method

Respondents

S-CWT and the DMT were administered to 119 clinical and non-clinical respondents between the ages of 18 and 60. Only participants with a regular primary S-CWT classification, as described below, were included. As a result, the size of the sample was reduced to 58 persons, 38 of whom were women and 20 men. Aside from 15 nonclinical volunteers from the university administrative staff, participants included psychiatric and psychosomatic patients, diagnosed with anxiety disorders, bronchial asthma, psoriasis, and eczema. Psychotic or neurological patients as well as colour-blind persons were excluded.

Instruments

The Serial Color-Word Test

Participants were given a page with 10 lines of color-words printed in incongruent hues and were asked to name the printed hue, disregarding color names. Instructions, administration, and calculations followed strictly the S-CWT manual (Smith *et al.*, 2001). Italian norms, stratified for age and gender, were employed for classification (cf. Rubino, Grasso, & Pezzarossa, 1990). Each protocol was assigned to six classifications: (1) primary types (based on R and V values for the five subtests), (2) R-types (based on R and V values for the five R*s*), (3) V-types (based on R and V values of the five V*s*), (4) IT_A, (5) IT_B, and, (6) R_{AD}. Primary, R-, and V-types have the same fourfold classification, comprising Stabilized, Cumulative, Dissociative, and Cumulative-Dissociative patterns (cf. Table 18.1). IT_A, IT_B, and R_{AD} are simply classified as high ($^+$) or low ($^{-}$). In this study, only rigorous classification criteria for primary types were applied, i.e., the same pattern on at least three subtests, and at least on two of the first three subtests. Table 18.2 presents the distribution of types in the final sample.

Table 18.2: *Distribution of Participants Across S-CWT types (N = 58).*

Primary types	R-types	V-types	I T_A	IT_B	R_{AD}
S (N= 14)	S_R (N= 15)	S_V (N= 14)	IT_A^+ (N = 26)	IT_B^+ (N = 27)	R_{AD}^+ (N = 30)
C (N= 10)	C_R (N = 14)	C_V (N= 17)	IT_A^- (N = 32)	IT_B^- (N = 31)	R_{AD}^- (N = 28)
D (N = 17)	D_R (N= 10)	D_V (N= 14)			
CD (N = 17)	CD_R (N = 19)	CD_V (N = 13)			

The Defense Mechanism Test

DMT involves the administration of two TAT-like pictures representing a central figure or hero (H) and a threatening peripheral person of the same gender as H (Pp). These stimuli are presented tachistoscopically at gradually increased exposure times. There are two series of 22 steps, from 5 msec. to 2 sec. Verbal and graphic reports are coded for evidence of defensive alterations, according to the classical psychoanalytic list of defense mechanisms. Administration and coding followed the DMT manual (Kragh, 1985). The DMT apparatus employed was the standard one produced by Persona in Sweden. A 0.5 grey filter was used throughout; no distracting stimulus was presented during testing. The following codings were found to be relevant to the present study: 1:42 (Stimulus-distal repression). Pp is an object. Particular attention is paid to excluding reports of objects not clearly in the position of Pp. Instances of two objects, one on each side of the H, and reports of repression combined with isolation (e.g., "a lighted reflector") are not included in 1:42 scores.

1. 1:42 (Stimulus-distal repression). Pp is an object. Particular attention is paid to excluding reports of objects not clearly in the position of Pp. Instances of two objects, one on each side of the H, and reports of repression combined with isolation (e.g., "a lighted reflector") are not included in 1:42 scores
2. 2:10a (Barrier isolation). H and Pp are isolated by a separating line or area. Only clear reports of 2:10a were coded.
3. 2:10b (Second variant of isolation between H and Pp). H and Pp are placed in different frames of reference (levels of reality or space).

4. 2:10c (Third variant of isolation between H and Pp). The distance between H and Pp increases (typically, Pp turns away from H).
5. 2:32 (Pp discontinuity). Pp disappears after having been reported in the preceding phase.
6. 3: (Denial). Threat is explicitly denied or minimized.
7. 4:10 (First variant of reaction formation). H and Pp have a mutual positive relationship.
8. 4:12 (Third variant of reaction formation). Pp is positive or tries to establish positive contact with H.
9. 4: (Reaction formation). The two variants above and 4:20 (the total mood is specified as agreeable).
10. 7:31 (A variant of introjection). H's gender is changed from correct to incorrect.
11. 8:71 (A variant of polymorphous identification). H is below 7 years of age.
12. 10:30 (Color regression). Color is seen even though the stimulus picture is black and white. Also weak reports are coded (e.g., "a brown table" or "a pink face").

Three codings that were not included in the manual were introduced: (a) WTP (without T-phase), Pp is not recognized as threatening even at the 22nd exposure; (b) STER (stereotypy), a single defensive variant is repeated in more than five phases directly following each other; and (c) BAPP (belated appearance of Pp), Pp is reported more than eight phases after the first reporting of H as a human figure. Furthermore, all defense scores for each DMT protocol were summed, to produce the number of defensive scorings (NDS). A sample of 20 protocols was independently scored by a psychologist with several years of experience in DMT coding. Interrater agreement on the 13 variants listed above was invariably high, ranging from .85 to 1.

Results

Variant 1:42 was the only repression score with a significant difference of distributions across the S-CWT types. Table 18.3 shows that it was rare among S and C participants and common in D and CD primary types. Moreover, 1:42 was more frequently associated with R_{AD}^{+} than with R_{AD}^{-} types.

Table 18.3: *Stimulus-Distal Repression (1:42) and S-CWT Types.*

Group	S + C	D + CD	*p* (two-tailed)
Participants with 1:42	2	15	.004
Others	22	19	
Group	R_{AD}+	R_{AD}^{-}	*p* (two-tailed)
Participants with 1:42	13	4	.048
Others	17	24	

Table 18.4 shows that IT_A^+ and overall Initial Types are significantly linked with isolation variants 2:10a and 2:10b. More specifically, a statistical trend is noticeable between IT_A^+ and 2:10a (barrier isolation). The disappearance of Pp (isolation variant 2:32) was significantly linked with several S-CWT patterns (see Table 18.5). This kind of percept-genetic defense was far more common among D and CD than among S and C participants. Somewhat surprisingly, 2:32 was more often reported by S_V subjects than by persons with the other V secondary classifications. In particular, the C_V type was rarely associated with 2:32. A significant relationship between R_{AD}^+ and 2:32 was also noted.

It can be seen from Table 18.6 that the failure to recognize the threatening character of Pp (WTP) was also significantly linked to the number of primary and secondary S-CWT classifications. As for 2:32, D and CD types were more often associated with WTP than was the case for S and C primary types. The same trend held true for D_R and CD_R, compared with S_R and C_R. A stronger probability level characterized the correspondence of D_V with WTP, compared with the other three secondary V types. Also, defense in this case was more often scored in protocols belonging to R_{AD}^+ than to R_{AD}^- patterns.

Table 18.4: *Isolation Variants and Initial Types.*

Group	IT_A+	IT_A^-	*p* (two-tailed)
Participants with 2:10a	9	4	.070
Others	17	28	
Group	IT_A+	IT_A^-	*p* (two-tailed)
Particip. with 2:10a and/or 2:10b	15	9	.032
Others	11	23	
Group	IT+	IT^-	*p* (two-tailed)
Particip. with 2:10a and/or 2:10b	21	3	.008
Others	18	16	

Table 18.5: *Disappearance of Peripheral Person and S-CWT Types*

Group	S+C	D+CD	*p* (two-tailed)
Participants with 2:32	4	21	.001
Others	20	13	
Group	S_V	$C_V+D_V+CD_V$	*p* (two-tailed)
Participants with 2:32	10	15	.026
Others	4	29	
Group	S_V	C_V	*p* (two-tailed)
Participants with 2:32	10	2	.001
Others	4	15	
Group	$R_{AD}+$	R_{AD}^{-}	*p* (two-tailed)
Participants with 2:32	17	8	.042
Others	13	20	

The primary C type was closely linked to Sign 4 (reaction formation). Moreover, Table 18.7 shows that among the R secondary types, the C_R pattern was significantly associated with the variant 4.10, where H and Pp are doing something together. The clearest evidence of reaction formation, i.e., that 4:12: Pp is friendly toward H, was again typical of the primary Cumulative type of adaptation. Furthermore, the most pathological S-CWT pattern, combining two high secondary V*s*, was characterized by a significant, if low, association with codings of reaction formation.

Among the many variants of introjection and of polymorphous identification listed in the DMT manual, only 7:31, involving H's change of gender from correct to incorrect, and 8:71, where H's age is below 7, presented significant associations with adaptive patterns. Clearly, both of these defenses were more frequently employed by participants classified as Dissociatives than by participants with other primary types (see Table 18.8).

Table 18.6: *Lack of Recognition of the Threat and S-CWT Types*

Group	S+C	D+CD	*p* (two-tailed)
Participants with WTP	5	19	.012
Others	19	15	
Group	S_R+C_R	D_R+CD_R	*p* (two-tailed)
Participants with WTP	7	17	.012
Others	22	12	
Group	D_V	S_V+C_V+CD_V	*p* (two-tailed)
Participants with WTP	11	13	.002
Others	3	31	
Group	R_{AD}+	R_{AD}^-	*p* (two-tailed)
Participants with WTP	18	8	.024
Others	12	20	

Table 18.7: *Reaction Formation (4:) and S-CWT Types*

Group	C	S+D+CD	*p* (two-tailed)
Participants with 4:	9	24	.036
Others	1	24	
Group	Two high secondary Vs	Others	*p* (two-tailed)
Participants with 4:	4	29	.012
Others	11	14	
Group	C_R	S_R+D_R+CD_R	*p* (two-tailed)
Participants with 4	6	3	.006
Others	8	41	
Group	C	S+D+CD	*p* (two-tailed)
Participants with 4:12	9	14	.001
Others	1	34	

Because of the low number of scores in the sensitivity-projection cluster, no information was obtained about the relationships of these important defenses with S-CWT types. The same was true for the most pathological variant of regression. Color regression (10:30), however, was more frequently linked to the CD type than to the other primary patterns, and the significance level was increased when CD was compared only with S. Table 18.9 shows association between CD_R and 10:30, but at a relatively low level of significance.

The belated appearance of Pp (BAPP) was more frequently coded in subjects with D or CD, CD_R and R_{AD}^+ types (see Table 18.10). The CD_R pattern was found to be clearly linked to the stereotyped repetition of the same defensive variant, especially when compared with the S_R type (see Table 18.11).

Last but not least, no one-to-one correspondence between any defense scores and S-CWT types was found. Table 18.12 shows that very low numbers of defense scores, at least 1 standard deviation below the mean, are characteristic of the DMT protocols of the minority of participants who were neither R_{AD}^+ nor IT^+. Table 18.12 also shows that, surprisingly, a greater number of participants with a S classification in comparison to participants with a CD classification had either a very high or a very low number of defensive scores. This was confirmed regarding R-types, for which CD_R corresponded to intermediate numbers of scores, whereas S_R was more frequent in the two extreme quartiles. The reverse was true for V-types; here the Cumulative-Dissociatives were significantly more extreme scorers than the Stabilizers.

Table 18.8: *Introjection Variants and Dissociative Type*

Group	D	S+C+CD	*p* (two-tailed)
Participants with 7:31	10	10	.022
Others	7	31	
Group	D	S+C+CD	*p* (two-tailed)
Subjects with 8:71	11	7	.001
Others	6	34	

Table 18.9: *Color-Regression and Cumulative-Dissociative Type*

Group	CD	S+C+D	*p* (two-tailed)
Participants with 10:30	8	6	.02
Others	9	35	
Group	CD	S	*p* (two-tailed)
Participants with 10:30	8	0	.006
Others	9	14	
Group	CD_R	$S_R+C_R+D_R$	*p* (two-tailed)
Participants with 10:30	8	6	.048
Others	11	33	

Table 18.10: *Belated Appearance of Peripheral Person (BAPP) and S-CWT Types*

Group	D+CD	S+C	*p* (two-tailed)
Participants with BAPP	19	5	.012
Others	15	19	
Group	CD_R	$S_R+C_R+D_R$	*p* (two-tailed)
Participants with BAPP	12	12	.030
Others	7	27	
Group	$R_{AD}+$	$R_{AD}-$	*p* (two-tailed)
Participants with BAPP	17	7	.022
Others	13	21	

Table 18.11: *Stereotyped Repetition of the Same Variant and S-CWT Types*

Group	CD_R	$S_R+C_R+D_R$	*p* (two-tailed)
Participants with STER	16	17	.006
Others	3	22	
Group	CD_R	S_R	*p* (two-tailed)
Participants with STER	16	5	.004
Others	3	10	

Table 18.12: *Number of Participants' (Ps) Defensive Scores (NDS) and their S-CWT Types*

Group	IT_A^- or/and $R_{AD}+$	IT_A^- and R_{AD}^-	*p* (two-tailed)
Ps with NDS > 35	12	0	.004
Ps with NDS < 10	4	6	
Group	S	CD	*p* (two-tailed)
Ps with NDS > 35or <10	9	2	.006
Ps with intermediate NDS	5	15	
Group	S_R	CD_R	*p* (two-tailed)
Ps with NDS > 35 or <10	8	3	.042
Ps with intermediate NDS	7	16	
Group	S_V	CD_V	*p* (two-tailed)
Ps with NDS > 35 or <10	2	8	.026
Ps with intermediate NDS	12	5	

Discussion

Primary Dissociation, either alone or in conjunction with primary Cumulation, exhibited the most striking correspondences with types of defense. It was strongly linked with stimulus-distal repression, disappearance of Pp, WTP, and BAPP. The latter three codings share a formal feature, i.e., the absence of something that ought to be present. This feature shows affinity to the appearance of sudden gaps that characterizes the dissociative style. Not all of the defense variants with discontinuity features showed this correlation, probably for the following interfering reasons: (a) 2:30 (structure disappears from the entire field) may be due to blinking and is often hard to distinguish from 2:31 (disappearance of H); it may have no specific meaning when coded between the very first phases; (b) 2:33a (threat disappears, after having been recognized) is not compatible with WTP; therefore the high ratio of WTP among D*s* and CD*s* automatically resulted in lowering the frequency of 2:33a; and (c) 10:10 (sudden breakdown of stimulus adequacy) was exceedingly rare in this nonpsychotic sample.

Although WTP and BAPP are not explicitly listed in the DMT manual, definitions close to these two categories are included by Kragh among the variants of isolation, which is the typical obsessive-compulsive defense. Present findings suggest a different interpretation of 2:32, WTP, and BAPP (for similar variants, the MCT manual employs the categories of regressive discontinuity and of depressive stereotypy; *cf.* Smith et al., 1982). Furthermore, the clustering of stimulus-distal repression together with these three codings points to some unexpected conceptual relationships: a common regulatory style encompassing the transformation of Pp into an inanimate object, the disappearance of Pp, its belated appearance, and its total lack of threatening character. Even more radically, one might wonder what is the nature of the well known link between primary Dissociation and stimulus-distal (phobic) repression.

By way of a hypothetical explanation we would like to advance the following considerations. Repression corresponds basically to the disappearance from consciousness of a drive derivative or of a traumatic event. Its most typical product is infantile amnesia. In other words, repression is the lack of something that ought to be there. Thus, its affinity to primary Dissociation and to 2:32, WTP, and BAPP comes into play. Only when displacement is added to repression can a perceptual defense like 1:42 - or for that matter, a phobic symptom - be activated. Apart from displacement, reports of 1:42, with their distance from the real stimulus, suggest an element of excessive imagination, reminiscent of Smith and Klein's (1953) comment about the Dissociative style: "D*s* are more autistically disposed than are C*s* and S*s*; i.e., at least intermittently they lean less upon objective supports or cues" (p.200).

When attention is shifted from the correspondences of 2:32 WTP and BAPP with primary Dissociation to the links between these defenses and secondary Vs, the following differences are worth noting: (a) Surprisingly, disappearance of Pp is typical of the S_V pattern and does not correspond to R-type; (b) WTP is strongly characteristic of the D_V pattern and is significantly linked to D_R and CD_R and to the concomitance of the two high secondary V*s*; and (e) BAPP is not associated with the V-types and is more frequent among subjects of the CD_R type. Thus, WTP can be considered a super-dissociative defense, and 2:32 a dissociative defense at a more superficial level, being an antidissociative strategy at a deeper, secondary level. BAPP is in an intermediate position, midway between 2:32 and WTP on the dissociation continuum. Clearly, on the basis of the present findings WTP can be considered to be the most pathological type of defense observed in the DMT. Unfortunately, it is unclear to what defense mechanism described in the psychoanalytic situation WTP corresponds. Is it close to denial, as distinguished from negation? The "lack of something that ought to be there" can be thought of as a defensive strategy, with varying serious and far-reaching consequences from the waiving of a wish or emotion through the cancellation of simple or complex memories to disregarding major portions of current external reality (see Fenichel, 1945). We hypothesize that this progression from repression to true denial may correspond to the escalation from primary dissociation without accompanying secondary dissociation toward concomitant primary R- and V-dissociation. While the foregoing considerations are equally valid for the primary types D and CD, two variants of introjection/identification characterized type D in particular: change of H's gender from correct to incorrect (7:31) and H's very young age (8:71). The instability of identity inherent in these codings accords well with primary Dissociation. The surprisingly strong link between D type and 8:71 may also deserve closer scrutiny, because 8:71 is as yet a poorly understood developmentally early mechanism. The resumption of earlier roles in order to escape the dangers connected with more advanced conflicts may constitute the natural counterpart of the danger of stepping backward, which is at the core of primary Dissociation in its purest form (D type).

As predicted, the CD type was significantly connected with color regression, that is, with the trend toward faulty reality testing. This finding provides validation for one of the most "psychotic" DMT defenses. However, the link between 10:30

and CD_R barely reached significance, and there was no significant correspondence between 10:30 and D_V, CD_V, or the two concomitantly high secondary V*s*. The low relationship of color regression with the level of secondary Dissociation may be indicative of a circumscribed, time-bound meaning of this perceptual sign of ego-regression. The cluster of "compulsive" defenses was found to be clearly divided into codings associated with IT^+ (barrier isolation) and those associated with Cumulation (reaction formation). The very low rate of reports coded for reaction formation among the participants with the two high secondary V*s* confirms that this defense (and especially its strong variant, 4:12) is the prototype of the C style, in opposition to the dissociative defenses discussed above. The IT^+, as a type of adaptation "stamped by attempts at a sudden pseudo-objective mastery of reality" (Nyman & Smith, 1961), seems to fit well with a defense like barrier isolation, which does not directly alter the disturbing percept but provides a safe distance from the threat. It is more difficult to grasp the common ground between the C type and reaction formation, even if the anxious, rigid overcontrol and the highly structured, actively defensive style reflected in cumulative patterns seem to share formal features with the reaction formation strategy. In the clinical S-CWT literature, IT^+ (especially IT_A^+) has been most frequently connected with the obsessive-compulsive personality, while the C type has been described as typical of patients with symptoms of anxiety coupled with averting defenses against insight. (Nyman & Smith, 1961).

The conceptual and ontogenetic closeness between "turning away of the threat," barrier isolation, intellectualization, and negation (MCT codings roughly corresponding respectively to 2:10c, 2:10a, 2:10b, and 3: in the DMT) was suggested by Smith and Danielsson (1982, p. 44). Present findings highlight unanticipated stylistic opposition of turning away of the threat and negation (IT^-) versus barrier isolation and intellectualization (IT^+). The higher frequency of stereotyped repetitions of the same coding among the participants of the CD_R type confirms the usefulness of this R-type as a sign of extreme rigidity and defective functioning (Smith et al., 1982, pp. 48-49) but indicates that C_R and CD are not wholly overlapping patterns, even though they have been frequently so considered.

Unexpectedly, the R_{AD}^+ type tended to correspond to dissociative defenses (1:42, 2:32, WTP, and BAPP). One way to make sense of this convergence between Dissociation and R_{AD}^+ is to realize that the latter represents the opposite of Cumulation of initial times.

Types based on initial times were the only ones with significant relationships with a great many defensive scorings (IT_A^+ or/and R_{AD}^+) and with very low NDS (IT_A^-or/and R_{AD}^-). In the absence of differences on these variables between Stabilizers and other types, it is impossible to determine whether it is more adaptive to have many or few defenses. It is easier to conclude that an intermediate NDS has advantages over an NDS at the either extreme, high or low. Strangely, however, both primary and R-Stabilizers were more extreme scorers than their CD counterparts, a finding that remains in search of a reasonable explanation. This paradoxical result is partially counterbalanced by the higher frequency of extreme scorers among CD_V as compared with S_V.

The complex and sometimes surprising relationships between the patterns of adaptation to interference and the DMT defenses reported herein underscore the heuristic value of studying defense mechanisms and strategies within the framework and tradition of cognitive controls. It may be added that only a portion of the information available about the S-CWT was utilized in this chapter. It remains for a more comprehensive investigation to consider the relationships between defense variables and the various combinations of primary, secondary, and initial S-CWT patterns. Very large numbers of participants are needed for the implementation of this ambitious research objective.

References

Almgren, P. E. (1980). Die Beziehungen zwischen Abwehrformen in der MetaContrast-Technik und verschiedenen Anpassungsstilen in zwei serialen Wahrnehmungstests (Relationships between varieties of defense on the Meta Contrast Technique and in two serial percptual tests). In U. Hentschel & G.J.W. Smith (Eds), *Experimentelle Persönlichkeitspsychologie* (pp. 94-106). Wiesbaden: Akademische Verlagsgesellschaft.

Andersson, A. L. (1967). Adaptive visual aftereffect processes as related to patterns of color-word interference serials. *Perceptual & Motor Skills,* 25, 437-453.

Andersson, A. L. & Bengtsson M. (1985). Perceptgenetic defenses against anxiety and a threatened sense of self as seen in terms of the Spiral Aftereffect Technique. *Scandinavian Journal of Psychology,* 26, 123-139.

Andersson, A. L., Nilsson, A., Ruuth, E., & Smith, G. J. W. (1972). *Visual aftereffects and the individual as an adaptive system.* Lund: Gleerups.

Andersson, A..L, & Weikert, C. (1974). Adult defensive organization as related to adaptive regulation of spiral aftereffect duration. *Social Behavior & Personality,* 2, 56-75.

Fenichel, O. *(1945). The psychoanalytical theory of neurosis.* New York: Norton.

Kragh, U. (1985). *Defence Mechanism Test manual.* Stockholm: Persona.

Kragh, U. & Smith, G. J. W.(1970). *Percept-genetic analysis.* Lund: Gleerups.

Nyman, G. E. & Smith, G. J. W. (1961). Experimental differentiation of clinical syndromes within a sample of young neurotics. *Acta Psychiatrica Neurologica Scandinavica,* 37, *14-31.*

Rubino, I. A., Grasso, S., & Pezzarossa, B. (1990). Microgenetic patterns of adaptation on the Stroop task by patients with bronchial asthma and duodenal peptic ulcer. *Perceptual & Motor Skills,* 71, 19-31.

Smith, G. J. W. & Danielsson, A. (1982). Anxiety and defensive strategies in childhood and adolescence. *Psychological Issues,* No. 52. Madison, CT: International Universities Press.

Smith, G. J. W. & Klein, G. (1953). Cognitive controls in serial behavior patterns. *Journal of Personality,* 22, 188-213.

Smith, G. J. W., Johnson, G., & Almgren, P. E. (1989). *MCT-The Meta-Contrast Technique. Manual.* Stockholm: Psykologi Förlaget.

Smith, G. J. W., Nilsson, L., & Johnson, G. (1964). Differentiation of character neurosis and symptom neurosis on the basis of differences between two serial experiments. *Scandinavian Journal of Psychology,* 5, 234-238.

Smith, G. J. W., Nyman, G. E., Hentschel, U., & Rubino, I. A. (2001). *Serieller Farb-Wort-Test (S-CWT) Manual.* Frankfurt a.M: Swets & Zeitlinger.

Stroop, J. R. (1935). Studies of interference in serial verbal reactions. *Journal of Experimental Psychology,* 18, 643-661.

Westerlundh, B. (1983). Personal organization of the visual field: A study of ambient to focal reports of threatening stimuli. *Archives of Psychology,* 135, 17-35.

Defense Mechanisms
U. Hentschel, G. Smith, J.G. Draguns & W. Ehlers (Editors)

Chapter 19

Intellectual Performance and Defense Mechanisms in Depression

Uwe Hentschel, Manfred Kiessling, Heidi Teubner-Berg and Herbert Dreier

Moodswings are an experience common to everyone, and to this experience also belong downward swings. Thus based on this common experience, diagnosing a depression should not be a major problem. A depressed mood is, however, very different from the clinical state of depression (cf. Willner, 1985), and here the criteria for a reliable diagnosis cannot always be derived from self-experience. In spite of a strong opposition to regarding psychiatric symptoms exclusively from a positivistic medical or biological point of view (Foucault, 1967; Szasz, 1972), there is a need for reliable diagnosis. Even if one does not adhere to Cattell's (1940) statement that nosology necessarily precedes etiology, the necessity of diagnosis is obvious when it comes to the evaluation of treatment, be it by psychopharmaca or psychotherapy.

Without knowing the specific condition of the group who gets a specific treatment, the effects of such treatment cannot be assessed. The similarity of the phenomena related to depression, at least as it expresses itself in the Western world, has made it possible to derive at a number of definitions with pretty much the same elements. Although since the introduction of the DSM in 1952 to DSM IV-TR (2000) the diagnostic system as a whole as well as many categories have been changed, the core definition of depression remained rather stable. In 1968, for example, it was defined in a global form as "an emotional state with retardation of psychomotor and thought processes, a depressive emotional reaction, feelings of guilt or criticism and delusion of unworthiness" (American Psychiatric Association, 1968, p. 36). Also a broader list of symptoms connected with it is not so difficult to agree upon (cf. Table 19.1).

The problem here is rather that not all symptoms are exclusively related to depression, but that they show considerable overlap with other illnesses (cf. Clare & Blacker, 1986), as, for example, in the Chronic Fatigue Syndrome. Powell, Dolan, and Wessely (1990) could show that attribution of the illness and self-esteem can be used as differential diagnostic criteria, with true depressives showing more self-blame and lower self-esteem, together with an internal, stable, and global attribution style characteristic for the helplessness-hopelessness syndrome (Abramson, Seligman, & Teasdale, 1978).

Table 19.1: *List of typical symptoms of depressive disorders*

Dysphoric, apathetic mood	
Negative self-image, hopelessness, anxieties	
	Feelings of shame and guilt
	Social withdrawal
	Suicidal thoughts
Somatic symptoms like:	
	Sleep difficulties
	Loss of appetite
	Loss of libido
	Fatigue
Difficulties in concentration, loss of interest	

Source: Based on diagnostic criteria and evidence from empirical studies (cf. Brown & Haris, 1978; Feighner et al., 1972; Hentschel et al., 1976).

This is at the same time, again, a good example of the need for a good diagnostic classification, since the two illnesses require different treatments. In the literature the relations of depression and pain also are discussed in many ways. Supported by empirical results, one possible conclusion is that pain could be a substitute for depression (Ahrens & Lamparter, 1989). Severe states of depression, on the other hand, seem to a large degree to exclude pain feelings (Von Auersperg, 1963).

By extending the differential diagnostic endeavor, it should be possible also to diagnose different forms of depression. Differences to be considered here concern forms like unipolar-bipolar, primary-secondary, and endogenous-reactive. For a differential diagnosis of endogenous versus neurotic depression, the psychopathologic phenomena alone are not sufficient (Hentschel, Schubö, & Von Zerssen, 1976; Schubö, Hentschel, Von Zerssen, & Mombour, 1975).

One could say that the general agreement is quite good as long as the diagnostic endeavors are restricted to a phenomenological level and that it is considerably lower or even absent when it comes to attempts to explain the reasons for depression. Is it better understandable in purely behavioral terms, as a change in behavior frequencies, where avoidance and escape are augmented and other activities reduced (Ferster, 1974)? Are the purely cognitive and attributional variables the central ones that lead to a negative view of oneself, the outer world and the future, or is an approach that uses a combination of behavior and cognition like the revised learned helplessness-hopelessness theory the most appropriate? Or should an explanation comprise even more person-related aspects and elements from the personal history , like the psychoanalytic explanation for depression, focusing on the lack of narcissistic supplies and the struggle of an orally fixated person against an introjected ambivalent or unconsciously hated object (Fenichel, 1946)?

The differences in the theoretical explanations of the same phenomena are striking, but nevertheless probably would not have evoked so much attention if they were not linked with different approaches of treatment.

For several reasons, however, theory testing seems to be more promising in the field of diagnostics than in the field of treatment. Even here there are no clear-cut criteria for the best approach if one does not look for parsimony alone, for example. Moreover, within all the basic approaches -the behavioral, the cognitive, and the psychoanalytic- there are different points of view and changing concepts over time, with the result that it is not easy to define some generally acceptable requirements for a criterion-related validity test, but still it is easier here than in treatment, where other sets of variables are added.

Because this book is concerned with defense mechanisms, the reader may have guessed that our preference goes to the psychodynamic approach, in spite of its greater complexity, which covers implicit elements like developmental stages, with sensible phases, fixation to the oral stage due to some trauma, and a later regression to this stage following a similarly frustrating critical event, finally resulting in a structural conflict in the patient.

None of these assumptions could be tested in our study, but the concept of defense mechanisms is related to the structural conflict concept and covers a dynamic aspect that reaches farther than a mere phenomenological classification. Not too much is known about how and when certain defense mechanisms are "learned". Their basic roots may be inherited. Empirical studies show, however, that this development is embedded in the general cognitive and emotional development (Smith & Danielsson, 1980), so that theoretical links also are probable to other elements of the psychoanalytic view of depression, the elaboration of which is beyond the scope of this chapter. Here a more straightforward line is followed by referring to the general psychological impact of the concept of defense mechanisms (i.e., their reality-relatedness). If one accepts the idea of putting defenses together in one dimension from immature to mature (Vaillant, 1974), including the concept of coping mechanisms, then all defense mechanisms at the *lower* immature end of this dimension should lead to a distortion of objective perception of reality. This is not true for the mature mechanisms like humor and sublimation, where something is added and/or transformed: Arieti (1976) speaks here of the magic synthesis of primary and secondary process thinking. At the lower (immature) end of the dimension, however, something is lacking (e.g., in repression, denial, regression, isolation) or transformed in such a way (reaction formation, turning against the self, projection) that an objective perception becomes impossible.

Psychoanalysis has never stated that there is a point-to-point relation between the diagnosis of symptoms on the one hand and defense mechanisms on the other, but it was always assumed that symptoms and diagnoses and clusters of defense would show some relation (A. Freud, 1936/1946).

In fact, explaining the resulting symptoms as a compromise in the structural conflict between the ego and the id or the superego, mediated by the functional construct of defense mechanisms, has added very much to a psychodynamic understanding of the psychic illnesses for which a basic phenomenological diagnostic system (Kraepelin, 1896) had already been created without the influence of psychoanalysis. Thus the assessment of defense mechanisms has an additional diagnostic value (Offer, Lavie, Gothelf, & Apter, 2000; Mullen, Blanco, Vaughan, Vaughan, & Roose, 1999; Akkerman, Lewin, & Carr, 1999; Kwon, 1999, 2002).

We wanted to regard defenses in relation to a field of reality-related performance (i.e., intellectual functioning). The basic hypothesis of our study was that depressive patients, in comparison to a control group, should show another pattern of intellectual functioning and defense mechanisms, that is, in a more concrete formulation, they would show a worse intellectual performance in interaction with more signs of defense. Originally, we wanted to test this with a mixed group of male and female depressive patients, and a corresponding control group, by means of an intelligence test, allowing for an estimation of the "intellectual potential" in comparison to the "actual performance".

For this purpose, we constructed an adapted German version of the Jastak test (Jastak, 1959). Defense mechanisms were measured by means of the Defense Mechanism Test (DMT, Kragh, 1969; see Chapter 7). The original design of the study calling for a mixed group of patients, and the rather simple, straightforward comparison of an experimental with a control group, had to be changed to accommodate the actual circumstances.

The hypothesis of an interaction of intellectual performance and defenses, however, could be kept.

Method

Respondents

Depressive inpatients were recruited from the Psychiatric University Hospital in Mainz. It soon became apparent that not enough male patients were admitted to the hospital during the planned period for the study, and the sample was restricted to female patients. This condition is in accordance with the clinical observation and results of epidemiologic studies that females prevail by far in the clinical group of unipolar depression (Weissman & Klerman, 1987), possibly to be traced back already to adolescence (Nummer, & Seiffge-Krenke, 2001). At the same time it is a loss, however, for the empirical study of defense mechanisms in depressive males. A matched control group of volunteers was formed to correspond to the 29 female depressed patients, so that the whole sample comprised 58 women.

Table 19.2: *Age ranges and education of the subjects in the study*

	Depressives (N = 29)	Original control group (N = 29)
Age	$M = 43.7$; $s = 9.9$; range, 22-67	$M = 46.3$; $s = 9.0$; range, 24-61
Education		
Elementary and middle school (Grundschule, Hauptschule)	21	15
Non-classical secondary school (Realschule)	5	9
Academic high school (Gymnasium)	1	3
University degree	2	2

Table 19.2 gives the age ranges and educational levels of the two groups. The most important criterion for selection of the respondents in the control group was not being in psychiatric treatment.

Diagnosis of Depression

All patients were rated by a psychiatrist on the Hamilton Depression Scale (Hamilton, 1960), which can be regarded as one of the standard rating scales for the assessment of affective disorders. A cut-off point of 24 was used to allow the inclusion of one patient in the experimental group.

The Tests Used: The DMT and the Jastak Test

The DMT and its scoring procedures are described in greater detail in Chapter 7. The apparatus used in this study was a projection tachistoscope made by Zak (Simbach, Germany). The stimuli consisted of DMT slides from the 1969 manual (Kragh, 1969), including a distracter slide before, between, and after the two test series. The slides were projected on a mirror, so that a viewing device as in the original DMT apparatus could be used. All other circumstances were as similar as possible to the standard test situation. The scoring was done according to the manual (Kragh, 1969).

Table 19.3: *Grouping of the DMT defense mechanisms as used in the analyses of variance*

Repression Denial
Isolation Reaction formation
Identification with the aggressor Turning against the self
Introjection of the opposite sex Introjection of another object
Projection Regression

To overcome the problem of too low frequencies in some of the original scales and to avoid too many statistical analyses, the defense mechanisms were grouped into clusters of two (cf. Table 19.3), a strategy that can be defended on theoretical grounds and has been used before (Hentschel, Kiessling, & Hosemann, 1991). Jastak published his intelligence test (the Jastak Test of Potential Ability and Behavior Stability) in 1959. His aim was to evaluate retarded or deviant children and adolescents by taking a measure of intellectual capacity (i.e., the highest subtest score). To say it the other way around, Jastak wanted to start from the idea of a homogeneous intelligence profile and from there determine where the greatest losses are. Even though the operationalization of the concept of capacity might not have been complex enough, the idea is fascinating and its application to the field of depression attractive.

Basically, we encountered two problems: the language problem (there is no German translation of the Jastak test) and a possible ceiling effect, since the original test was constructed for an age level up to 14.5 years. The language problem was solved by introducing subtests from other German intelligence tests that corresponded as much as possible to the respective original subtests. In a pretest with our new test, a ceiling effect did not occur. Table 19.4 gives examples from the subtests of our adaptation of the Jastak test, together with the sources and their reliability estimates (Cronbach's alpha), achieved in this study.

Changes in the Original Design of the Study

The strategy of having a mixed sample had to be abandoned as a result of the actual base rates of male and female depressive patients admitted to the hospital. The other major change came from the consideration that the female patients tested differed in their actual state. The interval between diagnosis and testing was not a constant one. Also the use of a cutoff point of 24 in the Hamilton scale leaves enough space for considerable differences in the severity of depression. According to the basic psychodynamic assumption, the degree of disturbance and the number and severity of defense mechanisms should be related. An overall test for all defense mechanisms between the original patient and control groups showed no significant difference. Since there are no norms for the DMT available, it could not be stated without any doubts whether this result should be ascribed to the experimental or the control group. The observation in the testing situation was that some of the patients who volunteered to be tested were not able to stand the 3-4 hours of testing and had to be sent back to their rooms without being tested, whereas others showed no obvious behavioral differences at all in comparison to the controls. This finding is in close correspondence to experimental research with depressive patients (Hentschel, 1980a,b), where in one study (Hentschel, 1980b) the time before leaving the hospital was used as a correction factor. These data were, however, not available in the present study. We therefore decided to cluster all respondents on the basis of their intellectual performance, giving up the idea of a clear-cut division of an experimental and a

Table 19.4: *Contents of the German adaptation of the Jastak intelligence test*

Source	Subtest	Cronbach's alpha
Jastak (1959)	Arithmetic: test the four basic arithmetic operations	.85
LPS (Horn, 1962)	Spelling: words with printing errors must be corrected	.96
MWT (Lehrl, 1977)	Vocabulary: to find a correct word among nonsense words	.94
IST (Amthauer, 1970)	Verbal reasoning: to find a word that is not conceptually related to the others	.65
Jastak (1959)	Social concept: to find the picture that does not fit in	.64

Source	Subtest	Cronbach's alpha
Jastak (1959)	Picture reasoning: to put pictures in an ordered sequence (temporal, local, social, physical)	.68
CFT (Weiß, 1971)	Space series:	.69

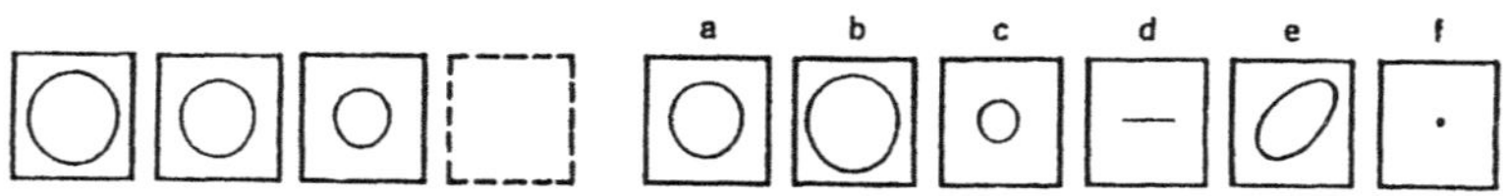

Jastak (1959)	Space completion: 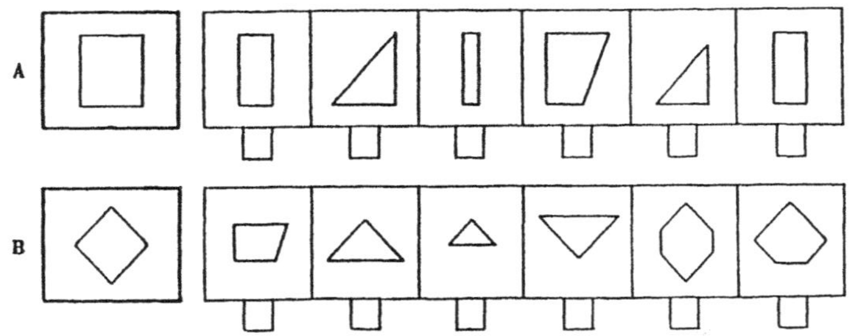	.57
Jastak (1959)	Coding: 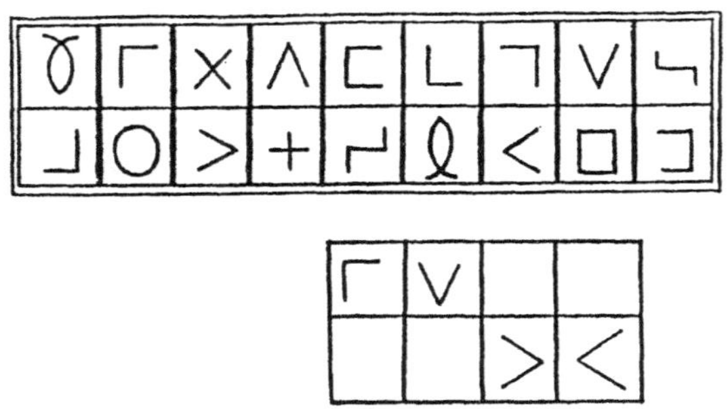	.96
IST (Amthauer, 1970)	Number series: inductive thinking with numbers	.91

control group, and replacing it by the idea of different groups on a continuum from severely disturbed to normal, conserving at the same time the basic hypothesis of an interaction of defense mechanisms with intellectual functioning: that is, that the lower level of performance in the intelligence test is connected with more signs of combinations of defense mechanisms, or of one particular mechanism, in different phases. In this study, the actual level of functioning hypothesis is preferred to the hypothesis of a relatively close relation of percept-genesis to ontogenesis. In percept-genetic theory, Ulf Kragh especially has postulated a possible correspondence between ontogenetic phases and percept-genetic phases. He was also able to demonstrate this phenomenon convincingly in a number of case studies (e.g., Kragh, 1970, 1986). The combination of the ontogenesis-percept-genesis correspondence hypothesis with the psychodynamic fixation hypothesis would mean that in depressive patients, more and/or more severe signs for defense mechanisms should appear in the early phases of the DMT series. According to the actual level of functioning hypothesis, more signs for defense mechanisms are expected on a more conscious level (i.e., the later phases with longer exposure times in the DMT series). The latter hypothesis is simpler and stresses more the principle of a possible distortion of the objective reality. To make testable our expectation that a worse performance in the intelligence test will be accompanied by more signs of defense in the later phases of percept-genesis, we partitioned the whole DMT series into three thirds: an early, a middle, and a late one.

Results

Clustering on the Basis of the Jastak Test

The intelligence test was used to divide the whole group into subgroups, from better to worse performance. With all subtests of the Jastak test, a cluster analysis was calculated, resulting in three-person clusters, the differentiation of which by means of discriminant analysis resulted in 96.6% in a correct reclassification of the cases. These clusters are graphically presented in Figure 19.1. Cluster 1 is mostly a control group cluster, cluster 2 is mixed, and cluster 3 consists mostly of depressive patients. To check the possible :differences of age between the clusters, an analysis of variance was calculated, showing no significant difference. Figure 19.2 gives three typical profiles from the different clusters, at the same time representing graphically the Jastak idea of varying discrepancies between the actual and the potential performance. The respective profiles of the three clusters as a whole are given in form of a frequency polygon in Figure 19.3.

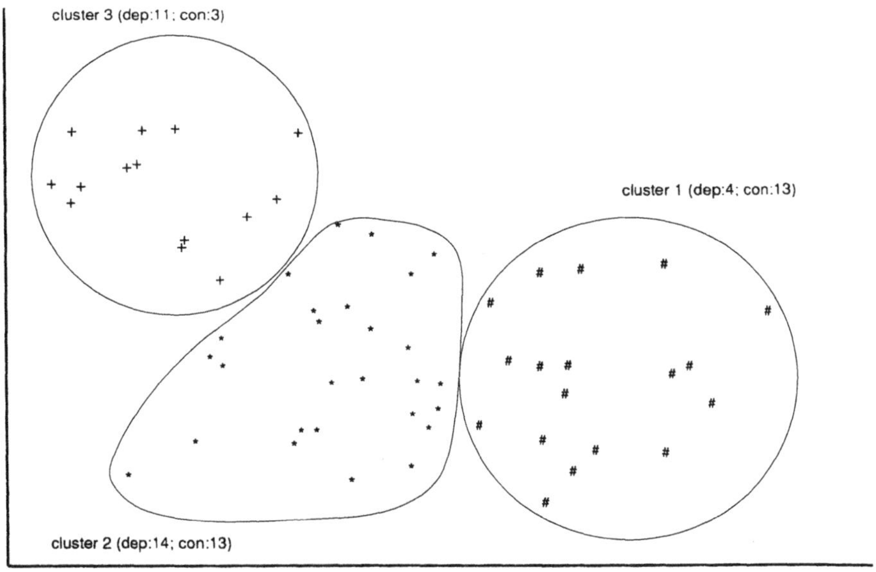

Figure 19.1: *The three-person clusters based on the Jastak test: Plane through the centers*

There is a clear difference in performance in all subtests, in most cases for the comparison of the three clusters, although in some cases only one cluster differs significantly from the other two. Differences that are not significant between all three clusters appear only in the subtests of arithmetic, space completion, and number series. To ensure that the main effects are not better explained in terms of a possible age and education effect in the specific subtest results, analyses of covariance were calculated for all subtests. In all cases, the reported main effects remained significant (cf. Table 19.4).

Defense in Interaction with Intellectual Performance

To test the interaction of defenses with intellectual performance, we chose to use analyses of variance, with the clusters as independent variables and the course of defenses in the three thirds of percept-genetic process as dependent variables (repeated measurement design).

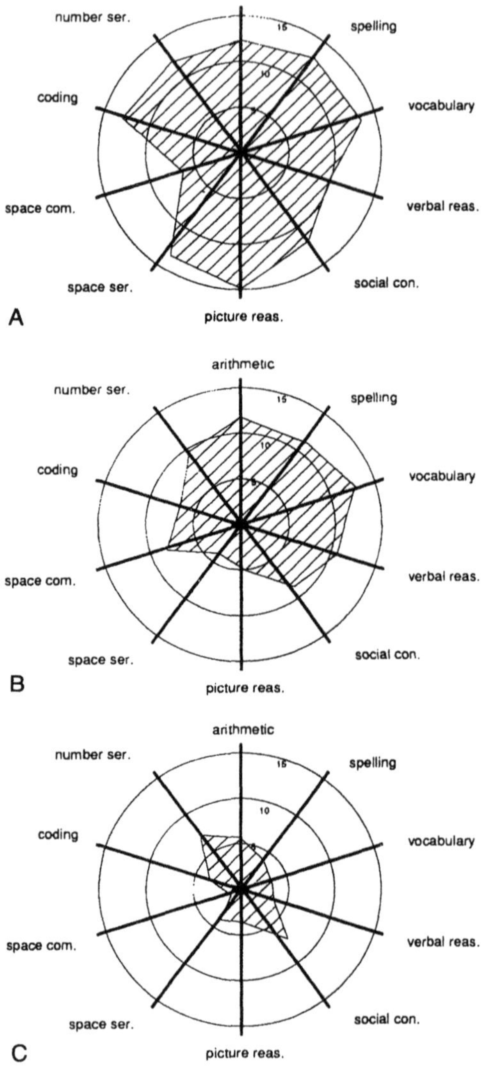

Figure 19.2: *Three examples, one for each cluster, for the Jastak Intelligence Profile. A. Cluster 1: Subject No. 25. B. Cluster 2: Subject No. 14. C. Cluster 3: Subject No. 9*

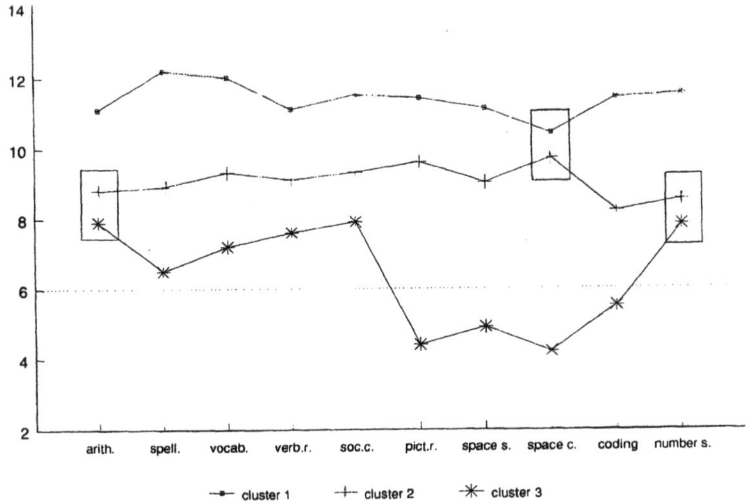

Figure 19.3: *Performance differences of the three clusters in the 10 subtests of the Jastak test*

Of the five analyses, one showed a significant result (cf. Table 19.5). It is the isolation/reaction formation group of defenses that is significantly related to the clusters as presented in Figure 19.4. There is no difference among the clusters in the first third in the DMT series; clusters 3 and 1 show a significant difference in the second third of the series, and in the last third cluster 1 again shows lower scores in isolation/reaction formation, this time in comparison with the two other clusters.

Table 19.5: *Analysis of variance with isolation/reaction formation as dependent variable over the three parts of the DMT series (repeated measurements)*

	F	*df*	*p*
Main effect clusters	1.68	2/55	n.s.
Repeated measurements	18.40	2/110	<.001
Repeated measurements x clusters	3.87	4/110	<.01

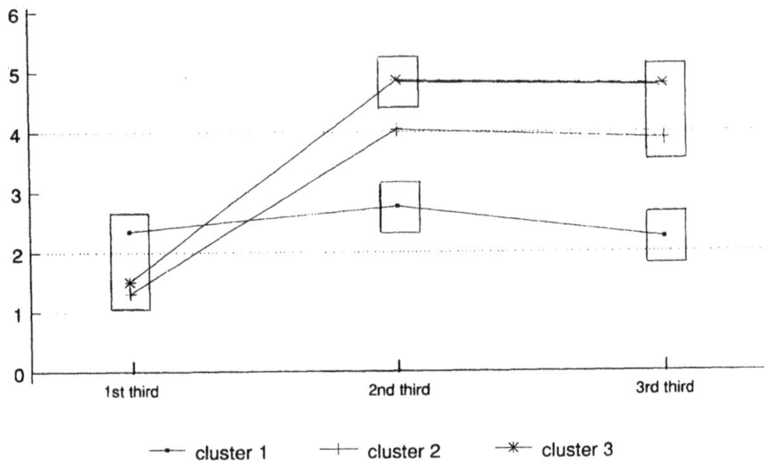

Figure 19.4: *Graphical representation of "isolation/reaction formation" in the three clusters over the three parts of the DMT series*

Discussion

Our results support the hypothesis of an interaction of defenses with intellectual functioning, clearly more related to the actual level of functioning in contrast to the also mentioned hypothesis of a possible parallelism between percept-genesis and ontogenesis. The conclusion would thus be that actual distortion of reality, to be inferred from the isolation/reaction formation combination, is greater for clusters 2 and 3 than for cluster 1. Through cluster 2 and the four persons each in clusters 3 and 1, there is considerable overlap between the patient group and the original normal control group, and this circumstance would seem to merit attention for further research.

Is it not possible to differentiate from depressive patients a certain subgroup of normal women, in a certain age range -most of them housewives- regarding their intellectual and emotional functioning, or were many of the depressive patients quite well recovered at the time of testing? The intellectual deficit visible from Fig. 19.3 seems to suggest that the question posed as the first alternative can be answered in the affirmative. The lowest performance is reached by respondents of cluster 3 in tasks that can be labeled as requiring fluid intelligence or speed (subtests 6, 7, 8, and 9).

In our basic hypothesis we did not specify which defense mechanism we expected to prevail in the more disturbed respondents. It is especially reaction formation as measured with the DMT that interferes with performance in high risk tasks, as piloting and diving (cf. Smith, Kragh, & Hentschel, 1980; Vaernes, 1982). The combination of isolation and reaction formation has been shown to be responsible for deficits in attention control under inadequate stimulation: that is, information underload and information overload (Hentschel et al., 1991). This effect, repeated now in depressive patients, requires some additional comments. A significant difference in the combination identification with the aggressor and turning against the self, which we did not find, would, according to psychodynamic theory, have been more self-evident. In an earlier study of Hentschel and Balint (1974) comparing psychopathological symptoms with defense ratings, depressive symptoms showed the strongest relation to ratings of introjection and turning against the self. We think that the result of our study in fact could have been influenced by a method effect. Isolation and especially reaction formation seem to have a very strong impact in many studies with the DMT, although it seems possible to differentiate clinical subgroups also by means of other signs of defenses in the DMT (Gitzinger, 1988). The number of defenses or empirical identifiable clusters remains, however, open for further discussions (Hentschel, & Kiessling , in preparation).

The DMT by its theoretical basis and intention is a psychodynamic test. Any summary of its empirical value will have to acknowledge its empirical validity and all attempts to restrict the results achieved by it to perceptual difficulties of the respondents (Ekehammar, Zuber, & Simonsson-Sarnecki, 2002) seem to be premature and do not have the necessary theoretical or empirical support. To clarify this hypothesis needs more studies, specifically designed to this point. A translation of defense mechanisms into ethological terms does not seem completely impossible (Kavaliers, & Choleris, 2001), but does not seem suitable for clinical purposes yet.

From a psychodynamic point of view, it is plausible to differentiate depression into problems of dependency, self-criticism, and efficacy (Blatt, 1974; Blatt, D' Afflitti, & Quinlan, 1979). The interaction of intellectual deficits and defenses that we have found seems to mirror more the efficacy and dependency aspects. On the basis of our data, it is not possible to decide whether the lack of representation of the self-criticism aspect in the DMT defense mechanisms corresponds to a relative lack of these phenomena in our sample, or whether it could be due to a possible method effect, as mentioned above. Zubin (1975) has criticized the dependence of most psychological testing for diagnostic purposes on motivation, attention, and interest, which usually leads to a mapping of deficits with largely unclear reasons for these deficits. He has proposed looking for more objective measures instead, also with the intention of finding performances in which the patients excel. This very interesting proposal should be given more sup- port than it has so far enjoyed, probably because most clinical researchers do not think in that direction. A possible compromise also could be the search for physiological indicators in combination with motivational variables (e.g., Munz, Winkow, Kessler, & Traue, 1989). The fact remains, however, that depression is an illness in which only few social advantages can be seen, and those so labeled seem to be of doubtful value in daily life (cf. Mahendra, 1987). The obvious deficits not only influence the test performance of these respondents, they have severe consequences for daily functioning too, which for the depressive patients in clusters 2 and 3 had led to a stay in the psychiatric hospital. We do not know any concrete details of the daily functioning of the control respondents in these two clusters, but we tend to infer that their performance also probably will be far from optimal. One can look at these results as only the reflection of deficits, or one can try to look for meaning and to see how the most severe symptoms are incorporated in the structure of the basic personality characteristics, of which Oliver Sacks (1982), for another group of patients, has given such impressing descriptions. He opted for an idiographic approach, but also from a nomothetic point of view, as in our case, one can focus on the obvious problems of the patients as meaning-related phenomena. The defense combination that we have found to be significantly higher for cluster(s) 3 (and 2), in the later phases in the percept-genetic process, also can be interpreted as serving the purpose of preventing the intrusion of aggression into the respondentsive reality of these respondents by isolating it or turning it into the misperception of a friendly act. The reality is distorted, but this also adds something to the world of these respondents, probably enabling them at least to keep their actual level of functioning as opposed to ending up in a completely empty experiential world. Interestingly enough, Berglund and Smith (1988) have found with another percept-genetic technique, the Meta-Contrast Technique (MCT) (see Chapter 7) that depressive patients without any defensive signs committed suicide significantly more often than those having a "protective shield" of defenses. Seen from the point of view of optimal functioning and well-being, it is beyond any doubt that it is highly desirable to achieve some change in this part of the internal milieu of our depressive patients, and at the same time to reduce their intellectual deficits, which in some way interact with their defensive structure. The way of striving for harmony, already present on a subconscious level, in spite of the need for therapy to achieve a better level of adaptation, evokes, however, respect as a deeply rooted human quality.

Acknowledgments. We thank a number of people for making this study possible: the medical staff of the Psychiatric University Clinic in Mainz, for giving permission to test patients; Dr. A. Westen for her helpful assistance in recruiting control respondents; and, of course, the patients and the control persons for their voluntary participation.

References

Abramson, L. Y., Seligman, M.E.P., & Teasdale, J .D. (1978). Learned helplessness in humans: critique and reformulation. *Journal of Abnormal Psychology, 87*,49- 74.

Ahrens, S. & Lamparter, U. (1989). Objektale Funktion des Schmerzes und Depressivitiit [The function of pain as an object and depression]. *Psychotherapie Psychosomatik Medizinische Psychologie, 39*,219-222.

Akkerman, K., Lewin, T. J., & Carr, V. J. (1999). Long-term changes in defensive style among patients recovering from major depression. *Journal of Nervous and Mental Disease, 187*, 80-87.

American Psychiatric Association (1952). *Diagnostic and statistical manual of mental disorders* (Ist ed.). Washington, DC: Author.

American Psychiatric Association (1968). *Diagnostic and statistical manual of mental disorders* (2nd ed.). Washington, DC: Author.

American Psychiatric Association (2000). *Diagnostic and statistical manual of mental disorders* (4th ed. Text Revision.). Washington, DC: Author.

Amthauer, R. (1970). IST, Intelligenz-Struktur-Test [*IST, Intelligence Structure Test]*. Göttingen: Hogrefe.

Arieti, S. (1976). *Creativity: The magic synthesis.* New York: Basic Books.

Auersperg, A. von (1963). *Schmerz und Schmerzhaftigkeit* [Pain and painfulness].Berlin: Springer .

Berglund, M. & Smith, G. (1988). Postdiction of suicide in a group of depression patients. *Acta Psychiatrica Scandinavica, 77,* 504-510.

Blatt, *S.l.* (1974). Levels of object representation in anaclitic and introjective depression. *Psychoanalytic Study of the Child, 29*,107-157.

Blatt, *S.l.,* D'Afflitti, *l.P.,* & Quinlan, D.M. (1979). *Depressive Experiences Questionnaire.* Yale University, New Haven, CT.

Brown, G. W. & Harris, T. (1978). *Social origins of depression: A study of psychiatric disorder in women.* London: Tavistock.

Cattell, R.B. (1940). The description of personality: 1. Foundation of trait measure- ment. *Psychological Review,* 50, 559-594.

Clare, A. W. & Blacker, R. (1986). Some problems affecting diagnosis and classi- fication of depressive disorders in primary care. In M. Shepherd, G. Wilkinson, & P. Williams (Eds.), *Mental illness in primary care settings* (pp. 7-26). London: Tavistock.

Ekehammar, B., Zuber, I., & Simonsson-Sarnecki, M. (2002).The Defense Mechanism Test (DMT) revisited: Experimental validationusing threatening and non-threatening pictures. *European Journal of Personality, 16,* 283-294.

Feighner, J.P., Robins, E., Guze, S.B., Woodruff, R.A., Jr., Winokur, G., & Munoz, R. (1972). Diagnostic criteria for use in psychiatric research. *Archives of General Psychiatry, 26,*56- 73.

Fenichel, 0. (1946). *The psychoanalytic theory of neurosis.* London: Routledge & Kegan Paul.

Ferster, C.B. (1974). Behavioral approaches to depression. In R. Y .Friedman & M.M. Kate (Eds.), *The psychology of depression* (pp. 29-53). New York: Wiley.

Foucault, M. (1967). *Madness and civilisation.* London: Tavistock.

Freud, A. (1946). *The ego and the mechanisms of defense.* Madison CT: International Universities Press. (Original work published 1936).

Gitzinger, I. (1988). *Operationalisierung von Abwehrmechanismen: Wahrnehmung- sabwehr und Einste/lungsmessung Psychoanalytischer Abwehrkonzepte* [Operationalization of defense mechanisms: Perceptual defense and measurement of attitude in psychoanalytic defense concepts]. Unpublished thesis, Freiburg.

Hamilton, M. (1960). A rating scale for depression. *Journal of Neurology, Neuro- surgery, and Psychiatry,* 23, 56-62.

Hentschel, U. (1980a). Kognitive Kontrollprinzipien und Neuroseformen [Cognitive styles and types of neurosis]. In U. Hentschel & G. Smith (Eds.), *Experimentelle Persönlichkeitspsychologie [Experimental personality psychology]* (pp. 227- 321). Wiesbaden: Akademische Verlagsgesellschaft.

Hentschel, U. (1980b). Zur Validität serial ausgewerteter Interferenztests [On the validity of serially scored interference tests] .In U. Hentschel & G. Smith (Eds.), *Experimentelle Persönlichkeitspsychologie [Experimental personality psychology]* (pp. 337-349). Wiesbaden: Akademische Verlagsgesellschaft.

Hentschel, U. & Balint, S. (1974). Plausible diagnostic taxonomy in the field of neurosis. *Psychological Research Bulletin. Lund University, 14*, No.2. Monograph Series.

Hentschel, U., & Kiessling, M. (in preparation). Groups of defense mechanisms that can be dicerned by the Defense Mechanism Test.

Hentschel, U., Kiessling, M. & Hosemann, A. (1991). Anxiety, defense and attention control. In R.E. Hanlon (Ed.), *Cognitive microgenesis: A neuropsychological perspective* (pp. 262-285). New York: Springer.

Hentschel, U., Schubö, W., & Zerssen, D. v. (1976). Diagnostische Klassifikationsversuche mit zwei standardisierten psychiatrischen Schätzskalen [Attempts at a nosological classification with two standardized psychiatric rating scales]. *Archiv für Psychiatrie und Nervenkrankheiten, 221*, 283-301.

Horn, W. (1962). *Das Leistungsprüfsystem [The performance test system]*. Göttingen: Hogrefe.

Jastak, J.F. (1959). *The Jastak Test (Junior Highschool Level)*. Minneapolis: Educational Publishers.

Kraepelin, E. (1896). *Psychiatrie* (5. Auflage) [Psychiatry (5th ed.)]. Leipzig: Barth.

Kragh, U. (1969). *Manual till DMT-Defense Mechanism Test* [Manual for the DMT-Defense Mechanism Test]. Stockholm: Skandinaviska Testförlaget.

Kragh, U. (1970). Pathogenesis in dipsomania. In U. Kragh & G. Smith (Eds.), *Percept-genetic analysis* (pp. 160-178). Lund: Gleerup.

Kragh, U. (1986). Life panorama under the microscope: A paradigmatic case study. In U. Hentschel, G. Smith, & J.G. Draguns (Eds.), *The roots of perception* (pp. 145-159). Amsterdam: North-Holland.

Kwon, P. (1999). Attributional style and psychodynamic defense mechanisms: toward an integrative model of depression. *Journal of Personality, 67*, 645-658.

Kwon, P. (2002). Hope,defense mechanisms, and adjustment: implications for false hope and defensive hopelessness. *Journal of Personality, 70*, 207-231.

Lehrl, S. (1977). *Mehrfachwahl-Wortschatz-Intelligenztest (MWT-B) [Multiple choice vocabulary intelligence test (MWT-B)]*. Erlangen: Straube.

Mahendra, B. (1987). *Depression: The disorder and its associations*. Lancaster, PA: MTP Press.

Mullen, L. S., Blanco, C., Vaughan, S. C., Vaughan, R., & Roose, S. P. (1999). Defese mechanisms in personality and depression. *Depression and Anxiety, 10*, 168-174.

Munz, D., Winkow, E., Kessler, M., & Traue, H.C. (1989). *The moderating effect of motivation and attribution on the behavior of depressives.* Paper presented at the 3rd European Conference on Psychotherapy Research, September, Bern.

Nummer, G., & Seiffge-Krenke, I. (2001). Können Unterschied in der Stresswahrnehmung und -bewältigung geschlechtsunterschiede in der depressiven Symptombelastung bei Jugendlichen erklären? *Zeitschrift für Kinder- und Jugendpsychiatrie und Psychotherapy, 29*, 89-97.

Offer, R., Lavie, R., Gothelf, D., & Apter, A. (2000). Defense mechanisms, negative emotions, anf psychopathology in adolescent patients. *Comprehensive Psychiatry, 41*, 35-41.

Powell, R. Dolan, R. , & Wessely, S. (1990). Attributions and self-esteem in depression and chronic fatigue syndromes. *Journal of Psychosomatic Research,* 34, 665-673.

Sacks, 0. (1982). *Awakenings.* London: Pan Books.

Schubö, W., Hentschel, U., Zerssen, D. v., & Mombour, M. (1975). Psychiatrische Klassifikation durch diskriminanzanalytische Anwendung der Q-Faktorenanalyse [Psychiatric classification by means of a discriminatory appli- cation of Q-factor analysis]. *Archiv für Psychiatrie und Nervenkrankheiten, 220*, 187-200.

Smith, G. & Danielsson, A. (1980). Ideenreichtum, Ich-Beteiligung und Effektivität bei einer Gruppe von Natur- und Geisteswissenschaftlern (Richness in ideas, ego-involvement and efficiency in a group of scientists and humanists). In U. Hentschel & G. Smith (Eds.), *Experimentelle Persönlichkeitspsychologie* [Experimental personality psychology]. Wiesbaden: Akademische Verlagsgesellschaft.

Smith, G., Kragh, U., & Hentschel, U. (1980). Perzeptgenetische Verfahren: Historische und methodologische Obersicht [Perceptgenetic techniques: His- torical and methodological overview]. In U. Hentschel & G. Smith (Eds.), *Experimentelle Persönlichkeitspsychologie* [Experimental personality psychology] (pp. 31-63). Wiesbaden: Akademische Verlagsgesellschaft.

Szasz, T. (1972). *The myth of mental illness.* London: Paladin.

Vaemes, R. (1982). The Defense Mechanism Test predicts inadequate performance under stress. *Scandinavian Journal of Psychology, 23*, 37-43.

Vaillant, G. E. (1974). *Adaptation* to life. Boston, Little, Brown.

Weiss, R. H. (1971). *Grundintelligenztest CFT* 3 *Skala* 3 *[Basic intelligence test CFT* 3 *Scale* 3]. Braunschweig: Westermann.

Weissman, M. M. & Klerman, G. (1987). Gender and depression. In R. Formanek, & A. Gurian (Eds.), *Women and depression: A lifespan perspective* (pp. 3-15). New York: Springer.

Willner, P. (1985). *Depression: A psychobiological synthesis.* New York: Wiley.

Zubin, J. (1975). A biometric approach to diagnosis and evaluation of therapeutic intervention in schizophrenia. In G. Usdin (Ed.), *Overview of the psychotherapies* (pp. 153-204). New York: Brunner & Mazel.

Defense Mechanisms
U. Hentschel, G. Smith, J.G. Draguns & W. Ehlers (Editors)

Chapter 20

Defense Mechanisms and Hope as Protective Factors in Physical and Mental Disorders

Louis A. Gottschalk, Janny Fronczek and Robert J. Bechtel

Whether defense mechanisms may serve as markers of increased vulnerability or resistance to illness is an issue that merits being more clearly and definitively addressed and investigated. Anna Freud (1936/1946) focused on defense mechanisms as tools used to relieve anxiety, and their presence might, hence, be seen as clues to some underlying psychopathological process. The ways in which defense mechanisms function to influence the course of illness have been rarely studied. On the other hand, hope is a state or trait that has been examined over many years in empirical studies to determine whether it is capable of influencing the onset or course of illness. French (1952) and Frank (1968) regarded hope as a personal incentive toward encouraging a person to cope better with inner psychological conflicts. Perley, Winget, and Placci (1971) found that elevated hopefulness derived from the content analysis of speech predicted patients who followed up recommendations that they seek psychiatric treatment. Gottschalk, Kunkel, Wohl, Saenger, and Winget (1960) found that hope scores derived from the content analysis of verbal samples predicted the duration of survival of patients with terminal cancer receiving irradiation treatment. Gottschalk, Mayerson, and Gottlieb (1967) and Gottschalk, Fox, and Bates (1973), moreover, found that high measures of hopefulness pointed to relatively favorable outcome in psychotherapy. Udelman and Udelman (1986) reported a significant correlation between hope scores and indicators of immune competence, namely, via mitogenic stimulation by concanavalin A and percentage of B cells. Gottschalk and Hoigaard-Martin (1986) found significantly higher affect denial scores and positive hope scores, derived from the content analysis of speech (Gottschalk 1979; Gottschalk & Gleser, 1969; Gottschalk, Lolas, & Viney 1986), for a group of women (N = 123) experiencing a mastectomy as compared to groups of women having a cholecystectomy (N = 74), women having a normal breast biopsy (N = 63), and physically healthy women. These findings prevailed, although the severity of the emotional impact, as adjudged from the anxiety and hostility scores from these women derived from their speech samples and the Symptom Checklist 90 Analogue (Derogatis, Lipman, Rickels, Uhlenhuth, & Covi, 1964) and the Global Assessment Scale (Endicott, Spitzer, Fleiss, & Cohen, 1976), revealed a stepwise increase in emotional disturbance going from measures obtained from the healthy through noncancerous to cancerous women.

Studies involving the Hope scale by Gottschalk (1974) have demonstrated that hope scores, derived from the content analysis of speech, correlate positively with content-analysis-derived markers of personal competence, such as good human relations and object relations, and negatively with markers of vulnerability or psychopathological problems, such as anxiety, hostility out, hostility in, depression, and social alienation-personal disorganization (see Table 20.1). These hope scores also correlate significantly positively with other measures of emotional well-being, such as, scores from the Anant Belongingness Scale (1967) and the Barron Ego Strength Scale (1953). Other empirical evidence that hope functions to strengthen tolerance to life stress (see also Table 20.1) is suggested by the finding that pretreatment hope scores -from out patients receiving crisis intervention psychotherapy- correlated significantly negatively with measures of psychiatric morbidity 6-10 weeks later (Gottschalk et al., 1973). And in a group of acute schizophrenic patients (N = 24), 48 hours after being given oral thioridazine (4mg/kg) -a major tranquilizer- hope scores improved significantly (1.79, $p < .05$) and total hostility outward (-1.73, $p < .05$), social alienation-personal disorganization (-2.27, $p < .05$), and depression scores (-1.83, $p < .05$) decreased significantly, all scores being obtained from the content analysis of 5-minute speech samples (Gottschalk, 1974: Gottschalk, Biener, Noble, Birch, Wilbert, & Heiser, 1975).

To pursue these issues, the following series of studies was undertaken to look at the relationships between the defense mechanisms of displacements, denial, and hope with illness behavior and mental disorder. Many of the Gottschalk-Gleser scales for measuring the magnitude of psychological states through the content analysis of verbal behavior (Gottschalk, 1979; Gottschalk & Gleser, 1969) include counting verbal references not only to the self having or experiencing an emotional state (e.g., I am scared), but also verbal references to others (animate or inanimate) having the emotional condition (e.g., he is afraid; the auto's engine died.). Other defenses or coping mechanisms in these scales include verbal references denying the state (e.g., I am not frightened) or assertions of hopefulness in the face of stressors (e.g., I am sure everything will come out satisfactorily; God will certainly protect me.).

Table 20.1: *Intercorrelations of Hope scale scores and other psychological states*

	Content analysis measures				
		Hostility			Social Alienation Personal Disorganization
Subjects	Anxiety	Out	In	Ambivalent	
Normative adult group (*N*=91)	-.19	-.26*	-.14	-.22*	-.30*
Normative children group (*N*=109)	-.46*	-.45*	-.36*	-.38*	-.61*
Crisis clinic outpatients (*N*=55)	–	–	–	–	-.63*
Medical in-patients (*N*=36)	–	–	–	–	-.75*
	Content analysis measures of human relations	Patients improvement		Anant Belongingness Scale	Barron Ego Strength Scale
Normative children's group (*N*=109)	+.51*	–		–	–
Crisis clinic outpatients (*N*=54)	+.68*	+.26*		+.29*	+.21*
Medical in-patients (*N*=25)	+.75*	–		–	–

Notes: * = statistically significant (two-tailed test) p<.05.
– = correlation not carried out because data not available.

Methods and Procedures

Content analysis scores obtained from earlier studies were reexamined focusing on the frequency of use of the verbal categories of the Gottschalk- Gleser Anxiety and three Hostility scales (Gottschalk, Hoigaard, Birch, & Rickels, 1979) involving displacement and denial (Gottschalk, 1976; Gottschalk & Gleser, 1969; Gottschalk et al., 1973, 1975, 1976). Of interest was how the percentage use of those verbal categories, such as displacement and denial, by different psychiatric groups compares to the frequency of use of direct verbal statements of experiencing affects (e.g., I am anxious). The effect of demographic factors, such as sex, age, and intelligence quotients, was also examined, as well as how the frequency of use of these various verbal categories designating anxiety varies with scores from the same subjects on the three Gottschalk-Gleser Hostility scales (Gottschalk et al., 1963; Gottschalk & Gleser, 1969), namely, Hostility Outward, Hostility Inward, and Ambivalent Hostility (which under certain circumstances appear to function as defense mechanisms against, e.g., anxiety, rather than merely expressions of solitary emotions of hostility (Gleser & Ihilevich, 1969; Ihilevich & Gleser, 1986).

Another approach was to determine the relative cerebral glucose metabolic rates associated with anxiety and hope scores during three states of consciousness, namely, during silent wakeful mentation, REM dreaming, and NONREM mentation, using Positron Emission Tomography (PET). The procedures and rationale used in these latter studies have been described more fully elsewhere (Gottschalk, Buchsbaum, Gillin, Wu, Reynolds, & Herrera, 1992). Briefly, 48 normal male subjects were screened by medical and psychiatric interviews, physical examinations, laboratory measures, normal sleep habits, and the absence of the use of medication for participation in PET studies to compare cerebral glucose metabolic rates during the states of sleep and wakefulness. The subjects were studied during the waking state, Rapid-Eye-Movement (REM), and Non-Rapid-Eye-Movement (NONREM) sleep, each state being con firmed by standard EEG and other criteria. Intravenous infusion with 18-F D-deoxyglyucose (FDG) was started when all the criteria indicated that the subjects were awake or in REM or NONREM sleep. Thirty-two minutes after the FDG injection, each subject was aroused and asked to give 5-minute tape-recorded reports of their dreams or mental events as well as free-associations to the content of these mental experiences. Other investigators have reported (Huang, Phelps, Hoffman, Sideris, Selin, & Kuhl, 1980; Sokoloff, Reivich, Kennedy, Des Rosiers, Patlak, Pettigrew, Sakurada, & Shinohara, 1977) that 30 minutes after a single intravenous injection of FDG, there is negligible error in estimates of localized cerebral glucose consumption, for most of the free desoxyglucose has been fixed and converted in the brain tissues to desoxyglucose-6-phosphate, the relative amounts of which can be detected 45-120 minutes later by the PET scanner. The typescripts of these reports were blindly content analyzed by the senior author using the Gottschalk-Gleser Anxiety and Hostility scales (Gottschalk & Gleser, 1969) and the Gottschalk Hope scale (1974).

Respondents

Six groups of respondents were involved in these investigations.

1. A group of normal young males, average age 25.3 ± 6.6 to 26.2 ± 5.8, consisting of three subgroups of sleeping or wakeful respondents (Gottschalk et al., 1991): the REM group (N = 10), the NONREM group (N = 10), and wakeful group (N = 10). In the collection of this group, clinical examinations and tests were done to exclude subjects with detectable mental or physical disorders.
2. One group was comprised of normative adult respondents of ages ranging from 20 to 50, gainfully employed and without known physical or mental disorders (Gottschalk & Gleser, 1969, pp. 71-72), consisting of 15 males (low 10 intelligence quotient, 80-100, N = 6; medium 10, 101-115, N = 3; high 10, 116 and up, N = 6; 10 determined by the Wonderlic test [1945]) and 15 females (low 10, N = 6; medium 10, N = 3; high 10, N = 6). Clinical examinations and tests were not carried out to exclude mental or physical disorders.
3. Another group consisted of normative school children (Gottschalk, 1976), that is, children without known physical or mental disorders, ranging in age from 6 to 16 years, both boys (N = 15) and girls (N = 15). For this group, clinical examinations and tests were not done to rule out the presence of mental or physical disorders.
4. A group of adult patients with psychoneuroses (Gottschalk et al., 1979, p. 41 f) and consisting of males (N = 10) and females (N = 10).
5. A group of emotionally disturbed criminal offenders imprisoned in Patuxent Institution in Patuxent, Maryland (Gottschalk, Covi, Uliana, & Bates, 1973), consisting of 44 males, average age 25.6 ± 6.15 and average educational level 8.25 ± 1.90 years.
6. A group of acute schizophrenic patients ranging in age from 21 to 55 years (Gottschalk *et al.*, 1975) and consisting of males (N=10) and females (N=12).

Table 20.2: *Anxiety scale*[a]

1. Death anxiety: References to death, dying, threat of death, or anxiety about death experienced by or occuring to:
   a. Self
   b. Animate others (2)
   c. Inanimate objects destroyed (1)
   d. Denial of death anxiety (1)
2. Mutilation (castration) anxiety: References to injury, tissues or physical damage, or anxiety about injury or threat of such experienced by or occuring to:
   a. Self (3)
   b. Animate others (2)
   c. Inanimate objects (1)
   d. Denial (1)
3. Separation anxiety: References to desertion, abandonment, lonelines, ostracism, loss of support, falling, loss of love object, or threat of such experienced by or occurring to:
   a. Self (3)
   b. Animate others (2)
   c. Inanimate objects (1)
   d. Denial (1)
4. Guilt anxiety: References to adverse criticism, abuse, condemnation, moral disapproval, guilt, or threat of such experienced by:
   a. Self (3)
   b. Animate others (2)
   c. Denial (1)
5. Shame anxiety: References to ridicule, inadequacy, shame, embarrassment, huminilation, overexposure of deficiencies or private details, or threat of experienced by:
   a. Self (3)
   b. Animate others (2)
   c. Denial (1)
6. Diffuse of nonspecific anxiety: References by word or in phrases to anxiety and/or fear without distinguishing type or source of anxiety:
   a. Self (3)
   b. Animate others (2)
   c. Denial (1)

[a] Numbers in parentheses are weight

Table 20.3: *Hostility directed outward scale: Thematic categories of destructive, injurious, critical thoughts and actions directed to others*

I	Hostility outward - overt[a]	II	Hostility outward – covert[a]
a 3	Self killing, fighting, injuring other individuals or threatening to do so.	a 3	Others (human) killing, fighting, injuring other individuals or threatening tot do so.
b 3	Self robbing or abandoning other individuals, causing suffering or anguish to others, or threatening to do so.	b 3	Others (human) robbing or abandoning other individuals, causing suffering or anguish to others, or threatening to do so.
c 3	Self adversely criticizing, depreciating, blaming, expressing anger, dislike of other human beings.	c 3	Others (human) adversely critizing, depreciating, blaming, expressing anger, dislike of other human beings
a2	self killing, injuring, or destroying domestic animals, pets, or threatening to do so	a2	Others (human) killing, injuring or destroying domestic animals, pets, or threatening to do so
b2	self abandoning, robbing domestic animals, pets, or threatening to do so	b2	Others (human) abandoning, robbing domestic animals, pets, or threatening to do so
c2	Self criticizing or depreciating others in a vague or mild manner	c2	Others (human) criticizing or depreciating other individuals in a vague or mild manner
d2	Self depriving or disappointing other humans beings	d2	Others (human) depriving or disappointing other human beings
		e2	Others (human or domestic animals) dying or killing violently in deathdealing situation or threatening with such
		f2	Bodies (human or domestic animals) multilated, depreciated, defiled
a1	Self killing, injuring, destroying, robbing wildlife, flora, inanimate objects, or threatening to do so	a1	Wildlife flora, inanimate objects, injured, broken, robbed, destroyed, or threatening with such (with or without mention of agent)
b1	Self adversely criticizing, depreciating, blaming, expressing anger or dislike of subhumans, inanimate objects, places, situations	b1	Others (human) adversely criticizing, depreciating, expressing anger or dislike of subhumans, inanimate objects, places, situations

c1	Self using hostile words, cursing, mention of anger or rage without referent	c1	Others angry, cursing without referent to cause or direction of anger. Also instruments of destruction not used threateningly
		d1	Others (human, domestic animals) injured, robbed, dead, abandoned or threatened with such from any source including subhuman, inanimate objects, situation (storms, floods, etc.)
		e1	Subhumans killing, fighting, injuring, robbing, destroying each other or threatening to do so
		f1	Denial of anger, dislike, hatred, cruelty, and intent to harm

[a] Numbers serve to give weight as well as to identify category; letters also help to identify category.

Measurement of Emotions and Defenses

Scores on the Gottschalk-Gleser affect scales are corrected for number of words spoken by deriving a score per 100 words spoken (Gottschalk & Gottschalk, 1969; Gottschalk, Winget, & Gleser, 1969), for discontinuity of frequency distributions of scores due to zero scores by adding 0.5 to the raw score, and for non-parametric frequency distribution of scores by square-rooting the adjusted score (see Tables 20.2-20.5, indicating the Anxiety, Hostility Outward, Hostility Inward, and Ambivalent Hostility scales).

These mathematical transformations of the scores permit comparisons of such scores across different occasions and individuals and lead to a frequency distribution of scores approximating a parametric distribution. The Gottschalk Hope scale also corrects for the number of words spoken by deriving a score per 100 words (Gottschalk, 1974) and in the present study 0.5 was added to the raw zero scores, but the final hope scores were not square-rooted (see Table 20.6, illustrating the verbal categories for the Hope scale). A minimum of 70 words has been recommended for a reliable sample (Gottschalk et al., 1969, p. 15).

Table 20.4: *Hostility directed inward scale: Thematic categories of self destructive, self-critical thoughts and actions*

I. Hostility inward[a]	
a4	References to self (speaker) attempting to kill self, with or without conscious intent
b4	References to self wanting to die, needing or deserving to die
a3	References to self injuring, mutilating, disfiguring self or threats to do so, with or without conscious intent
b3	Self blaming, expressing anger or hatred to self, considering self worthless or of no value, causing oneself grief or trouble, or threatening to do so
c3	References to feeling of discouragement, giving up hope, despairing, feeling grieved or depressed, having no purpose in life
a2	References to self needing or diserving punishment, paying for one's sins, needing to atone or do penance
b2	Self adversely criticizing, depreciating self; references to regretting, being sorry or ashamed for what one say or does; references to self mistake or in error
c2	References to feeling of deprivation in self, disappointment, lonesomeness
a1	References to feeling disappointed in self; unable to meet expectations of self or others
b1	Denial of anger, dislike, hatred, blame, destructive impulses from self to self
c1	References to feeling painfully driven or obliged to meet one's own expectations and standards

Table 20.5: *Ambivilant hostility scale: Thematic categories of destructive, injurious, critical thoughts and actions of others to self*

II. Ambivalent hostility[a]	
a3	Others (human) killing or threatening to kill self
b3	Others (human) physically injuring, mutilating, disfiguring self or threatening to do so
c3	Others (human) adversely criticizing, blaming, expressing anger or dislike toward self or threatening to do so
d3	Others (human) abandoning, robbing self, causing suffering, anguish, or threatening to do so
a2	Others (human) depriving, disappointing, misunderstanding self or threatening to do so
b2	Self threatening with death from subhuman or inanimate object, or death-dealing situation
a1	Others (subhuman, inanimate, or situation), injuring, abandoning, robbing self, causing suffering, anguish
b1	Denial of blame

Table 20.6: *Hope scale*

Weight		Content category
+ 1	H 1.	References to self or others getting or receiving help, advice, support, sustenance, confidence, esteem (a) from others; (b) from self.
+ 1	H 2.	References to feelings of optimism about the present of future by (a) others; (b) self.
+ 1	H 3.	References to being or wanting to be or seeking to be the recipient of good fortune, good luck, God's favor or blessing by (a) others; (b) self.
+ 1	H 4.	References to any kind of hope that lead to a constructive outcome, to survival, to longevity, to smooth-going interpersonal relationships (this category can be scored only if the word "hope" or "wish" or a close synonym is used).
- 1	H 5.	References to not being or not wanting to be or not seeking to be the recipient of good fortune, good luck, God's favor or blessing.
- 1	H 6.	References to self or others not getting or receiving help, advice, support, sustenance, confidence, esteem (a) from others; (b) from self.
- 1	H 7.	References to feelings of hopelessness, losing hope, despair, lack of confidence, lack of ambition, lack of interes; feelings of pessimism, discouragement by (a) others; (b) self.

[a] Numbers serve to give weight as well as to identify category; letters also help to identify category.

Statistical Procedures

The statistical procedures applied to testing the hypotheses put forward included nonparametric tests (e.g., Spearman, Kendall tau, etc.) to examine the intercorrelations between the frequency of occurrence of verbal category references involving the self and verbal category statements involving others (displacement) or denials across the different experiences reported and recorded from each subject while awake actually occurred when the individual was having REM dreaming, NONREM thoughts and feelings, or silent waking fantasies and reveries.

Results

1. In the group of normal male adults, the frequency of occurrence of verbal statements referring to the self being anxious, displacements of anxiety, and denials of anxiety were significantly and positively inter-correlated. In the group of normative adults, the frequency of occurrence of verbal references to the self being anxious and denials of anxiety were significantly positively correlated. The group of psychoneurotic adults showed a significant negative correlation between the occurrence of verbal references to the self being anxious and denials of anxiety (r = -.48, $p < .03$) and a negative nonsignificant correlation (r = -.30, $p < .15$) between verbal references to the self and

verbal displacements of anxiety to others. The groups of normative children, emotionally disordered criminals, and schizophrenic patients had no significant intercorrelations of any of these kinds (see Table 20.7). Hence, the phenomena of (verbal) displacements and denials of anxiety, particularly when they are not intense or of great magnitude, are associated with mental health, especially in adults, and are linked statistically (as adjudged from significant positive correlations) and psychodynamically (on the basis of observations with individual subjects or patients) with diverse hostile affects (Gottschalk, Fronczek, & Abel, 1993a). In patients with neuroses, the verbal denials and displacements tend to substitute for verbal statements concerning the self being anxious; hence, these variables are negatively intercorrelated, which illustrates and confirms that denial and displacement are used as defense mechanisms in the neuroses. (See also, Gottschalk, Fronczek, Abel, Buchsbaum, Fallon, 2001).

Table 20.7: *Intercorrelation between verbal statements referring to the self being anxious (a), others being anxious (b + c), denial of anxiousness (d), and their p-values*

Group 1. Normal male adults			Group 2. Normative adults		
Categories	a	b + c	Categories	a	b + c
b + c	.45		b + c	-.01	
	(.007)			(.472)	
d	.42	.65	d	.42	.23
	(.010)	(.000)		(.010)	(.107)
Group 3. Normative children			Group 4. Neurotic patients		
Categories	a	b + c	Categories	a	b + c
b + c	.17		b + c	-.30	
	(.182)			(.150)	
d	.10	.02		-.48	.16
	(.305)	(.448)		(.016)	(.256)
Group 5.			Group 6.		
Categories	a	b + c	Categories	a	b + c
b + c	-.08		b + c	.09	
	(.303)			(.349)	
d	.16	.18	d	-.01	.08
	(.153)	(.115)		(.499)	(.371)

2. Among normative children (from age 6 to 16), probably for developmental reasons, (verbal) displacements and denials of anxiety are not linked in any clear way, statistically, with other affects. How displacement and denial are

linked with hostility and other affects apparently needs to be determined in each single case.

3. In mentally disordered groups of adults, (verbal) displacements and denials may serve a defensive or coping function and substitute, to some extent, for disturbing affects (as adjudged from their relative infrequent significant positive intercorrelations).
4. In schizophrenic patients, the personal disorganization of the schizophrenic syndrome may serve to obscure the possible usefulness as a defense or coping mechanism of the expression of anxiety or hostility in various forms. In this connection, clinicians have uniformly observed that frequently the affects expressed by acute schizophrenic patients are driven by the content of their delusions and hallucinations (see Figures. 23.1 and 23.2).

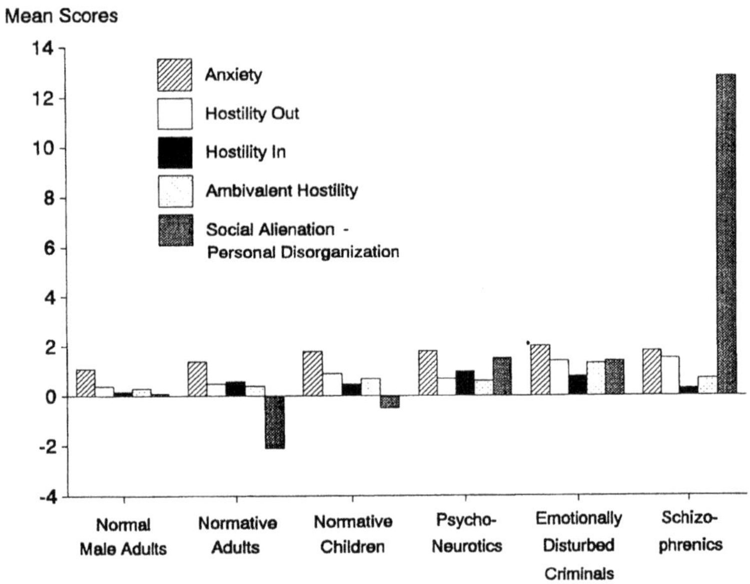

Figure 20.1: *Comparisons of mean affect and social alienation-personal disorganization scores for six groups of subjects*

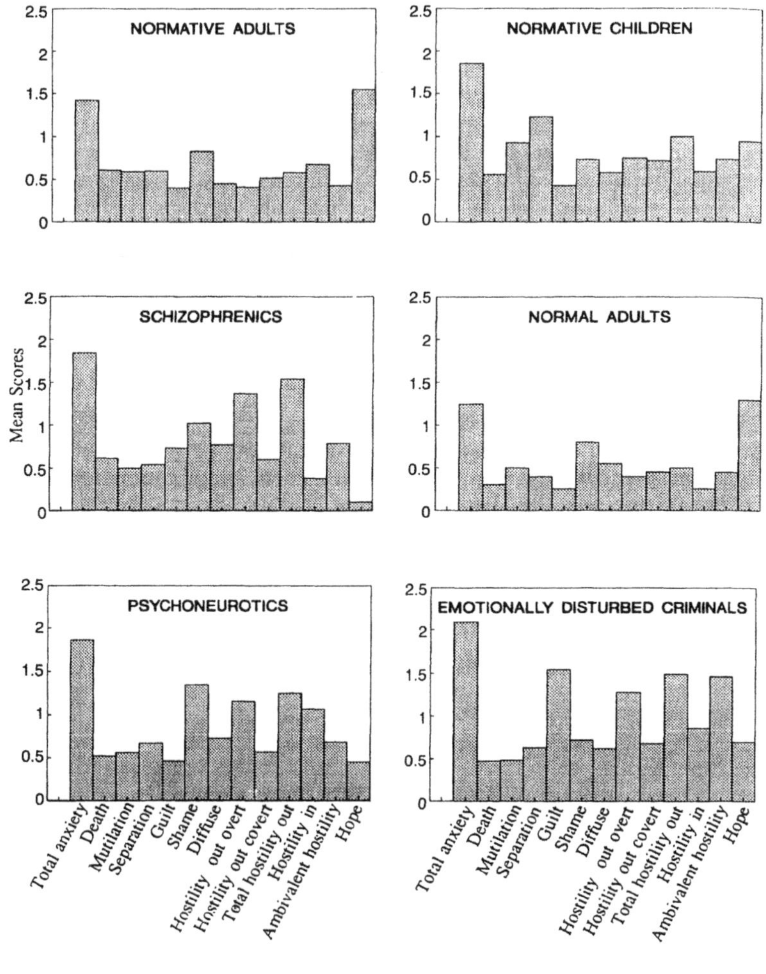

Figure 20.2: *Comparison of anxiety, anxiety subscales, and hostility scores for six groups of subjects*

5. The state of consciousness -namely, wakefulness, REM dreaming, and NONREM mentation- influences the intercorrelations between anxiety and hostility and localized cerebral glucose metabolic rates (Gottschalk et al., 1991a,b, 1992, 1993a,b). Furthermore, the same states of consciousness influence the cerebral areas, where significant inter-correlations occur between positive hope scores, negative hope scores, and total hope scores (the sum of positive and negative hope scores) with cerebral glucose metabolic rates (Gottschalk, Fronczek, Abel, & Buchsbaum, 1993b).
6. The direction of lateralization - right-sided versus left-sided hemispheric dominance - and the ratios of positive to negative significant correlations between cerebral glucose metabolic rates and total anxiety (a+b+c+d), self-anxiety (a), anxiety displacements (b+c), and anxiety denials (d) varies with the brain areas examined: that is, whole brain, medial and subcortical gray areas, and lateral cortical regions (see Table 20.8).
7. Based on the location of the largest number of significant correlations (positive or negative), there is left-sided lateralization for total anxiety during wakeful (silent) mentation in whole brain and right-sided lateralization for total anxiety, self references, and displacements in medial and subcortical gray regions and left-sided lateralization for anxiety denials in these brain regions. In lateral cortical cerebral regions, the lateralization differs in that there is left-sided dominance for total anxiety scores and self references, right-sided dominance for displacements, and no definite lateralization for denials of anxiety.
8. Denials of anxiety tend to have an opposite cerebral hemispheric dominance (or no lateralization, depending on the brain region) than affirmations of anxiety, which suggests a yes-no function for the two cerebral hemispheres.
9. The findings with respect to the intercorrelations of localized cerebral glucose metabolic rates with total anxiety, self-anxiety, anxiety displacement, and anxiety denial clearly indicate that the cerebral neurobiological representations of these anxiety variables have largely distinct and separate cerebral localizations. (For full details, see Gottschalk et al., 1991b,c,e.) Moreover, the significant increases or decreases in cerebral energy consumption (in the form of localized glucose metabolic rates) associated with changes in the verbal measures of anxiety involve brain areas known from other animal and human studies to subserve the functions of cognition, reasoning, memory, audition, vision, and emotions.
10. Positive hope and negative hope scores tend to have significant correlations with glucose metabolic rates in opposite cerebral hemispheres in medial cortical and subcortical gray as well as lateral cortical areas (see Table 20.8). And when these correlations involve similar identical cerebral locations, the

significant correlations between positive and negative hope with glucose metabolic rate are in opposite directions (Gottschalk et al., 1991d,e).

Figure 20.3 illustrates the brain areas targeted for glucose metabolic rates based on the neuroanatomical atlas of Matsui and Hirano (1987).

Table 20.8 aims to summarize the tendencies for hemispheric lateralization, based on the criterion of the largest number of significant intercorrelations (positive or negative), between anxiety and hope scores with localized cerebral glucose metabolic rates.

Table 20.8: *Hemispheric lateralization and number of significant positive (+) and negative (-) correlations between anxiety and hope scores during silent mentation with cerebral glucose metabolic rates*

	Whole brain				Medical cortical and subcortical gray				Lateral cortical				Sums			
	L		R		L		R		L		R		L		R	
Scores	+	-	+	-	+	-	+	-	+	-	+	-	+	-	+	-
Anxiety																
Total scores		1			1	2	2	3	1				2	3	2	3
Self reference (verbal)		1		1	1	3	2	3	1				2	4	2	4
Displacement	1	1	1	1	1	2	1	4	1		2		3	3	4	5
Denials	2	1		1	3	9	2	3	1	1		2	6	11	2	
Hope																
Total hope	1	2	1	1	1	2	4	1				1	2	4	5	3
Positive hope	1	1	1			3	2	2	1			1	2	4	5	3
Negative hope	2				2	1	1	1		2			4	3	1	1

During wakeful silent mentation in whole brain, positive hope scores correlate positively with glucose metabolic rates in the parietal lobe, left temporal cortex, occipital cortex, and right occipital cortex and negatively with glucose metabolic rate in the left temporal lobe. Negative hope scores correlate positively with glucose metabolic rate in the left frontal lobe and left temporal lobe (Gottschalk et al., 1991b). The precise significant correlations between cerebral glucose metabolic rates with anxiety and hope scores are reported in detail elsewhere (Gottschalk et al., 1991a,b, 1992, 1993b).

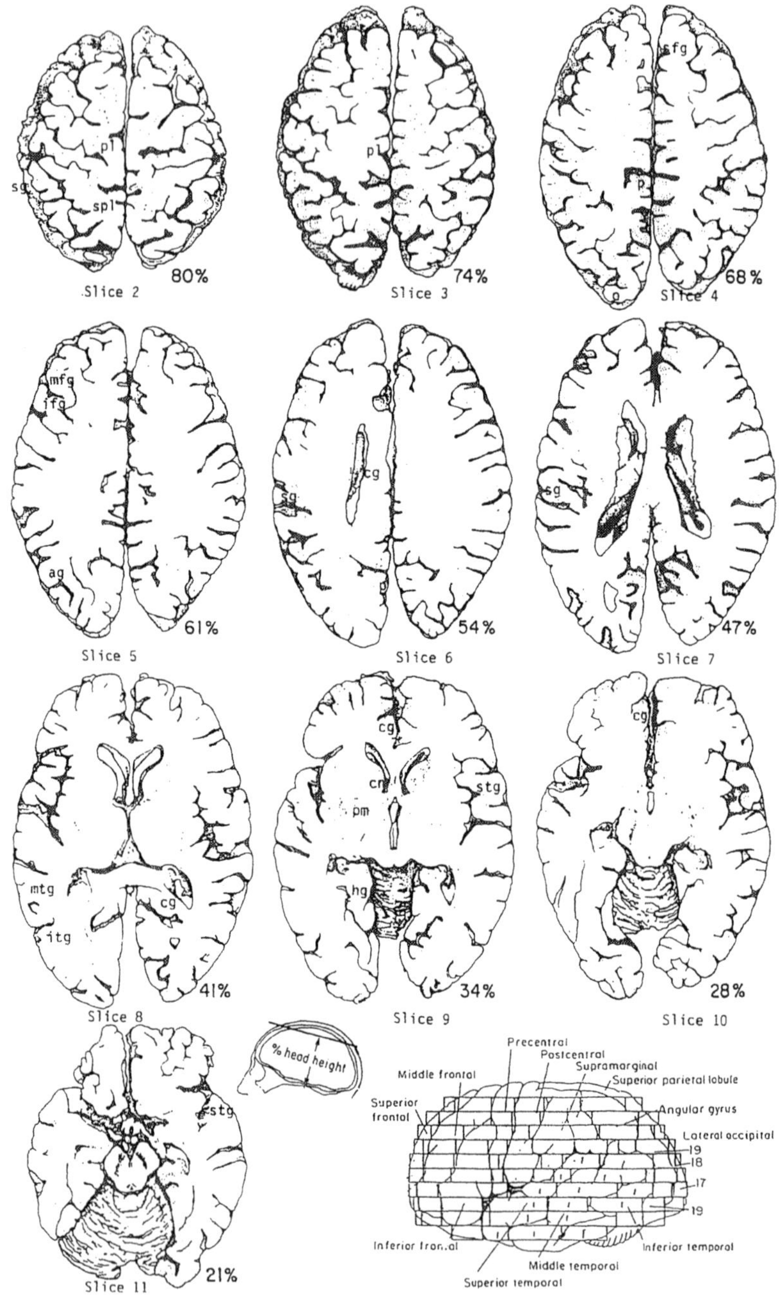
pl
sg
spl
80%
Slice 2
pl
74%
Slice 3
sfg
p
68%
Slice 4
mfg
ifg
ag
61%
Slice 5
cg
sg
54%
Slice 6
sg
47%
Slice 7
mtg
itg
cg
41%
Slice 8
cg
cn
pm
stg
hg
34%
Slice 9
cg
28%
Slice 10
stg
21%
Slice 11
% head height
Precentral
Postcentral
Supramarginal
Superior parietal lobule
Middle frontal
Superior frontal
Angular gyrus
Lateral occipital
19
18
17
19
Inferior frontal
Inferior temporal
Middle temporal
Superior temporal

←

Figure 20.3: *Brain slices and locations: drawing of brain levels from atlas of Matsui and Hirano showing slice number, percentage of head height above canthomeatal line, and location of statistically significant correlations with anxiety. Regions on cortical surface were assessed with the radial cortical peel computer algorithm (Buchsbaum, Gillin, Wu, Hazlett, Prager, Sicotte, & Dupont, 1989) and regions in the medial areas of the brain with square, stereotaxically placed regions of interest. All correlations with p < .05, two-tailed, of this exploratory analysis are given in Table 20.8. Abbreviations: spl = superior parietal lobule, sg = supramarginal gyrus, ifg = inferior frontal gyrus, sfg = superior frontal gyrus, pl = paracentral lobule, p = precuneus, cg = cingulate gyrus, ag = angular gyrus, ol = occipital lobe.*

Discussion

These findings, using the objective method of verbal behavior content analysis and the noninvasive method of measuring localized energy consumption in the living human brain by recording the relative cerebral glucose metabolic rates via positron emission tomography, provide novel perspectives on psychological defense and coping mechanisms and how these relate to psychopathological and neurobiological processes. At the same time, an introduction is given to the cerebral locations associated with the alerting and usually negative emotions of anxiety, hostility, and hopelessness and the positive emotion of hope. Our findings with respect to these psychological mechanisms and psychopathological processes can be easily discussed and possibly integrated with other bodies of know ledge on the subject.

Our findings, however, with regard to these psychological mechanisms and their ongoing neurobiological substrates as represented by cerebral glucose metabolic correlates, since they constitute a first look at such interrelationships, are almost beyond lengthy intelligent discussion. As with the first explorers of a new continent or of the Earth's moon, the easiest and most natural communication to others is to describe what one sees and, then, to wait for others to corroborate the existence of the initial phenomena observed. Along that approach, our initial observations regarding cerebral glucose metabolic correlates with the verbal-behavior-derived scores for anxiety, hostility, hope, and some of their defenses provide a new map of unexplored land that bears checking and replication. Since there is no extant empirical body of knowledge throwing light on the cerebral correlates of emotions and their defenses, our findings at this time need further scrutiny, reflection, and cautious assimilation. It is perhaps permissible to go one step beyond that position and with modest certainty claim that apparently brain circuits record yes-and-no matters, such as anxious thoughts and denials of anxious thoughts, in opposite cerebral hemispheres. And though not quite as uniformly, hopeful thoughts are more often processed in the opposite cerebral hemisphere than unhopeful thoughts. Moreover, the cerebral neurobiological representations - as adjudged from the locations of significant correlations with cerebral glucose metabolic rates - of total anxiety, self-anxiety, anxiety displacement, anxiety denial, hopefulness, and hopelessness have largely discrete and separate cerebral localizations. Beyond these observations, there is no more to say except to be prepared for new hypothesis generating on the relationships of brain functioning and psychological functioning.

With regard to emotions, defenses, and psychopathological processes, the findings in this study support the viewpoint that (verbal) displaceme`nts and denials of anxiety, when they are not of great magnitude, are associated with mental health, especially in adults, and are highly positively correlated in their frequency of occurrence with direct statements of the self being anxious. As the severity of the psychopathological processes increases, significant intercorrelations between assertions of the self being anxious and denials of anxiety become significantly negative in patients with neuroses. And as the psychopathological processes become even more severe - for example, in emotionally disordered criminals and in acute schizophrenic patients - such intercorrelations disappear entirely. Since the frequency of occurrence of verbal statements concerning the self being anxious and displacements and denials of anxiety all tend to increase with the severity of emotional and mental impairment, the magnitude of self-anxiety or displacements or denials of anxiety can all serve as signs of the severity of mental incapacity (see also Gottschalk et al., 1993a).

Hope scores, derived from the content analysis of speech, appear to serve a protective function in mental health. The greater the mental health of individuals, the higher their hope scores. This observation (see Table 20.1) is backed up by current findings that our group of normal young males, during wakefulness, had mean hope scores of +0.43 ± 1.02, our group of normative adults had mean hope scores of +0.73 ± 1.03, our normative children had mean hope scores of +.04 ± 1.251, our emotionally disordered criminals had average hope scores of -.49 ±1.49, and our group of acute schizophrenic patients had average hope scores of -.78 ± 1.64. With regard to the cerebral lateralization of positive and negative emotions, Tucker (1981) has reported that negative emotions, such as anxiety, are more often lateralized to the left cerebral hemisphere; whereas Sackeim, Greenberg, Weiman, Gur, Hungerbuhler, & Geschwind, (1982) and Campbell, (1982) observe that the left hemisphere is more frequently associated with positive emotions and the right hemisphere is more frequently associated with negative emotions. These conflicting hypotheses may be explainable by our own findings in that we find slight left-sided cerebral lateralization for total anxiety in the whole brain and right-sided lateralization for total anxiety, self-anxiety, and displaced anxiety in medial cortical and subcortical gray areas and left-sided lateralization for total anxiety in lateral cortical areas (see Table 20.8). We suggest that the determination of cerebral lateralization is influenced by the methods and criteria used for assessing such cerebral localization and, certainly, by the range and completeness of brain regions examined. Our use of positron emission tomography has allowed us to survey the whole brain as well as cortical and subcortical areas of interest, and our criterion of ascertaining lateralization by locating the brain areas where the majority of significant correlations are found between the magnitude of the emotions and localized cerebral glucose metabolic rates would seem to be more reliable than other methods used heretofore. Looking at the cerebral lateralization associated with positive and negative hope scores derived from verbal reports during wakeful silent mentation would tend to favor the hypothesis that negative hope scores (feelings and thoughts of hopelessness) are localized in the left cerebral hemisphere if one considers whole brain and lateral gray areas, but that there is less clear lateralization if one focuses on the medial cortical and subcortical gray areas. And if one considers the state of consciousness - that is, whether the subject is awake or asleep during the experiencing of these emotions - the constancy of cerebral lateralization during emotions disappears. Obviously, further studies to clarify these issues are in order.

Finally, we recommend the use of the content analysis of natural language as a very specific and reliable method of determining the occurrence of psychological defense mechanisms, such as displacements, denials, and hopefulness. No inferences are necessary to establish when such psychological dimensions are being used, for their occurrence is manifestly observable in the content of verbal behavior itself. Furthermore, other studies we have cited provide construct validation. Moreover, a computerized methodology for scoring speech samples and verbal texts has been perfected enabling clinicians and researchers to use this content methodology, and the software enables the user to apply the methodology to a wide variety of situations and subjects (Gottschalk, 1995, 2000; Gottschalk and Bechtel, 1995, 2002; Gottschalk, Fronczek, Abel, Buchsbaum, & Fallon, 2001).

Summary and Conclusions

This is a study examining, through the content analysis of verbal behavior, the extent to which the verbalization of an emotion, such as anxiety, correlates significantly with the frequency of verbalization of "defenses" against anxiety, such as displacements and denials of anxiety, across different groups of subjects, ranging from mentally and physically healthy individuals to emotionally disturbed criminals and schizophrenic patients. With the availability of positron emission tomography at our Brain Imaging Center, the opportunity was presented to examine, also, the relationship of verbalizations of anxiety, anxiety displacements, and anxiety denials as well as verbalizations of hopefulness and hopelessness to localized cerebral glucose metabolic rates. Since hope is often regarded as a defensive or protective state or trait against mental or physical disorders the exploration of its cerebral neurobiology with respect to glucose metabolic rate appeared to be a relevant undertaking.

With the exception of children, the more mentally healthy the group of subjects, the more likely were there to be significant intercorrelations between verbal statements of the self being anxious and displacements and denials of anxiety. Sex, intelligence, and age had no significant effects on the frequency of occurrence of the phenomena of displacements and denials in the spoken language of six groups of subjects.

Opposite cerebral hemispheres had significant intercorrelations between measures of the self being anxious and denials of such anxiety with cerebral glucose metabolic rates, and less consistently, measures of hopefulness and hopelessness revealed a similar phenomenon. There are quite different cerebral representations for verbalized self-anxiety, anxiety displacements, anxiety denials, hopefulness, and hopelessness during the same and different states of consciousness, specifically, silent wakeful mentation, REM dreaming, and NONREM mentation.

A discussion is offered of the bearings our findings have on the issues of cerebral lateralization of positive and negative emotions. We believe our findings provide more stringent criteria for determining such lateralization than previous studies in this area. Moreover, positron emission tomography provides an opportunity to survey all brain regions, instead of omitting possibly crucial areas, and it affords occasions for noninvasive cerebral neurobiochemical assessments in the living human subject. The computerization of the scoring of speech samples and verbal texts now enables the clinician and researcher to apply this content analysis methodology to subjects in a variety of life situations.

References

Anant, S. S. (1967). Belongingness, anxiety, and self-sufficiency. *Psychological Reports, 20,* 1137-1138.

Barron, F. (1953). An ego strength scale which predicts response to psychotherapy. *Journal of Consulting and Clinical Psychology, 17,* 327-333.

Buchsbaum, M. S., Gillin, J. C., Wu, J., Hazlett, E., Prager, L., Sicotte, N., & Dupont, R. (1989). Regional cerebral metabolic rate in human sleep assessed by positron emission tomography. *Life Sciences, 45,* 1349-1356.

Campbell, R. (1982). The lateralization of emotion: A critical review. *International Journal of Psychology, 17,* 211-229.

Derogatis, L. R., Lipman, R., Rickels, K., Uhlenhuth, E. H., & Covi, L. (1974). The Hopkins Symptom Checklist (HSCL): A measure of primary symptom dimensions. In P. Pichat (Ed.), *Psychological measurements in psychopharmacology: Vol. 7* (pp. 79-110). Basel: Karger.

Endicott, J., Spitzer, R., Fleiss, J., & Cohen, J. (1976). The global assessment scale. *Archives of General Psychiatry, 33,* 766-771.

Frank, J. (1968). The role of hope in psychotherapy. *International Journal of Psychiatry, 5,* 383-395.

French, T. M. (1952). *The integration of behavior: Vol. 1.* Chicago: University of Chicago Press.

Freud, A. (1946). *The ego and the mechanisms of defense.* New York: International Universities Press. (Original work published 1936)

Gleser, G. C. & Ihilevich, D. (1969). An objective instrument for measuring defense mechanisms. *Journal of Consulting and Clinical Psychology, 33,* 51-60.

Gottschalk, L. A. (1976). Children's speech as a source of data towards the measurement of psychological states. *Journal of Youth and Adolescence, 5,* 11-36.

Gottschalk, L. A. (1974). A hope scale applicable to verbal samples. *Archives of General Psychiatry, 30,* 779-785.

Gottschalk, L. A. (1995). *Content Analysis of Verbal Behavior. New Findings and Clinical Applications.* Hillsdale, New Jersey: Lawrence Erlbaum Associates.

Gottschalk, L. A. (2000). The application of computerized content analysis of natural language to psychotherapy research now and in the future. *American Journal of Psychotherapy.*54, 306-311.

Gottschalk, L. A. & Bechtel, R. J. (1995). Computerized content analysis of the content analysis of natural language for use in biomedical research. *Computer Methods and Programs in Biomedicine.* 47, 123-130.

Gottschalk, L. A. & Bechtel, R. J. (2000-2002). *PCAD 2000—Psychiatric Con-*

tent Analysis and Diagnosis. Corona del Mar, CA: GB-Software, 4607 Perham Road, Corona del Mar, CA 92625, pp. 75.

Gottschalk, L. A., Biener, R., Noble, E. P., Birch, H., Wilbert, D. E., & Heiser, J. F. (1975). Thioridazine plasma levels and clinical response. *Comprehensive Psychiatry, 16,* 323-337.

Gottschalk, L. A., Buchsbaum, M., Gillin, J. R., Wu, J., Reynolds, C., & Herrera, D. B. (1991a). Anxiety levels in dreams: Relation to localized cerebral glucose metabolic rate. *Brain Research, 538,* 107-110.

Gottschalk, L. A., Buchsbaum, M., Gillin, J. R., Wu, J., Reynolds, C., & Herrera, D. B. (1991b). Positron emission tomographic studies of the relationship of cerebral glucose metabolism and the magnitude of anxiety and hostility ex perienced during dreaming and waking. *Journal of Neuropsychiatry and Clinical Neuroscience, 31,* 131-142.

Gottschalk, L. A., Buchsbaum, M., Gillin, J. R., Wu, J., Reynolds, C., & Herrera, D. B. (1992c). The effect of silent mentation on cerebral glucose metabolic rate. *Comprehensive Psychiatry, 33,* 52-59.

Gottschalk, L. A., Covi, L., Uliana, R., & Bates, D. E. (1973). Effects of diphenylhydantoin on anxiety and hostility in institutionalized prisoners. *Comprehensive Psychiatry, 14, 503-511.*

Gottschalk, L. A., Fox, R. A., & Bates, D. E. (1973). A study of prediction and outcome in a Mental Health Crisis Clinic. *American Journal of Psychiatry, 190,* 1107-1111.

Gottschalk, L. A., Fronczek, J., Abel, L. (1993a). Emotions, defenses, coping mechanisms, and symptoms *Psychoanalytic Psychology 10,* 237-260.

Gottschalk, L. A., Fronczek, J., Abel, L., & Buchsbaum, M.S. (1993b). The cerebral neurobiology of hope and hopelessness, *Psychiatry. 56,* 270-281.

Gottschalk, L. A., Fronczek, J., Abel, L., Buchsbaum, M. S., Fallon, J. H. (2001). The neurobiology of anxiety, anxiety-displacement, and anxiety-denial. *Psychotherapy and Psychosomatics.* 70, 17-24.

Gottschalk, L. A. & Gleser, G. C. (1969). *The measurement of psychological states through the content analysis of verbal behavior.* Berkeley, Los Angeles: University of California Press.

Gottschalk, L. A., Gleser, G. C., & Springer, K.J. (1963). Three hostility scales applicable to verbal samples. *Archives of General Psychiatry, 9,* 254-279.

Gottschalk, L. A. & Hoigaard-Martin, J. (1986). The emotional impact of mastectomy. *Psychiatry Research, 17,* 153-167.

Gottschalk, L. A., Hoigaard, J. C., Birch, H., & Rickels, K. (1979). The measurement of psychological states: Relationships between Gottschalk-Gleser content analyses scores and Hamilton Anxiety Rating Scales score, Physician Questionnaire Rating Scales scores, and Hopkins Symptom Checklist scores. In L.A. Gottschalk (Ed.), *Content analysis of verbal behavior: Further studies* (pp. 41-94). New York: Spectrum.

Gottschalk, L. A., Kunkel, R. L., Wohl, T., Saenger, E., & Winget, C. N. (1969). Total and half body irradiation. Effect on cognitive and emotional processes. *Archives of General Psychiatry, 21,* 574-580.

Gottschalk, L. A., Lolas, F., & Viney, L. L. (Eds.). (1986). *Content analysis of verbal behavior. Significance in clinical medicine and psychiatry* (pp. 249-256). Heidelberg, Germany: Springer-Verlag.

Gottschalk, L. A., Mayerson, P., & Gottlieb, A. (1967). The prediction and evaluation of outcome in an emergency brief psychotherapy clinic. *Journal of Nervous and Mental Disease, 144,* 77-96.

Gottschalk, L. A., Winget, C. N., & Gleser, G. C. (1969). *Manual of instructions for using the Gottschalk-Gleser Content Analysis Scales: Anxiety, Hostility, and Social Alienation-Personal Disorganization.* Berkeley, Los Angeles: University of California Press.

Huang, S. C., Phelps, M. E., Hoffman, E. J., Sideris, K., Selin, C. J., & Kuhl, D. E. (1980). Noninvasive determination of local cerebral metabolic rate of glucose in man. *American Journal of Physiology, 238,* E69-E82.

Ihilevich, D. & Gleser, G. C. (1986). *Defense mechanisms. Their classification, correlates, and measurement with the defense mechanisms inventory.* Owosso, MI:DMT Associates.

Matsui, T. & Hirano, A. (1987). *An atlas of the human brain for computerized tomography.* Tokyo: Igaku-Shoin.

Persky, J., Winget, C. N., & Placci, C. (1971). Hope and discomfort as factors influencing treatment continuance. *Comprehensive Psychiatry, 12,* 557-563.

Sackeim, H. A., Greenberg, M. S., Weiman, A. L., Gur, R. C., Hungerbuhler, J. P., & Geschwind, N. (1982). Hemispheric asymmetry in the social expression of positive and negative emotions: Neurological evidence. *Archives of Neurology, 39,* 210-218.

Sokoloff, L., Reivich, M., Kennedy, C., Des Rosiers, M. S., Patlak, D. S., Pettigrew, K. D., Sakurada, 0., & Shinohara, M. (1977). The ['4C] deoxyglucose method for the measurement of local cerebral glucose utilization: Theory, procedure, and normal values in the conscious and anesthetized albino rat. *Journal of Neurochemistry, 28,* 897-916.

SPSS (1990). *SPSS reference guide.* Chicago: SPSS, Inc.

Tucker, D. M. (1981). Lateral brain function, emotion, and conceptualization. *Psychological Bulletin, 89,* 19-46.

Udelman, D. L. & Udelman, H. D. (1986). A preliminary report on antidepressant therapy and its effect on hope and immunity. In L.A. Gottschalk, F. Lolas, L. L. Viney (Eds.). (1986). *Content analysis of verbal behavior.*

Significance in clinical medicine and psychiatry. (pp. 249-256). Heidelberg, Germany: Springer-Verlag..

Uliana, R. L. (1979). Measurement of black children's affective states and the effect of interviewer's race on affective states as measured through language behavior. In L.A. Gottschalk (Ed.), *Content analysis of verbal behavior: Further studies* (pp. 175-233). New York: Spectrum.

Winget, C., Seligman, R., Rauh, J. L., & Gleser, G. C. (1979). Social Alienation- Personal Disorganization assessment in disturbed and normal adolescents. *Journal of Nervous and Mental Disease, 167,* 282-287.

Wonderlic, E. F. (1945). *Wonderlic Personnel Test Manual.* Norfield, IL: Wonderlic and Associates.

Defense Mechanisms
U. Hentschel, G. Smith, J.G. Draguns & W. Ehlers (Editors)

Chapter 21

Defense Mechanisms and Physical Health

Shulamith Kreitler

Why Expect Defense Mechanisms to Play a Role in the Context of Physical Diseases?

As is well known, defense mechanisms (DMs) have originated in the field of medicine, in which they have been recognized as a major means for combating diseases, in the form of nonspecific defense mechanisms (e.g., mechanical barriers, chemical inhibitors, enzymes and flushing acts) against pathogens or in the form of specific defense mechanisms (i.e., immune system components) against specific foreign organisms and substances. Though the DMs on the psychological level differ from the medical DMs in their nature, they resemble them in their function in regard to mental health. Could the psychological DMs also play a role in regard to physical health? There are serious considerations in favor of this assumption. First, DMs are a basic characteristic of human functioning and as such may be expected to play a role in any domain, including disease and health. A further, more specific reason is that health disorders are one of the more difficult states confronting human beings, mostly involving disability, reduced independence, role changes, physical suffering, and other hardships, often for prolonged periods of time. Situations of this kind tend to evoke emotions known to be defense-related, such as fear, anxiety, sadness and anger. There is evidence about the evocation of such emotions, for example, in patients with myocardial infarction, diabetes, asthma, and cancer (Couzijn, Ros, & Winubst, 1990; Maes & Schlosser, 1987; Pennings-Van der Aerden & Visser, 1990; Van Elderen, 1991). Moreover, health disorders may represent serious threats to the physical and even psychological existence of the individual, generating despair, hopelessness, helplessness and confusion of the kind that may be handled by defensive reactions (Morse & Johnson, 1991; Perretz & Reicherts, 1992). The fact that a situation has the potential for evoking DMs is a strong argument for expecting the involvement of DMs in the context of health. A further factor that has contributed to enhancing this expectation was the finding that despite the difficulties, individuals often adapted to the situation of sickness and after some time reverted to a normal state of well-being (e.g., Van Elderen 1991). Studies showed that most outpatients with diabetes, cancer, and rheumatic, renal or skin diseases report in most disease stages (except the initial and pre-terminal) stress levels and well-being degrees that do not differ from those of healthy individuals (Cassileth et al., 1984). These findings suggest that the decreases in distress may be attained by applying DMs. More direct suggestions were provided by studies showing that in healthy shift workers, up to 25% of the variance in the immunological indicators was explained by a combination of DM scores, perceived health (number of health complaints, e.g., sleep disturbances, allergies, breathing difficulties) and work problems (e.g., time pressure, troubles with management) (Vaernes et al., 1988).

Assumed Roles of DMs in the Context of Physical Diseases

Another way of approaching the issue of why are DMs expected to play a role in the context of physical diseases is to ask about the possible function of DMs in regard to physical health. One obvious function has already been presented above. It is likely that DMs play a role in coping with the distress and hardships of the disease itself after its occurrence. The common use of denial in cancer patients (Kreitler, 1999) or in the various neurological disorders involving brain injury (Frigatano & Schacter, 1991) exemplifies this role of DMs.

A second function of DMs consists in enabling individuals to avoid fear-provoking but relevant medical recommendations that could help in preventing diseases or at least minimizing their deleterious effects. Thus, denial of relevant information about testing for cancer prevents in many cases early detection of the disease that would contribute to prolonging life (Kreitler, 1999). Again, defensive coping that is based on attention avoidance, bunting, suppression and counter argumentation leads to overlooking HIV prevention measures in sexually active students (Blumberg, 2000).

A third less obvious function of DMs is related to the causes for the occurrence of a disease. DMs may affect disease occurrence in various ways. One possibility is represented by the conceptualization that underlying the somatic disease there is some kind of psychological conflict that is handled by means of DMs specific to that conflict. For example, asthma patients tend both to idealize their parents as well as to become liberated from them (Hentschel, 1999). Hence, DMs may be expected to be related to the physical symptoms. Another conceptualization emphasizes the failure of DMs in psychosomatic diseases so that the ego makes no contact with the dangerous inner elements that go on to get full expression (Levitan, 1989). Hence, weak and ineffective DMs may be expected in somatic diseases. A different conceptualization consists in suggesting that in psychosomatic diseases there is a split in the ego organization which is expressed as a disease, so that the disease itself serves as a defense for the fragile ego against the outside world (Winnicott, 1982). This conceptualization too leads to the expectation that of highly primitive DMs in somatic diseases. A similar approach is reflected in the assumption that the disease itself is the DM against the instinctual demands of the id (Bellini, 1973), for example, gastrointestinal disorders may cause the person to focus on his or her body or render him or her body unattractive enough to engage in sexual acts. A simpler formulation of the same concept is that repressed emotion or drives undergo by means of DMs transformation into physical symptoms, for example, aggression is transformed into chronic pain (Burns, 2000a). Another approach is suggested by an interesting study of the causes (organic and circumstantial) of falls in the elderly, which indicated that the fall is triggered by the individual's DM (Buffler & Seffert, 1989), i.e., the DM creates the disease. Recent psychophysiological studies lend support to the conceptualizations about the causal contribution of DMs to physical disease. The stress reaction that occurs when there is a discrepancy between the expected and the actual state of affairs involves the activation of endocrine, immunological and biochemical systems in the brain. Individuals with who cope directly and efficiently with the situation show the fast and short-lasting catecholamine response that brings the acute stress state to an end. However, individuals with high DMs, evoked by the meanings of the stimuli, may show a prolonged general activation that may develop into somatic disease (Eriksen et al., 1999).

Difficulties in Studying DMs in the Context of Physical Diseases

Beyond the difficulties of assessing DMs in general (Vaillant, 1998), there are two major problems characteristic for the study of DMs in the context of physical health and disease. The first has to do with the blurred boundaries between DMs and coping mechanisms. The issue of distinguishing between these two constructs has arisen also in other contexts (Cramer, 1998a; Haan, 1992), but it is particularly bothersome in regard to health where a large part of the research overlooks the distinction. In contrast to Vaillant (1998) who claimed that DMs and coping cannot be distinguished because the same mental mechanism can function as one or the other, Cramer (1998a) suggested to distinguish between DMs and coping strategies by means of the criteria of consciousness and intentionality. Accordingly, DMs and coping are assumed to represent adaptational mechanisms for managing adversity, functioning on two different levels, some (viz. DMs) less accessible to conscious and intentional decision making than others (viz. coping). Hence the difference consists more in the psychological processes involved than in the outcome. A further elaboration along these lines was undertaken by Kreitler and Kreitler (this volume). In addition to differing in consciousness, coping and DMs are assumed to differ in their function. Coping mechanisms are performance programs, often enacted overtly, for dealing with a clearly identified threat to the individual's psychological or physical survival. In contrast, DMs are conflict resolution programs, enacted mainly internally, for resolving a conflict between internally-represented forces in regard to issues concerning one's survival or well-being. This distinction may be of great significance in the context of physical health.

Another difficulty besetting the study of DMs in the context of health concerns the tendency to focus on defensiveness in general rather than on specific DMs. In a great many studies it has become habitual to refer to defensiveness or repressiveness or repression or even denial as general encompassing tendencies indicative of the individual's striving to handle threatening or stressful situations, without attempting to specify how precisely the self-protective defensiveness takes place. This practice may be due to mistrust of assessment tools of DMs, to theoretical biases (shunning the use of clinical or psychoanalytic terms such as projection or reaction formation, Cramer, 1998b), or to conceptual assumptions that place general defensiveness on a more primary or fundamental level than the specific later-evolving DMs (Weinberger, 1998). However it may be, relying on defensiveness in general may have retarded development of research into DMs in the context of health.

Finally, many studies deal with the role of repression in physical health, using the definition of repression as the defensive denial of unacceptable thoughts and negative affect, mainly anxiety, defined as low on anxiety (assessed by the Taylor Manifest Anxiety Scale) and high in defensiveness (assessed by the Marlowe-Crowne Social Desirability scale) (Weinberger, Schwartz & Davidson, 1979). The use of this measure is not fortuitous because from the very start findings made it likely that repression is related to somatic symptoms, increased susceptibility to certain illnesses and impaired immunological function (Weinberger et al., 1979). But the relation of repression to DMs is unclear.

DMs and Specific Physical Disorders

In this section representative studies of DMs in patients with specific physical disorders will be reviewed. The studies will refer to a variety of diseases, DMs and assessment methods. An attempt at grouping studies referring to the same kind of diseases will be made.

Pain

A study on migraine female patients using a DM inventory showed that the patients had higher scores on repression and self-aggrandizement than controls (Passchier et al., 1988). Chronic pain patients were found to be characterized by the DMs somatization and denial (assessed by the MMPI) (Monsen & Havik, 2001). Back pain patients used less coping and more defense than healthy controls. The DM Inventory revealed two defense clusters in this sample: cognitive defense and defensive hostility (Eriksen, Olff & Ursin, 1997).

Neurological Disorders

In a study of Alzheimer patients almost all patients were found to use DMs. Various DMs were applied in response to the threatening aspects of the onset of disease and the prospect of continuous deterioration, whereby the most frequently used DMs were partial or complete denial, dissociation of affect, vagueness and circumstantialities, and the less frequently used DMs were externalization, displacement, somatization and self-blame (Bahro, Silber, & Sunderland, 1995). Assessing DMs by means of the meta-contrast technique showed that Alzheimer patients exercised more complete denial with signs of anxiety, as compared with patients with frontotemporal degeneration, who manifested more projection with signs of depression (Johanson et al., 1990).

In patients with epileptic seizures the DMs of repression and isolation were found to be activated especially when the integrity of the identity is threatened (Mazza et al., 1994). Further, in terms of the Rorschach Index of Repressive Style, these same DMs were shown to be more frequent also in a sample of patients with multiple sclerosis than in healthy controls, especially in order to drive out of consciousness progression of the disease (Caviliglia et al., 1880).

Patients with Huntington Disease were found to use denial and to be unaware of their involuntary movements. The denial has unique characteristics since it refers specifically to the chorea but not to other aspects of their physical disorder, such as the physical slowing. Snowden et al (1998) assume that the denial has a physiological basis. The same phenomenon has been observed in Parkinson's disease (Snowden et al., 1998). Denial has been found also in regard to another neurological symptom (prosopagnosia) and in this case too has been interpreted not in dynamic terms but as a product of a functional dissociation between modular and central processes (Nachson, 1999).
Also in patients after brain injury the most common DM is denial in regard to the variety of neurological symptoms (amnesia, aphasia, motor dysfunctions etc.)

(Prigatano & Schacter, 1991). The denial may be complete or partial (e.g., the deficit is acknowledged but its impact underestimated), varies with the different types of brain injuries and is comprised of both cognitive and emotional components. The four main types of denial (or impaired self-awareness) are: frontal heteromodal syndrome (denial of deficits in planning, social judgment, and impulse control), parietal heteromodal syndrome (denial hemiparesis and of one side of one's environment), temporal heteromodal syndrome (denial of memory and language deficits) and occipital heteromodal syndrome (denial of deficit in recognizing objects) (Prigatano, 1999).

Gastrointestinal Disorders

In patients with Crohn's disease, denial and rationalization were found in all stages, while in the newly diagnosed patients the alexithymic and narcissistic defenses predominated, and in the more chronic patients the neurotic obsessive-compulsive and depressive defenses (assessed by the Clinical Assessment of Defense Mechanisms) (Küchenhoff, 1993). Comparing Crohn's patients with ulcerative colitis patients (16-90 years) showed that ulcerative colitis patients had lower levels of DMs (assessed by DMI) and reduced emotional stability (Costa et al., 1998).

A study with Chinese peptic ulcer patients administered the Defense Styles Questionnaire showed that they differed from healthy normal individuals in having weaker more defective DMs (Pan et al., 2000).

Rheumatic Disorders

A preliminary study with 11 rheumatic patients suggested that they had overwhelming anxiety over aggressive impulses, manifested also in the form of violent fantasies, and tended to apply the more archaic modes of defense, particularly feeling of omnipotence (Pipineli-Potamianou, 1976).

Patients with chronic fatigue syndrome were found to include a higher per cent (46%) of defensive high anxious individuals (MAS & Marlow Crowne) than healthy volunteers and chronic illness volunteers (Creswell & Chalder, 2001), i.e., they use ineffective DMs.

Diabetes

A Chinese sample of patients (30-69 years old) with type II diabetes mellitus was characterized on the basis of questionnaires as having immature DMs and avoidance of harmful events (Xu et al., 1996). On the basis of clinical interviews, type I diabetics were found to have a high level of suppression, and as compared to healthy controls - were lower on intellectualization and altruism, and did not differ from them in repression and rationalization (that were the highest DMs in both samples) (Jacobson et al., 1986).

Cardiovascular Disorders

In regard to hypertensives, the DM Inventory showed that they were significantly lower than healthy controls on the Turning Against Object but higher on Turning Against Self, Reversal and Principalization (Bekker, Hentschel & Reinsch, 1993). Several studies show an association between hypertension and inhibiting DMs (denial and repression) (Sommers & Greenberg, 1989), more specifically between systolic blood pressure (BP) (but not diastolic BP) and suppression in regard to anger, in males (Dimsdale et al., 1986).

In medical patients (cardiac patients after an MI or prior to bypass surgery and epileptic patients), high scorers on the Levine Denial of Illness Scale had lower BP reactivity in a stress interview than low scorers, although it is to be considered that denial of illness differs from repression (Warrenburg et al., 1989).

In healthy middle aged adults of both genders repressors showed greater systolic BP under both resting conditions and stress-inducing conditions of mental challenge (King et al., 1990). Yet a study based on archival data showed that in older adults there were no associations between repression and elevated BP or lipid profiles (O'Sullivan, 1999).

In patients with cardiovascular disease, confronted with the threat of death and the problems of increased dependence and reduced control, various DMs were observed, whose occurrence, stability and change depend on the premorbid personality and the extent of the physical damage (Ilic, Milic, & Stefanovic, 1997). In the first stage of the disease there is a tendency toward immature DMs, mainly denial, projection of hostility toward staff and family, and regression to the first level of primary oral dependence, manifested as marked dependence, passive receptive behavior and total reliance on the medical staff and their instructions (Ili & Apostolovi, 2002). While the denial helps to allay anxiety by disavowing feelings and thoughts that may be consciously intolerable (Hackett, Casem & Siverberg, 1974), aggression towards relatives and staff helps the patient to express anger against the unjust fate of having contracted the disease. More mature DMs may develop in the course of time, mainly suppression, humor and sublimation.

A psychodynamically-oriented study of middle-aged men, showed that extreme type-A individuals as compared with type-B persons had more insufficiency of repression, and more projection, reaction formation and denial, while a few had more disordered ego defenses (Venaelaeinen & Salonen, 1992).

In male cardiac patients undergoing rehabilitation, individuals scoring high on repressiveness scored lower on the Jenkins Activity Survey and the Cook-Medley Hostility scale than patients with high or low scores on negative affectivity; the scores of repression were stable over 3 months (Donollet, 1991).

Notably, Type A individuals use specific DMs – denial and projection - more than Type B individuals under high-stress conditions in which they also react with greater pulse rates and more changes in BP (Pittner, Houston & Spiridigliozzi, 1983).

A study with college students showed that though type-A individuals do not report more stress than type-B's their tendencies toward repression, limited awareness and narrow scanning contributed singly and together to increasing stress (Heilbrun & Renert, 1986).

Almost 15 years ago Mertens (1986) summarized the available data about the DMs of cardiovascular patients and concluded that their stereotypic DMs enable clustering them into two groups: the majority of patients (66%) use repression against their aggressiveness, whereas the others (34%) use the opposite DMs of acting out their aggressiveness. Accordingly, it is likely that not all psychological correlates diagnosed in cardiac patients appear in all patients, but rather that the former tend toward anxiety and depression, and the latter toward impulsiveness, hysteria and stress.

Some studies indicate that in the case of cardiovascular diseases DMs may play a role in regard to disease onset. DMs may be one factor that can contribute to increased coronary risk: Type A (assessed by Jenkins Activity Survey) when coupled with poor DMs increase risk for cardiovascular symptoms (Vickers et al.,

1981). More than a decade later Siegman (1994) concluded that expression of anger without using DMs is a risk factor for coronary heart disease.

Cancer

Women with papillomavirus-related precancerous cervical dysplasia and HIV-infected gay men undergoing long-term medical follow-up used defensive strategies (i.e., denial, mental and behavioral disengagement) especially if they tended to be highly vigilant and faced the threat of HIV (Miller et al., 1996).

A large body of research showed consistently that women with breast cancer use more than healthy controls the DM of repression in regard to affect (anger in particular) (e.g., Bahnson, 1981; Dattore, Shantz & Coyne, 1980; Gross, 1989; Hahn & Pettiti, 1988; Kneier & Temoshok, 1984; McKenna et al., 1999), and denial in general (Bahnson & Bahnson, 1969; Derogatis et al., 1979; Schonfield, 1975).

In breast cancer patients the repressive styles (Introversive, Cooperative and Respectful, assessed by the Millon Behavioral Health Inventory) were more frequent than in a sample of healthy women, and in metastatic breast cancer patients the score on the Respectful scale was even clinically significant (Goldstein & Antoni, 1989). Also in a further sample, women with breast cancer scored higher than healthy controls on scales assessing emotional defensiveness, i.e., tendencies to inhibit, deny, suppress and repress their emotions, regardless of age and whether they were in treatment or not (Fernandez-Ballesteros, Ruiz & Garde, 2000).

In breast cancer patients, ineffective DMs against aggressive impulses were found (Lilja et al., 1998). Another study showed that the DMs of breast cancer women were not repression of all emotions but rather repression of aggression and impulsiveness, manifesting a reaction to the disease rather than personality characteristics predisposing to breast cancer (Servaes et al., 1999).

In breast cancer patients repressive DMs appeared to be related to an advanced stage of the disease (Forsen, 1990). In general, denial in cancer patients seems to be more salient in the first and final stages of the disease than in the interim ones (Kreitler, 1999). Also age may play a role in regard to the incidence of DMs as shown by the finding that younger (premenopausal) patients were characterized by reaction formation more than the older patients (Lilja et al., 1998).

It has often been claimed that cancer patients tend toward denial. In evaluating this claim it is necessary to take into account studies that have examined the tendency toward denial after the onset of the disease, at about the time of diagnosis as well as prior to the onset (i.e., retrospective, quasi-prospective and prospective studies). A review of 55 such studies showed that the tendency for denial was indeed characteristic of cancer patients of various diagnoses: the claim was fully supported by 70.9% of the studies, partly by 14.5% and not supported by 14.6% (Kreitler, 1999; see also Kreitler, 2003).

There is evidence that repressiveness in breast cancer patients may be a reaction to the anxiety evoked by the disease rather than a personality tendency antedating the diagnosis. Comparing the repressiveness of women before and after a biopsy for breast cancer and for nonmalignant control surgery showed that prior to surgery all women had a comparable level of repressiveness, but that after surgery there was significant rise in the repressiveness of only those women who got the diagnosis of malignancy (Kreitler, Kreitler & Chaitchik, 1993). Hence, it is likely that the repressiveness reflected a rise in defensiveness against anxiety evoked by the diagnosis.

In the case of breast cancer patients, defensiveness was manifested also in the decision-making process regarding surgical treatment: most women did not delve into the process but halted as soon as possible and left the decision to their surgeons using satisficing (accepting the first tolerable alternative), complacency (accepting advice without questioning) and defensive avoidance (rationalizing and avoiding discussion) (Reaby, 1998).

Defensiveness affects also the screening tests. In the case of screening for cervical cancer, women (age 20-66) who used defensive avoidance tended to be over due for their pap test (White et al., 1994).

Tendencies toward similar DMs were found also in other groups of cancer patients. In colon cancer patients a tendency for denial was documented by means of a Cognitive Orientation Questionnaire (Figer et al., 2002). In adult and adolescent leukemia patients the most frequently used DMs are intellectualism, rationalization and minimization (assessed by the Defense Mechanisms Rating Scale) (Grulke et al. 2001). In adolescent cancer patients (12-18 yrs old) there was a significantly higher number of repressors (high defensiveness and low anxiety) than in a comparable healthy high school sample of children (Canning, Canning & Boyce, 1992). Also in children with cancer (7-16 yrs old), defensiveness was found to be higher than in healthy controls and attenuated their self-reported depression scores, increasing the discrepancy between their scores and the ratings of depression provided by their parents (Phipps & Srivastava, 1999).

Various Health Problems

A preliminary study with bronchial asthma indicated the salience of the DM identification with the aggressor (Gervais, 1966).

In patients with type II Raynaud's phenomenon, inhibition and narcissistic defenses were identified (by applying Shentoub's grid method for interpreting TAT stories) (Baudin, Consoli, & Bayle, 1990).

In elderly patients (71-76 yrs old) before the cataract operation, the stress caused by poor vision was correlated with the DMs of suppression, regression, isolation and denial, whereas after the surgical restoration of vision the most common DMs were suppression, intellectualization, isolation, humor and rationalization (Fagerstroem, 1992).

Pregnant women participating in a Tay-Sachs screening program coped with the threat of the situation by "affective defense" (which is akin to denial). (Ben-Sira & Padeh, 1978).

A study that compared orthopedically handicapped males and females to physically normal males and females on the DM Inventory showed that handicapped males used Turning Against Self and Reversal more than normal males and Turning Against Object less than normal males and females, whereas normal males showed equal preference for each of the DM clusters : Turning Against Object (i.e., externalized aggression), Turning Against Self, Projection, Principalization (i.e., rationalization), and Reversal (i.e., reaction formation) (Ramteke & Mrinal, 1984).

An interesting study focused on the role of DMs (assessed by the Plutchik questionnaire) in patients and healthy controls. In the healthy group the DMs were correlated more with MMPI scales and 16PF factors, whereas in the patient group there was only one stable correlation (between repression and depression on the MMPI). The strain of DMs was higher in the patient group than in the healthy controls; healthy women resembled in their DMs more the patient group than the healthy men (Rotenberg & Michailov, 1992-3).

In sum, the reviewed findings about the relation of DMs to physical disease support Hentschel's (1993) basic hypothesis that different psychosomatic illnesses will show different profiles in different personality domains, including DMs.

Age and Culture Effects

For evaluating the effects of DMs on various diseases, it is recommended to consider also the effects of culture and age on DMs. Repression was found to be more characteristic (prevalent) in African-American women than in Caucasian women with newly diagnosed Stage II and recurrent breast cancer, irrespective of religiosity and education level (Hunt, 2001). Some studies show that persons with feminine sex-role orientations use more repressive, self-blaming DMs which may affect the propensity toward breast cancer (Liste, 1999).

The use of DMs is also affected by age. In samples of men and women volunteers (with number of participants ranging from 182 to 477) aged 20 to 92, age was correlated positively with principalization, reversal, repression, denial, intellectualization and self-sacrifice, negatively with turning against object, projection and maladaptive action, and unrelated to turning against self, regression, displacement, projection, doubt, image distortion, and adaptive responding (Costa, Zonderman & McCrae, 1991). These findings contrast however with those of other studies that found with age decrease in immature defenses (projection, unrealistic fantasy) and increase in mature defenses (sublimation, suppression) (Valliant et al., 1986) and a general decrease with age of escapist coping strategies (Aldwin, 1991) and avoidance coping (Feifel & Strack, 1989). This difference may be due to the way in which the stressful situation is grasped by the older people (as controllable – and hence evoking problem-focused coping, or as uncontrollable and hence evoking emotion-focused coping) (Irion & Blanchard-Fields, 1987).

Effects of DMs on Disease Course

DMs appear to be not merely correlates of the disease but may also play a role in regard to the course of disease and prognosis. Thus, in female migraine patients self-aggrandizement was related to headache frequency and reduced temporal blood flow (Passchier et al., 1988). In patients with chronic fatigue syndrome improvement was associated with obsessional and healthy neurotic defense levels, as assessed by the Defense Mechanism Rating Scale (Salzstein et al., 1998).

In persons (16-62 years) who had undergone surgery for herniated lumbar disc, follow-up of 6 months after surgery showed that patients with poor operational outcome used the DMs of regression, rationalization, withdrawal and passive resignation (Fulde, Junge, & Ahrens, 1995).

It has been observed that the use of specific DMs affects the effectiveness of therapy. Thus, in patients with arterial hypertension the effectiveness of anti-hypertensive therapy was limited in those with the Disease Denial-Rationalization syndrome, who deny their hypertension and the need for therapy (Podell, Kent & Keller, 1976). In chronic pain patients who have undergone a 4-week pain program, the repressors recovered more poorly than the others, as assessed by scores of depression and pain severity. This finding indicates that repression may interfere with the patients' recovery (Burns, 2000a).

In patients with cardiovascular disease denial in the short run may not affect prognosis negatively if the patient follows treatment recommendations. In fact, inability to use denial in the coronary care unit was found to be related to early death (Froese et al., 1974; Hackett et al., 1968). However, in the long run, denial may have deleterious effects. Persistent denial was shown to be related to poor outcomes insofar as patients may ignore symptoms of an impending cardiac event, or fail to seek and comply with recommendations for treatment and rehabilitation (Froese et al., 1974). Accordingly, denial may contribute to mortality from coronary artery disease. In order to minimize the danger of cardiac death of these patients, family physicians are urged to screen those who are prone to inappropriate denial and use nonthreatening diagnostic and medical approaches in an attempt to reduce their anxiety (Fields, 1989).

Similar maladaptive effects of denial on disease outcomes were reported in diabetic and hemodialysis patients (Farberow, 1980; Goldstein, 1980).

In recent years interest has focused on the effects of denial on prognosis in cancer patients. A review of the relevant methodologically acceptable studies (n=24) showed that in 50% denial was related to a negative course of the disease, in 16.7% to a positive course, in 4.2% to mixed results, and in 29.2% it was unrelated to the course of disease (Kreitler, 1999).

Part of the negative effect of denial on the course of disease may be due to the fact that denial may cause the patient to delay addressing a doctor and thus getting on time the appropriate treatment (Katz et al., 1970; Kreitler, 1999).

There are only few studies that deal with the effects of other DMs on prognosis in cancer. In regard to breast cancer, daydreaming and self-comforting fantasies were related to bad prognosis (Jensen, 1987), whereas DMs against aggressive impulses were related to better prognosis (Lilja et al., 1998).

Effects of DMs on Adjustment to the Disease

There is evidence about the relation of DMs to adjustment to the disease and the accompanying treatments. In medically hospitalized patients, the use of effective defenses was related to better adjustment, and the defense mechanism ineffectiveness was related to psychological distress (independently assessed) (Katz et al., 1970; Knight et al., 1979; Wolff, Hofer and Mason, 1964). A study on the DMs used by individuals exposed to the stress of testing positive for AIDS showed that an active-resistant attitude led to more adaptive consequences than denial and passive resignation (Weiner, Nilsson-Schoennesson, & Clement, 1989). In patients who had undergone reconstructive vascular surgery for occlusive disease, those who were poorly adjusted 1 year post operatively differed from those who were better adjusted in being limited in DMs to magical thinking, repression and denial (Boyd, Yaeger & McMillan, 1973).

In chronic pain patients, the high scorers on repression (assessed by anxiety scores and defensiveness assessed by the Balanced Inventory of Desirable Responding) scored comparably with dysfunctional patients and higher than adaptive copers on somatic symptoms of depression, pain severity and perceived disability; they scored lower than dysfunctional patients and comparably with adaptive copers on depression, anxiety and anger; repressors also reported more pain severity and perceived disability relative to their negative affect whereas in the dysfunctional and adaptive copers no such disparities were evident. Hence, chronic pain patients who are repressors readily endorse physical symptoms yet report low levels of emotional distress (Burns et al., 2001). Another study with chronic pain patients (in which repression was assessed by the anxiety and Lie scales of the MMPI-2) found that repressors performed poorly on lifting capacity (Burns, 2000a).

In male cardiac patients undergoing rehabilitation (31-76 years), repression was related to lower subjective distress, manifested in fewer health complaints, but no relation was found between tendency toward repression and cardiovascular fitness as assessed by exercise stress testing (Denollet, 1991).

Cardiac, HIV/AIDS and breast cancer patients providing unrealistically positive reports of their well-being, had better health status (i.e., reported better status) (Helgeson & Taylor, 1993; Taylor et al. 1991, 1992; Wood, Taylor & Lichtman,

1985), although this indicated only subjective evaluation of adjustment was not correlated with outcome measures in terms of external criteria (Cramer, 1998a; Wood et al. 1985).

Studies of cardiac patients found inverse relations between the use of denial, as rated by clinician, and independent ratings of anxiety and depression (Froese et al., 1974; Hackett et al., 1968).

The evidence shows that in breast cancer patients short-term denial reduced psychological distress (Katz et al., 1970). Again, repression and avoidance at the stage of surgery for breast cancer predicted more negative emotions 6 to 8 months following chemotherapeutic treatment, but repression was associated with better adjustment to the illness (Galbadon, Mayoral & Paez, 1993). The same holds in regard to later phases of the disease. Repressive DMs were more salient in advanced stages of the disease and were related negatively to depression (Forsen, 1990).

In cancer patients, repressors (high defensiveness, low distress) reported fewer and less severe side effects of treatment and less information exchange (communication) with significant others (Ward, Leventhal & Love, 1988). In leukemic patients scheduled for bone marrow transplantation (BMT), DMs assessed prior to BMT were shown to affect adaptation in the BMT situation; adaptation was better when the patients had immature regression-supporting DMs than passive-aggressive DMs that tended to evoke negative reactions on the part of the health professionals (Grulke et al., 2001).

In Chinese cancer patients more patients than healthy controls (with hand injuries) had either very high or very low scores of death anxiety (assessed by Templer's Death Anxiety Questionnaire), whereby a certain level of death anxiety in patients with a life-threatening disease is considered to be a positive sign of coping. The patients with abnormally high or low death anxiety had higher scores on the two immature DMs Autistic Fantasy and Passive Aggression (assessed by Bond's Defense Style Questionnaire) (Ho & Shiu, 1995).

In children too DMs play a role in adjusting to disease, though not in disease course. Repression is a DM that serves adaptation also in children with cancer. It starts around the period of diagnosis and is maintained all through the treatment period, for at least 12 months (Phipps et al., 2001). In children with cancer (8-18 yrs old), defensiveness predicted better emotional adjustment (Grootenhuis & Last, 2001). Similarly, in adolescent cancer patients (12-18 yrs old), repression was associated with lower levels of reported depression and distress (Canning, Canning & Boyce, 1992).

Effects of DMs on Physiological Processes

It is likely that the health effects of DMs are related to the physiologic correlates of DMs. Several studies focused on physiological correlates of specific DMs. Most of the data refer however to denial or repression. In one study the neuroendocrine and cardiovascular responses associated with repression were investigated. The findings showed that repression is associated with greater adrenocorticotropic (ACTH) responses and higher systolic blood pressure levels, greater heart rate and rate-pressure product responses while performing stress-evoking tasks (e.g., public speaking, mental arithmetic), and with the highest discrepancy between these physiological responses and self-reported anxiety (Al'Absi, 1995). Another study showed repression is associated with elevated eosinophile counts, serum glucose levels, and decreased monocyte counts. These findings support the opioid peptide hypothesis linking the reduced emotional experience of pain and distress (repression) with the reduced resistance to diseases (Jamner, Schwartz & Leigh, 1988).

A major characteristic of individuals high on repression is that when they are put in potentially stressful situations they report low levels of distress but are physiologically very aroused (e.g., increased heart rate and BP) and manage to avoid experiencing much anxiety on the conscious level (Myers, 2000).

The manner in which DMs affect perception through brain processes has been studied by investigating letter recognition by means of a tachistoscope under three conditions (neutral, negative emotions, positive emotions) in individuals identified as high or low in repression (assessed by the DM Inventory). During both emotional conditions, the high repression group manifested significant performance enhancement in the right visual field; during the negative emotion, the high repression group manifested decrement in the left visual field while the low repression group manifested decrement in the right visual field (Waldinger & Van Strien, 1995). Plasma levels of the beta-carboline norharman were negatively correlated with the DMs of principalization and repression, and positively with coping strategies involving palliation (Verheij et al., 1997).

In young adults (mean age 32.9) resting plasma beta-endorphin levels were positively correlated with defensiveness in men but not in women; high self-deception was associated with naloxone-induced hyperalgesia, but not in low-deception subjects. These findings support the hypothesis that repression is associated with endorphinergic dysregulation (Jamner & Leigh, 1999). However in older subjects (59-79) defensiveness was correlated negatively with endorphin levels, and reached significance only in the women's sample (Kline et al., 1998).

In a sample of chronic pain patients, repressors had significantly higher sympathetic arousal (on the skin conductance measure) than non-repressors and than individuals with high anxiety at baseline, under stress, and during recovery (Stafford, 1997).

In women with breast cancer as well as healthy women, those who scored low on distress (and hence were suspect of using a repressive style) had lower cytotoxic activity than those reporting high levels of distress (Bovbjerg & Valdimarsdottir, 1993). Further, in cancer patients of different diagnoses decreases in distress were correlated with increases in absolute numbers of white blood cells and parallel increases in plasma levels of cortisol (Schedlowski et al., 1994) and increases in the number and cytotoxic activity of large granular lymphocytes as natural killer cells (Fawzy et al., 1990). Physiologic effects of this kind may affect positively the course of disease (Bovbjerg & Valdimarsdottir, 1998).

A Study on DMs and Coping in Cancer Patients

This section presents findings of a study with cancer patients that focused on exploring in some detail interrelations between DMs and coping on the one hand and two sets of characteristics on the other hand: first, demographic and medical ones, and second, quality of life effects. The number of participants was 252 (203 women, 49 males): mean age 57.39 years (*SD*=14.8), mean number of years of education 13.65 (*SD*=5.88), number of different diagnoses 19, the most frequent ones being breast cancer (*n*=126) and colon cancer (*n*=34); in all four disease stages; and different time durations since diagnosis (with 1 year as a cutting point, there were 130 over 1 year, with 5 years as a cutting point, there were 45 over 5 years). The data was obtained by administering to all participants the three following questionnaires: First, a questionnaire providing demographic and medical information. Second, 'The defensive coping questionnaire' (Kreitler & Kreitler, 2000), whose reliability and validity have been pretested and found to be highly satisfactory: it includes 48 items, representing defensive responses identified on the basis of interviews with cancer patients. Each item has 4 response alternatives (labeled very true, true, not true, not at all true; scored 4 to 1, respectively). The items are clustered (on the basis of factor analyses and clustering procedures) into 21 primary-level clusters (1.-21.), and then further into 6 secondary-level clusters (A.-F.). Each of the clusters is defined by the assumed goal or function expressed by the items, in line with the judgments of clinical psychologists. The primary level clusters were:

1. Fighting the disease,
2. Searching for new solutions,
3. Strengthening health,
4. Preoccupation with the disease,
5. Coming to terms with the situation,
6. Humor,
7. Drawing practical conclusions,
8. Denial,
9. Dissociation,
10. Distraction,
11. Focusing on others,
12. Looking for support,
13. Religiosity,
14. Relying on experts,
15. Changing oneself and one's personality,
16. Developing spirituality,
17. Focusing on emotions,
18. Self understanding,
19. Wish fulfillments,
20. Self improvement,
21. Despair and helplessness.

The secondary-level clusters are:

A. Focusing on the disease and strengthening health (clusters 1-4);
B. Coming to terms with the situation (clusters 5-7);
C. Denial (clusters 8-11);
D. Strengthening oneself and seeking support (clusters 12-14);
E. Psychological change (clusters 15-20);
F. Helplessness (cluster 21).

In addition, an index of activity reflected in the defenses endorsed by the patient was computed as well as the total number of different defenses the patient has at his or her disposal (i.e., items scored 3 or 4). The third tool was the Quality of Life (QOL) Questionnaire-Adult version (Kreitler & Kreitler, 1999). This inventory has high reliability and validity (range .80 to .97). It includes 60 items, each with 4 response alternatives scored 1 to 4, providing a total summative score (range 60 to 260) and scores on the following scales: functioning in the family, negative feelings, positive feelings, confusion and bewilderment, cognitive functioning, health worries, pain, friends and social ties, body image, sexuality, sense of mastery and independence, self image, meaningfulness, and stress.

Table 21.1: *Significant differences of medical characteristics in defensive coping variables*

Defensive Coping Varia bles[a]		*Means*	*SDs*	*t/F*[a]	*Sig.*
Diagnosis					
6. Humor	Breast	2.62	1.03	2.186	.034
	Colon	2.13	1.11		
10. Distraction	Breast	2.95	1.08	2.947	.004
	Colon	2.29	1.13		
11. Focusing on others	Breast	2.35	.81	2.038	.043
	Colon	2.03	.73		
16. Developing spirituality	Breast	2.61	1.09	3.208	.002
	Colon	1.94	1.03		
B. Coming to terms with the situation	Breast	2.78	.50	2.089	.038
	Colon	2.56	.53		
C. Denial	Breast	2.79	.48	2.468	.014
	Colon	2.53	.66		
E. Psychological change	Breast	2.66	.56	1.985	.049
	Colon	2.43	.53		
Stage of disease					
8. Denial	I	3.19	.60	2.621	.050
	II	2.88	.74		
	III	2.84	.72		
	IV	3.09	.59		
13. Religiosity	I	2.02	1.11	3.800	.011
	II	2.64	1.17		
	III	2.58	1.22		
	IV	1.93	.93		
Time since diagnosis					
1. Fighting the disease	Up to 1 year	2.43	.80	4.980	.000
	More than 1 year	1.91	.71		
1. Fighting the disease	Up to 5 years	2.23	.79	3.622	.000
	More than 5 years	1.74	.67		
4. Preoccupation with the disease	Up to 1 year	2.49	.77	3.710	.000
	More than 1 year	2.09	.76		
8. Denial	Up to 1 year	2.79	.75	-3.083	.002
	More than 1 year	3.09	.65		
10. Distraction	Up to 1 year	2.43	1.18	-3.653	.000
	More than 1 year	3.02	1.05		
12. Looking for support	Up to 1 year	2.81	1.17	2.445	.015
	More than 1 year	2.42	1.09		

Table 21.1 *continued*

19. Wish fulfillment	Up to 1 year	2.55	.69	-3.444	.001
	More than 1 year	2.90	.72		
A. Focusing on the disease and strengthening health	Up to 1 year	2.16	.52	2.795	.006
	More than 1 year	1.95	.55		
A. Focusing on the disease and strengthening health	Up to 5 years	2.07	.55	1.929	.050
	More than 5 years	1.89	.51		
C. Denial	Up to 1 year	2.57	.55	-3.787	.000
	More than 1 year	2.84	.47		

Note. The results presented in regard to breast and colon are based on contrasts by the Duncan test, performed following a significant F value of an Anova in which all diagnoses were included.
[a] Defensive coping variables preceded by numbers represent primary level clusters, those preceded by letters represent secondary level clusters.
[b] The values in regard to diagnosis and stage are F values, in all other cases – *t* values.

Table 21.1 presents significant differences in defensive coping related to medical variables. It shows the effects of diagnosis, stage and time since diagnosis. Patients with breast cancer score higher than those with colon cancer on the primary-level clusters of humor, distraction, focusing on others, and developing spirituality a well as on the secondary-level clusters of coming to terms with the situation, denial and psychological change. As expected, denial is higher in the first and fourth disease stages, whereas religiosity is higher in the second and third disease stages. Notably, the clusters of fighting the disease, preoccupation with the disease, looking for support and the secondary-level cluster of focusing on the disease and strengthening health are more salient when the time since diagnosis is short, whereas denial, distraction and wish-fulfillment become dominant after longer time durations since diagnosis. Notably, denial may co-exist with other defenses.

Table 21.2 presents significant differences in defensive coping related to demographical variables. Most of the differences relate to age and education. Notably, in all the defensive coping variables the younger patients score higher than the older: the primary-level clusters of fighting the disease, searching for new solutions, religiosity, changing oneself and one's personality, developing spirituality, focusing on emotions, and self improvement; the secondary-level clusters of focusing on the disease and strengthening health, strengthening oneself and seeking support and psychological change.

Table 21.2: *Significant differences of demographic variables and defensive coping variables*

Defensive Coping Variables[a]		*Means*	*SDs*	*t/F*	*Sig.*
Age					
1. Fighting the disease	AM 56	1.90	.78	-4.433	.000
	BM 56	2.33	.71		
2. Searching for new solutions	AM 56	1.61	.64	-3.538	.000
	BM 56	1.93	.73		
13. Religiosity	AM 56	2.08	1.13	-3.608	.000
	BM 56	2.60	1.09		
15. Changing oneself and one's personality	AM 56	1.86	.83	-5.805	.000
	BM 56	2.50	.85		
16. Developing spirituality	AM 56	2.34	1.13	-2.156	.032
	BM 56	2.66	1.10		
17. Focusing on emotions	AM 56	2.99	.71	-2.087	.038
	BM 56	3.17	.60		
20. Self improvement	AM 56	2.06	.85	-2.571	.011
	BM 56	2.35	.87		
A. Focusing on the disease and strengthening health	AM 56	1.89	.53	-4.051	.000
	BM 56	2.17	.53		
D. Strengthening oneself and seeking support	AM 56	2.59	.64	-2.625	.009
	BM 56	2.80	.61		
E. Psychological change	AM 56	2.50	.58	-3.120	.002
	BM 56	2.74	.55		
Index of Activity	AM 56	33.23	15.88	-3.647	.000
	BM 56	40.32	14.56		
Number of different defenses	AM 56	9.64	4.57	-4.008	.000
	BM 56	11.88	4.16		
	Years of education				
3. Strengthening health	AM 12	2.61	1.04	2.284	.023
	BM 12	2.19	1.13		
6. Humor	AM 12	2.64	1.08	2.538	.012
	BM 12	2.17	1.10		
14. Relying on experts	AM 12	3.05	.80	-2.688	.008
	BM 12	3.40	.70		
D. Strengthening oneself and seeking support	AM 12	2.66	.63	-2.440	.015
	BM 12	2.92	.57		

Table 21.2 *continued*

Marital status					
1. Fighting the disease	Married	2.10	.76	4.079	.003
	Single	2.02	.63		
	Divorced	2.17	.91		
	Widowed	1.83	.70		
	Separated	3.67	.58		
4. Preoccupation with the disease	Married	2.31	.76	2.565	.039
	Single	1.85	.73		
	Divorced	2.32	.81		
	Widowed	2.02	.76		
	Separated	2.67	1.53		

Note. AM = Above median; BM = Below median.

[a] Defensive coping variables preceded by numbers represent primary level clusters, thos- preceded by letters represent secondary level clusters.

[b] The values in regard to marital status are F values, in all other cases t values.

Not surprisingly, they also score higher on the activity index and on the number of different defenses. It is of interest to note that education level contributes to enhancing the defensive clusters of strengthening health, humor, relying on experts and strengthening oneself and seeking support. All these reflect active efforts on the part of the patient. Fighting the disease and preoccupation with the disease are particularly high in the patients who have been separated from their spouses, perhaps because they cannot rely on the help of the spouses but only on themselves. Notably, there were no differences in defensive coping variables between the genders.

Table 21.3, in the Appendix, presents significant differences in defensive coping related to QOL variables. The sheer amount of the presented information testifies to the close relations between the defensive and QOL variables. We will focus on a few dominant findings. It is notable that the primary-level and secondary-level clusters of denial are related significantly and positively to the summative score and to all QOL scales except the following two scales: family functioning and sexuality. This reflects the central role of denial in the context of living with a serious disease. Further, it may also indicate the diversified role of denial in this context: due to its salience, it may become intertwined with the most varied domains of life – ranging from cognition to emotions, from social relations to stress, encompassing self image, body image, mastery, meaningfulness, and health. In regard to each domain, the contribution of denial is positive. No fewer relations were obtained for the cluster of helplessness, which could be interpreted as reflecting the minimal degree of the use of defenses. Helplessness was correlated significantly and negatively with the summative score on QOL and all of its scales.

Each of the other defensive coping variables was related to several specific scales of QOL. Thus, patients who tended to use the defense of humor had an overall higher score on QOL as well as more positive feelings, more friends, and a more positive self image.

Positive effects were obtained also for the defensive measure of wish fulfillments. Patients who tended to use wish fulfillments had a higher score on the overall QOL, as well as on the scales of positive feelings, confusion, health worries, friends, body image, sense of mastery, self-image, meaningfulness, and stress.

On the other hand, patients who tended to use religion as a defensive measure had a lower overall score of QOL and more negative feelings, health worries, pain and stress. Hence, religion seems not to be an efficient defensive measure in this context.

Further, the defensive measure of changing oneself and one's personality was also related negatively to overall QOL and a broad range of scales (negative feelings, positive feelings, confusion, cognition, pain, sexuality, mastery, self-image, meaningfulness and stress). As could be expected, rejecting oneself to the point of changing oneself indicates a defensive measure that does not contribute positively to one's QOL. Even the defensive measure of self-improvement, which also indicates rejection of oneself, is related negatively to negative emotions.

The most convincing evidence for the important role of DMs in the context of coping with disease is based on the findings in regard to the clusters of "fighting the disease", "preoccupation with the disease" and "Focusing on the disease and strengthening oneself". It is to be noted that these three clusters are related negatively to the overall QOL as well as to a broad range of scales (to all except friends and meaningfulness): negative feelings, positive feelings, confusion, cognition, health worries, pain, sexuality, sense of mastery, self-image and stress, and the first two clusters also to body-image. Notably the three coping clusters indicate minimal denial and defensiveness, reflecting a head-on attack on the disease. The fact that they were related negatively to so many domains of

QOL implies that at least insofar as QOL is concerned defensiveness is preferable to no defensiveness, and denial to preoccupation with the disease.

In sum, the reported findings of the study about defensive coping indicate that defenses in general and specific measures in particular play an important role in the context of living with a serious disease as cancer. The general conclusion is that denial in its different forms contributes positively to the patient's QOL, and is often applied with other measures, such as humor and wish fulfillments whose contribution is also positive. Negative effects on QOL were observed for preoccupation with the disease, helplessness and changing oneself. In particular the former two reflect a minimal use of defensive measures.

General Conclusions

The review of studies and data presented in this chapter indicates the important role played by DMs in regard to disease. The effects of DMs may be detected in the cognitive, emotional, behavioral and physiological domains.

Denial in its various forms seems to be a most dominant DM, probably not only because it was studied most frequently. However, in addition it seems justified to conclude that specific DMs tend to be used by patients with particular diseases. This may be due either to the particular psychodynamic understructure of the disease or to the specific psychosocial problems related to the disease. Several DMs seem to have a broader range of application than others, e.g., wish fulfillment as compared with humor. Again, some DMs affect the patients' QOL negatively, e.g., changing oneself. Avoiding the use of DMs, manifested as preoccupation with the disease or as helplessness, is related to negative effects on the patients' QOL.

There is a broad range of issues in regard to which DMs are applied in the context of disease. These include daily life difficulties, loss of independence, impaired self-image and body image, and possibly fear of death. It is likely that each problem may call forth the use of different DMs.

It seems that DMs differ from coping strategies in the context of disease. While DMs target mainly internal conflicts, coping strategies seem to implement the solutions. The conflicts may refer to the dynamics underlying the disease, or to problems arising because of the disease (e.g., loss of independence, existential threat). Thus, it is likely that a specific DM may be related to different coping strategies, for example, denial may enable both an active and a passive coping strategy.

DMs emerged first in the medical domain of physical diseases. They were transported by Freud into the clinical domain of psychological and psychopathological disorders. In view of the important and varied roles that DMs were shown to play in regard to physical disorders, it is evident that the time has come to introduce DMs as a central construct in health psychology, the domain that integrates medicine with psychology.

References

Aldwin, C. M. (1991). Does age affect the stress and coping process? Implications of age differences in perceived control. *Journal of Gerontology, 46*, 174-180.

Al'Absi, M. N. (1995). Pituitary-adrenocortical and cardiovascular responses to extended mental and interpersonal stressors: The role of repressive-defensive coping style. *Dissertation Abstracts International*: Section B: The Sciences and Engineering, 56 (5-B), 2846.

Bahnson, C. B. (1981). Stress and cancer: The state of the art part 2. *Psychosomatics, 22*, 207-220.

Bahnson, M. B., & Bahnson, C. B. (1969). Ego defenses in cancer patients. *Annals of the New York Academy of Science, 164*, 546-559.

Bahro, M., Silber, E., & Sunderland, T. (1995). How do patients with Alzheimer's disease cope with their illness? A clinical experience report. *Journal of the American Geriatrics Society, 43*, 41-46.

Baudin, M. L, Consoli, S. M., Silla, M., & Bayle, O. (1990). Contribution a l'etude du phenomene de Raynaud par le test du TAT. *Psychologie Medicale, 22*, 19-25.

Bekker, F. J., Hentschel, U., & Reinsch, M. (1993). Attitudes toward illness and health and defense mechanisms in psychosomatic patients. In U. Hentschel, G. Smith, W. Ehlers & J. G. Draguns (Eds.), *The concept of defense mechanisms in contemporary psychology* (pp. 373-388). New York: Springer-Verlag.

Bellini, M. (1973). Gastric and intestinal somatization of psychic conflicts. *Medicina Psicosomatica, 18*, 3-23.

Ben-Sira, Z., & Padeh, B. (1978). "Instrumental coping" and "affective defense": An additional perspective in health promoting behavior. *Social Science and Medicine, 12,* 163-168.

Blumberg, S. J. (2000). Guarding against threatening HIV prevention messages: An information-processing model. *Health Education and Behavior, 27*, 780-795.

Bovbjerg, D. H., & Valdimarsdottir, H. B. (1993). Familial cancer, emotional distress, and low natural cytotoxiv activity in healthy women. *Annals of Oncology, 4*, 745-752.

Bovbjerg, D. H., & Valdimarsdottir, H. B. (1998). Psychoneuroimmunology: Implications for psycho-oncology. In J. C. Holland (Ed.) *Psycho-oncology* (pp.125-134). New York: Oxford University Press.

Boyd, I., Yeager, M., & McMillan, M. (1973). Personality styles in the postoperative course. *Psychosomatic Medicine, 35*, 23-40.

Buffler, P., & Seffert, P. (1989). La chute de la personne agée: Un trouble de conduite? [Falls in old age: A behavioral disorder?] *Psychologie Medicale, 21*, 1158-1160.

Burns, J. W., Kubilus, A., Bruehl, S., & Harden, R. N. (2001). A fourth empirically derived cluster of chronic pain patients based on the Multidimensional Pain Inventory: Evidence for repression within the dysfunctional group. *Journal of Consulting and Clinical Psychology, 69*, 663-673.

Burns, J. W. (2000a). Repression predicts outcome following multidisciplinary treatment of chronic pain. *Health Psychology, 19*, 75-84.

Burns, J. W. (2000b). Repression in chronic pain: An idea worth recovering. *Applied and Preventive Psychology, 9*, 173-190.

Canning, E. H., Canning, R. D., & Boyce, W. T. (1992). Depressive symptoms and adaptive style in children with cancer. *Journal of the American Academy of Child and Adolescent Psychiatry, 31*, 1120-1124.

Cassileth, B. R., Lusk, B. J., Strouse, T. B., Miller, D. S., Brown, L. L., Cross, P. A., & Tenaglia, A. N. (1984). Psychosocial status in chronic illness. *The New England Journal of Medicine, 311*, 506-511.

Caviglia, C., Crisi, A., Azzoni, A., Mazza, S., et al. (1990). The mechanism of repression and isolation in multiple sclerosis as regulators of personality system: a clinical study. *Schweizer Archiv für Neurologie und Psychiatrie, 14*, 206-215.

Costa, E., Papa, M., Gentili, G., Burla, F., & de Maria, S. (1998). I meccanismi di difensa nelle coliti inflammatorie croniche [Defense mechanisms in inflammatory chronic colitis]. *Medicina Psicosomatica, 43*, 139-148.

Costa, P. T., Jr., Zonderman, A. B., & McCrae, R. R. (1991). Personality, defense, coping and adaptation in older adulthood. In E. M. Cummings, A. L. Greene, & K. H. Karraker (Eds.), *Life-span developmental psychology: Perspectives on stress and coping* (pp. 277-293). NJ: Hillsdale, Erlbaum.

Couzijn, A. L., Ros, W. J. G., & Winubst, J. A. M. (1990). Cancer. In A. A. Kapstein, H. M. van der Ploeg, R. Garssen & R. Beunderman (Eds.), *Behavioral medicine* (pp. 231-247). New York: Wiley.

Cramer, P. (1998a) Coping and defense mechanisms: What's the difference? *Journal of Personality, 66*, 919-946.

Cramer, P. (1998b). Defensiveness and defense mechanisms. *Journal of Personality, 66*, 879-894.

Creswell, C., & Chalder, T. (2001). Defensive coping styles in chronic fatigue syndrome. *Journal of Psychosomatic Research, 5*, 607-610.

Dattore, P. J., Shantz, R. C., & Coyne, L. (1980). Premorbid personality differentiation of cancer and noncancer groups: a test of the hypothesis of cancer proneness. *Journal of Consulting and Clinical Psychology, 43*, 388-394.

Denollet, J. (1991). Negative affectivity and repressive coping: Pervasive influence on self-reported mood, health and coronary-prone behavior. *Psychosomatic Medicine, 53*, 538-556.

Derogatis, L. R., Abeloff, M. D., & Melisaratos, N. (1979). Psychological coping mechanisms and survival time in metastatic breast cancer. *Journal of the American Medical Association, 242*, 1504-1508.

Dimsdale, J. E., Pierce, C., Schoenfeld, D., Brown, A. et al. (1986). Suppressed anger and blood pressure: The effects of race, sex, social class, obesity and age. *Psychosomatic Medicine, 48*, 430-436.

Eriksen, H. R., Olff, M., Murison, R., & Ursin, H. (1999). The time dimension in stress responses: Relevance for survival and health. *Psychiatry Research, 85*, 39-50.

Eriksen, H. R., Olff, M., & Ursin, H. (1997). The CODE: A revised battery for coping and defense and its relations to subjective health. *Scandinavian Journal of Psychology, 38*, 175-182.

Fagerstroem, R. (1992). Defense mechanisms of elderly persons before and after a cataract operation. *Journal of Visual Impairment and Blindness, 86*, 361-363.

Farberow, N. L. (1980). Indirect self-destructive behavior in diabetics and Buerger's Disease patients. In N. L. Farberow (Ed.), *The many faces of suicide: Indirect self-destructive behavior* (pp. 79-88). New York: McGraw-Hill.

Fawzy, F. I., Kemeny, M. E., Fawzy, N. W. et al. (1990). A structured psychiatric intervention for cancer patients: II. Changes over time in immunological measures. *Archives of General Psychiatry, 47*, 729-735.

Feifel, H., & Strack, S. (1989). Coping with conflict situations: Middle-aged and elderly men. *Psychology and Aging, 4*, 26-33.

Fernandez-Ballesteros, R., Ruiz, M. A., & Garde, S. (1998). Emotional expression in healthy women and those with breast cancer. British *Journal of Health Psychology, 3*, 41-50.

Fields, K. B. (1989). Myocardial infarction and denial. *Journal of Family Practice, 28*, 157-161.

Figer, A., Kreitler, S., Kreitler, M., & Inbar, M. (2002). Personality dispositions of colon cancer patients. *Gastrointestinal Oncology, 4*, 81-92.

Forsen, A. (1990). Psychosocial aspects of breast cancer. *Psychiatria Fennica, 21*, 189-200.

Froese, A., Hackett, T. P., Cassem, N. H., & Silverberg, E. L. (1974). Trajectories of anxiety and depression in denying and nondenying acute myocardial infarction patients during hospitalization. *Journal of Psychosomatic Research, 18*, 412-420.

Fulde, E., Junge, A., & Ahrens, S. (1995). Coping strategies and defense mechanisms and their relevance for the recovery after discectomy. *Journal of Psychosomatic Research, 39*, 819-826.

Gabaldon, O., Mayoral, J. L., & Paez, D. (1993). Afectividad, apoyo social, represion, alexithymia y grupos de apoyo. *Boletin de Psicologia Spain, 41*, 35-41.

Gervais, L. (1966). Bronchial asthma and identification with the aggresssor. *Canadian Psychiatric Association Journal, 11*, 497-500.

Goldstein, A. M. (1980). The "uncooperative" patient: self-destructive behavior in hemodialysis patients. In N. L. Farberow (Ed), *The many faces of suicide: Indirect self-destructive behavior* (pp. 89-98). New York: McGraw-Hill.

Goldstein, D. A., & Antoni, M. H. (1989). The distribution of repressive coping styles among non-metastatic and metastatic breast cancer patients as compared to non-cancer patients. *Psychology and Health, 3*, 245-258.

Grootenhuis, M. A., & Last, B. F. (2001). Children with cancer with different survival perspectives: Defensiveness, control strategies, and psychological adjustment. *Psycho-Oncology, 10*, 305-314.

Gross, J. (1989). Emotional expression in cancer onset and progression. *Social Science and Medicine, 28*, 1239-1248.

Grulke, N., Bailer, H., Tschuschke, V., Bunjes, D., Arnold, R., Denziger, R., & Kaechele, H. (2001). Defense mechanisms in patients with leukemia undergoing bone marrow transplantation. *Archives of Psychiatry and Psychotherapy, 3*, 5-18.

Haan, N. (1992). The assessment of coping, defense and stress. In L. Goldberger S. Breznitz (Eds.), *Handbook of stress: Theoretical and clinical aspects* (pp. 258-273). New York: Free Press.

Hackett, T. P., Cassem, N. H., & Siverberg, E. L. (1974). Trajectories of anxiety and depression in denying and nondenying acute myocardial infarction patients during hospitalization. *Journal of Psychosomatic Research, 18*, 412-420.

Hahn, R. C., & Pettiti, D. B. (1988). Minnesota Multiphasic Minnesota Inventory-rated depression and the incidence of breast cancer. *Cancer, 61*, 845-848.

Heilbrun, A. B., & Renert, D. (1986). Type A behavior, cognitive defense, and stress. *Psychological Reports, 58*, 447-456.

Helgerson, V. S., & Taylor, S. E. (1993). Special comparisons and adjustment among cardiac patients. *Journal of Applied Social Psychology, 23*, 1171-1195.

Hentschel, U. (1993). Cognitive and affective aspects of information processing in psychosomatic disorders. In U. Hentschel, & E. H. E. Eurelings-Bontekoe (Eds.), *Experimental research in psychosomatics.* (pp. 127-144). Leiden, The Netherlands: DSWO Press.

Hentschel, U. & Nooijen, E. (1999). Defense mechanisms and introjected parents' images in patients suffering from psychosomatic symptom. An explorative study. *Psichiatria e Psicoterapia Analitica, 18*, 121-134.

Ho, S., M. Y. & Shiu, W. C. T. (1995). Death anxiety and coping mechanism of Chinese cancer patients. *Omega: Journal of Death and Dying, 31*, 59-65.

Hunt, M. E. (2001). Exploring the repressive coping styles of Caucasian and African-American women with newly diagnosed stage II and recurrent breast cancer: The impact of religiosity and under-reporting of stressful life events. *Dissertation Abstracts International: Section B. The Sciences and Engineering, 62 (3-B)*, 1580.

Ili, S., & Apostolovi, S. (2002). Psychological aspects of cardiovascular diseases. *Medicine and Biology, 9*, 138-141.

Ilic, S., Milic, I., & Stefanovic V. (1997). Psychological defense mechanisms of patients with end-stage kidney disease as adaptation factor to hemodialysis treatment. *The International Journal of Artifical Organs, 20*, 545-546.

Irion, J. C., & Blanchard-Fields, F. (1987). A cross-sectional comparison of adaptive coping in adulthood. *Journal of Gerontology, 42*, 502-504.

Jacobsn, A. M., Beardslee, W. R., Hauser, S. T., Noam, G. G., et al. (1986). Evaluating ego defense mechanism using clinical interviews: an empirical study of adolescent diabetic and psychiatric patients. *Journal of Adolescence, 9*, 303-319.

Jamner, L. D., & Leigh, H. (1999). Repressive/defensive coping , endogenous opioids and health: How a life so perfect can make you sick [comment]. *Psychiatry Research, 85*, 7-15.

Jamner, L. D., Schwartz, G. E., & Leigh, H. (1988). The relationship between repressive and defensive coping styles and monocyte, eosinophile, and serum glucose levels: Support for the opioid peptide hypothesis of repression. *Psychosomatic Medicine, 50*, 567-575.

Jensen, M. R. (1987). Psychobiological factors predicting the course of breast cancer. *Journal of Personality, 55*, 317-342.

Johanson, A., Gustafson, L., Smith G. J., Risberg, J. et al. (1990). Adaptation in different types of dementia and in normal elderly subjects. *Dementia, 1*, 95-101.

Katz, J. L., Weiner, H., Gallagher, T. F., & Hellman, L. (1970). Stress, distress, and ego defenses. *Archives of General Psychiatry, 23*, 131-142.

King, A. C., Taylor, C. B., Albright, C. A., & Haskell, W. L. (1990). The relationship between repressive and defensive coping styles and blood pressure responses in healthy middle aged men and women. *Journal of Psychosomatic Research, 34*, 461-471.

Kline, J. P., Bell, I., Schwartz, G. E., Hau, V., & Davis, T. (1998). Repressive and defensive coping styles predict resting plasma endorphin levels in the elderly. *Biological Psychology, 49*, 295-302.

Knight, R. B., Atkins, A., Eagle, C. J., Evans, N., Finkelstein, J. W., Fukushima, D., Katz, J., & Weiner, H. (1979). Psychological stress, ego defenses, and cortisol production in children hospitalized for elective surgery. *Psychosomatic Medicine, 41*, 40-49.

Kneier, A. W., & Temoshok, L. (1984). Repressive coping reactions in patients with malignant melanoma as compared to cardiovascular disease patients. *Journal of Psychosomatic Research, 28*, 145-155.

Kreitler, S. (1999). Denial in cancer patients. *Cancer Investigation, 17*, 514-534.

Kreitler, S. (2003). Psycho-oncology. In L. M. Cohen, D. E. McChargue & F. L. Collins, Jr. (Eds.), *The health psychology handbook* (pp. 325-358). Thousand Oaks, CA: Sage.

Kreitler, S., Chaitchik, S., & Kreitler, H. (1993). Repressiveness: Cause or results of cancer? *Psycho-Oncology, 2*, 43-54.

Kreitler, S., & Kreitler, M. M. (1999). The Quality of Life Questionnaire-adult version, children's version. Psychooncology Unit, Tel-Aviv Medical Center, Tel-Aviv, Israel.

Kreitler, S., & Kreitler, M. M. (2000). The Questionnaire of Defensive Coping. Psychooncology Unit, Tel-Aviv Medical Center, Tel-Aviv, Israel..

Küchenhoff, J. (1993). *Psychosomatik des Morbus Crohn*. Stuttgart: Enke.

Maes, S., & Schlosser, M. (1987). The role of cognition and coping in health behavior outcomes in asthmatic patients. *Current Psychological Research and Reviews, 6*, 79-90.

Mertens, C. (1986). Psychological etiology in cardiovascular disorders: Basic findings and new trends. *Acta Psychiatrica Belgica, 86*, 5-21.

Levitan, H (1989). Failure of the defensive functions of the ego in psychosomatic patients. In S. Cheren (Ed.), *Psychosomatic medicine: Theory, physiology and practice* (pp. 135-157). New York: International Universities Press.

Lilja, A., Smith, G., Malmstroem, P, & Salford, L. G. (1998). Attitude towards aggression and creative functioning in patients with breast cancer. *Perceptual and Motor Skills, 87*, 291-303.

Liste, K. H. (1999). Breast cancer, personality, and feminine role. *Patient Education and Counseling, 36*, 33-45.

Mazza, S., Pinkus, L., Caviglia, G., Crisi, A. et al. (1994). A psychological approach model to neurological chronic illness: Epilepsy and multiple sclerosis. *Archivio di Psicologia, Neurologia e Psichiatria, 55*, 791-795.

McKenna, M. C., Zevon, M. A., Corn, B., & Rounds, J. (1999). Psychosocial factors and the development of breast cancer: a meta-analysis. *Health Psychology, 18*, 520-531.

Miller, S. M., Rodoletz, M., Schroeder, C. M., Mangan, C. E., & Sedlacek, T. V. (1996). Applications of the monitoring process model to coping with severe long-term medical threats. *Health Psychology, 15*, 216-225.

Monsen, K., & Havik, O. E. (2001). Psychological functioning and bodily conditions in patients with pain disorder associated with psychological factors. *British Journal of Medical Psychology, 74 (Pt 2)*, 183-195.

Myers, L. B. (2000). Deceiving others or deceiving themselves? *Psychologist, 13*, 400-403.

Nachson, I. (1999). Self-deception in neurological syndromes. *Journal of Mind and Behavior, 20*, 117-132.

O'Sullivan, P. H. (1999). Relationships between defensive coping styles, resting blood pressure, and plasma lipid levels in a community based sample of older adults. *Dissertation Abstracts International: Section B: The Sciences and Engineering, 59 (10-B)*, 5583.

Pan, J., Mao, R., Tao, M., Zhang, J., Sun, Q., Tong, R., & Gao, J. (2000). Analysis of psychological defensive mechanisms and related factors in patients with peptic ulcer. *Chinese Mental Health Journal, 14*, 203-205.

Passchier, J., Goudswaard, P., Orlebeke, J. F., & Verhage, F. (1988). Migraine and defense mechanisms: psychophysiological relationships in young females. *Social Science & Medicine, 26*, 343-50.

Pennings-Van der Aerden, L., & Visser, A. Ph. (1990). Diabetes mellitus. In A. A. Kapstein, H. M. van der Ploeg, B. Garssen, P. J. G. Schreurs, & R.

Beunderman (Eds.), *Behavioral medicine* (pp. 247-263). New York: Wiley.

Phipps, S., Steele, P. G., Hall, K., & Leigh, L. (2001). Repressive adaptation in children with cancer: A replication and extension. *Health Psychology, 20*, 445-451.

Phipps, S., & Stivastava, D. K. (1999). Approaches to the measurement of depressive symptomatology in children with cancer: Attempting to circumvent the effects of defensiveness. *Journal of Developmental and Behavioral Pediatrics, 20*, 150-156.

Pipineli-Potamianou, A. (1976). Stress and anxiety in psychosomatic disease: a research on cases of rheumatoid arthritis. *Transnational Mental Health Research Newsletter, 18*, 1.

Pittner, M. S., Houston, B. K., & Spiridigliozzi, G. A. (1983). Control over stress, Type A behavior pattern, and response to stress. *Journal of Personality and Social Psychology, 44*, 627-637.

Podell, R. N., Kent, D., & Keller, K. (1976). Patient psychological defenses and physician response in the long-term treatment of hypertension. *Journal of Family Practice, 3*, 145-149.

Prigatano, G. (1999). *Principles of neuropsychological rehabilitation*. New York: Oxford University Press.

Prigatano, G. P., & Schacter, D. L. (Eds.) (1991). *Awareness of deficit after brain injury: Clinical and theoretical issues*. New York: Oxford University Press.

Ramteke, B. S., & Mrinal, N. R. (1984). Defense mechanisms in orthopaedically handicapped. *Indian Journal of Clinical Psychology, 11*, 53-59.

Reaby, L. L. (1998). The quality and coping patterns of women's decision-making regarding breast cancer surgery. *Psycho-Oncolgy, 7*, 252-262.

Rotenberg, V., & Michailov, A. N. (1992-1993). Characteristics of psychological defense mechanisms in healthy testees and in patients with somatic disorders. *Homeostasis in Health and Disease, 34*, 54-58.

Saltzstein, B. J., Wyshak, G., Hubbuch, J. T., & Perry, J. C. (1998). A naturalistic study of the chronic fatigue syndrome among women in primary care. *General Hospital Psychiatry, 20*, 307-316.

Schedlowski, M., Tewes, U., & Schmoll, H. J. (1994). The effects of psychological intervention on cortisol levels and leukocyte numbers in the peripheral blood of breast cancer patients. In Lewis, C. E., O'Sullivan, C., & Barraclough, J. (Eds.), *The psychoimmunology of cancer* (pp. 336-348). New York: Oxford University Press.

Schonfield, J. (1975). Psychological and life experience differences between Israeli women with benign and cancerous breast lesions. *Journal of Psychosomatic Research, 19*, 229-234.

Servaes, P., Vingerhoets, A. J. J. M., Vreugdenhil, G., Keuning, J. J., & Broekhuijsen, A. M.(1999). Inhibition of emotional expression in breast cancer patients. *Behavioral Medicine, 25*, 23-27.

Siegman, A. W. (1994). Cardiovascular consequences of expressing and repressing anger. In Siegman, A. W., & Smith, T.W. (Eds.) *Anger, hostility and the heart* (pp. 173-197). Hillsdale, NJ: Erlbaum.

Snowden, J. S., Craufurd, D., Griffiths, H. L., & Neary, D. (1998). Awareness of involuntary movements in Huntington Disease. *Archives of Neurology, 55*, 801-805.

Sommers-Flanagan, J., & Greenberg, R. P. (1989). Psychosocial variables and hypertension: A new look at an old controversy. *Journal of Nervous and Mental Disease, 177*, 15-24.

Stafford, S. L. (1997). Repressive coping, autonomic arousal, and needle EMG activity in myofacial pain patients. *Dissertation Abstracts International: Section B: The Sciences and Engineering, 58 (4-B)*, 2172.

Taylor, S. E., Helgerson, V. S., Reed, G. M., & Skokan, L. A. (1991). Self-generated feelings of control and adjustment to physical illness. *Journal of Social Issues, 47*, 91-109.

Taylor, S. E., Kemeny, M. E., Aspinwall, L. G., Schneider, S. C., Rodriguiez, R., & Herbert, M. (1992). Optimism, coping, psychological distress, and high-risk sexual behavior among men at risk for AIDS. *Journal of Personality and Social Psychology, 63*, 460-473.

Vaernes, R. J., Knardahl, S., Romsing, J., Askvaag, A., et al. (1988). Relations between environmental problems, psychology and health among shift-workers in the Norwegian process industry. *Work and Stress, 2*, 7-15.

Valliant, G. L., Bond, M., & Valliant, C. O. (1986). An empirically validated hierarchy of defense mechanisms. *Archives of General Psychiatry, 42*, 597-601.

Van Elderen, T. (1991). *Health education in cardiac rehabilitation*. Leiden, The Netherlands: DSWO Press.

Venaelaeinen, E. & Salonen, J. T. (1992). Characteristics of Type-A men in a psychodynamically oriented interview. *Nordic Journal of Psychiatry, 46*, 329-334.

Verheij, R., Timmerman, L., Passchier, J., & Fekkes, D. (1997). Trait anxiety, coping with stress, and norharman. *Psychological Reports, 80*, 51-59.

Vickers, R. A., Hervig, L. K., Rahe, R. H., & Rosenman, R. H. (1981). Type A behavior pattern and coping and defense. *Psychosomatic Medicine, 43*, 381-396.

Waldinger, M. D., & Van-Strien, J. W. (1995). Repression and cerebral laterality: A study of selective hemispheric activations. *Neuropsychiatry, Neuropsychology and Behavioral Neurology, 8*, 1-5.

Ward, S. E., Leventhal, H., & Love, L. (1988). Repression revisited: Tactics used in coping with a severe health threat. *Personality and Social Psychology Bulletin, 14*, 735-746.

Warrenburg, S., Levine, J., Schwartz, G. E., Fontana, A. F. et al. (1989). Defensive coping and blood pressure reactivity in medical patients. *Journal of Behavioral Medicine, 12*, 407-424.

Weimer, E., Nilsson-Schoennesson, L., & Clement, U. (1989). HIV-Infektion: Trauma und Traumverarbeitung. *Psyche, 43*, 720-735.

Weinberger, D. A., Schwartz, G. E., & Davidson, R. J. (1979). Low-anxious, high-anxious, and repressive coping styles: Psychometric patterns and behavioral and physiological responses to stress. *Journal of Abnormal Psychology, 88*, 369-380.

White, V. M., Wearing, A. J., & Hill, D. J. (1994). Is the conflict model of decision making applicable to the decision to be screened for cervical cancer? A field study. *Journal of Behavioral Decision Making, 7*, 57-72.

Winnicott, D. W. (1982). La enfermedad psico-somatica en sus aspectos positivos y negativos [Psychosomatic illness in its positive and negative aspects]. *Revista Uruguaya de Psicoanalisis, 61*, 11-22.

Wolff, C. T., Hofer, M. A., & Mason, J. W. (1964). Relationship between psychological defense and mean urinary 17-hydroxycorticosteroid excretion rates, Part 2: Methodologic and. Theoretical considerations. *Psychosomatic Medicine, 26*, 592-609.

Wood, J. V., Taylor, S. E., & Lichtman, R. R. (1985). Social comparison in adjustment to breast cancer. *Journal of Personality and Social Psychology, 49*, 1169-1183.

Xu, Z., Fan, X., Hu, P., Li, X., & Feng, J. (1996). Study of type II diabetes mellitus behavioral pattern. *Acta Psychologica Sinica, 28*, 315-319.

Appendix

Table 21.3: *Significant differences of quality of life variables and defensive coping variables*

Defensive Coping Variables[a]		*Means*	*SDs*	*t/F*	*Sig.*
QOL					
1. Fighting the disease	AM 193	1.93	.72	-3.431	.001
	BM 193	2.27	.81		
3. Strengthening health	AM 193	2.70	1.07	2.482	.014
	BM 193	2.35	1.04		
4. Preoccupation with the disease	AM 193	2.08	.62	-2.911	.004
	BM 193	2.38	.90		
6. Humor	AM 193	2.72	1.10	2.361	.019
	BM 193	2.38	1.07		
8. Denial	AM 193	3.24	.60	6.097	.000
	BM 193	2.72	.70		
10. Distraction	AM 193	3.29	.88	7.163	.000
	BM 193	2.35	1.12		
13. Religiosity	AM 193	2.15	1.18	-2.493	.013
	BM 193	2.52	1.08		
14. Relying on experts	AM 193	3.22	.73	2.371	.019
	BM 193	2.98	.83		
15. Changing oneself and one's personality	AM 193	1.99	.83	-3.176	.002
	BM 193	2.35	.92		
19. Wish fulfillment	AM 193	2.96	.70	3.842	.000
	BM 193	2.61	.72		
21. Despair and helplessness	AM 193	1.48	.50	-7.698	.000
	BM 193	2.07	.66		
C. Denial	AM 193	2.95	.41	6.306	.000
	BM 193	2.55	.55		
F. Helplessness	AM 193	1.48	.50	-7.698	.000
	BM 193	2.07	.66		
Family scale					
1. Fighting the disease	AM 21	1.98	.76	-2.430	.016
	BM 21	2.23	.78		
4. Preoccupation with the disease	AM 21	2.13	.65	-2.140	.034
	BM 21	2.35	.90		
9. Dissociation	AM 21	2.11	1.03	-2.651	.009
	BM 21	2.51	1.22		
10. Distraction	AM 21	3.06	1.05	3.582	.000
	BM 21	2.55	1.12		
21. Despair and helplessness	AM 21	1.57	.53	-5.460	.000
	BM 21	2.01	.71		
A. Focusing on the disease and strengthening health	AM 21	1.94	.51	-2.264	.025
	BM 21	2.10	.58		

F. Helplessness	AM 21	1.57	.53	-5.460	.000
	BM 21	2.01	.71		
Negative feelings scale					
2. Searching for new solutions	AM 32	1.61	.63	-3.764	.000
	BM 32	1.94	.73		
4. Preoccupation with the disease	AM 32	2.05	.67	-3.865	.000
	BM 32	2.46	.86		
6. Humor	AM 32	2.68	1.16	2.069	.040
	BM 32	2.39	1.00		
8. Denial	AM 32	3.18	.64	5.119	.000
	BM 32	2.73	.70		
10. Distraction	AM 32	3.01	1.12	2.865	.005
	BM 32	2.59	1.05		
12. Looking for support	AM 32	2.46	1.15	-2.620	.009
	BM 32	2.84	1.05		
13. Religiosity	AM 32	2.20	1.21	-2.161	.032
	BM 32	2.51	1.04		
14. Relying on experts	AM 32	3.27	.75	3.714	.000
	BM 32	2.90	.80		
15. Changing oneself and one's personality	AM 32	1.93	.85	-4.904	.000
	BM 32	2.48	.85		
18. Self understanding	AM 32	2.72	1.23	-3.732	.000
	BM 32	3.23	.85		
20. Self improvement	AM 32	2.04	.83	-3.193	.002
	BM 32	2.41	.90		
21. Despair and helplessness	AM 32	1.50	.52	-8.399	.000
	BM 32	2.13	.64		
A. Focusing on the disease and strengthening health	AM 32	1.88	.49	-4.586	.000
	BM 32	2.20	.57		
C. Denial	AM 32	2.86	.48	3.929	.000
	BM 32	2.60	.55		
E. Psychological change	AM 32	2.53	.59	-2.492	.013
	BM 32	2.72	.54		
F. Helplessness	AM 32	1.49	.52	-8.399	.000
	BM 32	2.13	.64		
Positive feelings scale					
1. Fighting the disease	AM 10	2.00	.76	-2.129	.034
	BM 10	2.22	.79		
2. Searching for new solutions	AM 10	1.67	.63	-2.206	.029
	BM 10	1.88	.76		
4. Preoccupation with the disease	AM 10	2.13	.72	-2.307	.022
	BM 10	2.37	.85		
6. Humor	AM 10	2.71	1.14	2.525	.012
	BM 10	2.34	1.00		
8. Denial	AM 10	3.16	.68	4.888	.000
	BM 10	2.73	.65		

10. Distraction	AM 10	3.08	1.05	4.016	.000
	BM 10	2.51	1.11		
14. Relying on experts	AM 10	3.25	.73	3.327	.001
	BM 10	2.91	.82		
15. Changing oneself and one's personality	AM 10	2.05	.86	-2.502	.013
	BM 10	2.34	.91		
19. Wish fulfillment	AM 10	2.97	.71	4.610	.000
	BM 10	2.54	.68		
21. Despair and helplessness	AM 10	1.56	.56	-6.341	.000
	BM 10	2.07	.66		
A. Focusing on the disease and strengthening health	AM 10	1.95	.51	-2.319	.021
	BM 10	2.11	.58		
C. Denial	AM 10	2.87	.42	4.184	.000
	BM 10	2.59	.54		
F. Helplessness	AM 10	1.56	.56	-6.341	.000
	BM 10	2.07	.66		
Confusion scale					
1. Fighting the disease	AM 6	1.92	.73	-4.580	.000
	BM 6	2.38	.78		
2. Searching for new solutions	AM 6	1.66	.63	-2.621	.010
	BM 6	1.91	.76		
4. Preoccupation with the disease	AM 6	2.13	.72	-2.536	.012
	BM 6	2.39	.85		
8. Denial	AM 6	3.12	.66	4.051	.000
	BM 6	2.75	.71		
10. Distraction	AM 6	3.03	1.10	3.549	.000
	BM 6	2.51	1.05		
14. Relying on experts	AM 6	3.21	.75	2.573	.011
	BM 6	2.94	.83		
15. Changing oneself and one's personality	AM 6	2.05	.89	-2.705	.007
	BM 6	2.37	.87		
18. Self understanding	AM 6	2.79	1.20	-2.843	.005
	BM 6	3.19	.89		
19. Wish fulfillment	AM 6	2.90	.72	3.084	.002
	BM 6	2.60	.71		
21. Despair and helplessness	AM 6	1.57	.56	-6.317	.000
	BM 6	2.09	.67		
A. Focusing on the disease and strengthening health	AM 6	1.92	.51	-3.401	.001
	BM 6	2.17	.57		
C. Denial	AM 6	2.83	.48	3.087	.002
	BM 6	2.62	.57		
F. Helplessness	AM 6	1.57	.56	-6.317	.000
	BM 6	2.09	.67		
Cognition scale					
1. Fighting the disease	AM 11	1.94	.72	-3.292	.001
	BM 11	2.27	.81		

2. Searching for new solutions	AM 11	1.66	.62	-2.185	.030
	BM 11	1.86	.76		
4. Preoccupation with the disease	AM 11	2.07	.64	-3.378	.001
	BM 11	2.41	.88		
8. Denial	AM 11	3.08	.70	2.308	.022
	BM 11	2.87	.68		
10. Distraction	AM 11	3.19	1.01	5.765	.000
	BM 11	2.40	1.07		
12. Looking for support	AM 11	2.42	1.07	-2.943	.004
	BM 11	2.85	1.13		
15. Changing oneself and one's per-	AM 11	2.06	.88	-2.017	.045
sonality	BM 11	2.30	.89		
21. Despair and helplessness	AM 11	1.57	.64	-5.511	.000
	BM 11	2.01	.59		
A. Focusing on the disease and	AM 11	1.91	.47	-3.274	.001
strengthening health	BM 11	2.14	.60		
C. Denial	AM 11	2.84	.49	2.898	.004
	BM 11	2.64	.54		
F. Helplessness	AM 11	1.57	.64	-5.511	.000
	BM 11	2.01	.59		
Health scale					
1. Fighting the disease	AM 6	1.83	.68	-5.755	.000
	BM 6	2.38	.79		
2. Searching for new solutions	AM 6	1.65	.65	-2.525	.012
	BM 6	1.87	.73		
3. Strengthening health	AM 6	2.75	1.05	3.394	.001
	BM 6	2.28	1.04		
4. Preoccupation with the disease	AM 6	2.05	.70	-3.582	.000
	BM 6	2.41	.82		
8. Denial	AM 6	3.22	.62	5.732	.000
	BM 6	2.73	.68		
10. Distraction	AM 6	3.14	.96	4.619	.000
	BM 6	2.49	1.16		
13. Religiosity	AM 6	2.09	1.14	-3.522	.001
	BM 6	2.60	1.09		
14. Relying on experts	AM 6	3.20	.75	1.980	.049
	BM 6	3.00	.82		
18. Self understanding	AM 6	2.68	1.23	-3.783	.000
	BM 6	3.22	.90		
19. Wish fulfillment	AM 6	2.91	.72	2.665	.008
	BM 6	2.66	.72		
21. Despair and helplessness	AM 6	1.52	.50	-6.451	.000
	BM 6	2.04	.69		
A. Focusing on the disease and	AM 6	1.89	.53	-3.797	.000
strengthening health	BM 6	2.15	.54		

C. Denial	AM 6	2.92	.45	5.369	.000
	BM 6	2.57	.55		
D. Strengthening oneself and seeking support	AM 6	2.61	.61	-2.215	.028
	BM 6	2.79	.64		
F. Helplessness	AM 6	1.52	.50	-6.485	.000
	BM 6	2.04	.69		
Pain scale					
1. Fighting the disease	AM 7	1.95	.73	-3.110	.002
	BM 7	2.26	.80		
2. Searching for new solutions	AM 7	1.67	.67	-2.008	.046
	BM 7	1.85	.71		
4. Preoccupation with the disease	AM 7	2.04	.67	-3.765	.000
	BM 7	2.42	.84		
8. Denial	AM 7	3.12	.66	3.331	.001
	BM 7	2.83	.70		
10. Distraction	AM 7	3.10	1.03	3.959	.000
	BM 7	2.54	1.13		
12. Looking for support	AM 7	2.44	1.13	-2.552	.011
	BM 7	2.81	1.08		
13. Religiosity	AM 7	2.10	1.16	-3.315	.001
	BM 7	2.58	1.08		
15. Changing oneself and one's personality	AM 7	2.04	.82	-2.379	.018
	BM 7	2.31	.94		
21. Despair and helplessness	AM 7	1.64	.61	-3.316	.001
	BM 7	1.92	.68		
A. Focusing on the disease and strengthening health	AM 7	1.91	.52	-3.277	.001
	BM 7	2.13	.55		
C. Denial	AM 7	2.86	.48	3.342	.001
	BM 7	2.64	.55		
D. Strengthening oneself and seeking support	AM 7	2.58	.61	-2.896	.004
	BM 7	2.82	.63		
F. Helplessness	AM 7	1.64	.61	-3.316	.001
	BM 7	1.92	.68		
Friends and social ties scale					
3. Strengthening health	AM 7	2.70	1.07	3.066	.002
	BM 7	2.26	1.03		
6. Humor	AM 7	2.68	1.13	2.194	.029
	BM 7	2.36	1.02		
8. Denial	AM 7	3.09	.69	3.073	.002
	BM 7	2.81	.67		
10. Distraction	AM 7	3.08	1.02	4.311	.000
	BM 7	2.45	1.14		
14. Relying on experts	AM 7	3.21	.75	2.438	.016
	BM 7	2.95	.83		
19. Wish fulfillment	AM 7	2.87	.74	2.215	.028
	BM 7	2.66	.70		

21. Despair and helplessness	AM 7	1.58	.56	-5.854	.000
	BM 7	2.06	.68		
C. Denial	AM 7	2.84	.52	3.407	.001
	BM 7	2.61	.50		
F. Helplessness	AM 7	1.58	.56	-5.854	.000
	BM 7	2.06	.68		
Body image scale					
1. Fighting the disease	AM 6	2.03	.76	-2.317	.021
	BM 6	2.31	.80		
3. Strengthening health	AM 6	2.71	1.04	5.076	.000
	BM 6	1.91	.92		
4. Preoccupation with the disease	AM 6	2.16	.75	-2.628	.009
	BM 6	2.47	.85		
8. Denial	AM 6	3.07	.66	3.898	.000
	BM 6	2.67	.72		
10. Distraction	AM 6	2.99	1.07	4.215	.000
	BM 6	2.28	1.06		
14. Relying on experts	AM 6	3.18	.78	2.809	.005
	BM 6	2.85	.78		
19. Wish fulfillment	AM 6	2.88	.71	3.893	.000
	BM 6	2.46	.72		
21. Despair and helplessness	AM 6	1.68	.61	-4.242	.000
	BM 6	2.09	.70		
C. Denial	AM 6	2.82	.51	4.050	.000
	BM 6	2.51	.49		
F. Helplessness	AM 6	1.68	.61	-4.242	.000
	BM 6	2.09	.70		
Sexuality scale					
1. Fighting the disease	AM 6	2.00	.79	-2.563	.011
	BM 6	2.27	.74		
2. Searching for new solutions	AM 6	1.69	.65	-2.101	.037
	BM 6	1.88	.75		
3. Strengthening health	AM 6	2.64	1.06	2.159	.032
	BM 6	2.32	1.07		
4. Preoccupation with the disease	AM 6	2.12	.71	-2.591	.011
	BM 6	2.41	.87		
9. Dissociation	AM 6	2.18	1.07	-2.028	.044
	BM 6	2.51	1.22		
10. Distraction	AM 6	2.96	1.10	2.436	.016
	BM 6	2.60	1.09		
14. Relying on experts	AM 6	3.18	.77	1.968	.050
	BM 6	2.97	.81		
15. Changing oneself and one's personality	AM 6	2.08	.88	-2.196	.029
	BM 6	2.34	.90		
19. Wish fulfillment	AM 6	2.87	.73	2.408	.017
	BM 6	2.63	.70		

21. Despair and helplessness	AM 6	1.68	.63	-2.986	.003
	BM 6	1.94	.66		
A. Focusing on the disease and strengthening health	AM 6	1.95	.53	-2.681	.008
	BM 6	2.14	.56		
F. Helplessness	AM 6	1.68	.63	-2.986	.003
	BM 6	1.94	.66		
Mastery scale					
1. Fighting the disease	AM 10	1.94	.75	-4.781	.000
	BM 10	2.43	.75		
4. Preoccupation with the disease	AM 10	2.13	.72	-2.678	.008
	BM 10	2.44	.87		
8. Denial	AM 10	3.11	.67	4.357	.000
	BM 10	2.70	.67		
10. Distraction	AM 10	3.10	1.02	5.871	.000
	BM 10	2.24	1.07		
12. Looking for support	AM 10	2.43	1.11	-4.111	.000
	BM 10	3.04	1.01		
14. Relying on experts	AM 10	3.18	.77	2.021	.044
	BM 10	2.95	.81		
15. Changing oneself and one's personality	AM 10	2.03	.87	-3.586	.000
	BM 10	2.47	.87		
19. Wish fulfillment	AM 10	2.88	.71	2.848	.005
	BM 10	2.59	.73		
21. Despair and helplessness	AM 10	1.60	.61	-6.154	.000
	BM 10	2.13	.61		
A. Focusing on the disease and strengthening health	AM 10	1.94	.51	-3.257	.001
	BM 10	2.18	.58		
C. Denial	AM 10	2.85	.49	4.661	.000
	BM 10	2.53	.52		
F. Helplessness	AM 10	1.60	.61	-6.154	.000
	BM 10	2.13	.61		
Self image scale					
1. Fighting the disease	AM 13	2.00	.75	-2.469	.014
	BM 13	2.25	.81		
4. Preoccupation with the disease	AM 13	2.15	.74	-1.999	.047
	BM 13	2.36	.84		
5. Coming to term with the situation	AM 13	2.93	.69	2.045	.042
	BM 13	2.75	.58		
6. Humor	AM 13	2.73	1.13	3.029	.003
	BM 13	2.29	.99		
8. Denial	AM 13	3.14	.67	4.540	.000
	BM 13	2.73	.66		
10. Distraction	AM 13	3.01	1.10	3.103	.002
	BM 13	2.55	1.07		
14. Relying on experts	AM 13	3.22	.75	2.863	.005
	BM 13	2.93	.81		

15. Changing oneself and one's personality	AM 13	2.08	.92	-1.975	.049
	BM 13	2.32	.83		
19. Wish fulfillment	AM 13	2.95	.74	4.478	.000
	BM 13	2.53	.64		
21. Despair and helplessness	AM 13	1.52	.53	-8.224	.000
	BM 13	2.16	.65		
C. Denial	AM 13	2.84	.53	3.438	.001
	BM 13	2.61	.49		
F. Helplessness	AM 13	1.52	.53	-8.224	.000
	BM 13	2.16	.65		
Meaningfullness scale					
3. Strengthening health	AM 8	2.68	1.14	2.496	.013
	BM 8	2.33	.96		
8. Denial	AM 8	3.09	.74	2.689	.008
	BM 8	2.85	.63		
10. Distraction	AM 8	2.99	1.16	2.429	.016
	BM 8	2.64	1.02		
14. Relying on experts	AM 8	3.25	.79	3.185	.002
	BM 8	2.93	.76		
19. Wish fulfillment	AM 8	2.92	.78	3.072	.002
	BM 8	2.63	.64		
21. Despair and helplessness	AM 8	1.54	.58	-6.232	.000
	BM 8	2.04	.64		
C. Denial	AM 8	2.82	.56	2.133	.034
	BM 8	2.67	.48		
D. Strengthening oneself and seeking support	AM 8	2.78	.65	2.146	.033
	BM 8	2.60	.59		
E. Helplessness	AM 8	1.55	.58	-6.232	.000
	BM 8	2.04	.64		
Active	AM 8	2.78	1.05	2.203	.029
	BM 8	2.46	1.24		
Active	AM 8	38.88	13.7	2.469	.014
	BM 8	34.07	17.0		
Number of coping strategies	AM 8	11.51	3.98	2.973	.003
	BM 8	9.85	4.86		
Stress scale					
1. Fighting the disease	AM 10	1.95	.70	-3.983	.000
	BM 10	2.36	.85		
3. Strengthening health	AM 10	2.67	1.05	2.827	.005
	BM 10	2.26	1.07		
4. Preoccupation with the disease	AM 10	2.13	.68	-2.307	.023
	BM 10	2.40	.92		
6. Humor	AM 10	2.68	1.08	2.309	.022
	BM 10	2.33	1.10		
8. Denial	AM 10	3.12	.65	4.258	.000
	BM 10	2.73	.71		

10. Distraction	AM 10	3.14	.95	5.840	.000
	BM 10	2.27	1.17		
12. Looking for support	AM 10	2.49	1.10	-2.366	.019
	BM 10	2.85	1.12		
13. Religiosity	AM 10	2.18	1.15	-2.817	.005
	BM 10	2.61	1.08		
15. Changing oneself and one's personality	AM 10	2.05	.87	-2.785	.006
	BM 10	2.39	.90		
19. Wish fulfillment	AM 10	2.89	.70	3.007	.003
	BM 10	2.60	.75		
21. Despair and helplessness	AM 10	1.61	.56	-5.263	.000
	BM 10	2.06	.72		
A. Focusing on the disease and strengthening health	AM 10	1.96	.48	-2.135	.035
	BM 10	2.13	.63		
C. Denial	AM 10	2.86	.46	4.185	.000
	BM 10	2.55	.58		
D. Strengthening oneself and seeking support	AM 10	2.63	.63	-2.245	.026
	BM 10	2.82	.62		
F. Helplessness	AM 10	1.61	.56	-5.263	.000
	BM 10	2.06	.72		
Index of Activity	AM 10	34.89	16.0	-2.323	.021
	BM 10	39.66	14.3		

Note. AM = Above median; BM = Below Median .

[a]Defensive coping variables preceded by numbers represent primary level clusters, those-preceded by letters represent secondary level clusters.

[b]All scores on QOL variables are cued in the positive direction, e.g., higher scores on health worries or stress scale indicate fewer health worries and lower stress.

Defense Mechanisms
U. Hentschel, G. Smith, J.G. Draguns & W. Ehlers (Editors)

Chapter 22

Patients Confronted With a Life-Threatening Situation: The Importance of Defense Mechanisms in Patients Facing Bone Marrow Transplantation. An Empirical Approach

Norbert Grulke, Harald Bailer, Heidi Caspari-Oberegelsbacher, Vera Heitz, Alexandra Juchems, Volker Tschuschke and Horst Kächele

Introduction

Patients facing a life threatening illness like leukemia and an aggressive medical treatment like bone marrow transplantation (BMT) (Atkinson, 1994; Forman, Blume, & Thomas, 1994) have to cope with multiple intense stressors: They are suddenly confronted with a highly threatening situation that turns their lives upside down. Typically, there is not enough time between the onset of symptoms, the determination of diagnosis, and the initiation of treatment. Thus, the time span for adjusting to the new situation is highly compressed. Patients have hardly realized what their diagnosis implies before they are confronted with very aggressive treatments like chemotherapy, radiation, and various invasive diagnostic or therapeutic procedures which often cause pain, nausea, vomiting, loss of hair, infections etc. Often they may not know for a protracted period of time whether the therapy has been successful. Patients undergoing BMT have to endure numerous inconveniences (Andrykowski, 1994; Neuser, 1989) such as germ-free isolation, physical inactivity, long periods of waiting for the new bone marrow to "take", and possible graft-versus-host disease. These side effects put success at risk – the mortality rate in BMT is up to 36%. Survival after one year depends on several factors including age, general health, and stage of disease and is reported to be about 50% for allogenic BMT when the donor is unrelated and 70-80% with a related donor (Andrykowski & McQuellon, 1998). Yet for most patients, BMT is the very last hope for survival. No doubt that such a situation challenges the person's mind and body to the utmost. Thus, specific defense and coping mechanisms are activated.

The impact of defense processes on coping with life-threatening diseases has been shown in many studies, especially in regard to cancer (Rowland, 1989), chronic hemodialysis (Gaus, Köhle, Koch, Beutel, & Muthny, 1996), myocardial infarction (Köhle, Gaus, & Waldschmidt, 1996), Crohn's disease (Küchenhoff, 1993), and eating disorders (Gitzinger, 1993). In general, denial emerged as one of the most prominent defense mechanisms of patients facing a chronic, malignant or other life-threatening disease (Beutel, 1988; Gaus & Köhle, 1990). However, only a few systematic studies on patients undergoing BMT have focused on how defense mechanisms influence the adaptation process. In a study on six BMT patients who were confronted with the anxiety-inducing decision on whether to perform BMT, Brown and Kelly (1976) reported that denial and displacement were their outstanding defense mechanisms. Furthermore, Patenaude and Rappeport (1982) described several defense mechanisms identified on four patients after BMT, such as minimization, withdrawal and denial, after the death of the patient "in the other bed". However, these retrospective studies with small numbers of patients discovered defense mechanisms only as a by-product of the general stress of coping with life threatening illness.

In order to find out more about the role played by defense mechanisms in extreme situations, the Ulm project on the aftermath of BMT (Kächele et al., 1988) was designed as a retrospective and prospective study with a focus on coping and defense mechanisms employed in adapting to this new situation. Because of advances in BMT, the treatment conditions have changed from the period of the retrospective study in 1986-1989 to that of the prospective study in 1990-1996. The focus of distress, however, remains the same. The aim of our research is to identify those mechanisms, which are preferably used by the patients. Proceeding from the assumption that defense is organized hierarchically at several levels, we shall also investigate any changes in defense organization during the several phases of treatment.

According to our conceptualization, defense is a major tool for regulating the relationship between the self and the object (Steffens & Kächele, 1988). Whenever a person suffers from an internal conflicts caused by an external stressor, his or her ego attempts to manage such internal struggles by means of defense mechanisms. Disease and therapy constitute external stressors, which can easily reactivate past unconscious conflicts or even provoke new dangerous and painful emotions, which by themselves trigger defensive maneuvers. Thus, a new balance has to be found between the intrapsychic object-related needs and wishes, on the one hand and the external demands of the disease and of its treatment consequences on the other hand.

The use of defense mechanisms changes the patient's thoughts, feelings and actions, and it can lead to a distorted perception of reality and to obliterating conflictual aspects of the self, thereby possibly modifying social relationships. All of these relationships may result in a less optimal adaptation to the therapeutic situation or may even weaken the person's tolerance of stressful situations. We should not forget, however, that these defensive operations also serve to protect the organism, as they enable it to master virtually overwhelming threats and anxiety, for example in life-threatening situations.

Several studies report about defense mechanisms in different syndromes. Perry (2001) found that patients with a personality disorder mainly used immature defense strategies and neurotic defenses. Borderline patients were found to have an even lower overall defensive function compared with other personality disorders. Interestingly, about a half of the defense mechanisms tended to form a stable repertoire, whereas the remaining ones were the result of variation and coincidence. Perry concluded that therapy would be more effective if it were adapted to patients' defense mechanisms. Tschuschke et al., (2002) compared defense mechanisms of patients with AML or CML with patients suffering from Crohn's disease and with neurotic patients. In comparison with these two groups, patients with leukemia showed the highest level of mature defense.

Below we report on portions of our own study in which we focused on the defense mechanisms used by the patients prior to BMT. To this end, we analyzed recorded interviews with patients, conducted immediately after signing the informed consent form. Apart from identifying the defense mechanisms used, we also related them to the results of the Symptom-Check-List SCL-90-R by Derogatis (Franke, 1996). Following this empirical approach, we shall illustrate the impact of our findings on adaptation to illness by presenting two prototypical cases.

Own Study

As defense mechanisms are by definition unconscious, their assessment by external raters would seem to be more appropriate than the use of patients' self-ratings (Hentschel, Smith, Ehlers, & Draguns, 1993). Thus, we used the German version of Perry's Defense Mechanism Rating Scales DMRS (Perry, Kardos, & Pagano, 1993; Tschuschke et al., 1994), which contain a defined hierarchy of seven levels of defense mechanisms. There are six sets of non-mature mechanisms (obsessional level, neurotic level, narcissistic defenses, disavowal level, borderline defenses, and action level), and one set of mature defense mechanisms, as exemplified by affiliation, altruism, humor, and sublimation In our study we only scored the six non-mature levels containing a total of 21 defense mechanisms Scoring was done on the basis of the German manual (translated and revised by Tschuschke et al. , 1994). We refrained from scoring the mature defense mechanisms because, in our view they are more likely to be coping strategies.

Our sample consisted of patients diagnosed with leukemia and scheduled for allogenic BMT at the University Hospital of Ulm. Patients were recruited between May 1990 and February 1994. Participants and non-participants did not substantially differ in sociodemographic or medical variables. A total of 58 patients were interviewed. The semi-structured interviews were audio taped shortly after the patient had signed the informed consent form. The interview was designed to cover all relevant aspects of the disease and BMT with such questions as: "When did the disease begin?" "What did you feel when you got your diagnosis?" "What changes did you notice in regard to your physical fitness?" "Has your relationship with your family or friends changed?" "What kinds of hopes or fears were you confronted with while facing BMT, during the isolation period, and in the patient-donor-relationship?" In the course of the interview, it was attempted to cover all episodes of BMT, but the length of the interviews varied as patients provided different amounts of information on their several episodes. Patients were interviewed in their own rooms on the BMT units. The audio taped interviews were rated by trained experts who were not identical with the interviewers. After identifying the various defense mechanisms we computed a score for each of them by dividing its frequency multiplied by 100 by the length of the interview in minutes, in order to take into account the variable duration of the interviews. Interrater reliability was satisfactory, with Kappa coefficients ranging from .45 to .97 (Denzinger, 1995).

On an average the patients were 36 years old, ranging from 16 to 55 years, male (67%), married (66%), with less than a completed high school education (55%). The patients were diagnosed with chronic myeloid leukemia (CML, 43%), acute myeloid leukemia (AML 41%), and acute lymphoblastic leukemia (ALL; 16%), 71% of them being in the first chronic phase or in the first complete remission, and 78% of the patients had a human leukocyte antigen (HLA) identical sibling donor.

Results

The most prevalent defense mechanisms were intellectualization (96.6%), minimization (86.2%), rationalization (81.0%) and isolation (75.9%). Dissociation was not used at all, and splitting and autistic fantasies were only used by two persons (3.4%). Most patients employed eight of the 21 defense mechanisms, with a range from three to 14 (see Table 22.1).

To make sure that no other variable is responsible for these differences, we correlated several demographic variables with the defense mechanism scores. Age, stage of disease, and HLA-status did not correlate with the scores for defense mechanisms, levels of defense or total scores. For gender, education, marital status, and diagnosis, we found only minor differences in defense- related measures. Females scored higher on narcissistic defense; patients with high school graduation or above scored higher on reaction formation, married patients scored higher for hypochondriasis, projective identification and had lower scores on minimization and ALL-patients obtained higher scores than other patient groups on turning against self and undoing. Yet it is likely that these results are due to chance since only seven out of 112 statistical tests reached significance, SCL-90-R showed no psychopathology. The GSI (General Symptomatic Index), which indicates overall psychic stress, was about 0.50 on the average which is slightly higher than the score for normal healthy persons (0.33), but substantially lower than for persons undergoing inpatient psychotherapy (1.29) in light of the German population norms (Franke, 1996). The elevation of the GSI score may be due to the demanding and life-threatening situation that the patients were facing. In order to find out whether there are subgroups of patients with a more or less "similar" defense structure we conducted a cluster analysis. Yet, in order to avoid intercorrelated factors adding excessive weight, we first ran a principal component analysis in which we eventually found a four-factor solution, explaining 43.8% of the total variance. The factor scores on these four components served as input for the cluster analysis (complete linkage with squared Euclidean distances) for which a three- cluster solution appeared to be appropriate. To assess the quality of clustering, a stepwise discriminant analysis was conducted with defense scores as discriminating variables. The two resulting discriminating functions allowed grouping all patients correctly into clusters.

Table 22.1: *Frequency of defense mechanisms with mean scores and standard deviation (SD), mean scores for levels of defense, and total scores (n=58)*

	Defense Mechanism	*Frequency (%)*	*Mean Score*	*SD*
(20)	intellectualization	96.6	20.7	14.4
(10)	minimization	86.2	7.1	5.2
(9)	rationalization	81.0	8.2	7.4
(19)	isolation of affect	75.9	5.1	5.5
(2)	passive aggression	67.2	5.8	6.1
(15)	repression	67.2	4.6	5.6
(13)	idealization	67.2	5.4	5.5
(7)	denial	60.3	4.1	5.6
(12)	devaluation	51.7	4.7	6.9
(8)	projection	46.6	2.8	3.8
(14)	omnipotence	39.7	3.7	6.5
(18)	displacement	29.3	1.4	2.8
(1)	acting out	24.1	1.1	2.2
(21)	undoing	22.4	.7	1.5
(3)	turning against self	17.2	.7	1.9
(17)	reaction formation	15.5	1.2	3.9
(4)	hypochondriasis	13.8	.8	2.5
(6)	project identification	6.9	.2	.7
(5)	splitting	3.4	.1	.7
(11)	autistic fantasies	3.4	.1	.4
(16)	dissociation	.0	.0	.0
	Level of Defense			
(VI)	obsessional level		8.8	5.4
(IV)	narcissistic defenses		4.6	4.0
(III)	disavowal level		4.5	2.7
(I)	action level		2.1	2.0
(V)	other neurotic level		1.8	2.1
(II)	borderline defenses		.2	.5
Total Score			3.7	1.6

Discussion

Whereas numerous earlier studies come up with denial as the most prominent defense mechanism, we found that intellectualization, rationalization, and minimization were the defense mechanisms with the highest scores and were used most frequently. What could be the reason for that?

The decision to undergo a BMT impels the patient toward high cognitive involvement. CML-diagnosed patients often do not feel sick or even affected. Yet, they are faced with the decision for or against an aggressive and demanding treatment with an uncertain outcome and no guarantee of success In this context such defenses as intellectualization, rationalization, and minimization appear to be helpful in facilitating difficult decisions under uncertainty while denial is only useful in reducing the impact of aversive memories. Thus, the findings obtained may be the result of the retrospective method.

Our exploratory multi-method approach yielded some noteworthy findings. The first discriminant function f1 could be labeled as "immature defense". The standardized canonical discriminant function coefficients for the immature defenses of acting out, turning against self, hypochondriasis, and splitting contribute substantially to this function with a positive sign, but the coefficient for passive aggression is negative and near zero. The canonical correlation coefficients support this interpretation of f1; immature and lower level defenses are positively correlated while higher level defenses, especially all three of the obsessional level defenses, carry a negative sign.

Function f2 is dominated by reaction formation and passive aggression. Given the fact that the patients are confronted with the prospect of BMT, the two main themes of the defense mechanisms associated with function f2 appear to be a search for a way of denying threat through denial and repression and replacing negative feelings and thoughts with positive ones through reaction formation and idealization. Passive aggression in this context allows a person to express negative impulses, normally behind a mask of friendliness and cooperation. In summary: Patients show no resignation, and they seem to be quite confident, friendly, and compliant, but inside they are full of doubts. For function f2 we suggest the label of "neurotic defense" despite the presence of passive aggression, which seems to play a special role within this function, yet seems to be distinct from the other mechanisms.

Yet, only few patients are representative of either of the two functions. The majority of patients show no distinctive, pathological or negative, structure of defensive mechanisms, which is in keeping with the prevailing clinical impression that most of the patients undergoing BMT appear quite "normal". Nevertheless, it is interesting to have a closer look at a couple of clear-cut cases.

Two Prototypical Cases

To illustrate the meaning of the two functions, we will describe two prototypical cases, representing function f1 (immature defense, cluster 3, patient, A in Figure 22.1) and function f2 (neurotic defense, cluster 2, patient, B in Figure 22.1). Apart from defense mechanisms, we shall report on social behaviors, coping strategies, and assessments by the staff, using registered scores. Listening to the audiotapes also contributed to our clinical understanding. Both cases were married women, diagnosed CML about two years prior to BMT. Patient A is 45 years old mother of two children who are 14 and 20 years of age. She has given up working as a reporter. Patient B is 29 years old, with no children, who was working full time in a white-collar job before being admitted to the hospital for BMT.

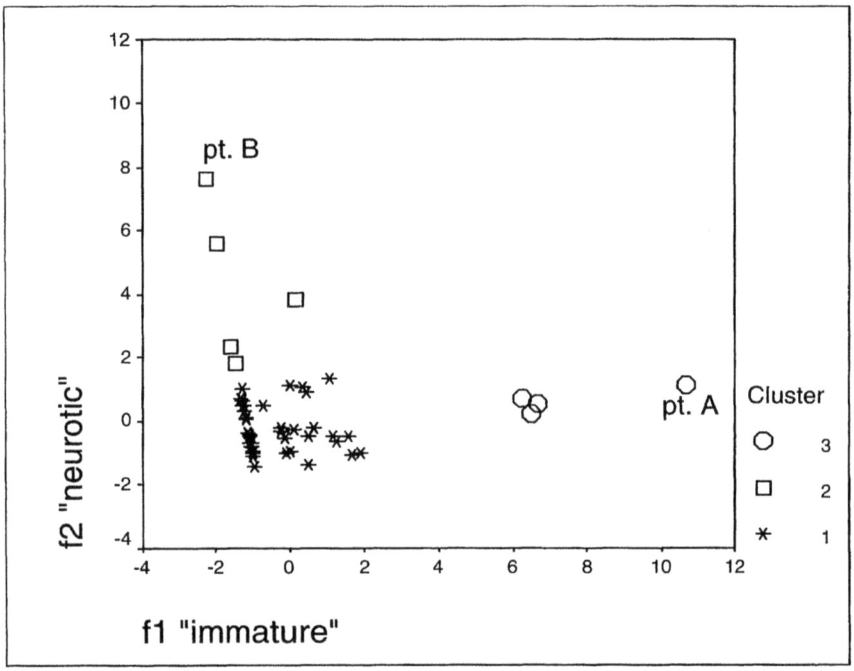

Figure 22.1: *Discriminant Scores on Function1 (immature defense) and Function 2 (neurotic defense) for the Cases of Clusters 1. 2, and 3; the two prototypical cases are identified as "pt. A" and "pt. B"*

Patient A

For patient A, 12 out of 21 defense mechanisms were noted. Compared to the norms, her overall defense score is below the average. She shows high devaluation, denial, and splitting. Her SCL-GSI score is 1.25, which virtually corresponds to the average score for psychotherapy inpatients with neurotic disorders (1.29). She scores high on SCL factors "obsessive-compulsive", "depression", and "anxiety". Resignation, passive receptivity, and distraction from the disease are the coping strategies that she uses more than the average. She received her transplant during the first chronic phase. Her physician assessed her chance getting cured as good, but her psychic resistance as less than good; similar ratings were given by the nursing staff.

The impression from her scores was somewhat modified by listening to the recorded interview. She reports on how shocked she was when her diagnosis was. Confirmed to her, being diagnosed with leukemia was tantamount of being condemned to death. As her brother was not a possible donor, an unrelated donor had to be found. No one could help her with the decision in favor of BMT, and she had to decide on her own. She hates nothing more than being told what to do. To make sure that she has chosen "the best from what doctors and others had to offer" she also looked for help outside of conventional medicine. Thus, she followed the advice of a non-medical practitioner who suggested a special form of diet, "My quality of life improved 100 percent", she reports. He told her about her horoscope and met her secret expectations. If she would manage the next five or six years, everything will turn out to be all right. For a long time, she says, she could not decide whether to undergo BMT or not. She believed that the time of her death was predetermined. Thus, she could not go wrong in deciding in favor of BMT. She also had psychotherapeutic help. A female friend recommended a female psychologist to her. At first she was skeptical, but then thought that "in the worst scenario I shall have wasted my time". Looking back, she considered these therapeutic contacts to be very helpful as they enabled her to talk about topics that she could not discuss with her husband or anybody else. All in all, she concluded: "I had a lot of good luck in my life".

Listening to the interview, one gets the impression of a somewhat childlike person who constructs her own reality. Thus, her position on f1 seems to be plausible. Perhaps f1 reflects a kind of regression from maturity to earlier stages of development, and in this sense to immature behavior.

Patient B

Patient B scored very high on repression, reaction formation, denial, and isolation. All in all, she displayed seven defense mechanisms and her overall defensive score was above the average. Her GSI of 0.10 is markedly lower than that for a "normal healthy woman" (0.39). Her highest score on SCL was 0.30 on "obsessive-compulsive" (average = 0.51). She used resignation as a coping strategy less than average and diversion, more than average. These results were confirmed by the reports of the nursing stuff. Her psychic resistance was judged to be quite good by the physician. However, her chances to be cured were only average, in spite of having an HLA-identical related donor and in spite of her receiving a transplant during her first chronic phase.

On the audiotape patient B was heard to be laughing when talking about her diagnosis. She said that the shock diminished when the doctor proposed BMT. From that moment on, she was full of hope and it was clear to her that she should undergo BMT. She tolerated medication well. She felt no need to talk with anyone about her disease, but acted as though nothing had happened. She was absolutely sure that the doctors would do their best and that she was in good hands. So, she did not think a lot about it, "There will always be a risk, and you have to face it." Concerning time in isolation, she expected no problems. Since she likes to be alone, she anticipated that she would have something to read and handicrafts to work with. So, she told her husband that he should not stay with her for the days of radiation and chemotherapy. "At the moment I can't imagine that it would get worse, I am not very sensitive to pain, I don't fear isolation", she said. "It will be a success, I've come here and I think I will leave cured."

The patient talked clearly and distinctly, without any resignation in her voice. She was reserved and showed barely any affect during the interview. This case illustrates function f2 quite well. The negative aspects of the disease and procedure are blocked away. A calculated optimism was displayed, but she did not sound optimistic on the audiotape

Patient B died 38 days after BMT. Patient A is still alive. At follow up, all four patients in Cluster 3 were living. In Cluster 1, 22 out of 49, and in Cluster 2, 3 out of 5 patients survived to date. There may be a trend for higher survival rates among Cluster 3 patients, but this impression needs further empirical investigation.

A Preliminary Attempt of Evaluating the Meaning of the Two Functions

What psychic symptoms are associated with high scores on one of the two functions (see Figure 22.1)? Patients scoring high on f1 (immature defense) are expected to show more psychic symptoms than low-scoring patients. High scorers on f2 (neurotic defense) may present fewer immature defense mechanisms than high scorers on f1 and persons with low scores on f1 and f2. On symptom measures we therefore expect high scores on f1 to be associated with a greater number of psychic symptoms, so that Group or Cluster 3 should have the most symptoms, followed by Group 1, and ending up with Group 2 having the least symptoms (group 3 > group 1 > group 2).

In order to substantiate the characterization of the groups, we looked at SCL scores for each group, as SCL is a measure of impairment of psychic symptoms. In Cluster 3, we found the highest scores on GSI and all of the 8 subscales of the SCL. Cluster 2 is characterized by the lowest scores, except on the subscale for "anger-hostility", on which Cluster 1 had the lowest average score. Because of the small number of cases in Clusters 2 and 3, significance testing of differences was not performed. However, the pattern of Group 2 < Group 1 < Group 3 was observed in eight out of nine cases, which is more than what would be expected by chance.

We can only speculate on the impact the defense mechanisms may have on how severe diseases are managed. Given the different functions and the psychic symptoms associated with them, one would hypothesize that high scorers on f1 are probably less successful in this respect than low scorers on f1 or high scorers on f2. Yet, the two cases described above appear to stand in contradiction to this expectation. Presumably, the answer to this question must be established empirically. As far as BMT is concerned, immature defense mechanisms may be adaptive: In the clinical setting, the patient has to follow routines and procedures as well as physicians' and nursing staff's orders, and is expected to take medication as prescribed. Thus, a lot of regressive behavior is demanded. This situation is not unlike that of a child who has to obey his parents. And if the patient is "good", he or she will get positive attention, emotional support, and other kinds of reinforcement. Therefore, patients scoring high on f2 and showing more passive aggression are expected to conform less to the regressive demands of the situation and may therefore arouse negative feelings, emotions, and/or attitudes towards them on the part of the staff, a process of which both parties are likely not to be aware.

Further research should also concentrate on the relationship between defense mechanisms and coping strategies. We think both of these constructs are relevant to the understanding of managing severe diseases. Understanding the defensive structure of patients may help in caring for them. However, it seems premature to give empirically derived directions for psychotherapeutic interventions. Whether BMT patients profit from a psychosocial intervention program is a question under scrutiny in an ongoing study (Grulke et al., 2000). For further research it would be interesting to investigate if and how defense mechanisms change over time from diagnosis through treatment to recovery or death.

Acknowledgement. This study was supported by Deutsche Forschungsgemeinschaft DFG. grant no. Ka 483/2-4.

References

Andrykowski, M. A. (1994). Psychosocial factors in bone marrow transplantation: a review and recommendations for research. *Bone Marrow Transplantation, 13.* 357-375.

Andrykowski, M. A., & McQuellon, R. P. (1998). Bone marrow transplantation. In J. C. Holland (Ed.), *Psycho-oncology* (pp. 289-299). New York. Oxford: Oxford University Press.

Atkinson, K. (Ed.), (1994). *Clinical bone marrow transplantation: a reference textbook.* Cambridge: University Press.

Beutel, M. (1988). *Bewältigungsprozesse bei chronischen Erkrankungen (Coping processes in chronic illness).* Weinheim: VCH Verlagsgesellschaft.

Brown, H. N., & Kelly, M. J. (1976). Stages of bone marrow transplantation: a psychiatric perspective. *Psychosomatic Medicine, 38*(6), 439-446.

Denzinger, R. J. (1995). *Abwehr und Coping bei erwachsenen Leukämiepatienten unter Knochenmarktransplantation.* (Defense and coping in adult leukemia patients undergoing bone marrow transplantation) Dissertation (Dr. hum. biol.). Universität Ulm.

Forman, S. J., Blume, K. G., & Thomas, E. D. (Eds.), (1994). *Bone marrow transplantation.* Boston: Blackwell Scientific Publications.

Franke, G. H. (1996). SCL 90-R: Symptom-Check-Liste Selbstbeurteilungs-Skala (S) von L.R. Derogatis (G. H. Franke, Trans.). In C. I. P. S. Collegium Internationale Psychiatriae Scalarum (Ed.), *Internationale Skalen für Psychiatrie* (International scales for psychiatry), (4th ed.), (pp. 161-167). Göttingen: Beltz Test Gesellschaft.

Gaus, E., & Köhle, K. (1990). Psychische Anpassungs- und Abwehrprozesse bei körperlichen Erkrankungen. (Psychic adaptation and defense processes in bodily diseases) In R. Adler, J. M. Herrmann, K. Köhle, & O.W.

Schonecke & T. von Uexküll & W. Wesiack (Eds.), *Uexküll - Psychosomatische Medizin,* (4th ed.) (pp. 1135-1151). München: Urban & Schwarzenberg.

Gaus, E., Köhle, K., Koch, U., Beutel, M., & Muthny, F. A. (1996). Organersatz und Transplantation - Beispiel: die Behandlung der chronischen terminalen Niereninsuffizienz (Organ replacement and transplantation, as exemplified in the treatment of chronic terminal kidney insufficiency). In R. Adler & J. M. Herrmann & K. Köhle & O. W. Schonecke & T. v. Uexküll & W. Wesiack (Eds.), *Uexküll - Psychosomatische Medizin* (5th ed., pp. 1206-1223). München: Urban & Schwarzenberg.

Gitzinger, I. (1993). Defense styles in eating disorders. In U. Hentschel & G. J. W. Smith & W. Ehlers & J. G. Draguns (Eds.), *The concept of defense mechanisms in contemporary psychology: Theoretical, research, and clinical perspectives* (pp. 404-411). New York Berlin Heidelberg: Springer.

Grulke, N., Bailer, H., Larbig, W., Prudlo, U., Domann, U., & Kächele, H. (2000). Supportive psychotherapeutic interventions for patients with leukemia undergoing allogenic stem cell transplantation. First results of a randomized and controlled study (abstract #308). *Psycho-Oncology, 9* (5 Suppl.), S77.

Hentschel, U., Smith, G. J. W., Ehlers, W., & Draguns, J. G. (Eds.), (1993). *The concept of defense mechanisms in contemporary psychology: Theoretical, research, and clinical perspectives.* New York Berlin Heidelberg: Springer.

Kächele, H., Arnold, R., Novak, P., Bergerhoff, P., Hertenstein, B., Paul-Hambrink, B., Schwilk, C., & Simons, C. (1988). *Die Knochenmarktransplantation - Folgen und Chancen, Langzeitstudie psycho-sozialer Aspekte. (Bone marrow transplantation - consequences and prospects) Arbeitsbericht 1986-1988* (Arbeitsbericht des Projektes A 15, SFB 129). Ulm: Universität Ulm - Klinikum, Abteilung Psychotherapie.

Köhle, K., Gaus, E., & Waldschmidt, D. (1996). Krankheitsverarbeitung und Psychotherapie nach Herzinfarkt - Perspektiven für ein biopsychosoziales Behandlungskonzept. (Coping with illness and psychotherapy after heart infarct – Perspectives for a biopsychosocial treatment concept) In R. Adler, J. M. Herrmann, K. Köhle, O. W. Schonecke, T. v. Uexküll, & W. Wesiack (Eds.), *Uexküll - Psychosomatische Medizin* (5th ed. pp. 798-809). München: Urban & Schwarzenberg.

Küchenhoff, J. (1993). Defense mechanisms and defense organizations: Their role in the adaptation to the acute stage of Crohn's Disease. In U. Hentschel & G. J. W. Smith & W. Ehlers & J. G. Draguns (Eds.), *The concept of defense mechanisms in contemporary psychology: Theoretical, research, and clinical perspectives* (pp. 412-423). New York Berlin Heidelberg: Springer.

Neuser, J. (1989). *Psychische Belastung unter Knochenmarktransplantation.* Frankfurt/Main: Peter Lang.

Patenaude, A., & Rappeport, J. M. (1982). Surviving bone marrow transplantation: The patient in the other bed. *Annals of Internal Medicine, 97*, 915-918.

Perry, J. C. (2001). A pilot study of defenses in adults with personality disorders entering psychotherapy. *Journal of Nervous and Mental Disease, 189*(10), 651-660.

Perry, J. C., Kardos, M. E., & Pagano, C. J. (1993). The study of defense in psychotherapy using the Defense Mechanism Rating Scales (DMRS). In U. Hentschel & G. J. W. Smith & W. Ehlers & J. G. Draguns (Eds.), *The concept of defense mechanisms in contemporary psychology: Theoretical, research, and clinical perspectives* (pp. 122-132). New York Berlin Heidelberg: Springer.

Rowland, J. H. (1989). Intrapersonal resources: Coping. In J. C. Holland & J. H. Rowland (Eds.), *Handbook of psychooncology - Psychological care of the patient with cancer* (pp. 44-57). New York, Oxford: Oxford University Press.

Steffens, W., & Kächele, H. (1988). Abwehr und Bewältigung - Mechanismen und Strategien. Wie ist eine Integration möglich? (Defense and coping – Mechanisms and strategies. How is integration possible). In H. Kächele & W. Steffens (Eds.), *Bewältigung und Abwehr - Beiträge zur Psychologie und Psychotherapie schwerer körperlicher Krankheiten* (pp. 1-50). Berlin. Heidelberg, New York, Tokyo: Springer.

Tschuschke, V., Denzinger, R., Gaissmaier, R., Körner, M., Mishara, A., & Vauth, R. (1994). *Klinische Ratingskalen für Abwehrmechanismen. Deutsche Version (revidiert im März 1994) der Defense Mechanism Rating Scales (DMRS), 5. Auflage, revidiert Mai 1990, von J. Christopher Perry.* (Clinical rating scales for defense mechanisms. German version (revised in March 1994) of Defense Mechanism Rating Scales (DMRS) 5th edition,. revised in May 1990, by J. Christopher Perry) Ulm: Abteilung Psychotherapie, Universitätsklinikum, Ulm.

Tschuschke, V., Weber, R., Oberegelsbacher, H., Denzinger, R., Anbeh, T., Dirhold, S. S., Kühn, A., & Kächele, H. (2002). Das Verhältnis von Abwehr und Coping bei unterschiedlichen Erkrankungen. (The relationship of defense and coping in various illnesses). *Zeitschrift für Medizinische Psychologie. 11*, 73-82.

Defense Mechanisms in Psychomatic Research

Defense Mechanisms
U. Hentschel, G. Smith, J.G. Draguns & W. Ehlers (Editors)

Chapter 23

Defense Mechanisms, Life Style, and Hypertension

Uwe Hentschel and Frits J. Bekker

Introduction

Descartes' dualistic theory of body and mind works quite well in daily life. It is well integrated into the health care systems of many countries and a large number of public health institutions. There remains, however a clear risk of reductionism. The concept of psychosomatic disorders originally has tried to formulate bridges between mind and body. Regarding this specific option, in recent years the clock seems to have been turned back somewhat, making it almost a taboo to speak of 'psychogenic mechanisms' in somatic diseases (cf. Van de Loo, 1993). However, the concept of psychosomatics is still alive and well, even if its original formulation might have changed in some regards.

As one looks at the potential conditions of body and mind interactions, one is basically confronted with the so-called Bieri trilemma (see Table 23.1).

Table 23.1: *The Bieri-trilemma* [1]

Mental phenomena are nonphysical phenomena
Mental phenomena have causal effects on physical phenomena
The causal relationships of physical phenomena form a closed system

Any two of the statements in Table 23.1 are easy to combine with each other. However, if the third is added, one ends up in a trilemma, although as A.E. Meyer (1987) has stated in his brilliant overview on problems with psychosomatic reasoning, many people active in the field would probably accept all three of them, thus implicitly ignoring the logical problem connected with it. It is very unlikely that for most of the psychosomatic diseases one specific hypothetical mental cause would be sufficient to explain the disease. There remains, however, the astonishing fact that for some of these diseases repeatedly psychological similarities between the patients suffering from them have been described in line with Wittgenstein's

[1] *From Bieri (1981), translated into English by the authors.*

(1984) term 'family resemblance', signifying overlapping features in contrast to the assumption that all instances of a concept have to have something common (Glock, 1996). Weiner (1979) has summarized several models for explaining distinct types of psychosomatic disorders. Even though, the examples which Weiner gives are quite persuasive, it becomes apparent from his examples and when the attempt is made to summarize them schematically (Hentschel & Eurelings-Bontekoe, 1993) that these models are more or less interchangeable. Thus, the explanation of illness-related subjective physiological reactions can be sought exclusively in external events or, with equal degree of success, in internal symbolic processes. And at no point, as A.-E. Meyer (1987) has argued, can it be convincingly explained where and when a mental phenomenon becomes somatic. Why then bother at all with mental phenomena in diseases with clear somatic symptoms? The answer is that leaving them out simply would lead to a starkly reductionistic view. There is some evidence that health and illness attitudes (Bekker, Hentschel & Fujita, 1996) are linked to health-related behavior; the role of different personality-related buffers between stress and psychological and somatic disorders is according to the overview by Cohen & Edwards (1989) on the whole suggestive, even if the results are somewhat inconsistent. It is, however, probably still more difficult to determine the exact role and place of the relevant variables in what Mirsky (1958) has called the chain of biopsychosocial events in the development of psychosomatic diseases. According to the theory of the functional circle (Funtionskreistheorie; Jakob von Uexküll, 1921) animals live in a circular interaction with their environment. Thure von Uexküll and Wolfgang Wesiak (1990) have adopted the theory of Jakob von Uexküll for a theoretical frame of reference for psychosomatic diseases with the distinction of two levels:

1. biological needs and supplies (Funktionskreis [functional circle])
2. psychological needs and cues (Situationskreis [situational circle]).

The information exchange of the organism with its environment through symbolic processes (perception, attitudes, and concept formation), usually under the control of pragmatic and communicative reality criteria, is normally characterized by an equilibrium. Whereas short term disturbances of this equilibrium are tolerable, long term disturbances may lead to a chronic increase of the internal arousal level of the organism's physiologic and endocrine systems. Thus, in this theory mental phenomena have a central place in the development of psychosomatic disorders. These mental phenomena basically are comparable with the ones that are represented in all the different models proposed by Weiner (1979) which Hentschel and Eurelings-Bontekoe (1993) in their schematic summary generally have given the label 'symbolic processes'. Shapiro has given a very comprehensive overview on hypertension research (Shapiro 1996). Readers may get the impression that in his brilliant outline he on the whole places more hope on progress in medical research and treatment, yet he definitely refrains from any reductionism by also providing a wealth of psychological information and placing the disease in a clear biopsychosocial context with reference to Mirsky (1958) and to Page's (1963) mosaic theory. He is skeptical about the concept of a 'hypertension personality', and given the evidence in the literature one simply has to agree with his view, as far as 'personality as a whole' or personality traits as exclusive or main causes are concerned. Among the psychological variables, Shapiro (1996) gives much weight to the role of stress as a potentially contributing variable to the development of hypertension. For the description of the development of hypertension he uses in accordance with Mirsky (1958) the three different phases: predisposition, precipitation and perpetuation. Stress is mainly involved in the latter two. Focusing on the view of the regulatory function of the autonomous nervous system, in hypertension a pathophysiological imbalance of the system due to a longerlasting increase in sympathetic activity, combined with a decrease in vagal activity may have take place (Recordati, 2003).

We do not want to argue for inclusion of personality variables as direct causal mechanisms in the development of hypertension but we would like to offer an additional hypothesis, in line with the basic assumptions of the functional circle theory, as already summarized, that *susceptibility to stress* might be a predisposing variable, which also seems compatible with the basic assumptions within a thermodynamic model of the nervous system (Recordati, 2003). Stressors were conceptualized by Selye (1950) as external variables but in transactional definitions of stress (cf. McGrath, 1970) the subjective reactions are the essential ones, i.e. in terms of Kahn (1970) the strain on the person evoked by the stressor which in the concept of Lazarus (1966) in turn is dependent on the primary and secondary appraisal. From a psychodynamic point of view the susceptibility to stress in general, and maybe even to certain categories of stress, may be related to character development. Furthermore, instead of regarding the person not only as a passive recipient of various stressors one could argue that certain persons also create situations that are more or less stressful. In longitudinal research on life events some empirical evidence for this view has been produced (Heady & Wearing, 1988). As for a possible link between personality variables and hypertension, we thus would like to direct the attention to the loop of the disposition 'to end up in (or actively create) stressful situations and a special manner to cope with them'. It is obvious that this line of thinking as far as potential contents are concerned could be seen as related to the psychoanalytic concept of hypertension (either in terms of personality [Dunbar, 1935] or a specific conflict [Alexander, 1939] centered around aggressive tendencies and dependence which was assumed to be rooted in an authoritarian father or in general overprotection). The difference of our view from both of these early psychoanalytic conceptions is, however, that the loop of stress susceptibility and stress handling, as proposed above, is a formal one and principally content-free or open to many contents. Keeping it content-free might be meaningful, however, only for the stress-related part (there is an endless number of different potential stressors). For the disposition part, however, specific psychological hypotheses - by preference within a broader theoretical frame of reference - are virtually indispensable. Such variables with a broader conceptualization, not directed at a specific personality nor at a group-specific conflict, have already been proposed in psychodynamic hypertension research. Bastiaans' (1963) formulation that hypertensive patients could be characterized by a 'law-and-order superego' could be taken as a good example. Such a formulation is not focused on a specific conflict but is applicable to a potentially wide range of conflicts, it is obviously personality-related, but does not aspire to cover personality as a whole. Thus, it provides more of an indication for a *style of adaptation* - in line with the concept of cognitive styles (cf. Hentschel, 1980; Sternberg & Grigorenko, 1997) than a characterological description or a specific behavior. There is another set of variables, partly related to the superego assumption, but comprising also other structural conflicts, generally to be seen as a kind of filter in all reality-related symbolic processes, i.e. defense mechanisms. As Vaillaint (1977) has shown, defense mechanisms can be taken as predictors for adaptation in many fields of behavior and indeed for life in general. We have started our study with the working hypothesis that hypertensives should differ in their defense mechanisms from normotensives and that other differences in personality-related variables - hypothetically interacting with defense mechanisms - should also be discernible on a descriptive level between these groups. The variables other than defense mechanisms that we were interested in encompass values and attitudes towards broad health- and illness-related dimensions. In the title of this chapter we have subsumed them as 'lifestyle'.

Method, Sample and Procedure

37 out-patients (mean age: 57 years) diagnosed as suffering from essential hypertension (stage 1 or 2; systolic > 140 mm hg.; diastolic 90-115 mm hg.) were examined by means of the Dutch version of the Inventory of Conflict Solving Strategies (FKBS; Hentschel & Bekker, in preparation; Hentschel, Kiessling & Wiemers, 1998). They were extensively interviewed on their attitudes and feelings with regard to many different aspects of life (family, job situation, health care etc.). By means of open-ended questions (see below) they were also asked to report some life events. These data were compared with the data from a group of 120 control persons. As the mean age of the control group was 13 years lower, we have con-

trolled age for all variables for which it seemed reasonable to hypothesize an influence of age.

Measurement of Defense Mechanisms

The FKBS has five main scales. (Turning against Object; Turning against Self; Reversal; Intellectualization and Projection, cf. also Chapters 1, 14) measured on two separate levels (feelings and possible actual reactions) and an overall score for the five scales.

Values and Attitudes Towards Health and Illness

In the interview (Hentschel, 1991; Hentschel & Kiessling, 1986; Hentschel & Bekker, 1987) the respondents were asked for their opinion on a number of topics pertaining for the health care system, hospitals, doctors, use of medicine, their wishes and satisfaction in regard to their job, social relations, and fear of death and dying (cf. Diggory & Rothman, 1961). The interview comprised, both open and closed questions, a number of quantified scales (for the results of this technique in cross-cultural comparisons cf. Bekker et al, 1996) and a projective story of two elderly ladies talking about the history and outcome of their psychosomatic disease. The answers were submitted to categorization and combined into scales.

Registration of Life Events

The respondents had to fill in on a line representing their life (the so-called Life Line, Hentschel & Kiessling, 1986; Hentschel, Sumbadze & Shubladze, 2000; Sumbadze, Witkamp & Hentschel, 1996) at least three events in the past and three events in the future which they thought to be important. These events were put into a number of categories, differentiated into normative (age- and history-graded) vs. nonnormative ones (cf. Baltes, Reese & Lippsitt, 1980; Platteel, 1988).

Aim of the Study

Given the converging reports in the literature of a more restricted world of hypertensive patients with signs of withdrawal and lower expressions of emotion, especially in showing hostility and anger and sometimes also lowered perceptual and cognitive performances (cf. Shapiro, 1996) in our inventory for registering defense mechanisms, the FKBS, lower scores on the scale Turning against Object were expected. In the same line of reasoning the tendency for passive submission and a rigid superego structure led us to expect higher values for the hypertensive patients on the FKBS scales Turning against Self, Reversal, and Intellectualization. No specific expectations were formulated in regard to Projection. Other studies with the FKBS have shown that the feeling/fantasy reactions seem the more sensitive level, probably because they are more projective. Therefore we decided to do the group comparisons on the basis of the feeling level. The interview comprised altogether almost 600 variables. Due to the sample size and also in regard to relevant group differences to be expected, a detailed comparison did not seem meaningful. Instead we selected on the basis of frequency analyses and several explorative factor analyses 24 variables which we thought to be relevant in the present context. So far, not very much is known about attitudes and concepts of hypertensive patients in regard to every day life topics. Therefore this part of the study is explorative and no specific hypotheses were formulated. The general expectation, however, was that the groups to be compared would show differences, possibly also in interaction with defense mechanisms. There were also no specific hypotheses for the Life Line, except the expectation that the group of patients would differ from the control group in their reports of life events. Regarding the report of life events by hypertensive patients the results are mixed, with either more (Lal, Ahuja & Madhukar, 1982) or fewer (Theorell et al., 1986) events reported. In the study of Melamed, Kushnir, Strauss & Vigiser (1997) a negative correlation between self-reported stressful life events and blood pressure was found, but in our study broader content-related categories will be used.

Results

The hypertensive patients score, as expected, significantly lower on TAO and significantly higher on TAS, REV, and especially INT. In the use of PRO the two groups do not differ.

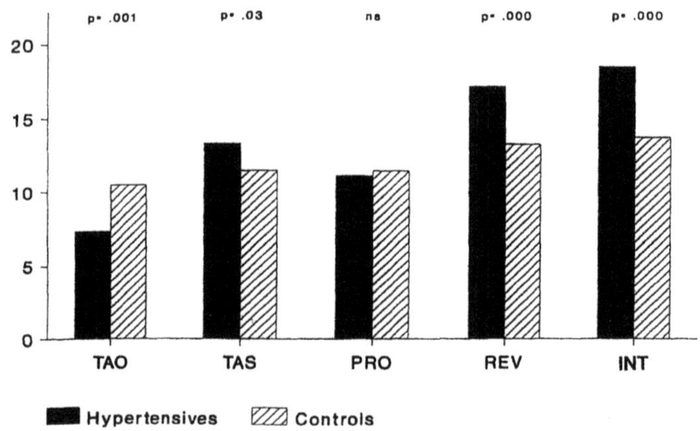

Figure 23.1: *Differences between the scores of hypertensives (N=37) and controls (N=120) on each of the five defense mechanisms*

The values presented graphically in Figure 23.1 comprise the means of the whole control group. As it is known from DMI studies that some defense mechanisms tend to increase or decrease with age (cf. Rohsenow, Erickson & O'Leary, 1978) we have repeated the statistical tests with a selected subgroup of the controls matched for age with the patients, resulting in not exactly the same means for the subgroup of controls but exactly the same significant differences between the groups compared. This result indicates that in conflict situations the hypertensive patients tend to direct aggression not against others but against themselves. Furthermore they ascribe positive characteristics to the frustrating person (REV) and use intellectualization (INT) to solve the conflict. The factor analysis of the 24 variables from the principal component analysis (with Varimax rotation) resulted in five factors with eigenvalues > 1, explaining 40 % of the total variance. The factor labels and variables with loadings >. 35 are presented in Table 23.2.

Table 23.2: *The five interview factors with their marker variables*

No.	Factor labels	Items and loadings
Factor 1	Health and medical care	The following items are important in keeping fit:
		.64 vacation
		.61 hygiene
		.60 conventional medical care vs. alternative ways of healing
		.53 entertainment
		.52 sports
Factor 2	Social relations (outside the family)	The following items are important in the vocational setting:
		.71 nice friends
		.60 interesting work
		.60 a good boss
Factor 3	Family and family life	In keeping fit it is important:
		.57 to have hobbies
		.55 to have good housing
		When suffering from a stomach ulcer it may help:
		.53 to change your life style
		It is important in the vocational setting:
		.52 to have shorter working hours
		An important goal in life is:
		.44 to raise children
Factor 4	Fear of death and dying	Thinking about my death I become anxious because:

Table 23.2: *Continued*

No.	Factor labels	Items and loadings
		.44 it could cause grief to my family and friends
		.81 I feel fear of death
		.80 I feel fear of dying
		.39 I have dreams about death
Factor 5	Social status	Important aspects of the vocational setting are:
		.75 social status
		.63 possibilities for promotion
		In keeping fit it is important:
		.51 to have sex

For the five factors factor scores were calculated and submitted to group comparisons between the patients and the control group by means of *t*-tests. The hypertensive group showed a higher mean on the first factor (health and conventional medical care) and the third factor (family and family life). The hypertensive patients obviously assign higher values to these two dimensions. No significant differences occured for factor 3 (social relations outside the family), 4 (fear of death and dying) and 5 (social status) (cf. Table 23.3).

Table 23.3: *Differences between the means of the factor scores of the control persons (C; N= 120) and the hypertensive patients (HT; N= 37)*

Factor	Group	*Mean*	*t-value*	*p*
1	C	- .15	- 3.97	.000
	HT	.47		
2	C	.07	1.32	ns.
	HT	- .24		
3	C	- .17	- 3.89	.000
	HT	.54		
4	C	.04	.86	ns.
	HT	- .12		
5	C	- .04	- .80	ns.
	HT	.12		

In addition to the main effects, we were also interested in possible interactions between the five dimensions and the five defense scales. To that end, two-way analyses of variance were carried out with the factor scores of the five dimensions as dependent variables and the groups (patients and controls) and the five defense scales (with a median splitting in high versus low) as independent variables. Significant interactions between the independent variables were found for factors 1 and 2.

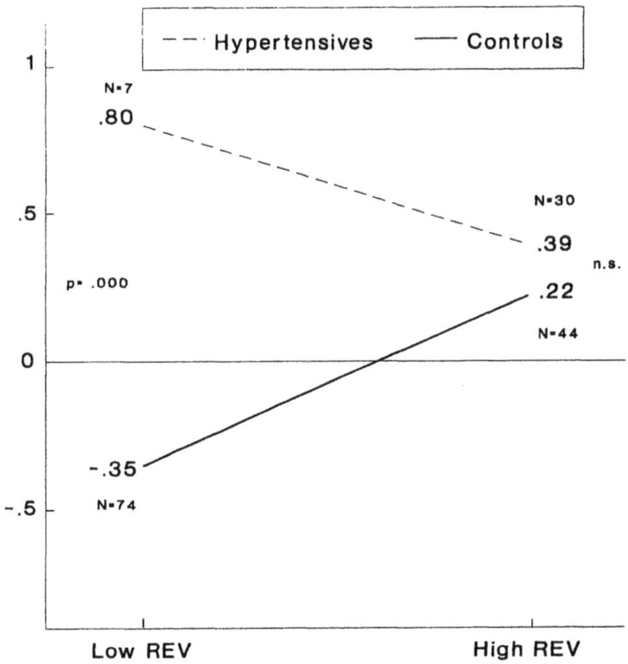

Figure 23.2: *Factor 1: Difference between hypertensives and control with regard to use of REV and attitude toward health and medical care*

As Figure 23.2 shows, control persons with a low REV score do not attach much importance to health and medical care. With a higher REV score this attitude becomes more important for that group. The hypertensive group shows an opposite pattern, i.e. with a low REV score these respondents attribute more importance to health and medical care and with a high REV score much less so. Intellectualization revealed a similar pattern, although the interaction did not become significant. The main effect for the difference between hypertensives and the controls regarding the importance of health and medical care has already been mentioned (cf. Table 23.3).This effect seems to be traceable to the groups with low REV and/or INT scores which among the hypertensive patients constitute a relatively small subgroup. For Factor 2, social relationships outside the family, an interaction was

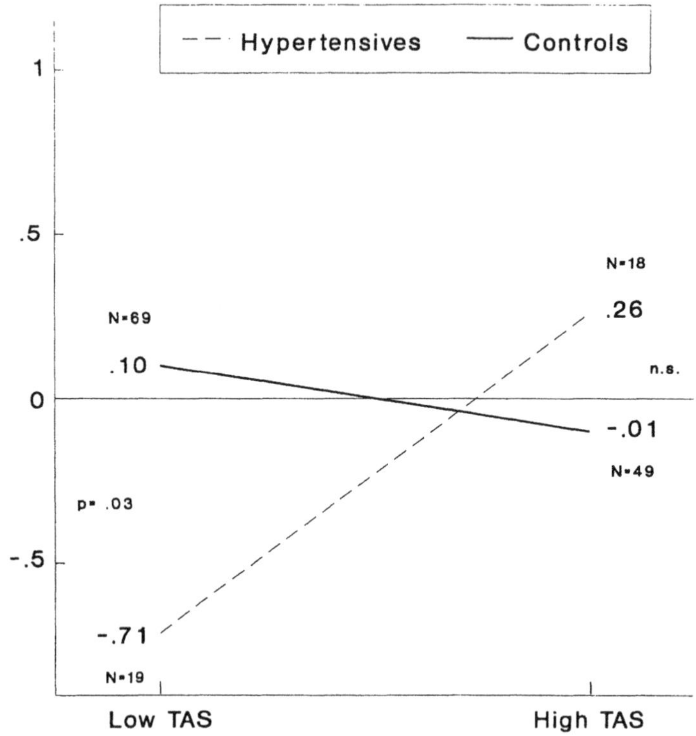

Figure 23.3: *Factor 2: Difference between hypertensives and controls with regard to use of TAS and attitude toward social relationships outside the family*

found between the groups and TAS ($p = .004$) which is shown in Figure 23.3. Hypertensives with low TAS scores do not attach much importance to these relationships whereas hypertensives with high TAS scores do. In the control group the value attached to social relationships outside the family did not change that much with high or low TAS scores. For the other interview factors there were no significant interactions found. As life events can be assumed directly or indirectly to be related to age we have used for the Life Line group comparisons the same age-controlled comparison group as for the FKBS aged-controlled comparison. For one hypertensive patient the Life Line data were missing.

Table 23.4: *Number of different life events of hypertensive patients (HT; N= 36) and control persons (C; N= 37) matched for age*

Life events	Total		Normative events		Chi-Quadrat/*p*	Nonnormative events		Chi-Quadrat/*p*
	HT	C	HT	C		HT	C	
Health	8	5	-	-		8	5	.37/*ns.*
Work	8	17	5	5	.08/*ns.*	3	12	4.31/< .05
Family	100	81	70	64	1.01/*ns*	30	17	9.46/< .005
Living situation	-	10	-	-		-	10	8.27/< .005
Personal	20	29	20	28	1.17/*ns.*	-	1	-/ns.

As can be seen from Table 23.4, hypertensives report more family-related life events and less events related to the living situation. If the categories are split up into normative and nonnormative events it becomes clear that these differences result mostly from the nonnormative events. For the nonnormative events the difference in the number of work-related events has also been found to be significant between the groups.

Discussion

The results of the study can be summarized as showing a relatively good concurrent validity in the differentiation of the hypertensive patients from the controls. With respect to defense mechanisms all hypotheses were supported: hypertensives when confronted with a projective, conflict-laden story are less inclined to react aggressively (TAO). They instead show a stronger disposition to blame themselves and direct aggressive reactions inward (TAS). They use more reaction formation (REV) and intellectualization (INT).

The results from the interview, the explorative part of the study, show that the group of hypertensives on the whole stresses the importance of health and health care more than the control group and they also are more family-oriented (Factor 3). The attitude and value factors showed some interaction with defense mechanisms. The interaction between health care and reaction formation shows that health and health-care are less important for hypertensive patients with high REV scores. This finding points to a possible tendency to reassure themselves and maybe also the interviewer in the sense of "don't worry, nothing is wrong with me". The other significant interaction between values and defenses was found between the importance of social relationships outside the family and TAS. Hypertensive patients who show a high tendency to put the blame on themselves stress also the importance of social relationships outside the family. This could be interpreted as some kind self-imposed duty in the sense of 'I have to....' . The self-reported life events on the Life Line show another aspect of the restricted experiential world of the hypertensives with fewer nonnormative events in the work sphere, and in the living situation category, and more family-related events. These results are on the whole in accordance with the so called 'hypertensive personality' which according to Shapiro (1996) is more a consequence than the cause of illness. As the study reported here is a retrospective one, nothing can be said about the hypothetical links in the causal chain.

In principle all of the differences found between the hypertensives and the controls could be consequences of hypertension. In the words of Shapiro (1996), "behavioral awareness of pressure reactivity results in a pattern of avoidance of those conflictual stimuli that would invoke reactions" (p. 43). In support for this conclusion he refers among other to Safar, Kamieniecka, Dimitru, Levenson and Pauleau (1978) who compared, normal controls, borderline, and pronounced hypertensives. In this study the Rorschach Test was used as a measure of personality differences. Borderline hypertensives were characterized by a combination of lack of fantasy, aggressive tendencies, and anxiety with somatic signs of increased lability of the autonomic nervous system. Pronounced hypertensives also had aggressive tendencies, deficencies in fantasy life, but no signs of neurotic symptoms and anxiety, which in the words of the authors could be characterized as "a more stereotyped approach to life" (p.629). The authors argue that between the borderline and perpetuation phase a shift had taken place from a psychologically steered mechanism to a somatically steered one. Unfortunately, there are to the best of our knowledge no prospective longitudinal psychological studies on hypertension which could test these results obtained with a cross-sectional design. Although the findings and arguments provided by the authors for a real shift between the different stages seem sound, there are, however, also indications for psychological similarities between the groups concerning the aggressive tendencies and the inadequacy of fantasy life. The results of the study by Nyklicek et al. (1997) that untreated hypertensives (in comparison to treated hypertensives and to normotensives) reported the lowest number of physical symptoms could be interpreted in keeping with the avoidance hypothesis. To make things more complicated, however, there was a gender difference between male and female treated hypertensives in reporting work-related irritations, with lower scores for the male and higher scores for the female group.

In another retrospective study on male hypertensive patients in comparison with asthma patients and controls, Hentschel and Nooijen (1999) found signs for reaction formation in the Defense Mechanism Test (see Chapters 1, 7, 8, 19, 27) and introjection of the other sex, indicating disturbed object relations with the father. In this study also attentional performance, adaptation to the color-word interference task by means of the Serial Color-word Test (Smith, Nyman, Hentschel, 1986; Smith, Nyman, Hentschel, Rubino, 2001; cf. also Chapter 18) and respiratory parameters (cf. Hentschel & Kiessling, 2001; van Praag, 1995; cf. also Chapter 27) were registered. The hypertensives could be adequately differentiated from the other two groups by using a limited number of variables (Hentschel & van Praag, 1997). However, as the study is retrospective, these indicators of concurrent validity may have reflected also the adaptation to the disease. We would argue, however, that this can be the case only in part. Due to the illness the avoidance reaction may increase while the performance may decrease. However, the internalized image of the parents is likely to remain rather stable over time, if measured reliably. Self-reported defenses are, although not completely insensitive for change, still rather stable traits (Hentschel, Kiessling & Wiemers, 1998; Hentschel, Sumbadze, Sadzaglishvili, Mamulashvili & Ulumberashvili, 1996; Smith, Kragh & Hentschel, 1980; Liedtke, Künsebeck & Lempa, 1990; 1991; cf. also Chapters 1, 7). From a differential point of view, defining personality as the unique pattern of all - relatively stable - traits (Guilford, 1959; see also Wiggins & Pincus, 1992), assuming interaction with external situations (cf. Magnusson, 1976) there is still room left for a hypothesized causal influence of mental phenomena on the development of hypertension. As the impressive study of Timio et al. (1988) shows, the external situation can have an overwhelming influence on this development. Living in a monastery, according to the results of Timio et al. (1988), prevents, as the hypothetically most important determinant, stressful events and keeps blood pressure stable. Choosing to spend one's life in a monastery is, however, very probably not unrelated to personality variables (cf. Very, Goldblatt & Monacelli, 1973; Gardiner, 1973) and it would also be very interesting to learn more about patterns of defense mechanisms of nuns or monks.

In contrast to many other diseases, sustained hypertension comprises the disregulation of a whole system. For this reason, looking for one or more isolated pieces of the puzzle will probably not lead to its completion. The idea of a long term process (e.g. Shapiro, 1996) seems more promising. The place of mental phenomena in the causal chain of the disease is far from being self-evident. A new way of conceptualizing clinical studies might be the use of recursive logics or of the so-called self-organization theories (Barton, 1994; Prigogine, 1978, 1980). These formulations provide more realistic explanations in cases in which the micro and macro systems do not follow the same rules (Neuser, 1991). Recordati (2003) has provided a dynamic model on how the general regulation of energy, matter and information may be organized by the autonomic nervous system with its two main divisions, the sympathetic (responsible for mobilization and utilization of metabolic energies) and the parasympathetic (responsible for self-protection and recovery), and in case of an enhanced and enduring sympathetic imbalance may contribute to the development of cardiovascular problems. Even within this approach it would be desirable to specify the concrete variables which can determine a longer-lasting shift to the sympathetic mode, and to construct appropriate models -probably rather recursive than linear ones- which could be applied in prospective studies. However, retrospective studies like ours are not futile either, in that they can point to the hypothetically important variables in the process. The variables in question encompass a wide range. Thus, a (poly)genetically determined predisposition of physiological reactions in combination with a family climate that in part, or over certain periods, may also be genetically influenced (Plomin, 1994) which can moderate the learning of psycho-emotional reactions to external stimuli (triggering/creating stressful situations and styles of coping with them). Hypothetically this can have an influence on precipitation, and stimulate further physiologic and consequent thereupon also behavior changes in perpetuation. The problem to be solved is not characterized by one, but manifold complexities (cf. Weiner, 1994), of which the process and change aspects belong to the most difficult ones. In our view, it would be advisable to gather more systematic data about the role of defense mechanisms in the earlier phases of the process. However, even in the phase of perpetuation defense mechanisms as well as other psychological moderator variables (Lee et al., 1992) for the hypertensive patients' compliance with the treatment still can have an important impact on the further course of the disease.

References

Alexander, F. (1939). Emotional factors in essential hypertension. Psychosomatic Medicine, 1, 173-179.

Baltes, P. B., Reese, H. W. & Lipsitt, L.P. (1980). Life-span developmental psychology. Ann. Rev. Psychol., 8, 65-110.

Barton, S. (1994). Chaos, self-organization, and psychology. American Psychologist, 49, 5- 14.

Bastiaans, J. (1963). Emotiogene Aspekte der essentiellen Hypertonie [Emotiogenic aspects of primary hypertension]. Verhandlungen Deutsche Gesellschaft für Innere Medizin, 69, 510-522.

Bekker, F. J., Hentschel, U. & Fujita, M. (1996). Basic cultural values and differences in attitudes towards health, illness and treatment preferences within a psychosomatic frame of reference. Psychother. Psychosom., 65, 191-198.

Bieri, P. (1981). Generelle Einführung [General introduction] In P. Bieri (Ed.), Analytische Philosophie des Geistes (pp. 1-18). Königstein: Hain.

Cohen, S. & Edwards, J. R. (1989). Personality characteristics as moderators of the relationship between stress and disorder. In R. W. J. Neufeld (Ed.), Advances in the investigation of psychological stress (pp. 235-283). New York: Wiley.

Diggory, J. C. & Rothman, D. Z. (1961). Values destroyed by death. Journal of Abnormal and Social Psychology, 63, 205-210.

Dunbar, F. (1943). Psychosomatic diagnosis. New York: Hoeber.

Gardiner,H. W. (1973). Catholic sisters and the Edwards Personal Preference Schedule.Journal of Psychology, 85, 97-100.

Guilford, J. P. (1959). Personality. New York: McGraw-Hill.

Glock, H. J. (1996). A Wittgenstein dictionairy. Oxford: Blackwell

Heady,B. & Wearing, A. J. (1988). Causing and controlling distress and happiness. Paper presented at the 'XXIV International Congress of Psychology', Sydney, Australia, August 28 - September 2, 1988.

Hentschel, U. (1980). Kognitive Kontrollprinzipien und Neuroseformen [Cognitive controls and forms of neurosis] In U. Hentschel & G. Smith (Eds.), Experimentelle Persönlichkeitspsychologie. Die Wahrnehmung als Zugang zu diagnostischen Problemen (pp.227-321). Wiesbaden: Akademische Verlags-gesellschaft.

Hentschel, U. (1991). Expectations in the health care system from a cross-cultural and group-specific approach. PPmP Disk Journal (Vol. 2, No. 2)

Hentschel, U. & Bekker, F.J. (1987). Interview: Ziekte en gezondheid [Interview: illness and health]. University of Leiden: mimeographed.

Hentschel, U. & Bekker, F.J. (in preparation). Vragenlijst voor konfliktoplossingsstrategieën - FKBS [Conflict-solving Strategy Inventory -FKBS].

Hentschel, U. & Eurelings-Bontekoe, E. H. M. (1993). Different perspectives in psychosomatic research. In U. Hentschel & E. H. M. Eurelings-Bontekoe (Eds.), Experimental research in psychosomatics (pp.1-17).Leiden: DSWO.

Hentschel, U. & Kiessling (1986). Interview: Krankheit und Gesundheit [Interview: illness and health]. University of Mainz: mimeographed.

Hentschel U. & Kiessling, M. (2001). Informationsverarbeitung und physiologische Reaktionen. External report for the Daimler-Chrysler Research Institute, Berlin. Mainz: GPS.

Hentschel, U., Kiessling, M. & Wiemers, M. (1998). Fragebogen zu Konfliktbewältigungsstrategien - FKBS [Conflict-solving Strategy Inventory -FKBS]. Weinheim: Beltz.

Hentschel, U. & Nooijen, E. (1999). Defense mechanisms and introjected parents' images in patients suffering from psychosomatic symptoms: an explorative study. Psichiatria e Psicjhotherapia Analitica, 18, 121-134.

Hentschel, U., Sumbadze, N., & Shubladze, S. (2000). The effect of the general I-E Locus of Control conviction on remembering and planning one's life: individual differences in life event reports of Georgian respondents. *Social Behavior and Personality, 28*, 443-454.

Hentschel, U. & Van Praag, T. (1997). Psychophysiological correlates and psychodynamic characteristics of hypertension and asthma patients. Paper presented at the "28th SPR Annual Meeting", Geilo, Norway, June 1997.

Kahn, R. L. (1970). Some propositions toward a researchable conceptualization. In J. E. McGrath (Ed.). Social and psychological factors in stress (pp. 97-103) New York: Holt, Rinehart & Winston.

Lal, N., Ahuja, R. C. & Madhukar, (1982). Life events in hypertensive patients. J. Psychosom Res., 26, 441-445.

Lazarus, R. S. (1966). Psychological stress and the coping process. New York: McGraw-Hill.

Lee, D., Mendes de Leon, C. F., Jenkins, C.D., Croog, S.H., Levine, S. & Sudilovsky, A. (1992). Relation of hostility to medication adherence, symptom complaints, and blood pressure reduction in a clinical field trial of antihypertensive medication. J. Psychosom. Res., 36, 181-190.

Liedtke, R., Künsebeck, H.-W., & Lempa, W. (1990). Änderung der Konfliktbewältigung während stationärer Therapie. Eine psychometrische Untersuchung zum Abwehrverhalten [Changes in coping with conflicts during inpatient psychotherapy] Zeitschrift ür Psychosomatische Medizin und Psychoanalyse, 36, 79- 88.

Liedtke, R., Künsebeck, H.-W., & Lempa, W. (1991). Abwehrverhalten und Symptomatik ein Jahr nach stationärer psyxchosomatischer Therapie [Defense and symptoms one year after inpatient psychosomatic therapy] Zeitschrift ür Psychosomatische Medizin und Psychoanalyse, 37, 185-193

Magnusson, D. (1976). The person and the situation in an interactional model of behavior. Scand. J. Psychol., 17, 253-271.

McGrath, J. E. (1970). A conceptual formulation for research on stress. In J. E.

McGrath (Ed.), Social and psychological factors in stress (pp. 10-21). New York: Holt, Rinehart & Winston.

Melamed, S., Kushnir, T., Strauss,E. Vigiser, D. (1997). Negative association between reported life events and cardiovascular disease risk factors in employed men: The CORDIS study. J. Psychosom Res., 42, J. Psychosom. Res., 42, 247-258.

Meyer, A.-E. (1987). Das Leib-Seele Problem aus der Sicht eines Psychosomatikers. Modelle und ihre Widersprüche. [The mind-body-dualism-problem from the viewpoint of a specialist in psychosomatics. Models and their inconsistencies]. Psychosom. Psychother. Med. Psychol., 37, 367-375.

Mirsky, I. A. (1958). Physiologic, psychologic and social determinants in the etiology of duodenal ulcer. Amer. J. Digest. Diss., 3, 285-314.

Neuser, W. (1991). Zur Logik der Selbstorganisation [On the logic of self-organization]. Paper presented at the colloquium "Gestaltkreis versus Systemtheorie" University of Oldenburg, December 1991.

Nyklícek, Vingerhoets, A. J. J. M., Heck, G. L. van, Kamphuis, P. L., Poppel, J.
W. M. J. van, & Limpt, M. C. A. M. van (1997). Blood pressure, self-reported symptoms and job-related problems in schoolteachers. J. Psychosom. Res., 42, 287-296.

Page, I. H. (1963). The nature of arterial hypertension. Arch. Intern. Med., 111, 103-115.

Platteel, D. 1988). De bloeddrukmeter als psychologische test? De relatie tussen essentiële hypertensie en (de omgang met) levensgebeurtenissen [The blood pressure instrument as a psychological test? The relationship between essential hypertension and (the coping with) life events]. University of Leiden: Unpublished master thesis.

Plomin, R. (1994). The Emanuel Miller Memorial Lecture 1993: Genetic research and identification of environmental influences. J. Child. Psychol. Psychiat., 35, 817-834.

Prigogine, I. (1978). Time, structure, and fluctuations. *Science, 201*, 77-785.

Prigogine, I. (1980). From being to becoming: Time and complexity in the physical science. San Fransisco: Freeman.

Recordati, G. (2003). A thermodynamic model of the sympathetic and parasympathetic nervous systems. *Autonomic Neuroscience: Basic and Clinical, 103*, 1-12.

Rohsenow, D. J., Erickson, R. C. & O'Leary, M. R. (1978). The Defense Mechanism Inventory and alcoholics. International Journal of the addictions, 13, 403-414.

Safar, M. E., Kamieniecka, H. A., Dimitru, V. M., Levenson , J. A.& Pauleau, N. F. (1978). Hemodynamic factors and Rorschach testing in borderline and sustained hypertension. Psychosom. Med., 40, 620- 630.

Selye, H. (1950). Stress: The physiology and pathology of exposure to stress. Montreal: Acta.

Shapiro, A.P. (1996). Hypertension and stress. A unified concept. Mahwah, N.J. : Erlbaum.

Smith, G., Kragh, U. & Hentschel, U. (1980). Perzeptgenische Verfahren: Historische und methodologische Übersicht [Percept-genetic procedures: Historical and methodological overview] In U. Hentschel & G. Smith (Eds.), Experimentelle Persönlichkeitspsychologie. Die Wahrnehmung als

Zugang zu diagnostischen Problemen (pp.31-63). Wiesbaden: Akademische Verlags-gesellschaft.

Smith, G., Nyman, E. & Hentschel, U. (1986). Manual till CWT - Serialt färgordtest. Stockholm: Psykologiförlaget.

Smith, G., Nyman, E., Hentschel, U. & Rubino, A. I. (2001). S - CWT. Serial Color-Word Test - Manual. Frankfurt: Swets Test Services.

Sternberg, R. J. & Grigorenko, E. L. (1997). Are cognitive styles still in style? American Psychologist 52, 700-712.

Sumbadze, N. , Witkamp, M. & Hentschel, U. (1996). Cultural differences in self-reported life events of the past as predictors for planned actions in the future. Poster presented at the "40. Kongreß der Deutschen Gesellschaft für Psychologie", Munich, September, 1996.

Theorell, T., Svensson, J., Knox, S., Waller, D. & Alvarez, M. (1986). Young men with high blood pressure report few recent life events. J. Psychosom. Res., 30, 243-249.

Timio, M., Verdecchia, P., Vananzi, S., Gentili, S., Ronconi, M., Francocci, B.,

Montanari, M. & Bichiszo, E. (1988). Age and blood pressure changes: a 20 year followup study in nuns in a secluded order. Hypertension, 12, 457-461.

Uexküll, J. von (1921). Umwelt und Innenwelt der Tiere. Berlin: Springer.

Uexküll, T. von & Wesiak, W. (1990). Wissenschaftstheorie und Psychsomatische Medizin, ein bio-psycho-soziales Modell [Theory of science and psychosomatic medicine, a bio-psycho-social model] In R. Adler, J. M. Herrmann, K. Köhle, O. W. Schonecke, T. von Uexküll & w. Wesiak (Eds.), Psychosomatische Medizin (pp. 5- 38). Munich: Urban & Schwarzenberg.

Vaillant, G. E. (1974). Adaptation to life. Boston: Little, Brown.

Van de Loo, K. J. M. (1993). The changing meaning of a concept: A short introduction to the psychosomatic approach. In U. Hentschel & E. H. M. Eurelings-Bontekoe (Eds.), Experimental research in psychosomatics (pp.XIII-XVII).Leiden: DSWO.

Van Praag, T. (1995). Adembeweging en persoonlijkheid[Respiratory movement and presonality]. Unpublished master thesis. University of Leiden.

Very, P. S., Goldblatt, R. B. & Monacelli, V. (1973). Birth order, personality development, and vocational choice of becoming a Carmelite nun. Journal of Psychology, 85, 75-80.

Weiner, H. (1979). Psychobiology and human disease. New York: Elsevier.

Weiner, H. (1994). "Das biopsychosoziale Modell" ein hilfreiches Konstrukt? [Is the biopsychosocial model still a useful construct?] Psychosom. Psychother. Med. Psychol., 44, 73-83.

Wiggins, J. S. & Pincus, A. L. (1992). Personality: structure and asssessment. Annual Review of Psychology, 43, 473-504.
Wittgenstein L. (1984). Letzte Schriften zur Philosophie der Psychologie [Last writings on the philosophy of psycholgy]. Frankfurt: Suhrkamp.

Defense Mechanisms
U. Hentschel, G. Smith, J.G. Draguns & W. Ehlers (Editors)

Chapter 24

In Defense of Obesity

Olof Rydén

Obesity - an Expanding Problem

Overweight - defined as a body mass index (BMI=kg/meter^2) of over 25 - is a widespread condition in the western world, affecting roughly half of the population, although with considerable variation between age groups, different social classes, and the genders (Paeratakul et al., 2002; Visscher et al., 2002). In a survey in England (Gregory et al., 1990), middle-aged women (50-64 years) were found to have the highest proportion of overweight (46%) and obesity (BMI>30; 18%). The high and continually increasing prevalence of overweight is more than a cosmetic issue: mortality and morbidity for a number of diseases, such as coronary heart disease, stroke and diabetes, increase with BMIs that exceed 25, and rise steeply for BMIs over 30 (as reviewed by Ashwell, 1994). Recently, fat distribution, rather than overweight per se, has been found to be a decisive risk factor. Central, or abdominal, as contrasted with peripheral distribution of fat (on the hips and thighs), is responsible for most of the increased risk (British Nutrition Foundation, 1992). The first, or "apple" type of fat distribution is characteristic of males whereas the second, or "pear" type is more common in females, although these differences gradually disappear as the level of overweight increases.

The Simple but Unattainable Curing of Obesity

In view of the increased health risks and the social stigma associated with fatness, the latter particularly among young women and in upper class populations, the high and increasing prevalence of obesity is a puzzling phenomenon since its treatment is essentially simple and easily understood: reduction in the intake of energy in the diet below the energy output (cf. Crowley et al., 2002). This can be accomplished by a variety of means aimed either at *increasing* the expenditure of energy through a) increased physical activity, or b) speeding up the rate of metabolism through drug treatment; or *decreasing* food intake through c) the application of more or less drastic dietary regimes; d) gastroplastic surgery, or e) through intestinal bypass surgery, leading to a decrease in nutrient uptake.

Despite the plethora of treatment options available, their poor long-term results are well documented even if success in weight reduction and weight maintenance does vary markedly among individuals. As known from the tabloid press and the scientific literature alike, each treatment option, be it the application of an inextensible nylon cord around the waist to prevent weight gain or the use of very low calorie diets (VLCD; < 800 kcal/day), has its successful adherents. However, most people who lose weight with any program tend to return to their pre-program weight within 5 years (NIH Technology Assessment Conference Panel, 1992). The best results thus far have been obtained by gastric surgery. Pharmacological treatment, resulting in a reduction in fat uptake, may be the treatment of choice in the future. There is considerable controversy regarding the psychosocial effects of various treatment modalities. Whereas a majority of evaluations emphasize the average patient's experience of psychosocial benefits, particularly after gastric restriction surgery (e.g. Halmi et al., 1980), 10-20% have been reported to suffer adverse effects, including psychiatric complications (Espmark, 1979; Larsen, 1990; MacLean et al., 1990; Rydén et al., 1989).

Origins of Obesity

Etiological factors in obesity at quite different levels of analysis have been identified, and hereditary (Meyer, 1995), cellular (Gurr et al., 1982) metabolic (Jequier & Schutz, 1985), psychological (Wolman, 1982), familial (Ganley, 1986; Weisz & Bucher, 1980; Maddi et al., 1997) and social as well as cultural (Rozin, 1982) factors have also been reported. It can be argued that all of these factors, by whatever mechanisms and processes, influence the regulation of body weight through a final behavioral pathway. Thus, overweight is always due to past or current overeating in relation to the individual's nutrient needs, a relevant question being: What leads to overeating?

Prehistoric Man - a Slim Hunter-Gatherer

If man's evolutionary past is taken as a starting point in seeking an answer to this question, the initial observation is that man has evolved to become the ultimate generalist omnivore, an opportunist, able to exploit temporary sources of food and to plan and carry out sophisticated forms of social hunting. Compared to our herbivorous phylogenetic predecessors, we became hunter-gatherers, able to select a diet that provides a balance of nutrients and sufficient calories to keep bodyweight (or growth rate) reasonably constant. In particular, the inclusion of meat in the diet provides a source of high-quality, easily digestible protein but also led to a large increase in foraging cost. Since animals to prey upon were low and scattered in abundance (and highly reluctant to become prey), man adopted an irregular pattern of feeding. The ability to store large amounts of energy in the adipose tissue is an adaptation to that pattern (Collier, 1989).

In association with its feeding ecology, Homo sapiens acquired a physiological-biochemical machinery that regulated its nutrient needs on a relatively short-term basis in order to maintain a constant internal milieu. In such terms, feeding patterns are expressions of cycles of physiological depletion and repletion that are experienced as cycles of hunger and satiety. Physiological variables such as levels of peptide hormones and blood glucose, serve as mediators in the defense of psychosomatic homeostasis.

Feeding Secures Nutrients and Safety

Complementing with anthropological observations this sketch of the feeding behavior and ecology of Homo sapiens before the rate of cultural evolution escalated with the advent of agriculture, it is clear that there has always been more to feeding than the mere securing of immediate energy needs. Parental feeding of offspring, and particularly breast feeding, constitutes the very core of relaxation, security, and attachment. Among adults, eating either signals or symbolizes a friendly, non-threatening attitude. Thus, long before adaptation to our historical cultural environments commenced, eating fulfilled emotional and social, as well as nutrient needs.

In the following, I will take the situation facing early man as a starting point with the aim of identifying causes of intentional versus unintentional gain or loss in weight. Obesity is, in this perspective, the result of unintentional weight gain and/or unsuccessful attempts to lose weight.

The Adaptive Challenge of Maintaining Body Weight

A major conclusion to be drawn from the ecological conditions facing the adult early man is that feeding served primarily to maintain, or prevent the loss of, body weight. Hunger and satiation mechanisms regulated the onset and termination of eating on each feeding occasion. Unintentional weight gain probably rarely reached maladaptive levels. Hence no regulatory mechanisms, aimed at maintaining body weight below an appropriate point, evolved. It is also reasonable to assume that unintentional weight loss due to a shortage of food, to strenuous physical activity, or to low temperature, was a much more common problem. In sum, man's adaptive potential was presumably employed to favor effective gathering of food as well as metabolic efficiency, not to counteract a maladaptive gain in weight.

In line with ecological arguments, intentional weight gain must primarily have been a response to previous, unintentional and perhaps threatening weight loss. Since an ample body weight is a sign of capacity and strength, intentional weight gain beyond the limits of physical agility would seem to represent a leap from "the wisdom of the body" to the more questionable "wisdom of the culture". This contention is supported by the observation that in human populations in which starvation is a reality, fatness is deliberately sought in order to demonstrate well-being and prosperity.

Intentional weight loss, finally, in the frame of reference employed here, is a recent challenge, restricted to populations with a sedentary life style and with highly nutritious food that is more or less constantly available. Thus, in modern, affluent societies, the same biological mechanisms which in our phylogenetic past were used to maintain body weight have become factors that counteract our efforts to control incipient weight gain and, in addition, jeopardize attempts to attain weight loss.

To sum up, whereas our somatic machinery has not been devised to avoid overconsumption by means other than that of controlling food intake on separate occasions of feeding, weight loss evokes powerful attempts to arrest the depletion of physiological reserves. The scene is thus set for a battle between biological mechanisms, on the one hand, which serve to maintain body weight, and psychological motives and social pressures, on the other hand, aimed at weight reduction.

In view of the preceding picture of man as a hunter-gatherer primate, somatically adapted to ecological conditions different from, or even the opposite to those prevailing in modern, highly affluent societies, it seems reasonable to change the question "what leads to overeating?" around to "Why are most people not overweight?" Three broad categories of conditions that counteract incipient weight gain can be discerned.

Condition of Strenuous Physical Activity, High Metabolism, High Muscular Tonus, or Low Ambient Temperature that Increase Energy Expenditure

Physical exercise is the standard recommendation for achieving an increase in energy expenditure. A more simple way of attaining this goal - hours being easier to count than calories - would be to reduce the number of hours spent indoors (where physical activity is low, food is readily available, and high ambient temperatures are the norm). Spending very few hours per day indoors (VFHI/day) would then be equivalent to a very a low calorie diet and could be called "outdoor therapy".

Situations or Factors that either Reduce Hunger or the Satisfaction Derived from Eating

Hunger strikes in which people may starve themselves to death, or eating disturbances such as anorexia nervosa, are examples of the strength of human motivation. Stress, depression, worry, falling in love and experiences of redemption are examples of emotional states that can interfere with normal eating and lead to drastic body weight loss. Needless to say, such factors do not readily lend themselves to manipulation and control, and are inappropriate to use as guidelines in weight reducing programs.

Deliberate Reduction in Food Intake in Response to Social Norms or because of Health Concerns

Here we are back to square one and are confronted with the simple fact that overweight people are not able to tolerate restriction on their food intake in order to lose weight, at least not on a long-term basis. Whereas there is general agreement on certain causes of such difficulties, such as alcoholism, psychoses or a sense of ambivalence, it remains unclear why some individuals do well and others poorly when trying to lose weight, and whether persons who easily become overweight are also those who are least successful in weight reducing programs. However, from an ecological viewpoint such as that just outlined, physiological signals of nutrient depletion represent a threat of starvation that elicits food-seeking behavior, which gradually becomes intensified. In phenomenological terms, frustration of the need for food represents not only a biological threat to one's very existence, but easily escalates as well representing a threat of the loss of social and emotional security. It appears that the more nutrient depletion is contaminated with emotional significance, the harder it is to tolerate.

Eating in Response to Displeasure

According to Bruch's ontogenetic approach to the origin of obesity (1969, 1973), the ability to interpret and respond correctly to "hunger" as the phenomenological correlate of physiological depletion is dependent on the early feeding-interaction with the mother. According to Bruch's model, the infant must experience, repeatedly and consistently, a fixed sequence of events: felt and expressed discomfort, the recognition of this signal by the mother, feeding, and relief from hunger. Children who are deprived of such experience by mothers who feed them in response to a variety of inappropriate external and internal stimuli are unable to differentiate accurately between various unpleasant physiological and emotional states and may thus overeat in response to virtually any internal arousal state. In particular, emotional distress becomes confused with hunger. Empirical results in line with Bruch's model have been obtained in studies of individuals at all levels of overweight. In a series of elegant experiments, Slochower (as reviewed in Slochower, 1983) has shown that mildly obese college students, in contrast to normal-weight subjects, overeat in response to unlabeled or "free-floating" anxiety, particularly if it is strong and uncontrollable, and that eating curbs their anxiety much as a sedative would. Similar findings in controlled studies of non-clinical groups have been reported by Cooper and Bowskill (1986), who found in students on a weight-reducing diet a clear association between dysphoric mood (depression, anxiety, loneliness) and overeating. Clinical studies of massively obese patients have yielded similar results, various negative emotions being found to initiate eating episodes that alleviate anxiety (Wolman, 1982; Holland et al., 1970; Rand, 1978; Maddi et al. 1997). Taken as a whole, these data support the idea that, in some individuals, eating may serve to reduce anxiety. According to Bruch's theory, this pattern is established in the early feeding interaction with the mother. However, it seems equally possible that, whatever the underlying etiology may be, individuals who are unable to readily label and differentiate between various unpleasant emotional and physiological states suffer a greater risk of overeating in response to such states.

Eating in Response to Idiosyncratic Motives

A complementary, psychodynamic view is that, in some individuals, food and eating may have acquired a highly idiosyncratic and subconscious significance, representing a hesitance to separate from parents, for example, or - in view of today's emphasis on a slim appearance - expressing an introaggressive motive of remaining unattractive, or serving as a substitute for inaccessible pleasures. If food deprivation threatens to unmask such hidden motives, the individual may well prefer to remain unaware of them at the cost of breaking the diet regime.

Psychological Defense: An Alternative to Eating in the Control of Anxiety

On the assumption that food and eating serve the purpose of alleviating painful emotional states, one hypothetical source of inter-individual differences in the ability to adhere to diet regimes, would be the individual's armamentarium of psychological defense. Defenses that effectively neutralize threatening stimulation would protect against anxiety and other painful emotions, such as depression or shame. Isolation would be particularly advantageous, since it essentially implies the ability to "keep things apart", that is to separate from each other affect and thought, or thinking and behavior. In a rare study of obese patients in individual psychotherapy, isolation was found to characterize those who lost weight successfully (Zukerfeld & Guido, 1983). On the other hand, a faltering defense strategy, permitting anxiety to become manifest, would increase the individual's difficulties in resisting the temptation to resort to eating in anxiety-evoking situations. Another feature that can be expected to be a hindrance when the individual is deprived of the habitual use of eating in order to attain a relaxed state is sensitivity, or an inclination to respond to marginal internal and external cues, and to experience such cues as personally meaningful. A sensitive disposition is often accompanied by increased psychic vulnerability and anxiety (Smith et al., 1975).

In a series of studies using the Meat-Contrast Technique (MCT; Smith et al., 1989), or the Defense Mechanism Test (DMT; Kragh, 1960; Kragh & Smith, 1970), described in Chapter 7 in this volume, the defensive organization was studied in moderately and grossly obese patients before and after conservative (by dietary regimes) or surgical treatment. The main aim of the studies reported here was to identify putative psychological predictors of a successful or unsuccessful outcome of treatment for obesity.

Psychological Features in Obese Patients Investigated Before and After Treatment

In an initial study of 21 grossly obese patients (mean body weight 126 kg, range 93-190 kg; 17 women, 4 men) testing took place a few days prior to surgery (Rydén & Danielsson, 1983). Apart from medical conditions (cardiovascular disease, severe diabetes), only psychiatric disorder and alcoholism were used as exclusion criteria. Thus, these patients represented a fairly unselected sample of the grossly obese population and were also exposed to preoperative stress. Hence, we expected that, to the extent that obese individuals possess characteristic defensive patterns, these mechanisms should be optimally accessible for examination.

As expected, the MCT-protocols of these patients showed reactions to the threatening picture-motif in the test which differed from those of various clinical and non-clinical groups studied earlier (Smith and Westerlundh, 1980; Smith et al., 1989) and which were similar to protocols of children in some respects (Smith & Danielsson, 1982). Above all, a common feature was an incapacity to ward off the threat effectively on a structural-symbolic, psychological level. These persons were left to defend themselves by maneuvers usually abandoned during childhood, such as reporting that the threat is irrelevant, or that the hero figure is sleeping or is eating (primitive denial, n=10), or by evasive measures such as trying to persuade the experimenter to describe the picture, resulting in empty protocols (n=10). Two patients even showed open behavioral responses (irresistible yawning or complaints of feeling cold) which are normal in children but are rarely found in adults (Smith & Danielsson, 1982). Ten subjects were scored for "leaking" mechanisms, implying that the defense fails and does not manage to disguise the threatening characteristics of the picture (Smith et al., 1989). The threat may be reported as partly visible, or reports of defensive structures may occur together with somatic manifestations of anxiety. Denial and projection, considered to be less for example sophisticated defenses in terms of their ontogenetically early emergence (Smith & Danielsson, 1976/77), were scored for 5 and 6 patients. The patients' insufficient capacity for defending themselves against emotional threat was evident in the prevalent signs of anxiety that were found (n=12). The patients' commonly interpreting the hero in childish or sex-inadequate terms (n=10) was seen as signifying arrest of development towards emotional maturity. More mature defenses, such as isolation and/or repression, were found in 13 of the patients, often in combination with infantile ones. Sensitivity, or disposition to respond to marginal external as well as internal cues, often accompanied by increased anxiety and a heightened psychic vulnerability, was scored in three patients.

Summing up, in these patients child-type modes of adjustment had not been abandoned but were functioning more or less extensively in combination with more mature ones. The patients also showed more signs of anxiety than did non-clinical controls (Smith et al., 1989). However, in interpreting these findings, one should consider possible effects of the impending operation. It has been shown (Janis, 1957) that major surgery constitutes a threat to the patient's physical and mental integrity. The abundant signs of anxiety and immaturity may thus at least partly reflect a temporary regression in the face of a major surgical operation.

In order to investigate this issue, the patients' defensive organization was reassessed 8-18 months after surgery (Rydén et al., 1989). We expected that MCT testing at that time would yield a picture showing adaptation to a long-term food deprivation, perhaps quite similar to their habitual state since these patients were constantly involved in often long-term efforts to diet.

Of the original sample, twelve patients were tested with MCT both before and after surgery. Two major changes were apparent (Table 24.1). Signs of regressive defense and/or of immaturity were found in twelve of the patients prior to surgery, but only in five following surgery. On the other hand, whereas prior to surgery no patient was scored for depression, following surgery eight patients received such scores. Two additional patients were tested prior to surgery, and another six after surgery.

Table 24.1: *Distribution of signs per person in MCT in a group of 12 grossly obese patients tested both before and after surgery (including patients tested only before (N=2) or only after (N=6) surgery within parentheses).*

	Regressive defense +immature identity		Depression	
	+	-	+	-
MCT before surgery	12 (12)	0 (2)	0 (1)	12 (13)
MCT after surgery	7 (8)	5 (10)	8 (11)	4 (7)
	p= .05 (p= .04)		p= < .001 (p= < .001)	

Fisher's exact test, two-tailed

When all the available MCT-protocols were compared, signs of regressive defense were found to have decreased from 86% to 44%, and signs of depression to have increased from 4% to 61%. Four patients developed depressive reactions severe enough to require professional intervention. Further analysis of all 18 postoperative MCT-protocols showed that combinations of repression, isolation, and/or projection were found in 11 of the patients. In all, these results suggest that preoperative stress did distort the patients' habitual mode of functioning. An additional stress effect may have been that habitual mild or moderate depressive tendencies were temporarily concealed and were replaced by alternative strategies aimed at averting anxiety.

It can be argued that correlations between psychological features and obesity can be expected in severely obese patients referred for surgery after innumerable unsuccessful attempts to lose weight by various forms of dietary treatment, but that it may be less obvious in other samples. Therefore, in a third study, we investigated 20 highly motivated and carefully selected patients (Mean BMI=41.1; 16 women, 4 men) about 3 weeks prior to surgery (Rydén et al., 1996). The patients were provided with oral and written information concerning the surgical procedure and its effects (above all that they would be able to eat only small quantities of food at a time for the rest of their lives) by the surgeon who emphasized the patients' own responsibility for the outcome. The information was given to groups of interested obese individuals, many of whom chose not to proceed further in the selection process. The MCT was used as well as two parts of the Percept-genetic Objects Relation Test (PORT). I.e. the Attachment theme and the Separation theme (Nilsson 1983; Nilsson & Svensson, 1999). Each theme is represented by pictures portraying a mother caring for and leaving her child respectively. The subject's vulnerability to each theme, and strategies for averting the anxiety possibly elicited by it, are identified through various distortions of the picture motif as detailed in the manual (Nilsson & Svensson, 1999). In addition, we conducted an interview and employed five questionnaires: The Three Factor Eating Questionnaire (EQ), assessing three aspects of eating behavior: 'restraint', 'disinhibition', and 'hunger' (Björvell et al., 1989); the Beck Depression Inventory (BDI; Beck et. al., 1961); and the Hopkins Symptom Check List (HSCL; Derogatis et al., 1973), quantifying various psychiatric dimensions, two of which were of particular interest here: Depression, and Interpersonal Sensitivity; MACL; and the Karolinska Scales of Personality (KSP), a self-report inventory constructed for identifying dimensions of vulnerability to various personality and psychiatric disorders (Somatic anxiety, Psychic anxiety, Muscular Tension, Social Desirability, Impulsiveness, Monotony Avoidance, Detachment, Psychastenia, Socialization, Indirect Aggression, Verbal Aggression, Irritability, Suspicion, Guilt, and Inhibition of Aggression (Schalling et al., 1983).

Inspection of the MCT-protocols of these more strictly selected patients showed the distribution of signs not to deviate from what could be expected in a non-clinical group, with one exception: that six of the patients showed signs of depression. In comparison to normal-weight reference groups our patients reported a higher level of hunger ($p<.001$) and more inhibited eating ($p<.001$) (EQ); greater impulsivity ($p<.05$, women) and a lower degree of socialization ($p<.01$, women) (KSP); and greater a degree of depression ($p<.001$) (HSCL). In these respects, they were similar to other obese groups investigated with the same instruments.

To sum up, this group of more strictly selected obese patients resembled previously tested obese samples in some respects but did not show the immature defensive organization found in our first group. Apparently, the fact that grossly obese individuals have one obvious external feature in common, does not allow the generalization to be made that they constitute a homogenous group with respect to their psychological features.

In order to test this conclusion, we extended our investigations to include a third group of obese subjects: 30 middle-aged (mean 51.4 years; 22 women, 8 men), socially well-adapted individuals, most of them mildly or moderately obese (16 subjects BMI 25-30; 13 subjects BMI 30-40; 3 subjects BMI>40), who had enrolled in a two-year lacto-vegetarian program, announced in local newspapers (Rydén & Johnsson, 1989). All of these subjects suffered from hypertension and their primary motive was to lower their blood pressure and be freed from their hypertension medicine. Only eight of them said that their primary motive was to lose weight. Thus this group represented a clearly overweight population but differed from patients referred to surgical or psychiatric clinics, who suffer more from their obesity, both socially and medically. These subjects were interviewed and were tested with the DMT. In addition, they filled out the Karolinska Scales of Personality (KSP), as well as the Mood Adjective Check List (MACL; Sjöberg et al., 1979), which consists of 71 mood scales, represented by six bipolar mood factors: hedonic tone, activation/deactivation, calmness/tension, extraversion/introversion, social orientation, and control/lack of control. The frequencies (always, sometimes, often) of self-rated eating behaviors (eating for consolation, night-eating, eating very large meals, eating incessantly, hunger increasing during meals, eating normally) were assessed by questionnaire. Our aims were first to determine the extent to which these individuals reported deviant eating behavior, and secondly to identify possible subgroups of individuals who differed in psychological characteristics associated with deviant eating behavior.

Night-eating was reported by 5 participants (all of them sometimes), eating very large meals by 16 (8 always-often, 8 sometimes), eating incessantly by 13 (6 always-often, 7 sometimes), eating for consolation by 12 (always-often), and hunger increasing during meals by 10 (4 always-often, 6 sometimes). The most common defense mechanisms were Isolation (n=18), Reaction formation (n=14), Repression (n=11), and Introjection (n=8). Identification with the Aggressor and Denial were scored in 4 and 3 subjects, respectively, and Introaggression in one subject. Canonical correlation analysis showed that Inhibition of aggression (r^2=.79), Psychic anxiety (r^2=.72) and Monotony avoidance (r^2=.67), independently of each other, were correlated with the whole set of food- and eating-related variables. Cluster analysis was performed to identify possible subgroups of patients differing in the relationships between the KSP-dimensions, mood, and the eating-related variables (Figure 24.1).

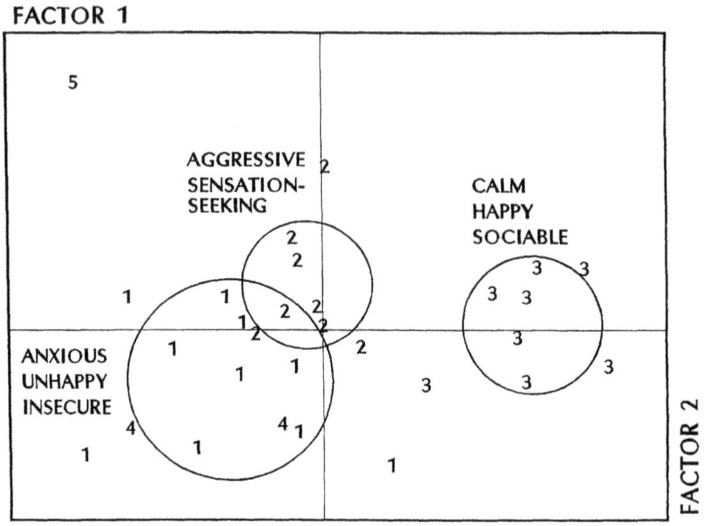

Figure 24.1: *Diagnostic features of three subgroups of moderately obese subjects as derived from cluster analysis of data from the Karolinska Scales of Personality and a Mood Adjective Check List. Factor 1 includes variables denoting anxiety and aggressiveness; Factor 2 expresses inhibition versus impulsiveness and internality versus externality. Number 4 and 5 denote individuals who constitute additional "clusters".*

Three subgroups, encompassing 26 of the subjects, were identified: one *anxious-unhappy-insecure* group (1, n=8) characterized by high somatic and psychic anxiety, high muscular tension, and feelings of low hedonic tone and of weak control; another *aggressive-sensation-seeking* group (2, n=10) with high levels of monotony avoidance and of verbal aggression; and a third, *calm-happy-sociable* group (3, n=8) with high scores on socialization and hedonic tone and with low scores on somatic anxiety, indirect aggression and irritability. Two of the remaining subjects (4, 4) were related to cluster 1 whereas one subject (5) had an extreme position in the diagram. In a complementary analysis, the clusters were related to the dichotomous DMT- and interview-variables. As shown in Table 24.2, subjects who were scored for immature defenses and reported regular alcohol consumption more often belonged to clusters 1 and 2, whereas subjects in cluster 3 more often used mature defenses and showed less problematic eating behavior. Interestingly, of the six subjects who had food-related professions, four belonged to cluster 3.

Table 24.2: *Psychological features characteristic of subjects belonging to clusters 1+2 (N=19) and 3 (N=8; cf. Figure 24.1).*

Feature	Cluster 1+2 vs. Cluster 3	*p*
Defenses (DMT)		
Repression and/or Isolation	10/8 8/0	.03
Denial, Id. with the aggr., Introaggr.	8/10 0/8	.03
Eats for consolation	11/7 1/7	.03
Eats incessantly	12/6 1/7	.02
Food-related profession	2/16 4/4	.05

Fisher's exact test, two-tailed

In sum, in this group of middle-aged individuals - for whom overweight can be expected to mainly be attributable to a sedentary life-style in combination with tolerance for moderate overweight - two different psychological concomitants to overeating emerged: one apparently involving the use of food as a sedative to ward off or neutralize negative emotions (cluster 1), and the other being related to impulsivity/externality (cluster 2). Experimental evidence that eating tends to be both initiated and reduced by dysphoric mood has been presented above. The second type of psychological vulnerability that was found to be related to overeating has also been shown to be related to sensation-seeking, smoking, and fluctuations of mood, particularly fits of violent temper (Schalling et al., 1983). Jönsson et al. (1986) found monotony avoidance to predict incapacity to maintain weight loss after jaw fixation. A complementary aspect of high monotony avoidance would be "stimulus-boundness", that is a propensity to be governed by chance external-contextual cues, e.g. to overeat in response to the mere presence of food, particularly if it is highly palatable. This feature agrees with the "externality hypothesis" of overweight (Rodin, 1982), according to which obese persons have a heightened sensitivity to external cues.

The third cluster contained eight individuals who showed a consistently well-adapted picture. Interestingly, four of the six subjects professionally involved in the preparation or selling of food belonged to this group. Presumably, the food-rich environment in which four of them spent their working days can partly explain their overweight. The distribution of defense mechanisms in the three groups agrees well with the assumption that less mature defenses tend to be found in subjects who report more overeating and vice versa.

Duckro et al. (1983), applying principal-component analysis to MMPI data obtained from 199 chronically obese patients, reported findings in basic agreement with our results. They derived three homogenous subgroups with features strikingly similar to those identified in our sample. One group was characterized as being unhappy and tense, with minimal assertiveness and self-confidence and with suppressed and self-directed anger; a second group was characterized by anger and hostile acting out; whereas the third group was not deviant from the norms.

Altogether, our findings suggest that certain psychological features - immature psychological defense, depression, anxiety and impulsivity/externality - which serve to explain overeating, are more common among obese than among normal-weight individuals and tend to be linked with difficulties in enduring food deprivation. Furthermore, these features can be expected to be more prevalent and more pronounced in samples of very obese patients who have been referred for psychiatric evaluation than in less obese individuals belonging to non-clinical samples. Accordingly, obese individuals who possess these features should suffer a greater risk of becoming treatment failures after either conservative or surgical treatment. Follow-up studies of patients who had undergone surgery and/or had participated in a fasting program were conducted to test this hypothesis.

Psychological Correlates of Differential Weight Loss after Treatment

Eighteen months after surgery, 21 patients who were investigated only a few days prior to surgery (Rydén & Danielsson, 1983) had lost on the average 34.4 kg (range 1-71 kg). Three groups that showed consistent and significant differences in weight loss after surgery, as confirmed by a significant time x group interaction in a two-way ANOVA, could be distinguished. Whereas two of these groups showed excellent (A; n=8, about 45 kg) or adequate (B; n=5, about 30 kg) weight loss, the seven patients in the third group (group C; 35% of the overall group) were judged as failures due to insufficient weight loss (about 20 kg and regaining their initial weight loss). No preoperative differences between the groups were found in terms of body weight, and surgical, morphological or biochemical variables. Inspection of preoperative MCT- data from patients who were available for both pre- and post-surgery analysis revealed that, contrary to our expectations, the groups could not be differentiated in terms of signs of immature defense or anxiety. However, signs of sensitivity and depression turned out to be ominous since they were more often found in group C (Table 24.3). Data from a preoperative clinical interview showed that, taken together, two of the variables, sensitivity and social phobia, in themselves differentiated group C from group A+B (p=.02). Further interview variables that characterized group C were the following: 'avoids taking about the operation, belittles it or believes that one will be reborn through it', and 'previous anxiety reactions'. A clear differentiation between group C and group A+B was obtained on the basis of these variables (5/1 vs. 1/12, p=.01). Finally, the physician's estimation of the patients' degree of responsible behavior on the hospital ward and degree of above average alcohol consumption yielded a similar C vs. A+B contrast (5/1 vs. 2/12, p.02).

Table 24.3: *Predictive signs in the MCT test differentiating patients who failed to lose weight successfully after surgery (C, N=5) from patients who showed adequate (B, N=3) or excellent (A, N=6) weight loss.*

	A	B	C
a. Anxiety and/or regressive defense;	5	3	1
b. All combinations with sensitivity;	1	0	3
c. Depression	1	0	4

a: b+c, A+B/C: Fisher´s exact test, p = .015 (two-tailed)

Analysis of the psychological sequelae following weight loss showed that the significant increase in signs of depression in the MCT test was unevenly distributed among the groups. The patients in groups A and B who managed to lose weight successfully showed more signs either of repression, isolation and projection or of depression (n=13) than patients in group C (n=1). Group C patients, on the other hand, with one exception, were the only to show signs of denial, as well as a C-phase without previous defense (n=3) (13/1 vs. 1/3, p=.001). Thus, the patients who did poorly employed an immature defense, or had no effective defense for averting anxiety.

Summing up, preoperative assessment of the patients' defensive strategies, as well as information obtained by interview and through observation of the patients' behavior in the hospital ward, provided a coherent picture that predicted treatment failure or success in terms of postoperative weight loss.

Since patients who did not lose weight satisfactorily could well be expected on a common sense basis to experience more severe psychological problems, the quite opposite findings here suggest that rapid and substantial weight loss involves problems of adaptation. In view of the immature or "leaking" defense which many patients resorted to when exposed to the stress of the forthcoming operation, indicating an immature identity or sense of self, a possible interpretation of the depressive reactions suffered more often by the successful patients is that these reactions served as defense against anxiety elicited by their separation from sources of satisfaction of their narcissistic needs, such as food or nurturing relationships (Sandler & Joffe, 1965; Wolman,1981).

A second attempt to predict the treatment results after surgery was made in follow-up three years after surgery. This study involved 20 obese patients who had been carefully selected (Rydén et al., 1996). By that time, 13 of the patients had attained satisfactory weight loss (loss of >50% of their preoperative excess weight, which had been defined as BMI >25; average weight at operation 117.2 (SD=5.2) kg); average weight at follow-up 84.0 (SD=6.7) kg, whereas seven of the patients had failed to achieve this (average weight at operation 117.7 (SD=5.0) kg; average weight at follow-up 103.8 (SD=6.7) kg). An interview revealed the effects to mainly have been positive, even among the supposedly unsuccessful patients. Fifteen of the patients reported, for example, that their mood had improved, and nine of the patients experienced an improved ability to assert themselves in social situations. Eight of the patients had increased their social activity, whereas six of the patients continued to lead a very restricted social life. The seven unsuccessful patients reported deviant eating behavior, especially addictive eating, frequent vomiting, or 'eating as they had before the operation' more frequently than the successful patients did ($p=.01$). Discriminant analysis showed that three variables from the preoperative investigation correctly classified 17 of the 19 patients available for analysis ($p=.004$). The seven unsuccessful patients scored higher on the Hunger factor of the Three-factor Eating Questionnaire, and lower on the KSP Verbal Aggression and Socialization scales. These features had previously been found in patients who dropped our from a long-term behavioral modification program for obesity (Björvell et al., 1989; cf. Rowe et al. 2000) and in patients who were unable to maintain weight loss after one year of jaw fixation (Jönsson et al., 1986). Apparently, difficulties in the psychological processing of aggression can interfere with the adaptation to food restrictions, independent of the treatment modality. Espmark (1979) found 69% of 105 extremely obese patients to be eridophobic, that is, to have difficulties in handling aggressive feelings. After surgical treatment more than 59% of these patients developed crisis reactions, often initiated by outbreaks of aggression followed by enhanced self-esteem. In these patients overeating may have served to neutralize feelings of aggression, which are threatening to an eridophobic individual.

Further analyses by use of discriminant analysis disclosed that high scores on KSP-Detachment (need for emotional distance from other people), and on the Hunger factor of the Eating Questionnaire, and signs on the percept-genetic MCT and PORT tests indicating high psychological vulnerability (as found in interpretation of drawings that expressed anxiety, insecure identity, or depression in the PORT, in conjunction with maladaptive or immature defenses in the MCT), predicted deviant eating behavior at follow-up (11 patients) (16/17 patients correctly classified, $p=.001$). It was also found that deviant eating was primarily related to KSP-Impulsivity and to KSP-Detachment, as well as to low ability to resist food intake (EQ-Restraint), whereas reduced well-being was associated with SCL-Depression, limited ability to form close relationships (KSP-Socialization), strong feelings of guilt (KSP-Guilt) and psychological vulnerability, as manifested in the percept-genetic tests. The small size of the subgroups makes conclusions regarding the predictive value of specific variables hazardous. However, the results suggest that when patients are more strictly selected - candidates who are ambivalent or have unrealistic expectations regarding the operation being excluded - percept-genetic data that cannot be used to predict weight loss in this study can predict disturbed eating behavior and mood effects. However, disturbed eating behavior and/or untoward mood effects may well jeopardize persistent maintenance of weight loss over a longer period of time.

In the final study of long-term effects of a 5-week fasting program at a health center, 20 grossly obese patients (mean weight 115.1 kg; BMI 39.6), were investigated (Rydén & Sörbris, 1986). Their average weight loss during fasting was 10.1 (SD=5.7) kg. In order to assess their weight fluctuation following treatment, three subgroups of patients were interviewed and were tested with the MCT approximately 1.5 years (n=14), 2.5 years (n=9), and 3.7 years (n=7) after fasting. Twelve of the patients later received surgical treatment and 10 of them were available, permitting the effects of fasting and surgery, respectively, to be compared. As expected, weight gain after fasting was positively related to the length of the follow-up period ($p<.01$). Large inter-individual variation in weight loss during fasting and in rate of weight gain after fasting was found. Some 75% of the weight loss during fasting could be accounted for in terms of prefasting body weight and uptake of T_3 (a thyroid hormone, Sörbris et al., 1982). Three sets of variables - deviant eating behavior, MCT-signs, and affective responses to fasting - could predict treatment outcome at follow-up. The less successful patients (in terms of weight at follow-up in relation to prefasting weight) more often reported eating for consolation ($p<.002$), night-eating ($p<.002$), and eating without satiation ($p<.02$). During fasting they reported being more fatigued ($p<.02$), and irritable ($p<.02$). Inspection of their MCT-protocols revealed both mature and immature defenses. Repression was found in 16 of the protocols, isolation in 14, sensitivity in 9, stereotyped iteration of response indicative of depression or dysphoria in 4, and C-phase without previous response, indicating evasiveness, in 4 protocols. The combination of sensitivity and/or evasiveness and lack of isolation (N=8) was more common in the less successful patients (7/7 vs. 1/13, $p<.02$).

Comparison of the treatment effects of fasting and of surgery showed that patients who were more successful in maintaining weight loss after fasting (n=5) were also more successful at this after surgery (cf. Olsson et al., 1984), whereas four of five patients who were less successful after fasting belonged to the group of treatment failures following surgery ($p=.05$). Thus, despite the large difference in weight loss attained generally during fasting and after surgery, differences between individuals remain. This finding suggests that when patients are under the constant surveillance of the staff at the fasting clinic, variations in weight loss can be attributed primarily to somatic variables. Later, when the patients are on their own, psychological features that distinguished the less from more successful patients - such as those relating to their defensive organization - appear to be related to their ability to endure sustained dietary restrictions, thus serving to explain the differences in weight gain found between fasting and follow-up.

Conclusions

Attempts to lose weight in order to improve health or adapt to ideals of having a slim physique constitute a challenge that runs counter to the ecological requirements of man's original environment as a hunter-gatherer. It is reasonable to assume that in such an environment the limited access to food, and the physical activity necessary to obtain it, together with the time spent in relatively low ambient temperatures, precluded the development of maladaptive weight gain. Furthermore, since physiological depletion, signaled by decreasing blood sugar levels, for example, is potentially life-threatening, it evokes strong behavioral responses, those of food seeking. On the other hand, when food supply is inadequate, physiological defenses, such as lowering of the body temperature and motoric sluggishness, are activated in order to reduce the depletion of nutrient reserves.

In sum, dieting can be expected to elicit somatic countermeasures, quite independent of its inherent psychological significance.

Furthermore dieting is particularly difficult since in modern urban environments, eating is such a ubiquitous behavior, fulfilling more than simply nutrient needs. Dieting creates free time that has to be filled by alternative activities. In this respect, dieting creates conditions similar to those involved in cessation of smoking. The habit of eating, or of smoking, is difficult to abandon, partly because it is an ingrained feature of our behavioral repertoire.

Given the more or less constant availability of food, individuals who are either prone to respond impulsively, who avoid monotony, or who are habitually responsive to external cues are more liable to eat when food is present. This tendency is strengthened by the influence of stress, which leads to the increase of the individual's response rate.

Efforts to reduce food intake moderately in order to prevent weight gain, or to adhere to more demanding diet regimes in order to lose weight, are made more difficult, as eating serves psychological or social ends. In particular, individuals who habitually use food and eating in order to alleviate painful feelings have to face these feelings when dieting, unless they can be neutralized by psychological defenses. Furthermore, individuals who have difficulties in differentiating between various disagreeable physiological and psychological states will be even more strongly exposed to unpleasant or painful feelings when dieting. Such difficulties may derive from an insufficient early mother-child interaction or may have other etiologies, such as an alexithymic disposition.

There are both clinical observations and experimental evidence to show that two propensities, in particular, are more common in overweight individuals than in normal-weight controls: an inclination to eat in response to unlabeled and uncontrolled anxiety, in particular; and a strong dependence on environmental stimuli in connection with impulsiveness, monotony avoidance, sensation-seeking, or extraversion. The common behavioral denominator here - an inclination to act at the spur of the moment in response to inner impulses or outer stimulation - has been variously interpreted as having its origin in lack of a firm inner reference, as being the effect of a faltering individuation process, and as a neuropsychological characteristic. The first alternative implies an immature defensive organization, whereas the second is neutral in this respect.

Since the obese individual with immature or ineffective defenses cannot readily neutralize painful feelings which s/he is liable to experience during food deprivation, s/he is left dependent on somatic or behavioral reactions, or is prone to experience depressive affects as a protection against anxiety. In such a predicament, the more food and eating serves an anxiety-curbing purpose, the more difficult food restrictions are to endure. Hence, success or failure after treatment for obesity should be predictable on the basis of the maturity of the individual's defenses. The results obtained in the series of studies reviewed support this conclusion.

References

Ashwell, M. (1994). Obesity in men and women. *International Journal of Obesity*, 18, Suppl. 1, S1-S7.

Björvell, H., Edman, G., Schalling, D. (1989). Personality traits related to eating behavior and weight loss in a group of severely obese patients. *International Journal of Eating Disorders*, 8, 315-323.

British Nutrition Foundation (1992). *The nature and risks of obesity*. London: British Nutrition Foundation.

Bruch, H. (1969). Hunger and instinct. *Journal of Nervous and Mental Disease*, 149, 91-114.

Bruch, H. (1973). *Eating disorders. Obesity, Anorexia nervosa and the person within*. London: Routledge & Kegan Paul.

Collier, G. (1989). The economics of hunger, thirst, satiety, and regulation. In L.H. Schneider, S.J. Cooper, & K.A. Halmi (Eds.), *The psychobiology of human eating disorders. preclinical and clinical perspectives.* Annals of the New York Academy of Science, Vol. 575, 136-154.

Cooper, P., & Bowshill, R. (1986). Dysphoric mood and overeating. *British Journal of Clinical Psychology, 25,* 155-156.

Derogatis, L. R., Lipman, R. S., & Covi, L. (1973). SCL-90. An outpatient psychiatric rating scale - preliminary report. *Psychopharmacology Bulletin*, 9, 13-28.

Duckro, P. N., Leavitt, J. N. Jr., Beal, D. G., & Chang, A. F. (1983). Psychological status among female candidates for surgical treatment of obesity. *International Journal of Obesity*, 7, 477-485.

Espmark, S. (1979). Psychological effects of ileojejunal and gastric bypass surgery - attitude of the patient and its effect on the individual, family and other relationships. In D. Maxwell (Ed.), *Surgical Treatment of Obesity*. London: Academic Press.

Ganley, R. M. (1986). Epistemology, family patterns, and psychosomatics: The case of obesity. *Family Processes*, 25, 437-451.

Gregory et al. (1990). *The dietary and nutritional survey of British adults*. London: HMSO.

Gurr, M. I., Jung, R. T., Robinson, M. P., & James, P. T. (1982). Adipose tissue cellularity in man: The relationship between fat cell size and number, the mass and distribution of body fat, and the history of weight gain and loss. *International Journal of Obesity*, 6, 419-436.

Halmi, K. A., Stunkard, A. J., & Mason, E. (1980). Emotional response to weight reduction by three methods: gastric bypass, jejunoileal bypass, diet. *American Journal of Clinical Nutrition*, 33, 446-451.

Janis, I. L. (1957). *Psychological stress. Psychoanalytic and behavioral studies of surgical patients*. London: Academic Press.

Jequier, E., & Schutz, Y. (1985). New evidence for a thermogenetic defect in human obesity. *International Journal of Obesity*, 9, Suppl. 2, 1-7.

Jönsson, B., Björvell, H., Levander, S., & Rössner, S. (1986). Personality traits predicting weight loss outcome in obese patients. *Acta Psychiatrica Scandinavica*, 74, 384-387.

Kragh, U. (1960). The Defense Mechanism Test: A new method for diagnosis and personnel selection. *Journal of Applied Psychology*, 44, 303-309.

Kragh, U., & Smith, G.J.W. (1970). *Percept-genetic Analysis*. Lund, Sweden: Gleerups.

Larsen, F. Psychosocial function before and after gastric banding surgery for morbid obesity. *Acta Psychiatrica Scandinavica*, 82, Suppl. 359, 1-54.

MacLean, L. D., Rhode, B. M., & Forse, R. A. (1990). Late results of vertical banded gastroplasty for morbid and superobesity. *Surgery*, 107, 20-27.

Maddi. S. R., Khoshaba, D. M., Persoco, M., Bleecker, F-. & VanArsdall, G. (1997). Psychosocial correlates of psychopathology in a national sample of the morbidly obese. *Obesity Surgery*, 7, 397-404.

Meyer, J. M. (1995). Genetic studies of obesity across the life span. In J.R. Turner, L.R. Cardon, & J.K. Hewitt (Eds.), *Behavior genetic approaches to behavioral medicine* (pp. 145-146) . New York: Plenum.

NIH Technology Assessment Conference Panel (1992). Methods for voluntary weight loss and control. *Annals of Internal Medicine*, 116, 942-948.

Nilsson, A. (1983). *The mechanisms of defense within a developmental frame of reference*. Lund: Gleerup.

Nilsson, A. & Svensson, B. (1999). PORT – *Percept-Genetic Object-relation test. A projective method for clinical use. Manual*. Department of Psychology, Lund University: Lund, Sweden.

Olsson, S- Å., Rydén, O., Danielsson, A., & Nilsson-Ehle, P. (1984). Weight reduction after gastroplasty: the predictive value of surgical, metabolic, and psychological variables. *International Journal of Obesity*, 8, 245-258.

Paeratakul, S., Lovejoy, J.C ., Ryan, D. H., & Bray, G. A. (2002). The relation of gender, race and socioeconomic status to obesity and obesity comorbidities in a sample of US adults. *Nature reviews. Drug discovery*, 1, 276-286.

Rand, S. S. W. (1978). Treatment of obese patients in psychoanalysis. *Psychiatric Clinics of North America,* 1, 661-672.

Rodin, J. (1982). *Obesity: Why the losing battle.* In B.B. Wolman (Ed.), Psychological aspects of Obesity. A Handbook. (pp. 30-87). New York: Van Nostrand Reinhold Co.

Rozin, P. (1982). Human food selection: the interaction of biology, culture, and individual experience. In L.M. Barker (Ed.), *The Psychobiology of Human Food Selection* (pp. 225-254). Westport, Connecticut: Connecticut Avi Publishing Co.

Rowe, J. L., Downey, J. E., Faust, M., & Horn, M. J. (2000). Psychological and demographic predictors of successful weight loss following silastic ring vertical stapled gastroplasty. *Psychological Reports*, 86, 1028-1036.

Rydén, O., & Danielsson, A. (1983). Personality features of grossly obese surgical patients - a preoperative study. *Archives of Psychology*, 135, 115-134.

Rydén, O., & Johnsson, P. (1989). Psychological vulnerabilities and eating patterns in a group of moderately obese patients. *The Journal of Obesity and Weight Regulation*, 8, 83-97.

Rydén, O., & Sörbris, R. (1986). Weight maintenance after fasting: a look at somatic and psychological parameters. *The Journal of Obesity and Weight Regulation*, 5, 166-180.

Rydén, O., Hedenbro, J. L., & Fredriksen, S. G. (1996). Weight loss after vertical banded gastroplasty can be predicted: a prospective psychological study. *Obesity Surgery*, 6 (3), 237-243.

Rydén, O., Olsson, S-Å., Danielsson, B. A., & Nilsson-Ehle, P. (1989). Weight loss after gastroplasty: psychological sequelae in relation to clinical and metabolic observations. *Journal of the American College of Nutrition*, 8, 15-23.

Sandler, J, & Joffe, W. G. (1965). Notes on pain, depression and individuation. *Psychoanalytic Study of the Child*, 20, 394-424.

Schalling, D., Edman, G., & Åsberg, M. (1983). Impulsive cognitive style and inability to tolerate boredom: Psychobiological studies of temperamental vulnerability. In M. Zuckerman (Ed.), *Biological bases of sensation-seeking, impulsivity, and anxiety* (pp. 123-145). Hilsdale, NJ: Erlbaum Ass.

Sjöberg, L., Svensson, E., & Persson L. O. (1979). The measurement of mood. *Scandinavian Journal of Psychology*, 20, 1-20.

Slochower, J. A. (1983). *Excessive eating. The role of emotions and environment.* New York: Human Sciences Press.

Smith, G. J. W., & Danielsson, A. (1976/77). From open flight to symbolic and perceptual tactics. A study of defense in preschool children. *Publications of the Royal Society of Letters at Lund*, 20, 5-41.

Smith, G. J. W., & Danielsson, A. (1982). Anxiety and defensive strategies in childhood and adolescence. *Psychological Issues*, Monograph 52. New York: International Universities Press.

Smith, G. J. W., & Westerlundh, B. (1980). Percept-genesis: A process perspective on perception-personality. In L. Wheeler (Ed.), *Review of Personality and Social Psychology*, Vol 1, (pp. 94-124). Beverly Hills: Sage.

Smith, G. J. W., Johnson, G., Almgren, P-E., and Johansson, A. (2001). *MCT - The Meta Contrast Tecnique. Manual.* Department of Psychology, Lund University, Sweden.

Sörbris, R., Aly, K-O., Nilsson-Ehle, P., Pettersson, BG., & Öckerman, P-A. (1982). Vegetarian fasting of obese patients: a clinical and biochemical evaluation. *Scandinavian Journal of Gastroenterology*, 17, 417-424.

Visscher, T. L., Kromhout, D., & Seidell, J. C. (2002). Long-term and recent time trends in the prevalence of obesity among Dutch men and women. *International Journal of Obesity and Related Metabolic Disorders*, 26, 1218-1224.

Weisz, G., & Bucher, B. (1980). Involving husbands in treatment of obesity - effects on weight loss, depression, and marital satisfaction. *Behavior Therapy*, 11, 643-650.

Wolman, B. B. (Ed.). (1982). *Psychological Aspects of Obesity. A Handbook.* New York: Van Nostrand Reinhold Co.

Wolman, B. B. (1981). Depression and obesity. In B.B. Wolman (Ed.), *Psychological aspects of Obesity. A Handbook* (pp. 88-103). New York: Van Nostrand Reinhold Co.

Zukerfeldt, R., & Guido, I. (1983, October). *Evolution of obese patients under psychotherapy.* Paper read at the 4th International Congress on Obesity, New York.

Defense Mechanisms
U. Hentschel, G. Smith, J.G. Draguns & W. Ehlers (Editors)

Chapter 25

An Experimental Study of Severe Eating Disorders (Anorexia Nervosa and Bulimia Nervosa)

Per Johnsson, Gudmund J.W. Smith and Gunilla Amnér

Introduction

Current formulations of the two major eating disorders, anorexia nervosa (A) and bulimia nervosa (B), focus on the interaction of multiple determinants (Johnson & Connors, 1987). A and B have been described as disorders with a variety of psychopathological backgrounds ranging from neurosis to psychosis and schizophrenia (Piran et al, 1985; Wonderlich et al, 1990). Hudson et al. (1983) found a 16 percent rate of borderline personality disorder in a sample of 49 patients with bulimia nervosa but no difference in the rates of this disorder between subjects with active and remitted bulimia.

Several findings differentiate restricters from bingers along personality disorder lines Thus, Piran et al. (1988) reached consensus in judging 77 percent of restricters as belonging to the DSM-III anxious-fearful cluster of personality disorders and 66 percent of anorectic bingers to show dramatic-erratic (borderline or histrionic) personality deviations. In a study involving normal-weight bulimics alone, Levine & Hyler (1986) found a 60 percent prevalence of the dramatic-erratic cluster of personality disorders. Wonderlich et al. (1990), using DSM-III-R Axis II criteria, reported findings only partially supportive of a dichotomy (cf. also Gartner et al, 1989).

In a long-term prospective study, Norring and Sohlberg (1991, 1993) followed the course and outcome of a group of 48 eating disordered patients. Using cluster analysis techniques on multiple measures of ego functioning, they found higher neurotic, lower neurotic, borderline, and borderline-psychotic organizations in both restricters and bingers. Etiologic theories concerning anorexia nervosa have predominantly stressed the involvement of ego weakness (1977), splitting, projection, and denial being the predominant modes of defense in the borderline group. Johnsson (1993) found that bulimics manifested immature isolation and depression defenses, whereas anorectics relied on sensitivity defenses as their main strategy. Poikolainen et al (2001) found that eating disorder patients had higher scores on sublimation, undoing, and passive aggression. Research on the role of defense styles clusters has found that, compared with controls, eating disorder patients have higher scores on immature defense styles (1990, 1991). Meyer and Waller (2000) found that subliminal presentation of abandonment cues led to activation of food- and shape-related schemata.

Eating disorders are disorders of the self. Since the child's genuine narcissistic needs are not met with empathy, these needs and affects are disavowed, repressed, or split off from the total self-structure (Geist, 1989). At some crucial point in his/her development, the individual invents a new restitutive system by means of which disordered eating patterns, rather than people, are used to meet self-object needs. Goodsitt (1984) has consistently viewed eating disorders as attempts to supply missing self-object functions.

One crucial aspect of the present group of patients with anorexia or bulimia is their alexithymia, and it was investigated in a separate study (1997). Alexithymia was studied by means of a projective test, the Identity Test (IT), described in more detail below. In this test the viewer is confronted with brief flashes of a picture of a face and is invited to describe his/her impression of the face. The presentations of the picture are paired with the subliminal messages "I", "I WELL", or "I ILL", which were designed to manipulate the viewer's impressions.

Alexithymia means literally "to have no words for emotions". The meaningful use of emotional words can be regarded as a sign of open communication between the more rational (conscious) and the more emotional (preconscious) stages of the user's constructive microprocesses. When this communication is obstructed, emotional conflicts run the risk of being somatized. Naturally, the requirement would be that the emotional words are meaningful to the person employing them. The present subjects do not generally avoid emotional words when asked to describe the face. However, they reveal that they do not really understand what the words imply. With respect to the use of strategies to avoid empathizing, the present patient group differed almost completely from the controls ($p < 0.000$).

A special scoring category indicating bewilderment when asked to describe the face involves reports of staring, begging or searching eyes. Such reports were given by 12 respondents. We interpreted this sign to mean that the subject was appealing for help and guidance. This interpretation was supported by the results of the Meta-Contrast Technique (MCT), to be described below. The young person depicted in that test was seen as "sad", "lonely", or "dejected" by ten of the 12 subjects with "eye" reports, but only by one of the remaining 16 subjects ($p< 0.000$).

The patients in the present group are actually extremely alexithymic. Since they do not experience the meaning of emotions, their reactions to them run the risk of being somatized. What other personality disturbances were associated with this alexithymia? In order to clarify this question, we employed an interview as well as the Tennessee Self Concept Scale and three percept-genetic methods.

Method

Participants

Twenty-eight inpatients were taken consecutively from a special ward for severe eating disturbances at the psychiatric clinic of the university hospital in Lund, Sweden. They were diagnosed according to the DSM-III-R criteria, as follows:

For anorexia nervosa:
1. Refusal to maintain body weight over a minimal weight for age and height;
2. Intense fear of gaining weight or becoming fat, even though underweight;
3. Disturbance in the way in which one's body weight, size, or shape is experienced;
4. Absence of at least three consecutive menstrual cycles.

For bulimia nervosa:
1. Recurrent episodes of binge-eating;
2. A feeling of lack of control over eating behavior during the eating binges;
3. Regularly engaging in self-induced vomiting, use of laxatives or diuretics, strict dieting, or rigorous exercise to prevent weight gain;
4. Persistent anxiety about body shape and weight.

Among the 28 patients, 15 were anorectic and 13 bulimic. Their ages varied from 20 to 49 years, with a mean of 27.1. The duration of the illness, based on their own information about the first appearance of eating irregularities, varied from 2 to 26 years, with a mean of 9.9. The bulimics had a somewhat earlier self-reported onset.

The reference group consisted of 21 women. With the exception of a few volonteers, most of them were selected at random from the telephone directory. They were 26 to 54 years old, with a mean of 38.3

The Interview

The interview was originally constructed by Hentschel and Kiessling (1989). The following items, among others, proved to be of particular relevance: patient's statement about onset of illness and present state of health; her most difficult period in life; report about nightmares, view on greatest threat to life, experiences of injustice, level of self-confidence, durability of decisions, meaning of life quality. We also inquired about attitudes towards aging.

Judging from previous work with patients suffering from Crohn's disease and ulcerative colitis (e.g., Smith et al, 1997), subjects' descriptions of their parents were crucial. A categorization of these descriptions will be presented later.

Case Descriptions

The subjects were asked to read the case stories of two elderly ladies discussing their health problems (Smith & van der Meer, 1993), and then to choose four statements among 12 to explain why one of them had regained her health more easily during the years and, similarly, why the other was less fortunate.

On the basis of findings in a previous study (1997) we constructed four groups of explanations:

- Psychological (e.g., I was very dependent: my mother used to say that Erna cannot do anything at all by herself).
- Doctor's orders (e.g., the internist who treated me wrote out a prescription for a fantastic medicine and then the symptoms quickly faded away).
- Surface psychology (e.g., I have always been very active and have a strong will; that enables me to get over illnesses quickly).
- Biological-deterministic (e.g., I come from a decidedly sound family; in our home illness was very rare.)

Single and Double Pair-Wise Comparisons

The following five factors were compared in pair-wise arrangements: (a) Freedom to guide your own life, (b) peace of mind, (c) appreciation by others, (d) chance to achieve something, and (e) physical health. The subjects were asked to mark which factor was most important for her in ten Type I comparisons, for example: a or b? In the Type II arrangement the pairings were changed in the following way: *a* versus *b* was rephrased as More of *a* but less of *b* versus Less of *a* but more of *b*, Thus, the respondent was placed in a situation where gains and losses were balanced. Previous studies (18) had demonstrated that the Type I comparisons are more likely to reflect conventional public attitudes while the Type II comparisons are more colored by the individual's private situation. Thus, when a factor was more often chosen in Type I than Type II comparisons, it was considered to be overvalued. The opposite outcome meant undervaluation. A zero difference was interpreted as a realistic adaptation.

The Identity Test (IT)

A full description of this test can be found elsewhere (Smith & van der Meer, 1995, Smith et al, 1993). A face is flashed on a screen in front of the subject, using the same device as in the MCT (below). By presenting subliminal verbal tags immediately prior to the face, the experimenter prepares the viewer for it and influences her perception. The face was indeterminate and invited a wide variety of interpretations with respect to age, gender, expression, and other variables.

When, after a series of increasing exposure times, the viewer had recognized the picture as a face, presentation time of .057 seconds was used for all respondents. The verbal tags were shown at .014 seconds, which made them undetectable in most cases (see below). There were four series of five exposures each with the following tags: (1) "I", (2) "I WELL", (3) "I ILL", (4) no tag. The order between 2 and 3 was randomized.

The instructor asked subjects to describe the pictures appearing on the screen and to give their impression of them. If a subject suspected some extra stimulation in the form of fragments of letters, the exposure time for the verbal tag was cut back one scale step and her report excluded from the protocol.

The Following Scoring Dimensions were Employed in the Present Study:

Anxiety, scored when the face was seen as blurred or darkened. When scored in the first series it was labeled anticipatory anxiety, implying that the viewer had reacted to the subliminal message and was ready to identify with the face. Anxiety in the last series was thought to reflect the insecurity felt when the guiding subliminal support was withdrawn.

Positive or negative reports, scored when the face had a happy, cheerful, or contented expression, or an unhappy or dejected one.

Use of emotional words, not scored when there was merely a happy expression on the face; the expression should grow out of a state of happiness.

Concentration from the onset (series 1) on trivial details, such as "bangs", "side parting", etc., to the exclusion of more comprehensive descriptions.

Reports of staring, begging, searching, etc. eyes. This sign was interpreted as a projection of the patient's own search for useful information about the face, i.e., basically about herself.

Validity of the IT

The test has been validated in several investigations (cf. e.g., Smith & van der Meer, 1995) demonstrating that the subliminal tagging was indeed effective.

The Meta-Contrast Technique (MCT)

The MCT has been described in detail elsewhere (Smith et al, 1989). It rests on the assumption that the micro-processes (percept-geneses) behind our everyday perception can be reconstructed by presenting stimuli "piecemeal", starting with subthreshold exposures. The succession of reports reflects a qualitative change, from subjectively colored impressions to reality adapted percepts. Presentations involve pairs of stimuli (A and B). Stimulus B depicts a young person sitting at a table with a small window in the background, stimulus A features an ugly/angry face. A is projected on the window in B. When, after a series of gradually prolonged exposures the subject has reported B correctly, the exposure time is reduced to a standard value (.06s). Unnoticed by the subject, exposures of A are introduced immediately before B and are gradually prolonged, while the exposure time of B is kept constant. The double exposures are repeated until A + B have been correctly reported.

The verbal reports were scored according to the MCT manual (19). Perceptual transformations of the correct picture content are thought of as the result of perceptual defensive strategies, or cognitive controls, activated to ward off the threat in A, directed at the person in B.

Advanced transformations. This mature type of defense is scored when the threat is interpreted as something relatively far removed from A (the face), e.g., a house, a tree, a bike, etc.

Projective strategies. Here the viewer does not let A become a perceptual structure in its own right (as in the above category) but interprets it indirectly via the B-perception. If reported B-changes do not endanger B's identity ("it is a new perspective now", "I see it from afar"), *sensitivity* is scored.

Depression. Here the micro-development of A seems to have got stuck over a series of at least five phases, e.g., the viewer reports "something in the window" without being able to proceed.

Validity of the MCT

The validity of the MCT scoring dimensions has proved to be high, as attested by the latest manuals (1989)

The Creative Functioning Test (CFT)

The CFT rests on the conception of creativity as a central personality characteristic, a way of functioning and of handling reality. To allow communication between logic and fantasy and to tolerate the anxiety evoked in the process is to function in a creative way.

Since this test will only play a minor role in the attempts to differentiate the subjects, we content ourselves with the following brief description (see 24). The viewer is introduced in a percept-genetic fashion to a picture of a still-life. If the stimulus is then presented at gradually shortened times, does the viewer hang on to the "correct" interpretation (being low-creative) or does he or she eventually indulge in reports of deviant themes (being creative)?

Validity of the CFT

The validity of the CFT has proved to be high, as shown in a recent monograph (Smith & Carlsson, 1990).

Reliability of the Tests

The IT, MCT, and CFT have all yielded high interrater correlations in previous investigations. In the present study in which the authors independently scored the protocols, there were only minor differences between their scores.

Tennessee Self Concept Scale (TSCS)

This scale was constructed to map self-perception. It consists of 100 self-descriptive questions of which 90 concern self-perception and 10 self-criticism. Answers to each question are graded from 1 (completely true) to 5 (completely false). The test includes the following subscales: Identity, Self-satisfaction, Behavior, Physical self, Moral-ethical self, Personal self, Family self, and Social self. The total number of points is then added. The sum of positive points shows the level of self-appreciation. The validity of TSCS has been tested in several ways: content validity, differentiation of groups, and correlations with other personality tests, such as MMPI. In general, it has been concluded that the validity of the test is substantial (Fitts, 1965; Faldt Ciccolo & Johnsson, 2002.

Statistics

Three statistical methods have been used: chi^2 computations to compare the distribution of scores in the patients, on one hand, and the control group, on the other, or, in anorectics and bulimics within the patient group; discriminant analysis between these pairs of groups; and cluster analysis in the patient group.

The chi^2 comparisons have not been corrected for continuity. If they were corrected, however, all listed probability values would remain significant. The discriminant analysis was followed out until 100 percent correct placement of the subjects was made. The cluster analysis was performed according to Ward, a method designed to optimize the minimum variance within clusters.

Results

Tables 25.1a and 25.1b give an overview of items differentiating the patient and control groups. Descriptions of parents are mainly negative in the patient group. In the collection of miscellaneous reports from the interview they appear insecure, tormented and self-accusing. In a manner consistent with that impression, in the pairwise comparisons they emphasize "peace of mind" and undervalue the possibility of "being appreciated" by others. Talk about aging seems to frighten them. However, the IT results demonstrate convincingly that they can react positively to subliminal encouragement. Most IT items concern the alexithymic avoidance strategies described in the introduction. The reference group is mostly characterized by rather prosaic views on life in the hereafter and on attributions of illness. The last two items about anxiety in the IT deserve a special comment. Slight anticipatory anxiety in the beginning of that test, when the subliminal "I" has just been introduced, has proved to be a positive, "non-alexithymic" sign. The viewer reacts preconsciously to the risk that crucial aspects of her own self are likely to be actualized. The anxiety reaction to the introduction of "I WELL" leaves room for speculation. Healthy subjects may see the message as a challenge.

Because of the negative attitudes to their parents, we tried to find out what mothers and fathers, in their daughters' eyes, really looked like. Descriptions of mothers could be arranged in the following four categories; with numbers of patients in parentheses.

a. A pretending mother with an inviting face to outsiders and a surly face turned towards the daughter, above all sensitive to other people's opinion of her, often with variable moods (20).
b. A cold, distant, unappreciative, or indifferent mother (6).
c. A weak, unstable, diseased mother (5).
d. Exclusively positive descriptions (3).

There were five categories for father descriptions.

e. A father unavailable because of a heavy workload and/or travel (4).
f. A silent, withdrawn father, often not trustworthy (8).
g. A strong, much respected father with integrity, often highly temperamental (8).
h. Exclusively positive descriptions (4).
i. Father died a long time ago, or father unknown (4)

Half of the mothers were placed in the Janus-faced category (a), and more than half of the fathers were assigned to categories where lack of close contact with the children is typical (e, f, g). Still, mothers seemed were less suited as objects of identification, not only those placed in category a but also in categories b and c. Even though they were seen as more trustworthy, the distant or absent fathers would have been of little help.

T-testing the differences between anorectics and bulimics yielded a rather meager harvest. Still, it is instructive to note the inner-directed view of life quality in anorectics, in contrast to the emphasis on comfort prevalent among bulimics. Anorectics feature the mature transformations of the threat in the MCT that in other groups of subjects has re-presented creativity, at least to some degree. The early onset of disease reported by bulimics may have to do with their definition of onset, typically a very distinct episode of binge-eating. In anorectics early symptoms could possibly be more difficult to establish. While we found positive reactions to "I WELL" in the IT among all patients, we find a heightened sensitivity to "I ILL" only in the group of bulimics.

Table 25.1a: *Point-wise chi-square tested comparisons of the patient and reference groups*

Typical of patients		*p*-value
Parent relations	Negative description of mother	.02
	Negative description of father	.02
	Negative relation father	.01
Miscellaneous Most difficult time, NOW		.01
from interview Nightmares, NOW		<.01
	Not feeling close to childhood	<.01
	Threat to life from inside myself	<.01
	Has often been wronged	<.01
	Lacking self-confidence	<.001
	Often regrets decisions	<.001
Illness	Negative to swollen looks	<.01
	Least afraid of AIDS	.02
Aging & death Elderly should withdraw		<.02
	Negative to aging	<.01
Pairwise comp. High on "Peace of mind"		.02
	Low on achievement	<.02
	Undervalues appreciation	.01
MCT	Tendency to depression	<.02
IT	Positive in "I WELL"	<.001
	Most positive in "I WELL"	<.01
	"Bangs" in introduction	<.05
	Incomprehensible doubleness	.001
	Emotional words	<.01

Table 25.1b: *Point-wise chi-square tested comparisons of the patient and reference groups*

Typical of controls		*p*-value
Miscellaneous	Has not been wronged	<.01
From interview	Never regrets decisions	.000
Aging & death	Does not believe in a live hereafter	<.02
Cases	Many choices of biological alternatives	.02
	Many choices of doctor's orders alternatives	<.01
Pairwise comp.	Low on appreciation	.01
IT	Anxiety in "I WELL"	.01
	Anxiety in introduction	<.01

Table 25.2: *Point-wise chi-square tested comparisons of anorectics and bulimics*

Typical of anorectics		*p*-value
Life quality	Personal development	.01
Most feared disease	AIDS	<.02
MCT	Mature transformations of threat	.01
Typical of bulimics		
Important for work	Short hours	<.02
Onset of disease	Early	<.01
IT	Negative in "I ILL"	<.01

A stepwise discriminant analysis was also performed to separate anorectics from bulimics. By the sixth step, 100 percent of the subjects had been correctly placed. The important steps were: early onset of disease (B), life quality = personal development (A), freedom to guide your own life (A), anxiety in the IT, the "I ILL" series (A), short working hours important (B), life over when I have achieved everything (A).

The discriminant analysis tells approximately the same story as the point-wise comparisons. There is, however, one small and possibly instructive difference, in the reaction to the "I ILL" series. Bulimics react by projecting negative impressions on the face, anorectics by showing anxiety. This could be taken as the difference between object-directed and self-directed reactions, an interpretation supported by the importance that the anorectics place upon the freedom to guide their own lives.

In cluster analysis, a second cluster of eight appeared to capture the essence of the patient group. These young women believe that their health is bad and that their mothers are untrustworthy. They do not expect to be appreciated by others. Upon additional analysis we found among them more of the staring, begging eyes in the IT, mentioned in the introduction ($p < 0.01$). And these appealing young women were generally low in creativity ($p < 0.05$). Their low TSCS scores fit well into this picture.

Discussion

The relatively small number of patients reflects the exclusiveness of the ward where only very sick patients were admitted. Thus, our subjects do not necessarily represent a broad spectrum of anorectics and bulimics. One consequence of this restriction is the difficulty in forming meaningful statistical clusters where all significant differences are represented. With this in mind, we shall, nevertheless, attempt to formulate some relevant conclusions. The alexithymic signs in these patients' IT protocols were dealt with in the introduction.

Why can these people not verbalize their feelings? The pertinent question to ask, according to Krystal (1988), is how feelings are understood when, at the same time, they are regarded as dangerous. Apparently, for the alexithymic person feelings represent undifferentiated, ghostlike monsters lurking at the preconscious level. The maturation, i.e., differentiation, of feelings has been halted before the point of possible verbalization.

Signs of anxiety were not particularly prominent in the MCT. Johnsson's (1993) study of eating disturbances produced similarly negative results. Apparently, anxiety is tightly bound up in the symptomatology of these patients. They even lack anticipatory anxiety in the first IT series.

Differences between anorectics and bulimics are sparse, no doubt partly because of the limited size of these subgroups. The fact that anorectics respond with signs of anxiety in the "I ILL" series (in IT) but bulimics with negative descriptions of the face seems to parallel Johnsson's (1993) MCT findings. His anorectics were clearly more sensitive, his bulimics more depressive. In another series of percept-genetic testing using two motifs (mother leaving or approaching the child) in a test named PORT (Nilsson, 1995) Johnsson found that the bulimics more often saw distressed persons in the pictures whereas it was typical of anorectics to scrutinize the faces of the mother figures.

It seems that anorectics are more inclined toward subtle manipulations of the stimulus motif because of the unpleasant subliminal message, whereas bulimics project the unpleasantness in a more global manner on the face, thereby distancing themselves from their own illness. Their attention to the mother's face in the PORT may indicate that anorectics, in spite of all, try to appeal to her. For the bulimics, mother may be hostile or indifferent in any case. This could be a reflection of what has been assumed to be maternal overinvolvement in anorectics (Johnson, 1991) and underinvolvement in bulimics (Stern, 1985).

On the whole, anorectics seem to be both more mature and more self-involved than bulimics. On the MCT, anorectics' defenses are more mature; in the interview they emphasize personal development, whereas bulimics find short working hours more important.

Parent descriptions in eating disorders are indeed deviant, but deviant in another way than in other pychosomatic groups studied by us (Smith et al. 1995). In ulcerative colitis and Crohn's disease it was a question of clear-cut positive or negative attitudes toward the parents. In eating disorders, parent descriptions are generally negative, particularly towards the mother. Yet, the mother may be ingratiating - towards other people, but not toward her daughter. The father does not seem to be of much help. In many families with an anorectic child. As noted by Bemporad and Ratey (1985), the parental relationship is deeply troubled by mutual difficulties with intimacy and trust, yet masked by a facade of smooth functioning. The child's illness may be an attempt to protect the parental relationship. This must necessarily lead to grave problems of identification. Therefore, these patients "fail to recognize the meaning of their affects" (Krystal, 1988, p. 71).

A particularly pathetic subgroup, containing both anorectics and bulimics, was sorted out through cluster analysis. The "begging eyes" in the IT are particularly typical for them. They regard their own health as bad. And they undervalue the importance of "peace of mind". It is instructive that symptoms of depression are common both in anorectics (2) and bulimics (Walsh et al, 1985). Many have argued that binge eaters are recruited from among those who somehow learn to regulate negative emotions by using eating as a tension reduction method (Fairburn & Cooper, 1987; Herman & Polivy, 1988; Hsu, 1990).

One inevitable question concerns what is the cause and what is the effect in the development of these women. Are the parents to blame or is the description of them slanted and untrue? A closer scrutiny of the family background, like the one attempted in a study of diabetics (Rydén et al, 1993), is planned by the present authors. At this stage we may concede that biological determinants have probably also been at work even if we cannot regard them as omnipotent. Since identity formation, involving beliefs about the nature, consistency, and value of the self, appears to be more difficult for girls than for boys (Simmons & Blyth, 1987; Striegel-Moore, 1993), gender may be considered as a powerful, biological factor. But it is also obvious that biology and psychology are closely intertwined her

Acknowledgements. The present study was supported by the Research Council for the Humanities and Social Sciences, by Clas Groschinsky's Memorial Fund, the Söderström-König Foundation, and the funds of the Psychiatric Clinic at the Lund University Hospital.

References

Bemporad, J. R., & Ratey J. (1985). Intensive psychotherapy of former anorexic individuals. *American Journal of Psychotherapy, 39*, 454-465.

Fairburn, C. G., & Cooper Z. (1987). Behavioral and cognitive approaches to treatment of anorexia nervosa and bulimia nervosa. In P.J.V. Beamont, G.D. Burrows, & R.C. Casper (Eds.), *Handbook of eating disorders* (pp. 271-298). Amsterdam: Elsevier

Faldt Ciccolo, E. B, & Johnsson, P. (2002). Personality and Self-concept in subgroups of patients with anorexia nervosa and bulimia nervosa. *Social Behavior and Personality, 30*, 347-358.

Fitts W. H. (1965). *Manual: Tennessee Self Concept Scale*. Nashville, Tenn: Counsellor Recordings and Tests.

Gartner A. F,. Marcus, R. N., Halmi, K., & Loranger, A. W. (1989). DSM-III-R Personality disorder in patients with eating disorders. *American Journal of Psychiatry,146,* 1585-1591.

Geist, R. A. (1989). Self psychological reflections on the origins of eating disorders. In J. Bemporad, & D.B. Herzog (Eds), *Psychoanalysis and eating disorders* (pp. 5-27). New York: Guilford Press.

Goodsitt, A. (1984). Self-psychology and the treatment of anorexia nervosa. In D. M. Garner & P.E. Garfinkel. (Eds), *Handbook of psychotherapy for anorexia nervosa and bulimia* (pp. 55-82). New York: Guilford Press.

Hentschel, U., & Kiessling, M. (1989). *Interview: Krankheit und Gesundheit.* Mimeo: University of Mainz.

Hsu, L. K. G. (1990). *Eating disorders*. New York: Guilford Press.

Johnson, C. (1991). Treatment of eating disordered patients with borderline and false/narcissistic disorders. In C. Johnson (Ed.), *Psychodynamic treatment of anorexia nervosa and bulimia* (pp. 165-193). New York: Guilford

Johnson, C. & Connors, M. (1987). *The etiology and treatment of bulimia nervosa: a biopsychosocial perspective.* New York: Basic Books.

Johnsson, P. (1993). Anorexics and Bulimics compared vis-à-vis defense, proximity, and separation. In U. Hentschel, G. Smith , W Ehlers & J. Draguns (Eds), *The concept of defense mechanisms in contemporary psychology* (pp. 389-401). New York: Springer-Verlag.

Krystal, H. (1988) *Integration and self-healing. Affect-trauma-alexithymia.* Hillsdale, NJ: The Analytic Press.

Levine, A. P., & Hyler, S. E. (1986). DSM-III personality diagnosis in bulimia. *Comprehensive Psychiatry, 27,* 47-53.

Masterson, J. F. (1977). Primary anorexia nervosa in the borderline adolescent - an object-relations view. In P. Hartocollis (Ed.), *Borderline personality disorders* (pp. 475-494). New York: International Universities Press,

Meyer, C., & Waller, G. (2000). Subliminal activation of abandonment- and eating-related schemata: Relationship with eating disordered attitudes in a nonclinical population. *International Journal of Eating Disorders, 27,* 328-334.

Nilsson, A. (1995). Differentiation between patients with schizophrenia and borderline disorders in the Percept-genetic Object-Relations Test. PORT. *British Journal of Medical Psychology, 68,* 287-309.

Norring, C., & Sohlberg, S. (1991). Ego functioning in eating disorders: prediction of outcome after one and two years. *International Journal of Eating Disorders, 10,* 1-13.

Norring, C., & Sohlberg, S. (1993). Outcome, recovery, relapse, and mortality across six years in patients with clinical eating disorders. *Acta Psychiatrica Scandinavica, 87,* 437-444.

Piran, N., Kennedy, S., Garfinkel, P. E., &Owens, M. (1988). Affective disturbance in eating disorders. *Journal of Nervous and Mental Disease, 173,* 395-400.

Piran, N., Lerner, P., Garfinkel, P. E., Kennedy, S. H., & Brouilette, C. (1988). Personality disorders in anorexia nervosa patients. *International Journal of Eating Disorders, 9,* 607-615.

Poikolainen, K,. Kanerva, R., Marttunen, M., & Lönnqvist, J. (2001). Defense styles and other risk factors for eating disorders among female adolescents: A case-control study. *European Eating Disorders Review, 9,* 325-334.

Rydén, O., Johnsson, P., Nevander, L., Sjöblad, S., & Westbom, L. (1993). Co-operation between parents in caring for diabetic children: Relations to metabolic control and parents' field-dependence - independence. *Diabetes Research and Clinical Practice, 20*, 223-229.

Simmons, R. G., & Blyth, D. A. (1987). *Moving into adolescence. The impact of pubertal change and school context.* New York: Aldine Press.

Smith, G. J. W., & Carlsson I (1990). The creative process. *Psychological Issues, Monograph 57.* Madison, CT: International Universities Press.

Smith, G. J. W., Johnson. G., & Almgren, P.E. (1989). *MCT - The Meta Contrast Technique.* Psykologiförlaget: Stockholm.

Smith. G. J. W., & Lund, A. (1954). *Women workers in industry.* Studieförbundet Näringsliv och Samhälle: Stockholm.

Smith, G. J. W., & van der Meer, G. (1993). Causal attributions of disease as related to dynamic personality variables. In U. Hentschel, G.J.W. Smith, W. Ehlers. J.G. Draguns JG (Eds), *The concept of defense mechanisms in contemporary psychology* (pp. 135-145). New York: Springer-Verlag

Smith, G. J. W., van der Meer, G., Ursing, B., Prytz, H., & Benoni, C. (1995). Psychological profile of patients suffering from Crohn's disease and ulcerative colitis. *Acta Psychiatrica Scandinavica, 92*, 187-192.

Smith, G. J. W., van der Meer, G., Johnsson, P., & Franck, A. (1997). Alexithymia in patients with eating disorders: an investigation using a new projective technique. *Perceptual and Motor Skills, 83*, 247-256.

Steiger, H., Goldstein, C., Mongrain, M., & Van der Feen, J. (1990). Description of eating-disordered, psychiatric, and normal women along cognitive and psychodynamic dimensions. *International Journal of Eating Disorders, 9*, 129-140.

Steiger, H., & Houle, L. (1991). Defense styles and object-relations disturbance among university women displaying varying degrees of ´symptomatic´ eating. *International Journal of Eating Disorders, 10*, 145-153

Stern, D. N. (1995) *The interpersonal world of the infant.* New York, Basic Books.

Striegel-Moore, R. H. (1993). Etiology of binge eating: A developmental perspective. In C.G.Fairburn, & G.T. Wilson (Eds.), *Binge eating. Nature, assessment and treatment* (pp. 144-172). New York: Guilford Press.

Walsh, B. T., Roose, S. P., Glassman, A. H., Gladis, M. A., & Sadik, C. (1985). Depression and bulimia. *Psychosomatic Medicine, 47,* 123-131.

Wonderlich, S. A., Swift, W. J., Slotnick, H. B., & Goodman, I. (1990). DSM-III:R Personality disorders in eating disorder sub-types. International *Journal of Eating Disorders, 9*, 607-615.

Defense Mechanisms
U. Hentschel, G. Smith, J.G. Draguns & W. Ehlers (Editors)

Chapter 26

Defense Organizations and Coping in the Course of Chronic Disease: A Study on Crohn's Disease

Joachim Küchenhoff

Acute and severe somatic illnesses inflict severe psychological stress for the patient. The disturbance of bodily well-being has a serious impact on the narcissistic investment of the body. Thus a vital dimension of self-coherence is called into question. Being confronted with the diagnosis of a chronic disease implies that future life perspectives have become insecure, since the patient must live with the danger of possible relapse. He or she faces unusual dependencies on medical professionals and medical treatment. Therefore confrontation with an acute or chronic illness constitutes a challenge to the personality and its adaptive resources. From a psychoanalytic perspective, this constitutes a challenge to the defensive repertoire. One important aim of defense is to regulate the individual narcissistic balance that is endangered by the disease (Küchenhoff 2000a). It is therefore important to study the relationship of defense to the course of and adaptation to a disease.

The relevant research issues that have increasingly become influential in present day psychosomatic research as a whole and in the research on Crohn's disease can be summarized as follows:

1. What is the impact of illness experience on the defense organization during an acute relapse of the chronic disease?
2. Do defense organizations change in adaptation to the course of the disease?
3. What relationships can be found between defensive and (cognitive) coping strategies in the disease process?

The Heidelberg Research Project on Crohn's Disease

The Heidelberg Research Project on Crohn's Disease (Küchenhoff, 1993 a, 2000b) was a longitudinal study that analyses the interrelation of personality, defense and coping in the course of Crohn's disease (CD). CD is a severe and chronic relapsing illness mainly of the gastrointestinal tract; the patients suffer from abdominal pain, bloody diarrhoea, fistula formation and severe impairment of general health. Various extraintestinal manifestations may complicate the picture. Personality, disease process and adaptation to the disease are interrelated in a complex manner. However, numerous empirical studies on the personality of CD patients have not taken into account the changing course of the disease (e.g. Cohn et al, 1970). Meanwhile, it has been shown that some psychological factors have erroneously been regarded as traits whereas they clearly depend on the somatic state (cf. e.g. Leibig, Wilke, & Feiereis, 1985). Therefore, research designs have to be longitudinal or have to differentiate patients by disease activity measurement. In the Heidelberg research project on CD patients were seen three times: in the acute phase, during remission and three years after the first interview (cf. Table 26.1).

This chapter presents data on defense and coping from phase 1 and 2. At phase 1, all patients were acutely ill. In order to avoid selection biases all patients were referred by medical departments co-operating with the research team. Acuteness in generally approved medical terms means that the patients have surpassed 150 on a disease activity scale especially designed for CD, the so-called Best Index or CDAI. Remission is defined by a CDAI lower than 100 and the absence of acute inflammation in coloscopy. Former experience with CD varied across the sample, some patients fell ill for the first time („new" patients), others were chronically ill the criterion for chronicity being a CD course of more than 1,5 years. The comparison of both groups is relevant to the first research issues of hat impact the long-lasting adaptation to the disease might have on the defense. Other characteristic features of the sample are summarized in table 26.2. 118 CD patients took part in the study, 78 were available for the phase 2 investigation; a dropout analysis did not show significant differences between drop-outs and co-operating patients. At both phases, all patients were asked to answer questionnaires assessing personality, coping, satisfaction with life etc. Psychodynamic interviews were performed that were tape recorded and used for the clinical assessment of defense mechanisms (CADM) (Ehlers et al., 1995) (cf. Chapter 17).

Three experienced psychoanalysts listened to three 10 minute periods and noted an individual rating; these were compared and discussed, each individual defense mechanism was considered and the result achieved by consensus was noted (Küchenhoff, 1991). Defense mechanisms do not work in isolation, but form patterns or defense organizations (Lichtenberg & Slap, 1971). Evaluation of these complex defense organizations allows an analysis that is closer to clinical reality. Therefore, a factor analysis on the defense ratings in phase 1 was performed yielding a three factor solution (cf. Table 26.3). Factor 1 was labelled

„defense of affect“ because isolation, reaction formation and rationalisation as well as denial were prominent, like in patients with obsessive-compulsive personalities (internal consistency 0.68). Factor 2 summarizes „primitive“ defense mechanisms, mainly splitting and projective identification (internal consistency 0.81). Factor 3 combines turning-against-self and projection, whereas regression is inversely correlated to the factor. The factor can best be interpreted by describing defensive styles that defend aggressive conflicts by blaming oneself or others, but without repression of affects. Therefore it was labelled „defense of aggression“ (internal consistency 0. 42). Cognitive coping attitudes were assessed by the Freiburg coping inventory FKV. For statistical analyses, uni- (t-test) and multivariate (correlation, cluster and path analysis) procedures were used. The interviews were partially submitted to content analyses (cf. Küchenhoff, 2000b).

Table 26.1: *The Heidelberg study on Crohn's disease*

	t1: acute illness	t2: remission	t3: 3 years after t1
	Crohn's Disease Activity Index > 150	Crohn's Disease Activity Index < 150	CDAI variable
	n = 118	n = 78	n = 55
medical data	x	x	x
questionnaire:	x	x	x
• personality inventory			
• coping questionnaire FKV			
• satisfaction with life questionnaire			
Interviews	x	x	

Table 26.2: *Sample*

		t 1 n = 118	t 2 n = 78
Sex	Male	36	25
	Female	82	53
Age	Average	29.9	30.3
	Range	17-71	18-71
social class	lower middle	12	14
	upper middle	46	28
	upper class	26	9
medical history	New	38	
	Chronic	80	

Table 26.3: *Factor analysis of defense mechanisms*

Defense mechanisms	Factor 1	factor 2	factor 3
Turning against self	- 0.463	0.241	0.405
Regression	0.054	0.195	-0.427
Depression	- 0.526	0.062	0.152
Displacement	0.171	0.329	0.117
Isolation	0.520	0.116	0.272
Rationalisation	0.743	0.030	0.022
Reaction formation	0.480	0.192	0.302
Denial	0.436	0.132	0.008
Projection	0.116	0.078	0.510
Splitting	-0.092	0.656	0.054
Projective identification	-0.190	0.636	0.171

Results

According to psychodynamic concepts of dealing with traumatic or stressful life events (van der Kolk et al., 1996) such as the onset of a severe, potentially life threatening disease, one should expect the defense mechanisms to vary with the course of the disease and with its acuity: the more unexpected and the more severe the disease onset, the more denial or primitive defense mechanisms like splitting or projective identification might be activated; these may serve as emergency mechanisms (Laub & Auerhahn 1993): in traumata, the ego might not be able to overcome anxiety or other affects by the usual „neurotic" defense, i.e. mechanisms of a countercathectic type like repression. In this case, more primitive and genetically earlier defense formations might be activated. These are characterized by alterations in self and object representations, like splitting and projective identification. If the acute and severe somatic illness is experienced as a trauma, then primitive defense mechanisms might be additionally employed. Preliminary studies on 53 CD patients suggested that for a considerable number esp. of „new" patients, „primitive" defense mechanisms are important (Küchenhoff, 1993 b). With the complete data, it is possible to refine this suggestion. First of all, the overall effect of former experience with CD on defense is far less than might be expected. In a group-statistical comparison of new and chronic patients there is no significant difference in regard to defense mechanisms. More astonishingly, there are no significant differences in defense mechanisms activated by all patients in phase 1 and phase 2 (acute illness v. remission). This result seems to contradict the preliminary results. On the other hand, group-statistical analyses tend to mask subgroup effects. Therefore, to be able to assess the changing patterns of defense in subgroups of patients over time, a cluster analysis on the defense factors in phase 1 and 2 was performed. A three-cluster solution was chosen (Figure 26.1). Cluster 1 (n=38) is characterized by the dominance and stability of the „defense of affect" factor. These patients show hardly any change in their defense organization over time. This cluster contains the largest number of patients; this result is in accordance with our preliminary study on data of phase 1 where we had expected that obsessive-compulsive like defense characteristics were predominant in CD patients and would not vary with the disease process.

The cluster 2 (n=21) patients as well show stabile defense organizations; they differ from cluster 1 in the dominance of the „defense of aggression" factor. Obviously, in terms of defense organisations, the CD patients do not constitute a homogenous group. And in the majority of patients, the defense organizations are not challenged or significantly altered by the varying somatic state. Taking the heterogeneity and the relative stability of defense organizations into account, the small cluster 3 (n=9) might be especially important. In cluster 3, there is a considerable change over time. These patients activate „primitive" or borderline-like defenses, but only in phase 1; these seem to subside in phase 2. It might not be a „considerable amount" of patients that use primitive defense mechanisms, but these patients' defense repertoire nevertheless changes in adaptation to the disease process and is unstable. This minority deserves special attention. According to Moser's theory of a hierarchical layering of defense organizations, they cannot cope with the acute stage of the disease by their usual defenses, but they have to take resort to emergency mechanisms. Again, it is worth while noting that on the other hand the occurrence of primitive defense mechanisms in severely ill patients does not herald borderline personality disorders, but a temporary loss of ego strength and a concomitant ego regression. Socio-demographic and qualitative interview data allow to detail the characteristics of the subgroup. It is a rather homogenous group. All patients of cluster 3 are female. All of them have fallen ill for the first time at an early age (average 14.8 years). In the interviews it became evident that these young females did not only fell ill in the vulnerable period of puberty, but suffered from additional psychic conflicts. All of them reported on a weak or bad relationship to their fathers, who had died early, did not care at all etc. As a consequence, their mothers were strongly idealised; separation and individuation thus became more difficult.

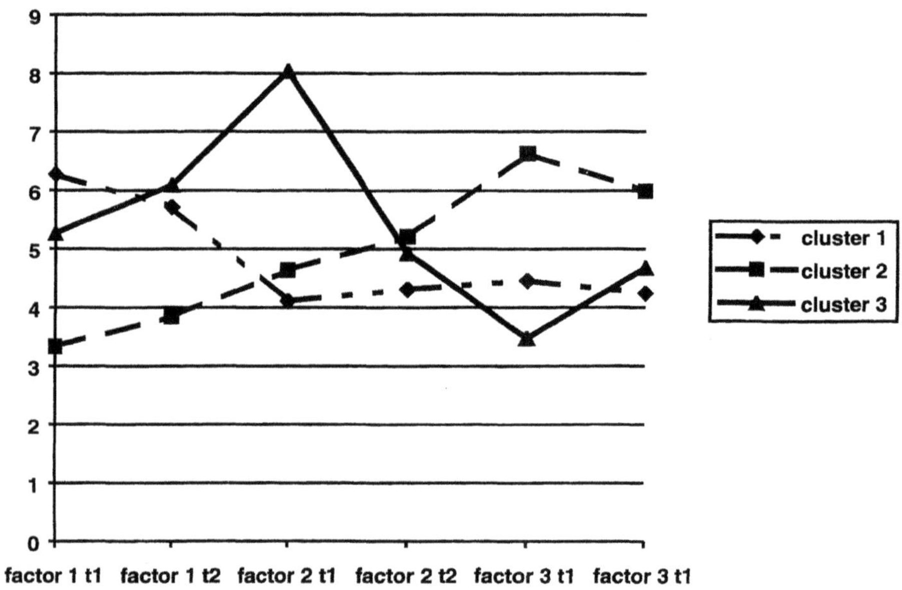

Figure 26.1: Three *patient clusters (see text) with results on 3 defense factors over time: factor 1 = defense of affects; factor 2 = primitive defense; factor 3 = defense of aggression; t1 = acute phase of CD; t2 = remission.*

Case Example

Mrs. X, a young woman of 17, fell ill for the first time when she was ten. When she entered the project she had to overcome a severe, indeed life-threatening relapse. Neither she nor her parents had dared much about the warning symptoms of diarrhoea and protein losses, instead of addressing a doctor they went abroad for holidays where Mrs. X nearly dies; she had to be transferred to an intensive care unit in Heidelberg. There she was well liked by the hospital staff, but her mother was not; she used to stay in the ward up to 16 hours a day accompanying her daughter virtually everywhere. When I talked to her I realised that she could not differentiate between herself and her child, between her own and her daughter's body; she spoke of Mrs. X's complaints as if she had them herself, as if they shared one body (McDougall, 1989). Mrs. X found it very hard to express her own feelings and affects. Nevertheless, she communicated them by arousing a great deal of interest, compassion and sorrow in me (projective identification). Splitting was evident in the description of her parents; whereas her mother was idealised her father was devaluated. In the course of the interview she described some of her problems. Shortly before she was born, her parents had started a small restaurant that left no time or attention for the child. Being left alone in the afternoons she spent her time playing around in the restaurant. Only her grandmother looked after her, but she died shortly before the actual relapse. The fact that she had a vaginal fistula that had not been operated on for years did not allow a stabile female identity to develop; she avoided social contacts, especially with boys. The atmosphere in the phase 2 interview was very different; she claimed to be happy and in a good mood again, she denied any familial quarrels or anxieties about the disease. Whereas I realised that in fact she felt much better I felt the interview to be sterile, devoid of shared affects. Eventually, she had reestablished her „usual" form of defense. In the majority of CD patients, defense organizations as measured by the CADM seem to be stabile traits of their personalities. For most patients, a potentially traumatic event like the onset or a relapse of a chronic disease like CD does not provoke emergency mechanisms. Instead, the „usual" defense organizations suffice in dealing with the stress imposed upon them by diagnosis and somatic ailments. This result contrasts with the transactional coping concept (Lazarus 1966) that claims that coping mechanisms (in the broad sense of the term) do not exist in a preformed way within the personality but are provoked by a crisis. The cognitive coping attitudes as measured by the FKV do not vary significantly in phase 1 and 2, either (for further details see Küchenhoff 1993 a). Is it possible to reconcile these data with the transactional concept? Studying the interaction of defense and coping, we were able to show by applying path analyses that it is the very interplay of defense and coping that is co-ordinated during acute stress like the acute phase of CD, and only then. E.g., patients with a dominant defense of aggression tend to cope actively in acute stress, whereas primitive defense is followed by depressive and evading coping styles (Küchenhoff & Manz, 1993). In remission, this co-ordination of defense and coping dissolves, i.e. no significant path models between the defense and coping factors can be found. They seem to be independent of each other again. Maybe the dynamic factor postulated in the transitional coping concept can be found in this interplay of defense and coping.

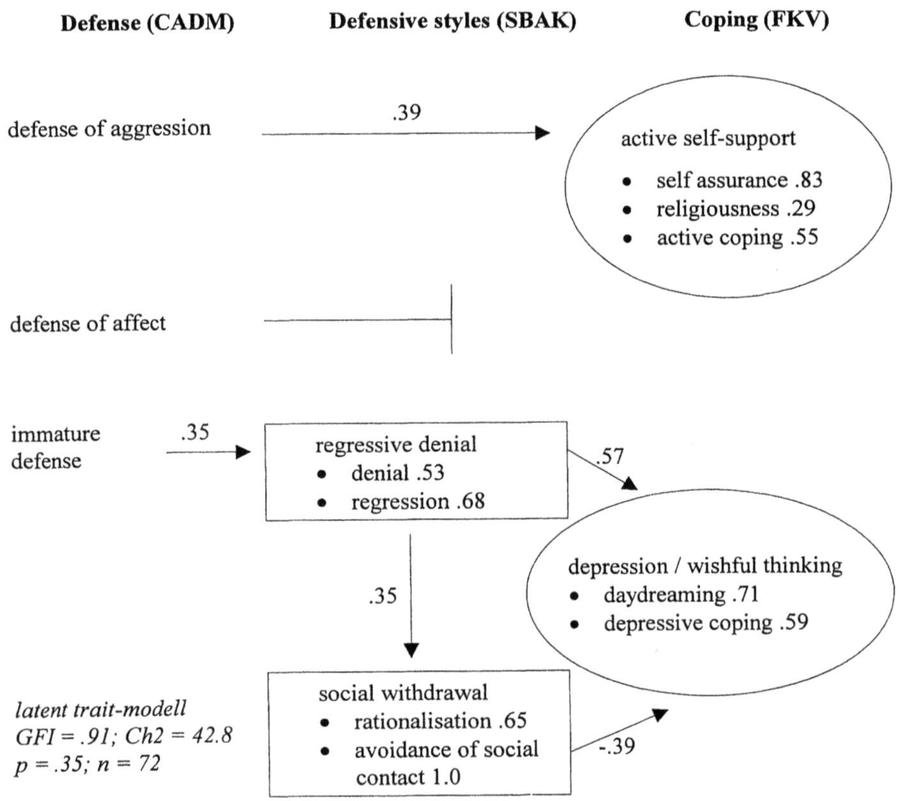

Figure 26.2: *Path analysis acute phase model of the interplay between defense and coping*

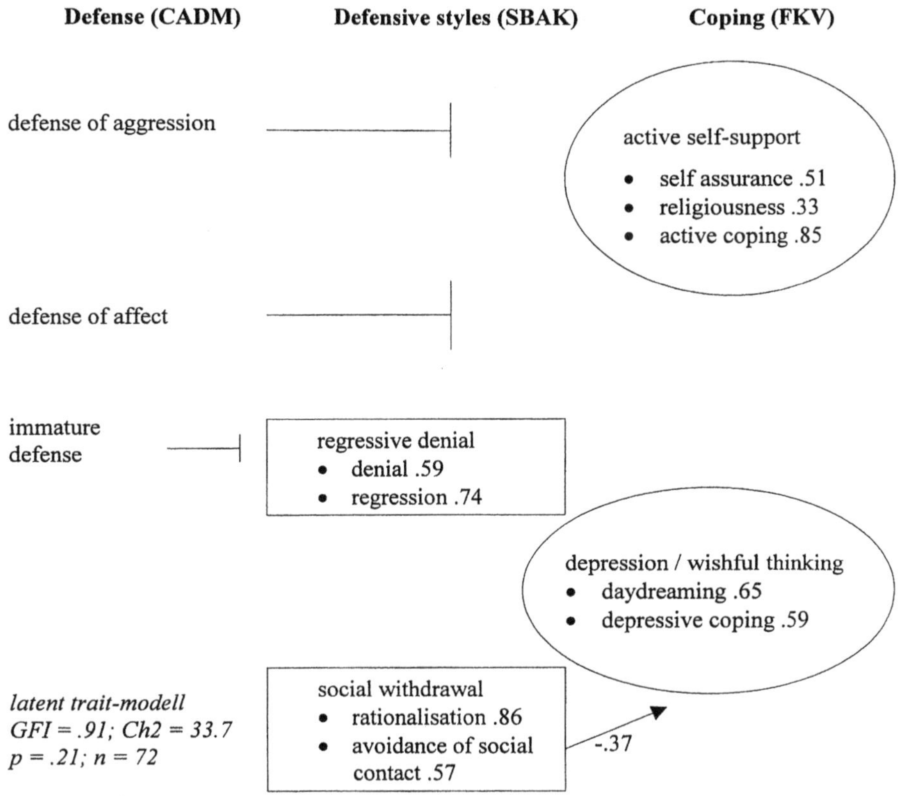

Figure 26.3: *Path analysis: remission phase model of the interplay between defense and coping*

Thus, patients with a dominant defence of aggression tend to cope actively during acute stress, whereas immature defence is followed by depressive and evading coping styles. In remission, this co-ordination of defence and coping dissolves, i.e. no significant path models between the defence and coping factors can be found. Once again, they are independent of each other. Perhaps the dynamic factor postulated in the transitional coping concept can be found in this interplay of defence and coping. As most coping research have shown, active coping is a positive influence on the course of the disease. One factor contributing to the ability to cope actively is what we have called defence of aggression;

this is a rather stabile defence organisation in patients with a well integrated personality structure who need not mobilise immature defence mechanisms in the acute phase. This command of aggressive affects, this ability to control impulses, predisposes to active coping - whereas a more obsessive-compulsive like defence does not motivate coping.

Summary

The CADM is a complex rating method; it needs an intensive expert training in assessing defense mechanisms, and a fair amount of time to do the actual rating. But the effort is worth while; the results presented above underline the CADM's usefulness in the research on adaptation to chronic diseases. The empirical analysis of defense during the course of Crohn's disease shows that the defense organisations are relatively stabile. On the whole, they are not significantly influenced by former experiences with the disease nor by the actual somatic state. They seem to be traits rather than states (cf. Spielberger, 1966). Another important result of the analysis is the relative heterogeneity of CD patients in terms of defense organization, and thus of psychic conflicts and personality features. While the majority of patients in our sample answer the stress of acute illness by their customary defensive repertoire, a subgroup is forced to mobilise „primitive" defense mechanisms as an emergency mechanism, their ego is overwhelmed by the acute stress. All patients in this subgroup are young females having fallen ill during puberty and suffering from familial and psychic conflicts. Thus, the analysis of defense helps to identify a small but clinically important subgroup that can be regarded as a risk group needing intensified psychosocial and medical care.

References

Cohn, E., Lederman, I., & Shore, E. (1970). Regional enteritis and its relation to emotional disorders. *American Journal of Gastroenterology*, *54*, 378-387.

Ehlers, W., Hettinger, R., & Paar, G. (1995). Operational diagnostic approaches in the assessment of defense mechanisms. *Psychotherapy and Psychosomatics*, *42*, 156-163.

Küchenhoff, J. (1991). Zur Theorie und Methodik der Fremdeinschätzung von Abwehrprozessen [Clinical rating of defense processes: theory and methodology]. *Psychotherapie, Psychosomatik, medizinische Psychologie, 41*, 216-223.

Küchenhoff, J. (1993a). *Psychosomatik des M.Crohn. Zur Wechselwirkung seelischer und körperlicher Faktoren im Krankheitsverlauf* [Psychosomatics of Crohn's Disease. The interaction of psychological and somatic factors during the course of the disease]. Stuttgart: Enke.

Küchenhoff, J. (1993b). Defense mechanisms and defense organizations: Their role in adaptation to the acute stage of Crohn's disease. In U. Hentschel, G. Smith, W. Ehlers, & J.Draguns (Ed.), *The concept of defense mechanisms in contemporary psychology*. (pp.412-424). Berlin Heidelberg New York: Springer.

Küchenhoff, J., & Manz, R. (1993). Zum Zusammenspiel von Abwehr und Coping im Krankheitsverlauf [The interaction of defense and coping in the course of chronic disease]. *Psychotherapie, Psychosomatik, medizinische Psychologie, 43*, 318-324.

Küchenhoff, J., Manz, R., & Mathes, L. (1995). Was beeinflußt den Krankheitsverlauf des M.Crohn? [Influences on the course of Crohn's disease]. *Nervenarzt,66*, 41-48.

Küchenhoff, J. (2000a). Abwehr [Defense]. In W.Mertens & B. Waldvogel (Ed.) *Handbuch psychoanalytischer Grundbegriffe* [A comprehensive textbook on basic psychoanalytic terms]. (pp. 6-11). Stuttgart: Kohlhammer

Küchenhoff, J. (2000b). Coping and its influence on the course of Crohn's disease. In J. von Wietersheim (Ed.) *Psychological factors in inflammatory bowel disease*. Proceedings of the 22nd Ulm Workshop. (pp. 103-121). Ulm

Lazarus, R.S. (1966). Psychological stress and the coping process. New York: McGraw-Hill.

Laub, D., & Auerhan, N. (1993). Knowing and not knowing massive psychic trauma. *International Journal of Psychoanalysis, 74*, 287-302.

Leibig, T., Wilke, E., & Feiereis, H. (1985). Zur Persönlichkeitsstruktur von Patienten mit Colitis ulcerosa und Morbus Crohn [On the personality structure in patients with ulcerative colitis and Crohn's disease]. *Zeitschrift für psychosomatische Medizin und Psychoanalyse, 31*, 380-392.

Lichtenberg, J.D. & Slap, J.W. (1971). On the defensive organization. *International Journal of Psychoanalysis, 52*, 451-457.

McDougall, J. (1989). *Theatres du corps* [Theaters of the body]. Paris: Gallimard

Spielberger, Ch.D. (ed.) (1966). *Anxiety and Behaviour*. New York: Academic Press.

Van der Kolk, B., McFarlane, A., & Weisaeth, L. (Ed.) (1996). *Traumatic Stress*. New York: Guilford.

Defense Mechanisms in Neuropsychological Contexts

Defense Mechanisms
U. Hentschel, G. Smith, J.G. Draguns & W. Ehlers (Editors)

Chapter 27

Defense Mechanisms and Their Psychophysiological Correlates

Uwe Hentschel, Gudmund Smith and Juris G. Draguns

Introduction

Mind-brain problems continue to fascinate, challenge, and frustrate psychologists. Many of them regard a physiological explanation of their findings as inherently more fundamental and definitive than a psychological one. We do not share this standpoint nor do we believe that the search for physiological causes constitutes the road royal for psychological theorizing. Nonetheless, we consider the interplay between behavioral and experiential manifestations of defense mechanisms and any of all of their physiological, biochemical, and endocrine concomitants a vitally important problem that has been neglected for an appallingly long time. Fundamental adaptive strategies, which defense mechanisms are, must be investigated in all of their modes of expression if their role in human functioning is to be understood.

In the last few decades, many prominent contributors have addressed this complex and thorny issue. Let us just mention Howard Shevrin and his experiments on subliminal excitation, Charles Fisher, William Dement, and Edward Wolpert and their research on dreams, and Ludwig von Bertalanffy who explicitly formulated his general systems theory in order to forge links between psychoanalysis and biology. Brain-imaging techniques such as the registration of cerebral blood flow used by Niels Lassen, and David Ingvar for mapping cortical activity, represent another physiological approach to a problem area shared by psychology and neurology. On the basic issues pertaining to the interrelationship of mind and brain positions remain as divergent as ever. Thus, Dennett (1991), a philosopher, held that the mind is independent of the machine that created it and that little can be learned about the mind by studying anatomy and physiology. Eccles (1989), a neurophysiologist, strenuously objected to the inherent reductionism in many views that posit a mind-brain unity. In his view, higher mental functions cannot be reduced to biology and chemistry. On the opposing side of the argument, Searle (1997) was equally adamant in maintaining that consciousness is as much a function of the brain as digestion is a function of the stomach.

Ever since Sigmund Freud's (1954) *Project for a scientific psychology,* written in 1895 but published much later, came to the attention of the psychoanalytic community, interest in possible neurological counterparts of psychological processes has also been brewing among psychoanalysts. Two signs of this trend are the launching of a new periodical, *Neuropsychoanalysis,* and the publication of a book by Kaplan-Solms and Solms (2000) on the same topic. However, Freud's *Project* was the object of a critical review by Brown (2000). It is interesting to note that Brown not only objected to the obsolete neurological groundwork of the *Project* but was even more critical of the psychoanalytic meta-theory which he found to be lacking in clinical referents.

In spite of the growing interest in mind-brain problems among psychoanalysts, there is little in their publications that specifically deals with defense mechanisms. Even in a comprehensive book like "*Clinical studies in neuro-psychoanalysis*" (Kaplan-Solms & Solms, 2000) defense mechanisms are only indirectly treated, among the functions of the ego. Freud's energy concept as well as his attempts to arrive at neuropsychological definitions remained ultimately a psychological construction, even though it featured analogies to physical concepts. Thus, repression was described as countering a cathexis by an anticathexis or in psychological terms, as the counteraction of two ideas or intentions (cf. Rychlak, 1973). By using exclusively psychological terms, the mind-body dichotomy is kept alive in psychoanalysis, even if physical analogies are sometimes invoked. This may be one of the reasons why neuropsychology, always on the lookout for maximally direct links between brain mechanisms and behavior, has not yet included defense mechanisms into its repertoire of relevant variables.

In this chapter, we do not expect to narrow the mind-body gap, a topic to be pursued in a dialogue between philosophers, biologists, and neuroscientists. As psychologists, we only aspire to account for the present state of knowledge on the link between the defense mechanisms and physiological indicators.

Neuropsychology, Physiology and Defense Mechanisms: Is There an Empirical Link?

On a theoretical basis, a relationship between physiology and psychology on the plane of defenses is highly plausible. Yet, the existence of such a connection remains to be established on the basis of systematic and programmatic empirical research. At this point, we can only point to fragments of relevant evidence, in the hope that collectively they will contribute toward the emergence of a coherent picture. Moreover, all defense mechanisms may be physiologically rooted, but not necessarily to the same extent. Repression, for example, is likely to feature a greater number of physiological correlates and displacement, more numerous behavioural indicators. In several current texts in psychophysiology (Bradley, 2000), we have failed to find an index entry for defense mechanisms. The closest term that was included was Pavlov's 'defensive reaction' or 'defensive reflex' that constitutes the avoidance counterpart to the orienting reaction, a concept that, at most, shows some overlap with defense mechanisms. At this point, defense mechanisms continue to be detached from the psychophysiological research enterprise, and one can only speculate on the reasons for this separation. On the part of psychoanalysis, affinity to neuropsychology has been reactivated. The exchange of ideas has been resumed, and the time is ripe for including defenses in this endeavor.

Pending a conceptual resolution of the mind-body dichotomy, physiological indicators of defense may be construed as one of the several interfaces between the mind and the brain. In the optimal case, defenses help to protect the individual from external as well as internal dangers. Moreover, they accomplish this task largely outside of the person's scope of awareness. In the worst scenario, they fail to reduce the person's distress or the individual ends up paying a high price for securing, for example, protection from forbidden impulses but developing a neurotic symptom in the process. Chances of getting effective relief from suffering are higher with mature than with immature defenses, but even mature defenses can fail. There is also probably a higher degree of awareness and conscious control in mature defenses. Humor and suppression, for example, can be used deliberately.

Coping and Physiological Reactions

Physiological reactions appear to provide the most direct connection between the concepts of defense and those of coping. Coping devices represent conscious attempts to optimize personally relevant outcomes. According to Lazarus and Launier (1978) coping includes an evaluation of the situation in two steps. Primary appraisal results in the categorization of the stressful situation as harmful, not dangerous, or even positive. Secondary appraisal is concerned with the person's options to react to the stressor directly, through problem-oriented coping, or internally, by means of emotion-focused coping. In the early stages of their research, Lazarus and coworkers presented films of stressful scenes of surgical operations and occupational accidents. Denial and intellectualization were found to be prominent mechanisms in lowering the intensity of both emotional and physiological reactions, principally in the form of heart rate and skin conductance (Lazarus & Opton, 1966). Discrepancies between the various indicators were also noted. Weinstein, Averill, Opton and Lazarus (1968) presented a more detailed overview of the discrepancy between feelings and physiologic indicators, which is also discussed in Chapter 11. As the experimenters' interest shifted to life stress, such as coping with disabling or life-threatening illness and medical treatment, their theory moved into a more behavioral direction (Lazarus & Folkman, 1984). Its recent elaborations assign a central place to emotions in determining the person-environment relationship within an inclusive cognitive-motivational-relational framework. Cognitive components refer to appraisal and motivational ones to goals (Lazarus, 1993). In Lazarus' words, " to change an emotion one must change the appraisal" (Lazarus, 1993, p. 35), and "not only does coping belong within the rubric of finding solutions but it also falls within the realm of motivation" (p.36). Lazarus opted for this comprehensive frame of reference in order to put "an emphasis on a broader, richer and clinically more useful concept, emotion" (p. 36).

Empirical Evidence for the Relationship Between Defense Mechanisms and Physiological Variables

Our theoretical conception remains clearly within the scope of describing and where possible, explaining individual differences in defense mechanisms and physiological indicators as well as their interrelationship. Typically, we shall proceed from defenses as predictors to physiologic reactions as dependent variables. This approach differs from the attempts to formulate psychobiological personality models by Eysenck (1967) on the basis of extraversion-introversion and neuroticism, by Gray (1981), centered on rewarding systems; and by Zuckerman (1991) who tried to integrate the above variables and added sensation seeking. Our pathway is consistent with Lazarus' conception in as much as we proceed from the centrality of emotions.

From a neuropsychological point of view, emotions are characterized by three components, physiological, with central and autonomic as well as biochemical reactions; cognitive, including attention, memory, and plans; and overt behaviors, like verbalizations, facial expressions, and posture (Kolb & Whishaw, 1996). Not only can defenses be inferred from some of these emotional reactions, but they also exercise influence upon emotions, by moderating or steering their expression. Therefore, knowledge of a person's defensive structure may improve predictions on how emotions are experienced and expressed (cf. Chapter 1). Although the conscious emotional component does not get full representation, it can be asserted that most defenses have an impact on emotions.

Neuropsychological Variables and Defense

Activation Theory and Defense

Grzegolowska-Klarkowska (1976, 1980, 1991) proposed a biologically based theory that posits informational discrepancy as a principal antecedent for activating defense mechanisms. Its basic tenet is that information discrepancy increases cerebral activation by promoting discharges from the ascending reticular activating system (ARAS). On the psychological level, information discrepancy is often experienced as anxiety, frequently triggered by experiences, which the person finds difficult to integrate. In general, excessive levels of activation are experienced as unpleasant. Thus, the person is motivated to work toward restoring a tolerable, if not optimal, activation level. According to Grzegolowska-Klarkowska (1980) defense mechanisms come into play in reducing information discrepancy and thereby lowering activation. The first line of defense consists of denial and repression, both of which interfere with the encoding of threatening or excessive information in long-term memory. The second group of defenses, which includes intellectualisation, projection, rationalization, and reaction formation, transforms, and thereby reduces the impact of the information that has already been encoded. Activation of defense can produce a variety of outcomes. In the optimal case, defenses successfully accomplish their primary purpose, i.e. they reduce discomfort and distress. Quite often, however, defenses lessen a person's cognitive efficiency in the process by restricting cue utilization, impairing working memory, and interfering with attention deployment.

Grzegolowska-Klarkowska's theory is formal, reductionistic, and content-free. Defenses against instinctual drives, central to Freudian theory, are regarded as a special case of information discrepancy and of the resulting excessive activation. Paulhus and Suedfeld (1988) proposed a complex dynamic model of self-deception which extends the scope of defense mechanisms to the socio-cognitive arena. This formulation is compatible with activation theory, as it is recognized that information discrepancy can be brought about by intrapsychic, interpersonal, and/or physiological factors. Empirically, Grzegolowska-Klarkowska (1980) was able to demonstrate that physiologically induced ARAS arousal selectively impaired the recall of threatening verbal texts, both in comparison with the performance of a placebo control group and with the respondents' own baseline established before drug ingestion.

Lateralization and Defense

Another variable that may be germane to defensive reactions is the difference in information processing between the two hemispheres. In general, the right hemisphere excels in analyzing complex visual material (Kolb & Whishaw, 1996), which may complicate the interpretation of the results of percept-genetic experiments. Assuming, however, a comparable representation of the threatening stimuli in the two hemispheres on the two major defense-evoking percept-genetic instruments (the Defense Mechanism Test (DMT) and the Meta-Contrast Technique (MCT), cf. Chapter 7), research has focused on the preponderance of the type of defense in one hemisphere as evoked in visual half-field experiments. This objective was pursued by Ingegerd Carlsson in a series of experiments on hemisphericity, defense, and creativity.

In her initial study, Carlsson (1989a) presented the MCT (see Chapter 7) to the right visual field of 23 student respondents and to the left visual field of 22 of their counterparts, randomly assigned to their respective condition. She thus had 22 respondents with a probably better stimulus representation in the right hemisphere and 23 respondents with a better representation in the left hemisphere. The hypotheses were: 1) that the more primary process-related defense mechanisms, i.e., projection and regression, should be evoked in the right hemisphere condition and 2) that the more secondary process-related defenses, i.e. repression and isolation, would be elicited in the left hemisphere condition. The second hypothesis was supported by the results. Lateralization was more pronounced in female than male respondents.

In another study Carlsson (1989b) conducted a similar experiment with 169 student respondents who were randomly assigned to three conditions (left visual field [42 respondents], right visual field [43 respondents] and the usual MCT presentation [84 respondents]). In keeping with the hypothesis, the right hemisphere group obtained higher scores for regression (followed by the left hemisphere group and the control group). No significant differences were found for projection and sensitivity. In contrast, the left hemisphere group scored significantly higher for repression (followed by the controls and the right hemisphere group). For isolation, there was only a trend toward the hypothesized relationship. To a considerable degree, this study provided cross-validation of Carlsson's initial results.

On the basis of theoretical considerations and unsystematic impressions, many creativity investigators hold the view that better interhemispheric communication is characteristic of creative individuals (cf. Arieti, 1976). In another study, Carlsson (1990) extended this hypothesis to defense preferences. In this experiment, 84 students were given the MCT under the two visual half-field conditions, with 42 respondents in each group. All respondents also took the Creative Functioning Test (CFT, Smith & Carlsson, 2001). On the basis of the CFT results, respondents were placed in one of three groups: noncreative, medium creative, and highly creative. Whereas the left hemisphere subgroup of noncreative respondents had significantly more signs of isolation and repression, there was no such difference in the creative group. Moreover, highly creative respondents had significantly more hemisphere-nonspecific defenses than their noncreative counterparts. These findings demonstrate that defenses evoked by visual stimuli obey in part the rules of hemisphere-specific information processing. However, the results also indicate that personality variables, such as creativity in this case, as well as gender can override the effect of hemisphere specificity (cf. Carlsson, 2002).

As defenses in general tend to be quite stable within the personality organization (see Chapters 1 and 7), the two contrasting hemisphere conditions are probably indicative of the limits for a shift in the person's most typical defense mechanism. It is therefore worth noting that not all respondents with the highest scores for projection and regression under the right hemisphere condition remained in this group when stimuli were presented in the usual manner. Carlsson´s studies thus have implications for the method of presentation as well as for considering defenses as stable personal characteristics.

It would be interesting to see this research paradigm extended to clinical samples.

Other Measures of Central Processes in Relation to Defense

Other methods for studying central variables in relation to defensive processes include the Electroencephalogram (EEG), regional Cerebral Blood Flow (rCBF), Positron Emission Tomography (PET scans), and functional Magnetic Resonance Imaging (fMRI). EEG results are available from a study of a sample of respondents at a United States Air Force base (Sterman & Olff, 1991). EEG was recorded at rest, under eyes closed and eyes open conditions, and in the course of presenting the Defense Mechanisms Test (DMT): before the exposure of the test stimulus [pre-ex], during the exposure [during ex], and after the exposure [post-ex]. On the basis of the first recognition of the threat in the DMT picture by the respondents, DMT series was partitioned into pre-threat, threat, and post-threat segments. Seven respondents received low DMT ratings for all defenses and six, high ratings. These two groups were compared in their 8-12 Hz activity during both the rest period and the recording periods of the DMT (pre-ex, during ex and post-ex). A decrease of 8-12 Hz spectrum magnitude was found to be related to task demands (Sterman & Suyenobu, 1990). There was no difference in the rest period (eyes open condition) between the two groups. While the high defense group showed a greater attenuation of the 8-12 HZ activity (mainly at the mid-line, medial central, and parietal cortical sites) during the exposures, increasing over the three test sections (pre-threat, threat, post- threat), this pattern was reversed for the low defensive group. The attenuation effect was also present to a high degree for the post-exposure period. These results were interpreted by their authors as indicative of an increase in cognitive workload and seen as resulting in the availability of fewer resources for efficient decision-making in the high defense group.

rCBF measures were recorded together with a percept-genetic defense test (Johanson, Risberg, Silfverskiöld & Smith, 1986). In that study they were analyzed only with regard to anxiety, which forms a separate category in the Meta-Contrast Technique (MCT, see Chapter 7). There are also several MCT studies with cancer patients. In a study of brain tumors (Lilja et al., 1992) patients with highly malignant (HM) tumors (n = 17) were compared with patients with tumors of low malignity (LM) (n = 8), before and, for a subgroup, also after surgery. The HM group showed more pathological regression, moderate projection, and immature repression before surgery. After surgery, more signs of isolation were found in this group, whereas the LM group relied more on symbolic repression. While there was no difference in frontal rCBF preoperatively, postoperative rRCBF's were lower in the HM group in the midfrontal and inferior frontal areas of the right hemisphere. These rCBF results were discussed by Lilja et al. mainly in reference to the patients' general emotional functioning and their anxiety level and not in terms of the specific defenses as scored on percept-genetic instruments. However, in a study using the MCT of defensive strategies in patients with organic dementia, Johanson (1990) demonstrated an association between frontal disturbance and relative immaturity of the defenses mobilized in the test situation.

Results of glucose metabolic rates registered by means of PET scans during silent mentation are available for the Gottschalk-Gleser affect scales, including displacement and denial of anxiety (see Chapter 20). These results vary across brain regions. However, a clear tendency is detectable for a distinct neurobiological representation of separate cerebral locations for the different anxiety variables, with, for example, a greater number of left hemispheric correlates for denial. The authors are cautious in interpetating their results, and they recognize that the determination of lateralization is dependent on methods and criteria as well as on the brain regions studied.

There are to our knowledge no fMRI studies involving defenses.

Cardiovascular and Skin Conductance Reactions in Relation to Defense

In contrast to the more sensitive EEG registration during percept-genetic experiments, the simultaneous measurement of cardiovascular and skin conductance reactions during percept-genetic tests does not lend itself well to bringing forth individual differences in defensive reactions. This is so because subliminal presentation of threat extends over protracted periods, and it is exceedingly difficult to specify the duration of time before and after the onset of threat in order for the reactions to be compared. There are, however, differences in cardiovascular and skin conductance reactions between groups categorized with regard to defenses as determined by percept-genetic instruments.

Godaert, Haagenaars, Olff, and Brosschot (1991) studied stress reactions in respondents high or low in their overall scores of the DMT. Twenty-seven male secondary school teachers were included in the experimental group. The stress task of 30 minutes in duration required the participants to explain an unsolvable puzzle to another person, who was in fact a confederate of the experimenter. Respondents with higher defense scores showed heightened cardiovascular activity at rest as well as under stress. Heart rate variability as operationalized by interbeat interval variance over different frequencies showed greater variability in the middle range of frequencies, which was interpreted by the authors as a shift in the sympathetic-parasympathetic balance toward greater sympathetic reactivity. Hentschel and Kiessling (1990) worked with a stepwise hypothesis. It was hypothesized that problem solving performance in the Symbol-Maze Test (SMT, cf. Chapter 14) would be hampered by higher defense levels as measured by the FKBS (Fragebogen zu Konfliktbewältigungsstrategien, cf. Chapters 14 and 23). The crucial hypothesis predicted that these groups would also show differences in their physiological reactions related to information processing. On the SMT there are decision points marked with symbols for permitted and forbidden turns instead of blind alleys, which the respondent has to learn while going through the maze. The SMT comprises eight mazes with 25 decision points each. Wrong decisions are signalled by a low tone as feedback; for good decisions the feedback signal is no tone. As the noise signal by itself may stimulate physiological reactions, good decisions were recorded in order for the comparison of pre-decision and post-decision periods in heart rate and skin conductance. Respondents were 60 students of social work.

Respondents with higher scores on Turning Against Self (TAS) and Intellectualization (INT) performed more poorly on problem solving tasks on the SMT. When the heart rates and Skin Conductance Reactions (SCR's) were compared for the median-split TAS and INT groups, a contrasting pattern was found. Respondents with high TAS scores compared to respondents with low TAS scores after a correct decision in the SMT had both lower SCR's and heart rates. Respondents with high INT scores had higher heart rates and SCR's, compared with their low INT counterparts. Analyzed as separate measures, only the SCR results reached significance while heart rates only showed a nonsignificant trend, probably because of their great variance. It is not easy to interpret these results on the basis of general theories of information processing and physiological reactivity (Lacey, 1959; Sokolov, 1969). Trying, however, to infer what people with high TAS and high INT scores may have thought might yield plausible leads for future exploration. High TAS scorers may have felt: "***I*** am not able to solve this," and may have experienced relief after arriving at a correct decision. High INT scorers may have thought: "This ***task*** is too difficult." Subsequently, they were surprised to find that their decision was correct.

In Chapter 15 Cramer reports a study on three defenses (denial, projection and identification), measured by the Thematic Apperception Test (TAT), and cardiovascular and skin reactions (diastolic blood pressure and skin conductance level [SCL]) during stressful tasks. The use of identification was found to be related to lower SCL and higher blood pressure. Projection resulted in lower SCL and denial, in higher SCL, and in temporary elevation in blood pressure. Cramer explained her results on the basis of differences in complexity between the three defenses (identification, projection, denial, in descending order) as well as in relation to the activating versus inhibiting behavioral consequences of identification and denial, respectively.

Respiration and Defense

Respiration is a variable under automatic, unconscious, as well as under voluntary, conscious, control. It can exercise influence on other physiological variables such as heart rate (cf. Harver & Lorig, 2000). Registration of respiratory variables can be accomplished by a variety of methods. Among others, one gauge, around the person's chest, or two gauges, around his or her chest and abdomen, can be used, connected to a polygraph or computer (cf. Stern, Ray, & Davis, 1980). Respiration has been studied in relation to a great many psychological variables, such as state of wakefulness, attention, conditioning, emotion, and personality (cf. Harver & Lorig, 2000; Wientjes, 1993). The link to defense, however, is a new topic of investigation. Van Praag (1995) developed and calibrated a mechanical recording device with two gauges as well as a computerized recording and analysis program (Van Praag, 1996).

The normal respiration cycle is divided into three phases, which in the ideal case are equal in duration. They are: inspiration, expiration, and pause. These variables are measured in terms of respiration volume per minute (comparable but not identical to an exact registration of the minute ventilation); speed of expiration (comparable to steepness) at the beginning of the expiration period (1/2 second after the start of the expiration phase); cycle length (1/cycle length x 60 = frequency); duration of inspiration and expiration pauses; and the proportion of thoracic respiration to the whole cycle. Seventy respondents (17 men and 51 women) took part in a study on physiological reactions to stress. With regard to defense, Hentschel and Kiessling (2000) factor analyzed the FKBS and used the resulting four factor scores, Intellectualization/Reversal (INT/REV), Projection (PRO), Turning Against Self (TAS) and Turning Against Objects (TAO) as predictors and the respiration parameters as dependent variables in an ANOVA design with repeated measurements (specific defense scores [high-low] *x* sex *x* specific respiration parameter [repeated] under rest and stress). The stress situation was a cognitive overload task, requiring participants to respond as fast as possible to various signals on the PC screen. The relation of the respiration parameters to the experimental conditions was in general as expected: Inspiration and expiration pauses were longer under resting conditions while frequency, thoracic respiration, and respiration volume per minute increased with stress. There were also interactions with gender, which makes it difficult to provide a comprehensive formulation of the defense-respiration relationship. At the risk of disconfirmation, it can be proposed that some defenses, such as INT/REV and PRO, interfere with the reflection of change in the experimental condition (high defense scores result in lower respiration volume under stress for these respondents), because these mechanisms help to lessen the stress or prevent an adequate adaptation to the actually changed condition. High scores for TAO result, especially for men, in greater relaxedness in the rest condition, as indexed by longer expiration pauses, and increased steepness in the expiration phase under stress. This pattern of response may reflect a healthy way of "taking a breather" in this situation. PRO exhibits an opposite pattern, with high scorers showing shorter expiration pauses under rest, as well as a generally higher respiration frequency and lesser steepness in expiration under stress. All of these indicators probably point to a less adequate adaptation of these respondents to the stress situation.

Endocrine Parameters and Defense Mechanisms

It is even more difficult to come up with a comprehensive summary of research on defenses and endocrine parameters. The number of potentially relevant substances, their differences in the timing of release, their potential interactions and the variety of physiological systems and mechanisms involved at different levels stand in the way of identifying trends and detecting commonalities in the available body of research. In order to make our task more manageable, we shall restrict coverage in this segment to reactions to stress in interaction with defenses and coping. Concomitantly, we shall leave out all details of measurement and methods of analysis of endocrine substances.

Most research on psychoendocrinological reactions to stress has been done with the pituitary-adrenal cortical system. Rose (1984) noted in his review that in many studies stress was defined as an external variable and that individual differences were often ignored or tended to be regarded as a problem. Defense mechanisms may provide a good basis for the formation of groups. Such a research strategy shifts emphasis to individual differences in the impact of stressful events upon the endocrine system (Kahn, 1970), consistent with the transactional definition of stress (cf. Lazarus, 1993).

Ellertsen, Johnsen and Ursin (1978) extracted three factors in endocrine reactions in men (n = 44), who were successful applicants for parachutist training. These factors were: cortisol, testosterone, and catecholamine. Vaernes, Ursin, Darragh, and Lambe (1982) studied stress reactions of 62 army cadets with no prior swimming experience, who had to qualify for a swimming proficiency certificate. They were able to replicate the three endocrine factors found earlier by Ellertsen et al. Defense was measured among other methods by means of the DMT, and the combination of three DMT defenses (repression, isolation and reaction formation [DMT DEF]) correlated significantly with the catecholamine factor at post-jump measurement. When scores for anxiety were added, high overall defenses on the DMT correlated positively with the testosterone factor at post-jump.

Vaernes and Darragh (1982) studied reactions to a dive of 60 meter hyperbaric pressure in 29 male trainee divers. They found moderate positive correlations between DMT DEF and cortisol and prolactine and moderately high negative correlations between identification with the other sex and cortisol. These latter respondents also performed better on a reasoning task during the dive, whereas the performance of respondents with high DMT DEF scores and a bad prognosis score on the DMT (DMT PROG) was impaired.

Olff et al. (1991) related defenses to endocrine variables both before and after the interpersonal stress task used by Godaert et al. (1991). Fifty high school teachers took part in the experimental condition and 36 served as controls. The mean of interaction terms was formed for the weighted sum scores of the two DMT series (DMT TOT) and the prognosis score of the DMT (DMT PROG) with the stress condition. Significant partial correlations, controlling for main effects and baseline values, were found with changes in cortisol, ACTH, prolactine, endorphine, and norepinephrine. Cortisol changes were negatively related to DMT TOT, and ACTH changes showed a negative relationship with both DMT scores and mastery-oriented coping. Change in norepinephrine was positively related to DMT TOT, and emotion-focused coping exhibited a negative relationship with prolactine change.

Endresen and Ursin (1991) reported results on correlations between defenses as measured by the LSI (cf. Chapter 17) and endocrine variables in large samples selected for varying degrees of job stress. Their detailed results, showing connections between defenses and cortisol and immune globulines (B-cell line), cannot be reported here. Correlations were low for the whole sample, even though they were consistent and significant. They were higher for job-specific subgroups. Endresen and Ursin (1991) interpreted their results in part on the basis of genetic selection, but emphasized interactions between defenses and particular job situations in determining endocrine reactivity.

De Leeuwe, Hentschel, Tavenier, and Edelbroek (1992) tried to predict endocrine reactions of computer operators to a stressful information overload task, which consisted of playing a high level computer game while listening to a short story. As endocrine parameter a norepinephrine metabolite (3-methoxy-4-hydroxy-phenylglycol, MHPG) was chosen. Blood plasma values of MHPG can be regarded as a central norepinephrine indicator (De Met & Halaris, 1979; Kopin, 1985). There are a number of animal studies indicating a positive relationship between stress and MHPG level (Korf, Aghajanian & Roth, 1973), but not many studies on humans. The study by Linnoila et al. (1985) has shown, however, that findings with human respondents, namely a decrease of MHPG concentration with the pharmacological treatment of depression, are similar to those with animals. From the pool of 63 men and 20 women in the study by de Leeuwe et al., groups of stress-resistant and stress-nonresistant respondents were blindly selected, consisting of 17 and 13 persons, respectively. This selection was based on FKBS scores, a neuroticism scale (Hentschel & Klintman, 1974), and a scale measuring achievement motivation vs. fear of failure from the PMT (Hermans, 1976). The stress nonresistant group of respondents had higher blood plasma values of MHPG. A post-hoc stepwise regression analysis for the FKBS on the MHPG values resulted in R = .57, including as predictors the three FKBS scales TAS, INT, and REV. As there was no baseline measurement in this study, the higher MHPG level in the stress nonresistant group could have other causes than coping with the stress task, although the two groups also differed significantly in signs of stressful behavior during this task.

Discussion

In interpreting studies presented in this chapter, we are faced with a problem. As yet, there is no way of knowing whether the physiological changes observed during stressful conditions dissipate over a short time span or whether they may affect the health of the respondents over a protracted period of time. Specifically, it is not known whether it is good or bad in the long run to react to stress with decrease in the cortisol level, or to show an elevated MHPG level or higher blood pressure for a period of time after exposure to a stressful task. In a similar manner, we lack information on whether or not changing the respiration pattern in accordance with task demands or reacting with attenuation of the 8-12 Hz activity as an indicator for a higher workload during a test procedure could have enduring consequences for a person's health. Thus, there is room for doubts concerning the direct usefulness of such indicators in applied health psychology. One may ask, however, whether there are other potential applications and whether general conclusions can be derived from these results.

Defense mechanisms were first described in a clinical context (cf. Chapter 1). Adding psychophysiological indicators extends the scope of defensive operations considerably. First, the traditional chain of inference from symptom to defense can now be reversed. Historically, clinical research and theorizing proceeded, for example, from obsession to isolation and from hysteria to repression. The opportunity is at hand for retracing this pathway from physiological responses to the manifestations of defense (cf. Hentschel & Kiessling, 1990). Thus, accelerated heartbeat may be a harbinger of free-floating anxiety associated with panic states and with other anxiety disorders together with the defenses related to them. Such psychophysiological indicators may also reflect an individual's characteristic information processing features. All of these considerations argue for according central physiological variables a key role in future research.

On the theoretical plane, the challenge is to relate individual differences discussed in this chapter to differences in information processing, and eventually to integrate them into a comprehensive conceptual framework that would be anchored in biological "hardware." Earlier in this chapter, we envisaged defenses as a mind-body interface. Can this view be reconciled with the tradition of psychoanalysis? Grzegolowska-Klarkowska (1991) has discussed the various implicit meanings of psychoanalysis as viewed by other theorists, ranging from hermeneutic reconstruction to biological explanations. Erdelyi (1985) speculated that Freud would have used the computer analogy in his theorizing, if it were an option in his lifetime. However, psychoanalytic constructs have turned out to be very different from computers, even on the metaphoric plane. Analogously, psychoanalytic formulations do not lend themselves easily to translation into biological or psychophysiological parameters. Content-related individual differences, on the other hand, can be construed as social representations in Moscovici's (1961) sense, dependent on the shared experiences and learning histories of a group. Defenses, however, do not provide direct information on 'what' is learned or represented, but rather about 'how' things are experienced. Nonetheless, there is no way of avoiding or disregarding content-related differences. Psychoanalysis remains inescapably a content-related theory, although in a very special sense. Rapaport (1973) made a substantial contribution by construing the central elements of psychoanalytic theory in terms of six perspectives: empirical, organismic, economic, structural, adaptive, and psychosocial. Historically, defenses were mainly viewed from the structural and dynamic perspectives. Defense mechanisms may, however, be regarded as a central construct within psychoanalytic theory because they fit virtually all of the different viewpoints identified by Rapaport. Defense mechanisms are unthinkable outside of their embeddedness in the genetically determined hierarchy of developmental challenges and dangers and in the developmental progression of the sense of reality (Gedo & Goldberg, 1973). Thus, they defy being reduced to content-free information processing parameters. In order to process information meaningfully, they have to have both aspects, referring to 'what' and to 'how'.

It is debatable, however, whether the whole theoretical framework of psychoanalysis, including the heavy burden that the meta-psychological constructs necessarily carry, is needed for the operational definition of defense mechanisms and for their empirical investigation. Research on coping, stemming from the same conceptual roots, has to a great extent left this ground behind. This state of affairs goes a long way to explain why coping enjoys much greater acceptance within academic psychology than does defense. The main question is, how well is the construct supported by the theory, or to use a more precise term, how good is the construct validity within the theory. There are indeed some indications that, with some of the operationalizations of defenses, compatibility with the basic psychoanalytic assumptions is made difficult. As long as the psychodynamic perspective is retained, however, and constructions are not reduced to mere cognitive operations, the psychoanalytic origin of defenses continues to be acknowledged. There is, moreover, in our view no good substitute for the original theoretical basis of these constructs. Critique of some of the theoretical psychoanalytical constructs is not necessarily applicable to the theory as a whole and neither should it be transferred automatically to the other constructs within the theory.

The constructors of cognitive computer models often introduce artificial mistakes in order to make their models more realistic. Human respondents make such errors by themselves, not only due to the restricted human cognitive capacities but also because of the intrinsic affective-emotional embeddedness of human information processing. Human beings are just no objective registration and measurement apparatuses, neither with regard to their introspective window, nor with regard to their view of the outside world. Dixon's (1981) model of processing stimuli through the entire perceptual process (cf. Figure 27.1) takes fully into account the preconscious origins of even the seemingly automatic and momentarily experienced subjective states (Dixon, Hentschel & Smith, 1986). It is incumbent upon generalizable theories of human information processing to include this preconscious component. Dixon's model does not make an explicit provision for defense mechanisms, but they can be easily accommodated as supraordinate constructs with an impact upon the diverse domains of human reactivity, including physiological ones.

One of the main conclusions to be drawn from stress research is that it is not the objective situation that determines a person's reaction to stress, but the individual with his or her personal history. Coping and defense mechanisms seem to belong to the promising grouping variables, which enable us to classify these reactions into clusters on the basis of similarity. Such mechanisms can also be differentiated on an empirical basis. Physiological variables should be included among the essential components of the comprehensive information process. It is well worth noting that psychological measures of defense mechanisms which show minimal intercorrelations converge in yielding similar correlates with physiological variables (cf. Endresen & Ursin, 1991). This finding suggests a more restricted and less differentiated pattern of biological reactions compared with the psychological ones. In regard to the strategies for validation of coping and defense measures, this discrepancy requires that the selection of the range of criteria for the various defense and coping instruments be kept as constant and systematic as possible (cf. Hentschel, Ehlers, & Peter, 1993).

In addition to the studies focused on stressful and threatening situations, physiological indicators have also been recorded in research on sensory deprivation and information overload (see Goldberger, 1993; cf. also the role of defenses in situations of suboptimal stimulation in Chapter 14 and some of the studies reported above). In most cases, physiological variables cannot serve as substitutes for the specific defensive or coping reactions of the respondents. Specific physiological reactions are traceable to diverse causes. Heart rate deceleration, for example, can be traced to information intake, relief, change in the state of wakefulness, and a variety of other factors. Endocrine reactions to stress seem to be somewhat more robust in reflecting situation-person interactions (Vaernes & Darragh, 1982) while interpretations of autonomic reactions appear to be much more relevant to individual differences. Consequently, autonomic indicators are often unpredictable when investigated by conventional methods.

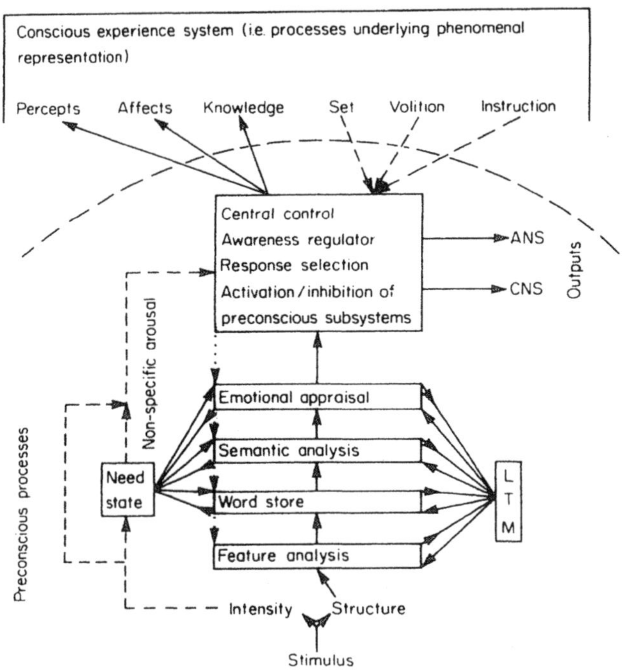

Figure 27.1: *Relationships between conscious and preconscious processors implied by the data from studies of unconscious perception (from Dixon, 1981)*

There is just no substitute for knowing the functional context and, above all, the psychological reaction tendencies of the specific individual. Given the hitherto available results, defense mechanisms and cognitive styles have proven to be valuable tools for describing and explaining individual differences including physiological reactions, both to specific stress tasks and in adapting to the challenges of life in general.

Two recent, provocative and promising, formulations may help integrate many of the findings in this chapter. On the basis of the extension of fMRI to psychotherapy research, Strauman (2003) provisionally concluded that psychological disturbance can be viewed as a possible result of disjunction between psychological and physiological reactions. Conversely, mental health can be construed as restoration of balance between these two classes of reactivity. Perhaps defense mechanisms with their physiological concomitants represent the person' s attempts, successful or not, of re-attaining this equilibrium. It should be kept in mind, however, that these fascinating possibilities emerged in the course of observations that are still in progress. Caution is indicated lest definitive conclusions are prematurely derived.

LeDoux's (2002, 2003) proposed model of the synaptic self also emphasizes the adaptive significance of coordination among and integration of various psychological functions. LeDoux (2003) views the self as a network of memories, implicit and explicit, conscious and unconscious. The common denominator of mental disorders is construed to be the reduction of synaptic plasticity. In LeDoux's (2003) words: "Most of us, most of the time are able to piece together synaptic connections that hold our self together. Sometimes, though, thoughts, emotions, and motivations come uncoupled. When this happens, the self is likely to begin to disintegrate, and mental health to deteriorate" (p. 302). This formulation is consonant with Grzegolowska's-Klarkowska's (1980) position that identifies informational discrepancy as the main trigger for defense mechanisms. Within LeDoux's synaptic model, it can be inferred that anything that threatens the coherence of the self may activate defensive operations.

We started this book with a vignette of a solitary, homeless woman on a Berlin underground train struggling to cope with the help of a succession of defense mechanisms. We conclude this chapter by recalling the same episode, of a person under stress, seeking to adapt, interact, and communicate by marshalling her available resources in order to forestall imbalance, disintegration, and consequent helplessness.

References

Arieti, S (1976). *Creativity*. New York: Basic Books.

Bradley, M. M. (2000). Emotion and motivation. In Cacioppo, J. T., Tassinari, L. G., & Berntson, G. G. (Eds.), *Handbook of psychophysiology* (2nd. ed) (pp. 602-642). Cambridge: Cambridge University Press.

Brown, J. (2000). *Mind and nature*. London: Whurr.

Carlsson, I. (1989a). Lateralization of defence mechanisms: Differing influences on perception with left and right visual field presentation of anxiety arousing stimulation. *European Journal of Personality, 3,* 167-179.

Carlsson, I. (1989b). Lateralization of defence .mechanisms in a visual half-field papadigm. *Scandinavian Journal of Psychology, 30*, 296-303.

Carlsson, I. (1990). Lateralization of defence mechanisms related to creativity. *Scandinavian Journal of Psychology*, 31, 241-247.

Carlsson, I. (2002). Anxiety and flexibility of defense related to creative functioning. *Creativity Research Journal*, 14, 341-349.

De Leeuwe, J. N., Hentschel, U., Tavenier, R., & Edelbroek, P. (1992). Prediction of endocrine stress reactions by means of personality variables. *Psychological Reports, 70*, 791-802.

De Met, E. M., & Halaris, A. E. (19979). Origin and distribution of 3-methoxy-4hydroxyphenylglycol in body fluid. *Biochemical Pharmacology, 28*, 3043-3050.

Dennett, D,C. (1991). *Consciousness explained.* Boston : Little Brown.

Dixon, N. F. (1981). *Preconscious processing*. Chichester: Wiley.

Dixon, N. F., Hentschel, U., & Smith, G. (1986). Subliminal perception and microgenesis in the context of personality research. In A. Angleitner, A. Furnham, & G. van Heck (Eds.), *Personality psychology in Europe (*Vol. 2) (pp. 239-255). Lisse: Swets & Zeitlinger.

Eccles, J (1991). *Evolution of the brain (reaction of the self*). New York: Routledge.

Ellertsen, B. Johnsen, T. B., & Ursin, H. (1978). Relationship between the hormonal responses to activation and coping. In H. Ursin, E. Baade, & S. Levine (Eds.), *Psychobiology of stress. A study of coping men* (pp. 105-122). New York: Academic Press.

Endresen, I. M., & Ursin, H. (1991). The relationship between psychological defence, cortisol, immunoglobulins, and complements. In M. Olff, G. Godaert, & H. Ursin (Eds.), *Quantification of human defence mechanisms* (pp.262-272). Heidelberg: Springer-Verlag.

Erdelyi, M. H. (1985). *Psychoanalysis: Freud's cognitive psychology.* New York: Freeman.

Eysenck, H. J. (1967). *The biological basis of personality.* Springfield, Il: Thomas.

Freud, S. (1895). Project for a scientific psychology. In Freud, The origins of psychoanalysis, 1887-1902 (pp 341-445). New York: Basic Books, 1954.

Gedo, J. E., & Goldberg, A. (1976). *Models of the mind. A psychoanalytical theory.* Chicago: University of Chicago Press.

Godaert, G., Hagenaars, J., Olff, M., & Brosschot, J. (1991). Defensiveness and cardiovascular reactions. In M. Olff (Chapter 7), *Defence and coping: Self-reported health and psychobiological correlates* (pp. 123-130). Utrecht: Isor.

Goldberger, L. (1993). Sensory deprivation and overload. In L. Goldberger, & S. Breznitz (Eds.), *Handbook of stress. Theoretical and clinical aspects* (2nd. ed) (pp. 333-341). New York: Free Press.

Gray, J. A. (1981). A critique of Eysenck' s theory of personality. In H. J. Eysenck (Ed.). *A model for Personality* (pp. 246-276). New York: Springer-Verlag

Grzegolowska-Klarkowska, H.J. (1976) An activation theory approach to defence mechanisms. *Polish Psychological Bulletin, 7,* 225-233.

Grzegolowska-Klarkowska, H.J. (1980) Use of defence mechanisms as determined by reactivity and situational level of activation. *Polish Psychological Bulletin,11,* 155-168.

Grzegolowska-Klarkowska, H. J. (1991). Defence and activation theory: An example of reinterpretation and reductionism in explaining the process of psychological defence. In M. Olff, G. Godaert, & H. Ursin (Eds.), *Quantification of human defence mechanisms* (pp.252-261). Heidelberg: Springer-Verlag.

Harver, A., & Lorig, T. S. (2000). Respiration. In Cacioppo, J. T., Tassinari, L. G., & Berntson, G. G. (Eds.), *Handbook of psychophysiology* (2nd. ed) (pp. 265-293). Cambridge: Cambridge University Press.

Hentschel, U., Ehlers, W., & Peter, R. (1993). The measurement of defense mechanisms by self-report questionnaires. In U. Hentschel, G. Smith, W. Ehlers, & J. G. Draguns (Eds.), *The concept of defense mechanisms in contemporary psychology* (pp. 53-86). New York: Springer-Verlag.

Hentschel, U. & Kiessling, M. (1990). Are defense mechanisms valid predictors of performance in cognitive tasks? In G. van Heck, S. Hampson, J. Reykowsky, & J. Zakrzewski (Eds.), *Personality psychology in Europe* (Vol. 3) (pp. 203-219). Amsterdam: Swets & Zeitlinger.

Hentschel, U., & Klintman, H. (1974). A 28-variable semantic differential: I. On factorial identification of content. *Psychological Research Bulletin, 14,* No. 4.

Hermans, H. (1976). *Prestatie Motivatie Test (PMT)* [Achievement Motivation Test]. Amsterdam: Swets & Zeitlinger.

Johanson, A., Risberg, J., Silfverskiöld, P., & Smith, G. (1986). Regional changes in cerebral blood flow during increased anxiety in patients with anxiety neurosis. In U. Hentschel, G. Smith, & J. G. Draguns (Eds.), *The roots of perception. Individual differences in information processing within and beyond awareness.* (pp. 353-360). Amsterdam: North Holland.

Johanson, A. (1990). Adaptation in different kinds of dementia and in normal elderly.*Dementia*, 1, 95-101.

Kahn, R. L. (1970). Some propositions toward a researchable conceptualization. In J. E. McGrath (Ed.), *Social and psychological factors in stress* (pp. 97-103). New York: Holt, Rinehart & Winston.

Kaplan-Solms, K., & Solms, M. (2000). *Clinical studies in neuropsychoanalysis* London: Karnac Books.

Kolb, B., & Whishaw, I. Q. (1996). *Human neuropsychology* (4th. ed.). New York: Freeman, Worth.

Kopin, I. J. (1985). Catecholamine metabolism: basic aspects and clinical significance. *Pharmacological Review, 37*, 333-364.

Korf, J., Aghajanian, G. K., & Roth, R. H. (1973). Stimulation and destruction of the locus coeruleus: opposite effects on 3-methoxy-4hydroxyphenylglycol sulphate levels in the rat cerebral cortex. *European Journal of Pharmacology, 21*, 305-310.

Lacey, J. I. (1959). Psychophysiological approaches to the evaluation of psychotherapeutic process and outcome. In E. A. Rubenstein, & M.B. Parloff (Eds.), *Research in Psychotherapy* (pp. 160-208). Washington: American Psychological Association.

Lazarus, R. S. (1993). Why we should think of stress as a subset of emotion. In L. Goldberger, & S. Breznitz (Eds.), *Handbook of stress. Theoretical and clinical aspects* (2nd. ed) (pp. 21-39). New York: Free Press.

Lazarus, R. S., & Folkman, S. (1984). *Stress, appraisal, and coping*. New York: Springer.

Lazarus, R. S., & Launier, R. (1978). Stress-related transactions between person and environment. In L. A. Pervin, & M. Lewis (Eds.), *Perspectives in interactional psychology* (pp. 287-327). New York: Plenum.

Lazarus, R. S., & Opton, E. M. (1966). The use of motion picture films in the study of psychological stress: A summary of experimental studies and theoretical formulations. In C. Spielberger (Ed.). *Anxiety and behavior* (pp. 225-262). New York: Academic Press.

Le Doux, J. (2002). *The synaptic self.* New York: Macmillan.

Le Doux, J. E. (2003) The self: clues from the brain. In J. E. LeDoux, J. Debiec, & H. Moss (Eds.), *The self: From soul to brain* (pp. 295-304). New York: New York Academy of Sciences.

Lilja, Å., Hagstadius, S., Risberg, J., Salford, L., Smith. G. J. W., & Öhmann, R.. (1992). Frontal lobe dynamics in brain tumor patients: A study of reginal cerebral blood flow and affective changes in brain tumor patients before and after surgery. *Neuropsychiatry, Neuropsychology and Behavioral Neurology, 5*, 294-300.

Olff, M., Brossschot, J. F., Godaert, G., Benschop, R. J., Ballieux, R. E., Heijnen, C. J., & Ursin, H. (1991). In M. Olff (Chapter 9), *Defence and coping: Self-reported health and psychobiological correlates* (pp. 151-169). Utrecht: Isor.

Paulhus, D.L. & Suedfeld.P. Self-deception: A dynamic complexity model. In J.S. Lockard & D.L. Paulhus (Eds.) *Self-deception: An adaptive mechanism*. New York: Prentice Hall.

Rapaport, D. (1960). *The structure of psychoanalytic theory: A systematizing attempt*. New York: International Universities Press.

Rose, R. M. (1984). Overview of endocrinology of stress. In G. M. Brown, H. H. Koslow, & S: Reichlin (Eds.), *Neuroendocinology and psychiatric disorder* (pp. 95-121). New York: Raven.

Rychlak, J. F. (1973). *Introduction to personality and psychotherapy. A theory-construction approach*. Boston: Houghton Mifflin.

Searle, J.F. (1997). *The mystery of consciousness*. New York: New York Review of Books.

Smith, G. J. W., & Carlsson, I. (2001). *CFT- Creative Functioning Test*. Lund: Department of Psychology.

Sokolov, E. N. (1969). The modeling properties of the nervous system. In M. Cole & I. A. Maltzman (Eds.), *Handbook of contemporary Soviet psychology* (pp. 672-704). New York: Basic Books.

Sterman, M. B., & Olff, M. (1991). Topographic EEG correlates of perceptual defensiveness. In M. Olff (Chapter 6), *Defence and coping: Self-reported health and psychobiological correlates* (pp. 115-122). Utrecht: Isor.

Sterman, M. B., & Suyenobu, B. Y. (1990). Topographic and hemispheric EEG spectral density characteristics during standardized control and performance conditions. *Psychophysiology, 27*, 67.

Stern, R. M., Ray, W. J., & Davis, C. M. (1980). *Psychophysiological recording*. New York: Oxford University Press.

Strauman, T. (2003). Using functional Magnetic Resonance Imagining in psychotherapy research: A cautionary yet confident tale. Paper presented at the 34th Annual Meeting of the Society for Psychotherapy Research in Weimar, Germany, June 2003.

Vaernes, R. J., & Darragh, A. (1982). Endocrine reactions and cognitive performance at 60 metres hyperbaric pressure. *Scandinavian Journal of Psychology, 23*, 193-199.

Vaernes, R., Ursin, H., Darragh, A., & Lambe, R. (1982): Endocrine response patterns and psychological correlates. *Journal of Psychosomatic Research, 26,* 123-131.

Van Praag, T. (1995). Adembeweging en persoonlijkheid [Respiratory movements and personality]. Leiden University: unpublished Master thesis.

Van Praag, T. (1996). Physiocope. Manual. Leiden University: mimeographed.

Weinstein, J., Averill, J. R., Opton, E. M., & Lazarus, R. S. (1968). Defensive style and discrepancy between self-report and physiological indexes of stress. *Journal of Personality and Social Psychology, 10,* 406-413.

Wientjes, C. E. J. (1993). *Psychological influences upon breathing: Situational and dispositional aspects.* Den Haag: Cip-Data.

Zuckerman, M. (1991). *Psychobiology of personality.* Cambridge: Cambridge University Press.

Index

A

B

C

D

E

F

G

H

I

J

K

L

M

N

O

P

T

U

V

W

Contributors

Gunilla Amnér, PhD, Department of Psychology , University of Lund, Box 213, S-22100 Lund, Sweden

Harald Bailer, PhD, Department of Psychosomatic Medicine and Psychotherapy, University Hospital of Ulm, Schillerstrasse 15, D-89077 Ulm, Germany

Robert J. Bechtel, PhD, GB Software, 4607 Perham Road, Corona del Mar, CA 92625, USA

Frits J. Bekker, PhD, Department of Psychology, University of Leiden, 2300 RB Leiden, The Netherlands

Heidi Caspari-Oberegelsbacher, PhD, Department of Psychosomatic Medicine and Psychotherapy, University Hospital of Ulm, Schillerstrasse 15, D-89077 Ulm, Germany

Hope R. Conte, PhD , Albert Einstein College of Medicine of Yeshiva University, Bronx, NY 10461, USA

Phebe Cramer, PhD, Department of Psychology, Williams College, Williamstown, MA 01267, USA

Juris G. Draguns, PhD, Department of Psychology, The Pennsylvania State University, University Park, PA 16802, USA

Herbert Dreier, MPs, Department of Psychology, University of Mainz, D-55099 Mainz, Germany

Wolfram Ehlers, MD, PD, Birkenwaldstr. 132, D-70191 Stuttgart, Germany

Janny Fronczek, Department of Psychonomics, University of Amsterdam, 1018 WB Amsterdam, The Netherlands

Louis A. Gottschalk, PhD, Department of Psychiatry and Human Behavior, College of Medicine, University of California, Irvine, CA 92717, USA

Norbert Grulke, MD, PhD, Department of Psychosomatic Medicine and Psychotherapy, University Hospital of Ulm, Robert-Koch-Strasse 8, D-89081 Ulm, Germany

Vera Heitz, Department of Psychosomatic Medicine and Psychotherapy, University Hospital of Ulm, Schillerstrasse 15, D-89077 Ulm, Germany

Melissa Henry, MPs, Department of Psychology, Université du Québec à Montréal, Canada

Uwe Hentschel, PhD, Department of Psychology, University of Leiden, 2300 RB Leiden, The Netherlands

Arn Hosemann, PhD, E.R.P. Eastern Relationship, Grabbeallee 62a, Berlin, D-13156, Germany

Per Johnsson, PhD, Department of Psychology , University of Lund, Box 213, S-22100 Lund, Sweden

Alexandra Juchems, MD, Department of Psychosomatic Medicine and Psychotherapy, University Hospital of Ulm, Schillerstrasse 15, D-89077 Ulm, Germany

Horst Kächele, MD, Department of Psychosomatic Medicine and Psychotherapy, University Hospital of Ulm, Am Hochstraess 8, D-89081 Ulm, Germany

Manfred Kiessling, MPs, Gesellschaft zur Förderung persönlichkeits- und sozialpyschologischer-Forschung (GPS), University of Mainz, D-55099 Mainz, Germany

Paul Kline, PhD, DSc, Washington Singer Laboratories, Department of Psychology, University of Exeter, Exeter EX44QG, UK (deceased)

Carl-Walter Kohlmann, PhD, Department of Psychology, University of Education, Oberbettringer Str. 200, D-73535 Schwäbisch Gmünd, Germany

Hans Kreitler, PhD , Department of Psychology, Tel-Aviv University, 69978 Tel Aviv, Israel (deceased)

Shulamith Kreitler, PhD, Department of Psychology, Tel-Aviv University, 69978 Tel Aviv, Israel

Joachim Küchenhoff, PhD, Psychiatric University Hospital, University of Basel, CH-4051 Basel, Switzerland

Falk Leichsenring, PhD , Department of Psychosomatics and Psychotherapy, University of Göttingen, von Sieboldstr. 5, D-37075 Göttingen, Germany

Fernando Lolas, MD, Regional Program on Bioethics PAHO/WHO, Avda. Providencia 1017, Piso 7, Providencia P.O. 27141, Santiago, Chile

J. Christopher Perry, MD, The Institute of Community & Family Psychiatry, Sir Mortimer B. Davis - Jewish General Hospital, 4333 Chemin de la Cote Ste-Catherine, Montréal, Québec H3T 1E4, Canada;

Robert Plutchik, PhD, Albert Einstein College of Medicine of Yeshiva University, Bronx, NY 10461, USA

I. Alex Rubino, MD, Percept-Genetic Laboratory, Tor Vergata University, I-00141 Rome, Italy

Olof Rydén, PhD, Department of Psychology , University of Lund, Box 213, S-22100 Lund, Sweden

Barbara E. Saitner, PhD, Gottesweg 131, D-50935 Cologne, Germany

Andreas Schwerdtfeger, PhD, Department of Psychology, Johannes-Gutenberg University, Mainz, 55099, Germany

Alberto Siracusano, MD, Percept-Genetic Laboratory, Tor Vergata University, I-00141 Rome, Italy

Hans Sjöbäck, PhD, Department of Psychology , University of Lund, Box 213, S-22100 Lund, Sweden (deceased)

Gudmund J. W. Smith, PhD, Department of Psychology, University of Lund, Box 213, S-22350 Lund, Sweden

Heidi Teubner-Berg, MPs, Gesellschaft zur Förderung persönlichkeits- und sozialpyschologischer-Forschung (GPS), University of Mainz, D-55099 Mainz, Germany

Volker Tschuschke, PhD, Department of Medical Psychology, University of Cologne, Joseph-Stelzmann-Strasse 9, D-50924 Cologne, Germany

Bert Westerlundh, PhD, Department of Psychology , University of Lund, Box 213, S-22100 Lund, Sweden

www.ingramcontent.com/pod-product-compliance
Ingram Content Group UK Ltd.
Pitfield, Milton Keynes, MK11 3LW, UK
UKHW021514071026
15470UKWH00031B/358